a synopsis of American History

a synopsis of American History

Fifth Edition

Charles Sellers
Henry May
University of California at Berkeley

Neil R. McMillen
University of Southern Mississippi

HOUGHTON MIFFLIN Company/Boston

Dallas   Geneva, Illinois   Hopewell, New Jersey   Palo Alto   London

Printed in the U.S.A.

Library of Congress Catalog Card Number: 80–50978

ISBN: 0–395–30735–X

Preface

A *Synopsis of American History* is a brief summary, with an emphasis on politics, designed for those who are beginning the study of the subject. Our purpose in offering a much briefer book than the average textbook is not to cut down the *amount* a student reads, but to increase the diversity. The *Synopsis,* together with other materials assigned by the instructor and suggested in the bibliographies and historiographical essays, should help the student to get some idea of the wide variety of American historical writing. At the same time, the student can acquire some knowledge of the chronological order without which history makes no sense. The brief chapter bibliographies are restricted to books that are readily available and readable, and they provide no more than a bare introduction to the study of each period.

In our opinion, political history affords the clearest organization of American history. Surprisingly often, American politics reflects with fair accuracy underlying tendencies in economic, social, and intellectual life. In general, we have said little about social and intellectual history, not because we consider these fields unimportant, but because they are best studied in primary sources and specialized books and because they do not lend themselves to summary.

To supplement the political emphasis, 18 essays on "Conflicting Historical Viewpoints" are included. These essays point out areas of past and present political controversy and show the development of historical thinking about some of the critical events in American history.

In reducing this big story to such a small space, we have found it impossible to avoid expressing opinions. While we have tried to keep partisanship to a minimum, we have allowed ourselves to suggest interpretations. Appropriate reading in other books—the whole purpose of the *Synopsis*—should enable students to accept or reject our interpretative statements.

We wish to thank a number of colleagues who, in one edition or another, read all or parts of this book and made many valuable suggestions. These suggestions we have tried to follow insofar as they were consistent with the philosophy of the book.

In its first two editions, the *Synopsis* was the work of Charles Sellers (Chapters 1–15) and Henry May (Chapters 16–31). Neil R. McMillen joined the enterprise in 1974, assumed responsibility for the third, fourth, and fifth revised editions, and wrote the essays on "Conflicting Historical Viewpoints."

This fifth edition of *A Synopsis of American History* is available as a single volume or as a two-volume set. Chapters 1–16 comprise Volume One, *Through Reconstruction;* Chapters 15–32 comprise Volume Two, *Since the Civil War.*

C.S.
H.M.
N.R.M.

Contents

Conflicting Historical Viewpoints

Special Tables

Maps

Beginnings
1607–1700

1

When Christopher Columbus broke through the water barrier to the New World and became the first European to set foot on San Salvador, he opened a momentous chapter in the history of the Old World as well as the New. Already, a static and status-bound Europe was responding to new intellectual stirrings, growing trade, and competition among emerging nation-states in overseas exploration and commerce. The dramatic European discovery of the New World frontier accelerated these beginning currents of change into a 400-year revolution. The very knowledge of the existence of seemingly limitless space and resources in America set off a prolonged economic boom, quickened the spirit of enterprise, generated mounting pressures against the rigidities of the social order, and hastened Europe's entrance into the modern world of individualism, capitalism, and liberal democracy.

The development of America took place in the midst of this profoundly important transformation of the Atlantic world. The central characteristics of the emerging "modern" epoch, as the term is used here, were the increasing importance of individual autonomy and the growing faith that human beings could win secular salvation —wealth and "happiness"—through individual enterprise. By the nineteenth century, when modernity in this special sense reached its fullest development, this emphasis on the individual had given rise to the social philosophy known as *liberalism*. In its original meaning, liberalism was the conviction that the good of everyone would be served if all were left as free as possible to pursue their individual ends. In the economic sphere, liberal doctrines lent support to *laissez-faire* capitalism. In the political sphere, liberal doctrines encouraged a majoritarian democracy with some protection for the rights of minorities.

EUROPE DISCOVERS THE NEW WORLD

Although October 12, 1492 is the traditional date for the discovery of the Americas, Columbus was a relative latecomer to the New World. Many centuries before the

Italian adventurer sailed west from Spain in search of trade routes to the Orient, Asian nomads entered the North American wilderness. The combined work of geologists, archeologists, and anthropologists suggests that this migration from the east was possible as early as the beginning of the Ice Age (perhaps 50,000 years ago). The mainstream of migration to the Americas, however, began some 11,000 years ago and continued for several centuries. Very likely these earliest discoverers traveled the "land bridge" across the Bering Straits; some may have entered the New World by crossing the Pacific Ocean to other points of entry. But however they came, the New World's first settlers were dispersed in a relatively brief time throughout the western hemisphere, from Alaska to Tierra del Fuego.

In our own millennium, the New World was rediscovered by eleventh-century Scandinavian sailors. Although the exploits of these colorful Northlanders are also largely unknown, there is substantial evidence that Viking explorers sailed brightly painted, high-prowed ships from their settlements in Greenland to the North Atlantic coast of the Americas. About the year 1000, Leif Ericson led an expedition to "Vinland," a location possibly near Cape Cod but more likely in Newfoundland. During the next 10 to 20 years—four centuries before the French "discoverer" Jacques Cartier gave the region its name—other Viking parties probably scouted the vast reaches of the Gulf of St. Lawrence. These tentative Viking probings, however, had no lasting impact on North America. Whatever settlements the Norse established quickly disappeared. Theirs was an apparently isolated adventure without direct implication for future explorations in the great age of discovery.

Curiously it was Spain and not seafaring Portugal that was in the forefront of the bold exploration of the New World. Pioneers in the use of ships for trade and exploration, Portuguese mariners under the patronage of Henry the Navigator directed their swift, seaworthy caravels south along the coast of western Africa in search of gold and a passage to India. Some 25 years after Henry's death and 5 years before Columbus's first voyage to America, Bartholomeu Diaz rounded the Cape of Good Hope. In 1498 Vasco da Gama reached India, and two years later India-bound Pedro Cabral was blown off course and happened upon the coast of Brazil. By that time, however, Spain had already seized the initiative in New World exploration. In fact Columbus, who had developed his considerable navigational skills in the service of the Portuguese, turned for the support of his first New World voyage to Ferdinand and Isabella of Spain only after being refused by the King of Portugal. Buoyed by the success of Columbus, the Spanish crown soon dispatched Vasco de Balboa, who discovered the Pacific (1513), and Ferdinand Magellan, whose expedition completed the first circumnavigation of the globe (1519-1522). By the early years of the sixteenth century Spanish settlers occupied portions of Haiti, Cuba, Puerto Rico, Jamaica, and Panama. Soon thereafter (1519-1521), the resourceful Hernando Cortes, in the name of the Spanish crown, subdued the Aztec empire of Montezuma to claim the vast treasure of Mexico. In the 1530s, Francisco Pizarro, following a nine-year seige, defeated the Incas to give Spain the even richer prize of Peru.

Initially, when the explorations of Juan Ponce de Leon, Francisco Coronado, and Hernando de Soto uncovered no gold or silver, the Spanish showed little interest in the region north of Mexico. Yet by the time the French and English began planting their North American colonies, the Spanish had already staked out Florida and present-day New Mexico and Arizona. A century later Spain added Texas, and in the eighteenth century extended its missions and fortresses (*presidios*) to California. Always secondary to Peru and Mexico in the Spanish scheme of things, these northern outposts served largely as buffers against hostile Indians and rival European powers. As the coming years would prove, these settlements were the most vulnerable New World possessions of an Old World nation rapidly declining in power and wealth.

The empire of New Spain in the south had its French and Dutch counterparts in the north with New France and New Netherland. Although the French and Dutch also sailed west in search of riches, they found it not in gold and silver but in fish and furs. Following the failed efforts of explorers Giovanni de Verrazano (1524), Jacques Cartier (1534), and Henry Hudson (1609), both nations abandoned their hope of a short cut to China and turned early in the seventeenth century to the less spectacular enterprise of colony building. In 1655 New Netherland managed to absorb a tiny Swedish outpost (New Sweden) along the Delaware River, but the colony soon became New York when the Dutch lost out to their commercial and colonial rivals, the English. The French proved more tenacious, but they too were to be driven from the continent in the eighteenth century.

The English also looked westward for a water route to the East. From the fifteenth-century voyages of John Cabot and John Rut to the eighteenth-century adventures of James Cook and Alexander Mackenzie, Britain searched for the elusive Northwest Passage. Failing here, the English became colonizers. Oddly, the area they eventually exploited was the last major segment of the New World frontier to attract Europeans. In the sixteenth century, while the Portuguese concentrated on Brazil, the Spanish on Central and South America, and the French on Canada, most of the intervening expanse of temperate and fertile country lay untouched while England slowly readied herself for overseas expansion.

English colonization in America differed in character and consequences from that of other European nations. England was closer to having a tradition of individual rights and social mobility, and the English exhibited earlier and more fully that spirit of individual enterprise that was to be a major force in the modernization of the European world. Henry VII and Henry VIII had destroyed the power of the feudal nobility, already weakened by the War of the Roses, and had established a strong centralized state. In so doing, the Tudor monarchs had encouraged the growth of the business middle classes, the merchants and entrepreneurs who were to be major agents of the modernizing process. Moreover, Henry VIII had welcomed the Protestant Reformation in England, and Protestant theology, with its spiritual individualism, reinforced the individualistic, enterprising spirit of English middle-class life. All of these influences culminated in a burst of national vigor and creativity in the late sixteenth century under the last of the Tudors, Elizabeth I. It was at this point that the English turned their eyes toward the New World.

A second crucial difference between England and the other major colonizing nations was that England entered into her colonizing ventures as a poor country. Though the Elizabethans dared to challenge the might of Catholic Spain, they were only on the threshold of holding major-power status, and the Queen's treasury had insufficient funds to support the New World ventures that seemed vital to England's grand strategic design. Private enterprise had to be enlisted, and the English responded to this national purpose with a mixture of patriotism, Protestant religious zeal, thirst for adventure, and greed.

Sir Humphrey Gilbert, one of the first individual colonizers, died in his effort to found a colony in Newfoundland in 1583. Gilbert's half-brother Sir Walter Raleigh then took up the task. But the colonists Raleigh planted on Roanoke Island in present North Carolina in 1585 gave up and returned to England after a year, and a second group of settlers sent out in 1587 disappeared before a relief expedition reached Roanoke three years later. These failures demonstrated that a colonizing venture was beyond the financial capacity of any single individual. Raleigh solved this problem by organizing a "joint-stock company" to finance his second colonial venture. The joint-stock device, forerunner of the modern corporation, dated back to the time of Henry VIII when English merchants had pooled their capital and shared the risks of trade with Russia by buying shares in the "stock" or capital of the self-governing Muscovy Company. Applied to America, this device not only made English colonization possible, but insured that it would be carried out under the direction of private entrepreneurs seeking private profits as well as national ends.

The private entrepreneurial aspect of English colonization and the individualistic character of English society interacted with the New World environment to produce important consequences. Everywhere in the New World, the absence of established institutions left people free to build new social orders, and rich resources afforded a field for enterprise that led English Americans toward individualism and modernity.

The ready source of gold and silver that the Spanish found in their America reinforced the authoritarian social structure they had brought with them. The fur trade played a like role in French America. The English colonizers at first also sought gold or a northwest passage that would open to them the Pacific and the riches of the fabled Orient. They, too, attempted to impose on their colonies a rigid form of social organization designed to promote corporate rather than individual ends. But the English New World, the temperate zone of North America, yielded no ready riches. Instead, it proved superbly fitted for the humbler pursuits of farming, fishing, and trade, tasks better adapted to individual than corporate enterprise.

Paradoxically, the English colonies flourished because they failed in their original corporate aims and thus left fields of enterprise open for individual English colonists. It was under these circumstances that English America surged into the forefront of the Atlantic world's drift toward modernity. This movement, with interesting variations, can be seen in the two colonial societies established in the first half of the seventeenth century, one on Chesapeake Bay and the other in New England.

THE CHESAPEAKE COLONIES: VIRGINIA AND MARYLAND

Following Queen Elizabeth's death in 1603, her successor, James I, made peace with Spain, thus freeing English human and economic resources for American ventures. In

1606, King James issued charters to two joint-stock companies to colonize the land that Raleigh had named Virginia in honor of the virgin Queen Elizabeth. The more important of the two Virginia companies, with headquarters at London, promptly sent out an expedition. Reaching Chesapeake Bay in April, 1607 after a voyage of four months, the 100-odd adventurers proceeded up the great river that they named for King James and founded the first permanent English settlement in the New World at Jamestown.

Hunger, hostile Indians, and disease took many lives in the early years before the settlers learned to cope with the strange environment. At one point the colony was almost abandoned. Much trouble arose from the organization and aims of the enterprise. Anxious for quick profits from gold or a northwest passage, the settlers were slow to settle down to the mundane agricultural labor necessary for the colony to sustain itself. Their reluctance arose partly from the fact that all the original settlers were employees of the company and their labor was exacted under military discipline by an autocratic governor.

By 1618, officials of the Virginia Company frankly recognized that there would be no quick profits and shifted to a policy of making Virginia so attractive to immigrants that it would grow rapidly and yield eventual profits through the company's control of trade. The famous "headright" system was inaugurated whereby a person received 50 acres for every individual that person transported to America. The "cruell lawes" of former years were replaced by the "free lawes" of England, and the settlers were authorized to send delegates to a representative assembly. In 1619, as the first representative body in the New World, the democratically elected Virginia House of Burgesses organized itself on the model of the English House of Commons and claimed the right of local self-government.

The shift in company policy was a graceful adaptation to social fact: the fortunes of the colony were increasing only as people found opportunity to pursue their individual ends rather than the corporate ends of the company. John Rolfe, best known as the Virginian who helped gain peace with the Indians by marrying Pocahontas, daughter of the local chieftain, made a greater contribution to Virginia by developing, around 1613, a strain of Indian weed tobacco that achieved instant popularity in England. As the craze for tobacco in England created a flourishing market and high prices, Virginians poured all their energies into growing tobacco for individual profit, and company enterprises were left to languish.

The company made one final effort to recruit immigrants to staff its corporate enterprises, but the cost of promotion was too great, and the lure of tobacco quickly drew the new workers away. The company fell into factional bickering, and in 1622, after the death of Pocahontas's father, a new and more bellicose chieftain led the Indians in a devastating massacre of the English settlers, extending to the very gates of Jamestown. This disaster so discredited the company that the King revoked its charter in 1624, and Virginia became henceforth a royal colony. While the governor and his council were appointed by the crown, the Virginians' representative assembly was left unmolested, and the King interfered in Virginia affairs less than the company had.

The high profits from tobacco brought quick recovery from the effects of the Indian massacre and made Virginia a land of opportunity for the disadvantaged and discontented. The poorest of the English could come as the indentured servant of a Virginian who would pay the ocean passage. Labor was so dear and land so cheap that, when the three to five years of servitude were through, he or she could often buy a farm, plant tobacco, and perhaps even acquire indentured servants of his or her own. The most enterprising and affluent of the early settlers accumulated both labor and land in abundance by importing indentured servants and acquiring headrights in the process. While these more successful planters filled the offices of colony and county government, Virginia society remained so fluid during most of the seventeenth century that the planters could not be said to constitute an aristocracy or ruling class.

For one class of immigrants, the Virginia environment produced not self-fulfillment but enslavement. In 1619, the year of the first representative assembly in British North America, a Dutch trading ship dropped anchor at Jamestown with the first cargo of Africans. The original English settlers had brought with them the traditional European prejudice against blacks, but there was no provision in English law for treating Negroes differently from other indentured servants. However, it was easier to take advantage of blacks. Torn forcibly from their African cultures and languages, they had few means of resisting oppression in the alien culture of Virginia. Conspicuously distinguishable from European servants, they could not run away and melt into the free population. Gradually, masters began holding black servants for life and claiming the labor of their children. By the middle of the seventeenth century, Virginia law was modified to define a separate status of permanent and absolute slavery for Africans. America was to be a land of opportunity for Europeans only. In fact, it was through the exploitation of cheap black labor in the tobacco fields that some white Virginians began to amass great fortunes in the later seventeenth century.

While whites flourished in Virginia, a similar pattern of colonial life was being established under very different auspices farther up the shores of Chesapeake Bay. In 1632, King Charles I, successor of James I, granted to George Calvert, Lord Baltimore, proprietorship of the feudal domain of Maryland lying between the Potomac River and the 40th parallel. The Calverts were a noble Catholic family who envisioned Maryland as a refuge for their fellow Catholics from Protestant England. The first settlement was established at Saint Mary's in 1634, and soon both Protestants and Catholics were immigrating to Maryland to grow tobacco in emulation of the Virginians.

Lord Baltimore enjoyed absolute political power and ownership of the soil, but in order to attract settlers and make the colony a success, it was necessary to share both soil and power with the inhabitants. Large manorial grants were made to some, mostly Catholics, who presided over large numbers of servants and tenants and came to constitute a kind of gentry. Most of the population were yeoman farmers, perhaps employing a few servants and leasing their lands from the proprietor on a basis nearly equivalent to ownership in return for a nominal *quitrent*, the fixed rent payable to a feudal superior. The Calverts appointed a governor, but eventually allowed the inhabitants to elect an assembly that soon asserted its right to initiate legislation. The most notable piece of legislation was the Act of Toleration of 1649, assuring religious liberty to both Protestants and Catholics.

NEW ENGLAND: PLYMOUTH AND MASSACHUSETTS BAY

Meanwhile, far to the north of the Chesapeake colonies, a different kind of English colonization was taking place on the less hospitable coast of New England. The New England colonies were a direct outgrowth of a renewal of religious conflict in England. The more intense Protestants had never been satisfied with the moderate English Reformation as it was institutionalized in the Church of England. Calling themselves Puritans, they demanded a further purification of the English church through the elimination of bishops and the simplification of church services. The essence of Puritanism was a heightened sense of God's sovereignty and humanity's dependence on divine grace, and the Puritans strove zealously to live strictly in accordance with God's will.

Queen Elizabeth's astuteness had prevented the growing Puritan spirit from causing trouble during her reign, but her successors, the Stuart monarchs James I (1603–1625) and Charles I (1625–1649), invited conflict. James bluntly told the Puritans that they would either conform to the usages of the Church of England or be "harried out of the land." His son Charles married a French Catholic princess and supported efforts to compel religious conformity.

Early on, James harried one little band of particularly fervid left-wing Puritans out of England to Holland. Not finding Holland to their liking, these Pilgrims turned their eyes toward America. With support from a group of London merchants, they and additional recruits from England set sail in 1620 in the *Mayflower* bound for Virginia. Poor navigation brought them to the American coast at Cape Cod, and rather than brave further winter storms on the Atlantic, they established nearby the settlement of Plymouth. Before landing they subscribed to the Mayflower Compact, an agreement to govern themselves by majority will that was inspired by radical Puritan notions of church government. The Pilgrim settlement at Plymouth developed into a small agricultural colony, which was important as the first English community in New England but was soon overshadowed and eventually swallowed up by a larger Puritan migration.

The main Puritan migration to New England was made possible when a group of well-to-do and influential leaders obtained from King Charles in 1629 a charter for the Massachusetts Bay Company authorizing settlement in the area north of the Plymouth colony. In a bold move, the leaders resolved to make this charter of a joint-stock company the constitutional basis for a holy commonwealth beyond the King's reach by moving charter and company officers across the Atlantic. All over England, Puritans subscribed funds and volunteered themselves, and in the summer of 1630, a fleet of 17 vessels carried nearly 1,000 people to establish a series of towns around Boston harbor. As conditions for Puritanism worsened in England, these original settlers were followed by thousands more. Within little more than a decade, New England had 20,000 people.

However foreign the Puritans' ideals may seem to later generations, their enterprise for a holy commonwealth was certainly one of humanity's nobler dreams. If one accepts the Puritans' premises that God is sovereign, that one's primary duty is to do His will, and that the major issue of life is whether one receives God's grace, then it is hard to resist their conclusion that society should be constructed around a divine plan for salvation.

The Puritans' theory of civil government was similar to their congregationalist theory of church government, and both were based on the idea of covenant. A true church was a group of the "visible elect" (those who appeared by their lives to be true recipients of God's grace) who had entered into a covenant with God and each other to obey the divine will and establish a church to preach His word. It was then the business of the church members to choose as minister a man especially qualified by character and education to interpret divine will. (Women were, of course, generally denied education and were not eligible for the clergy.) This theory contained an element of democracy in that all members participated in the covenant, the choice of a minister, and the admission of new members; an element of aristocracy in that the minister once chosen should be accorded the authority due his special qualifications for interpreting God's will; and an element of monarchy in that God's will was sovereign.

The Puritans similarly believed that their holy commonwealth was founded on an implicit covenant with God and each other and that civil magistrates derived their authority from their special qualifications for interpreting God's will for the society. The Puritan commonwealth took its form from the corporate charter of the Massachusetts Bay Company. The stockholders or "freemen" of a joint-stock company met annually as a "Great and General Court" to decide major company policies and to elect the company's executive officers, a governor and a board of assistants. When the Puritan leaders transferred the charter from England to Massachusetts Bay in 1630, only a handful of magistrates, the governor John Winthrop, and a few freemen of the company who were also assistants, went along.

In their zeal to protect the religious objectives of the holy experiment, these few magistrates sought at first to make all rules, judge all cases, and govern alone. But within a year, a number of the leading settlers demanded a voice in government, and the magistrates decided that henceforth all church members should be considered freemen and allowed to attend the annual General Court to elect the governor and assistants. Within three years, the General Court had forced the magistrates to concede it a share in the lawmaking power. As the population increased and the General Court became unwieldy, the practice was adopted of having the freemen in each town elect two deputies to represent them in the General Court. The evolution of the General Court as a representative legislative body was completed in the 1640s when the deputies and magistrates began meeting separately.

The Puritan commonwealth was theocratic in the sense that God's will was sovereign, but not in the sense that ministers were given direct political power. The real power of the clergy arose from their authority as interpreters of God's will. With respect to civil matters, this function was ordinarily performed by the magistrates, but when they disagreed with the deputies, the magistrates could usually call the powerful authority of the clergy to their support. Nearly everyone believed that it was the duty of the state to support the church, to require church attendance by members and nonmembers alike, to enforce a strict morality, and to do anything else that would increase the chances of salvation for every member of the community.

The pattern of settlement reflected the religious aims of the holy commonwealth. Individuals were not permitted to buy land wherever they wished. The General Court insisted on compact settlement in contiguous towns. When population increase warranted, the General Court would authorize a group of people to settle a new town adjacent to one already established. Families were given house lots in a compact village within the town's boundaries from which they went daily to work the outlying agricultural lands they were allotted. The church was located in the village center, and villagers and the town and church officials were encouraged to guard, warn, and reprove each other against moral lapses. Everyone was allowed to participate in the town meeting, which elected town officials and decided town policy.

Deeply believing that a trained intelligence was required to discern God's will, the Puritans were zealous advocates of education. The family was the basic educational unit. Every father was required to see that his children and servants mastered reading, writing, and arithmetic and that the boys learned a trade. Fathers were responsible, too, of course, for the religious and moral training and behavior of their families. In 1647, the General Court ordered every town of 50 houses to maintain an elementary school, and some of the larger towns supported public secondary schools as well.

Puritan theory required not only a decently educated general population but also a highly educated magistracy and clergy. More than 100 graduates of Oxford and Cambridge came to Massachusetts Bay in its first decade to fill this need. In 1636, the General Court established at Cambridge a college modeled on the English universities and named after John Harvard, a young English clergyman who bequeathed to it his library and half his estate. Bright boys from ordinary farm families attended Harvard, and about half of the graduates became ministers.

RHODE ISLAND, CONNECTICUT, NEW HAMPSHIRE

It was inevitable that the holy commonwealth's efforts to maintain social discipline and a uniform doctrine would lead to friction in a population filled with gifted, intense, and devout individuals. The most embarrassing troublemaker in the early days was a brilliant young minister named Roger Williams, who challenged the principle of religious uniformity. Williams was really a radical Puritan who had arrived at the modern principle of separation of church and state on the not so modern ground that enforcement of religious uniformity impeded the soul in its search for religious truth. Such a view clearly threatened the commonwealth, and Williams's close friend Governor Winthrop warned him of his impending arrest in time for him to escape. Making his way south to Narragansett Bay in 1634, he became the father of the colony of Rhode Island, where he proclaimed the policy of complete religious freedom and inaugurated a democratic system of self-government. Receiving a charter from the English government in 1644, Rhode Island attracted dissenters from Massachusetts and Europe, flourished as a farming and trading community, and was a thorn in the sides of its orthodox Puritan neighbors.

Another New England colony came into being when the strong-minded Reverend Thomas Hooker and members of his congregation in Cambridge became excited over the fertile Connecticut River Valley, 100 miles inland from the Massachusetts Bay settlements. Rivalry between Hooker and the other leaders probably figured in the fact that the magistrates departed from their rule of compact settlement and allowed the Cambridge people to go. Traveling overland in 1636, Hooker's followers founded Hartford and organized their own colony of Connecticut on the model of Massachusetts Bay. Other Puritan groups founded settlements at Saybrook and New Haven on the coast and maintained an independent status for a quarter of a century before merging with Hooker's valley settlements as the united colony of Connecticut.

Massachusetts Bay sought to maintain control over the sporadic settlements that grew up to its north. In 1679, the towns beyond the Merrimac River obtained a charter making them the separate royal colony of New Hampshire, but the Maine area beyond continued to be ruled from Boston.

ENGLISH STRIFE AND AMERICAN AUTONOMY

The Stuart monarchy of Charles I had little liking for the stiff-necked independence of Puritan New England, but Charles had his hands too full with Puritanism in old England to undertake any punitive measures across the broad Atlantic. English Puritans had become increasingly important leaders in Parliament's struggle against the arbitrary policies of the Stuarts. The long and bitter conflict culminated in civil war in the 1640s. Oliver Cromwell's Parliamentary army defeated the royalist forces, King Charles was beheaded in 1649, and Cromwell became the dominant figure in a Puritan Commonwealth.

Under these circumstances, the English colonies on the Cheasapeake Bay and in New England had been left to develop as they pleased. The Virginians cared little who ruled in England so long as they were left alone to grow tobacco and pursue their individual fortunes. In Maryland, however, the Protestant majority took advantage of the English Civil War to overthrow the Calverts and the Catholic ruling class and to repeal the Act of Toleration.

The New Englanders became more independent than ever. The leaders of Massachusetts Bay regarded their holy commonwealth as "a city set upon a hill," a model that England and eventually the whole world would follow. The early success of the Puritan cause in the English Civil War reinforced their faith that they were leading the way to a world organized under the will of God. With redoubled zeal to maintain a pure and undefiled commonwealth, they sought to eliminate religious error wherever it appeared. The Quakers caused the Puritans the greatest trouble. These adherents of the Religious Society of Friends represented a kind of radical Puritanism of lower-class origin that enjoined each person to follow the divine promptings of the "Inner Light" in his or her own soul. The antiauthoritarian Quakers felt impelled to bear witness to their faith in the most hostile places, and many of them came to Massachusetts Bay for this purpose. Although they were banished, they returned at the first opportunity. The authorities tried whipping, then cutting off ears, then the threat of hanging, but still the banished Quakers returned. Finally four were hanged.

But suddenly New England lost its sense of cosmic significance. The Puritan Commonwealth collapsed in England, and the Stuart monarchy returned to power in the Restoration of 1660. The new Stuart king, Charles II, restored Maryland to the Calverts and sought to strengthen his control over the other colonies, but the habit of independence had become so deeply ingrained that he encountered strong resistance. Though the New England magistrates and clergy ceased their persecutions and grudgingly began to tolerate Quakers, Anglicans, and other dissenters, they stubbornly sought other ways to maintain their autonomy and power in loyalty to the ideal of the holy commonwealth. But by now, this ideal was being weakened from within as well as from without.

PURITANISM VERSUS MODERNITY

The Chesapeake colonists had reacted to the New World environment and the lure of profits from tobacco culture by moving easily and happily toward a society of individual enterprise and liberal institutions. In New England, an equally autonomous society had developed, but here institutionalized Puritanism was a brake against the pull of the New World environment toward modernity.

In emphasizing God's sovereignty and humanity's dependence, Puritanism (only somewhat more forcibly than Protestantism generally) was profoundly antagonistic to the modern spirit of optimism and confident individualism. Yet at the same time, Puritanism gave a powerful psychological impetus to individual striving. The Puritans were "moral athletes" who believed that "right living" was the best evidence (although no guarantee) that one enjoyed God's grace. Right living included working as hard and being as successful as possible in whatever worldly calling or business God had placed one. With these convictions, it was not surprising that Puritans were highly successful in their temporal pursuits, especially under the favoring circumstances offered by the New World environment.

Despite its scarcity of fertile soil, New England prospered from the beginning. The cod fisheries developed early into a source of profit. Even greater opportunities were opened up by trade with the English colonies in the West Indies. These tropical islands devoted themselves exclusively to the production of tobacco and sugar for the European market, and New England hastened to supply them with foodstuffs, lumber, and livestock. In the process, the New Englanders built a flourishing merchant marine, and this in turn stimulated a shipbuilding industry.

By the middle of the seventeenth century, the Puritan colonies contained a growing class of successful and wealthy merchants and entrepreneurs. Such people found it increasingly difficult to put salvation ahead of worldly prosperity and to feel helplessly dependent on the grace of an omnipotent God. They did not consciously part from orthodoxy, but nevertheless there was a gradual ebbing of the intense piety that had sustained the early commonwealth. This became apparent when the children of the first generation of church members increasingly failed to give sufficient evidence of God's grace to be received into full membership themselves. Stubbornly retreating before the relentless tides of heterodoxy and secularism, the churches compromised; to retain influence, they opened their membership under a "half-way covenant" to those baptized children of church members who led exemplary lives and accepted the orthodox doctrines but who were still unable to testify to a convincing subjective experience of grace. Having thus blurred the distinction between the "elect" and all others, some churches soon went even further by permitting communion without public confession of faith.

Meanwhile, some of the more successful and less pious New Englanders began to argue that religious persecution discouraged immigration and hampered growth and prosperity. These settlers also chafed under the orthodox leadership and disapproved of the continued defiance of royal authority. Thus when the British government finally lost patience with Massachusetts Bay, it found some allies among the Puritans. In 1684, Charles II annulled the Massachusetts charter, and the following year his brother and successor, James II, placed all the New England colonies, along with recently acquired New York and New Jersey, under the Dominion of New England. All legislative bodies were suspended, and the Dominion was arbitrarily ruled by a royally appointed governor, Sir Edmund Andros, and his council. But James's equally arbitrary rule at home was arousing opposition. When the King was overthrown in the "Glorious Revolution" of 1688, a series of popular demonstrations ousted the Dominion authorities in the American colonies.

In 1691, the Massachusetts Bay authorities had to accept from the new English monarchs William and Mary a charter that seriously compromised the ideal of the holy commonwealth. The legislative power of the General Court was restored, but henceforth the governor was to be royally appointed, and property ownership replaced church membership as a qualification for voting. Under the new charter, the anticlerical elements gained increasing political influence and finally succeeded even in taking control of Harvard College.

The clergy sought to stem the ebbing of their spiritual and political authority by ever more fervent reminders of God's power and wrath and unwittingly contributed to the Salem witchcraft hysteria of the early 1690s. Before this frenzy subsided, 2 dogs and 19 innocent people died on the gallows, an old man was pressed to death by rocks, and some 150 others awaited (but would not suffer) a similar fate. Although belief in witches was almost universal throughout Christendom and although Europe was only then emerging from three centuries of witch mania, the revulsion against the Salem outrages further undermined the prestige of the orthodox leadership. In all likelihood, the New England hysteria owed more to tensions resulting from a changing social and political order than to clerical excesses, but the tragic episode was another major setback for the Puritan hierarchy. By the turn of the century, the social and political leadership of the Puritan colonies was clearly passing into the hands of the enterprising merchant class that constituted the advance guard of modernity.

FOR FURTHER READING

A. L. Rowse's *Elizabethans and America* (1949) and Samuel Eliot Morison's *The European Discovery of America* (1971) are notable introductions to English explorations. Wallace Notestein describes *The English People on the Eve of Colonization, 1603–1630* (1954), and R. C. Simmons, in *The American Colonies* (1976), provides a readable introduction to colonial history. The authoritative account of the early colonies is Charles M. Andrews's *The Colonial Period of American History* (4 vols., 1934-1938), but W. W. Abbot's *The Colonial Origins of the United States* (1975) is a good, very brief account. The early history of the Chesapeake colonies is traced in Wesley Frank Craven's *The Southern Colonies in the Seventeenth Century* (1949), and Philip L. Barbour ably recounts *The Three Worlds of Captain John Smith* (1964). Darrett B. Rutman, in *American Puritanism* (1970), and Everett Emerson, in *Puritanism in America* (1977), provide good introductions to early New England faith and practice. Both Edmund S. Morgan's *Visible Saints* (1963) and Richard Gildries's *Salem Massachusetts* (1975) help to explain the transformation of the Puritan commonwealth into a Yankee province. Other major works include Perry Miller's classic two-volume study of *The New England Mind* (1939, 1953)* and Samuel Eliot Morison's volumes on the *Builders of the Bay Colony* (1930)* and *The Intellectual Life of Colonial New England* (1956).* There is no substitute, however, for the splendid contemporary account written by Governor William Bradford, *Of Plimouth Plantation, 1620–1691* (1966).* Edmund S. Morgan has written a brief biography of Governor John Winthrop under the title of *The Puritan Dilemma* (1958);* Robert Middlekauff surveys three generations of Puritan intellectuals in *The Mathers* (1971); and John Demos examines family life in Plymouth colony in *A Little Commonwealth* (1970). Chadwick Hansen has analysed *Witchcraft at Salem* (1969), as have M. L. Starkey in *The Devil in Massachusetts* (1949) and Paul Boyer and Stephen Nissenbaum in *Salem Possessed* (1974).

---

*Available in paperback edition.

Britain's North American Empire 1660–1763

2

Before 1660, the English had little or no conception of a colonial empire. The isolated American settlements were rarely thought of, and the British government had been too distracted by political chaos to devise any systematic scheme of beneficial relations between colonies and mother country. The end of civil strife brought a new interest in America. Under the Stuart Restoration, the whole North American seaboard, from Maine south to Spanish Florida, was organized for settlement and exploitation, and an emerging theory of empire began to be embodied in a set of colonial policies.

THE PROPRIETARY COLONIES

The expansion of English settlement in North America was prompted partly by a desire to gain strategic advantages against other colonizing nations and partly by a desire to reward favored courtiers who had sided with the Stuarts during the Civil War. In 1663, Charles II granted a group of eight English noblemen the vast domain stretching south from Virginia to the borders of Spanish Florida. This grant of Carolina was modeled on the proprietary grant of Maryland to the Calverts, and the eight Lords Proprietor were given title to the soil as well as political authority over the area. Carolina already contained a small population that had spilled over from Virginia into the area of Albemarle Sound. In 1670, an expedition from the British West Indies colony of Barbados established another settlement several hundred miles down the coast at Charleston.

Anxious to encourage immigration and make profits from rising land values, the Proprietors promised religious toleration and adopted a liberal land system, including headrights. Settlers in each of the two settled sections were allowed to elect an assembly and make laws in conjunction with a governor and council appointed by the Proprietors. Coastal sandbars blocked off the northern settlements from good ocean transportation, and this area came to be populated by small landowners whose isolation and independence made them difficult to govern. The southern settlements around Charleston, on the other hand, quickly developed profitable staple productions for export, first deerskins and naval stores and then rice and indigo. Great plantations grew up on the tidal estuaries, and the planters came to constitute a tightly knit ruling class. They had their headquarters in Charleston, where they spent the malarial summer months in breeze-swept town houses.

While Carolina was a buffer against the Spanish to the south, the British were eliminating another competitor farther north: the Netherlands, the European nation most like England in the enterprising qualities of its people. Early in the sixteenth century, the Dutch merchant marine dominated the spice trade with the Far East. Though their Far Eastern ventures absorbed so much of their slender resources and work force that they had little left for the New World, the Dutch were interested in finding a more direct water passage to the spice islands through North America. It was the search for such a northwest passage that led Henry Hudson in 1609 up the river that bears his name.

The Hudson River proved to be no northwest passage, but it did lead into the heart of the fur-rich Iroquois country, and by 1624, the Dutch had established trading posts that grew into the colony of New Netherland. New Amsterdam at the tip of Manhattan Island became a cosmopolitan trading center; a scattering of Dutch farmers spread out over Long Island, Staten Island, and across the Hudson from Manhattan; along the Hudson vast manors were granted to wealthy patroons who exercised feudal authority over their tenants. Yet the preoccupation of the Dutch with the Far East, the authoritarian patroonship system, and the petty tyranny of its governors prevented New Netherland from flourishing like its English neighbors.

The English resented this Dutch intrusion into what they regarded as their domain. In 1664, Charles II granted the area between the Delaware and Connecticut rivers to his brother, the Duke of York, who ascended the throne in 1685 as James II. James promptly organized a fleet and sailed for New Amsterdam, which surrendered without a shot. He found his proprietary domain, which he renamed New York, to be larger than he desired, and he transferred the area lying between the Delaware and the Hudson to two of his favorites as the proprietary grant of New Jersey. The New Jersey proprietors later divided the grant into eastern and western sections and sold their rights to other proprietors; West Jersey eventually came into the hands of a group of Quakers who included William Penn.

William Penn was responsible for filling one of the last gaps in the continuous band of English settlement along the Atlantic coast of North America. The son of a British admiral who was a close friend of the Duke of York, Penn was converted to Quakerism and spent time in prison for his religious convictions. On missionary tours of continental Europe, he began dreaming of a refuge in America where not just Quakers but the persecuted and poor of all sects and countries could live in peace. The Stuarts had owed Penn's father a large sum of money, and this debt helped persuade Charles II to grant the son in 1681 the province of Pennsylvania, extending west and south from the Delaware River to Maryland.

Penn promptly began advertising his province, offering complete religious freedom, representative government, and the most generous land policy of any of the
American colonies. The quick response from English Quakers, the Welsh, and persecuted German sects made Pennsylvania the most rapidly growing and populous
area in British America. Penn himself went there in 1682 for several years, laid out
the city of Philadelphia between the Delaware and Schuylkill rivers, and inaugurated
a government that enforced the most humane code of laws in the world. Separate
assemblies were provided for the Philadelphia area and the area of the "Three Lower
Counties" of Delaware below Philadelphia; both had the same governor who was
appointed by the Proprietor. The preponderant Quakers continued for decades to
govern the province in the generous spirit of Penn's "Holy Experiment," and Pennsylvania became for European liberals the preeminent symbol of a tolerant and prosperous New World society.

Thus, by 1682, Great Britain's North American empire had been almost completely rounded out. Georgia, the last remaining American colony of Great Britain, was
not established until 1732. In that year, a group of English philanthropists persuaded
the British government to appoint them Trustees of the area south of the Savannah
River to be used as a refuge for imprisoned debtors and the unemployed. The leading
Trustee and first governor, James Oglethorpe, sailed with a contingent of settlers in
1733 and founded Savannah. While the benevolent Trustees tried to insure a moral
society of small farmers by limiting each settler to 50 acres of land and prohibiting
the importation of rum and slaves, these restrictions had to be relaxed to enable
Georgia to compete for settlers with its prosperous neighbor, South Carolina. However, the colony remained only a small outpost against Spanish Florida.

The failure of the Georgia restrictions was merely the final demonstration that
corporate purposes, however high-minded, could not survive among the English in the
New World. This lesson was forced upon the Virginia Company early, and the holy
commonwealth of the Puritans resisted it only a little longer. The proprietary colonies
founded after 1660 all promised religious toleration, representative government, and
cheap land—policies designed to attract settlers by guaranteeing individual rights and
opportunity. The characteristics of the English and the free environment of the New
World led irresistibly toward a society permeated with the spirit of individual enterprise.

THE NAVIGATION ACTS AND THE COLONIAL ECONOMY

While the proprietary colonies were eschewing corporate purposes in the New World,
officials in London were developing a series of policies designed to implement the
larger corporate purposes suggested by an emerging concept of British empire. These
policies were based on the theory of political economy known as *mercantilism* that
was generally accepted throughout Europe. Mercantilism presupposed that nations
were engaged in a continuous struggle for supremacy. Economic strength was valued
for the military and strategic advantages it yielded and was to be measured primarily
by the accumulation of *bullion,* or uncoined gold or silver. As nations lost gold and

silver by buying things from other nations, the most self-sufficient nations were considered the strongest and healthiest.

Colonies held an important place in mercantilist thinking. No one questioned that colonies should exist to benefit the mother country, which they could do by furnishing those non-European commodities—like sugar, tobacco, rice, molasses, cotton, indigo, naval stores, and furs—that the mother country would otherwise have to buy from a rival nation. Colonies could also contribute to the prosperity of the mother country by providing a market for its manufactures. Finally, an extensive trade with colonies would support a large merchant marine, and in a period when merchant ships and seamen were easily converted to naval purposes, this increased the fighting strength of the mother country.

These mercantilist principles were applied to the British colonies through a series of Acts of Trade and Navigation passed by Parliament between 1660 and 1672 and augmented by subsequent legislation. The Navigation Acts contained three major requirements: (1) All trade between England and her colonies must be carried in British boats. (2) All European goods imported into the colonies—with a few special exceptions—must pass through England, thus benefiting English businesses that handle these items of foreign manufacture. (3) Certain "enumerated articles" produced by the colonies (primarily tobacco at first, but later nearly every export) must be shipped first to Britain or British colonies, even if destined for ultimate resale in other European countries.

The exclusion of Dutch merchants from the Chesapeake tobacco trade and the loss of the direct European market for North American tobacco contributed to a period of stringency in Virginia and Maryland in the late seventeenth century. Yet the effects of the Navigation Acts were by no means uniformly bad for the Americans, who, at least until the end of the French and Indian War (1763), generally agreed that the advantages of the loosely administered British imperial policy outweighed its disadvantages. The British colonies were given a monopoly of the tobacco market in the mother country, and bounties were paid to colonial producers of indigo and naval stores. The exclusion of foreign-built and -owned ships from the trade between England and the colonies was a great boon to the New England shipbuilding industry and merchant marine. Indeed, the Navigation Acts were the "cement of empire," a positive force that bound colony to mother country.

Certainly by the first half of the eighteenth century, the colonial economy was in a highly prosperous state. European demand for tobacco, sugar, rice, indigo, and naval stores rose even faster than the production in the southern and West Indian colonies could expand. As these colonies grew and concentrated ever more exclusively on the profitable staples, they provided an ever greater market for wheat, flour, ground vegetables, salt fish and meat, lumber, and livestock from the middle colonies and New England. Philadelphia and Baltimore became flour milling and exporting centers, and New York exported the furs brought into Albany by the far ranging Iroquois.

New England produced few or no staples for the mother country and at first did not seem to fit the mercantilist prescriptions for usefulness. But the New Englanders quickly made themselves indispensable to the operation of the imperial economic system. Carrying provisions from the mainland to the West Indies, they picked up cargoes of sugar and then proceeded to England where they loaded their vessels with manufactured goods for America. In another variation of this "triangular trade," they brought molasses from the West Indies to New England, manufactured it into rum, took the rum to West Africa and traded it for slaves, and then carried the slaves for sale to the West Indies or the southern colonies. Similarly they carried Chesapeake tobacco or Carolina rice to England, bringing back manufactured goods. Prospering greatly from this trade and from shipbuilding and fisheries, New England also became the heaviest consumer of British manufactured goods.

As the colonial economy matured, British officials found additional regulations necessary to maintain mercantilist aims. To prevent New England rum makers from importing their supplies from non-English sources, Parliament passed the Molasses Act in 1733, levying a prohibitive duty on foreign molasses or sugar imported into British possessions. But New England evaded the duty by systematic smuggling, and the rum trade continued to flourish. To prevent colonial producers from competing with British manufacturers, Parliament passed a series of acts between 1699 and 1750 forbidding colonists to export woolen cloth and beaver hats or to expand their production of finished iron products.

The most serious economic problem of the colonies—money supply—was greatly aggravated by British restrictions that grew out of the mercantilist preoccupation with bullion for the mother country's treasury. Because gold and silver coin was the only recognized money and because the colonists could neither import British coin nor mint their own, they had to rely on Spanish coin acquired in the West Indian trade. Even this was an unstable money supply for it was constantly drained away to offset colonial trade deficits with England. Thus, there was never an adequate money supply for an intercolonial exchange of goods and services.

Under these circumstances, the colonial governments finally resorted to issuing paper money. These issues were to be redeemed within a certain period and were accompanied by new taxes designed to yield a sufficient fund to pay for redemption. But if too much paper money were issued or if redemption were delayed, the paper money depreciated in value and creditors complained. Moreover, colonial paper money was worthless in England and caused trouble to English merchants who tried to collect from American debtors. The British government first sought to remedy the situation by instructing the colonial governors to veto all but the most soundly backed paper money issues. This failing, Parliament in 1751 forbade the New England colonies, where the worst abuses occurred, to issue any further paper for payment of debts.

ADMINISTERING THE EMPIRE

While British officials were groping toward a concept of empire, administrative agencies for colonial planning and control were haphazardly evolving in the British government. Soon after the Restoration, the King's principal advisory body, the noble Privy

Council, designated a committee known as the Lords of Trade to consider colonial matters. But not until the Glorious Revolution of 1688 and the accession of William and Mary did colonial officials in London seriously consider the creation of a centralized empire of politically uniform and dependent colonies directly supervised by the imperial government. A supplementary Navigation Act in 1696 set up a system of admiralty courts in America to enforce commercial regulations and punish smugglers. This same legislation created in England a Board of Trade and Plantations (a group of bureaucratic experts on colonial matters) to advise the Privy Council through the Lords of Trade. While the Board of Trade had little direct power, it did attain considerable importance as the one agency of the British government that systematically considered all colonial matters. Gradually and over many years, the Board of Trade was able to implement some consistent policies of colonial control.

One basic aim of the Board was to convert all the corporate and proprietary colonies into royal colonies. This process, begun with Virginia in 1624 and New Hampshire in 1679, became a deliberate objective upon the accession of William and Mary. Massachusetts Bay, Plymouth, and Maine were organized into the province of Massachusetts under a royal governor in 1691. That same year the Calverts' Maryland proprietary was royalized, and in 1692, Penn's Pennsylvania and Delaware suffered the same fate. But the new policy was too weak to withstand the political influence of such powerful Proprietors: Penn's domain was restored within two years, and the Calverts finally got theirs back after being converted to Protestantism in 1715. Despite these setbacks, the colonial converters persevered, extracting East and West Jersey from their Proprietors and uniting them as the royal province of New Jersey in 1702. The Carolina Proprietors gave up South Carolina in 1719 and North Carolina ten years later, and in 1752 Georgia fell under royal control. Only the strong English respect for property and charter rights enabled Connecticut and Rhode Island to maintain their corporate status and Penn and the Calverts to regain their domains.

The British government had several means of control over a royal colony. Most important was appointment of the governor, who was sent out with a set of detailed instructions drafted by the Board of Trade and who had an absolute veto over the acts of the colonial assembly. Moreover all colonial legislation was sent to the Board of Trade for careful scrutiny, and anything objectionable could be disallowed by the Privy Council. The Privy Council was also a court of appeal from decisions of colonial courts.

Through these means, the Privy Council and the Board of Trade sought to restrain the provincial governments from acts harmful to either English merchants or the royal prerogative. But this restraint was not burdensome. Sir Robert Walpole, who became the king's chief minister in 1721, believed that it was in England's interest to let the colonies flourish without interference; his policy of "salutary neglect" continued until the 1760s.

Under these circumstances, the provinces became virtually self-governing. All had a similar form of government. Except in Rhode Island and Connecticut, which continued to elect all their officials, and in Massachusetts, where the assembly elected the council, the governor and council were appointed by the king or the Proprietor for indefinite terms. The council and an elected lower house formed a bicameral assembly. The assembly could convene only when called by the governor, who could suspend its sessions or dissolve it at will. The governor's veto could not be overridden. But whatever the governor's legal authority, he had practical difficulties in resisting the assembly's will. Lax imperial administration, either through design or neglect, permitted colonial assemblies gradually to exercise powers and privileges that in practice, though not by law, shifted the center of colonial control from the executive to themselves. Although intended to be dependent assemblies, they became, in effect, little Houses of Commons and claimed broad Parliamentary authority over local affairs. They particularly insisted on the well established English principle that citizens could be taxed only by consent of their representatives. The governors were paid by the colonies, and an assembly's refusal to levy taxes or appropriate funds for the governor's salary was a powerful political weapon.

Disputes between governors and assemblies were legion. Often incompetent and invariably caught between the conflicting demands of the London officials and the local assemblies, the governors could satisfy neither group. The ablest among them achieved some success only through the astute distribution of favors and by horsetrading with leaders of the assembly. At times, a governor could fill the council with influential provincials who would side with him against the lower house. But except in the few areas of special concern to the Privy Council, the assemblies usually had their way.

As the decades wore on, Americans increasingly assumed that they had an inalienable right to self-government through their assemblies. The recurrent disputes with the governors taught them political sophistication and political skills that were to be invaluable when this right was challenged. Serious conflict with Crown and Parliament was to be avoided only so long as imperial authorities did not demand that colonial practices coincide with imperial policies.

THE ANGLO-FRENCH WARS

While the English colonies were growing strong and prosperous along the eastern seacoast of North America, the French were developing a different kind of empire to the north and inland. In 1608, one year after the founding of Virginia, Samuel de Champlain began a French settlement at Quebec on the St. Lawrence River. For years Champlain devoted himself to exploring the interior far up the St. Lawrence and into the Great Lakes country and to developing a flourishing fur trade with the Algonquin and Huron Indians of the region. The French fur traders were soon joined by a band of dauntless Jesuit missionaries who ranged far and wide over the wilderness of the north country preaching Christianity to the Indians. By the middle of the seventeenth century, there was a narrow zone of agricultural settlement along the St. Lawrence where humble French *habitants* worked peasant-style on the manorial grants of a rather down-at-the-heels class of feudal *seigneurs*.

Despite the fewer numbers of the French in America, their vigorous exploration and the good relations they had achieved with their Indian allies made them a formidable barrier to English westward expansion. Only the powerful Iroquois confederation in upper New York, hostile to the French-oriented Huron and Algonquin tribes, shielded Dutch New Netherland and the English colonies from contact with the French. But after the rise of Louis XIV in the 1660s, the French pushed their Canadian enterprise more vigorously and assisted their Indian allies in making war on the Iroquois. Meanwhile Louis sought to make France the dominant power in Europe as well as to expand her colonial empire in America and other parts of the world. England joined a series of alliances designed to block French ambitions, and the result was a series of four great wars (1689–1763) fought mainly in Europe but also between the French and English in America.

In the first three encounters—King William's War, 1689–1697; Queen Anne's War, 1702–1713; King George's War, 1744–1748—the French and their Indian allies raided the New England and New York frontiers. Beginning with Queen Anne's War, the Spanish were allied with the French, so that there was skirmishing along the southern as well as northern British frontier. The only American territorial change that resulted from the first three wars was the transfer of Nova Scotia, Newfoundland, and the Hudson Bay country in the far north from France to England in 1713.

Meanwhile, during the intervals of peace, the French moved into the Mississippi Valley behind the English settlements. Around 1700, they set up posts in the Illinois country on the northern Mississippi and established themselves at Biloxi and Mobile on the Gulf Coast near the great river's mouth. New Orleans was founded as the capital of French Louisiana in 1718.

The final phase of the conflict between Britain and France in North America was the French and Indian War (known in Europe as the Seven Years' War). This conflict began when a group of Virginians sent agents across the Appalachians and into the upper Ohio Valley for the purpose of Indian trade and land speculation. The French responded by building a chain of small forts on the upper Ohio. Young George Washington, sent out in command of a force of Virginia militia in 1754, arrived barely too late to prevent construction of Fort Duquesne at the forks of the Ohio on the future site of Pittsburgh. He was driven off by the French, and the war began—though it was not officially declared for two more years.

All the major European powers were quickly drawn into the fighting. At first things went badly for the British in America and elsewhere. General James Braddock's army was routed within a few miles of Fort Duquesne, throwing the whole frontier open to several years of pounding by the French and Indians. The British seemed to have no overall strategy, and the colonies could not be persuaded to contribute very loyally or enthusiastically to the war effort. Delegates from eight of the colonies, meeting at Albany in 1754, approved Benjamin Franklin's farsighted plan for intercolonial defense and unity, but this early plan for voluntary union failed to win the support of either the crown or the colonial assemblies. (Its implications, however, were not lost on a later generation of rebels who, during the imperial crisis that followed the war with France, would again entertain plans for a closer union.)

The situation changed dramatically in 1757 when the vigorous William Pitt assumed direction of the British war effort. Making the conquest of Canada his paramount aim, Pitt organized a series of offensives that culminated in the capture of Quebec by General James Wolfe in 1759. By the time the war ended in Europe, the British were victorious everywhere. In the Peace of Paris (1763), Britain gained French Canada and Spanish Florida, as well as acquisitions in India and elsewhere. Louisiana was transferred from France to Spain.

No one had more reason to rejoice than the British Americans. Suddenly freed from the greatest threat to their security, they now looked west upon an unbounded arena of opportunity lying open to their enterprise. It did not yet occur to them that their new security and confidence might weaken their attachment to the mother country whose emergence as the world's most powerful nation they were now so loyally celebrating.

FOR FURTHER READING

The final volume of Charles M. Andrews's *The Colonial Period of American History* (4 vols., 1934–1938)*, Oliver M. Dickerson's, *The Navigation Acts and the American Revolution* (1951), and Michael Kammen's *Empire and Interest* (1970) are significant analyses of British policy and administration. Jack P. Greene has studied the struggles between colonial governors and assemblies in *The Quest for Power: The Lower House of Assembly in the Southern Royal Colonies, 1689–1776* (1965), and in *"Unite or Die"* (1971), Harry M. Ward has analyzed intercolonial relations from 1690 to 1763. The 13 volumes in *History of the American Colonies* series, edited by Milton M. Klein and Jacob E. Cooke, are designed for both the serious student and the layperson. See, for example, Michael Kammen's *Colonial New York* (1975), and Joseph E. Illick's *Colonial Pennsylvania* (1976). *The Middle Colonies* (1938) are described by Thomas J. Wertenbaker. Max Sevelle's *Empires to Nations* (1974) is a significant comparative analysis of European expansion and the development of eighteenth-century "Euroamerican" societies. Catherine O. Peare has written a good biography of *William Penn* (1957)*; Frederick B. Tolles deals with the changing role of Philadelphia's Quaker merchants in *Meeting House and Counting House* (1948).* Francis Parkman's *France and England in America* (8 vols., 1851–1892)* is still the classic account of the development of French Canada and the great struggle for empire in North America. The final phase of that struggle and the period after the French and Indian War are delineated authoritatively in Lawrence H. Gipson's *The British Empire before the American Revolution* (15 vols., 1936–1970).

---

*Available in paperback edition.

A New Society

3

Within the loose institutional framework of Britain's North American empire, a distinctly new kind of society had been taking shape. Inside this new society, the typical European was being subtly altered. "What then is the American, this new man?" the French immigrant Crèvecoeur was asking by the 1770s.

THE AMERICANS

Crèvecoeur's American, in the first place, belonged to a numerous and rapidly multiplying people. The American population grew from about a quarter of a million in 1700 to two-and-a-half million by 1775. The majority of these Americans were of English origin. But English immigration slowed in the latter part of the seventeenth century, and the continuing predominance of English stock owed much to the fecundity of Anglo-American parents.

The spectacular population increase of the eighteenth century was also based on a quickening of non-English immigration. Since the founding of Pennsylvania in the 1680s, Penn's advertising attracted a steadily mounting flow of impoverished peasants from the war-ravaged states of the German Rhineland. By the 1770s there were around 200,000 industrious German farmers in the North American colonies, and in Pennsylvania they constituted a third of the population.

An even larger tide of immigration began flowing in the first decades of the eighteenth century from Ulster in northern Ireland. These Protestants of Scottish origin, called Scotch-Irish by their descendants to distinguish them from the indigenous Catholic population of the rest of Ireland, had been transplanted to Ulster in the early seventeenth century as part of the English government's campaign to subdue Ireland. By the beginning of the eighteenth century, they were suffering from English restrictions on Irish trade and industry, increasing farm rents, and various civil disabilities against their staunch Presbyterianism. Under these circumstances, Scotch-Irish by the thousands crossed the Atlantic. Concentrated along the frontier as pioneer farmers and aggressive Indian fighters, they made up one-twelfth of the entire population by the 1770s.

Smaller groups from Europe included the Dutch and the French Huguenots. New Netherland had 8,000 Dutch residents at the time of its transfer to English control, and their descendants remained a substantial segment of New York's population. The Huguenots, or French Protestants, began leaving France when the revocation of the Edict of Nantes in 1685 ended religious toleration in that predominantly Catholic country. They did not come to America in large numbers, but their enterprising qualities made many of them successful and prominent. Probably the largest number came to South Carolina, where they were quickly assimilated to Anglicanism and emerged as a major element of the mercantile-planting elite.

Whether English or non-English, the European immigrants of the eighteenth century came mainly from the lower or middling orders of Old World society. Probably half or more of the settlers in the middle colonies crossed the Atlantic as indentured servants. Some were actually kidnapped and sold to America by dealers in human merchandise. Thousands more—orphans, pauper children, and prisoners—were sent abroad by public authorities. Not a few of them chose emigration as a welcome alternative to long imprisonment or execution for minor offenses. Some 40,000 English convicts were transported to North America in the six decades before the Revolution, and in Maryland, convicts made up the bulk of the servant class.

But whatever their legal status, most Europeans who embarked on the long voyage to America were the younger and more vigorous people from their home communities. Once free of indenture, even the lowliest among them was free to rise. Colonel John Lamb, a wealthy merchant and prominent political leader in New York in the 1770s, was the son of a man who had been taken from the gallows in England and transported to America, where he established himself as a solid citizen and laid the basis for his son's later success.

The African slaves, however, came most unwillingly and had no chance to rise, whatever their vigor or ability. By the late seventeenth century, the very prosperity of the European immigrants was creating a growing demand for cheap and easily exploited labor. Yankee and European ship captains hastened to supply this demand. Slavery became established in all the colonies, but the readiest market for the black men and women who survived the horrors of the middle passage from Africa or the West Indies was found in the southern states. There large gangs of Africans could be employed efficiently in the exhausting but routine plantation tasks of tobacco, rice, and indigo culture. By the eve of the Revolution, there were about 600,000 blacks in British North America. In South Carolina they comprised nearly half of the population; in Virginia, fully 40 percent.

AMERICAN ENVIRONMENTS: NEW TOWNS AND THE OLD WEST

The acceleration of immigration and economic activity in the eighteenth century created a diversified society in the American colonies. Towns began to play an increasingly important role in colonial life. The early upsurge of commercial activity in New England was accompanied by a trend toward urbanization as Boston, Newport, and Salem became flourishing trading centers. Philadelphia and New York emerged later as major urban centers but eventually outstripped their predecessors. By the 1770s, Philadelphia's population of nearly 40,000 made it the second largest city in the British empire. New York was the second biggest city of British North America followed by Boston, Charleston, and Newport, the last having a population of around 7,000. The Chesapeake tobacco country, where oceangoing ships could sail directly up to the individual planter's wharf for trade, was the only area that did not develop a major urban center.

Though the colonial towns never contained more than a tenth of the total population, they exercised great influence. Here were published the newspapers, pamphlets, and almanacs that were almost the only means of general communication in the colonies. Here flourished the artisan class of shoemakers, weavers, hatters, cabinet-makers, and adepts of countless other trades who satisfied most of the colonists' needs. Here sat the principal courts, and here the lawyers emerged as an influential professional group. The towns in short became the focal points of the economic, intellectual, and political life of the colonies.

While towns were developing along the coast, the pressure of the population increase was forcing a line of settlement far inland. In this hinterland or "Old West," a new kind of society took shape by the middle of the eighteenth century. The distinguishing characteristic of this settlement was that it lay beyond the "fall line," the point where the rivers descended over rapids into the level coastal plain and became navigable. In the absence of good roads or other transportation facilities, the Old West lay too far inland to produce goods for market and thus became an area of pioneer subsistence farming, isolated from the coastal settlements and the Atlantic world. Nevertheless, to those who peopled it, the Old West seemed an agrarian paradise where the ease of acquiring farms of their own promised a degree of security, well-being, and independence that would have been unthinkable in the land-hungry Europe they had left behind.

New England's Old West included the northern and western hill towns and lay away from the coast and the deep inland extension of coastal society along the navigable Connecticut River. The old Puritan pattern of town planting broke down in New England as the provincial governments began disposing of blocks of new towns to land speculators who in turn sold farms to actual settlers.

South of New England, New York's Hudson River was a magnificent highway north into the interior. The Mohawk River, flowing east from the Great Lakes country into the Hudson at Albany, afforded the colonies their only easy avenue through the Appalachian mountains to the Ohio and Mississippi valleys. But fur-trading interests blocked settlement along the Mohawk until the early eighteenth century when the British government sponsored the resettlement of Germans above Albany.

The main current of German settlement flowed through Philadelphia and on inland to fill the broad and fertile lower valley of the Susquehanna. Beyond the Susquehanna, it washed up against the series of Appalachian ridges that run from the northeast through central Pennsylvania. Diverted down the valleys to the southwest, the Germans settled interior Maryland and crossed the Potomac into Virginia. Here some drifted southeast of the first great Appalachian range, the Blue Ridge, into the rolling Virginia Piedmont, but the main current moved on southwest up the Shenandoah Valley behind the Blue Ridge. By the 1750s, some Germans were pushing southeast from the upper Shenandoah across the Blue Ridge and down into the North Carolina Piedmont.

The German migration was followed and overlapped by the migration of the more aggressive Scotch-Irish. The Scotch-Irish filled in the gaps left by German settlements and then surged beyond them to the west and south. In Pennsylvania these hardy Indian fighters crossed ridge after ridge and filled valley after valley until by the 1770s they were on the waters of the Ohio occupying the area around Pittsburgh. Farther south, in the Carolinas, the Scotch-Irish pushed the Piedmont frontier up against the mountains; while in Virginia they pressed southwest through the mountain valleys toward the headwaters of the Tennessee River.

COLONIAL SOCIETY

The people of the Old West—the Yankee farmers of the New England hill towns, the Germans on the Mohawk, and the Germans and Scotch-Irish in the great curve southwest against the Appalachians from the Susquehanna to Georgia—soon complained of grievances against the older colonial settlements along the coast. The older areas continued to dominate the provincial governments by refusing to give the new settlements the representation to which their population entitled them. In Pennsylvania, the three oldest counties had only one-third of the province's population but elected two-thirds of the assemblymen. The frontier people complained that unrepresentative, Quaker-dominated assemblies were indifferent to such western problems as the need for an aggressive policy against the Indians. The most extreme case of indifference to frontier needs occurred in South Carolina where the new settlements were separated from the old coastal planting society by a wide belt of sandhills. Though the up-country people in the new settlements came to be a majority of the free population, the low-country people not only refused them any representatives whatever in the assembly, but also neglected to provide them with courts or local law-enforcement officers.

Not remarkably, the failure to give representation or consideration to the rapidly growing frontier settlements led to sporadic tensions and occasional outbreaks of violence. As early as 1676, Nathaniel Bacon led an armed rebellion in Virginia against the governor, Sir William Berkeley, who had ruled the province autocratically for 25 years in alliance with the wealthiest planters. Similar tensions among New Yorkers figured in Jacob Leisler's rebellion at the time of the Glorious Revolution. Great landlords periodically faced mob violence from their tenants in New York, New Jersey, and elsewhere. There was a bitter struggle between debtor and creditor interests in Massachusetts over an inflationary Land Bank scheme in the 1740s. In 1764, the Paxton Boys, an armed mob of frontier men, marched on Philadelphia in anger at the pacific Indian policy of the eastern-dominated Pennsylvania assembly. The most spectacular of these outbreaks occurred in North Carolina where the oppressive policies of the local ruling class finally goaded the people of the interior into systematic mobbing of the courts. The governor had to march an army against the insurgents, or the Regulators, as they called themselves, and in a ragged engagement at Alamance in 1771 dispersed them.

The tension between the old and new settlements was only a phase of a more general tension that accompanied the emergence of somewhat sharper class distinctions in the eighteenth century. The English who came to the New World in the seventeenth century had brought with them the traditional European notion that people should defer to their betters in a society of ranks and orders. Old World distinctions, however, made little sense in a fluid society of mobile individuals, and, consequently, class and property qualifications for voting were almost unknown in the early assemblies. Yet the very atmosphere of equal opportunity that eroded Old World notions made for new forms of inequality. In an environment of growing wealth and expanding opportunities, social and economic disparities widened as some inevitably became more successful than others. Eventually, a disproportionate share of wealth from trade and commercial farming fell into the hands of the most enterprising New England merchants and southern planters. As a result, the relatively simple society of roughly equal yeomen in the seventeenth century became a more highly stratified and differentiated society in the eighteenth.

This process of stratification was abetted by the British government, which actively encouraged the growth and political influence of a colonial elite. After the Glorious Revolution London authorities replaced religious qualifications for voting with a property qualification in the new Massachusetts charter, and property qualifications became general in the colonies. Usually a voter had to be a "freeholder," the owner of 50 acres or a town lot. Royal governors generally sought to secure the support of the wealthiest colonials by bestowing important appointments and other favors on them. The provincial councils became the political strongholds of the very rich, while the assemblies were usually controlled by the merely well-to-do. Thus the eighteenth-century provincial governments were generally dominated by a local ruling class, the wealthiest members of which sometimes sided with the governors in disputes with the assemblies.

Yet too much can be made of socioeconomic conflict in eighteenth-century America. Unquestionably, this was a "deferential society." Marked by extremes in standards and styles of life, fundamentally elitist in character, it was governed by men of privilege whose influence was usually, though not invariably, derived from wealth and property. Prerevolutionary America compared very favorably to older and more highly structured contemporary Europe. Although hardly democratic by twentieth-century standards, this highly mobile New World society offered remarkably broad economic opportunities, relatively little poverty, and much class fluidity. Except for the anomaly of slavery and pervasive restrictions on the rights enjoyed by women, there was no real social stratification in the Old World sense. Even the property restriction on suffrage was hardly restrictive in a society of extensive land ownership.

In some colonies, where the franchise was open to a vast majority of free male adults, there is evidence to suggest that suffrage was more widespread than the willingness to use it. To be sure, this remarkable breadth of franchise owed much to the availability of inexpensive land and very little to either constitutional theories or modern democratic notions. Even in a society that readily acquiesced to government by aristocrats, colonial rulers could not entirely ignore the needs and aspirations of the general population. Certainly, few historians would argue today that class tension was a principal, or even an important, cause of the Revolution. By the 1760s and 1770s, most scholars now agree, the Americans had already made significant progress toward a more representative social and political order for men. It would be some two centuries, however, before American women won even token admission to this circle of privilege.

THE ENLIGHTENMENT

By the eighteenth century, the Atlantic world's advance into modernity had produced a new climate of thought known as the Enlightenment. The people of this optimistic age believed that a benevolent Creator had laid down certain "natural laws" regulating all phenomena for the purpose of producing human happiness. Human beings, it was believed, had been endowed by the Creator with powers of observation and reasoning that would enable them to understand and live by these natural laws and thus achieve happiness.

This faith of the Enlightenment received a strong impetus from Sir Isaac Newton's description of the physical world as a harmonious system of bodies regulated by simple natural laws (*Principia Mathematica,* 1687). Another English thinker, John Locke, persuasively applied the Newtonian kind of analysis to the moral and political spheres. In *An Essay Concerning Human Understanding* (1690), Locke analyzed the processes of observation and reasoning that enabled human beings to understand what kinds of behavior were conducive to happiness or, in other words, consistent with the Creator's natural laws for human behavior. Following Locke, thinkers of the Enlightenment exalted "reason" as the faculty that could lead humanity toward virtue, happiness, and perfection. Analyzing politics (*Two Treatises on Government,* 1689), Locke maintained that natural law ordained a government that rested on the consent of the governed and that respected the inherent "natural rights" of all.

Enlightenment thought was the theoretical expression of the emerging spirit of modernity. Though British North America was too young and too busy a society to give much attention to metaphysical speculation, its people, at the forefront of the movement into modernity, gladly embraced Lockean ideas as explaining what already seemed to them self-evident. Many of the better educated drifted gradually and often unconsciously from the tenets of orthodox Christianity toward *Deism,* the worship of a wise and kindly but impersonal Creator who is best served by right living.

The influence of Enlightenment thought can be seen everywhere in eighteenth-century American life. The aesthetic principles of rational simplicity, order, and balance were exemplified in the "colonial" or "Georgian" architecture of the period. American writers imitated the simple elegance of the English authors Addison and Steele and sought to persuade their readers by rational argument.

The Enlightenment gave a great impetus to the maturing cultural and intellectual life of the colonies. Beginning with the Boston *News-Letter* (1704), newspapers sprang up everywhere; by 1765 there were 25, and every colony except Delaware and New Jersey had at least one. A hungry market developed for pamphlets on every conceivable topic. Artisans organized clubs for discussion and intellectual self-improvement. Booksellers flourished, many wealthier persons developed fine private libraries, and, following the example of an enterprise launched by Benjamin Franklin in Philadelphia, subscription libraries were established in most of the towns.

By placing such a high value on intellect, the Enlightenment reinforced the religious impulse toward higher education. This combination of influences resulted in the creation of nine colleges by the 1770s. Harvard (1636) was joined by Virginia's William and Mary (1693), Connecticut's Yale (1701), and the Philadelphia Academy, which was originally founded as a secondary school by Benjamin Franklin and became in the 1750s the most modern and secular of the colonial colleges. Five other new colleges owed their founding most immediately to a great religious movement that seemed at first to oppose the spirit of the Enlightenment and modernity.

THE GREAT AWAKENING

The drift toward modernity had steadily eroded the seventeenth-century piety that the settlers had brought to all the early colonies and of which Puritanism was merely the most intense form. Religious observances were as strictly enforced in early Anglican Virginia as in New England, but the prosperity from tobacco soon converted Anglicanism into a bland and undemanding adornment of Virginia's genial country life. It was this kind of Anglicanism that became the established or official religion, supported by public taxation, in all the southern colonies and the three lower counties of New York. Anglican religious zeal was apparent only where the missionaries sent out by England's Society for the Propagation of the Gospel were at work and in New England where the Anglicans were an unpopular minority. Perhaps the most conspicuous example of the erosion of piety in the New World was the quick conversion of the Huguenots, those French counterparts of the Puritans, to the polite Anglicanism of the South Carolina planter class. Even the Pennsylvania Quakers, growing wealthy as a result of godly industry, frugality, and honesty, arrived at a point where the counting house seemed to overshadow the meeting house.

The decline of piety can be clearly traced among the theologically sophisticated and articulate Puritan Congregationalists of New England. By the end of the seventeenth century, the Reverend Cotton Mather, the last great defender of the orthodox order, was talking more about the necessity of right living in this world than about humanity's dependence on God for salvation in the next. The wealthy Boston merchants who founded the Brattle Street Church in 1699 did not require an account of conversion for full membership and chose a minister who preached a "free and catholic" version of Christianity emphasizing morality over piety. As the eighteenth century advanced, the most influential ministers in Boston, Charles Chauncy and Jonathan Mayhew, drifted into the "Arminian" heresy, which diminished human dependence on God by regarding humans as capable of contributing to their own salvation by right living.

But a people conditioned to piety did not adjust easily to the clear, rather bland atmosphere of the dawning Enlightenment. The embers of the old intense faith still smoldered and, in the 1730s and 1740s, were fanned into a bright blaze of religious enthusiasm that burned up and down the length and breadth of the colonies. This American Great Awakening was only part of a general movement in the Protestant world including such parallel phenomena as an upsurge of Pietism in Germany and the Wesleyan revival in England. Beginning as an effort to reassert the earlier extreme piety against the rationalism and optimism of the Enlightenment, these awakenings appealed frankly to the emotions and ended by unconsciously accommodating Christianity to the modern spirit.

The American Great Awakening began in different places. As early as the 1720s, the Reverend Theodore J. Frelinghuysen touched off emotional revivals of religious feeling among the Germans in New Jersey's Raritan Valley. Nearby a group of ardent Presbyterian ministers began trying to stimulate intense religious feeling in place of the cold formalism of Calvinist orthodoxy. And at Northampton, Massachusetts in 1734, a gifted Congregationalist minister, Jonathan Edwards, stirred up a series of revivals by his powerful appeals to the religious emotions. All of these streams merged into a general revival movement throughout the colonies when England's great evangelist George Whitefield made the first of his American tours in 1739–1740.

The Great Awakening was emotional, popular, and anti-intellectual. The revivalists were often poorly educated, and their fervent exhortations sometimes touched off extravagant reactions—barking, having the "jerks," falling down—by their audiences. Revivalists maintained that a heart open to the divine spirit was more important than a highly trained intellect, and they stirred up much strife by accusing conservative, educated clergy of spiritual coldness. People responded with enthusiasm, and the more popular Protestant denominations—the Baptists, the "New Light" Presbyterians, and later the Methodists—grew enormously as a refreshing religious pluralism swept across the colonies. In appealing for an emotional response to God's grace, the revival preachers often unconsciously suggested that salvation was available to all and that the individual played an important part in the process. The Methodists came to espouse these Arminian (and modern) heresies quite consciously.

Despite its anti-intellectual character, the Great Awakening prompted the establishment of three colonial colleges designed to train ministers for revivalist wings of the sponsoring denominations: the Presbyterians' College of New Jersey (Princeton, 1746), the Baptists' College of Rhode Island (Brown, 1764), and the Dutch Reformed Rutgers (1766). Two other colonial colleges were founded under nonrevivalist church auspices: Anglican King's College in New York (Columbia, 1754) and Congregationalist Dartmouth (1769), which began as an Indian school in New Hampshire. For all of its anti-intellectualism, this eighteenth-century resurgence of religious enthusiasm contributed mightily to the nation's educational development.

The Awakening had as one of its major leaders the most gifted intellectual in colonial America, Jonathan Edwards. This brilliant Congregationalist minister burned with a personal sense of God's majesty and power that would have been exceptional even among the first-generation Puritans. But he also had an understanding of the intellectual implications of Newtonian-Lockean thought that was equaled by few if any of his generation in either Europe or America. In a series of treatises, he impressively utilized the most advanced thought of his day to reconstruct the old Puritan vision of God. In a very real sense, this remarkable theologian was a transitional figure, a bridge between two ages, who sought to recast and modernize Puritanism in the light of eighteenth-century rationalism.

Few in Edwards's generation really understood what he was trying to do. His fellow revivalists gladly adopted his advanced principles of human psychology, which recognized the importance and legitimacy of emotion. But most Americans had moved too far into modernity to share, even in seasons of religious exaltation, his vision of the beauty and fitness of God's awful sovereignty and the sinner's helpless dependence on the miracle of divine grace.

"THIS NEW MAN"

Crèvecoeur's "new man," then, was a product of New World opportunity, whether the opportunity to acquire a farm of one's own in the Old West, to grow rich planting tobacco, to trade with the West Indies, or to achieve dignity and independence as an artisan in one of the growing colonial towns. According to Crèvecour, Americans welcomed the optimistic tendencies of Enlightenment thought as something their New World experience had made self-evident. In politics, they stoutly defended the English tradition of individual rights and aspired to control the representative institutions of provincial government in the interest of their group. In religion, they tended consciously toward Deism or Arminianism if educated; otherwise they reveled in the emotionalism of the Great Awakening while moving less consciously away from the orthodox piety of their ancestors.

"The American, this new man" takes a fully developed form in the *Autobiography* of Benjamin Franklin. This son of a Boston candlemaker sat in Cotton Mather's congregation as a boy, assimilated Enlightenment thought while working on his brother's newspaper and while sowing wild oats in London, and returned to win wealth and prestige as a Philadelphia printer while still in his forties. Retiring from business, this wise, humane, and practical man spent the rest of his life in scientific experiments that explained the nature of electricity, in developing a host of practical devices and projects for the benefit and improvement of his fellow citizens, and in public service culminating with attendance at the birth of a new nation.

The fascination of Franklin lies largely in the fact that he showed to perfection so many traits that were characteristic of his compatriots. "*He* is an American," wrote Crèvecoeur, "who, leaving behind him all his ancient prejudices and manners, receives new ones from the new mode of life he has embraced, the new government he obeys, and the new rank he holds. . . . Here the rewards of his industry follow with equal steps the progress of his labor. . . . Here religion demands but little of him. . . . The American is a new man, who acts upon new principles; he must therefore entertain new ideas, and form new opinions. From involuntary idleness, servile dependence, penury, and useless labor, he has passed to toils of a different nature, rewarded by ample subsistence.—This is an American."

FOR FURTHER READING

J. Hector St. John de Crèvecoeur recorded his impressions of American life in the eighteenth century in *Letters from an American Farmer* (1782).* European immigrants to America in the colonial period are described in Marcus Lee Hansen's *The Atlantic Migration, 1607–1860* (1940)*, while Abbott Emerson Smith's *Colonists in Bondage* (1947) deals with indentured servants. Herbert S. Klein's *The Middle Passage* (1978) offers a comparative history of the Atlantic slave trade. The development of slavery and of white attitudes toward blacks in America are analyzed in Winthrop D. Jordan's *White over Black: American Attitudes toward the Negro, 1550–1812* (1968). Daniel J. Boorstin presents a suggestive interpretation of the unique institutions and attitudes that emerged in the New World environment in *The Americans: The Colonial Experience* (1958).* The development of colonial towns is described in Carl Bridenbaugh's *Cities in the Wilderness, 1625–1742* (1938),* while Edward M. Cook, Jr., *The Fathers of Towns* (1976), examines community leadership in eighteenth-century New England. The best introduction to the Old West, as well as to Frederick Jackson Turner's famous "frontier thesis," is the first three chapters of his volume of collected essays, *The Frontier in American History* (1920).* The Old West of the southern colonies is described, along with the tidewater societies of Virginia and South Carolina, in Carl Bridenbaugh's *Myths and Realities: Societies of the Colonial South* (1952)*; Wilcomb Washburn's *The Governor and the Rebel* (1957) is a recent critical interpretation of Bacon's rebellion. Richard M. Brown examines the *South Carolina Regulators* (1963). Leonard W. Labaree's *Conservatism in Early American History* (1948)* traces the growing influence of the upper classes in colonial politics, while Carl Bridenbaugh deals with the mechanic classes of the towns in *The Colonial Craftsman* (1950). Jackson T. Main's *Social Structure of Revolutionary America* (1965) and Robert E. Brown's *Middle-Class Democracy and the Revolution in Massachusetts* (1955) are major revisionist studies of colonial social, economic, and political developments. The intellectual and theological transformation of New England Congregationalism may be followed in Conrad Wright's *The Beginnings of Unitarianism in America* (1955)*. Alan Heimert has written an arresting interpretation of

---

*Available in paperback edition.

Religion and the American Mind: From the Great Awakening to the Revolution (1966), and Henry May examines the nature, development, and impact of *The Enlightenment in America* (1976). Edward H. Davidson's *Jonathan Edwards* (1968) is a brief biography, and Perry Miller's *Jonathan Edwards* (1949)* is a brilliant interpretation. James West Davidson's *The Logic of Millennial Thought* (1972) is a challenging essay on early American eschatological thought. Carl Van Doren has written the best biography of *Benjamin Franklin* (1941),* but a sense of Franklin's quality is best derived from his own fascinating *Autobiography* (many editions).*

1. EVENTS LEADING TO THE REVOLUTION

British Actions		*American Actions*
Revenue (Sugar) Act—laying duties for revenue.	1764	
Stamp Act—revenue stamps.	1765	Mob action. Nonimportation agreements.
Repeal of Stamp Act. Declaratory Act—asserting right of Parliament to legislate for colonies in all respects.	1766	Nonimportation suspended.
Townshend duties—revenue duties on various articles.	1767	Mob action. Nonimportation agreements.
Repeal of Townshend duties, except duty on tea.	1770	Boston Massacre. Suspension of nonimportation.
	1772	Committees of correspondence organized.
Tea Act—giving East India Co. monopoly on colonial tea trade.	1773	Mob action. Boston Tea Party.
Intolerable acts: 1) closing port of Boston. 2) restricting self-government in Massachusetts. 3) allowing royal officers to be tried in England. 4) allowing royal troops to requisition private buildings for quarters. Quebec Act—continuing nonrepresentative government in Quebec, tolerating Roman Catholicism in Quebec, and incorporating Ohio Valley in Quebec.	1774	First Continental Congress 1) rejects Galloway's plan of union. 2) adopts Continental Association, establishing committees of safety to enforce commercial nonintercourse with England. 3) encourages Massachusetts to establish revolutionary government and prepare for military defense.
Lexington-Concord—British troops skirmish with Massachusetts militiamen.	1775	Committees of safety seize control. Second Continental Congress— appoints Washington to command continental army at Boston.

Toward Revolution
1763–1775

4

At the close of the French and Indian War in 1763, the inhabitants of British North America considered themselves patriotic and loyal British subjects. Under British rule, the colonies had become flourishing and prosperous societies, affording to ordinary individuals well-being and opportunities without parallel in Europe and perhaps anywhere in previous human history. The British navigation laws had, by and large, fostered colonial prosperity; British fleets and armies had defended colonials against their Spanish, French, and Indian enemies; and a benevolent (or careless) home government had allowed them to develop representative institutions and to regulate their domestic affairs with only minor interference. Nourished on the British Whig tradition stemming from the Glorious Revolution of 1688, the American colonists thought of their political rights and liberties as British rights and liberties.

Yet within 12 years, these same loyal British subjects were at war with the mother country. Although their relations with Britain until 1763 were relatively harmonious, the crisis of the next dozen years taught them that they had long since developed a deep attachment to the society they were creating in the colonies. Somewhat to their own surprise they learned that they really valued the British connection only as far as, and as long as, it was compatible with their desire to preserve and perfect their free and semiautonomous American society. In one of history's most notorious instances of bad timing, British officials had chosen to tighten the lax administration of the Empire at the very moment when American colonials were beginning to feel their own separate identity. Colonial cries of imperial despotism and oppression were doubtless unwarranted, but the stiffening of British policy was at best untimely. The result was not only a deepening hostility to Great Britain, but a heightened sense of common purpose that would turn colonists into Americans.

THE NEW IMPERIAL POLICY

When Britain emerged victorious from the great Anglo-French wars, there were a number of conditions that supported a new and more vigorous imperial policy. First,

King George III, enthroned in 1760, was an ambitious and conscientious monarch who desired to play a larger role in governmental affairs than had his predecessors. Through manipulation of royal patronage and maneuvering of Parliamentary elections he tried to reestablish the royal influence that earlier monarchs had exercised by right. Unfortunately, the King and his ministers proved to be less flexible and astute in dealing with the colonists than their easygoing predecessors had been. Yet probably any British ministry would have sought to strengthen the imperial system at this time. During the war, the colonists had irritated the British by their reluctance to furnish troops, supplies, and money and in too many cases had actually prospered by trading with the enemy. Moreover, the Empire had been greatly enlarged, and more efficient regulation seemed necessary everywhere if the colonial territories were to serve their purpose of benefiting the mother country.

The most pressing immediate problem was that of revenue to pay off the crushing debt incurred during the war and to support the increased costs of defending and administering the enlarged empire. Compared with English landowners, the colonists were virtually untaxed, and in London it seemed only fair that they should bear some of the heavy tax burden required for the defense of American territory.

The new imperial policy that grew out of these conditions was inaugurated by the ministry of George Grenville in the years 1763–1765. A permanent military force was established in the American colonies, the control over Indian relations was transferred from the colonial governments to imperial officials, settlement on the western frontier was restricted and placed under imperial regulation, and the colonial assemblies were forbidden to issue paper money. Particularly important was the Revenue Act of 1764 (often called the Sugar Act) that for the first time avowedly levied import duties for revenue rather than regulation of trade and provided machinery that insured that the duties would really be collected.

Most disturbing was the duty on molasses from the French West Indies. For years New England merchants had been evading an earlier duty levied under the Molasses Act of 1733 in order to import molasses for manufacture of rum. The new molasses duty was half of the old, but it was rigorously enforced, and the effect was to cripple the flourishing commerce of New England. Shocked by the sudden vigor of imperial control after decades of salutary neglect, the colonists quickly took the position that they could not rightfully be taxed except by their own representatives.

Either underestimating the strength of colonial opposition or not caring how strong it was, Grenville pushed through Parliament in 1765 the even more provocative Stamp Act. This measure required the colonists to purchase revenue stamps and affix them to all kinds of legal and commercial documents, newspapers, almanacs, playing cards, dice, and liquor licenses. This was taxation (without representation) in a highly visible and odious form. Moreover, it offended most those who were most influential in shaping colonial opinion—merchants, lawyers, printers, and tavern keepers. An explosion of protest indicated not only how averse the colonists were to taxation of any kind, but also how attached they were to the representative tradition of British Whiggery and to the home rule they had enjoyed with so little interference.

Colonial mobs blocked a sale of stamps and intimidated stamp agents into resigning. A more effective reaction, in the long run, was a nonimportation agreement sponsored by the colonial merchants that led to a boycott of British goods. This had such an effect on British manufacturers and exporting merchants that Parliament was persuaded in 1766 to repeal the Stamp Act. But Parliament did not surrender its claim to tax the colonists, for repeal was accompanied by a Declaratory Act asserting Parliament's right to legislate for the colonies in any and all respects.

That this was no idle claim was shown the very next year, 1767, when Charles Townshend, Chancellor of the Exchequer, pushed through Parliament the so-called Townshend Acts levying duties for revenue on a new class of previously untaxed articles. The new taxes were rendered more unpalatable by provisions for further strengthening the enforcement and collection machinery and by the stipulation that revenues from the act would be used to pay the salaries of royal officials in the colonies, thus robbing the colonial assemblies of their most potent weapon, the power to withhold salaries from uncooperative royal officers. Again the Americans resorted to mob action and the proven weapon of nonimportation, and again, in 1770, Parliament backed down, repealing all the duties except the one on tea.

Most of the colonists were willing to accept this action as settling the controversy, and the next few years brought a period of prosperity and relative peace between colonies and mother country. Except for New England merchants and, later, wealthy Virginia planters—two of the most powerful and articulate segments of the population—the trade regulations adopted after 1763 imposed no significant hardship on the colonial economy. Yet the British ministers were badly deceived if they supposed that imperial relations were as cordial as they had once been. During the seven years of controversy, the Americans had become increasingly conscious of their separate identity and common interest. They had been able to defy the home government successfully, and they were now more committed than perhaps they themselves realized to the principles of self-government without Parliamentary intervention.

THE RADICALS

Especially dangerous to continued harmony was a small but well organized and ably led group of American radicals who, since the 1760s, had opposed any British effort to tax or regulate colonial affairs. Most of these radicals were the ones who had led the more violent phases of the agitation against the Stamp Act and the Townshend duties, and their hostility toward the British was often combined with a democratic resentment of their more aristocratic fellow Americans. In Virginia, for example, Patrick Henry's radical opposition to the Stamp Act was simultaneously a challenge to the control of the House of Burgesses by the most conservative wing of the planter oligarchy. In Boston the radical leader Samuel Adams, though strongly backed by the wealthy merchant John Hancock, drew most of his support from artisans and shopkeepers who welcomed an opportunity to strike at aristocratic Bostonians with close royal ties. Charleston artisans, manual workers, and other middling types constituted most of the radical group in their city, although their leader was the young aristocrat Christopher Gadsden.

Americans of every social level had joined in the protest against the Stamp Act and Townshend duties, but the wealthier and more conservative of them had been dismayed by the excesses of mob action. These more conservative American Whigs were satisfied when Parliament repealed all the offensive duties except the one on tea, while the radicals insisted on continuing the agitation against the tea duty. The most dangerous of the radical leaders was that superb organizer, agitator, and propagandist Samuel Adams. Through his control of the Boston town meeting, Adams kept Boston in an uproar even as quiet returned to other areas. By exploiting incidents like the "Boston Massacre" of 1770 (where an unruly crowd goaded a small party of British soldiers into firing and killing three persons), Adams poured out a constant stream of distorted propaganda designed to keep the colonists alarmed over encroaching British tyranny.

Simultaneously, Adams and his allies were creating a radical organization. Operating from his base in the Boston town meeting, Adams induced other Massachusetts towns to establish "committees of correspondence" to promote intercolonial resistance to imperial policy. The idea spread and, shortly, dissident Virginians urged the establishment of a provincial committee of correspondence in every colony. Naturally these committees came to be dominated by those with relatively radical attitudes. While the radicals were unable to dispel the complacency that prevailed in the prosperous years 1770–1773, they created an organization that could seize the initiative whenever an opportunity arose.

THE SECOND CRISIS

Opportunity came when the British ministry of Lord North, in all innocence, undertook to aid the British East India Company by pushing through Parliament the Tea Act of 1773. The company was given the exclusive privilege of selling its tea directly to American consumers without paying the English export tax, thus increasing the company's profits, lowering the price of tea to Americans, eliminating widespread smuggling and evasion of the American tea duty, and depriving American importing merchants of any share in the tea trade.

The resentment of the conservative American merchants drove them again into alliance with the radicals, and the radicals made the most of this opportunity to renew violent agitation. Convinced that the British were using lower tea prices to seduce Americans into surrendering their liberties, the radicals again resorted to mob action which was climaxed by the famous Tea Party in Boston. Boarding the vessels that had arrived with East India tea, Samuel Adams's followers dumped Boston's entire consignment overboard. These defiant and destructive acts were shocking to many Americans, but patriot leaders and the public in general agreed that to accept the Tea Act was to risk conceding Parliament's right to tax the colonies for revenue.

The British government, on the other hand, was now convinced that only punitive action could bring the rebellious colonists to heel. Promptly, Parliament passed a series of four "Coercive Acts" (known to Americans as the "Intolerable Acts"), closing the port of Boston until the Bostonians paid for the tea they had destroyed, drastically reducing the representative and self-governing features of the Massachusetts provincial government, allowing royal officials to be tried in England when accused of crimes in the colonies, and permitting the British army to requisition American buildings as quarters. However logical and necessary these measures appeared to a London government faced with colonial insubordination, they confirmed American suspicions of Britian's despotic designs. A fifth measure followed that, although not punitive in nature nor actually one of the Coercive Acts, proved no more tolerable to the colonists. Through the Quebec Act of 1774, Parliament added to the Canadian province western territory claimed by several of the colonies, continued the autocratic rule in Quebec that had prevailed under the French, and afforded complete religious toleration to the province's Catholic population.

These measures threw the radical propaganda machine and committee organization into high gear. "The cause of Boston is the cause of all British America" was the message trumpeted everywhere during the spring and summer of 1774. Food, fuel, and money were collected for the relief of the beleaguered Bostonians, local nonimportation agreements sprang up on all sides, and a proposal for a continental congress to coordinate resistance won quick endorsement from the assemblies or from extralegal meetings of the assemblies in most of the colonies.

THE FIRST CONTINENTAL CONGRESS

In September, 1774, an extralegal Congress of delegates from every colony except Georgia assembled in Philadelphia. Because the delegates had been chosen at the height of the anti-British excitement following the Intolerable Acts, the already organized radicals gained a majority in the Congress over the confused and unorganized conservatives. Nevertheless, the conservatives were ably led and made a strong fight for moderate measures. The most promising conservative proposal was Joseph Galloway's plan for establishing a colonial union under a royally appointed president-general and a council representing the colonial assemblies, with the latter having power to legislate for the colonies and to veto Parliamentary legislation affecting the colonies. But when the Congress narrowly refused to endorse this plan, the radicals were given a green light to proceed with more aggressive measures.

After a hard fight, they persuaded Congress to adopt the Continental Association, a detailed plan for nonimportation, nonconsumption, and nonexportation of goods between the colonies and Great Britain. To enforce the plan, Congress authorized every county or town to elect extralegal committees of safety. These committees were to circulate the Association among all citizens for endorsement and then to single out violators for boycott and for denunciation as "enemies to the rights of British America." Goods imported in violation of the Association could be seized, and the work of the local committees was to be coordinated in each colony by a provincial Congress and a provincial committee of safety.

During the winter and spring of 1774–1775, the radicals began vigorously implementing this revolutionary scheme in every colony. A drastic decline in British imports quickly demonstrated the Association's effectiveness as an instrument of economic warfare; it was probably even more important as an instrument of political persuasion and coercion.

While nearly all Americans favored efforts to secure concessions from the British government, perhaps only a minority supported the aggressive tactics of the radicals. Many were decidedly hostile to any action that threatened to break the British connection, and many more were simply confused or indifferent. But the Association and its committee system gave the organized and purposeful radicals a highly efficient means of committing the passive and often hostile majority to their program.

Though the committees were supposed to be elected, they were frequently in fact self-constituted bodies of the local radical leaders and in some cases were merely the old committees of correspondence continued under a new name. Where public denunciation failed to secure compliance with the Association, committees did not hesitate to employ threats and even physical violence. As the revolutionary crisis deepened, the committees increasingly assumed the powers of government, fixing prices, levying fines, and taking charge of local militia units.

Yet radical control was far from complete by the spring of 1775. The mercantile and officeholding aristocracy put up strong opposition in the northeastern port towns; up-country Carolina farmers were disposed to side with the royal governors against the provincial politicians who had oppressed them in the past and who were now leading the radical movement; and everywhere there were wide areas still so unexcited over British oppression that the radicals had made little headway. An additional impulse was needed and once again Samuel Adams's Massachusetts radicals supplied it.

WAR

British despotism was anything but a remote and idle threat to the Massachusetts radicals during the winter and spring of 1774–1775. As part of the British plan to crush the spirit of insubordination in Massachusetts, additional troops were sent to Boston, and their commander, General Thomas Gage, was designated military governor of the province. With the endorsement of the Continental Congress, the radicals took the momentous step of establishing a revolutionary provincial government under the old suspended charter and began training troops and collecting military supplies.

The inevitable clash came on the morning of April 19, 1775, when General Gage sent a detachment of British soldiers from Boston to seize the powder and arms that had been collected at nearby Concord and to arrest Samuel Adams and John Hancock. Warned by Paul Revere and William Dawes, the farmer "minutemen" of Lexington and Concord boldly challenged the British regulars, and by the time the harassed soldiers had run the gauntlet of farmers' muskets on the road back to Boston, they had lost 273 dead, wounded, and missing.

Instantly the radicals sent special riders flying through the colonies with exaggerated accounts of the massacre of innocent Massachusetts farmers by bloodthirsty British soldiers. Everywhere there was a burst of patriotic indignation, enabling the radical-dominated committees of safety to gain complete control. Royal governors were driven from their posts, troops were drilled, and royal forts and powder magazines were seized.

On May 10, a Second Continental Congress was hastily assembled in Philadelphia. As a gesture to the timid, this radical-dominated body sent an "Olive Branch Petition" to the king as a final appeal for a peaceful settlement. When this petition was refused, the last vestiges of loyalty to the crown dissolved. Rapidly, a once-respected monarch was becoming, in Tom Paine's memorable words, a "royal brute." With all other acceptable avenues of resistance now closed, Congress prepared for war. The thousands of armed New Englanders who had rushed to besiege Gage's redcoats from the hills overlooking Boston were taken under the aegis of the Congress. And George Washington, who came to Philadelphia in the blue uniform of the Virginia militia, was named to command the emerging continental army. As resistance became rebellion, the 2.5 million British subjects in 13 New World colonies were awash in sentiments that would rapidly make them a single and independent people—Americans.

CONFLICTING HISTORICAL VIEWPOINTS

1. What Caused the American Revolution and How Revolutionary Was It?

Nineteenth-century historians rarely quarreled about the origin and nature of the Revolution. The war for American independence, they concluded, was a just and truly revolutionary struggle against the tyrannical and reactionary British imperial system. The colonial triumph ushered in a new era of human liberty, fraternity, and democracy. Indeed, to George Bancroft, author of the authoritative and justly celebrated History of the United States *(12 vols., 1834–1882), the Americans were God's chosen people and their revolution was part of the "grand design of Providence," a noble prelude to the "regeneration" of humankind.*

In the 1890s, the patriotic distortions of this traditional view were challenged by two schools of historical interpretation: the imperialist and the progressive. Influenced by a turn-of-the-century spirit of Anglo-American accord, such imperialist historians as Charles McLean Andrews (The Colonial Background of the American Revolution, *1924) were more critical of colonial behavior than English policy. The quarrel with England, they argued, could be interpreted correctly only within the broad context of the British empire as a whole. Examining the imperial as well as the colonial point of view, they sympathetically concluded that the British Trade and Navigation Acts were not oppressive and that Parliament's efforts to tax the Americans were justifiable.*

While imperialist scholars sought for the origins of the Revolution in political and constitutional issues within the empire, the progressives focused on social and economic issues within the colonies themselves. Products of the reform mentality of the late nineteenth and early twentieth centuries, these liberal scholars addressed not only the question of home rule but the question of who should rule at home.

Indeed, as Carl Becker, the greatest of the progressive historians, expressed it in History of Political Parties in the Province of New York (*1909*), *the American Revolution was actually two revolutions in one. The first, an external revolution, involved a conflict of economic interests between Great Britain and the American colonies. The second, an internal revolution, involved a class conflict between the "haves" and "have-nots" of colonial society. Such distinguished historians as Lawrence Gipson* (The British Empire before the American Revolution, 15 vols., *1936–1970*) *and Merrill Jensen* (The Founding of a Nation, *1968*) *still analyze the Revolution from the imperialist and progressive persuasions. But in recent decades new directions in historical thought have challenged these older viewpoints. In the 1950s, for example, so-called consensus historians, apparently mirroring the conservatism of the Cold War period, disputed progressive notions of class conflict. Arguing that American society was far more democratic, affluent, and fluid than the progressives had believed, such consensus histories as Robert E. Brown's* Middle-Class Democracy and the Revolution in Massachusetts (1955) *and Daniel J. Boorstin's* The Genius of American Politics (1953) *concluded that the Revolution was essentially a conservative movement waged to protect traditional American rights and liberties from a changing and increasingly arbitrary British policy.*

Edmund S. Morgan (The Birth of the Republic, *1956*), *Bernard Bailyn* (The Ideological Origins of the American Revolution, *1967*) *and other scholars who stress the causal importance of ideas have also discounted internal social and economic cleavage theories. Colonial patriots, Bailyn wrote, although not unmindful of their pocketbooks, were genuinely alarmed by the changing course of imperial policy and deeply affected by the antiauthoritarian tradition of English thought. Possessed of "real fears, real anxieties, [and] a sense of real danger," they viewed their opposition to Parliamentary taxation as a struggle of liberty against the corrupting force of power. Thus the new intellectual history has returned to the nineteenth-century conclusion that constitutional rights and lofty ideals lie at the heart of the American revolution. Although embracing neither Bancroft's patriotic and religious excesses nor his undue criticism of British policy, it finds the old master correct when he argued that the colonists revolted in the name of liberty.*

Recently, radical or New Left scholars have contributed yet another dimension to the debate. Not without justification they indicted their fellow historians for overemphasizing the attitudes and behavior of social and economic elites to the neglect of the great mass of human society. In the radical view, the Revolution can be correctly interpreted only from "the bottom up," the vantage point of colonial nonelites. Regardless of the perspective, however, there is little likelihood of unanimity of historical opinion.

FOR FURTHER READING

John C. Miller's *Origins of the American Revolution* (1943)* offers a narrative overview of the events leading to conflict. Robert M. Calhoon's *Revolutionary America* (1976) is a brief interpretation of the period from 1763 to 1787. John R. Alden has

---

*Available in paperback edition.

assessed the role of *The South in the Revolution, 1763-1789* (1957). Both J. Franklin Jameson, *The American Revolution Considered as a Social Movement* (1926) and A. M. Schlesinger, Sr., *The Colonial Merchants and the American Revolution* (1918) are dated but still command attention. J. R. Pole's *Political Representation in England and the Origins of the American Republic* (1966) is a work of great importance, and Pauline Maier's *From Resistance to Revolution* (1972) provides a new synthesis of the role of colonial radicals in the development of hostilities. Bernhard Knollenberg traces *The Origins of the American Revolution;* Edmund S. and Helen M. Morgan brilliantly analyze *The Stamp Act Crisis* (1953); Hiller B. Zobel surveys *The Boston Massacre* (1970); and Benjamin W. Labaree details *The Boston Tea Party* (1964). John C. Miller's *Sam Adams* (1936) is a readable biography of an important figure, and Larry R. Gerlach's *Prologue to Independence* (1976) expertly studies New Jersey's path to the American Revolution.

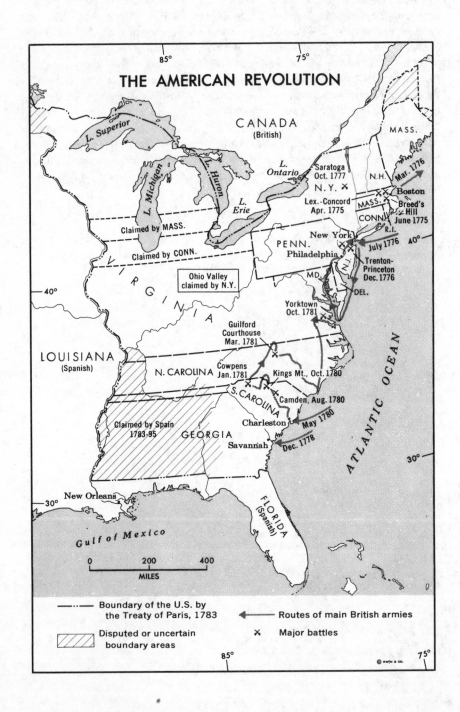

THE AMERICAN REVOLUTION

CANADA
(British)

L. Superior

L. Michigan

L. Huron

L. Ontario

L. Erie

Claimed by MASS.

Claimed by CONN.

Ohio Valley
claimed by N.Y.

VIRGINIA

LOUISIANA
(Spanish)

N. CAROLINA

Claimed by Spain
1783-95

GEORGIA

New Orleans

Gulf of Mexico

FLORIDA
(Spanish)

MASS.

N.H.

Mar. 1776

Saratoga
Oct. 1777

N.Y. ✕

Lex.-Concord
Apr. 1775

✕✕ Boston

MASS. ✕ Breed's
Hill
June 1775

CONN.

R.I.

New York

July 1776

40°

PENN.

Philadelphia

N.J.

Trenton-
Princeton
Dec. 1776

MD.

DEL.

Yorktown
Oct. 1781

Guilford
Courthouse
Mar. 1781

Cowpens
Jan. 1781

Kings Mt., Oct. 1780

S. CAROLINA

Camden, Aug. 1780

Charleston

May 1780

Savannah

Dec. 1778

ATLANTIC OCEAN

30°

0   200   400
MILES

— · — Boundary of the U.S. by
the Treaty of Paris, 1783

⬛ Disputed or uncertain
boundary areas

⬅ Routes of main British armies

✕   Major battles

© RAND & CO.

85°   75°

Independence Achieved
1775–1783

5

THE FIRST YEAR OF WAR

The military struggle began slowly, and during the first year no really decisive engagements occurred. In June, 1775, shortly before Washington arrived to take command of the poorly organized American forces on the hills surrounding Boston, General Gage managed to drive his besiegers from one of their strongest positions, Breed's Hill. But the misnamed Battle of Bunker Hill cost the British some 40 percent of their force, and these frightful losses demonstrated that the Americans could not easily be dislodged. During the months that followed Washington methodically converted his untrained militia into a disciplined army and tightened the ring around the British.

With Gage's army encircled in Boston, the ebullient Americans undertook, during the winter of 1775–1776, a two-pronged offensive against Canada. The valiant forces led by Richard Montgomery and Benedict Arnold surmounted great hardships and won some early successes, but in the end the reluctance of the Canadian population to join the rebellion forced a retreat.

In the first year of the war, perhaps the most important struggle was within the colonies themselves. Because neither the British nor the American leaders were prepared to compromise, few doubted that the issue could be resolved by means short of full-scale war. But many colonists remained deeply loyal to the British and, despite the coercion of the Revolutionaries, unwilling to wage open war against the mother country. Nearly 100,000 of these Loyalists were forced into exile, while those who remained suffered ostracism, disfranchisement, confiscation of property, and other penalties for their loyalty to the King. Still, the American Revolution produced none of the wholesale imprisonments or executions of dissidents that have marked other revolutions, and the penalties imposed on the Loyalists do not seem disproportionate to the threat they represented to the success of the Revolutionary cause.

In March, 1776, General Gage finally abandoned the increasingly difficult task of holding Boston and sailed away with his army and hundreds of Loyalists to the

British stronghold at Halifax, Nova Scotia. His departure did not mark a decisive American victory, but instead the approaching end of a year of stalemate in which each side had consolidated its position and prepared for the real struggle yet to come. During that fortunate year of respite a new American nation animated by fresh and exciting ideals had been coming to birth.

"CONCEIVED IN LIBERTY"

Until months after the Revolutionary War began, few Americans admitted that they sought independence from England. Yet the pressure of events increasingly forced them into independent acts and steadily prepared them for an open break.

The question of independence was connected in an indirect, but important, way with the acceleration of democratic tendencies inherent in the Revolutionary movement. While "home rule" was the primary issue in the Revolution, a political upsurge of the "lower orders" of the social hierarchy raised the important secondary issue of "*who* should rule at home?" The Liberty Boys who rioted against the Stamp Act or the Townshend duties were making a bid for political status. Perhaps more important, the Revolutionary agitation opened an avenue by which ambitious persons of the "middling sort"—Samuel Adams, Patrick Henry, and their counterparts in other colonies—could rise to power and influence. The Revolutionary movement offered such "new men" an opportunity to gain power by espousing radical measures and appealing indirectly to the inchoate democratic aspirations of those heretofore without influence in government.

The success of these "new men" was due in considerable measure to a favorable climate of ideas. The Revolutionary era was one of those periods in history when ideas have had great consequences. All Americans, including the most conservative and aristocratic, believed that the Glorious Revolution of 1688 and its great Bill of Rights had guaranteed to every British citizen certain rights—especially rights of liberty and property—upon which no monarch or government could rightfully infringe. The colonies pegged their opposition to the New Imperial Policy on the claim that it was an arbitrary violation of these rights. "Liberty and Property" became the slogan of the Revolutionary movement.

These Whig slogans carried democratic implications that could be applied to government within as well as outside of the colonies. When the colonial leaders argued for the Whig principle of "no taxation without representation" in imperial relations, inadequately represented Americans required no great imagination to apply the same argument to domestic affairs or even to expand it into the more general principle that government should be representative of the governed, meaning *all* the governed.

These democratic implications of the British Whig tradition were powerfully reinforced by the larger stream of thought of the Enlightenment. Confident that the Creator desired human happiness, the people of the eighteenth century were drifting toward the notion that all people were equal in their "natural rights" and that the only just end of government was to maintain a state of society in which every person could enjoy his or her rights to the fullest possible extent. Since liberty was the most precious of these rights, government should be restricted to the smallest possible compass that would enable it to keep individuals from invading each other's liberty, and since all persons were potentially rational, government should rest on the consent of the governed. The second of John Locke's *Two Treatises on Government* (1689) was a most trenchant justification of revolution on the basis of the natural-rights argument.

During the later stages of the Revolutionary crisis, the colonial leaders broadened the basis for their claim to autonomy from their rights as British citizens, according to the Whig tradition, to their rights as human beings, according to the natural-rights tradition. Directly or indirectly, Americans were thinking in Lockean terms as they decided for revolution, drafted their Declaration of Independence, and established a new governmental system.

This is not to say that the Americans rebelled against England because they deliberately sought to extend democracy at home. Rather, large segments of the population rallied to the movement for colonial autonomy more enthusiastically than they might otherwise have done because they were aroused by the democratic implications of Revolutionary rhetoric. Moreover, in the process of creating broad support for their movement, the Revolutionary leaders were compelled to seek the participation of groups that had previously played little part in public life. Consequently the new provincial congresses that were organized in the early months of the war had a far broader membership than the colonial assemblies and councils that they succeeded.

This rise of the lower orders affected the ways in which members of the old colonial ruling group reacted to the Revolutionary crisis. Many of the gentry were alarmed into being Loyalists. A larger number (conservative Whigs) continued to furnish leadership to the Revolutionary movement but resisted independence. They hoped to win colonial autonomy while restoring the British connection as a means of preserving the predominance of the aristocrats within the colonies. A third segment of the gentry (radical whigs) were so deeply infected with the Revolutionary ideology that they worked closely with the "new men" who spoke for the lower orders, espousing independence and paving the way for a new distribution of political power.

It was this last group, especially Richard Henry Lee of Virginia and Samuel and John Adams of Massachusetts, who controlled the Continental Congress in the early years of the war. On the question of independence, they were aided by the drift of events. The British government showed little disposition to conciliate the Americans and every disposition to wage vigorous war against them. The importance of aid from Britain's ancient enemy France became increasingly apparent, and it was hoped that independence might pave the way for a French alliance. Finally, Americans of all classes were gradually beginning to sense the exciting possibility of building a new and independent society based on natural rights and the implicitly democratic principles of Revolutionary rhetoric. How rapidly this feeling had spread was demonstrated by the tremendous public response to Thomas Paine's pamphlet *Common Sense*, published in January, 1776. Advocating both independence and democracy, Paine's slashing pamphlet sold several hundred-thousand copies.

A new American, who emigrated from England only in 1774, Paine did not create the sentiment for independence; he merely crystallized an unspoken but rapidly growing attitude. Once catapulted into the arena of open debate, the idea of independence rapidly overcame conservative opposition. On July 2, the Continental Congress resolved that "these United States are, and of right ought to be, free and independent states"; two days later the Declaration of Independence was adopted.

Drafted by Thomas Jefferson, with the help of Benjamin Franklin and John Adams, this memorable document was for the most part a long and exaggerated catalog of British violations of American rights. Designed in large part as propaganda for world consumption, the Declaration offered no subtle interpretations of events. It was the hapless George III—not Parliament, the source of most colonial grievances —who was made the villain of the piece. What made the Declaration a momentous factor in history, however, was its opening section, which distilled in a few sentences of enduring prose the essence of the Lockean, natural-rights theory of government: "We hold these truths to be self-evident, that all men are created equal, that they are endowed by their Creator with certain inalienable Rights, that among these are Life, Liberty, and the pursuit of Happiness. That to secure these rights, Governments are instituted among Men, deriving their just powers from the consent of the governed. That whenever any Form of Government becomes destructive of these ends, it is the Right of the People to alter or abolish it." Much of subsequent American history was to be a working out of the implications of the principles so ringingly enunciated here.

THE NEW STATE CONSTITUTIONS

By the time the Declaration of Independence was adopted, four of the colonies had already applied its liberal principles in the drafting of new state constitutions. Shortly, all the other states followed suit, except Rhode Island and Connecticut, which continued to operate under their unusually liberal colonial charters. The very drafting of written constitutions was unprecedented and significant. With British authority destroyed, Americans were free to perform in literal fact the act that lay at the root of all legitimate government according to Lockean theory: they entered into a "social contract." The new state constitutions were conceived of as voluntary compacts among all the people, creating governments of limited and explicitly defined powers. In several states, the people elected special conventions to draft the fundamental compacts; in several others, the constitutions were submitted for popular ratification; but in a majority of cases, the existing provincial congresses themselves drafted and promulgated the new constitutions.

However adopted, the new constitutions uniformly reflected the distrust of governmental power, especially executive power, that arose from the Enlightenment's liberalism and from the colonists' experience with British authority. Most states followed the distinguished example of Virginia by including a Bill of Rights specifying in detail those rights of the citizen—freedom of speech, freedom of the press, trial by jury, and the like—that no government could rightly abridge. All the constitutions sought to minimize the danger of arbitrary power by building "checks and balances" and a "separation of powers" into the very structure of government. The executive, legislative, and judicial functions were exercised by separate bodies, and, except in Pennsylvania and Georgia, the legislature was divided into two houses that were expected to act as checks on each other.

The "checks and balances" principle, however, was tempered by memories of the long struggles between the colonial assemblies and the royal governors. The new constitutions made the legislatures dominant and the governors—in most cases, elected annually by the legislatures and denied veto or appointive powers—relatively impotent.

Along with restrictions on the power of government, the new constitutions also manifested a marked tendency toward more representative government. Both of these impulses were reflected in the common provision that the voters should exercise close supervision over the legislators through annual elections. Although the state constitutions did not grant universal white male suffrage—Massachusetts actually raised its property qualifications for voting—and although none of the states granted any form of female suffrage, these new charters generally extended the privilege of voting, either by reducing the colonial freehold (property) requirement or by opening the polls to most taxpayers. While it would be easy to exaggerate the internal changes wrought by the rebellion, it seems certain that these new constitutions and the Revolutionary circumstances that produced them brought additional political democracy to the Americans.

THE ARTICLES OF CONFEDERATION

As the Continental Congress still had no regular constitutional authority, it began working on a plan for a confederation that would provide sufficient powers to conduct the war and to unite the states once victory was achieved. After protracted debate, the Articles of Confederation were finally approved by Congress in 1777, though a dispute over the western lands claimed by some of the states delayed final ratification until 1781.

The Articles of Confederation established not a government, but a confederation of sovereign states. Because the Revolution was being fought to abolish central control and because liberty was deemed safe only when government was kept close to where the governed could watch it, the Confederation was given only the powers to: (1) conduct foreign affairs by negotiating treaties and making war and peace, (2) control Indian affairs, (3) set standards of coinage, weights, and measures, (4) settle disputes among the states, and (5) conduct a postal service. It could not raise money or troops except by requisitions on the states. It had no power to make laws binding individual citizens and no means of enforcing its will on either citizens or states. Each state was to have a single vote in the Confederation Congress, the votes of nine states were required to approve all important measures, and the Articles could be amended only with the approval of Congress and the legislature of every state. The Articles did not even provide an executive agency to carry out whatever policies Congress might succeed in adopting.

THE CAMPAIGNS OF 1776–1777

The Declaration of Independence had just been adopted and the constitution-making process was well under way in the states and the Congress when the British launched the American war in earnest. In July, 1776, the greatest military force Britain had ever sent abroad sailed into New York harbor in hundreds of ships carrying 32,000 soldiers under the command of Sir William Howe. Anticipating the British strategy, Washington had moved his army to the vicinity, but his greatly outnumbered forces were easily pushed off Long Island, out of Manhattan, steadily through New Jersey, and across the Delaware River into Pennsylvania.

The 43-year-old Washington was a great leader but probably no great military genius. Indeed he lost more battles than he won. Yet his courage and tenacity under these disheartening circumstances kept his army intact and the American cause alive. When he assumed command, his troops were largely without uniforms and without a semblance of unified command. Pay was low; both enlistments and rations were short. The men were eager to return to family and farms. The officers were often elected and poorly qualified for leadership. War materials, always in short supply in this undeveloped country, had to be captured or imported from Europe. Yet by good fortune and force of will, this sober, aristocratic Virginian prevailed. With the assistance of such foreign advisers as the Baron von Steuben and the Marquis de Lafayette, he built a force of some 8,000–10,000 regulars. (There were an additional 7,000 short-term militia.) Wisely avoiding decisive engagements, he waited until the British ceased offensive operations for the winter, and on Christmas night, 1776, he daringly ferried his troops back across the icy Delaware and fell upon unsuspecting British forces at Trenton and nearby Princeton, New Jersey. With these small but brilliant victories to buoy American hopes, he went into winter quarters at Morristown.

The following summer of 1777 was the time of greatest military peril for the infant American nation. From Canada, General John Burgoyne launched a British offensive by way of Lake Champlain toward Albany and the lower Hudson Valley. Sir William Howe had the opportunity to move up the Hudson from New York City to join Burgoyne and cut the colonies in two. Instead, the indecisive Howe succumbed to the temptation of occupying the rebel capital at Philadelphia, brushing aside what resistance Washington's outnumbered army was able to offer at the Battle of Brandywine.

Freed from the threat of Howe to their rear, the American commanders in the Hudson Valley, Horatio Gates and Benedict Arnold, were able to put up a stubborn resistance against Burgoyne's advance from the north. Far from his base of supply and harassed on every side by farmer militia, the British commander was finally forced to surrender his entire army at Saratoga in October, 1777. The importance of this victory and the narrowness of the American escape from a crushing military catastrophe cannot be exaggerated. Thanks to a combination of British lethargy and American valor, it now appeared for the first time that the rash bid for independence might succeed.

THE FRENCH ALLIANCE AND
THE SOUTHERN CAMPAIGNS

Yet even the victory at Saratoga could not make up for the feebleness of the American war effort. Driven from Philadelphia to York, Pennsylvania, Congress struggled ineffectually during the winter of 1777–1778 with the problems of supply and funds as the paper money with which it was trying to finance the war became more and more worthless. Meanwhile, cold and hunger in the winter camp at Valley Forge decimated Washington's ragtag army. Too often local American farmers and merchants traded their goods for British coin supplied by enemy forces encamped in nearby Philadelphia.

Across the Atlantic, however, the Saratoga victory was bearing fruit. From the beginning of the conflict, the Americans hoped that France would avenge her recent defeat at British hands by giving them aid. As soon as independence was declared, the Congress sent Franklin to Paris to seek an alliance. The French government proved willing to furnish supplies and funds secretly, but it wanted assurance that the Americans had a real chance of winning before siding with them openly. Saratoga furnished this assurance, and in February, 1778, the treaty of alliance was signed. As a result, France's ally Spain was also pulled into the war with Britain, and, soon afterwards, the Netherlands were drawn into the conflict because of their insistence on continuing trade with the French and the Americans. Spain and the Netherlands furnished much needed loans for the American war effort, but France became the main source of both the money and the munitions that enabled the Americans to keep fighting. In addition, the French sent an army and a powerful naval force, without which victory would have been impossible.

Military activity was at a stalemate for a year following Saratoga as the British prepared for another offensive, this time aimed at the southern colonies. Landing at Savannah, Georgia in December, 1778, the British army under the aggressive Lord Cornwallis easily took Charleston and occupied most of South Carolina. When the Americans finally marched against him in August, 1780, they were soundly defeated at Camden, and Cornwallis was able to push his invasion northward. By this time, however, the American forces in the South were under the able command of Nathanael Greene. At King's Mountain and at Cowpens, severe defeats were inflicted on contingents of Cornwallis's army, and in March, 1781, the British army sustained heavy losses in a hard fought but inconclusive battle at Guilford Court House, North Carolina. The seriously weakened Cornwallis, despairing of subduing the vast and hostile southern interior, withdrew his army to Yorktown on the peninsula between the York and James rivers in tidewater Virginia, where he waited to be evacuated by the British fleet.

But it was not the British fleet that appeared. By a miracle of good fortune and good timing, Washington and the French commanders were able to march the combined Franco-American army down from the north just as the French fleet appeared off the Virginia coast. Thus caught between a hostile army and a hostile navy, Cornwallis had no alternative but to surrender on October 17, 1781.

THE TREATY OF PEACE

Cornwallis's surrender finally convinced the British that the effort to subdue the Americans was too difficult and too expensive to continue. Although the British armies had usually been able to advance at will and to defeat American armies when they could catch them, such success brought them little closer to their goal. The country was too vast, the population was too deeply committed to resistance, and the cost of supporting a large army 3,000 miles away was becoming an intolerable burden on an already debt-ridden treasury. The debacle at Yorktown forced Lord North to resign his ministry, and a new ministry came to power prepared to negotiate with the Americans.

Already, John Adams, Benjamin Franklin, and John Jay were in Europe to negotiate a peace treaty, but a settlement was delayed for some time by the crosscurrents of international politics. The Franco-American alliance committed each party to continue fighting as long as the other was fighting, and the Franco-Spanish alliance committed France to continuing the war until Spain won Gibraltar from England. This seemed to mean that the Americans could not make peace with England until Spain regained Gibraltar. But when the American commissioners uncovered evidence that the French were arranging that the Spanish and British control the northern and southern portions of the American land between the Allegheny Mountains and the Mississippi, the Americans felt absolved of their obligation to negotiate in concert with the French.

Seeing an opportunity to detach the Americans from French influence, the British accepted an American proposal for separate Anglo-American negotiations. By thus playing off one power against the other, the American commissioners won an exceedingly favorable treaty. Besides recognizing the independence of the United States, the British also acquiesced in giving up a generous extent of territory, stretching from the Atlantic to the Mississippi and from the Canadian border on the north to the Florida border on the south. These terms were agreed upon by late 1782, but peace did not come officially until Spain and France ended hostilities in early 1783. In this general settlement, Florida was transferred from Britain to Spain to compensate for Spain's failure to win Gibraltar.

FOR FURTHER READING

John C. Miller's *Triumph of Freedom* (1948)* and John R. Alden's *A History of the American Revolution* (1954) are useful general accounts of the American Revolution. There are two excellent briefer military histories of the war: Howard Peckham, *The War for Independence* (1958),* and Willard M. Wallace, *Appeal to Arms* (1951). R. Arthur Bowler examines *Logistics and the Failure of the British Army in America* (1975). Also excellent for military and naval history are two biographies: Douglas S.

---

*Available in paperback edition.

Freeman, *George Washington* (7 vols., 1948–1957) and Samuel Eliot Morison, *John Paul Jones: A Sailor's Biography* (1959). The treatment of rebel prisoners of war is the concern of Larry G. Bowman in *Captive Americans* (1976). William C. Stinchcombe writes about *The American Revolution and the French Alliance* (1969), and in *The Peace-makers: The Great Powers and American Independence* (1965), Richard B. Morris analyzes the maneuvers that led up to the Treaty of Paris. James Henderson's *Party Politics in the Continental Congress* (1975) closely examines congressional politics during a crucial period. For the political thought that influenced the development of new political institutions during the Revolutionary years, see Carl L. Becker's *The Declaration of Independence* (1922)* and Clinton Rossiter's *Seedtime of the Republic* (1953), which has been republished in two volumes under the titles *The First American Revolution** and *Political Thought of the American Revolution.** William Nelson's *American Tory* (1961), Wallace Brown's *The Good Americans* (1969), and Robert McCluer's *Loyalists in Revolutionary America* (1973) supplement the standard account of *The Loyalists in the American Revolution* (1902) by C. H. Van Tyne. Bernard Bailyn brilliantly delineates *The Ordeal of Thomas Hutchinson* (1974). Elisha P. Douglass, in *Rebels and Democrats* (1955),* describes the conflict between the democratic-minded and the elite-minded in the formation of the new state governments; Jackson T. Main analyzes *The Upper House in Revolutionary America* (1967); and Merrill Jensen offers a controversial analysis of the drafting of *The Articles of Confederation* (1940).* Charles S. Sydnor describes the political leadership of the Virginia gentry in *Gentlemen Freeholders* (1952, republished as *American Revolutionaries in the Making**). Jeffrey J. Crow in *The Black Experience in Revolutionary North Carolina* (1977) fills an important void for one state.

A Nation Emerges
1780–1788

6

The new nation brought into being by the Revolution covered a thinly populated but vast expanse of territory six times the area of England and Wales combined. Ninety-five percent of its 3 million people lived in the countryside. Most of them were near the seacoast, but even here they were so dispersed that there were only six cities with more than 8,000 inhabitants. Philadelphia, with some 40,000, was largest, followed by New York, Boston, Charleston, Baltimore, and Salem. Transportation facilities from one part of this far-flung republican empire to another were rudimentary, and communication was so infrequent that the letters carried by the postal service amounted to only one per capita per year.

Nevertheless, the shared experience of the Revolution had given Americans a sense of national pride and optimism about the future of their experiment in liberty. But because not all Americans agreed about what that future should be, the decade of the 1780s was one of conflict. It was also, as time would prove, the richest period of American political and constitutional thought.

THE AGRARIAN-MINDED AND
THE COMMERCIAL-MINDED

One fundamental division was between what might be called the *agrarian-minded* and the *commercial-minded* portions of the population. The great majority of the people were small farmers. Measured against the Europe that they or their peasant forebears had left behind—the Europe of arbitrary government, heavy taxes, military conscription, state churches, and rigid social distinctions—America seemed a virtual paradise. In America, the dream of land ownership—the key to security, independence, and dignity—could be realized by the great majority.

To these small landowners, secure on their acres, far from cities, often illiterate or semiliterate, the American utopia was already at hand. Provincial and typically adhering to the more orthodox brands of Protestantism, they regarded the farmer's way of life as morally superior to all others. They were deeply suspicious of cities, of change, and of those ambitious and probably evil people in cities who grew rich by commercial manipulations. This agrarian mystique was also shared in good part by many southern planters and by many of the great landlord families in New York's Hudson Valley.

Less numerous but equally influential were the people who saw America's future in terms of general economic growth and national strength. This commercial-minded-ness was centered in the cities and especially among the merchant and professional classes, the best educated and most cosmopolitan parts of the population. Included also were a good many farmers and planters who lived close enough to transportation and cities to produce commercial crops for foreign and domestic markets.

The division between the commercial-minded and the agrarian-minded merged into the other major political division of the 1780s: there was a tendency for the agrarian-minded to be democratic-minded and for the commercial-minded to resist democratic tendencies. However, the two alignments did not coincide completely. Thomas Paine, for example, was among the most effective advocates of both democ-racy and commercial expansion, while much of the leadership for the agrarian forces was provided by elitist gentry from the great landholding families.

With some important exceptions, then, the political struggles of the 1780s in-volved two rough groupings. On one side were those who favored leadership by the gentry, vigorous and more centralized government, and policies designed to foster national strength and economic growth through encouragement to entrepreneurs. On the other side were persons resentful of any pretensions to superiority, deeply suspi-cious of all government, and mistrustful of even their own elected representatives. They consequently wanted government kept as decentralized as possible, as inactive and inexpensive as possible, and subject to the check of frequent and democratic elections.

CONFLICT WITHIN THE STATES

The state governments were the principal arenas of conflict between the two groups. The conflict was in part a straight struggle for control, as in Pennsylvania where displaced conservatives warred unrelentingly against the ultrademocratic constitution of 1776 and the power it gave to western farmers and the lower orders of Philadel-phia.

Religion was frequently another divisive issue. In New England (outside Rhode Island where religious freedom had always prevailed), the Congregationalists were persuaded to surrender only part of the exclusive privileges they had enjoyed by law before the Revolution; but in New York and the southern states, the members of the formerly established Anglican church were reduced to an equal footing with those other denominations. In Virginia, the Anglicans of the wealthy and conservative tidewater area managed to stave off this movement until 1786 when James Madison's coalition of liberal gentry, back-country Baptists, Methodists, and Presbyterians pushed through the legislature Jefferson's Statute for Religious Freedom.

The greatest cause of alarm to conservatives was the democratic legislatures' apparent disregard for property rights. In some states, property-minded persons fought against wholesale confiscations of the property of Loyalists, and they were even more alarmed by the movement for debtor laws and state-issued paper money.

Paper money had been used during the colonial period with both good and bad results, but the collapse of the Continental currency during the Revolution had utterly discredited the whole idea with merchants and creditors. Yet the return to a specie (gold and silver) currency at the end of the Revolution, the collapse of the brief boom that followed, and the ensuing depression of 1785–1786 produced a severe deflation. People who had borrowed money during inflationary times found that they had to repay their debts in money that was worth much more than the money originally borrowed and at a time when money of any kind was hard to obtain.

Under the pressure of desperate debtors, seven state legislatures authorized issues of paper money, while in several other states, creditors and merchants barely averted such demands. The paper issues were relatively beneficial where taxes were levied to support them, but in other instances, the old story of rapid depreciation was repeated. Some states tried to compel creditors to accept the paper money in payment of debts; and creditors were said to flee the state of Rhode Island to avoid payment in depreciated paper.

The conflict became most violent in Massachusetts, where debtors and small farmers of the interior simply could not find enough of the scarce specie to pay their debts and heavy state taxes. As the courts began imprisoning large numbers of defaulting debtors or foreclosing on their farms, armed mobs started breaking up sessions of the courts. By the winter of 1786–1787, the interior was swarming with a virtual insurrectionary militia whose principal leader was a Revolutionary veteran named Daniel Shays. Finally, a state army of 4,000 marched into the area and quelled the disorders after a series of minor skirmishes. But meanwhile exaggerated accounts of "Shays's Rebellion" had further alarmed property-minded conservatives in all the states.

PROBLEMS OF THE CONFEDERATION

Already, in the early 1780s, conservatives sought to erect a bulwark against the localism and democratic irresponsibility of the states by strengthening the Confederation government. Under the leadership of Robert Morris, a Philadelphia merchant who had grown wealthy from war contracts, they had persuaded Congress to appoint full-time executives to superintend departments of finance, war, foreign affairs, and marine. Morris himself became superintendent of finance, but exercised great influence in all areas. Continental paper money was abandoned, and Morris sought to finance the government by borrowing, partly from American citizens. In the process, he encouraged the creation of a powerful class of public creditors who had a vested interest in a government strong enough to pay its debts.

Yet the Confederation government could neither pay its debts nor effectively carry on its ordinary operations as long as it had to depend for income on voluntary contributions by the recalcitrant states. Morris's whole program hinged on getting the states to approve the "Impost of 1781," a proposed amendment of the Articles of Confederation that would give Congress the power to levy limited import duties to pay the Confederation debt. But Rhode Island refused to ratify, and all further efforts to give Congress any taxing power failed to get the required unanimous approval of the states. Meanwhile, the coming of peace dissipated the atmosphere of emergency, and the drive to add vigor to the Confederation government stalled.

Through the mid-1780s, national-minded persons could only grumble helplessly at the impotence of the Confederation in many areas. Lacking any means of enforcing its policies either on the states or directly on their citizens, the Confederation was unable to deal effectively with unseemly quarrels among various states over boundaries, western lands, and state-levied tariffs and trade restrictions.

The Confederation's weakness was most evident in foreign relations. Partly because the United States could not enforce uniform commercial regulations in its own territory or threaten uniform retaliatory regulations against other countries, it was unable to secure favorable commercial treaties with the leading European powers. More serious, Spain and Great Britain threatened the territorial integrity of the new nation in the Southwest and Northwest respectively.

Spain had lost Florida to Great Britain at the end of the Seven Years' War in 1763 but had gained formerly French Louisiana (the entire western watershed of the Mississippi and the "island" of New Orleans east of the river). Then, in 1783, Spain regained Florida, making her the dominant power on the southwestern borders of the United States. Moreover, Spain would not be bound by the 31° northern boundary of Florida specified by the Anglo-American treaty, but occupied territory north of that line and claimed the greater part of the Southwest. These claims she actively buttressed in the 1780s by gaining control over the southwestern Indians and restricting the Mississippi River trade through New Orleans. When the Confederation proved powerless to protect new settlements in the Tennessee-Kentucky area against the Indians or to secure them a right to trade down the Mississippi, many of the settlements sought the protection of Spain, and for a time there was a serious danger that the western settlers would cooperate in making the entire Southwest a Spanish territory.

Great Britain understandably treated her former subjects with great contempt, closing her West Indian possessions to American trade, restricting American trade with England, refusing to enter negotiations for a commercial treaty, and not even sending a minister to the new nation. Most threatening of all, she continued to occupy military posts along the northern frontier within territory she had ceded to the United States, and from these posts she retained dominion over the Indians of the northern Ohio Valley and encouraged them to resist the advance of American settlement.

The British found justification for these actions in the failure of the American states to live up to their obligations under the Treaty of Paris. Congress technically complied with the treaty by urging the states to restore confiscated property to Loyalists, but it could not force the states to do so. Nor could it prevent the states from violating the treaty by impeding the collection of debts that Americans owed to British merchants. The Confederation authorities could counter British complaints on these points only by demanding payment for several thousand slaves that the British armies had carried away from the southern states.

THE CONFEDERATION AND THE WEST

For all its weaknesses, the Confederation had one magnificent achievement to its credit: the creation of a great national domain west of the Appalachian Mountains and the formulation of a system for land sales and territorial government by which this West and later Wests would become a spectacularly expanding "empire for liberty."

Even before the Revolution, pioneers had crossed the mountains to form pockets of settlement in a few areas. New Englanders had moved up and across the Connecticut River to populate the green hills of Vermont. Resisting the claims of New York and New Hampshire to the area during the Revolution, Ethan Allen and his "Green Mountain Boys" created an independent republic that was not admitted as one of the United States until 1791.

Farther south, other pioneers had established themselves on the upper waters of the Ohio River in the Wheeling-Pittsburgh area, and still others had pushed southwestward through the valleys of the Virginia mountains to found the Watauga settlement on the headwaters of the Tennessee River in what was to become the northeastern corner of Tennessee. During and immediately after the Revolution, these outposts became staging areas for further advances of settlement into the country north of the Ohio, through Cumberland Gap into the Bluegrass region of what would later be central Kentucky, and over the Cumberland Plateau into the Nashville basin of what would later be central Tennessee.

Seven states laid claim to various parts of the trans-Appalachian empire. Virginia, making the most of the vague boundaries specified by its colonial charter, claimed Kentucky and all the territory north of the Ohio River. New York had a shadowy claim to the Ohio Valley resting on Indian treaties, while Massachusetts and Connecticut argued that their boundaries extended indefinitely westward, cutting across the Virginia claim. Farther south the two Carolinas and Georgia asserted that their boundaries extended all the way to the Mississippi.

Even before the war was over, under heavy pressure from landless states, Congress had urged that these western claims be ceded to the Confederation to create a great common domain. Virginia led the way in 1781 by offering its lands north of the Ohio, and by the end of the 1780s all except one of the landed states had followed suit. Georgia finally ceded its western lands in 1802, while, in 1792, Virginia passed the sovereignty over its remaining western territory directly to the new state of Kentucky that was created from it.

Congress lost no time in providing for land sales and a governmental system in the new public domain. The Ordinance of 1785 established a "rectangular" system of survey. Land was to be divided into squares one mile from north to south and one mile from east to west. "Townships" six miles square were to be laid off, each of which would contain 36 one-mile-square (640-acre) "sections." As the line of settlement advanced, these sections were to be auctioned off to the highest bidders, with a minimum price of two dollars an acre.

A year earlier, in the Ordinance of 1784 (drafted by Thomas Jefferson), Congress had declared that territorial governments in the public domain should evolve as quickly as possible into new states fully equal to the original states. The process by which this was to happen was altered by the so-called Northwest Ordinance of 1787, adopted to meet the wishes of the Ohio Company, a group of New England land speculators who were promoting a settlement in the Muskingum Valley of what was to become southeastern Ohio. The Ordinance of 1787 established a Northwest Territory in the area north of the Ohio and east of the Mississippi rivers; this area was to be administered first by a governor appointed by Congress. When the population of the territory reached 5,000, the people were to elect a representative assembly and a nonvoting delegate to Congress. Eventually the Old Northwest was to be divided into not less than three and not more than five states, and when the population of any of these proposed states reached 60,000, it could be admitted to the union on an equal footing with the original states. During the territorial stage, civil liberties and religious freedom were guaranteed, a system of free public education was called for, and slavery was excluded. Thus Congress laid down the pattern of territorial evolution by which the United States was to become a continental nation of equal states.

THE MOVEMENT FOR A STRONGER GOVERNMENT

Although many Americans may have been satisfied with the limited successes and modest potency of the Confederation, others grew steadily more disgusted with its weakness and more desperately determined to secure a strong national government in its place. The unpaid public creditors constituted a standing lobby for change. Merchants wanted a uniform commercial policy that could force concessions from the great trading nations. The artisan class and infant industrial sector wanted a uniform tariff policy that would protect them from the competition of British manufactures. The elite of many of the states dreaded the possibility of popular control. Creditors and wealthy persons cried out for protection against debtor legislation, paper money, and the assaults of the unpropertied on property. Frontier people demanded more vigorous defense against the Indians and their British and Spanish abettors. And the more cosmopolitan and national-minded patriots wanted their country to assume a position of greater strength and dignity among the nations of the world. Quite obviously the reasons for the discontent were nearly as numerous as the people who advocated a stronger government. But overriding all else was a pervasive fear among the nation's political leaders that the Confederation, as originally constructed, could not adequately protect American interests in a hostile world and that the excesses of the Revolutionary era threatened the interests of authority and stability in the name of popular liberty.

As the 1780s wore on, events pushed some of these national-minded elements into an almost revolutionary mood. Robert Morris's drive to strengthen the Confederation from within had stalled when the urgency of war was removed in 1783; all further attempts to remedy the inadequacy of the Articles by amendment failed. More important, the brief economic boom that followed peace collapsed into a commercial and financial depression in the mid-1780s, and inevitably merchants, financiers, and artisans began to think that their distress was related to the Confederation's weakness. As a result of the depression, the panic of conservatives over paper money and debtor legislation reached its peak; in the autumn of 1786, the conservatives' worst fears of the lower orders and anarchy seemed confirmed by the exaggerated accounts of Shays's Rebellion.

By this time, a concerted movement was under way to bypass the prescribed method for amending the Articles and to create a stronger government through constitutionally questionable means. The movement was initiated by a small group of national-minded people, particularly George Washington and James Madison in Virginia and Alexander Hamilton in New York. Washington shared the fears of anarchy held by other members of the upper classes, but his nationalism was more than a class prejudice. His views reflected his position as the preeminent personal symbol of American nationality, and he cared deeply about the strength, dignity, and perpetuity of the nation he had done so much to bring to birth.

Hamilton and Madison were younger men. After serving as Washington's aide-de-camp during the Revolution, Hamilton had become a highly successful lawyer in New York, where he had married into one of the leading families and had proved himself a staunch defender of property rights. But Hamilton was not primarily a servant of propertied interests. Instead he was obsessed with the need for vigor and strength in government and sought to ally wealth with government in the interest of strong government rather than wealth.

Madison was a nationalist on more theoretical grounds. A close friend of Jefferson and, like him, a member of the liberal wing of Virginia's planting gentry, the 36-year-old Madison had combined study of ancient and modern governments with a quiet but increasingly influential role in Virginia politics. His nationalism was a matter of intellectual conviction, stimulated by his association with Washington and buttressed by his wide reading and disinterested reflection on political problems. Although, until his death in 1836, he generously and accurately protested that the Constitution was not "the offspring of a single brain" but "the work of many heads and many hands," he, more than any other framer, was the father of that document.

In 1785, on Madison's initiative, a conference of commissioners from Virginia and Maryland met at Mount Vernon and Alexandria to consider improving navigation of the Potomac. Madison and Washington persuaded the commissioners that other states should be brought into the consultation, and the Virginia legislature invited all the states to send delegates to a convention at Annapolis in 1786 to deliberate on "a uniform system in their commercial regulations." When delegates from only five states appeared at Annapolis, Hamilton, a delegate from New York, persuaded the convention to send out a call for another convention in Philadelphia in May, 1787, to "devise such further provisions as shall appear . . . necessary as to render the constitution of the federal government adequate to the exigencies of the union."

The call for the Philadelphia convention was grudgingly endorsed by the Confederation Congress with the explicit stipulation that any amendments it proposed must be endorsed by all the states as the Articles required. During the spring, delegates were selected by the legislatures of every state save debtor-dominated Rhode Island. With only a few exceptions, those who were satisfied with the Articles as they stood refused to serve as delegates, thus permitting people who were inclined to a stronger government to represent even those states where they were in a minority. The legislature of Hamilton's New York, dominated by his opponents, permitted him to be a delegate only as a member of a three-man delegation controlled by two staunch opponents of change.

THE CONSTITUTIONAL CONVENTION

Except for the two New Yorkers and a few scattered delegates from other states, the convention was composed of delegates from the national-minded side of the political spectrum. Predominantly lawyers, merchants, and planters, the 55 delegates were males drawn heavily from urban and seaboard areas and from the upper classes; no women were permitted to serve as delegates. Collectively they presented an impressive showing of youth, education, ability, and disinterested patriotism. From the circumstances of their selection, the crucial political decision that faced the convention—whether the government should continue to be a weak "confederated" government with some additional powers to raise revenue and regulate commerce or whether it should become a "national" government acting directly on the citizens of the states—was settled before the delegates ever met.

Had this not been the case, Madison could never have scored such a resounding victory for a national plan at the very outset of the convention. The Virginia delegation arrived in Philadelphia some days before the convention opened, and Madison had his fellow Virginians hard at work on a "Virginia Plan" that became the basis for the convention's early deliberations. By accepting the Virginia Plan as its basis for deliberation, the convention made the momentous decision that it would propose not simply amendments to the Articles but an entirely new frame of government. It also indicated that it favored a government radically different from the Confederation.

The two principal features of the Virginia Plan were its grant of sweeping powers to the central government and its requirement that representation in the national legislative body be in proportion to population. It was the second feature that raised the only fundamental disagreement in the convention's proceedings, for delegates from the small states rightly feared that basing representation on population would allow the large states to control the new government. Consequently the small-state delegates presented a "New Jersey Plan" to amend the Articles rather than draft an entirely new constitution. The heart of the New Jersey Plan was the continuance of a one-house Congress in which each state would have one vote. By adhering to the form of the Articles, the small-state delegates were also proposing a confederated government of limited powers, though their plan did give Congress the power to levy import duties, regulate commerce, and admit new states. Yet it was the matter of representation rather than the question of nationalism that was at the bottom of the disagreement, and a compromise was finally effected by proposing a two-house Congress where representation in the lower house was apportioned by population and where the influence of the small states was safeguarded in an upper house composed of two senators from each state. Once the small states won this concession, their delegates showed less zeal in defending a confederated structure. From this point on, the convention was able to work out the detailed powers and structure of the new government without serious disagreement.

Though the delegates were predominantly nationalists and though many of them feared the influence of popular majorities, they were also political realists who recognized that whatever they proposed would have to be accepted by a society that was considerably more confederationist and democratic than the convention itself. Consequently, and to Hamilton's discomfort, the document that resulted from their deliberations was a compromise between the two poles of political thought. Its basic feature was the creation of a "federal" system in which powers and responsibilities were distributed between the state and national governments. While the powers given Congress were specified with the implication that only these powers could be exercised, the specified powers were quite ample. The new government was to have virtually unlimited authority to levy taxes, borrow money, regulate domestic and foreign commerce, conduct foreign relations, and maintain an army and navy. Moreover, the states were specifically forbidden to engage in diplomatic negotiations, maintain armies, or—closing the door on debtor legislation and paper money—"emit Bills of Credit, make any Thing but gold and silver Coin a Tender in Payment of Debts; pass any . . . Law impairing the Obligation of Contracts. . . ." Finally, and most important, the new national government was to operate directly upon the citizens rather than upon the states, and the proposed national constitution and laws and treaties made in pursuance of it were declared to be "the supreme Law of the Land."

Following the eighteenth-century doctrine of separation of powers and fearful of a concentration of power anywhere in government, the convention was at pains to create, in addition to Congress, a strong and independent executive and judiciary so that the three branches would act as "checks and balances" on each other. The vesting of the executive function in a single president with ample authority was a particularly important departure from existing practices in the states and the Confederation. The president was given a veto over congressional legislation (unless repassed by two-thirds of both houses); he was to appoint judges and other officers (with consent of the Senate); he was given primary responsibility for foreign relations and the making of treaties (with the advice and consent of two-thirds of the Senate); and he was to be commander in chief of the armed forces.

The convention spent much of its time working out the methods for choosing the personnel of the legislative, executive, and judicial branches. Nearly all the delegates recognized that popular majorities must have a voice somewhere in the governmental structure they were planning, but they were equally anxious to erect ample safeguards against the workings of popular passions and temporary enthusiasms. Popular majorities were allowed direct sway in the House of Representatives, whose members were to be elected every two years by those who were qualified to vote for the popular branches of the legislatures in the respective states. But laws passed by the House of Representatives also had to be approved by the Senate, and the senators were to be chosen for six-year terms by the state legislatures. Even after passage by both houses of Congress, laws still needed the approval of the president, and the convention worked long and hard before devising a method of selecting the president that would leave him independent of state legislatures, Congress, and popular majorities. The result was that famous invention, the electoral college. Each state was to appoint, as its legislature directed, as many electors as it had members of Congress, and the electors were then to elect a president who was to serve for four years. Finally, the members of the judiciary were to be appointed by the president for life.

The system as a whole seemed admirably contrived to frustrate direct popular control of all branches of the government at any one time and to ensure that the various branches would pull in such different directions as to hobble effective government. The convention did not foresee that the rise of political parties would quickly subvert its intentions in both respects, and indeed the government under the Constitution would probably have proved unworkable if it had operated exactly as its architects intended that it should.

RATIFICATION

In September, 1787, nearly four months after it convened, the Convention lifted the veil of secrecy with which it had covered its debates and presented its handiwork to the country. Only then did people outside the convention discover that the delegates had vastly exceeded their authority. Not only had they drafted a substantially new framework for government, instead of a revision of the existing Articles, but they provided for its ratification by only nine of the thirteen states.

The work of a relatively small but vigorous and talented group of continental-minded leaders who called themselves "Federalists" (rather than the more straightforward "Nationalists"), the Constitution won quick and decisive ratifications in the small states of Delaware, New Jersey, and Connecticut, whose powerful neighboring states had taken advantage of them under the Confederation, and in the small and exposed frontier state of Georgia. Two states, Rhode Island and North Carolina, were so well satisfied with the virtually independent course they had been pursuing that they refused even to consider ratification until after the new government was in full operation.

The crucial struggles occurred in the great states of Pennsylvania, Massachusetts, Virginia, and New York, which had been able to take care of themselves under the confederated system. Anti-Federalist delegates were probably in a majority when the ratifying conventions of several of these states opened—certainly overwhelmingly so in New York—but ratification finally carried in all of them. Rhode Island, the last to approve, did so in 1790. Federalist superiority in initiative, organization, and debate counted heavily in these close contests as did the strategy of agreeing to recommend whatever amendments the Anti-Federalist delegates wished to propose. Most of all, the Federalists had the advantage of a concrete proposal. Their opponents were forced, as one conceded, to ratify "this or nothing." Nor were Federalists opposed to unscrupulous tactics: in New York, Governor John Hancock was cynically won over by the implied promise of high national office; in Pennsylvania, Anti-Federalist legislators were physically dragged to their seats in a quorum-shy Assembly so that a ratification convention could be called. Thus not only was the Constitution adopted by extraconstitutional means, without the test of a mass plebiscite or even of Congressional ratification, but the Federalists' tactical advantages may well have given them victory over a potentially opposed but ineffectively organized majority in the country.

Allowing for the multitude of particular interests affecting people's attitudes toward the Constitution, there seems to have been a general pattern of division. The urban and seaboard areas were almost solidly in favor of the document, not just because particular interests were stronger here, but because in these wealthier, more commercial, more cosmopolitan areas, general commercial and elitist concerns were more prevalent. Conversely, the Constitution tended to be strongly opposed in the more provincial backcountry areas of small farms because of the greater prevalence of agrarian and democratic concerns. The numerically predominant small farmers, who comprised the backbone of Anti-Federalism during the ratification controversy, were well satisfied with things as they stood and saw little need for stronger government.

Until fairly recently, the Anti-Federalists were often described as small-minded, provincial obstructionists who in their petty, self-interested particularism lacked the continental vision of the Federalists. Recent scholarship, however, suggests that for all their political weakness and disunity, the Anti-Federalists should not be so easily dismissed. Because they chose to align themselves against some of the nation's most formidable and revered political thinkers—Washington, Franklin, Madison, Hamilton, Marshall, and Jay—it does not follow that they were "men of little faith," that they lacked virtue, or that their arguments were not well-founded. To be sure the Anti-Federalists were very often more state-centered, less cosmopolitan, and less educated than their opponents, and they were usually more suffused with the traditions of localism. Despite the centralizing pressures of the 1770s and 1780s, fears of concentrated governmental authority and loss of individual liberty remained central to popular American thought. It was in this tradition, then, that the Anti-Federalists opposed the Constitution. In an important, if limited, sense, they were the conservators of a national heritage and truer than the Federalists to the spirit of 1776. In their fear of the tyranny of centralized authority, in their continued fidelity to localist conventions, in their belief that republicanism could survive only in a small and homogeneous society, the Anti-Federalists had their roots firmly planted in Revolutionary assumptions. The Constitution, as they affirmed, represented a profound departure. Their spokesperson, Patrick Henry, characterized it as "a revolution as radical as that which separated us from Great Britain." Compared to such European imperialist nations as England or France, the Founding Fathers had crafted a relatively decentralized regime.

Yet, in the context of the American experience, the product of their labor represented a major leap toward national consolidation.

Finally, it should be noted that the agrarian- and democratic-minded majority might have defeated the Constitution had it been effectively mobilized. The fact that the majority did not mobilize suggests that the opposition was not terribly intense. Politics beyond the local and state level was still a matter of indifference to most farmers. Only a small proportion of the eligible voters bothered to vote at all for delegates to the ratifying conventions, and when the Constitution went into effect, it was readily accepted by all elements of the population. Within little more than a decade, under a Constitution whose operations had been transformed by political parties that the framers did not envisage, the hitherto apathetic agrarian- and democratic-minded majority would come into its own.

CONFLICTING HISTORICAL VIEWPOINTS

2. How Democratic Was the Constitution?

American exceptionalism has been one of the basic presuppositions of our national experience. America was a land peculiarly blessed; its people were God's chosen people, the embodiment of the promise of human perfection. In the words of John Adams, the nation's founding marked "the opening of a grand scheme and design in Providence for the illumination and emancipation of the slavish part of mankind all over the earth." More particularly, the Constitution was an instrument of heaven's will; its framers, Jefferson said, were themselves "demi-gods". Early students of American history were in full agreement. In fact, there was no article of American faith more sacred to nineteenth-century nationalist historians than the document of 1787. In his History of the Formation of the Constitution *(2 vols., 1882), pious, patriotic George Bancroft concluded that the nation's fundamental law fulfilled the promise of the Revolution. It was inspired by the scriptures, he believed, and drafted with providential blessings. Much the same conclusion was reached by John Fiske, who portrayed the document as one of the supreme achievements of human intelligence. In full agreement with Bancroft, his older contemporary, Fiske viewed the Articles of Confederation as an unfit instrument for national government. In his* The Critical Period of American History *(1893), he described the half-dozen years following the Revolutionary War as "the most critical moment in all of the history of the American people." The period of national crisis passed, he believed, only upon the creation of a strong central government. To both Bancroft and Fiske, the Founding Fathers were men of noble purpose and unquestioned devotion to the national welfare.*

A later generation of scholars, however, was more critical of both the Constitu-

tion and its framers. In his path-breaking study, An Economic 'Interpretation of the Constitution *(1913), the progressive historian Charles Beard offered the then shocking argument that the Founding Fathers were not selfless patriots but self-serving plutocrats: "men whose property interests were immediately at stake." The product of their labor represented not the culmination of the democratic revolutionary spirit of 1776, but a counterrevolution. Thus, through the instrument of the Constitution, Beard averred, a few conservative men of property affected a "coup d'état" to protect their economic self-interest and check the growth of popular democracy.*

Although Beard confessed that his work was "fragmentary" and his conclusions "tentative," his interpretation won prompt and almost universal acceptance. Among the many latter-day Beardians, none did more to fill out and document the Columbia University scholar's interpretation than Merrill Jensen. In The Articles of Confederation *(1940) and* The New Nation *(1950), Jensen carefully supported Beard's contention that the Confederation government was not one of "stagnation, ineptitude, bankruptcy, corruption, and disintegration." In his view, the democratic radicalism that waxed with the Declaration of Independence waned with the Constitution. The framers engineered a "conservative counterrevolution" that served to "thwart the will of 'the people'."*

More recently, Beard's critics have all but discredited his economic interpretations. Robert E. Brown (Charles A. Beard and the Constitution, *1955) and Forrest McDonald* (We the People, *1958), for example, have questioned Beard's use of the evidence and nearly all of his conclusions. Neither scholar accepted his class-conflict theories and Brown argued cogently that the Constitution was an essentially middle-class democratic document ideally suited for essentially middle-class democratic America. Other scholars have offered different conclusions, 'and both Jackson Turner Main* (The Antifederalists, *1961) and Lee Benson* (Turner and Beard, *1960) have found elements of Beardian conflict in the alignment of mercantile capitalists versus agrarians during the period of struggle over the Constitution. Yet most historians of the present generation (Main and Benson included) agree that Beard's thesis is seriously deficient. As the intellectual historian Gordon Wood writes in his important* Creation of the Republic *(1969), the notion that the ideas and behavior of the founders were determined by material consideration is "so crude that no further time should be spent on it." Wood does not reject the progressive view of the Constitution as an intrinsically aristocratic document designed to curb the democratic excesses of the Revolution. But he does suggest that the struggle between Federalist and Antifederalist was actually a struggle over what kind of democracy America would have—an elitist, nationally oriented democracy or a popular, locally based democracy.*

The Founders, then, may not have been Jefferson's "demi-gods" nor Bancroft's agents of Providential will. Yet most modern scholars agree that the product of their labors was basically democratic and that they themselves were people of great stature and vision whose devotion to nation transcended pocketbook concerns. It should be noted, however, that democracy in this context did not apply to blacks, the "slavish part" of John Adams's own nation, or to women. The creative energies of the framers were lavished on the foundation of a republic for white males, not on extending the benefits of liberty to blacks or women. A half-century after ratification, when the abolitionist William Lloyd Garrison proposed to burn the Constitution in the name of liberty, he did so on the unassailable ground that it perpetuated slavery. Although subsequent generations of Americans celebrated the framers' work as a charter for political freedom, it should not be forgotten that in 1787 it was not such a charter for blacks, women, or Indians.

FOR FURTHER READING

An excellent beginning point for any study of the political and constitutional significance of the American Revolution is R. R. Palmer's *Age of the Democratic Revolution* (1959). Part one of John R. Howe's *From the Revolution through the Age of Jackson* (1973) provides a convenient summary of current scholarly interpretations of the period. The classic interpretation of the Constitution itself is found, of course, in *The Federalist* (many editions), essays by Hamilton, Madison, and Jay. But several modern-day studies—Clinton Rossiter, *1787: The Grand Convention* (1966); Catherine Drinker Bowen, *Miracle at Philadelphia* (1966), and especially Charles Warren, *The Making of the Constitution* (1947)—may prove more useful to the student. The second and third volumes of Irving Brant's biography of *James Madison* (6 vols., 1941–1961) give an excellent detailed view of both the Confederation period and the Constitutional convention. David B. Davis, in *The Problem of Slavery in an Age of Revolution* (1975); Edmund S. Morgan, in *American Slavery, American Freedom* (1975); and Staughton Lynd, in *Class Conflict, Slavery and the United States Constitution* (1968), offer differing perspectives on a common problem. Both E. James Ferguson, in *The Power of the Purse* (1961), and Forrest McDonald, in *E Pluribus Unum* (1965), develop the financial dimensions of union; Paul C. Nagel, in *One Nation Indivisible* (1964), explores the concept of union in American thought.

2. PRESIDENTIAL ELECTIONS AND MAJOR EVENTS, 1789–1800

1789	**George Washington** elected without opposition.
1790–1791	Hamiltonian program enacted.
	Funding the national debt.
	Assumption of state debts. Bargain involving location of the national capital.
	First Bank of the United States.
	Excise taxes.
1792	**George Washington** reelected without opposition.
1793	Wars of the French Revolution begin.
	Washington's Neutrality Proclamation.
1794	Whiskey Rebellion
1795	Jay's Treaty with Great Britain.
1796	Pinckney's Treaty with Spain.
	John Adams (Federalist) elected over Thomas Jefferson (Republican).
1797–1798	American commissioners to France insulted.
1798	Undeclared naval war with France begins.
	Alien and Sedition Acts.
1798–1799	Virginia and Kentucky Resolutions.
1800	Convention of 1800 resolves differences with France.
	Thomas Jefferson (Republican) elected over John Adams (Federalist).

Federalists and Republicans
1789–1800

7

The new Constitution as written and ratified was merely a grand outline of government. An actual government was created only as the Constitution was put into practice, through adaptation and conflict, in the 1790s. During this stormy decade there were three major developments that lastingly affected the nature of the federal government. First, precedents were set with regard to the composition and functioning of the various branches of government. Second, the real and potential scope and authority of the new government were enormously broadened by Alexander Hamilton's vigorous program of exercising to the limit every power granted or even implied by the Constitution. Finally and most important, Hamilton's policies provoked a growing opposition around which a political party formed. By the end of the decade a two-party system was well established, and had a most profound influence on the way the new government operated.

LAUNCHING THE NEW GOVERNMENT

It was only natural that friends of the Constitution should be chosen to put it into effect. To no one's surprise, the first electoral college agreed unanimously on Virginia's George Washington for president. To provide geographical balance while avoiding the suspect Samuel Adams and John Hancock, the electors turned for vice-president to that sturdy patriot and nationalist, Massachusetts's John Adams. When the first Congress tardily assembled in New York's City Hall in April, 1789, both houses were dominated by Federalists.

While the senators squabbled behind closed doors about titles and ceremonial procedures, James Madison was pushing through the House of Representatives a series of laws that would put the new government into practical operation. Income was provided by a tariff act levying import duties at a moderate rate designed for revenue purposes only. An organization for the executive branch was provided by the

creation of departments of state, treasury, and war. The Judiciary Act of 1789 specified that the Supreme Court should consist of six justices, that there should be a district
court for each state, and that two Supreme Court justices sitting with a district judge
should constitute an intermediate court of appeals. The Act also provided for an
Attorney General and explicitly specified that any decision in the state courts that
questioned federal as opposed to state powers could be appealed to the Supreme
Court, thus authorizing the Supreme Court to pass on the constitutionality of state
laws.

Finally, this first Congress considered the 78 amendments to the Constitution that
had been proposed by the state ratifying conventions. Somewhat reluctantly, the
House approved 17 of these, the Senate approved 12 of the 17, and by 1791, a
sufficient number of states had ratified 10 of the 12. These first 10 amendments, now
known as the Bill of Rights, guaranteed citizens that the federal government would not
invade such rights as trial by jury and freedom of religion, speech, and the press. All
proposed amendments that substantially modified the powers of the federal government had been carefully omitted from the approved list, and disgruntled anti-Federalists could take only small comfort from the Tenth Amendment, which "reserved to
the States respectively, or to the people" all powers not mentioned by the Constitution.

Meanwhile President Washington was enhancing the dignity of the new government through formal and ceremonial behavior that some critics thought too high-
toned for a republic. Also, during the first years of his administration, he contributed
to the popularity of the new regime by taking exhausting tours through all parts of the
country. The president influenced the course of events most by his appointments,
especially of Alexander Hamilton as Secretary of the Treasury and Thomas Jefferson
as Secretary of State. Washington consulted with them regularly, along with his
Secretary of War and Attorney General, and soon the Cabinet, nowhere mentioned
in the Constitution, emerged as a major governmental institution.

THE HAMILTONIAN PROGRAM

Alexander Hamilton had no sooner taken office than he became the master spirit of
the administration; indeed he thought of himself as Washington's prime minister. This
remarkable man burned with a vision of national greatness. Aiming at a powerful,
unified nation, he detested the localistic tendencies of the states. Convinced that
vigorous leadership by the able few, especially in the executive branch of the government, was the only way to build a powerful nation, he feared the turbulence and
irresponsibility of the democratic masses. Astutely aware of the relationship between
political power and economic power, he was determined to promote the rapid economic growth of the country and to forge firm ties, political and economic, between
the government and the wealthy.

Hamilton was far from satisfied with the Constitution as an instrument for national
power and economic growth. Yet he recognized that it was the best that could be
secured, and he came into office resolved to strengthen it by stretching its provisions

and by vigorous administration. Seizing from Congress the initiative for public policy, he outlined in a series of four reports a brilliant, tightly integrated program for the achievement of his objectives.

Hamilton first proposed that the long unpaid continental debt, having a face value of over $50 million, be funded at par—that is, that the old and greatly depreciated securities be called in and exchanged for new federal bonds on which interest would be regularly paid and which upon maturity would be redeemed at full value. This would not only dramatically restore American public credit, but would at the same time bolster the private credit of American entrepreneurs and make it easier for them to obtain the European capital needed for a rapidly growing economy. Gilt-edged federal bonds could form the basis for investment capital. Moreover, the whole class of wealthy investors (or speculators) in continental securities would be greatly enriched, for many of them had obtained their securities from the original holders for as little as 20 or 25 cents on the dollar. On all these grounds, funding would have the political effect of attaching the wealthy to the idea of a strong federal government.

Hamilton next proposed that the federal government assume, in similar fashion, over $20 million in unpaid debts incurred by the various states during the Revolution. This would have the advantage of attaching the large class of state creditors to the federal government rather than to the states, thus strengthening the prestige of the former at the expense of the latter.

Funding and assumption of debts required additional revenue, and Hamilton recommended that this be raised by increasing tariff duties and by levying a direct excise tax on spirituous liquors. He frankly advocated the latter tax both as a means of increasing the government's power to collect a tax and of demonstrating that power to the fiercely independent whiskey-making farmers of the interior.

The capstone of Hamilton's financial system was his proposal for a national bank. The bank was to be chartered for 20 years as a mixed public-private corporation controlled by private investors who were to purchase four-fifths of the $10 million worth of capital stock. Investors could pay three-fourths of their stock subscriptions in the form of federal bonds and one-fourth in gold or silver coin (specie). On the basis of this capital the bank was to issue specie-redeemable bank notes for loans to borrowers. The fact that these notes were to be receivable for all dues to the government would tend to keep up their value. Such an institution, Hamilton argued, would provide an ample and uniform circulating medium, a source of credit for businesses, and a profitable investment for capitalists. More particularly it would convert into fluid and expandable capital the funded Continental and state securities. In all these ways, it would be another instrument for binding the wealthy to the federal government. A final advantage of the bank, Hamilton believed, was that it was nowhere authorized in the Constitution; it could be chartered only under a "broad construction" of that instrument and would help to establish a doctrine of "implied powers."

One major element in Hamilton's economic vision remains to be mentioned. As a pioneer student of what today would be called the economic growth of under-developed countries, he was far ahead of his time in recognizing the importance of promoting manufacturing. A major factor in his financial proposals was the desire to provide capital for industrial development. The last of his four great reports was devoted wholly to this subject, calling for tariff rates that would give "infant indus-tries" a competitive advantage in the domestic market until they could become well established.

To win congressional support for these proposals Hamilton fought with every political weapon at his command. The more agrarian-minded sections of the country had taken immediate alarm, and the first battle came over funding the Confederation debt. Critics objected particularly to the windfall profits of speculators who had acquired Continental securities at greatly depreciated rates. Indeed the opposition was so strong in Virginia that Madison parted with Hamilton, proposing that current holders be paid at only the depreciated rate with the remainder going to the original holders. Nevertheless, Hamilton's will prevailed. The commercial-minded Federalists in the first Congress passed the measure as originally proposed.

Assumption of state debts aroused even stronger opposition, especially from states like Virginia that had already paid off many of their own debts, and again Madison was in opposition. This time the measure was stalled, until Hamilton adroitly connected it with the simultaneous controversy among New York, Pennsylvania, and the southern states over the permanent location of the national capital. At a dinner with Hamilton, Jefferson agreed that he and Madison would draw off some of the opposition to assumption and that in return the national capital would be moved for ten years to Philadelphia and then permanently to a ten-mile-square tract to be selected by Washington on the Potomac River between Virginia and Maryland.

Hamilton's revenue proposals met their strongest opposition not in Congress but among backcountry farmers who violently resisted the tax on whiskey, their only easily transported and salable product. By 1794 this resistance culminated, in Pennsyl-vania, in a Whiskey Rebellion, and only when Washington sent an army of some thousands into the disaffected area were the armed mobs dispersed and order re-stored.

The serious constitutional objections to the national bank gave even Washington pause, and before signing the bill he requested written opinions from members of his Cabinet. Arguing the doctrine of implied powers, Hamilton pointed out that the Constitution authorized Congress to "make all laws which shall be necessary and proper for carrying into Execution" the specifically enumerated powers. "Necessary" should be construed, he thought, as meaning *"needful, requisite, incidental, useful, or conducive to,"* and he argued that powers "ought to be construed liberally in advancement of the public good." Jefferson, a strict constructionist, on the other hand, contended that all powers not expressly granted (restricting "necessary" to the narrowest sense) were reserved by the Tenth Amendment to the states or the people, and hence he believed the bank was unconstitutional. Washington finally followed the opinion of Hamilton and signed the bank bill.

Hamilton's proposals for encouraging manufacturing were the only part of his program that failed in Congress. Manufacturing was still in an infant state in the country, most of it carried on by independent artisans and in people's homes, and there was no strong interest group to back Hamilton's plans. Indeed, the wealthy mercantile capitalists who were his strongest supporters on other measures were opposed to tariff barriers that would impede the flow of international trade.

On the whole Hamilton had been brilliantly successful, and his policies gave to the new government a vigor and direction that profoundly affected its future development. At the same time, however, the forceful financier had provoked a rising opposition from agrarian-minded people. By 1791, there was a recognizable group in Congress opposed to the Hamiltonian policies, and Madison and Jefferson were beginning to work together to organize resistance to the New Yorker's influence. Already some spoke of a Republican or anti-Federalist "interest" as opposed to the Federalist "interest" of Hamilton and his followers. At the time of Washington's reelection in 1792, this nascent Republican party was strong enough to garner 50 electoral votes for New York's George Clinton for vice-president against John Adams's 77.

THE WARS OF THE FRENCH REVOLUTION

The outbreak of the French Revolution in 1789 was greeted with enthusiasm by most Americans for it confirmed their faith that their own Revolution had blazed a trail to liberty that all humanity would eventually follow. But widespread "Bastille fever" lasted only so long as the revolution in France remained relatively moderate. As the great upheaval moved into a new and more somber phase, American ardor cooled and public opinion divided sharply. The people who tended toward Federalism in domestic politics were shocked by the execution of Louis XVI and the wholesale guillotining of political opponents. When the revolutionary agitation spread to other countries, followed by French revolutionary armies, conservative Americans were driven into hysterical fears of mob rule, atheism, and Jacobinism at home. On the other hand, more democratic-minded Americans, those who tended toward Republicanism in domestic politics but often deplored the worst excesses of the "reign of terror," remained steadfast in their support of the goals of the French Revolution. Jefferson, for one, did not applaud the beheadings, but he believed that "the liberty of the whole earth" depended on the triumph of *liberté, égalité,* and *fraternité* in France. To Jefferson and his followers, the conservative reaction was proof that their Federalist opponents were really monarchists.

The French Revolution precipitated a great European war, lasting with brief interruptions from 1793 until 1815 and pitting France against a series of European coalitions headed by Great Britain. American leaders of all persuasions agreed that their infant nation should avoid becoming directly involved on either side, but there were sharp differences in sympathies. The Hamiltonians favored the British, partly out of a preference for British conservatism as opposed to French radicalism and partly because the large trade with Great Britain enriched the merchant class and provided 90 percent of the tariff revenues essential to Hamiltonian financial policies. Jefferson and his friends, more sympathetic to French aims, argued that the country owed its independence to the Franco-American alliance of 1778, which was still in force, and urged a neutrality that would be benevolent toward France.

Actually France did not want to invoke the alliance to bring the United States into the war as a belligerent. The powerful British navy was sweeping French merchant ships from the seas, and the French hoped that if the United States remained neutral, American merchant ships could supply her with foodstuffs and raw materials. Britain, too, as she devoted more of her resources to war, relied increasingly on American shipping. As a result, commercial interests and producers of exports in the United States entered upon a period of unparalleled prosperity.

Washington's proclamation of American neutrality in 1793 made considerable sense economically, but it did not begin to solve all the problems created by the European war. Existing American grievances against Great Britain over the northwest posts, incitement of the northwestern Indians, and discrimination against American trade were compounded in 1794 when Great Britain moved to cripple the newly flourishing American commerce on the high seas. Determined to starve France into submission, the British navy suddenly seized some 300 American ships under newly promulgated rules that forbade neutrals to carry grain or flour to France, to carry any French-owned goods whatever, or to engage in trade with the French West Indies. Adding insult to injury, British naval commanders began stopping American merchant ships and forcibly taking off crew members thought to have deserted from the British navy, including some who were American citizens.

Despite a storm of indignation, Hamilton was determined to avoid a break with Great Britain at all costs. Jefferson had already resigned in disgust at Hamilton's domination of the administration and interference in the affairs of the State Department, leaving no one in the Cabinet strong enough to oppose the iron-willed Treasury Secretary. The only diplomatic weapon against the British the United States had was the threat to join the Armed Neutrality of smaller European trading nations that was forming to resist British restrictions on international trade. Chief Justice John Jay was sent to London to negotiate, but Hamilton undercut his mission by assuring the British minister that the United States would not join the Armed Neutrality.

As a result Jay had to accept whatever terms the British offered. The British did agree to pay indemnities for seized American shipping and to withdraw by 1796 from their posts within the northwestern boundary of the United States. In return, Jay had to agree that the United States pay old claims of British merchants against American citizens and tacitly accept the restrictive British definitions of the rights of neutrals in international trade. Not a word was said about British impressment of American sailors, British interference with the northwestern Indians, or indemnity for the slaves carried away by British armies.

Hamilton's outraged opponents charged that these terms were a humiliating surrender to British power; in the violent debate over Jay's treaty during 1795, the emerging line of division between Federalists and Republicans finally crystallized. The only alternative to accepting the treaty, argued the Hamiltonians, was war with England and ratification of the treaty by the Senate guaranteed a return of commercial prosperity and gave the young nation a further period of freedom from European embroilments during which it could further strengthen its independence and institutions.

In another area of diplomacy, the Washington administration was able to capitalize on Spain's involvement in the European wars to achieve a brilliant diplomatic triumph. When Spain shifted in 1795 from the British to the French side and when the Jay Treaty appeared to align the United States with Great Britain, the Spanish authorities recognized that their possessions on the southwestern border of the United States had become exceedingly vulnerable. Consequently, the American minister Thomas Pinckney had little difficulty negotiating a treaty, ratified in 1796, that granted all the American demands: the fixing of the Florida boundary at the 31st parallel, free navigation of the Mississippi and a right of "deposit" (the right to bring goods down the Mississippi and land them while awaiting oceangoing ships) at New Orleans for American citizens, and a Spanish promise to restrain the Indians along the frontier.

Thus by the end of Washington's second term, the Jay and Pinckney treaties had eased America's difficulties with two of the three European powers with which the United States was dangerously involved. Washington's policy of preserving American neutrality had strengthened the nation's independence and yet afforded it opportunities to capitalize on the involvements of European nations. Whether this policy could be pursued in the face of difficulties with a third European power, France, was the major problem facing Washington's successor, John Adams.

THE TRIALS OF JOHN ADAMS

Washington's determination to retire at the end of two terms inopportunely deprived the Federalists of their greatest political asset just as the Jay Treaty controversy unfolded. Consequently the election of 1796 was the first hard fought and closely contested presidential election. Hamilton had made too many bitter enemies to be a successful candidate, and his ultracommercial and elitist views were too extreme even for many Federalist voters. Vice-President John Adams, to whom the party leaders now turned, represented a more moderate federalism. The Republican opposition, almost without discussion, accepted Jefferson as their candidate. After a vituperative campaign, Adams barely edged Jefferson, 71 electoral votes to 68; Jefferson became vice-president.

At the time of Adams's election, the French were enraged by the Jay Treaty. Truculently they ordered seizure of American ships carrying British goods, and this time it was the Hamiltonians who beat the drums for war. Resisting Hamiltonian pressure, however, Adams sent a special commission of three men to France to try to settle the difficulties. When the French treated the commissioners insultingly and made impossible demands, including bribes, the war spirit again flamed high in the United States. By the spring of 1798, the President and Congress were making preparations for war, and an undeclared naval war broke out between French and American vessels on the high seas. Yet Adams was never quite swept away by the war fever, and in early 1799, against bitter Hamiltonian opposition, he resolved to make one last effort for peace. Another three-man commission was sent to France and this time an agreement was reached that recognized American principles of neutral rights and abrogated amicably the Franco-American alliance of 1778.

John Adams must be credited with courage and disinterestedness for single-handedly resisting the war hysteria at the cost of his own popularity and the political success of his party, but there was one respect in which he went along with the Hamiltonian extremists. As in other periods of national crisis, the popular mood was highly suspicious of dissenters and foreigners, and the Federalists were all too ready to regard the Republicans as traitorous sympathizers with the nation's enemies. Indeed the ideas of free speech, a free press, and the legitimacy of partisan opposition were not yet firmly established. Under the circumstances, the Federalists, including President Adams, capitalized on the war hysteria by pushing through Congress in 1798 four measures known as the Alien and Sedition Acts. Three of these laws lengthened the minimum residence requirements for new American citizens from 5 to 14 years and authorized the president to deport any alien he thought dangerous and to imprison dangerous aliens during war. The fourth, the Sedition Act, prescribed fines up to $5,000 and imprisonment up to five years for persons who conspired to oppose measures of the government, who promoted riots or unlawful assemblies, or who published "any false, scandalous, and malicious writing" against the government or its officials.

No aliens were deported under the new laws, although many left the country in fear of prosecution. But partisan Federalist district attorneys and judges used the Sedition Act to secure indictments against 15 Republican editors; 10 were convicted, one of them a congressman from Vermont.

No one in the United States was more alarmed by the Alien and Sedition Acts than Thomas Jefferson. Seeking some means of arousing protest, he drafted a set of resolutions and sent them by a friend to Kentucky where the legislature adopted them. Meanwhile Madison had secured adoption of similar resolutions by the Virginia legislature. These Kentucky and Virginia resolutions of 1798 took the position that the Alien and Sedition Acts, being contrary to the Constitution, were null and void. These resolutions called on the other states to join in asking Congress to repeal them.

THE REVOLUTION OF 1800

The Kentucky and Virginia resolutions opened the campaign for the return match between Adams and Jefferson in the presidential election of 1800. Again there was a close, hard fought contest. The Republicans had been greatly weakened by the charge of Francophilism during the war hysteria, but with the passing of the threat of war, the reaction against the Alien and Sedition Acts gave hope of a Republican comeback. Moreover, the Federalists were weakened by mounting friction between the Adams and Hamilton wings of the party and by unpopular taxes levied to support the war-preparedness program. This time Jefferson edged ahead of Adams, 73 electoral votes to 65.

This "revolution of 1800" inaugurated no revolutionary change in public policy nor even, as yet, a revolutionary shift in the balance of strength between the parties. But the working of the constitutional system had been transformed beyond the intention of the framers by the growth within it of a system of two opposing political parties, representing divergent constituencies, holding divergent ideologies, and proposing divergent policies. The potentially overwhelming majority of the Republicans was not yet fully mobilized for political action in pursuance of its democratic- and agrarian-minded objectives. But already that party had overcome the great initial advantages of its competitor and won a majority. Thus the revolutionary principle of peaceful competition and transfer of power between parties was established. Meanwhile, the Federalists, though often out of tune with the slowly awakening majority, had given the new government a vigorous start, steered it safely through the shoals of international war, and presented it thriving and intact to the party of Thomas Jefferson.

FOR FURTHER READING

The most influential interpretation of the difference between Federalists and Republicans has been Charles A. Beard's *The Economic Origins of Jeffersonian Democracy* (1915).* Joseph C. Charles has written a series of suggestive essays on partisan divergence in *The Origins of the American Party System* (1956).* John C. Miller's *The Federalist Era* (1960) is a useful and sympathetic overview of the Federalists, while Marcus Cunliffe's *George Washington: Man and Monument* (1958)* and James T. Flexner's *George Washington and the New Nation* (1970) are excellent interpretative studies of the first president. Manning J. Dauer has distinguished between two wings of the Federalist party in *The Adams Federalists* (1953), and Broadus Mitchell's sympathetic *Alexander Hamilton: The National Adventure* (1962) is the best biography of this extraordinary figure. On the Republican side, Eugene P. Link has described those forerunners of the Republican party, the *Democratic-Republican Societies* (1942); Noble E. Cunningham has analyzed the development of the Republican party organization in *The Jeffersonian Republicans: The Formation of Party Organization, 1789–1801* (1957)*; and Alfred F. Young has carefully studied *The Democratic Republicans of New York: The Origins, 1763–1797* (1967). A political scientist, William N. Chambers, has written a suggestive analysis of the role of *Political Parties in a New Nation: The American Experience, 1776–1809* (1963)*; and a sociologist, Seymour M. Lipset, in *The First New Nation* (1963),* has made a suggestive comparison between the problems faced by American leaders in the 1790s and the problems faced by leaders of the new nations of the twentieth century. Both James M. Smith, in *Freedom's Fetters* (1956)*, and Leonard Levy, in *Legacy of Suppression* (1960), focus on the Alien and Sedition Acts; Charles R. Ritcheson's *Aftermath of Revolution* (1969) offers a bold new interpretation of early British policy toward the United States; and Samuel Bemis's *Jay's Treaty* (1923) is still unsurpassed.

---

*Available in paperback edition.

3. PRESIDENTIAL ELECTIONS AND MAJOR EVENTS, 1800–1823

1800	**Thomas Jefferson** (Republican) elected over John Adams (Federalist).
1803	*Marbury* vs. *Madison.* John Marshall's Supreme Court declares a law of Congress unconstitutional. Louisiana Purchase.
1804	**Thomas Jefferson** (Republican) reelected over Charles C. Pinckney (Federalist).
1804–1806	Lewis and Clark expedition.
1805–1807	Mounting seizures of American shipping under British Orders in Council and Napoleon's Decrees.
1807	*Chesapeake-Leopard* affair. Embargo Act.
1808	**James Madison** (Republican) elected over Charles C. Pinckney (Federalist).
1809	Nonintercourse Act replaces Embargo Act.
1810	Macon's Bill No. 2 replaces Nonintercourse Act.
1811	Recharter of First Bank of the United States defeated. Power of northwestern Indians broken at Tippecanoe.
1812	**James Madison** (Caucus Republican) reelected over DeWitt Clinton (Independent Republican).
1812–1815	War of 1812.
1814–1815	Treaty of Ghent.
1816	**James Monroe** (Republican) elected over Rufus King (Federalist).
1817	Rush-Bagot Agreement with Great Britain demilitarizes the Great Lakes. Andrew Jackson invades Spanish Florida.
1818	Convention of 1818 settles outstanding differences with Great Britain.
1819–1821	Transcontinental Treaty with Spain acquires Florida.
1820	**James Monroe** (Republican) reelected without opposition.
1823	Monroe Doctrine enunciated.

The Jeffersonian Republic in a Threatening World 1800–1823

8

Thomas Jefferson wisely recognized the political foolhardiness, if not the practical impossibility, of trying to erase the legacy of Hamiltonian measures that he inherited. The national bank was allowed to run its course undisturbed until its 20-year charter expired in 1811, and the funded federal debt continued to be honored. Yet there was a significant shift in the tone and direction of public policy. The government had just moved to the new Washington City. In sharp reaction to the formality and ceremony that his more aristocratic predecessors had cultivated, Jefferson invested the muddy little capital on the Potomac with an almost ostentatious simplicity. This lack of pretension symbolized his deliberately negative policy: to avoid ambitious measures, to keep the federal establishment as plain and simple as possible, to practice the most rigorous economy, and, thus, to pay off as rapidly as possible the federal debt that Hamilton had designed as semipermanent.

In taking this line, Jefferson was not only following his own agrarian and democratic preconceptions, but also proving himself a shrewd reader of the mood of the country. The Hamiltonian system, for all its brilliant success, had been premature, resting on the transitory and fortuitous ascendancy of a commercial-minded minority that was out of tune with the bulk of the population. Even in the Federalist stronghold of New England, religious and sectional considerations had contributed more to that party's strength than commercial-mindedness, and the Adams brand of Federalism was more popular than the Hamilton brand. Despite a flourishing overseas commerce that was gradually pulling more farmers and planters into producing staples for market, the country as a whole remained wedded to the vision of a simple, unprogressive, democratic utopia, dominated by self-sufficient and, therefore, independent and virtuous farmers. Jefferson's reasonable behavior in office and the eloquence of his statements and policies in behalf of the agrarian, democratic ideal won him overwhelming political strength, even in New England.

During these Jeffersonian years Americans appeared to believe that their utopian republican order might endure without change forever. They failed to realize that history will not leave societies, much less utopias, alone. The only problems that most of them saw were those arising out of the continuing international conflict. These were indeed to be severe problems for Jefferson and his successor Madison and would lead ultimately to war. Yet it was not war that was to undermine the republican utopia, but the unsuspected forces of westward expansion and economic change that were already gaining momentum.

VESTIGES OF FEDERALISM

Jefferson's disciplined majorities in Congress had moved promptly to repeal the whiskey tax, the unpopular war preparedness taxes, and the parts of the Alien and Sedition Acts that had not already expired. The only serious battle over remnants of Federalism arose in connection with the judiciary.

The federal courts were staffed entirely by Federalists serving for life, and some of the judges had conducted themselves with flagrant partisanship. In the last days of the Adams administration, the Federalists had sought to strengthen their judicial bastion with an act establishing a series of new courts, and President Adams had spent his last hours in office signing commissions for the "midnight judges" and other officials who were to staff the new courts. Adams had made his most important contribution to perpetuating Federalist principles a month earlier by appointing as Chief Justice of the Supreme Court John Marshall, a Virginian of the Washington rather than the Jefferson-Madison stamp, whose nationalistic ideas were to dominate the Court from 1801 until 1835.

The Republicans had no sooner assumed power than they repealed the act establishing the new courts, and Jefferson ordered his Secretary of State, James Madison, to withhold the commissions of Adams's "midnight" appointees. The stage was set for a showdown when one of these appointees applied to the Supreme Court for a *writ of mandamus* ordering Madison to deliver his commission. Chief Justice Marshall's famous decision in the case of *Marbury* vs. *Madison* was handed down in 1803. Marshall knew that he had no means of forcing Madison to deliver the commission so he skillfully sidestepped a direct confrontation with the administration while he gained an advantage in another quarter. Declaring that the petitioner was entitled to his commission, he contended nevertheless that the Supreme Court was not empowered to act in this kind of case. It had been given such jurisdiction by the Judiciary Act of 1789, but Marshall argued that in this respect the Judiciary Act contradicted the constitutional definition of the Court's jurisdiction. Therefore, said Marshall, this section of the Judiciary Act was unconstitutional and consequently void. The Court for the first time asserted the power, nowhere explicitly given it, to invalidate an act of Congress on constitutional grounds.

Even before Marshall's decision, the Republicans had begun a campaign to neutralize the Federalism of the judiciary. Incensed by the prosecutions under the Sedition Act and fearful of keeping any branch of the government from popular control, Jefferson favored making the judiciary amenable to political influence. This he thought might be accomplished by congressional impeachment of the more notorious judges. The Republicans had little difficulty getting one drunken and incompetent district judge removed from office. In a key case, however, they failed to get enough votes to impeach Supreme Court Justice Samuel Chase. This failure preserved the principle of an independent judiciary and left Chief Justice Marshall free to develop the Supreme Court into a fortress of nationalistic and anti-Jeffersonian influence.

AN EMPIRE FOR LIBERTY

Early in Jefferson's administration, the exigencies of international war again presented the United States with a splendid diplomatic opportunity. Napoleon had just forced Spain to return Louisiana (in Spanish hands since 1763) to France, hoping to use it as the granary for a growing French empire in the western hemisphere. Under Spanish control, Louisiana had been no great threat to the United States, but the prospect of having Napoleonic France astride the Mississippi with an economic stranglehold on the whole interior of the country was another matter. Promptly, Jefferson sent James Monroe to aid the American minister in Paris, Robert R. Livingston, in securing American interests at the mouth of the Mississippi. If possible, they were to purchase the isle of New Orleans, that small portion of Louisiana that lay east of the lower Mississippi.

By the time the negotiations opened in 1803, the collapse of the French expeditionary force in the West Indies and the resumption of the European war after a brief truce had caused Napoleon to abandon his plans for a French empire in America. To the astonishment of the American negotiators, the French offered to sell not only New Orleans but the whole of Louisiana, the entire western watershed of the Mississippi. A price of $15 million was quickly agreed upon, although the Americans were exceeding their instructions. When the news reached Washington, Jefferson, the strict constructionist, worried briefly about the lack of specific constitutional authorization for such purchases of territory, but his doubts were easily dissipated in his enthusiasm for so vast an extension of his agrarian "empire for liberty." Advising Congress to ratify quickly, lest Napoleon change his mind, he seemed to embrace the Hamiltonian doctrine of implied powers.

Even before the Louisiana Purchase was consummated, Jefferson had evinced his interest in the western country by beginning preparations for the exploration led by Meriwether Lewis and William Clark. Between 1804 and 1806, Lewis and Clark's party ascended the Missouri River to its sources, crossed the Rocky Mountains, and descended the Columbia River to the Pacific, returning with a wealth of information about the vast domain the United States had acquired.

During these years, a strong tide of migration was running westward out of the original states; the line of regular settlement had not yet reached the Mississippi River. The first of the new states (Vermont, 1791; Kentucky, 1792; Tennessee, 1796; and Ohio, 1803) were becoming populous commonwealths, while the French-Spanish settlements around New Orleans were attracting sufficient immigrants from the older states to enter the union as the state of Louisiana in 1812.

Thomas Jefferson and his party showed a special solicitude for the agrarian, democratic West. One demonstration of this solicitude was the provision made that a percentage of the public land proceeds from the new state of Ohio would be used to construct a great National Road from Cumberland, Maryland on the Potomac River across the mountains to Wheeling, Virginia on the Ohio. From there, the National Road was eventually extended through Ohio and Indiana and surveyed as far as St. Louis.

The new western states returned Jefferson's solicitude with overwhelming support for the Republican party. And so, increasingly, did the other states. In 1804, Jefferson was elected to a second term by a resounding victory over Charles Cotesworth Pinckney, 162 electoral votes to 14.

THE PERILS OF NEUTRALITY

During Jefferson's second administration the European war entered a more desperate phase. Napoleon's authority was extending over the whole of continental Europe, while the British were achieving unchallenged supremacy on the high seas. As the great land power and the great naval power moved into their final mortal struggle, each increasingly sought to cripple the other through economic warfare, and Americans, the leading neutral traders, were caught in the middle.

Out of self-interest and principle the United States had asserted an advanced doctrine of neutral rights, claiming the right to trade unmolested with all belligerents. This doctrine had been tenable in connection with the limited warfare of the sixteenth and seventeenth centuries, and it was supported by the code of international law that won considerable acceptance during that period. But the wars of the French Revolution brought a new kind of general warfare, precursor of the total war of the twentieth century, ranging populations against populations. This new warfare was waged by mass armies with sweeping ideological and nationalistic objectives, in place of the earlier small professional armies seeking limited national goals.

Under these circumstances, it was not realistic to expect belligerents to respect the doctrines of neutral rights that the United States sought to maintain. The Federalists had earlier recognized the realities of the world power situation in accepting Jay's Treaty as an alternative to war. Faced with these same realities, Jefferson was just as anxious as the Federalists had been to avoid American involvement in the war but more reluctant to compromise American principles of neutral rights. Believing that the belligerents needed American trade too much to risk war with the United States, he embarked on the difficult task of using American commerce (the strength of which he overestimated) as a weapon to coerce the belligerents into respecting neutral rights.

During Jefferson's first administration, American shippers had been able to pile up such tremendous profits as to more than offset their losses from seizures under the temporarily relaxed British and French restrictions. But in 1805, in the *Essex* case, the British admiralty courts outlawed the most lucrative part of this trade, involving goods shipped from the French West Indies to France by way of the United States. This was but the first in a series of British decisions blockading the Continent to stem the flow of commodities useful to the French war effort. As a result, seizures of American shipping mounted alarmingly. Even more intolerable to American pride was an increase in British impressments of sailors from American ships.

Congress responded in 1805 by barring certain British goods from American ports, and the Jefferson administration sought to use this Nonimportation Act as a counter in negotiations in London. The British were willing to relax their restrictions on the French West Indian trade, but since they refused to renounce altogether the right of impressment, Jefferson would not submit the resulting treaty to the Senate for ratification. British indignities culminated in 1807 when the British naval vessel *Leopard* opened fire on the unsuspecting American naval vessel *Chesapeake,* stopped her, and impressed at cannon's mouth four seamen.

Like Adams before him, Jefferson had to resist the clamor for war, meanwhile pushing through Congress the Embargo Act of 1807. This extreme measure of economic coercion forbade American ships to sail for Europe. Jefferson hoped, of course, to force the British to terms by denying them desperately needed American goods and shipping. Unfortunately the effects of the embargo were felt more severely by American commercial and exporting interests than they were by the British. New England, its economy prostrate and its people bitter, moved back into the Federalist orbit. Finally even Jefferson concluded, just before he left office in the spring of 1809, that the embargo could no longer be sustained. Congress repealed the Act, and it was left to James Madison to seek some better solution to the prickly problem of neutral rights.

MADISON TRIES HIS HAND

By the time of Madison's election, French depredations on American commerce were becoming as serious as those by the British. Napoleon had responded to the British blockade of the Continent with a series of decrees declaring the British Isles blockaded. Though he did not have the naval power to enforce a blockade, he could and did order the seizure of American ships reaching French ports after having submitted to British regulations. Such seizures reached wholesale proportions early in the Madison administration.

Shifting from one expedient of economic coercion to another, Madison and his congressional followers tried supplanting the embargo with a Nonintercourse Act (1809), freeing American shippers to trade with all nations except France and England and promising to resume trade with whichever of these nations would first remove its restrictions. Profits of trade were so high, however, that American shippers preferred to take their chances on the British and French trade even under the restrictions, and in 1810 Congress supplanted the Nonintercourse Act with a measure known as Macon's Bill No. 2. This overingenious measure reopened the whole world to American trade but declared that whenever either of the major belligerents rescinded its restrictions on neutral shipping, nonintercourse would be reinvoked against the other.

American embarrassment was compounded by the pathetic eagerness of the Madison administration to seize upon any indication that its policy of economic coercion was working. Under the Nonintercourse Act, the president used favorable

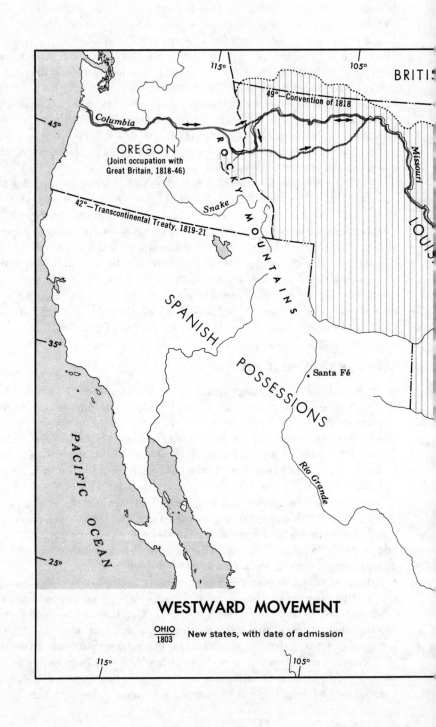

45°

115°   105°

                                              BRITIS

Columbia   49°—Convention of 1818

OREGON
(Joint occupation with
Great Britain, 1818-46)

42°—Transcontinental Treaty, 1819-21

Snake

ROCKY MOUNTAINS

LOUIS

Missouri

35°

SPANISH POSSESSIONS

• Santa Fé

PACIFIC OCEAN

Rio Grande

25°

WESTWARD MOVEMENT

OHIO
1803   New states, with date of admission

115°   105°

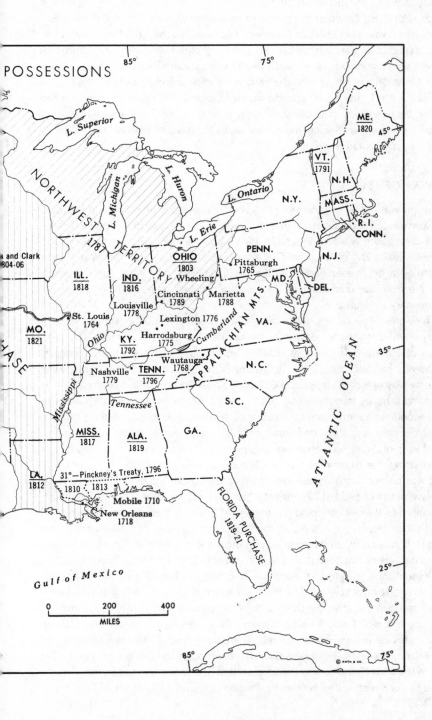

POSSESSIONS

85°
75°

L. Superior

NORTHWEST

L. Michigan

L. Huron

L. Ontario

TERRITORY
1787

L. Erie

ME.
1820
45°

VT.
1791

N.H.

MASS.

R.I.
CONN.

N.Y.

PENN.

OHIO
1803

Pittsburgh
1765

Wheeling

N.J.

MD.

DEL.

s and Clark
804-06

ILL.
1818

IND.
1816

Cincinnati
1789

Marietta
1788

Louisville
1778

St. Louis
1764

Lexington 1776

Harrodsburg
1775

Ohio

APPALACHIAN MTS.

Cumberland

VA.

35°

MO.
1821

KY.
1792

Wautauga
1768

N.C.

HASE

Nashville
1779

TENN.
1796

S.C.

Tennessee

Mississippi

MISS.
1817

ALA.
1819

GA.

LA.
1812

31°—Pinckney's Treaty, 1796

1810   1813

Mobile 1710

New Orleans
1718

FLORIDA PURCHASE
1819-21

ATLANTIC OCEAN

25°

Gulf of Mexico

0   200   400
MILES

85°
75°

© RMⁿⁿ & CO.

negotiation with a too pliable British minister as a pretext for announcing resumption of trade with Great Britain, only to have to eat his words when the British minister's work was disavowed in London. Napoleon exploited Macon's Bill No. 2 with even greater cynicism. A carefully ambiguous French promise to rescind the obnoxious decrees against neutral shipping hoodwinked Madison into reinvoking nonintercourse against Great Britain, whereupon the French resumed seizing American ships.

Thus by 1811, the pacific, agrarian-minded diplomacy of economic coercion had been tried in every way that could be imagined, all to no avail. The nation had never seemed so powerless to avert indignities, and the only alternatives seemed to be humiliating submission or war.

THE WAR OF 1812

Submission was utterly unacceptable to a remarkable group of vigorous young men who were elected to the Congress that convened in December, 1811, and who came to be known as the War Hawks. Led by the captivating Henry Clay of Kentucky and the intellectually impressive John C. Calhoun of South Carolina, the War Hawks represented a new generation of Republican politicians who were eager to wrest leadership from the tired hands of Madison and his dispirited companions of the Revolutionary generation.

These new Republicans were nationalistic, not only in their patriotic love of country but also in their freedom from the agrarian localism that animated the companions of Jefferson. This was especially true of Clay, whose Kentucky Bluegrass constituency had been drawn into flourishing hemp production for the international market by way of New Orleans, and Calhoun, whose South Carolina up-country was undergoing a heady transformation into a land of cotton plantations. Such areas of recent economic boom shared the cosmopolitanism, progressivism, and nationalism of the older commercial-minded areas and might be characterized as agrarian-commercial in spirit. From such areas was beginning to emanate a new-style Republican nationalism whose spokesmen par excellence were Clay and Calhoun.

It was no accident that the advocates for the agrarian-commercial areas were War Hawks in 1811 and 1812. In the older, strictly commercial areas of the Northeast, merchants and shipowners could run the risk of British and French seizures and still make great profits; they opposed both the Republican measures of economic coercion and the talk of war. But in the agrarian-commercial enclaves of the South and West, exhilarating booms had been stalled by the disorganization of international trade. As loyal Republicans, people in these areas had been willing to give the policies of economic coercion a trial, but now their patience had run out. Only war could save the national honor and enable the march of progress and prosperity to resume.

Embarrassingly, Great Britain and France had been equally obnoxious, and the United States could hardly take on both. There were special reasons for hostility to Great Britain. The British officials in Canada were thought to have encouraged Indian unrest in the Old Northwest and the organization of an ominous Indian confederacy, headed by Tecumseh and his brother the Prophet, to oppose the advance of American settlement. Though a frontier army destroyed Tecumseh's power at Tippecanoe in 1811, the bumptious Republicans of the Ohio Valley clamored for the conquest of Canada.

Similarly the Southwest was calling for the conquest of Spanish Florida, and Spain was again allied with Great Britain in the European war. Through Spanish Florida ran the rivers on which the people of the Georgia, Alabama, and Mississippi country depended for trade. The Spanish authorities were also suspected of encouraging Indian hostility, and their territory was a haven for the runaway slaves of the Americans. The United States asserted a doubtful claim under the Louisiana Purchase to West Florida, roughly the territory between Mobile Bay and New Orleans. Already by 1810, the Madison administration had taken advantage of a "revolution" by immigrants from the United States to annex part of this area. War with Great Britain would provide an opportunity to complete the conquest of Florida.

Thus the stalling of economic booms in several agrarian-commercial areas, resentment of British tampering with the Indians, and a desire for Canada and Florida made the war fever especially intense in a great arc running along the frontier from northern New England out through Kentucky and Tennessee to South Carolina and Georgia. Yet more important than any of these specific grounds for war was the widespread desire, especially among younger Republicans of the War Hawk stripe, to avenge the national honor and dignity. The callous impressments of American sailors made Great Britain the inevitable enemy.

By the spring of 1812, the Madison administration, not knowing what else to do, was ready to go along with the agitation for war. In June, on the President's recommendation, a declaration of war was pushed through a seriously divided Congress. Two days before the declaration, the British government in London decided to repeal all its restrictions on neutral trade. The Republican diplomacy of economic coercion had finally accomplished its purpose, barely too late to save the country from a disgraceful war.

The War of 1812 was a military debacle. But for British preoccupation with Napoleon, it would have been an utter disaster. Feeble administration in Washington and feebler generalship in the field brought defeat after defeat. Grandiose western boasts about the easy conquest of Canada eventuated in the disgraceful surrender of the American army at Detroit. In 1814, the defeat of Napoleon enabled the British to pay serious attention to the American war. One invading army easily captured Washington and burned the public buildings. Another, marching down from Canada to cut the country in two along the line of the Hudson, would have succeeded if its timid general had not been unduly discouraged by the success of a small American flotilla in maintaining naval control of Lake Champlain along his line of march. A final formidable force, fresh from victories over Napoleon, was sent to seize New Orleans with the aim of wresting much of the West from the United States. This seasoned army was annihilated by Andrew Jackson and his western militia in the only significant American triumph of the war. Americans were able to take pride in the naval victories of individual ships, but these could not prevent the mighty British navy from establishing unquestioned control of the seas along the American coasts.

Much of the American weakness arose from internal dissension. Southerners had little enthusiasm for the conquest of Canada, and Northerners had little for the conquest of Florida. The whole war was bitterly opposed in commercial areas, especially New England. New England banks and capitalists would not lend money to rescue the bankrupt federal treasury, the New England governors refused to supply troops, and in December, 1814, a convention of the New England states met at Hartford to seek redress against the tyranny of the federal government. Some participants advocated the secession of New England, but the more moderate majority contented itself with proposing constitutional amendments that would protect the interests of their section.

The unfortunate war had hardly started when the Madison administration began efforts to end it, but it was 1814 before a group of British and American commissioners got down to negotiating in earnest at Ghent in Belgium. The treaty they finally agreed on in December simply restored the state of things existing at the beginning of the war without mention of neutral rights, impressment, or any of the other questions that had been in dispute between the two countries. The United States escaped without loss of territory only because the British were too war weary at the end of their long struggle with Napoleon to go on fighting. Indeed, had the British defeated Jackson as expected at New Orleans in January, 1815, two weeks after the peace terms were agreed upon at Ghent, they would probably have insisted on territorial concessions before ratifying the treaty.

THE CENTURY OF SECURITY

However ignominious the War of 1812 seemed at the time, the independence of the United States was not really secure until it had been fought and, by great good luck, survived. It also began a century such as no other western nation has ever had the good fortune to enjoy, a century in which it would develop free from any external threat.

This marvelous security was guaranteed primarily by British domination of the seas. By the end of the War of 1812, Great Britain was ready to accept the permanence of the United States and to look for advantage in encouraging trade between the two countries. Seeing great commercial opportunities throughout the Americas, British ministries observed with satisfaction the crumbling of the Spanish Empire, the last great colonial empire in the New World, and resisted any efforts by other European powers to extend their influence across the Atlantic.

This happy turn in British-American relations was signaled by the amicable settlement of the outstanding questions between the two countries shortly after the War of 1812. The Rush-Bagot Agreement of 1817 provided for demilitarization of the Great Lakes, and in the Convention of 1818, American fishing rights in Canadian waters were specified, the northern boundary of the United States was set at the 49th parallel from the head of the Mississippi to the Rocky Mountains, and the two countries agreed to joint occupation of the Oregon country beyond the Rockies for a period of ten years. In 1827 the joint occupation agreement was extended indefinitely until such time as either nation should give a year's notice for terminating the arrangement.

The Anglo-American rapprochement facilitated another diplomatic achievement of this period: the liquidation of American difficulties with Spain through the acquisition of Florida. After acquiring West Florida as far east as the Pearl River (the area now a part of the state of Louisiana) through "revolution" in 1810, the Madison administration took advantage of the war to annex, in 1813, another chunk extending beyond Mobile Bay east to the Perdido River (the coastal areas of the present states of Mississippi and Alabama). Following the war, Spain was wracked by political turmoil at home and revolution in her South American colonies. Forays on American territory by Florida Indians intensified southwestern demands for annexation and furnished the pretext that Spain was not living up to her obligations under Pinckney's Treaty. When Andrew Jackson was sent to pacify the Indians along the Florida border in 1817, he moved on into Florida and seized the whole northern Gulf Coast area.

The administration in Washington could not sanction this rash and unauthorized occupation, but Secretary of State John Quincy Adams finally persuaded his Cabinet colleagues that Jackson should not be censured. Instead Adams told the Spaniards that the incident revealed their inability to maintain their treaty obligations along the Florida boundary, indicating the propriety of ceding Florida to the United States. Under this implied threat of forcible seizure, Spain yielded. By a treaty signed in 1819 but not ratified until 1821, Florida was ceded to the United States in exchange for the sum of $5 million. In the process, the Americans won undisputed control of the territory to the Rocky Mountains as well as a window on the Pacific. Sometimes called the Transcontinental Treaty, this remarkable agreement defined the boundary between the United States and the Spanish possessions to the southwest as running from the Gulf of Mexico up the Sabine River (the western boundary of the state of Louisiana), then west and north of the Rockies, then west along the 42nd parallel to the coast.

The Florida treaty was consummated during the administration of James Monroe, who had succeeded Madison in 1817 and who was to provide the classic definition of America's diplomatic position in the Century of Security. The Monroe Doctrine was enunciated in the president's annual message to Congress in December, 1823 and contained two principal parts. The first was the assertion that the American continents were no longer open to colonization by European powers. The second was a warning against any interference by European powers with the revolutionary new nations of Latin America or any extension of the political systems of Europe to the Americas.

In part, recent scholarship suggests, the document was the product of domestic politics, of Secretary of State John Quincy Adams's concern with the forthcoming presidential elections. But international considerations very likely predominated. The noncolonization declaration was prompted by an expansion of the sphere of Russian activity down the northwest American coast from Alaska, and in 1824, the Russians agreed to limit their interests to the area north of 54°40', leaving the United States and Great Britain as the only claimants of the Oregon country between that line and the Spanish-Mexican boundary at 42°.

The other part of the Monroe Doctrine was prompted by the fear that the major continental powers might unite in an effort to subdue Spain's rebellious American colonies. The British foreign secretary had suggested that the United States join his country in opposing any such action, but Secretary of State Adams and President Monroe decided that it would be better for the United States to make a unilateral statement, knowing that British seapower would back up the policy. The European powers had no enthusiasm anyhow for the reconquest of Spanish America against British opposition so the Doctrine had little effect on the immediate situation. But it did clarify, for Americans and for others, the idea of the proper relation between the Old World and the New that was to be the basis for American diplomacy during the Century of Security.

CONFLICTING HISTORICAL VIEWPOINTS

3. What Caused the War of 1812?

*The American war cry of 1812, "free trade and sailors' rights," moved the eccentric Virginian, John Randolph, to quip: "men shall not live by bread alone, but mostly by catch phrases." Catchy or otherwise, the phrase appealed to the people of Randolph's generation, who believed that the second Anglo-American war was fought for national honor and neutral maritime rights. With their president, James Madison, they traced the origins of conflict to "the continued British practice of violating the American flag on the great highway of nations, and of carrying off persons sailing under it." Actually, in his war message to Congress, Madison had mentioned other causes as well, but the maritime interpretation captured the American imagination. And throughout the century, laypersons and scholars alike believed that British commercial interference lay at the heart of the conflict. Histori-*ans as diverse as John Bach McMaster (History of the People of the United States, 8 vols., 1883–1913) and Alfred T. Mahan (Sea Power in Its Relations to the War of 1812, 1905) stressed impressment of sailors, the interruption of trade, and the Royal Navy's blockade. Even Henry Adams (History of the United States, 9 vols., 1889–1891), *who found the exclusive emphasis on maritime matters oversimple, offered only a slightly modified version of the standard interpretation.*

Following World War I, however, a generation of scholars, disillusioned by the failures of American wartime idealism, looked for causes less lofty than patriotism and principle. For example, Louis Hacker (Mississippi Valley Historical Review, March, 1924), *then an economic determinist, identified conflict in the war hawk's lust for Canadian land. Julius Pratt* (The Expansionists of 1812, 1925), *on the other hand, emphasized southern yearnings for the Floridas and a western desire to drive Britain from Canada as a solution to the Indian problem. A third scholar, George Taylor* (Journal of Political Economy, 1931), *linked westerners to seaboard griev-ances by noting that the farmers of the interior, hardly less than New England merchants, were economically dependent on foreign trade.*

More recently, pocketbook and sectional considerations have fallen from favor. Since World War II, a growing number of scholars have returned to arguments of national honor and free seas. Bradford Perkins (Prologue to War, 1961), Reginald Horsman (The Causes of the War of 1812, 1962), and Norman Risjord (William and Mary Quarterly, April, 1961), with varying degrees of emphasis, have led us back to the maritime causes stressed by nineteenth-century historians. Indeed, most historians today agree that England's policies of impressment and commercial restriction left its former colonies with but two alternatives: submission or war. As Risjord put it, "war was the only alternative to national humiliation and disgrace."

FOR FURTHER READING

Henry Adams's *History of the United States during the Administrations of Jefferson and Madison* (9 vols., 1889–1891) is a classic of American historical writing. Much material that has come to light since Adams wrote is utilized in two distinguished multivolume biographies: Irving Brant, *James Madison* (6 vols., 1941–1961); and Dumas Malone, *Jefferson and His Time* (4 vols., 1948–1970). Merrill D. Peterson's *Thomas Jefferson and the New Nation* (1970) is an excellent one-volume biography; Marshall Smelser's *The Democratic Republic* (1968) views Jefferson as a "Whiggish moderate"; Forrest McDonald's *Presidency of Thomas Jefferson* (1976) offers a latter-day Hamiltonian critique; Leonard Levy's *Jefferson and Civil Liberties* (1963) savagely explores "the darker side" of the sage's life; and John Chester Miller's *Wolf by the Ears* (1977) considers the anomaly of Jefferson the slave master. Noble Cunningham has written a study of *The Jeffersonian Republicans in Power* (1963)*; and Richard E. Ellis's *The Jeffersonian Crisis* (1971) carefully analyzes judicial politics and reform in the young republic. David H. Fischer's *The Revolution of American Conservatism* (1965) examines Federalist efforts to adapt to a more popular style of politics, and Linda K. Kerber's *Federalist in Dissent* (1970) assesses Federalist ideology in the period of Republican ascendancy. For the Lewis and Clark expedition and western development during the Jeffersonian era, see Bernard De Voto's *Course of Empire* (1952),* and his edition of *The Journals of Lewis and Clark* (1953); and Alexander De Conde's *This Affair of Louisiana* (1976). On the coming of the War of 1812, A. L. Burt, in *The United States, Great Britain, and British North America* (1940), offers a spirited defense of the maritime thesis; Harry L. Coles's *The War of 1812* (1965) is a good history of the military aspects of the conflict. Much about the period can be learned from Bernard Mayo's account of the earlier career of one of the leading War Hawks in *Henry Clay, Spokesman of the New West* (1949). The Treaty of Ghent and postwar diplomacy are splendidly delineated in Samuel Flagg Bemis's *John Quincy Adams and the Foundations of American Foreign Policy* (1949); Dexter Perkins's *Hands Off: A History of the Monroe Doctrine* (1941)* is the standard account of that subject; and Ernest R. May's *The Making of the Monroe Doctrine* (1976) emphasizes the role of domestic politics on external policy.

---

*Available in paperback edition.

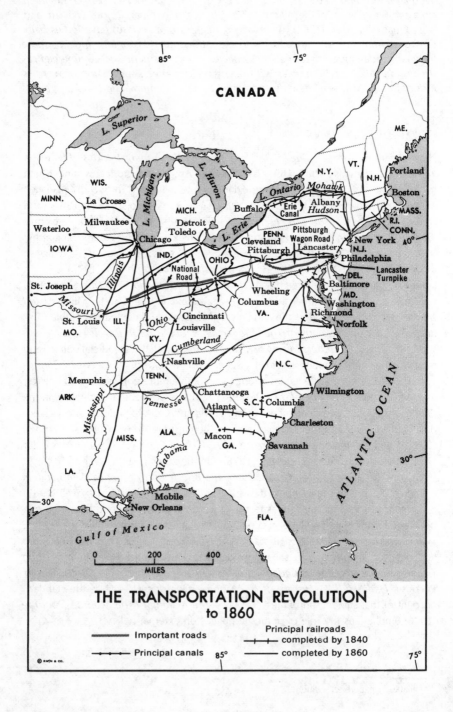

THE TRANSPORTATION REVOLUTION
to 1860

Important roads

Principal canals

Principal railroads
completed by 1840
completed by 1860

The Market versus the Agrarian Republic

9

The Century of Security into which the Republican leaders ushered the country was also a century of exceptional growth and development in the United States. Freedom from all entanglements with the Old World, except a free and peaceful trade, was deemed essential to the simple, and therefore virtuous, republic that Jefferson and his colleagues sought to perfect. Yet this freedom and security helped to foster a spirit of enterprise and rapid change that undermined the agrarian ideal.

The spirit and direction of American life became so strikingly different after the War of 1812 that the period around 1815 must be regarded as one of the major turning points in American history. The change was not quite so abrupt as it may appear—war has a way of temporarily damming up latent tendencies in a society and accelerating others so that they all seem to burst forth at the end of the conflict and as a result of it. In this case, economic changes were primary.

THE MARKET REVOLUTION

The American economy has developed through three main stages: the staple-exporting, national market, and industrial stages. The economy of the colonial period was a *staple-exporting economy,* in which people either concentrated on producing tobacco, grain, and other staples for overseas markets or on the carrying trade or were largely self-sufficing in their economic activities. About the middle of the eighteenth century, population flowed heavily into the interior where poor transportation prevented staple production, and the self-sufficing sector of the economy began to grow relative to the staple-exporting and, therefore, commercial sector. It was this development that set the stage for the struggle between commercial-mindedness and agrarian-mindedness in the last quarter of the century.

From the point of view of economic development, the important thing about the staple-exporting economy was its static quality, its lack of any tendency to self-acceleration or change. The overseas markets for American staples were seriously disturbed by the Revolution, and with the steady growth of the self-sufficing sector toward the end of the century, the economy was becoming, if anything, more set in its ways. This unprogressive, staple-exporting economy, with its sizeable self-sufficing sector, supported the stable agrarian utopia of Thomas Jefferson.

How, then, did this economy become a dynamic *industrial economy?* The "industrial revolution" that brought factories, large-scale enterprises, and rapid technological change did not really gain full momentum in the United States until after the Civil War. But the critical shift in the pace, direction, and spirit of the economy had occurred decades before as a result of the "market revolution," which brought most American economic activity into the orbit of an intricately intermeshed national market system. Between the *staple-exporting economy* of the eighteenth century and the *industrial economy* of the late nineteenth century there intervened a *national market economy,* which did not until the 1850s become significantly industrial.

The essence of the market revolution was a vast extension of the division of labor or, in other words, specialization of economic activities. Areas and individuals that formerly had been self-sufficing or that had engaged in mixed enterprises began to concentrate on the one product or service they could produce most efficiently, selling it for money and then buying with that money the other goods and services they needed. Areas and individuals that had formerly engaged in only barter or limited local trade were inexorably drawn into a national and international market system linked together by the mysterious mechanisms of money and credit. It was the resulting gains in efficiency and productivity that overnight jolted the formerly static economy into rapid growth. And it was in this atmosphere of rapid growth and ready profits that an economically conservative population became deeply infected with the spirit of enterprise, progress, and economic individualism.

The market revolution seemed to spring full blown from the War of 1812. With a staple-starved Europe paying high prices for American products, a long dammed-up flood of European imports pouring into American harbors, and settlers swarming over the newly opened lands of the West, the country was swept into an unprecedented four-year boom (1815–1818). Lured by high profits and easy credit into venturing their all on enterprises ranging from farms to steamboats, countless Americans were drawn for the first time into the money-market nexus. This spectacular boom ended in the even more spectacular bust of 1819 and the depression of the 1820s, to be followed by another boom-bust cycle in the 1830s.

The short-term boom-bust cycle of 1815–1819 arose immediately out of war and peace, but it had roots in the market revolution and in the greater interdependence of the economy that the market revolution produced. The market revolution itself was rooted in certain long-term developments that began before and continued long after the War of 1812. One of these was the accumulation of investment capital from the high profits of the American carrying trade during the Napoleonic Wars. Others will be discussed in the following sections.

THE ADVANCE TO THE MISSISSIPPI

A major stimulus to the growth of the American economy after 1815 was the rapid settlement and economic development of the West up to and across the Mississippi River. Much of this area was not open to settlement until William Henry Harrison destroyed the Indian power in the Northwest and Andrew Jackson crushed the Creeks and Cherokees of the Southwest during the War of 1812. Following the war, the broken tribes yielded to repeated demands for additional cessions of territory. In the 1820s, John C. Calhoun, Monroe's Secretary of War, inaugurated a policy of resettling the remaining Indians beyond the Missouri River, and by the middle 1830s, this objective had been substantially accomplished.

With the return of peace in 1815, a flood of settlers poured west to take up rich lands under the liberal Harrison Land Act of 1800. A tract of as little as 160 acres could be bought for $2.00 an acre, with a minimum down payment of 50 cents an acre and four years to pay the remaining $1.50 an acre. Overnight great plantations appeared on the fertile river lands of Alabama and Mississippi as planters from the worn soils of eastern Virginia, the Carolinas, and Georgia moved west with slaves, stock, and plantation gear. Along the line of the Mohawk Valley and the Great Lakes came a torrent of refugees from the stony hill farms of northern and western New England, blanketing the productive plains of northern Ohio, Indiana, and Illinois with townships, churches, and school houses on the New England pattern. The older western states of Kentucky and Tennessee became thickly settled, and from them and from farther south and east a stream of immigrants moved into southern Ohio, Indiana, and Illinois, establishing a pattern of life that differed from the New England-based style in the northern sections of those states.

During the boom years, this great migration attained staggering proportions. Federal land sales, which had risen from 67,800 acres in 1800 to over 500,000 acres in 1813 abruptly shot to 1,306,400 acres in 1815 and reached a peak of 3,491,000 acres in 1818. Even during the depressed '20s, the tide continued to run strongly. The population of the country beyond the Appalachians doubled between 1810 and 1820 and again between 1820 and 1830. In quick succession, five new states came to be: Indiana (1816), Mississippi (1817), Illinois (1818), Alabama (1819), and Missouri (1821). The typical western migrant was no solitude-loving Daniel Boone, but a person of enterprise, bent on self-improvement through shrewd investment, hard work, and a ride on a rising market. The market revolution in its early stages fostered the western boom that stimulated migration, and the great migration in turn accelerated the market revolution.

COMMERCIAL AGRICULTURE

The most important feature of the market revolution was the spectacular expansion of commercial agricultural production, with cotton leading the way. The development in England during the latter part of the eighteenth century of machinery that could manufacture cotton cloth cheaply had created a heavy demand for cotton. Cotton production was restricted for a time by the difficulty of separating the fibers from the seeds, but after Eli Whitney perfected in 1793 a gin that performed this task, cotton plantations mushroomed across the interior of Georgia and South Carolina. Checked for a time by the embargo and the War of 1812, the cotton boom roared ahead with the return of peace and the opening of the rich southwestern lands to cultivation. Production rose from 146,000 bales in 1814 to 209,000 bales in 1815 and 349,000 bales in 1819. Within a few years after 1815, a wide belt extending from North Carolina around to Louisiana had been converted into the world's largest cotton-producing area, and cotton was the country's leading export.

Unlike the staple-exporting sector of the colonial economy, the new cotton sector was intimately tied to the national as well as the international market system. While the bulk of the cotton shipped from New Orleans, Mobile, and Charleston went to Europe, much of it went by way of northeastern ports, especially New York. The proceeds of the crop paid for imports from Europe that found their way back to all parts of the United States through northeastern mercantile houses. Importations from Europe were financed to a great extent through the services of merchants in the Northeast in shipping and selling the South's cotton crop, through the South's purchases of northeastern manufactures, and through the foodstuffs and livestock shipped by the farmers in the Northwest to southern cotton planters. For some decades after 1815, the ever-mounting cotton exports were the most important factor in the growth of the economy.

Cotton production was merely the biggest segment of an expanding commercial agriculture. Tobacco cultivation in the old tidewater area of Virginia and Maryland never recovered from its post-Revolutionary slump, but new tobacco belts developed along the North Carolina-Virginia border and in sections of Kentucky, Tennessee, and Missouri. Not until the 1840s, however, did tobacco production flourish and become highly profitable. Rice culture benefited from improved seed selection and methods of cultivation but did not expand beyond its long-established locale in the coastal region of South Carolina and Georgia. The development of an improved variety of ribbon cane fostered a booming sugar-plantation economy in Louisiana following the War of 1812, and hemp, used especially for baling cotton, similarly afforded a profitable commercial crop for areas in Kentucky and Missouri.

While the great export staples were concentrated in the South, other sections were not lacking in an extensive commercial agriculture produced at first for the national market. Areas of commercial wheat production expanded steadily west from Pennsylvania's Susquehanna Valley to New York's Mohawk and Genesee valleys to Ohio, Indiana, and Illinois. In the decade after 1815 a mounting stream of wheat, flour, corn, pork, beef, and livestock began pouring from the Old Northwest into the East and South. Cincinnati became the country's leading center of flour milling and meat packing, and by the 1840s, the flood of cheap wheat and flour from the fertile Northwest was becoming a major item in American exports to Europe.

Farmers on the less productive soils of the Northeast, forced out of cereal and meat production by the cheap western products, turned to producing perishables—fruits, vegetables, poultry, and dairy products—for the growing eastern cities. Improved breeds of wool-bearing sheep and increased demand from an expanding woolens industry made wool production a profitable enterprise in many parts of the Northeast as well as the Northwest.

Thus within a brief space of time, mainly following the War of 1812, countless self-sufficing or general farmers had responded to the lure of cash returns held out by a mushrooming national and international market system and were concentrating on those staples that they could produce most efficiently. Little of this would have occurred, however, had it not become possible to transport bulky products cheaply from one part of the country to another.

THE CONQUEST OF DISTANCE

So important were the dramatic improvements in transportation facilities in the early nineteenth century that some historians have called the market revolution a transportation revolution. Like the great westward migration, the transportation revolution was part cause and part effect of the broader market revolution.

During the colonial period, production for market had been confined to areas along navigable waterways, and at the beginning of the nineteenth century, almost the only other transportation was by wagon or pack team over primitive dirt roads. As late as 1816, a ton of goods could be shipped 3,000 miles from England for what it cost to transport the same goods 30 miles overland in America. The cost of moving a bushel of wheat from Buffalo to New York City in 1817 was three times the market value; the cost of moving corn was six times the market value for corn; and the cost for oats was twelve times the market value. Cheaper transportation was an obvious prerequisite to a national market economy.

The first attempts to solve the problem were through improved roads. In 1794, a company chartered by the Pennsylvania legislature opened between Lancaster and Philadelphia the first major turnpike, or graded and paved road on which tolls were charged. So dramatically did it lower wagoning rates and stimulate commercial development and so profitable did it prove that a wave of turnpike construction followed. By the War of 1812, most of the major cities in the Northeast were connected by turnpikes; but not until after the war did the turnpike craze reach its peak and spread into the West. One major turnpike led west from Baltimore to Cumberland, Maryland; from here, the federal government began constructing the National Road. By 1818, this great highway had reached Wheeling, Virginia on the Ohio River, and by 1833, it extended to Columbus, Ohio. The National Road quickly became a major artery of east-west trade, while elsewhere the turnpikes reduced transportation costs and brought previously isolated areas into the market.

More important than better roads, especially in the West, was the introduction of the steamboat. Flatboating down the Ohio and Mississippi rivers to New Orleans had transported some production to market from the early days of settlement, but this mode of transportation was extremely slow even downriver while upriver shipping by oar-driven keelboat was so slow, backbreaking, and expensive as to inhibit any extensive commerce. A new era was predicted when Robert Fulton operated the first commercially successful steamboat, the *Clermont,* on the Hudson River in 1807. By 1812, a few forerunners of the classic shallow-draft sternwheeler had appeared on the Mississippi. The development of western steamboating came with a rush at the end of the war, and by 1820 there were 60 steamboats on the Mississippi-Ohio system (by 1860 there would be more than 1,000) and others on the river systems of Alabama and Mississippi. Steamboat freight rates were only 5 to 10 percent of what keelboats had charged to haul goods upriver and only 25 to 30 percent of what it had cost to flatboat goods down the river, and there were proportionate gains in speed of shipment. Able to operate far up the network of tributaries that laced the West, the shallow-draft sternwheeler made possible the production of cotton, wheat, and other bulky commercial commodities in widespread areas that could not otherwise have entered the national market.

While the steamboat was accelerating the market's conquest of the West, another transportation development was providing a direct water link between East and West. In 1817, the New York legislature, prodded by Governor DeWitt Clinton, authorized the construction of a canal from Albany on the Hudson River west along the Mohawk Valley to Buffalo on Lake Erie, and by 1825 the 364-mile Erie Canal was completed. Traffic on the new canal was so heavy that tolls equaled the cost of construction within nine years. Given cheap water communication with New York City and Europe, a flood of commodities from the whole Great Lakes region soon flowed eastward along the canal, meeting a return flow of eastern and European goods destined for the entire West.

The success of the Erie Canal prompted Pennsylvania to build a competing system linking Philadelphia with Pittsburgh on the Ohio, and in the 1830s and 1840s the states of the Old Northwest completed a series of canals connecting the Great Lakes with the Ohio and the Mississippi Rivers.

The development of a railroad network in the 1840s and 1850s gave added efficiency to a transportation system that had already succeeded in bringing most parts of the country within the orbit of the irresistible market. Baltimore began constructing its railroad west toward the Ohio River in 1828, and in the next decade several thousand miles of short lines were built. Not until the 1850s, however, did the railroad boom reach its height. It was in this decade that the great trunk lines connecting East and West were completed, and by 1860 the country had more than 30,000 miles of railroad.

In 1815, the shipment of goods from Cincinnati to New York by keelboat and wagon had required more than 50 days. In 1850, they could be sent by steamboat to New Orleans and thence by packet to New York in 28 days, by the Ohio and Erie canals and the Hudson River in 18 days, and by railroad in 6 to 8 days. In 1815, overland freight rates by wagon had ranged from 30 to 70 cents per ton per mile. By the 1850s, the railroads were charging 2 to 9 cents per ton-mile and the canals around one cent per ton-mile. Behind these simple figures lay a revolutionary transformation of American life.

ENTERPRISE AND PUBLIC POLICY

The transportation revolution and the market revolution would have come much more slowly if the Americans of the early republic had followed the *laissez-faire* notions of political economy that are often mistakenly ascribed to them. Instead, as the market advanced and the spirit of enterprise quickened, the people demanded that their governments ally themselves with private enterprise to speed the march of progress.

The most notable alliance of public and private enterprise at the state and local level was in the field of transportation, where progress demanded undertakings too vast for individuals or even groups of individuals. The early turnpike companies raised much of their capital from stock subscriptions by the states and towns through which they ran. The great canals were built directly by states, while other states spent large sums on improving navigable rivers. Governmental aid to transportation reached its peak in the construction of railroads. No one has yet calculated how many millions of dollars towns, cities, and states expended for all these purposes, but it is certain that the revolutionizing transportation network could not have gotten far without this governmental aid.

The turnpike, steamboat, and railroad companies were the forerunners of the modern corporation. These early corporations were born out of the theory of "mixed enterprise," the idea that government should ally itself with agrarian enterprise to accomplish ends beneficial to the public. In the simple days of the staple-exporting economy, all enterprise had been carried on by individuals or partnerships. Economic combinations of many individuals or their capital in large enterprises were thought to be dangerous to the public interest and were frowned upon by the law. Only where some great public purpose was to be accomplished were they thought justified and then only when chartered by special act of the legislature.

Such corporate charters usually facilitated the raising of capital by granting the privilege of "limited liability," making stockholders in the corporation (unlike members of partnerships) liable for debts of the corporation only to the extent of the stock they held. Charters also usually granted, either explicitly or implicitly, monopolies or semimonopolies, as when a company was given the exclusive right to develop a certain transportation route. Thus the early corporate charter was thought of as a privilege conferred by government in order to enlist private enterprise for the accomplishment of a public purpose.

The corporate device found much of its early use not only in transportation but in banking, and the rapid growth of banking was another of the major factors in the acceleration of economic development. The banking system before the War of 1812 had consisted of the Hamiltonian national bank, chartered by Congress, and a small number of private banks that were called *state banks* because they were chartered by state legislatures. In theory at least, stockholders bought stock in these banks by paying in gold and silver. On the basis of this "specie" capital, the banks made loans, with the interest they collected from their borrowers providing profits that could be paid back to the stockholders as dividends. What made the banks extremely profitable was the fact that they could safely lend out more than their capital. Instead of lending specie, a bank gave borrowers *bank notes,* or pieces of paper resembling modern paper money, each bearing a promise that the issuing bank would redeem the note on demand with a specified sum of specie. These bank notes then circulated as money in the vicinity of the bank and, as long as people had confidence in the bank, were not returned for redemption in specie. Thus the bank could safely print, lend, and collect interest on considerably more bank notes than it had specie to cover.

Though at first conservatively managed and restrained by the national bank, the state banks were potentially capable of expanding the supply of credit and investment "capital" almost infinitely and, thus, of stimulating feverish economic activity. This began to happen when the national bank's demise in 1811 and the economic stimulus of the war prompted enterprising politicians and businesses to secure legislative charters for a large number of new state banks designed to operate on more generous and lucrative principles than their predecessors. The bank mania reached its peak after the war, and the rapid multiplication of banks and bank credit contributed greatly to the boom-and-bust cycle of 1815–1819. Bust was again followed by boom, and the expansion of bank credit reached even greater heights than in the 1830s. In spite of the violent short-term fluctuations that the banks fostered, they also contributed greatly to the spectacular long-term prosperity of the economy through their active stimulation of its growth.

REPUBLICAN NATIONALISM

The spirit of enterprise was strong in the new generation of Republican leaders who had pushed Madison into war in 1812 and who dominated a transformed Republicanism after the war. Federalism, despite a momentary comeback in embargo days, was so weakened by the steady swelling of the Republican electorate and so discredited by secession discussion at the Hartford Convention before the war that in 1816 only three states voted for the Federalist presidential candidate. To succeed Madison, the Republicans picked James Monroe, the last prominent Virginian of the Revolutionary generation, and in 1820 Monroe was reelected without opposition.

Monroe himself retained some of Jefferson's agrarian-minded and strict-constructionist scruples and rejoiced that the death of Federalism had ushered in an "Era of Good Feelings" when parties should no longer be necessary. In truth, the younger men surrounding the president had moved, in the enterprising atmosphere of the boom years, so far toward the nationalist and commercial-minded views of the Federalists that Federalism had become superfluous. Monroe's State Department was headed by that ardent nationalist John Quincy Adams, who had deserted the party of his father, President John Adams, over the embargo issue. Monroe's Secretary of the Treasury, William H. Crawford of Georgia, worked for a new national bank. Presiding over the War Department was John C. Calhoun, vigorous champion of a strong army, protective tariffs, and federal road and canal construction. And in Congress, the dominant figure was Speaker of the House Henry Clay, who for a generation would symbolize a broad program of federal action—he would call it the "American System" —to aid enterprise and speed progress.

These people were preaching Hamiltonianism shorn of its elitist overtones. The onrushing market revolution was democratizing business, and the rapid spread of the spirit of enterprise through all levels of society made the new Republican nationalism more dynamic than the old Federalist nationalism of conservative merchants and financiers.

The war was no sooner over than several problems growing out of wartime developments were attacked in the spirit of Republican nationalism. The overexpansion of state banks had led to a financial crisis early in the war. Outside New England, the overextended banks had had to "suspend specie payments" (stop redeeming their bank notes in gold or silver coin on demand), and their notes had depreciated; the resulting financial chaos had contributed greatly to the government's difficulties in carrying on the war. To get the federal government out of its financial troubles and to furnish a sound paper currency and credit system as a basis for orderly business growth, the younger Republicans pushed through Congress in 1816 a charter for a Second Bank of the United States.

This institution, with headquarters in Philadelphia and branches elsewhere, was to have a capital of $35 million as compared with the $10 million of Hamilton's national bank. It was to be the depository for all federal funds, and its bank notes were declared receivable for all sums due the government. It was to serve public purposes by making loans to the government and also by regulating the state banks, aiding them to resume specie payments at the earliest possible moment, and thereafter keeping them on a sound basis by sustaining them in periods of financial stringency and by restraining them in periods of boom. Its power to do this came from its large capital and from the fact that it was constantly receiving large quantities of state bank notes in its role as federal depository. By promptly presenting these notes to the state banks for redemption during booms, it could force them to curtail their issues, while by expanding its own loans and note issues during bust periods, it could ease any pressure on the state banks. Yet this was to be essentially a private, profit-making institution with the government subscribing only one-fifth of its capital and designating only one-fifth of its directors.

Beginning operation in 1817, the Second Bank helped secure a general resumption of specie payments and then succumbed to the boom spirit itself. Inefficient and often dishonest officers so overextended the bank's own loans and note issues that it lost all power to restrain the expanding state banks. The inevitable reaction, the Panic of 1819, was much more severe than it might otherwise have been because the national bank suddenly reversed its policy and saved itself by ruthlessly applying pressure against its debtors and the state banks. Not until Nicholas Biddle became the bank's president in 1823 did it begin to realize its great potential as a balance wheel and regulator for the economy as a whole.

A second problem growing out of the war was the desperate situation of American manufacturers. Most American manufacturing before the War of 1812 had been of the "domestic" variety—spinning, weaving, shoemaking, hatmaking, and countless other enterprises carried on in the homes or shops of independent artisans. Large-scale industrial production would develop only in response to the market revolution and the vast national market it created. Yet even before 1812, small cotton textile factories had begun to spring up in New England, iron works were attaining some size in Pennsylvania, and other enterprises in cities like New York and Philadelphia were outgrowing their independent-artisan origins and beginning to employ substantial numbers of journeyman artisans on a wage basis. By cutting off imported European manufactures, the war stimulated a rapid growth in this manufacturing activity. But when the war ended, British manufacturers dumped on the American market their stored-up surplus of products at cut-rate prices, threatening the promising American manufacturing establishment with sudden death.

In the mood of generous nationalism that followed the war, Republican members of Congress from all sections of the country responded to the plight of the beleaguered northeastern manufacturers by passing the first tariff act designed primarily to protect American producers from foreign competition. The Tariff of 1816 required foreign imports that competed with such leading American manufactures as cotton, woolen cloth, and iron to pay import duties ranging around 20 to 25 percent of their value. Additional protection was granted to iron and textiles in 1818 and 1819.

One of the greatest ambitions of the national-minded Republicans was frustrated by the lingering constitutional doubts of Presidents Madison and Monroe. In the closing days of his administration, Madison vetoed as unconstitutional Calhoun's Bonus Bill of 1817, a measure reserving $1.5 million, which the new national bank paid the government for its charter, for beginning a great national system of roads and canals. Although he recognized that internal improvements were necessary to encourage national expansion and to cement the national union, Madison's strict-constructionist background asserted itself. While Calhoun found justification for the measure in the "general welfare" clause, Madison reluctantly concluded that, without a constitutional amendment, federal expenditures for internal improvements were unlawful. With this judgment, his successor, solemn, middle-of-the-road James Monroe, agreed fully.

JUDICIAL NATIONALISM

In the congenial atmosphere of Republican nationalism following the War of 1812, the Federalist nationalism of Chief Justice John Marshall and the Supreme Court he dominated came to full fruition. Having asserted the court's authority on constitutional questions in *Marbury vs. Madison* back in 1803, Marshall now used this authority in a series of remarkable decisions to establish his Federalist and nationalist views on questions of property rights, constitutional interpretation, and federal and state powers.

In *Dartmouth College vs. Woodward* (1819), the Court overruled an attempt by the New Hampshire legislature to change the college's colonial charter. Marshall's court had already made itself the defender of property rights against state legislatures in an earlier case, and now Marshall declared that charter rights, too, were sacred. This decision was to become increasingly significant with the growing importance of chartered corporations in American economic life.

The biggest corporation of Marshall's day, the Second Bank of the United States, was involved in his most far-reaching decision, *McCulloch vs. Maryland* (1819). This case arose from Maryland's attempt to tax out of existence the bank's branch at Baltimore. The power to tax was the power to destroy, he argued, and no state could be allowed to destroy an instrument of the federal government. Perhaps the most important part of this decision was Marshall's argument, based on the doctrine of implied powers, that Congress had acted constitutionally in chartering the bank. Here he echoed Hamilton's argument to President Washington at the time the first national bank was chartered, maintaining that if the end Congress sought to attain was sanctioned by the Constitution, then "all means which are appropriate, which are plainly adapted to that end" are constitutional.

Among various other decisions affirming federal over state powers, one may be singled out as particularly important. In *Gibbons vs. Ogden* (1824), the court invalidated a monopoly that New York had granted over steamboat service between New York and New Jersey. In giving Congress the power to regulate interstate commerce, Marshall declared, the Constitution meant that *only* Congress should have such power. Furthermore he defined "interstate commerce" so broadly as to include the carrying of passengers or any other variety of commerce between states. Marshall's sweeping extension of the commerce clause not only invalidated the New York monopoly as an invasion of Congress's exclusive power to regulate, but also laid the basis for the vast future extensions of federal regulatory powers.

Thus in the first flush of the market revolution, the spirit of enterprise and nationalism seemed pervasive everywhere in American life—in the entrepreneurial undertakings of countless citizens, in the efforts of the states to hasten progress through transportation projects and corporate charters, in the tariff and banking legislation of Congress, in the diplomacy of President Monroe's Doctrine, and in the decisions of the Supreme Court. The only marring note seemed to be the doubts of old-fashioned Virginia presidents about federal appropriations for roads and canals, and even this slight barrier to progress would be removed when one of the younger, national-minded Republicans entered the White House in 1825. Yet an unprogressive, agrarian society had not—could not have—changed so totally and quickly as this one momentarily appeared to have done. Two decades of crisis and conflict were to elapse before Americans would be at ease in the new world of enterprise.

FOR FURTHER READING

A good introduction to American economic history is Stuart Bruchey's *The Roots of American Economic Growth, 1607–1861* (1965),* while the indispensable starting point for this period is Douglass C. North's somewhat technical but rewarding analysis of *The Economic Growth of the United States, 1790–1860* (1961).* These may be

---

*Available in paperback edition.

supplemented with the detailed accounts of the factors of economic growth in George R. Taylor's *The Transportation Revolution, 1815–1860* (1951)* and Paul W. Gates's *The Farmer's Age: Agriculture, 1815–1860* (1960).* Special aspects are well treated in the following: Louis C. Hunter, *Steamboats on the Western Rivers* (1949); Carter Goodrich and others, *Canals and American Economic Development* (1961); Samuel Eliot Morison, *The Maritime History of Massachusetts, 1783–1860* (1921)*; Robert G. Albion, *The Rise of New York Port, 1815–1860* (1939); Robert W. Fogel, *Railroads and American Economic Growth* (1964); and Albert Fishlow, *American Railroads and the Transformation of the Ante-Bellum Economy* (1965). For western development, Frederick Jackson Turner's famous essay on "The Significance of the Frontier in American History" is reprinted, along with many of the arguments it has evoked from other historians, in George R. Taylor, ed., *The Turner Thesis Concerning the Role of the Frontier in American History* (rev. ed., 1956, Amherst Problems in American Civilization).* Francis Philbrick's *The Rise of the West* (1965) is a refutation of the Turner thesis; Ray A. Billington has written the best account of *Westward Expansion* (1949); Malcolm Rohrbough's *Land Office Business* (1968) and Francis Prucha's *Sword of the Republic* (1969) are important works on early white settlement of the west; Reginald Horsman's *The Frontier in the Formative Years* (1970) is a skillful synthesis; and Richard C. Wade describes early western cities in *The Urban Frontier* (1959).* *Flush Times of Alabama and Mississippi* (1853) by Joseph Baldwin is an absorbing contemporary account of the boom years in the Southwest. George Dangerfield has written two accounts of the political history of the era of Republican nationalism: *The Era of Good Feelings* (1952)* and *The Awakening of American Nationalism* (1965).

Depression Decade:
Sectionalism and Democracy
1819–1828

10

The Panic of 1819 was the first severe economic crisis ever to seriously affect the American people as a whole. Part of an international economic dislocation following a long period of war, it was especially intense in the United States because of the reckless expansion of banks, credit, and entrepreneurial investment that preceded it. When the prices of cotton and other commodities suddenly plummeted on the world markets, countless Americans faced the loss of their homes, farms, workshops, and other property because they could not meet the debts they had incurred to finance their entrepreneurial ventures. The banks suspended specie payments, and bank notes, the only circulating medium, skidded toward worthlessness in the hands of their holders. Merchants went bankrupt, city workers lost their jobs, and the economy ground to a standstill. The paralysis maintained its grip through the early 1820s, and not until after mid-decade did prosperity return.

The economic effects of the Panic were no more momentous than its psychological and political effects. In rapid succession, the American people had been drawn from the settled ways of the old agrarian order into a national market economy of dizzying prosperity, unlimited optimism, and headlong change and then suddenly plunged into privation and despair. The shock of this experience made the 1820s a decade of soul-searching and tension. The postwar mood of generous nationalism evaporated as sections and interest groups became narrowly concerned with their own welfare and jealous of rival sections and interest groups. There was a striking revival of Jeffersonian orthodoxy as prodigal agrarians eschewed the fleshpots of the market and resolved to return to the old ways of frugality and honest toil. Class antagonisms sharpened as impoverished farmers and urban workers blamed political and business leaders—above all, the banking fraternity—for the disaster. And finally, there was a growing interest in politics, a dissatisfaction with the political leadership that had allowed hard times to come, and a demand for new leaders who would be more responsive to the popular will in using government to relieve the distress.

4. PRESIDENTIAL ELECTIONS AND MAJOR EVENTS, 1816–1828

1816
James Monroe (Republican) elected over Rufus King (Federalist).
Tariff of 1816, the first deliberately protectionist tariff act.

1816
Second Bank of the United States chartered.
Madison vetoes Calhoun's Bonus Bill for internal improvements.

1817–1825
Erie Canal constructed.

1818
National Road reaches the Ohio River.

1819
Dartmouth College vs. *Woodward.* John Marshall's Supreme Court
defends charter rights against state legislation.
McCulloch vs. *Maryland.* John Marshall's Supreme Court upholds the
constitutionality of the national bank.
Panic of 1819 forces a general suspension of specie payments and
inaugurates a long and severe economic depression.

1820
Land Act of 1820. Lower land prices and abolition of credit system.
Missouri Compromise.
James Monroe (Republican) reelected without opposition.

1824
Tariff of 1824. Higher protection.
Gibbons vs. *Ogden.* John Marshall's Supreme Court extends the federal
power to regulate interstate commerce.
John Quincy Adams (Republican) elected over Andrew Jackson,
William H. Crawford, and Henry Clay (all Republicans).

1826
Anti-Masonic movement begins.

1828
Tariff of Abominations. Extremely high protective duties.
Andrew Jackson (Democratic Republican) elected over John Quincy
Adams (National Republican).

POLITICAL SECTIONALISM

The resurgence of sectional rivalries was dramatically demonstrated by the heated congressional controversy in 1820 over admitting Missouri as a slave state. Slavery had been a source of conflict in the constitutional convention and on several occasions since, but it had not yet become a major issue. The Quakers had been bearing testimony against human servitude for some time, and by 1804 every state north of Delaware had provided for the ultimate emancipation of slaves within its borders. But there was as yet no strong general movement against slavery as a moral and political evil, for most persons of goodwill, both north and south, continued to indulge Jefferson's hope that it would eventually disappear everywhere through the gradual operation of economic and moral forces.

Thus when northern members of Congress sought to amend the Missouri admission bill to require the gradual emancipation of Missouri slaves, they were acting less from moral repugnance at the institution than from a revival of the traditional northeastern resentment at southern political domination. Much of the South's political power was derived from the constitutional provision that three-fifths of its slaves be counted in apportioning congressional representation and electoral votes. Northeasterners seized upon the Missouri question as a means of blocking the extension of this political injustice throughout the Louisiana Purchase. Southern members of Congress, on the other hand, reacted violently to this attack on their vulnerable system of labor. Admission of Missouri as a free state would upset the even balance between slave and free states and destroy the protection that this gave the South in the Senate against any future antislavery measures.

A Missouri Compromise was finally reached because of the simultaneous movement to make the geographically separate eastern appendage of Massachusetts (now Maine) a separate state. Maine was admitted as a free state, Missouri was admitted as a slave state, and no further slave states were to be created from that part of the Louisiana Purchase lying north of latitude 36°30' (the latitude of the southern boundary of Missouri).

What many northern members of Congress had in mind when they opposed the admission of any more slave states was illustrated at this same session of 1820 by the fate of a bill to extend further tariff protection to the hard-pressed manufacturers. Representatives from slave-holding states voted almost five to one against this measure in the House and provided most of the votes that killed it in the Senate. By 1824, when the manufacturers tried again for higher duties, the South was opposed 57 to one in the House. This time the Northeast was heavily in favor, the only opposition there coming from representatives of international merchants and shippers who resisted any diminution of international trade. But now western farmers had been convinced that the growth of manufacturing might create a flourishing home market for their unprofitable products, and western representatives provided the margin by which the tariff bill squeaked through Congress. The Tariff of 1824 raised duties on textiles to 33.3 percent, sharply increased the rate on iron, and won rural support with duties on raw wool and hemp.

RELIEF AND DEMOCRACY

Manufacturers were not the only ones who had learned from the doctrines of Republican nationalism to look to government for aid. Thousands of western settlers were now unable to complete their payments for public lands under the credit system inaugurated by the Land Act of 1800. In response to their outcries, Congress forgave interest charges, extended payment periods, and allowed delinquent purchasers to retain an amount of land proportionate to the payments they had made. At the same time, in the Land Act of 1820, it abolished the credit system while lowering the minimum price of public lands from $2 to $1.25 an acre. The minimum tract that could be purchased had recently been reduced to 80 acres, and all these changes enabled a settler to buy a farm for as little as $100 cash.

But it was to the state governments that the people looked for relief from the most desperate problem created by the Panic, the disappearance of money and the collapse of the pyramid of debt that had been built up during the boom. People could neither collect the debts owed them nor pay the debts they owed, property could not be sold, and a sweeping liquidation through foreclosures and bankruptcies threatened the whole community.

Legislatures, especially in the hard-hit South and West, responded to the demands of their aroused constituents by various schemes to circumvent the constitutional prohibition against issuing paper money or making anything except gold and silver legal tender. Some states established "banks" or "loan offices" to print state-backed paper money for loan to desperate debtors. Usually these measures were coupled with "stay laws" requiring creditors who refused to accept the state-backed paper money to delay executions on their debtor's property. Relief was also provided through "property laws" whereby a "disinterested" jury composed of the debtor's neighbors set a minimum value below which property could not be forcibly sold to satisfy a debt.

The violent political struggles over debtor relief laws and the closely related banking question accelerated the drift toward a more democratic political system in many of the states. A few socially complex states like New York and Pennsylvania were already far along the road toward a well-developed two-party or bifactional system in which evenly matched candidates campaigned against each other with the aid of party newspapers and stable party organizations expert in the techniques of garnering votes. Under such circumstances voter interest and participation were high, and public policy was responsive to majority wishes.

In most of the country, however, widespread interest in politics had appeared only sporadically before the 1820s. Having little sense that government—at least the remote state and national governments—affected them much anyhow, most people were willing to leave politics to those well-to-do and socially superior men in their communities who had something to gain from political power, whether land grants or bank charters or simply office. This resulted in a *personal-factional* political system in which a group of leaders allied through personal or family ties normally maintained unchallenged predominance in a county or other district. In the legislatures, representatives from the various local oligarchies formed shifting alliances, again based on personal or family ties.

This system was sanctioned by Jeffersonian political theory. Jefferson had never maintained that the people as a whole should decide public policy but only that the people were wise enough and virtuous enough to select the wisest and most virtuous among them as political leaders. Candidates pretended that they did not seek office and certainly did not electioneer; they only reluctantly consented to serve when called upon by their fellow citizens. The voters did not tell their chosen representatives—who were, of course, always male—what to do once elected, and certainly the representatives did not seek votes by promising to do thus and so. Instead, according to Jeffersonian theory, these unusually wise and virtuous men should be left free to reach wise and virtuous decisions through rational debate and compromise with each other in legislatures and Congress.

The personal-factional system was best adapted to homogeneous communities where conflicts of interest were not very important. It mustered enough genuine wisdom and disinterestedness to function satisfactorily until the market revolution began multiplying the number of specialized economic roles and competing interest groups in the community, while at the same time making people more conscious of the connection between enterprise and public policy. This caused no difficulty during the boom years when there seemed to be enough for everybody. But the Panic made people suddenly aware of their separate and competing interests at the very moment they began looking to government for mutually contradictory kinds of aid. With debtors clamoring for stay laws and loan offices while creditors denounced them, the Jeffersonian notion of a harmony of interests served by wise and virtuous leaders could no longer be sustained. Voters wanted to know where candidates stood on questions of vital concern to them, and the more alert politicians began telling the voters what they thought a majority wanted to hear.

As elections began to be transformed into popular referenda on public policy, a current of discontent with the established political leadership manifested itself. The main target of popular resentment was the banking system, which was blamed for causing the collapse by its reckless overexpansion of credit. While the banks were refusing to pay their own debts by not redeeming their notes in specie and while the depreciation of bank notes was the most conspicuous source of loss to the whole community, the banks were foreclosing on the property of their debtors, continuing to pay dividends, and extending special accommodations to their favored borrowers. The state banks managed to shift some of the resulting resentment to the national bank against which they had similar complaints. But in the eyes of many newly aroused voters, the blame belonged to the banking system as a whole along with the politicians and business people who had fostered and profited from it. Moreover, these same politicians and business people were often leading the opposition to debtor relief.

As voters came to the polls in increasing numbers to repudiate the established leaders, a new style of democratic politics began to supplant the personal-factional system. The new-style democratic politicians not only promised what the voters wanted, but also portrayed themselves as fighting the battle of the plain people against a group of unscrupulous aristocrats. The old loose and shifting factional groupings in state politics began to stabilize as "democratic" and "aristocratic" alignments. In Kentucky, and to a lesser extent in some other southern and western states, something very like a two-party system developed out of the violent conflict over debtor relief.

In the East, where debtor relief was not such a pressing problem, other issues led to similar results. In New York, DeWitt Clinton capitalized on some high-handed maneuvers by the long entrenched "Albany Regency" candidates to make a smashing political comeback as gubernatorial candidate for the "People's Party." In the same state in 1826, the disappearance and presumed murder of a man who had revealed the secrets of the Masonic order caused an astonishing anti-Masonic outburst, which became a political movement and eventually a short-lived political party. Since Masonic lodges were usually composed of the most prominent men in their communities and since many of the dominant politicians were Masons, the anti-Masons attacked the order as a secret, aristocratic conspiracy against the rest of the community.

The urban counterpart of anti-Masonry was the labor movement that began to flourish late in the 1820s. By fostering larger and more specialized units of production, the market revolution was making it more difficult for artisans to follow the traditional progression from apprenticeship through the wage-earning journeyman status to independent proprietorship. The depression and unemployment highlighted the insecurity of the permanent wage-earning status in which more and more workers were finding themselves. Journeyman workers organized labor unions and called strikes against the ten-hour day. On the political front, they joined with small entrepreneurs, whose middle-class status was likewise threatened, to form workers' parties in Philadelphia and New York City. Under the banner of "Equal Rights," these parties advocated free public education, opposed imprisonment for debt, and agitated against banks and other monopolies through which a favored few could exploit the many.

Amid the frustrations and conflicts of the 1820s, the long drift toward popular sovereignty in the United States was reaching its culmination. From the beginning of settlement, the cheapness of land and the demand for labor had created an atmosphere of universal opportunity and rough social equality that was quickly reflected in the quasi-democratic political institutions of the colonies. The Revolution, consigning the destiny of Americans to their own hands, had cut off elitist tendencies and firmly established the ideal of equal political rights, but only for white males. In the following decades, state after state had alleviated restrictive male suffrage requirements and other denials—often more symbolic than real—of the Revolutionary ideal. Meanwhile the egalitarian tendency of American life had been reinforced by the process of western settlement, and the new western states had been free to adopt constitutions reflecting the increasingly democratic tone of the country.

Yet it remained for the market revolution to democratize enterprise, to give a final push to the egalitarian tendency, and to arouse a hitherto apathetic electorate to the importance of public policy and politics. The boom-bust cycle made this popular political awakening more abrupt than it might otherwise have been. Appearing first at the local and state levels, the new-style democratic politics began to manifest itself at the national level in the presidential election of 1824.

THE ELECTION OF 1824

An institutional symbol of the established personal-factional system was the presidential caucus. Every four years, the Republican senators and representatives met in caucus at Washington to designate their party's presidential candidate, and since 1800 the caucus designation had been tantamount to election. As the election of 1824 approached, the foreordained choice of the caucus was William H. Crawford of Georgia, Monroe's Secretary of the Treasury and the favorite of the large congressional delegations representing Virginia and New York. Crawford's strongest support came from areas that had been relatively immune to the postwar boom and the Republican nationalism that accompanied it (landlocked North Carolina, the worn-out plantation country of eastern Virginia, and the conservative Dutch farming counties along the Hudson River), and he ran as the candidate of a resurgent Jeffersonianism.

This time, however, the caucus system itself was challenged by the sectional and personal rivalries that had rendered Monroe's second term anything but an "Era of Good Feelings." Secretary of State John Quincy Adams came forward as the presidential choice of New England and Speaker Henry Clay as the choice of the West. In addition, Secretary of War John C. Calhoun proposed to take his state of South Carolina away from Crawford in the South and counted on his record of support for tariffs, internal improvements, and the national bank to give him Pennsylvania's electoral vote and additional nationwide backing. All of these anti-Crawford candidates, in fact, were unrepentant champions of Republican nationalism. Calhoun led them in attacking the caucus as undemocratic, and the refusal of their supporters to attend it resulted in Crawford's being nominated by only a minority of the Republican members of Congress.

The ultimate beneficiary of all these currents was none of these candidates but Andrew Jackson, hero of the Battle of New Orleans. In order to gain an advantage in a local factional struggle, some Tennessee politicians had pushed through their legislature a resolution nominating Jackson for president, never expecting him to be a serious candidate. But there was a surprising response to the nomination from quarters that politicians had not heretofore taken seriously. No one knew where the Tennessee general stood on public issues. To people disenchanted with the old leaders, it was enough that he was a popular hero, the people's man against the established leadership. The strength of this sentiment became apparent when a grass-roots movement swept the Pennsylvania Republican convention out of the control of the leaders who had intended to endorse Calhoun and forced them to pledge Pennsylvania for Jackson. Calhoun promptly withdrew from the presidential race, running unopposed for vice-president and carrying South Carolina into the Jackson camp.

When the election took place, Jackson led the four-man field in both popular and electoral votes, but no one had a majority. The Constitution directed that the House of Representatives, voting by states, should choose among the three highest candidates. This eliminated Clay, low man in electoral votes, and Crawford was also removed from serious contention by a physical collapse. This left Clay to wield his great influence in the House on behalf of either Jackson or Adams. Clay chose Adams, and Adams was elected by the narrowest of margins.

THE TRIBULATIONS OF THE SECOND ADAMS

John Quincy Adams was among the ablest and most patriotic presidents but was also one of the least successful. Partly through circumstances and partly through insensitivity to public sentiment, he defied and was overwhelmed by the most powerful political currents of the 1820s.

The Jackson supporters regarded Adams's election, in any case, as a flouting of the people's will. But when he appointed Henry Clay as Secretary of State, traditional stepping-stone to the presidency, their fury knew no bounds. The cry of "Bargain and Corruption" rang throughout the land, touching off a four-year campaign to vindicate popular sovereignty by placing Jackson in the White House.

Adams compounded his difficulties by underestimating the depression-bred reaction against Republican nationalism. Adams and Clay sought to build a National Republican party, based on a coalition of the Northeast and the Ohio Valley and dedicated to Clay's "American System" of protective tariff, national bank, and internal improvements. In addition, the president's first annual message called for a national university and federally sponsored scientific research and exploration, while cautioning Congress against being "palsied by the will of our constituents."

The Adams-Clay program outraged the neo-Jeffersonian Crawford supporters, now led by New York's Martin Van Buren, and drove them into alliance with the Jackson and Calhoun factions. Calling itself the Democratic Republican party, this Jacksonian coalition for four years blocked the president's program in Congress and harassed him in every way possible. The only significant legislative product of these four years was a tariff act passed in 1828. With both parties trying to win presidential votes by juggling complicated tariff schedules, this "Tariff of Abominations" pushed duties on both manufactured and agricultural products to absurdly high levels and satisfied almost no one.

The presidential election of 1828 was marked by the return of the two-party system to national politics and by an abusiveness on both sides that was unmatched since the last closely contested two-party election in 1800. Questions of public policy were hardly discussed, the real issue being whether the people's man Jackson should prevail over the seasoned statesman and old-style political leader Adams. This was enough to produce a substantial increase in the number of voters and a substantial majority for Jackson.

FOR FURTHER READING

Murray N. Rothbard focuses on the *The Panic of 1819* (1962). The best general account of the 1820s is Frederick Jackson Turner's *The Rise of the New West, 1819–1829* (1906).* Even more suggestive, though it deals only with the southern states, is Charles S. Sydnor's *The Development of Southern Sectionalism, 1819–*

---

*Available in paperback edition.

1848 (1948). Glover Moore has carefully examined *The Missouri Controversy, 1819–1821* (1953). James Sterling Young, in *The Washington Community, 1800–1828* (1966), explains how the very organization of governmental activity and institutions in Washington reflected the pervasive fears of a vigorous national government. Some idea of the political transformations going on in the states in the 1820s may be gained from Dixon Ryan Fox's *The Decline of Aristocracy in the Politics of New York* (1919)* and from Charles Sellers's *James K. Polk, Jacksonian: 1795–1843* (1957). The presidency and subsequent political career of John Quincy Adams are splendidly narrated by Samuel Flagg Bemis in *John Quincy Adams and the Union* (1956). Robert V. Remini has written a lively scholarly account of *The Election of Andrew Jackson* (1963).*

5. PRESIDENTIAL ELECTIONS AND MAJOR EVENTS, 1828–1840

1828	Andrew Jackson (Democratic Republican) elected over John Quincy Adams (National Republican). Tariff of Abominations.
1830	Jackson vetoes the Maysville Road Bill.
1832	Tariff of 1832 remedies the worst abuses of the Tariff of Abominations but fails to satisfy the South Carolina Nullifiers. Jackson vetoes the bill to recharter the Second Bank of the United States. Andrew Jackson (Democratic Republican) reelected over Henry Clay (National Republican). South Carolina nullifies the tariff laws.
1833	Compromise Tariff gradually reduces all tariff duties to 20 percent. Force Act authorizes president to use military to enforce the laws. Jackson transfers the federal deposits from the national bank to selected state-chartered deposit banks.
1836	Jackson issues Specie Circular requiring specie for purchase of federal lands. Distribution Act distributes the federal surplus among the states. Martin Van Buren (Democrat) elected over William Henry Harrison, Daniel Webster, and Hugh Lawson White (all Whigs).
1837	Panic of 1837 forces a general suspension of specie payments and initiates a severe and prolonged economic depression. Van Buren proposes the independent treasury system.
1838	New York Free Banking Act is a forerunner of general incorporation laws: one of the many efforts by the states to reform and regulate banking.
1840	Independent treasury system finally approved by Congress after three years of debate. William Henry Harrison (Whig) elected over Martin Van Buren (Democrat).

The Jacksonian Era
1828–1840

11

With Andrew Jackson's inauguration, the forces of egalitarianism swept over the federal government. Though Jackson had risen to become master of a large plantation and one of the leaders of his state, he had never abandoned the egalitarian habits of his earlier surroundings in small-farmer North Carolina and frontier Tennessee. On Inauguration Day, he opened the White House reception to an unruly mob of the high and the low, shocking the older official society but unmistakably announcing the new regime's conviction that common people were as good as aristocrats.

The same point was made with more substantial effect by Jackson's extension of the "spoils system" and his frank advocacy of "rotation in office." The new president was accompanied to Washington by a host of new-style democratic politicians demanding office as a reward for their support. Jackson took the position that any honest citizen could discharge the duties of a government office as well as any other. Furthermore, public offices should not be the property of their holders for life. They should be passed around, with a preference shown for friends of the administration that the people had elected. The numerous removals and appointments that Jackson made on these principles somewhat impaired the efficiency of government service but also made it more representative of and responsive to the country as a whole. Moreover, the spoils system helped make possible the new-style political parties through which the popular will could be translated into public policy.

Jackson was the first president to operate on the principle that the people themselves should decide public policy. Arguing that the president was the only federal official elected by the people as a whole, he was supremely certain that his policies represented the popular will. And so great was the popular confidence he inspired that the people, or a majority of them, usually agreed.

By assuming this role of democratic tribune, Jackson greatly increased the power of the presidency relative to Congress. All of his predecessors combined had vetoed only nine congressional measures, usually on the grounds that they were unconstitutional. Old Hickory used the veto 12 times against legislation he thought inexpedient as well as legislation he thought unconstitutional. And by taking his differences with Congress to the voters, he was highly successful in making recalcitrant legislators compliant or in replacing them.

JACKSONIAN POLICIES

Though the people's candidate had been elected, it was by no means clear what policies a people's administration would follow. Jackson himself had little political experience, and it was supposed that much would depend on whether Calhoun or Van Buren controlled his administration and became his heir for the presidential succession. Calhoun wanted to base the Jacksonian Democratic-Republican party (which gradually came to be called simply the Democratic party) on an alliance between the South and the West, which would reduce tariffs for the South and liberalize federal land policy for the West. A most embarrassing issue for Calhoun's plans was that of internal improvements, which the West favored and the South increasingly opposed.

Van Buren, on the other hand, wanted to resurrect the old Jeffersonian coalition between southern planters and the "plain Republicans" of the Northeast. Such a coalition could unite on neo-Jeffersonian grounds to oppose internal improvements (New York wanted no federally financed competition for its Erie Canal) and the national bank (New Yorkers resented the bank as a Philadelphia institution that gave New York City's rival an undeserved financial dominance). The one issue that was dangerous to Van Buren's plans was tariffs, over which Northerners and Southerners were disagreeing with mounting vehemence.

Although the Calhoun supporters had seemed to have the upper hand in the party, Jackson's inauguration produced a sudden reversal. Calhoun's friends were almost frozen out of the cabinet, while Van Buren himself was made the Secretary of State. Relations between Jackson and Calhoun steadily deteriorated until the South Carolinian was finally driven from the party. This result was produced in good part by Van Buren's astute use of the information that Calhoun, while a member of Monroe's cabinet, had advocated punishing Jackson for his rash invasion of Spanish Florida. The New Yorker was aided, too, by the "Eaton imbroglio," when the socially prominent women of Washington tried to ostracize the somewhat disreputable wife of Jackson's old friend and Secretary of War John Eaton. Calhoun's wife, Floride, was among the ladies who angered the president by snubbing Peggy Eaton, while the widower Van Buren was free to treat her with conspicuous gallantry.

But more fundamental than any of these considerations was the fact that the old general found Van Buren more congenial than Calhoun, both personally and in political outlook. Jackson came to Washington without a very well-thought-out position on the major issues. But he did have some deeply rooted political instincts that he trusted implicitly, and it was these that determined the policies of his administration. His instinctive egalitarianism has already been noted. Joined to this was an instinctive neo-Jeffersonian agrarian-mindedness.

Jackson himself had once engaged in extravagant land and commercial speculations based on credit. The bankruptcy that ended these operations and the long struggle to pay off his debts and regain solvency through farming were experiences that were most decisive for his political outlook. A thoroughly chastened advocate of the virtues of agriculture, hard work, and economy, abhorring debt and fearing the get-rich-quick atmosphere fostered by easy credit, he interpreted the boom-bust cycle of 1815–1819 as reproducing his own personal experiences on a national scale. Consequently, when he assumed the presidency, his one clearly defined objective was to administer a simple, economical government and to pay off the national debt as rapidly as possible.

Jackson's mood was more congenial with Van Buren's neo-Jeffersonianism than with the Republican nationalism that had heretofore been Calhoun's trademark. The influence that this gave Van Buren became most apparent when the advocates of a nationwide federal road system managed in 1830 to push through Congress the Maysville Road Bill. Though this bill only provided that the federal government should buy stock in a company building a turnpike from Maysville to Lexington in Kentucky, it was regarded as the test measure for the whole internal improvements program. Expenditures for internal improvements would delay Jackson's cherished project for paying off the national debt, and Van Buren had little difficulty persuading him that the measure should be vetoed. The veto message not only condemned the Maysville project, but suggested that all federal expenditures for internal improvements were perhaps either unwise or unlawful. Yet, though it retarded for several decades the dream of a nationally financed transportation network, the effect of the Maysville veto was more symbolic than practical. While it was a declaration that the Jacksonians favored not only frugal government but limits on federal powers, Jackson himself authorized some $10 million in improvement bills, including some for local projects.

THE TARIFF AND NULLIFICATION

Clearly, Jackson and Van Buren were not ready to assault all the works of Republican nationalism. To undertake a thorough downward revision of the Tariff of Abominations would be to delay payment of the public debt and to disrupt the North-South alliance that Van Buren sought to perfect. Consequently, the president urged his first Congress to handle the question with "utmost caution," and the resulting tariff revisions of 1830 hardly touched the more abominable features (the outrageously high duties) of the system.

At this point South Carolina exploded. No state had enjoyed a more uninterrupted prosperity from colonial days to 1819 than South Carolina. First rice, indigo, and sea island cotton had created a wealthy ruling class in the low country, and then the upland cotton boom had spread comparable riches through the rest of the state. No state, except perhaps Kentucky, was harder hit or more permanently damaged by the depression of the 1820s. The disruption of business coincided with the rise of more efficient cotton-producing areas in the Gulf states, and, to make matters infinitely worse, a growing anxiety over the slavery issue made South Carolina particularly sensitive about state rights. South Carolina's reaction to its economic prostration was the more violent because of the long period of heady prosperity that had preceded it and because no state had developed a prouder or touchier group of political leaders.

Until the depression, the Republican nationalism of Calhoun and his friends had been ascendant in South Carolina. The hard times enabled a rival "state rights" faction to blame Calhoun's favorite policies for all the state's woes. By the mid-'20s, the state-rights advocates had stirred up a storm of resentment against the protective tariff and were close to winning political control of the state. Calhoun and his friends were forced to retreat from Republican nationalism as rapidly and unobtrusively as possible. When Congress passed the Tariff of Abominations in 1828, the Calhoun supporters confounded their state-rights rivals by outdoing them in violent agitation against protection and by adopting an even more radical version of the state-rights doctrine.

The famous Doctrine of Nullification was announced in the South Carolina Exposition and Protest of 1828, secretly written by Calhoun and issued as a report of a legislative committee. The Nullifiers maintained that the Constitution was a compact among states that retained their essential sovereignty and that had delegated only limited and clearly specified powers to the federal government. The states themselves were the only proper judges of whether their common agent, the federal government, had exceeded the powers delegated to it by the constitutional compact. If a state judged that some federal law was a violation of the compact, it could declare it null and void, whereupon the federal government must desist unless and until three-fourths of the states, through the amending process, explicitly granted it the nullified power.

The South Carolinians counted on the Jackson administration to push tariff reform, and only after its failure to do so in 1829–1830 did Calhoun's friends begin a campaign in the state for actual nullification. The Jacksonian Congress responded by eliminating some of the worst excesses of the Tariff of Abominations in 1832, but the rates were still decidedly protectionist. Meanwhile Calhoun had openly broken with Jackson and put himself at the head of the Nullifiers; the Nullifiers won the two-thirds majority in the state legislature necessary to call a state convention; and in November, 1832, the state convention declared the tariff laws null and void and forbade their enforcement in South Carolina.

When Congress met in December, Jackson called for thorough tariff reform but at the same time announced his determination to enforce all federal laws throughout the land, by military means if necessary. It was this situation that produced the Compromise Tariff of 1833. Snatching from the Jackson party the credit for tariff reform, Clay and Calhoun united to push through a measure by which all tariff rates were to be reduced by gradual steps over a ten-year period to a uniform rate of 20 percent. Congress also complied with Jackson's demand that it simultaneously pass a Force Act, authorizing him to use the armed forces to uphold the laws. The South Carolina convention then reassembled and rescinded its nullification of the tariff laws but got in the last word by nullifying the Force Act.

The seemingly inconclusive outcome should not obscure the important long-range effects of this dangerous crisis. The fact that the Nullifiers could claim victory

—the tariff had been reformed—heightened their uncompromising attitude toward the federal government and gave them complete dominance over South Carolina. From this time on, the state and its magnetic leader Calhoun sought to unite the South in radical resistance to "federal tyranny," and the incessant agitation from this source was a major factor in producing the eventual secession of the southern states.

In the shorter run, nullification and disunion were discredited. Every other southern legislature denounced the South Carolina doctrine, the aged Madison denied that it derived from the Kentucky and Virginia resolutions of 1798, and the country as a whole responded enthusiastically to the nationalistic sentiments that Jackson expressed in opposing the Nullifiers. In fact, Jackson's zeal for preserving the Union led him to embrace a nationalistic interpretation of the Constitution that greatly embarrassed Van Buren and other state-rights Jacksonians. Heretofore the state-rights idea had been associated with democratic-mindedness in American politics, but now that the people's candidate was in the White House proclaiming federal preeminence over the states, federal power seemed less threatening. Perhaps the most significant result of the nullification crisis was the decline of state-rights sentiment in the face of a rising democratic nationalism.

INDIAN REMOVAL

Yet Jackson was not always a single-minded champion of federal prerogatives, as indicated by his handling of claims of the Cherokee nation, one of the Five Civilized Nations. A practical westerner who was not inclined to romanticize the "noble savage," the Tennessee president winked when the state of Georgia expropriated Cherokee lands in defiance of a federal court ruling. In *Cherokee Nation vs. Georgia* (1831) and *Worcester vs. Georgia* (1832), the Marshall court sided with the Indians, invalidating the state's claim to Cherokee territory. But Jackson refused to enforce the ruling, reportedly saying: "John Marshall has made his decision, now let him enforce it."

That which followed—the forced removal of these native Americans to territory beyond the Mississippi—is one of the darker chapters in the nation's history. Amid scenes of indescribable suffering, some 4,000 of the 16,000 refugees died in 1838 and 1839 of cold, hunger, and disease along the 800-mile-long route known in Cherokee memory as the "Trail of Tears." By 1839, three more of the remaining Five Civilized Nations—Choctaw, Chickasaw, and Creek—had been forcibly removed to the West under the congressional acts of 1830 and 1834. In 1843, the fifth nation, the resisting Seminoles of Florida, were all but exterminated by federal troops. Meanwhile, the Black Hawk War (1832) had ended effective Indian resistance to white settlement in the Old Northwest.

All told, more than 60,000 Indians were forced onto western reservations, thereby opening up millions of acres of fertile eastern land to land-hungry whites. Emerging as it did at the peak of the nullification crisis, the federal restraint implicit in Jackson's Indian policy may have confused some Jackson watchers. But southerners, westerners, and land speculators were delighted to find a president who shared their views of the Indian's place in an expanding nation. In fairness to Jackson—who, as nearly all historians agree, was no champion of Native American rights—the policy of dispossession and relocation that he so vigorously enforced was begun well before his election. Moreover, given the social values of the age and a context of growing conflict between Indian nations and eastern states, it did not appear an unreasonable solution to the "Indian problem." Convinced that assimilation was impossible and that autonomous Indian enclaves were impractical, if not unconstitutional, Jackson seems genuinely to have believed that his was a "just and humane policy" that placed the Indian "beyond the reach of injury or oppression." That it proved to be none of these things is indisputable; that other, more enlightened alternatives were open to him is less certain.

THE BANK WAR

Simultaneously with the nullification controversy, another great conflict had begun to take shape, this one between Andrew Jackson and the Second Bank of the United States. Jackson's experience with debt and depression had made him distrustful of all banks. On the bank question, his democratic-mindedness merged with his agrarian-mindedness to produce the conviction that banks fostered an unhealthy atmosphere of speculation, created boom-and-bust cycles, and transferred wealth from the many to the few. The national bank was open to special objection because it concentrated so much power in private hands and because it violated the Jeffersonian principles of strict construction and limited government. Jackson's views in all these respects reflected the resurgent agrarian-mindedness and neo-Jeffersonianism produced by the depression, as well as the antibank animus of the emerging worker's movement.

Actually, since Nicholas Biddle had become president of the bank in 1823, it had acted to restrain the numerous state-chartered banks from the tendencies Jackson feared, and most businesses and politicians had become convinced that the bank was indispensable to a soundly growing economy. Yet the opponents of banking in general saw the national bank as the head of the whole odious system, and the only part of the system that the federal government could readily reach. As a new boom gathered strength in the early 1830s, they were aided by an incongruous ally—entrepreneurial democracy.

Once again, as in the boom years following the War of 1812, the glittering promise of profits held out by a rapidly expanding market economy was creating a host of new entrepreneurs. For these business people, easy credit was the key to success, and the more reckless of the state-chartered banks became the citadels of the entrepreneurial spirit. By restraining the state banks from overexpansion, the national bank curtailed the profits and dimmed the prospects of the state banks and their borrowers. Consequently, the new entrepreneurs, the more speculative elements of the economy, regarded the bank as an aristocratic and repressive institution, representing established wealth and using its privileged position to hobble newcomers who attempted to join the race for success.

Both the new entrepreneurs and the agrarian-minded had been heavily attracted to Jackson's Democratic party. Both groups opposed the bank on somewhat egalitarian grounds, but their common hostility to Biddle's institution could not indefinitely conceal the fact that their ultimate objectives were diametrically opposed.

When Jackson became president, Biddle was already thinking about getting a bill passed to renew the bank's charter, which was due to expire in 1836. Jackson dismayed the bank's supporters when he questioned its constitutionality and expediency in his first message to Congress. Their dismay turned to alarm when it became clear that Jackson would be a candidate for reelection in 1832. The old Adams-Clay alignment, calling itself the National Republican party, was planning to run Clay against Jackson, and Clay was urging Biddle to press for recharter before the election. Clay argued that this would force Jackson to approve a recharter bill, for a veto would be a damaging issue against him in the election. Biddle finally agreed, and in July, 1832 a recharter bill passed Congress by substantial majorities.

Jackson promptly returned the measure to Congress with a veto message declaring the bank unconstitutional and demagogically denouncing the foreign ownership of much of the bank's stock. At the heart of his message was an eloquent paragraph expounding the Jacksonian social philosophy. The president granted that natural inequalities existed in every society. "But," he said, "when the laws undertake to add to these natural and just advantages artificial distinctions, to grant titles, gratuities, and exclusive privileges, to make the rich richer and the potent more powerful, the humble members of society—the farmers, mechanics, and laborers—who have neither the time nor the means of securing like favors to themselves, have a right to complain of the injustice of their government."

Jackson's hostility to the bank was genuine, but his veto message was at least in part designed to make the bank an election issue. The bank supporters did not have the votes in Congress to override the veto, but they confidently expected that both the veto and its author would be repudiated in the ensuing presidential election. When the returns were in, Jackson's estimate proved to be the shrewdest as he won 219 electoral votes to Clay's 40.

Yet the bank was far from dead. Jackson rightly feared that Biddle was determined to use the bank's great economic and political power to push a recharter bill through Congress over his veto. Equally determined to cripple the bank, the president resolved to remove the government's mounting deposits from its vaults. Federal receipts were booming along with the economy, the national debt had been paid off, and a federal surplus of millions of dollars was beginning to accumulate. These surplus federal deposits greatly extended the bank's lending ability, profits, and power. It took the administration a year to find a way of removing surplus deposits from the bank. After discharging two consecutive uncooperative Secretaries of the Treasury and after protracted negotiations with nervous state bankers, Jackson announced in September, 1833 that henceforth the Treasury would deposit the federal funds in selected state banks, so-called deposit banks or pet banks.

Enraged by the removal of deposits, Biddle recklessly threw the full economic power of the national bank against the government. Deposit removal and Jackson's hostility made some contraction of the bank's loans necessary, but Biddle resolved to force such a severe loan contraction and to create such widespread distress that Congress would be compelled to restore the deposits and eventually recharter the bank. As a result, the "Panic Session" of Congress was under intense pressure during the winter of 1833–1834 to restore the deposits to relieve the country from mounting bankruptcies, unemployment, and distress. But Jackson's antibank majority held firm; Biddle was finally forced to relax the pressure, and the bank's doom was sealed— partly because Biddle's panic helped to prove Jackson's case against the bank's immense power.

BOOM AND BUST AGAIN

The destruction of the national bank was only a Pyrrhic victory in the Jacksonians' larger campaign to reform banking in general. Jackson and many of his principal followers were "hard-money" people who wanted all bank notes driven from circulation, leaving only gold and silver coin as a circulating medium. Their attack on the national bank was only the first step in their deflationary, agrarian-minded program, and they hoped to use the state-bank deposit system to reform the state banks. The deposit banks would be required, as a condition for receiving the deposits, to cease issuing notes in denominations under $5 or accepting such notes in their transactions with other banks. Gradually the prohibition would be extended to notes under $10 and then $20. Driving small notes from circulation would create a steady demand for specie for small transactions, and all banks would have to reduce their loans and note issues in order to have enough specie on hand to meet the demand.

But this scheme did not have time to get under way before it was overwhelmed by a massive inflation. The Jacksonians had destroyed the national bank's stabilizing influence on the economy just at the moment when powerful inflationary forces were pushing the country into a boom even more wildly speculative than the one that followed the War of 1812. With the national bank's restraining influence removed, the state banks expanded their loans, note issues, and profits; new state banks were chartered by the hundreds; the deposit banks themselves got out of control; and the wave of inflation and speculation rolled ominously higher toward its inevitable cresting and crash.

The hard-money supporters could only shout futile warnings. Their Jeffersonian constitutional scruples prevented them from attempting direct federal regulation of the state banks. Regulation at the state level was equally impossible because the uneasy alliance between hard-money (or agrarian-minded) Democrats and enterprise-minded Democrats began breaking down as soon as their common enemy, the national bank, was finally defeated.

Nevertheless, in 1836, Jackson attempted a drastic remedy with his Specie Circular. The flood of bank notes had stimulated an especially frantic speculation in public lands, and the Circular directed that thenceforth lands must be paid for in specie or specie-redeemable bank notes. Coming too late, the Specie Circular succeeded only in putting a strain on the vastly overextended structure of credit. The strain was increased by the Distribution Act that Jackson had reluctantly signed a few weeks before. Congress had decided to distribute the bulging federal surplus, approaching $40 million, among the states; the federal deposit banks were suddenly called upon to transfer vast sums to the state treasuries. Finally, in the spring of 1837, only weeks after Jackson left office, a financial crisis in England set off a wave of bankruptcies in the United States, the banks suspended specie payments, and the Panic of 1837 brought the whole towering pyramid of credit crashing down.

Jackson's hand-picked successor Van Buren was left to cope with a severe and prolonged depression. Aligning himself with the hard-money wing of the Democratic party, Van Buren proposed that the government sever its connections with all banks and keep its funds in its own "independent treasury" offices. He further proposed that the government accept and pay out only gold and silver coin, which would have some deflationary effect by creating a constant demand for specie. But in the main the proposal meant that the federal government would wash its hands of responsibility for the economy. Because of the split between hard-money and soft-money Democrats, Congress wrangled over the independent treasury throughout Van Buren's term. The bill was finally passed in 1840.

Meanwhile, the depression had forced most state legislatures to attempt some kind of banking reform. A few states prohibited banks entirely, others gave a monopoly of the banking business to a state-owned or mixed public-private bank, and most states adopted stricter regulations to prevent an overextension of credit by private banks. New York's widely imitated Free Banking Act of 1838 sought to provide state regulation and at the same time to divest banks of the monopolistic special privileges they enjoyed through their legislative charters. Foreshadowing general incorporation laws for all kinds of enterprises, it provided that anyone who complied with certain regulations could engage in the banking business. Thus by the early 1840s, the country had reached a practical compromise on the banking question: banks would continue to stimulate economic growth, but they would be restrained through free competition and state regulation rather than through a national bank.

The long and hotly contested struggle over banking was important in two respects. On the most obvious level, it reflected the efforts of an economy newly swept forward by the market revolution to develop a credit and currency system that would sustain growth and broaden opportunity without causing disastrous boom-and-bust cycles. But at a deeper level, it reflected the psychological ambivalence of a conservative, agrarian society toward the whole new world of rapid change and growth into which it had been suddenly thrust. During the first great boom, 1815–1819, the country as a whole succumbed with uncritical enthusiasm to the new spirit of enterprise. The depression of the 1820s produced an equally decided reaction in the other direction—against banks, easy credit, paper money, and entrepreneurial ambition. Thus the return of prosperity and the second great boom, 1834–1837, evoked more ambivalent reactions. Some again saw unlimited opportunity and clamored for unlimited credit; others, the neo-agrarians who remembered the 1820s, championed hard money; still others, perhaps the majority, oscillated between the two extremes. By the time of the second great depression following 1837, the ever-advancing market had sufficiently undermined agrarian-mindedness and the boom-bust cycle had sufficiently chastened the enterprise-minded to make a rough consensus possible. The American people had finally made their adjustment to the new world of enterprise created by the market revolution.

THE NEW POLITICS

Just as the Jacksonian era saw the evolution of financial institutions and practices to serve the emerging spirit of enterprise, so did it see the evolution of political institutions and practices to serve the emerging spirit of egalitarian democracy. The basic feature of the new politics was the two-party system, which had flourished briefly and imperfectly around 1800 and which reemerged to reach its full development only in the 1830s.

Carrying to the national level the new-style democratic politics that had emerged in the states during the 1820s, the Jacksonians created a strong political party and forced their opponents to imitate their organization and techniques for wooing a mass electorate. The anti-Jacksonians were at first an ill-organized coalition of Clay-Adams National Republicans, Nullifiers, and—out of hostility to the Van Buren organization in New York—the democratic-minded anti-Masons. These elements were unable to unite to stem the Jacksonian tide in the presidential election of 1832, but they were already beginning to learn the lessons of Jacksonian politics. In fact the anti-Masons had anticipated the Democrats in calling a national party convention representing the grass-roots elements of the party to replace the discredited caucus method of nominating candidates.

A powerful, unified opposition party developed only in 1833–1834 when Jackson's removal of deposits caused the defection of many business-minded Democrats and enabled his opponents to unite on the platform of resistance to executive tyranny. Taking the name "Whigs" to identify themselves with earlier defenders of liberty, they stood for sound business enterprise and a program of Republican nationalism. Though the Whigs drew increasing support from all sections and classes, they appealed especially to the wealthier and more established members of the business community, to the manufacturing interests, and to the larger southern planters whose staple crops involved them extensively in the commercial network. Calhoun's Nullifiers cooperated with the Whigs for a few years but after 1837 returned to the Democratic party.

In 1836, the new Whig party sought to capitalize on political sectionalism by running three presidential candidates, hoping to throw the election into the House of Representatives. But the magic of Jackson's popularity was sufficient to win his candidate, Van Buren, a slim majority over all three Whigs. The Whigs' day finally came in 1840 when the Democrats were discredited by the depression and when the Whigs outdid the Democrats at the game of democratic politics. Running the popular old Indian fighter William Henry Harrison as the people's candidate against the "aristocratic" Van Buren, the Whigs whipped up enthusiasm with monster rallies, torchlight parades, songs, and log-cabin symbolism to win a sweeping majority.

The presidential election of 1840 also produced by far the largest outpouring of voters yet seen. Only 27 percent of the estimated eligible voters had voted for president in 1824; the Jackson-Adams contest of 1828 had raised the figure to 56 percent; but the contest of 1840 brought out 78 percent of the eligible electorate, a proportion that may never have been equaled since. This dramatic rise in political interest was a result of the full development of the two-party system. By 1840 the two parties were almost equally strong not only at the national level but also in every section, in most of the states, and in a majority of counties. This meant closely contested elections for all offices from sheriff to president with no efforts being spared to woo hesitant voters. Each party maintained an elaborate network of stridently partisan newspapers in Washington, the state capitals, and countless villages and towns. Rival orators stumped every neighborhood for months before every election. Competing systems of party committees at county, state, and national levels issued a constant stream of broadsides and pamphlets, organized parades and rallies, and made sure that no voter stayed away from the polls on election day. This incessant political activity not only brought voters to the polls in droves, but also made politics a leading form of American recreation, while providing the population with a massive political education.

But the parties were as much affected by the voters as they affected the voters. The new-style democratic politicians of both parties developed an acute sensitivity to shifts in public opinion and became expert in building coalitions that would yield a majority or near-majority. The Whigs continued to appeal more strongly to business interests, the well-to-do, manufacturers, and large planters, while the Democrats attracted smaller farmers, workers, and frontier areas. But both parties needed additional support to achieve a majority, and both quickly learned the techniques for constantly adjusting their positions to changing public moods. As a result the parties tended not to differ sharply in normal times and to maintain a nearly even balance of strength. From Jackson's day to our own, with only brief interruptions, this two-party system has remained a reasonably sensitive instrument for translating majority opinion into public policy while moderating the sharpness of conflict among the diverse groups that compose American society.

CONFLICTING HISTORICAL VIEWPOINTS

4. What Was Jacksonian Democracy?

In his Life of Andrew Jackson *(3 vols., 1860), the nineteenth-century historian James Parton concluded that the seventh president was "a patriot and a traitor. . . . A democratic autocrat. An urbane savage. An atrocious saint." On this note of paradox, scholarly investigation of Jacksonian politics began and to the present day Old Hickory's administration remains among the most controversial in American history.*

Parton, the earliest and most distinguished nineteenth-century Jackson scholar, represented the patrician school of historians. Sons of affluent and often aristocratic eastern families, deeply suspicious of popular democracy and the common folk, these early historians viewed Jacksonianism as the degradation of American govern-

ment. Jackson, they affirmed, was an illiterate backwoods barbarian, the agent of the unwashed and ignorant masses.

Soon after 1900, a generation of reform-minded scholars challenged this decidedly conservative "Whig" interpretation. Countering the antidemocratic views of the patricians with prodemocratic views of their own, these progressive historians generally celebrated Jackson as the champion of the popular will. Thus, in his distinguished Life of Andrew Jackson *(2 vols., 1911), John Spencer Bassett praised the rustic Tennessee president for his "brave, frank, masterly leadership" of a broad democratic movement. Generally agreed on the nature of Jacksonian democracy, the progressives nevertheless often argued about its origins. In* The Frontier in American History *(1920) and* The United States, 1830–1850 *(1935) Frederick Jackson Turner, one of the earliest of the great progressive scholars, emphasized the influence of frontier democracy in the development of Jacksonianism. In Turner's view, Jacksonian Democracy was a sectional rather than a class movement. It was inspired and sustained, he believed, by the pioneer societies of the new states of the West and Southwest. To Arthur M. Schlesinger, Jr., on the other hand, Jacksonianism was "a problem not of sections but of classes." In his Pulitzer Prize-winning* Age of Jackson *(1945), the younger Schlesinger included eastern wage earners as well as western farmers among the supporters of the Old Hero. The movement, he argued, pitted "noncapitalist groups, and laboring men, East, West, and South" against "capitalist groups, mainly Eastern."*

In recent years, the critics of the progressive interpretation, particularly of Schlesinger's labor thesis, have been numerous. Bray Hammond (Banks and Politics in America, *1957) and Edward Pessen* (Jacksonian America, *1969), for example, denied that Jackson's was a working-class movement. Arguing that his supporters were not common people at all but incipient entrepreneurs, Hammond characterized the Jacksonians as "newer, more aggressive . . . businessmen" who clashed with "an old and conservative merchant class." According to Pessen, Old Hickory was antilabor, and workers opposed him at the polls. Marvin Meyers* (The Jacksonian Persuasion, *1957) and John W. Ward* (Andrew Jackson, Symbol for an Age, *1955), on the other hand, have fastened on symbolism and psychology to explain the Jacksonian phenomenon. In differing though complementary studies, these scholars concluded that in Jackson Americans found neither a champion of class nor section, but the embodiment of old-fashioned republican virtues. But the ultimate refutation of the Schlesinger interpretation—and all others for that matter—came from Lee Benson, who argued in* The Concept of Jacksonian Democracy *(1961) that Jacksonianism existed only as a figment of the historical imagination. Indeed, if historians followed the advice of this historical quantifier, they would forget altogether about the concept of Jacksonian Democracy.*

Benson's thesis has some support, but the imminent demise of Jackson studies is most unlikely. Today, more than two centuries after the Old Hero's birth, the man and the movement continue to provoke lively controversy.

FOR FURTHER READING

Robert V. Remini's *Andrew Jackson* (1966)* is both brief and excellent; James C. Curtis's *Andrew Jackson* (1976) is a provocative and unflattering psychohistorical

portrait; and Glyndon G. Van Deusen's *The Jacksonian Era, 1828–1848* (1959)*
provides a generally whiggish overview of the entire period. Richard McCormick's
Second American Party System (1966) describes party formation in the Jacksonian
era; Robert V. Remini has analyzed *Andrew Jackson and the Bank War* (1967); Peter
Temin focuses on *The Jacksonian Economy* (1969); and Edward Pessen's *Riches,
Class, and Power Before the Civil War* (1973) provides a valuable social portrait of
the era. William W. Freehling has written the *Prelude to Civil War: The Nullification
Controversy in South Carolina* (1966)* and Charles M. Wiltse focuses on *John C.
Calhoun: Nullifier, 1829–1839* (1949). Other important biographies of Jackson's
contemporaries include: William N. Chambers, *Old Bullion Benton: Senator from the
New West* (1956); Thomas P. Govan, *Nicholas Biddle: Nationalist and Public Banker*
(1959); Glyndon G. Van Deusen, *The Life of Henry Clay* (1937)*; and Glyndon G.
Van Deusen, *Thurlow Weed, Wizard of the Lobby* (1947). The consequences of
Jackson's Indian policies may be traced in Thurman Wilkins's *Cherokee Tragedy*
(1970) and Arthur DeRosier's *Removal of the Choctaw Indians* (1970). Bernard W.
Sheehan's *Seeds of Extinction* (1973) thoughtfully analyzes the evolution of preremo-
val white attitudes and policies; and Francis Paul Prucha's *American Indian Policy in
the Formative Years* (1962) is an important revisionist work. A firsthand impression
of Martin Van Buren can be gained from his *Autobiography* (published in the *Annual
Report of the American Historical Association,* 1918); and James Curtis's *The Fox
at Bay* (1970) examines Van Buren's presidency. The analyses of Jacksonian America
by European observers are extremely illuminating. Here the classic is Alexis de
Tocqueville's *Democracy in America* (2 vols., 1835–1840)*; but also fascinating are:
Michael Chevalier, *Society, Manners, and Politics in the United States* (1839)*;
Francis J. Grund, *Aristocracy in America* (1839)*; Harriet Martineau, *Society in
America* (1837)*; and Frances Trollope, *Domestic Manners of the Americans*
(1832)*. The Bank War can be analyzed in Frank Otto Gatell's *The Jacksonians and
the Money Power, 1829–1840* (Berkeley Readings in American History, 1967).*

---

*Available in paperback edition.

Romanticism, Reform, Slavery

12

The country had no sooner developed a two-party system for reflecting the majority will while moderating conflict than it ran head-on into the one conflict that could be neither resolved by majority will nor moderated: the conflict over Negro slavery. The age of enterprise and egalitarianism that produced the two-party system had also brought Americans to their highest pitch of confidence about the possibilities for individuals and for optimism about the future of their society. It was a reforming age, abounding in schemes for wiping out the remaining blemishes that marred the full perfection of humanity. It was a utopian age, spattered with perfectionist communities and looking forward to the early perfection of the whole society. Such an age was bound to find intolerable the most glaring affront to the liberal principles of the Declaration of Independence. Yet Negro slavery was so deeply rooted as a social and economic institution that the slaveholders, though themselves heirs of the American liberal tradition, could not surrender it.

ROMANTICISM

Underlying the reformist spirit of the age was a new configuration of ideas and attitudes called *Romanticism.* A vast and complicated movement in the intellectual and literary history of the western world, Romanticism took different forms and suggested different conclusions for different countries, periods, and individuals. As used here, the term denotes the central tendencies of thought in the United States in the first half of the nineteenth century.

Romanticism grew out of the eighteenth-century Enlightenment and was akin to it. Both assumed that the world was designed for human happiness, both emphasized human ability, and both were little concerned with the rights of women. In America, at least, both led in the direction of optimism, individualism, and liberal political principles. But Romanticism was a reaction against the Enlightenment's mechanical view of the natural world and its emphasis on intellect. Where the Enlightenment ascribed human competence to the ability through reason to understand the natural laws by which a watchmaker Creator regulated both the physical and moral universes, Romanticism distrusted intellect and valued human emotional and intuitive qualities. Regarding the natural world as the embodiment of a divine spirit, Romanticism held that the natural and the spontaneous were good and that the highest truth was derived through the instantaneous spiritual intuition of the individual.

American Romanticism reached its most sophisticated and self-conscious form in the Transcendentalism of Ralph Waldo Emerson and the group of New England intellectuals he inspired. While most of Emerson's contemporaries were probably unaware of Transcendentalism or Romanticism as an explicit body of doctrine, the pervasive Romantic assumptions were apparent in every aspect of American life. The overwhelming theme of popular literature and the popular stage was the primacy of feeling over intellect. In more serious writing, James Fenimore Cooper celebrated the moral perfection and superior wisdom of the "natural" but untutored woodsman Leatherstocking and the "noble savage" Chingachgook, while Nathaniel Hawthorne and Herman Melville explored, from a Romantic standpoint, some of the darker implications of Romantic doctrine. The landscape painters of the Hudson River School sought to capture on their canvases the emotion of the "sublime" evoked by natural scenes. Architects turned from the intellectually satisfying simplicity, harmony, and proportion of the eighteenth century's "colonial" or "Georgian" style to exotic and more titillating models—Gothic, Moorish, and Egyptian. Even in laying out gardens and parks, Americans abandoned formal patterns and tried to reproduce artificially the wildness and irregularity of nature, as in Frederick Law Olmsted's design for Central Park in New York City.

The influence of Romanticism extended far beyond intellectuals, writers, and artists. Jacksonian egalitarianism was reinforced by some widely accepted Romantic assumptions. The Enlightenment's emphasis on reason and education, its insistence that reason was more highly developed in some people than in others, had prevented even the more liberal people of the eighteenth century from endorsing full egalitarianism and popular sovereignty. Thus Jefferson had relied on a "natural aristocracy" to rule, trusting the people to elect the "natural aristocrats" to office, yet not trusting them to dictate public policy. But when intuition rather than reason was seen as the source of truth, the situation changed. The Romantic doctrine of democracy was expounded most boldly by the Jacksonian politician and distinguished historian George Bancroft: "if the sentiment of truth, justice, love, and beauty exists in every one, then it follows, as a necessary consequence, that the common judgment in taste, politics, and religion is the highest authority on earth." Indeed, by Jackson's time, the semiliterate farmer who lived simply and close to nature was often regarded as being superior in virtue and real wisdom to a city dweller whose "natural" impulses had been stifled by the artificialities of education and culture.

Jackson's enormous popularity may be attributed in considerable measure to the prevalence of such attitudes. The contest between Jackson and John Quincy Adams in 1828 was widely interpreted as pitting a "natural" man of virtue, a product of the

American frontier, against the well-educated, highly cultured, and therefore suspect Adams, who had the additional disadvantage of having spent much of his early life in the artificial surroundings of an overcivilized and decadent Europe. To Harvard-trained John Quincy Adams, Jackson was "a barbarian who could not write a sentence of grammar and hardly could spell his own name." But the people found in him the embodiment of all the natural wisdom of the common folk. In the presidential election of 1840, the Whigs turned the tables by using, in naked parody, the Jacksonian political formula. Deftly exploiting a hard-cider and log-cabin symbolism, they presented William Henry Harrison, "the Ohio Plowman," as the representative of the "hardy yeomanry" whose "primitive" qualities contrasted sharply with the city-slicker airs of the Jacksonian candidate, Martin Van Buren. The voters who responded enthusiastically to these appeals had never heard of Romanticism as a body of doctrine, but the smashing victory they gave Harrison at the polls demonstrated their unconscious conversion to some key Romantic assumptions.

ROMANTIC CHRISTIANITY

Apart from political behavior, extensive popular acceptance of Romantic assumptions was most evident in religious behavior. Well into the nineteenth century, the story of religion in the United States was a story of the gradual erosion of the originally dominant Puritan-Calvinist strain of Protestant Christianity. In an increasingly self-reliant, optimistic, and individualistic society, it continually became more difficult to sustain a view of life that emphasized the awful sovereignty of God, the sinfulness and helplessness of humanity, and the necessity for salvation by God's miraculous and arbitrary grace.

Under the impact of the eighteenth-century Enlightenment, some members of the more sophisticated classes had abandoned the inscrutable, omnipresent God of the Calvinists for Deism's remote and kindly Creator. Others had moved in the same direction more gradually, retaining the outward forms and language of orthodox Christianity but coming to believe that a reasonable God was favorably disposed toward all people, that people were sufficiently endowed with reason to be capable of goodness, and that the objective of a religious life ought to be goodness in this world rather than God's arbitrary salvation in a world to come. Such opinions spread rapidly even among the direct descendants of seventeenth-century Puritanism, the New England Congregationalists. However, violent controversy broke out between the liberal and orthodox factions. By the end of the century, the liberal Congregationalists, who tended to be the wealthier and better educated, were breaking off to form separate churches and taking the name Unitarians.

While Unitarianism was a minority movement in the churches, Christian orthodoxy unquestionably was at a low ebb in the last quarter of the eighteenth century. The mighty orthodox counteroffensive, the Great Awakening of the 1730s and 1740s, had spent its force; the Revolution had brought with it the spiritual and moral laxity usual in wartime; Deism was growing popular and militant; and the orthodox themselves had become listless and had begun to acquiesce in compromises with the spirit of the age.

It was under these circumstances that the orthodox clergy resorted to the emotional techniques of the Great Awakening to launch another vigorous counteroffensive known as the Great Revival. Really a series of revival movements beginning around the turn of the century, the Great Revival kept the country in religious ferment for 25 years, obliterating the last traces of Deism and bringing a majority of Americans into the Protestant churches. America did not return to Calvinism, for in the process of capturing America, Protestant Christianity was itself captured and transformed by the Romantic optimism and individualism of American culture.

One phase of the Great Revival began with a series of spectacular "camp meetings" in Kentucky. These week-long extravaganzas of religious enthusiasm spread rapidly over the West, spawning a host of poorly educated but highly effective revival preachers. Traveling up and down the West, these emotional revivalists left in their wake a host of new churches, mainly of the less sophisticated popular denominations, Baptists and Methodists.

Meanwhile President Timothy Dwight of Yale and his protégé Lyman Beecher were showing the conservative clergy in the East how to use a more restrained revivalism as a technique for combating Unitarianism and maintaining the hegemony of orthodox Congregationalism. At the same time, the Congregationalists were cooperating with the Presbyterians in a joint campaign to evangelize the frontier areas of western New York and the Old Northwest. The revival movement and the western missionary effort both culminated in the 1820s in the spectacularly successful evangelism of Charles Grandison Finney. This former lawyer combined emotional intensity with some shrewdly devised new techniques—cottage prayer meetings preceding his revival meetings, the full participation of women, the "holy band" of zealous young helpers to pray individually with the religiously smitten—to produce an explosion of emotional piety that entrenched a revivalistic "Presbygationalism" in the western regions. Although he was ordained a Presbyterian minister, Finney's "New School" Calvinism led him far from the hell fire and damnation of an orthodox past. Preaching neither God's inscrutable sovereignty nor humanity's ineradicable depravity, he embraced the doctrine of free will and laced his sermons with a perfectionism that directed his followers not only to personal salvation but social reform.

Most of the revivalists started from positions they would have regarded as theologically orthodox, but like Finney they were more interested in the effectiveness, the preachability, of what they were saying than in its theological correctness. They quickly found that it was easiest to evoke the desired emotional response by preaching that God was anxious to save sinners, that sinners need only accept God's love. Many Presbyterians and the more conservative Protestants of all denominations in the South resisted this tendency, but the main body of American Protestantism moved gradually and unconsciously toward a Romantic theology. Love was viewed as the essence of the Christian life. God was love, freely offering his love to all who would accept it. Conversion was the emotional experience of acceptance and loving response. In some versions, as with many Methodists and in the theology that Finney himself taught, conversion was viewed as carrying with it a kind of spiritual perfection. The tone of this Romantic Protestantism was clearest perhaps in hymns like "O Love That Will Not Let Me Go" and its juvenile counterpart "Jesus Loves Me."

UTOPIANISM AND HUMANITARIANISM

Wherever the Great Revival burned—and especially in the frequently ravaged "burned-over district" of western New York—it left behind a bed of glowing embers ready to be fanned into all kinds of extravagant perfectionist and utopian movements. Most of these movements were millennialist, expecting Christ's early return to establish the Kingdom of God on earth. There was an excited outburst of expectation when the Reverend William Miller calculated from biblical prophecies the time of Christ's return, but believers were disillusioned when the event did not occur, either in the originally predicted spring of 1844 or, after Miller had corrected his calculations, on October 21 of that year.

Various groups that looked forward to an early millennium sought in the meantime to gather together those who had been "perfected" through conversion into communities that would be without sin or blemish. Because they emphasized the primacy of love in all relationships and the freedom from sin that comes with salvation, these perfectionist utopians had particular difficulty with conventional notions about the proper relations between the sexes. One group, led by John Humphrey Noyes, established a flourishing community at Oneida, New York that rejected private property for common ownership and exclusive marriage for a carefully regulated system of "complex marriage." A more successful group, the Shakers, solved the problem of exclusive love by practicing celibacy in their many communities. The most durable of all these movements was Mormonism, which derived from Joseph Smith's claim that he had discovered in upstate New York some golden plates containing new revelations from God, and which for a time sanctioned the practice of polygamy.

In addition to the religiously oriented utopian movements, the Romantic age produced many secular utopian communities. Perhaps the best known was Brook Farm at Roxbury, Massachusetts, which was supported by many people on the fringes of the Transcendentalist movement. A more ambitious community at New Harmony, Indiana was founded by Robert Dale Owen, son of the English textile manufacturer and social reformer Robert Owen. The most extensive movement in secular communitarianism was inspired by Charles Fourier, a French social philosopher who had calculated rationally the optimum size and organization for the ideal socialistic community, which he called a "phalanx." Attracting the support of the prominent New York editor Horace Greeley, the Fourierists established some 40 or 50 phalanxes in the United States. In general, the secular utopias did not fare as well as those that had a religious motivation to keep their members loyal to the communitarian ideal. Many of the latter survived late into the nineteenth century, dwindling away only as the ebbing of religious revivalism dried up their source of recruits.

The perfectionist impulse that produced the utopian communities also inspired a broader series of movements aimed at wiping out every individual and social evil that the age could identify. Much of this reformist activity was devoted to previously neglected classes of unfortunates. Dorothea Dix led the crusade that persuaded state legislatures to establish institutions for the care of the mentally ill. A related movement induced a number of states to undertake extensive programs of penal reform, emphasizing rehabilitation rather than merely punishment of criminals. For the first time, facilities were developed for educating the deaf, dumb, and blind. Indeed, the great movement for publicly supported common schools for all children got its real start in this perfectionist age, with Horace Mann's ambitious program in Massachusetts leading the way.

The reform movements that had the greatest impact were those most closely associated with the Great Revival. In the early stages of his revivalist campaign in Connecticut, Lyman Beecher devised the technique of organizing through local churches voluntary societies of lay members to promote various moral and evangelical objectives. By the late 1820s, these local societies had developed into a group of regional and national federations with paid agents to organize new local societies, raise funds, and carry out the various objectives of the federations. The American Home Missionary Society, which hired evangelists to carry the Great Revival into the West, was one of the first of the national federations. It was soon joined by other national societies that devoted themselves to such religious objectives as foreign missions, distributing Bibles and religious tracts, promoting Sunday schools, and saving sailors. Leadership and financing for all these societies came from the same group of revivalistic "Presbygational" ministers and philanthropists led by Beecher and Finney.

The developing Romantic theology of the Great Revival soon inspired a reform impulse that went beyond the evangelical objectives of the earliest societies. Finney in particular was preaching that conversion caused a disposition of "disinterested benevolence" in the converted, and his revivals left behind numbers of converts anxious to find some object on which to lavish their disinterested benevolence. The first object to be discovered was the drunkard.

The fantastic consumption of alcoholic beverages in the early republic unquestionably constituted a serious social problem. Lyman Beecher had early been shocked by the extent of drunkenness at ministerial ordinations, and as the revival spirit spread, he helped inspire the organization of local temperance societies, which aimed at moderation rather than complete abstinence in the consumption of alcohol. When this proved ineffective, Beecher began campaigning for total abstinence, and in 1826 the American Society for the Promotion of Temperance was organized with total abstinence as its goal. Sending evangelists through the country to persuade people to sign a pledge of total abstinence, the Society claimed 5,000 local branches with 1 million members by 1834.

Turning to politics, the temperance forces secured a local option law in Massachusetts in 1838 and the first statewide prohibition law in Maine in 1846. Soon most of the northern states had legislated against alcohol. In contrast to twentieth-century prohibitionism, the nineteenth-century movement was much weaker in the South, where only the border states of Delaware and Tennessee resorted to legislative prohibition.

The temperance movement was merely the first of the reform movements inspired by the Great Revival. By the 1830s, the headquarters for the benevolent societies had shifted from Boston to New York City, where Finney had been established as pastor of a great "free" church (charging no pew rents) for the poor and where resided the two leading financial angels of the general benevolence movement, the merchant brothers Arthur and Lewis Tappan. Into New York every May poured an army of the benevolent-minded from every part of the country to attend a series of annual conventions of all the societies. New societies were continually being organized for every conceivable purpose: to promote peace, to stop the carrying of mails on Sunday, to stop the wearing of corsets.

WOMEN'S RIGHTS

Animated by the same humanitarian and moral impulses as men, women played significant roles in the reform movements of the age. Very often, however, their effectiveness was severely limited by the fears and prejudices of the men with whom they sought common cause. Angelina and Sarah Grimké, for example, left their South Carolina home and went north to aid in the antislavery cause. But their efforts to speak in its behalf were often opposed by male abolitionists and frequently howled down by audiences unaccustomed to such "unladylike" endeavors. In 1840, Lucretia Mott, Elizabeth Cady Stanton, and a half-dozen other American women traveled to London to attend the World Anti-Slavery Convention only to be excluded because of their sex. In the 1850s, Susan B. Anthony had much the same experience in the temperance movement, where "ladies" were expected to be seen but not heard. The irony of such discrimination by men and by organizations dedicated to humanitarian causes was not lost on this generation of women. With Angelina Grimké, not a few of them would ask: "What can a *woman* do for the slave when she herself is under the feet of man and shamed into silence."

The sexual prejudices of the male reformers were mirrored and magnified by the larger society they sought to uplift. In the eyes of the law, women were perpetual minors, the wards of male guardians without whom they had no separate legal identity. Denied the right to vote, hold office, or sit on juries, they enjoyed few property guarantees, suffered gross educational and job discriminations, found divorce a virtual impossibility, and were legally subject even to corporal punishment by their husbands. Until 1850, nearly every state permitted wife beating "with a reasonable instrument" (defined by one Massachusetts judge as a "stick no bigger than my thumb"). Men also enjoyed a virtual monopoly on property rights. Except in Mississippi (after 1837) and New York (after 1845), women who owned real estate—generally only single women could—did so only through the authority of a male guardian.

Confronted by such disabilities, women (usually of the upper-middle class) organized for their own relief, often combining women's rights with temperance, abolition, public education, and prison reforms. Except for some highly significant breakthroughs in the fields of literature and education, their successes were few; throughout the period, feminism remained little more than an attitude shared by a few intrepid social pioneers. Sarah Grimké's *The Equality of the Sexes* (1838) and Margaret Fuller's *Women in the Nineteenth Century* (1844) were important early women's manifestoes. Amelia Bloomer's sensible but much ridiculed crusade for dress reform, Lucy Stone's repudiation of marriage laws that gave a husband "injurious and unnatural superiority" over his wife, and Stanton and Mott's Seneca Falls declaration of women's independence ("We hold these truths to be self-evident: that all men *and women* are created equal") symbolized a heightening feminist consciousness. But the work of these early feminists scarcely touched the lives of the vast majority of the nation's women. Sisterhood was not powerful in antebellum America. For all the vigor of their protest, the Susan B. Anthonys and the Angelina Grimkés of that era organized more effectively for causes other than their own. Despite the reform enthusiasms of the age, nineteenth-century concerns were nearly always restricted to the rights of *men*, not women.

ABOLITION

While the women's movement probably owed little to evangelical Christianity, religion was clearly a principal engine of abolition. Before 1830, the organized antislavery movement had been small and ineffectual, drawing its support mainly from those persons, notably Quakers, with strong religious scruples against human bondage. A scattering of manumission societies, principally in the upper South, sought to encourage owners to free their slaves, and Benjamin Lundy had maintained for some years an antislavery journal. In addition, the American Colonization Society had been seeking without much success to promote the migration of free Negroes to Africa, a conservative approach to the problem that aroused the suspicion of both the defenders and critics of slavery.

Only when the British Parliament's widely publicized debates over emancipation caught the attention of the leaders of the American benevolence movement did antislavery begin to become a major force on this side of the Atlantic. In 1830, the Tappan brothers helped organize an antislavery society in New York. The following year young William Lloyd Garrison left Benjamin Lundy's employment to set up his own militant antislavery newspaper, *The Liberator,* in Boston. Over the years to come, Garrison and the small group of zealous antislavery reformers he inspired in New England were to furnish an uncompromising ideology for the growing antislavery movement, while the Finney-Tappan benevolence movement was to commit its mass of support, stretching west from New York, almost wholly to the cause.

At first antislavery was only one among the many causes espoused by the Tappans and their associates. A turning point came when one of Finney's ablest young converts and apprentice evangelists, Theodore Dwight Weld, became wholly committed to the antislavery cause. In 1833, Weld enrolled at Lane Seminary in Cincinnati, a school that had just been established under Lyman Beecher's presidency to train Finney's converts for the ministry. Proselytizing among his fellow students, Weld provoked the famous Lane Debate, a revivalistic discussion of slavery that lasted for 18 days and nights and ended with the conversion of virtually the entire student body to the abolitionist cause. Meanwhile the Tappan and the Garrison groups had come together in uneasy alliance to form the American Anti-Slavery Society, which now employed Weld and his fellow Lane converts as agents. During the mid-1830s these and others conducted a whirlwind evangelistic campaign through New England, New

York, Pennsylvania, and the Old Northwest, which resulted in the conversion of some whole communities to antislavery and the organization of over 1,000 local antislavery societies with more than 100,000 members.

The abolitionism preached by Weld and his associates emphasized the moral evil of slavery and the religious duty of good people to align themselves against it. In fact, most abolitionists were intensely pious people, driven by religious sentiments that portrayed good works as the result of salvation. At first they naively hoped to persuade slaveholders to abandon the institution by sending into the South tons of pamphlets portraying the sin of holding human beings in bondage.

Despite the rapid growth of the movement, abolitionism remained highly unpopular in much of the North. Many Northerners who had no great fondness for slavery feared that antislavery agitation endangered the Union. Still others were deeply infected with the same race prejudice that bolstered slavery in the South. Prominent abolitionists had to face hostile mobs, and one editor, Elijah Lovejoy, was actually killed for his antislavery views.

Yet the abolitionists gained support far beyond their own ranks when they moved into politics in the mid-1830s with a petition campaign asking Congress to abolish slavery and the odious slave trade in the District of Columbia. Many Northerners who shied away from the constitutionally difficult question of abolition in the slave states were glad to support the abolitionist petitions with reference to the national capital over which Congress had unquestioned jurisdiction. Northern opinion was generally indignant when Congress responded to southern pressure in 1836 by adopting a "gag rule" refusing to consider petitions relating in any way to slavery. At this point, ex-President John Quincy Adams, serving out the remainder of his life in the House of Representatives, took up the cause. Originally not an abolitionist, "Old Man Eloquent" was infuriated by this denial of the constitutionally guaranteed right of petition. Supported by a growing body of northern opinion, he carried on a dogged fight against the gag rule until it was eventually repealed in 1844. Though the North was still far from abolitionized, the steady agitation of the question was gradually conditioning increasing thousands of voters to view the slaveholding section of American society with hostility.

THE SOUTH AND SLAVERY

Meanwhile white Southerners were being forced to reexamine their attitudes toward their "peculiar institution." Christianity and the liberal principles of the Declaration of Independence affected Southerners just as much as Northerners. During the latter part of the eighteenth century, many of the South's outstanding leaders had emancipated their slaves, denouncing slavery as incompatible with the ideals of the Revolution. Thomas Jefferson and other liberal Southerners had counted on the gradual operation of economic forces to eliminate slavery in the South as was already being done in the North. As late as the Missouri debate in 1820, southern members of Congress refused to defend slavery in the abstract, arguing instead that the unfortunate institution had been inherited and was difficult to eradicate.

Yet southern opinion had already begun to shift in a direction that would ultimately lead to civil war. The fundamental cause for change was the market revolution. Until the end of the eighteenth century, the stronghold of slavery had been in the Chesapeake tobacco region of Virginia and Maryland. The economic depression in this region following the Revolution had encouraged the spread of antislavery sentiment and afforded some grounds for Jefferson's hope that the institution might wither away. But farther down the coast the great plantations of South Carolina had continued to flourish; with the perfection of the cotton gin in 1793, high profits stimulated the rapid spread of plantation slavery into the up-country. South Carolina was the only state that permitted a resumption of the barbarous foreign slave trade before its prohibition by Congress in 1808.

The most spectacular expansion of plantation slavery came during the boom years following the War of 1812 when it flooded over the newly opened lands of Alabama, Mississippi, and Louisiana. Taking deep root as a flourishing economic system, the chief source of wealth, and a spur to enterprise, slavery became increasingly impossible for white Southerners to surrender. The cotton boom in the lower South dampened antislavery tendencies in the upper South by creating a heavy demand at high prices for the surplus slaves of the declining tobacco kingdom. Nonslaveholders, too, came to feel that they had a stake in the institution. Only about one-fourth of the white families in the South ever owned slaves, and even among the slaveholding minority only 12 percent owned as many as 20 slaves. But the South was as deeply infected as any other part of the country with the spirit of enterprise that the market revolution generated, and in the South the acquisition of slaves was becoming the primary and almost the exclusive means of raising one's economic and social status.

At the same time, another factor was reinforcing the white South's growing economic attachment to slavery. Thomas Jefferson had assumed that deep antipathies between whites and blacks would make emancipation unthinkable without some plan for removing the emancipated slaves from the United States. This conviction that the two races could not live side by side in freedom received a powerful impetus in the 1790s when the slaves on the nearby French West Indian island of Santo Domingo rose in rebellion, murdering or forcing into exile thousands of their former masters. From this time on, the more the white South became attached to slavery as an economic institution, the more it feared its slaves and, consequently, the more it insisted on slavery as an institution for controlling this dangerous population. Alarms over threatened slave insurrections became more frequent, some with a basis in fact and others arising more from imaginations made excitable by fear and guilt.

A real insurrection finally came in August, 1831 when a slave named Nat Turner led an uprising in Southampton County, Virginia. Over 60 whites were killed before the rebels were crushed. A wave of hysteria washed over the whole domain of slavery, and the Virginia legislature was frightened into the Old South's only full and free debate over the peculiar institution. Not a voice was raised to justify slavery in the abstract, and proposals for gradual emancipation were barely defeated.

The entire South sensed that a fateful choice had been made. The fears of slave insurrection had culminated just at the time when slavery was becoming too entrenched as an economic institution to be surrendered and at the very moment when the American antislavery movement was launching a massive propaganda barrage against slavery, appealing to Christian and liberal values that white Southerners shared. Slowly and reluctantly, Southerners faced the fact that, if slavery were to be retained, they could no longer ease their consciences with hopes for its eventual disappearance or tolerate the expression of such hopes in their midst. Southern minds must be nerved for a severe struggle in defense of the institution to which they now saw themselves committed. So southern leaders of the Calhoun school began trying to convince themselves and others that slavery was a "positive good," while southern legislatures abridged freedom of speech and the press, made manumission difficult or impossible, and imposed tighter restrictions on both slaves and free Negroes.

Proslavery arguments never succeeded in relieving the majority of white Southerners from varying degrees of moral uneasiness or feelings of guilt. Like all people unsure of their ground but unable to change it, Southerners responded to attacks on slavery with mounting vehemence. Even in the 1830s, when both Southerners and Northerners were still preoccupied with the Jacksonian political issues, the abolitionists' petitions provoked such violent congressional debates that the gag rule had to be imposed. Within another decade, the explosively emotional quarrel over slavery would move to the center of the political stage, there to remain until blood was shed.

CONFLICTING HISTORICAL VIEWPOINTS

5. How Brutal Was Slavery?

In his monumental studies, American Negro Slavery *(1918) and* Life and Labor in the Old South *(1929), Ulrich B. Phillips set forth the classic defense of slavery as a labor system beneficial to both master and slave. A tireless researcher and a prolific writer, Phillips uncovered a wealth of new material and contributed enormously to our factual knowledge of the "peculiar institution." But the work of this Georgia-born scholar was seriously flawed by racial prejudice. The Negro slave, he believed, was innately inferior and naturally submissive. In his view the plantation was a school in which primitive and uncouth blacks were purged of their African savagery and offered the blessings of western civilization and Christianity.*

This sympathetic interpretation of a benign and paternalistic institution dominated American historical writing for nearly three decades. But in the increasingly enlightened climate of racial opinion following World War II, historians began reassessing traditional assumptions about the antebellum South's labor system. In American Negro Slave Revolts *(1943), Herbert Aptheker, a Marxist historian and a passionate civil rights advocate, portrayed a rebellious and discontented slave work force that contrasted sharply with the carefree darky of Phillips's idyll. The most sweeping revision, however, was Kenneth Stampp's broad synthesis,* The Peculiar Institution *(1956). A distinguished liberal scholar who argued that "Negroes are, after all, only white men with black skins," Stampp viewed slavery as a harshly cruel system degrading to both exploiter and exploited. The typical slave, he concluded, hated both the institution and the master.*

Not all of Phillips's critics agreed with Stampp. In Slavery *(1959), Stanley Elkins, for example, offered a controversial study that blended Stampp's harsh criticism of slavery with Phillips's view of the slave as contented Sambo. Using social science and comparative history techniques, Elkins concluded that the labor system of the Old South was so brutal and dehumanizing that it infantilized its victims. According to this interpretation, the typical slave was, thus, childlike, docile, and convinced of his own inferiority.*

In the 1970s, historians have rejected Elkins's conclusions and moved beyond Stampp's. Increasingly the direction has been away from the study of slavery as an institutional problem toward an analysis of day-to-day life in the quarters. Masters now attract less scholarly attention than slaves. John Blassingame's Slave Community *(1972), for example, offers a fascinating view of plantation life and labor from the vantage point of the bondsperson; Eugene Genovese's* Roll, Jordan, Roll *(1974) brilliantly portrays (as its subtitle promises) "the world the slaves made"; Herbert Gutman's* The Black Family *(1976) emphasizes the close, multigenerational ties and the settled monogamous unions that characterized slave family life; Lawrence Levine's* Black Culture and Black Consciousness *(1977) imaginatively examines the folk expressions of a creative slave society that was anything but degraded or pathological; and Dena J. Epstein's* Sinful Tunes and Spirituals *(1977) explodes the notion that African expressive culture was shattered by the slavery experience. Although not understating the unjust and often unspeakably cruel dimensions of the institution, these scholars conclude that slaves were not simply acted upon by whites and that slavery permitted its victims a heretofore unsuspected degree of cultural autonomy and sense of community. Most of all these writers comprehend and appreciate the adaptive capacities of the Afro-Americans.*

The most provocative recent study is Robert Fogel and Stanley Engerman's Time on the Cross *(1974), a book that has attracted perhaps more public interest and more scholarly criticism than any other work of history in memory. A computer study by two gifted "cliometricians,"* Time on the Cross *contends that slave labor was more efficient and productive than free labor and that slaves lived comparatively well-provisioned, secure, and comfortable lives. "Over the course of his lifetime," the authors argue, "the typical slave field hand received about 90 percent of the income he produced." These conclusions, although less novel than the authors claim, provoked a storm of controversy. Many blacks found them offensive, and many scholars—including most historical quantifiers—faulted the data and research procedures upon which they were based. An example of scholarly criticism of* Time on the Cross *can be found in Herbert Gutman's* Slavery and the Numbers Game *(1975), which finds particular fault with Fogel and Engerman for their neglect of the beliefs and behavior of the slaves themselves.*

FOR FURTHER READING

In the absence of an adequate general account of Romanticism in American thought, much can be learned from the splendid segment of a study left uncompleted by Perry Miller, *The Life of the Mind in America from the Revolution to the Civil War* (1965).

An older work by Octavius B. Frothingham is still the fullest account of *Transcendentalism in New England* (1876); in *American Transcendentalism* (1974) Paul F. Boller offers a good, brief portrayal of leading New England intellectuals; and Henry Steele Commager's *Theodore Parker: Yankee Crusader* (1936)* describes a major figure on the fringes of the Transcendentalist movement. A general account of religion, utopianism, and reform in this period is Alice Felt Tyler's *Freedom's Ferment: Phases of American Social History to 1860* (1944)*; Daniel Boorstin, in *The Americans, the National Experience* (1965), sets these and other social movements in a broad historical context. For the Great Revival in the East and revivalism's connection with perfectionism and reformism, see Whitney R. Cross, *The Burned-over District* (1956)* and Timothy L. Smith, *Revivalism and Social Reform in Mid-Nineteenth Century America* (1957).* The flavor of revivalism in the West is reflected in the *Autobiography* (1856)* of Peter Cartwright; while the beginnings of Mormonism are traced by Fawn M. Brodie in *No Man Knows My History: The Life of Joseph Smith* (1945).

Outstanding studies of the Old South include: the early chapters of W. J. Cash, *The Mind of the South* (1941)*; Clement Eaton, *The Growth of Southern Civilization, 1790–1860* (1961)*; Clement Eaton, *The Freedom-of-Thought Struggle in the Old South* (1964)*; Clement Eaton, *The Mind of the Old South* (rev. ed., 1967)*; Frank L. Owsley, *Plain Folk of the Old South* (1949)*; and William R. Taylor, *Cavalier and Yankee: The Old South and American National Character* (1961).* Some aspects of slavery not included in the essays above are analyzed in: David Brion Davis, *The Problem of Slavery in Western Culture* (1966); Winthrop D. Jordan, *White Over Black: American Attitudes toward the Negro, 1550–1812* (1968); William K. Scarborough, *The Overseer* (1966); and Robert S. Starobin, *Industrial Slavery in the Old South* (1970). Differing views on the origins of abolitionism are offered by Gilbert H. Barnes, in *The Anti-Slavery Impulse* (1933)* and by Louis Filler, in *The Crusade Against Slavery* (1960). Benjamin Quarles has written about the *Black Abolitionists* (1969); Bertram Wyatt-Brown is the author of *Lewis Tappan* (1969); Gerde Lerner examines *The Grimke Sisters from South Carolina* (1967); Aileen Kraditor, in *Means and Ends in American Abolitionism* (1969), emphasizes variety and conflict within the abolitionist movement; Merton L. Dillon, in *The Abolitionists* (1974), considers the impact of an articulate minority on the larger community; and Richard H. Sewell's *Ballots for Freedom* (1976) is a history of antislavery politics. The interpretations of a number of scholars on various aspects of abolitionism are presented in a volume of essays collected by Martin Duberman, *The Anti-Slavery Vanguard* (1965).* A leading proslavery theorist is described by Harvey Wish, in *George Fitzhugh: Propagandist of the Old South* (1943).

---

*Available in paperback edition.

Manifest Destiny
and Sectional Conflict
1840–1852

13

Though the Whig and Democratic leaders continued to battle each other in the early 1840s over tariffs, the national bank, and internal improvements, these old issues no longer excited Americans as they had in Jackson's day. The market revolution had completed its psychological conquest of the country, and with hard times receding, an enterprising generation was engrossed in the pursuit of wealth and status.

For countless thousands, the pursuit led west toward the perennial American goal of cheap land and a fresh start. But now, for the first time in the American experience, there seemed a limit to the supply of cheap, fertile land. In the South the tide of settlement rolled up to the boundary of the Mexican province of Texas. Farther north it was nearing the treeless Great Plains, which were thought unfit for cultivation.

Yet neither political nor geographical boundaries were to halt the 200-year advance of the American frontier. Since the 1820s, American settlers had been pouring into Texas, where in 1836 they rebelled against Mexican authority, defeated a Mexican army, and set themselves up as an independent republic looking toward union with the United States. During the same period, wagon trains from the Missouri frontier had been crossing the plains along the northern borders of Texas and pushing on to trade with the ancient Spanish-Mexican settlement of Santa Fe on the upper Rio Grande. Still farther north, fur traders had followed in the tracks of Lewis and Clark, exploring the Rocky Mountains and bringing back tales of new promised lands beyond in the Oregon country and Mexican California. Meanwhile, the enterprising merchants of Boston and Salem and New York were sending their ships around Cape Horn at the southern tip of South America to pick up hides on the California coast and were becoming excited about the possibility of dominating trade with the Orient from the magnificent Pacific harbors at San Diego, San Francisco, and Puget Sound.

While Americans were discovering the far West, romantic assumptions were intensifying their faith in the superiority and glorious destiny of their free institutions. Rapidly the idea grew that it was the "manifest destiny" of these free institutions to

6. PRESIDENTIAL ELECTIONS AND MAJOR EVENTS, 1840–1852

1840   **William Henry Harrison** (Whig) elected over Martin Van Buren (Democrat).

1841   Vice-President **John Tyler** becomes president on death of Harrison.
Whig Congress repeals the independent treasury system.
Land Act of 1841: preemption principle allows settlers to buy public lands they occupy at minimum price.
Tyler vetoes successive bills chartering a national bank and is disowned by the Whig party.

1842   Tariff of 1842, a Whig measure, extends substantial protection to American manufactures.
Webster-Ashburton Treaty with Great Britain settles the Maine boundary and other disputed matters.

1844   Tyler's treaty for the annexation of Texas defeated in the Senate.
James K. Polk (Democrat) elected over Henry Clay (Whig).

1845   Texas annexed by joint resolution of Congress.

1846   Democratic Congress reinstitutes the independent treasury system.
Tariff of 1846 substantially reduces rates.
Polk's veto of Rivers and Harbors bill checks policy of internal improvements.
Oregon controversy with Great Britain compromised.
Polk precipitates Mexican War by insisting on extreme Texas boundary claim.
Wilmot Proviso proposed to bar slavery from any territories acquired from Mexico.

1848   Treaty of Guadelupe Hidalgo ends Mexican War, with the United States paying Mexico for a vast cession in the Southwest.
Zachary Taylor (Whig) elected over Lewis Cass (Democrat) and Martin Van Buren (Free Soiler).

1849   Gold Rush to California.

1850   Vice-President **Millard Fillmore** becomes president on death of Taylor.
Compromise of 1850: (1) California admitted as free state; (2) Utah and New Mexico territories organized on principle of squatter sovereignty; (3) Texas surrenders claims to area in New Mexico, and United States assumes Texas debt; (4) slave trade abolished in the District of Columbia; (5) a more stringent Fugitive Slave Law enacted.

1852   **Franklin Pierce** (Democrat) elected over Winfield Scott (Whig).

spread over all the vast, thinly inhabited, and lightly held territories between the Mississippi Valley and the Pacific Ocean.

The growing enthusiasm for territorial expansion further confused an already tangled political situation, while raising an ominous question. The decade of the 1840s opened with the Whigs and Democrats still battling inconclusively over old issues that no longer stirred the voters, and both parties were for different reasons somewhat demoralized. Under these circumstances the issue of expansion was a godsend to ambitious politicians with various axes to grind. But it was a dangerous issue. The controversy over slavery was making the country edgy. The mounting hostility between North and South was becoming too apparent to be wished out of consciousness. A great crusade to fulfill the manifest territorial destiny of the United States might reunite Americans in enthusiastic patriotism. But it could also incite a disastrous sectional conflict over the territorial spoils.

TIPPECANOE—AND TYLER TOO

Such possibilities were still far from most people's minds as the Whigs took over the national government following their great victory in the presidential election of 1840. President Harrison called a special session of Congress to pass the traditional Whig program—repeal of the independent treasury system, a new national bank, a higher protective tariff, and a scheme for distributing the federal land revenues among the states. Yet the Whigs were the unluckiest of the major political parties. Within a month after his inauguration, "Old Tippecanoe" died, leaving the Whig program at the mercy of the vain, stubborn vice-president, John Tyler of Virginia.

Tyler had left the Democratic party when Jackson threatened to coerce the South Carolina Nullifiers in 1832, and he retained much of the old-fashioned Virginian attachment to state rights. He went along with Clay in repealing the independent treasury system, but after indicating a willingness to approve a national fiscal agency, he vetoed two successive bills chartering a new national bank. By other vetoes, Tyler made it clear that Clay could have either a higher protective tariff or distribution but not both. Clay chose increased protection for manufacturers, and the Tariff of 1842 raised duties generally to the levels that had existed before the Compromise Tariff of 1833. Meanwhile, in a futile effort to secure distribution, the Whig Congress included in the Land Act of 1841 the principle of *preemption.* Preemption enabled any head of a family to settle on 160 acres of the public domain before they were offered for sale at the customary auction and then to bid them in at the minimum price of $1.25 an acre.

Thus the stubborn Virginia president frustrated every part of the Whig program except the higher tariff and caused Clay to accept a preemption system for which he had no great enthusiasm. The overwhelming majority of the Whig members of Congress, both northern and southern, turned on Tyler in fury and read him out of the Whig party. Every member of his cabinet resigned, Secretary of State Daniel Webster tarrying only a little longer than the others. Webster's delay was partly to enable him to complete the negotiations with England that led up to the Webster-Ashburton

Treaty of 1842, compromising a dispute over the boundary between Maine and Canada. Bereft of party support, Tyler took up the issue of expansion, hoping that it might enable him to run for president in 1844. Secretly, his administration began negotiating with the Texas authorities for a treaty of annexation.

The Texas question had long been regarded as a threat to the delicate sectional balances that held the two parties together as national organizations. From the moment of the Texas Revolution in 1836, antislavery people had been denouncing it as a plot by southern filibusterers to extend the area of slavery, and even Jackson, despite his warm friendship for the Texas leader Sam Houston, had delayed recognition of the new republic until after Van Buren was safely elected. Van Buren had similarly avoided the question of annexation during his administration as being too dangerous to the harmony of the Democratic party.

Thus, by pushing the Texas question to the fore, Tyler hoped to embarrass greatly the old party leaders and either run for president as the candidate of a pro-Texas third party or displace Van Buren as the Democratic nominee. The potential for sectional conflict over the Texas issue was increased when Tyler brought in Calhoun as his Secretary of State to complete the secret negotiations for an annexation treaty. The treaty was signed and sent to the Senate in April, 1844. Along with it, Calhoun sent a copy of a dispatch he had written to the British minister, Richard Pakenham, denouncing British interference in Texas, defending slavery as a positive good, and justifying annexation mainly as a measure in defense of slavery. Calhoun's Pakenham letter, irritating even moderate antislavery people, doomed the treaty to defeat in the Senate and produced violent political turmoil on the eve of the presidential nominating conventions.

THE PRESIDENTIAL ELECTION OF 1844

Clay and Van Buren had both seemed assured of nomination by their respective parties, and both wished to keep the Texas issue out of the campaign. At the end of April, hard on the heels of Calhoun's Pakenham letter, they published simultaneous letters opposing immediate annexation. Shortly thereafter, Clay was nominated by the Whig convention, but Van Buren's Texas letter aroused a storm of opposition against him at the Democratic convention.

Although a majority of the delegates to the Democratic convention had originally been instructed for Van Buren, the late developing Texas excitement had produced, especially in the southern and western states, a decided popular reaction in favor of a pro-Texas candidate. Van Buren's Texas letter was the signal for pro-Texas and anti-Van Buren factions to join forces in a last-ditch fight to block his nomination. Their strategy was to insist on a two-thirds majority for nomination. Many delegates who felt bound by their instructions to vote for Van Buren on the early ballots were nevertheless able to vote for the two-thirds rule that made his nomination impossible.

But if Van Buren could not muster a two-thirds majority, neither could his leading rival, Lewis Cass of Michigan. The deadlock might have destroyed the Democratic party if the convention had not finally hit upon a compromise candidate. James K. Polk had recently suffered two successive defeats in campaigns for governor of Tennessee, but he was almost the only Democrat of any prominence who could command the confidence of all the feuding factions. The hard-money Van Buren wing of the party respected him as a protégé of Jackson and able leader of the Democratic forces in the House of Representatives during the Bank War, while as a slaveholding Southerner and outspoken advocate of immediate annexation, he was acceptable to the expansionist, anti-Van Buren wing.

Having nominated Polk by acclamation, the convention adopted a platform calling for "the reoccupation of Oregon and the reannexation of Texas, at the earliest practicable moment." The Oregon question had recently generated considerable enthusiasm in the Northwest, but even there it had been overshadowed by the Texas question. The Oregon plank seems to have been included primarily to remove the sectional sting from the inescapable Texas issue.

The ensuing election reflected the nearly equal division of popular strength that the matured two-party system had by this time produced. In the closest presidential race to this time, Polk received 49.6 percent of the popular votes to 48.1 percent for Clay. Polk's majority margin in the electoral college was provided by New York, where the diversion of a small number of normally Whig votes to an antislavery third-party candidate swung the balance in favor of the Democrats.

The pro-Texas people interpreted this narrow victory as a mandate for annexation. Just before Polk's inauguration in early 1845, Congress approved, by joint resolution rather than treaty, the admission of Texas as one of the United States.

THE POLK ADMINISTRATION

Polk was one of the hardest working and most effective men ever to occupy the White House. Unimaginative, undramatic, and without much prestige when he entered office, he was nevertheless spectacularly successful in getting what he wanted from a deeply divided Democratic party and Congress and from other countries. And he wanted a great deal.

Polk was first of all an old-fashioned, doctrinaire Jacksonian Democrat. He wanted an independent treasury system reinstituted, and from his first Congress in 1846, he got it. He wanted a drastic downward revision of the tariff, and the same Congress gave him a tariff act incorporating the antiprotectionist principle of moderate rates designed chiefly for revenue and expressed in uniform percentages—with only moderate discrimination in favor of the most important American manufactures. He wanted an even further reduction in the already circumscribed federal expenditures for internal improvements, and his vetoes of long sanctioned appropriations for river and harbor improvements were sustained. Thus, under Polk, the traditional Democratic policies were finally established, to remain substantially unchanged until the Civil War.

While cleaning up this unfinished Democratic business, Polk was simultaneously moving aggressively along the new line of expansionism. With the Texas issue settled, he wasted not a moment in turning his attention to the Oregon country. This vast

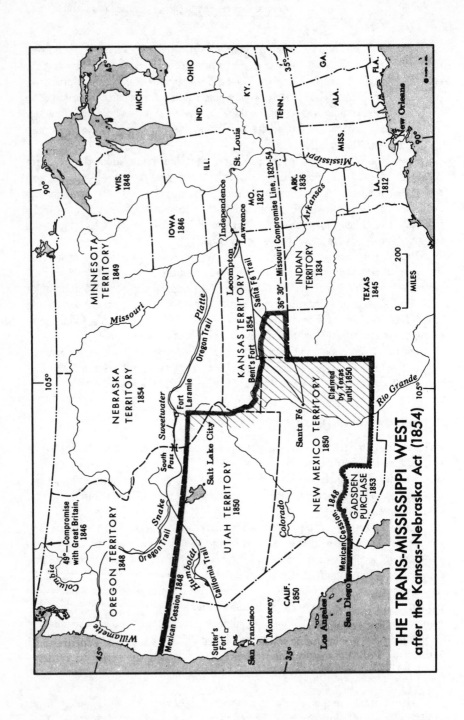

THE TRANS-MISSISSIPPI WEST after the Kansas-Nebraska Act (1854)

expanse of territory—stretching from the Rockies to the Pacific and from the border of Mexican California at 42° on the south to Russian Alaska at 54°40' on the north —had been jointly occupied by the United States and Great Britain with the proviso that either nation could terminate the joint occupation by giving one year's notice. In the early 1840s, American settlers began finding their way to Oregon in substantial numbers and disputing possession of the land with the well-established British posts of the Hudson's Bay Company. This migration had created considerable interest in Oregon in the states of the upper Mississippi Valley, northwestern Democrats had begun agitating for a more vigorous assertion of American claims to the country, and the Democratic platform had declared that "Our title to the whole of the Territory of Oregon is clear and unquestionable."

Polk's inaugural address echoed the Oregon plank in the Democratic platform, but he felt bound to renew once more his predecessors' offer of a compromise boundary along the 49th parallel, an offer the British had rejected several times. When the British minister rudely rebuffed this proposal without even referring it to his government, Polk took a more bellicose line. Calling on Congress to give notice of the termination of joint occupancy, he asserted the American claim to the whole of the territory.

For a time war threatened, but both sides were ready for any face-saving solution along the 49th parallel. Polk allowed intimations to reach the British that if they made a proper proposal he would submit it to the Senate for advice. Such a proposal came in June, 1846, and the Senate advised its acceptance. The 49° boundary already established east of the Rockies was extended west to the Pacific with a short detour down the Strait of Fuca to leave Britain the whole of Vancouver Island.

THE MEXICAN WAR

Polk's bold Oregon game with the British was rendered more dangerous by his bellicose diplomacy in another quarter. For a time, he seemed to be courting simultaneous wars with Great Britain and with Mexico. The principal prize in the latter case would be Mexican California with its splendid Pacific harbors. There can be little doubt that Polk was determined to secure the vast domain between the southwestern borders of the United States and the Pacific and that he deliberately provoked war when the Mexicans refused to sell it.

Having won its independence from Spain in 1821, Mexico was a proud young republic with a political system so unstable that any government compromising the national honor was sure to be driven from office. The Texas Revolution had been a severe blow to Mexican pride. Stubbornly refusing to recognize Texan independence, the Mexicans regarded the annexation of Texas by the United States as an act of aggression and had broken off diplomatic relations.

It was at this point that Polk entered the White House. One of his first acts was to order an American army to the western frontier of Texas to ward off any attack by Mexico while the formalities of annexation were being completed. He was less justified in authorizing the army to advance beyond the traditional Texan boundary at the Nueces River and in announcing his determination to enforce the unfounded Texas claim that its territory extended to the Rio Grande River. Then he sent a minister to Mexico with an offer that the United States would assume the unpaid claims of American citizens against Mexico for property losses during the Mexican Revolution in return for Mexican acceptance of the Rio Grande boundary. In addition, the envoy was to try to purchase New Mexico and California.

Since the Mexicans had not indicated any willingness to reopen regular diplomatic negotiations, it should not have been surprising that they refused to receive Polk's minister. Nevertheless Polk chose to regard this rebuff as a cause for war. He had already ordered the American army to advance to the Rio Grande, and he prepared to ask Congress for a declaration of war. The Mexicans saved him the trouble by precipitating hostilities. A Mexican force encountered an American patrol just east of the Rio Grande, and in the ensuing skirmish 16 Americans were killed or wounded. Polk got the news just in time to modify his war message. Mexico, he told Congress, "has invaded our territory and shed American blood upon the American soil." War was declared on May 13, 1846.

The Mexican War, whatever its morality, was militarily the most successful of American wars. General Zachary Taylor led the army on the Rio Grande into north central Mexico and at Buena Vista in February, 1847 won a brilliant victory over a superior Mexican force commanded by General Santa Anna. Shortly thereafter, another American army under General Winfield Scott landed at Vera Cruz on the Gulf Coast and by September had occupied the enemy capital, Mexico City. Meanwhile Colonel Stephen Kearney had led another American army across the plains from Missouri, seizing Santa Fe on the upper Rio Grande and then moving on west across the mountains and deserts to establish American authority in California.

When General Scott captured Vera Cruz, President Polk sent Nicholas P. Trist, chief clerk of the State Department, to accompany Scott's army and seize upon any opportunity for negotiating a peace that would give the United States the territory it wanted. The fall of Mexico City reduced that country to political chaos, and by the time Trist found a government stable enough to negotiate, he had infuriated President Polk by insubordinate behavior. Defying an order to return home, Trist went ahead and negotiated the Treaty of Guadelupe Hidalgo, signed in February, 1848. By this treaty, Mexico recognized the Rio Grande boundary and ceded New Mexico and California, while in return the United States was to assume the claims of its citizens against Mexico and pay Mexico $15 million. Since these were the terms Polk had instructed the repudiated diplomat to secure, he signed Trist's treaty, and the Senate ratified it.

TOWARD THE FIRST SECESSION CRISIS

Despite the brilliance of its military victories and the vastness of its territorial acquisitions, the United States emerged from the Mexican War more deeply divided and distracted than ever. The enthusiastic expansionism of people like President Polk had been partly an effort to find a cause that would unite all Americans in a new burst of patriotic nationalism and furnish a vaccine against the insidiously spreading infection of sectional enmity. But the infection had already taken too firm a hold, and the remedy served to intensify rather than alleviate the disease.

The enthusiasm for expansion was most widespread in the Northwest and the Southwest and among Democrats; in the East and among Whigs, the transparently aggressive character of the Mexican War had made it unpopular with many from the beginning. The Whigs carried on a constant criticism of the administration's war policy, and Northern Whigs began to denounce the war as a southern project for expanding the area of slavery. Northern voters were told, too, that a slavery-dominated Democratic party had demonstrated its indifference to the interests of the free states by reducing the tariff, cutting off appropriations for rivers and harbors, and surrendering the American claim to the whole of Oregon. The war helped to crystallize in thousands of northern minds the conviction that the area of slavery and the political power of slavery must not be allowed to expand.

In the summer of 1846, while Congress was debating a bill appropriating money for negotiations with Mexico, a Pennsylvania Democrat named David Wilmot offered an amendment declaring that slavery should be forever barred from any Mexican territories to be acquired. The Wilmot Proviso, though defeated when first introduced, infuriated southern members of Congress and provoked a struggle of such mounting violence that within three years it would bring the country to the brink of secession and civil war.

The end of the Mexican War made it indispensable to enact some legislation for government in the new territories, but no legislation could be passed without settling the status of slavery there. Northerners dominated the House of Representatives and insisted on the Wilmot Proviso while Southerners, relying on a Senate still evenly balanced between slave and free states, asserted their right to migrate with their property, including slaves, into the territory they had helped to win. President Polk urged that the Missouri Compromise line of 36°30' be extended to the Pacific as the boundary between slave and free territory, telling Northerners that slavery could never get a foothold in the arid Southwest no matter what Congress provided. But Polk made the serious blunder of announcing that he would under no circumstances accept a second term. Having expended his patronage in getting his ambitious program through his first Congress, he was less and less able to control Democrats in Congress as his term neared its end, and the extremists, both North and South, defeated his and all other efforts to reach a compromise solution.

It was in this atmosphere that the presidential election of 1848 occurred. The free-soil issue had split both parties deeply along sectional lines. The rift was potentially deeper among the Whigs because antislavery sentiment was stronger in the northern wing of their party, but they successfully obscured their differences by again adopting the strategy of nominating a military hero. This time he was General Zachary Taylor, the hero of Buena Vista, a plain, honest old soldier who owned a plantation and slaves in Louisiana. Democratic differences were more conspicuous because Polk's no-second-term position had prompted a prolonged intraparty struggle over the nomination. At the cost of great bitterness, the Democratic convention finally nominated Senator Lewis Cass of Michigan, hated by the Van Burenites for his role in blocking their chieftain's nomination four years previously.

The major party nominations provoked the formation of a formidable antislavery third party. Deeply suspicious of the slaveholding Taylor, the more fervently antislavery Whigs organized a Free Soil party with the Wilmot Proviso as their platform. They were quickly joined by the "Barnburners," or Van Buren Democrats, who were just as anxious for revenge against Cass and the rival "Hunker" faction of the New York Democratic party as they were to stop the spread of slavery. The new party nominated Van Buren for president and Charles Francis Adams, Whig son of John Quincy Adams, for vice-president.

Taylor's personal popularity, his nonpartisan posture, the special appeal that his slaveholding status gave him in the South, and the Barnburner secession from Cass in the North made the outcome a foregone conclusion. "Old Rough and Ready" did not have to say where he stood on the territorial question, while Cass advanced a compromise solution of great future significance but little immediate appeal to the more zealous defenders of the southern and northern positions. This compromise was the doctrine of popular sovereignty by which the settlers in the territories would be left to settle the status of slavery for themselves. Taylor won handily, while the Free Soilers garnered a substantial popular vote and elected nine representatives.

THE COMPROMISE OF 1850

By the time Taylor took office in March, 1849, the discovery of gold in California had attracted a horde of unruly immigrants and created a desperate need for legislation providing government in the new territories. Meanwhile, Southerners had been further infuriated by proposals in Congress to abolish slavery and the slave trade in the District of Columbia. Calhoun was passionately exhorting Southerners to abandon the old parties and unite in a new sectional party to defend the South's rights and safety. The more radical Southerners were demanding that the South secede if the Wilmot Proviso were applied in any form to any territory, and a number of southern governors and legislatures took measures looking toward secession in such an eventuality. In this crisis, the new president, to the shock of those Southerners who had supported him because he was a slaveholder, encouraged the Californians to bypass the territorial stage, to draw up a state constitution without congressional authorization, and to apply directly for admission as a free state. Thus Taylor's first Congress met in December, 1849 to find a free California waiting on its doorstep and passions running so high that members carried Bowie knives and revolvers and the House of Representatives took three weeks and 63 ballots to elect a Speaker.

The aged Henry Clay now stepped forward to rally the forces of moderation and compromise, presenting a series of proposals as an "omnibus" settlement of all the disputed questions arising from the slavery issue: (1) California was to be admitted as a free state. (2) The remainder of the Mexican cession was to be organized into two territories, Utah on the north and New Mexico on the south, leaving the status of slavery for their inhabitants to settle. The Utah territory was to provide a government for the large body of Mormons who had migrated to the shores of the Great Salt Lake in 1846 after being driven out of their settlements in Missouri and Illinois. The New Mexico territory involved an additional complication because Texas claimed that its territory extended to the upper Rio Grande, embracing Santa Fe and half of the old Spanish-Mexican province of New Mexico. Clay therefore further proposed that: (3) Texas should give up its claims to the New Mexican area in return for which the United States would assume the Texas public debt; (4) the slave trade but not slavery should be abolished in the District of Columbia; (5) the old federal Fugitive Slave Law of 1790, the enforcement of which had been increasingly defied and impeded in the North, should be strengthened.

Southerners complained that Clay's compromise would cost the South its equal strength in the Senate while making only the single concession to the South of a stronger fugitive slave law. Formidable opposition also came from President Taylor and the bulk of the northern Whigs, who were determined that the advance of slavery should be decisively halted. Even after Taylor died in July, 1850 and was succeeded by the procompromise Vice-President Millard Fillmore, Clay was unable to gain a majority for his omnibus proposal. Only when the Illinois Democrat, Stephen A. Douglas, took command and broke Clay's omnibus bill into separate proposals did the various compromise measures pass.

The success of the compromise depended on the willingness of the aroused lower South to accept it. In Georgia, Mississippi, and other states, party lines broke down as Whigs and moderate Democrats joined forces to defeat the advocates of secession. The country breathed sighs of relief, and the majority of politicians everywhere committed themselves to the compromise measures as a "final solution" of the slavery controversy.

In the presidential election of 1852, the Democratic nominee, Franklin Pierce of New Hampshire, won because of his allegiance to the compromise. Again the Whigs had turned to a military hero, nominating General Winfield Scott. But Whigs in the South could no longer sustain themselves as copartisans of the increasingly antislavery northern Whigs. With southern Whigs being forced into the Democratic party, the Whig party was already dying as a national entity, and Scott was its last presidential candidate.

FOR FURTHER READING

Frederick Merk has written an important work on *Manifest Destiny and Mission in American History* (1963); Ray A. Billington is the author of the best general account of *The Far Western Frontier, 1830–1860* (1956)*; and Henry Nash Smith's *Virgin Land* (1950)* is a brilliant interpretation of the meaning of the West for the American imagination. The trade between Missouri and Santa Fe is described by a participant in Josiah Gregg's *Commerce of the Prairies* (1844)*; the fur trade is vividly and

---

*Available in paperback edition.

soundly reconstructed in Robert G. Cleland's *This Reckless Breed: Trappers of the Southwest* (1950) and in Bernard De Voto's *Across the Wide Missouri* (1947)*; and Francis Parkman's account of his experiences along *The Oregon Trail* (1849)* is a classic. Bernard De Voto has written a distinguished book about the momentous developments on the western and expansionist fronts during *The Year of Decision, 1846* (1943)*; Marquis James's *The Raven* (1929)* is a vivid biography of the Texas leader Sam Houston; Frederick Merk has collected essays on *The Oregon Question* (1967); and Norman Graebner is the author of *Empire on the Pacific* (1955). The political history of the 1840s is best followed through three biographies: Robert Seager, II, *And Tyler Too: A Biography of John & Julia Gardiner Tyler* (1963); the third volume of Charles M. Wiltse, *John C. Calhoun* (3 vols., 1944–1951); and Charles Sellers, *James K. Polk, Continentalist: 1843–1846* (1966). Alfred H. Bill, in *Rehearsal for Conflict* (1947), describes the war with Mexico; and Holman Hamilton's *Zachary Taylor* (2 vols., 1941, 1951) covers both the war and the Taylor administration. Allan Nevins's biography of *Frémont, Pathmarker of the West* (1955) throws light on many aspects of western exploration and the Mexican War; Nevins's *Ordeal of the Union* (2 vols., 1947) is a full analysis of the developing sectional controversy of the late 1840s; Chaplain Morrison's *Democratic Politics and Sectionalism* (1967) closely examines the Wilmot Proviso; and Holman Hamilton's *Prologue to Conflict: The Crisis and Compromise of 1850* (1964)* explains the temporary resolution of the controversy.

A House Dividing
1843–1860

14

Hoping that the Compromise of 1850 had finally settled the slavery controversy, the American people again turned their energies to the march of enterprise. The 1850s were a decade of unprecedented economic growth and prosperity, the climax of the market revolution and the beginning of the industrial revolution. Yet the very process of economic growth and physical expansion provoked a renewal of sectional conflict that could be resolved only by civil war.

CULMINATION OF THE MARKET REVOLUTION

The exuberance of the forces generating the market revolution had also generated boom-and-bust cycles that had periodically inhibited the country's full potential for economic growth. Not until the years between 1843 and 1857 did the developed market economy have a chance to show what it could do in an extended period without a major depression.

The results were spectacular. Between 1844 and 1854, the total value of all commodities produced rose by 69 percent, the highest gain for any decade until the 1880s. Accompanying this rise in gross production was an equivalent gain in the efficiency of production with output per worker increasing by 10 percent in the 1840s and 23 percent in the 1850s, the latter increase again to be unequaled until the 1880s. This rapid economic growth was in part simply a further acceleration of the market revolution in its various aspects after a slackening of pace during the depression of 1837–1843.

Commercial agriculture resumed its growth at a faster rate than ever. By 1846, the formerly protectionist Northwest was exporting so much wheat to foreign markets that it turned toward free trade and provided the votes by which the tariff reductions of that year were passed. By 1850, the Northwest exceeded the Northeast in wheat production, and this was only a prelude of things to come. The advance of the

7. PRESIDENTIAL ELECTIONS AND MAJOR EVENTS, 1852–1860

1852	**Franklin Pierce** (Democrat) elected over Winfield Scott (Whig). Harriet Beecher Stowe publishes *Uncle Tom's Cabin*.
1854	Kansas-Nebraska Act repeals Missouri Compromise and organizes Kansas and Nebraska territories on principle of squatter sovereignty.
1856	**James Buchanan** (Democrat) elected over John C. Fremont (Republican) and Millard Fillmore (American).
1857	*Dred Scott* vs. *Sanford*. Roger B. Taney's Supreme Court declares that Congress cannot bar slavery from the territories.
	Buchanan fails to force the admission of Kansas to statehood under the proslavery Lecompton Constitution.
	Hinton Rowan Helper publishes *The Impending Crisis of the South*.
1858	Lincoln-Douglas Debates. In his contest with Abraham Lincoln for Senator from Illinois, Stephen A. Douglas argues, in his "Freeport Doctrine," that slavery cannot survive in a territory without positive supporting legislation.
1859	John Brown's raid on Harper's Ferry.
1860	Radical Southerners break up the Democratic party by withdrawing when the Charleston convention refuses to endorse their demand for a congressional slave code.
	Abraham Lincoln (Republican) elected over Stephen A. Douglas (Northern Democrat), John C. Breckinridge (Southern Democrat), and John Bell (Constitutional Unionist).
1860–1861	Seven states of the lower South secede and organize the Confederate States of America.

agricultural frontier north into Wisconsin and west across Iowa into eastern Kansas and Nebraska, coupled with the widespread use of Cyrus McCormick's mechanical reaper, pushed northwestern wheat production from some 30 million bushels in 1850 to almost 100 million bushels in 1860. Meat packing and the production of corn and hogs expanded almost as spectacularly.

Similarly in the South, the cotton crop increased by 60 percent in the 1840s and 100 percent in the 1850s. Sugar production in Louisiana rose fourfold between the mid-1830s and 1859. The increasing productivity and profitability of southern agriculture were reflected in the rising price of slaves. In the 1790s, a prime field hand could have been bought for $300; by 1840, the price had risen to $1,000; by 1860, it ran up to $1,500.

The impressive growth of a regionally specialized commercial agriculture was closely related to the perfection of a national system of transportation and communication providing facilities for swift, cheap, and efficient interregional and international exchanges of goods and services. Turnpikes, canals, and steamboats had been effective enough for the earlier stages of the market revolution, but not until the 1850s was the transportation system brought to full efficiency by the creation of a great railroad network.

Although railroad construction had received a start in the 1830s, only local lines had been completed before the depression of 1837–1843 stalled further progress. As late as 1848, the country had only 6,000 miles of track. Mileage doubled in the next four years and reached 30,000 by 1860. By 1857, the country had invested a billion dollars in railroads, two-thirds of that during the preceding seven years.

Particularly important was the completion in the early 1850s of five great trunk lines connecting the Atlantic ports of Boston, New York, Philadelphia, Baltimore, and Charleston with the Ohio and Mississippi valleys by way of Albany and Buffalo, Pittsburgh, Wheeling, and Atlanta and Chattanooga. From these terminals the eastern trunk lines rapidly developed new western railroads to the emerging transportation and commercial centers of Chicago, St. Louis, and Memphis. By 1855, a passenger could travel in two days from one of the Atlantic cities to Chicago or St. Louis for a fare of $20. Radiating out from the trunk lines were a series of feeder lines bringing cheap transportation and commercial production to virtually every part of the country.

The flood of products harvested by an expanded agriculture and brought to the coast by a perfected transportation system helped push American exports from $144 million worth of commodities in 1850 to $334 million worth in 1860. Imports climbed to an even higher level, the trade deficit being bridged by exports of California gold, which rose from $5 million in 1850 to $58 million by the end of the decade. This swelling of foreign commerce brought with it a vigorous revival of the American carrying trade.

Another element in the economic expansion was the upsurge of immigration from abroad, especially from Ireland and Germany after the potato famine created widespread destitution in 1846. Immigrants to the United States had not numbered more than 10,000 a year before 1825 but exceeded 100,000 in the mid-1840s and reached an annual level of around 400,000 in the early 1850s. Between 1844 and 1854 nearly

3 million new Americans arrived from abroad. Many of these people supplied the labor for the factories that were springing up in the East; others did the hard, dirty work in railroad and canal construction. The Germans established strong colonies in such northwestern cities as Cincinnati, St. Louis, and Milwaukee, while still other immigrants swelled the tide of agricultural migration into Wisconsin, Iowa, and beyond.

THE RISE OF INDUSTRY

The impressive economic gains of the late 1840s and the 1850s were more than a matter of growth along established lines. The rounding out of the vast and lucrative national market set the stage for the industrial revolution in the United States. A new sector of the economy was moving into the dynamic role. Earlier, the profits of the American carrying trade during the Napoleonic Wars had provided the initial impetus that jarred the economy out of its static staple-exporting phase. Then the swelling flood of commercial crops, cotton above all others, had fueled the transportation revolution and the creation of a national market economy. Now, from the 1850s on, industry was to be the primary stimulant for a sustained and massive expansion of production that would create the most abundant economy that history had yet known.

Large-scale factory production had been developing gradually since the War of 1812, but not until the 1840s did the expansion of the industrial sector spurt ahead. The value of manufactured products in 1850 for the first time exceeded the value of agricultural products, and between 1850 and 1860 the value of manufactured goods nearly doubled from just over $1 billion to just under $2 billion. Probably the best measure of industrial growth is the increase in the difference in value between raw materials used and final manufactured products. Between 1839 and 1849, this difference—or the value added by American manufacturing—is estimated to have risen by 157 percent; between 1844 and 1854 it rose by 134 percent. These ten-year increases were not to be equaled in any subsequent decade of the nineteenth century.

Cotton textile manufacturing had been the pioneer industry in the United States. In 1791, the successful Rhode Island merchant Moses Brown had employed Samuel Slater, who understood the recently developed English textile machinery, to set up a small spinning plant. Soon there were a number of such small enterprises putting out the yarn they spun to be woven into cloth on hand looms in homes. When imports of English cloth were cut off during the War of 1812, the infant American textile industry spurted ahead to meet the demand.

Besides giving American manufacturers a temporary monopoly of the domestic market, the war also caused large amounts of capital to be diverted from the disrupted shipping business to manufacturing. Beginning in 1813, a group of wealthy Boston merchants led by Francis Cabot Lowell poured the unprecedented capital of $600,000 into the Boston Manufacturing Company at Waltham, Massachusetts. This was the first really large-scale and completely integrated manufacturing enterprise in the United States. The Waltham operation included every step in the manufacturing process from raw cotton to the final printed cloth, with the most advanced machinery used at every stage. The healthy profits at Waltham encouraged the promoters to erect similar plants at Lowell and other places in New England where water power was available.

The example of the Waltham system hastened the development of large plants using power-driven machinery in other industries: woolens, flour, shoes, carpets, stockings, and paper. The assembly-line or continuous-process system was even adopted for nonmachine operations, as in the great pork butchering and packing establishments that grew up at Cincinnati and, later, Chicago. The small, scattered iron works of the colonial period expanded, with the adoption of the rolling mill and the substitution of coal for charcoal fuel, into larger-scale enterprises. The demand for iron created by the railroad boom helped quadruple the output of pig iron between 1842 and 1860.

By the 1840s stationary steam engines had been developed to the point where they could substitute for water power in industrial production. This strengthened the tendency for industry to locate in cities, and industrial growth contributed greatly to urbanization. In 1820, only 6 percent of the American people had lived in places of 2,500 or more population. By 1860, the figure had risen to nearly 20 percent, and New York had become the first city to pass the 1,000,000 mark. The greater part of this urban growth had occurred during the 1840s and 1850s. Much of it was produced by the increased volume of international and interregional trade that funneled through the cities, but industrial development was becoming almost as important. In five of the fifteen largest cities in 1860, more than 10 percent of their population engaged in manufacturing, while some of the newer and smaller cities like Newark, Lowell, and Lynn were almost wholly industrial.

The steady trend toward concentrating production in larger and larger industrial units had undermined the independence of the old artisan class and created a growing new working class of permanent wage earners. This shift in the status and prospects of working people had given rise in the 1820s and 1830s to a number of labor unions of skilled artisans in such crafts as printing, shoemaking, and the building trades. The craft unions had organized city federations in New York and Philadelphia, worker's parties had entered local politics, there had been strikes for the ten-hour day, and in 1834 a National Trades Union had been formed.

This early labor movement was swept under by the Panic of 1837, but as prosperity returned in the 1840s, so did the craft unions. Strikes became numerous and successful enough so that the ten-hour day was general by the middle 1850s. Again a National Trades Union was organized, and again in 1857 a depression wiped out labor's organizational gains. This time, though, several nationally organized craft unions survived the debacle.

The union movement largely bypassed the growing body of unskilled or semi-skilled workers who staffed the new mechanized factories. For several decades after the establishment of the Waltham plant, the New England cotton mills recruited their labor force mainly from young New England girls, who lived in paternalistically managed company boarding houses and worked in the mills until they married. This system broke down after the Panic of 1837, and from this time on, the labor force for all kinds of factories was recruited increasingly from unskilled immigrants. Factory hours were long, and factory wages provided only a mean living. Not for many decades would the industrial worker begin to share in the vastly expanded wealth created by the industrial revolution.

CONFLICT AGAIN

With North and South riding the greatest tide of prosperity either section had ever known, it may seem strange that the decade of the 1850s ended in civil war. Indeed direct conflicts of economic interest between the sections over national legislation seemed at the lowest ebb since the Panic of 1819. Southerners were no longer frustrating the Northwest's demands for federal aid to internal improvements; between 1850 and 1860, the federal government granted 18 million acres of the public lands to aid construction of 45 railroads in ten states. The tariff issue no longer engaged passions as northern industry continued to flourish under the low rates of 1846.

Yet the very lushness of prosperity and growth was fostering imperial visions in the two sections: in the South, visions of an expanding cotton-slavery empire and in the North visions of an expanding free-soil empire. As these competing expansionist impulses headed toward a collision, they were inevitably intensified by the moral dimensions of the slavery question.

The South's growing insecurity over the institution of slavery was particularly dangerous. By the 1850s, the North was rapidly outstripping the South in population and potential political power, while Northerners were demonstrating their deepening disapproval of slavery by blocking enforcement of the stringent new Fugitive Slave Law, one of the few concessions to the South in the Compromise of 1850. These circumstances help explain the mounting stridency with which southerners proclaimed the merits of slavery—and explain more specifically the South's hysterical reaction to two famous books published during the 1850s. The first, Harriet Beecher Stowe's novel *Uncle Tom's Cabin* (1852), was a sentimental portrayal of slavery's brutal impact on some appealingly drawn slave characters. The second, Hinton Rowan Helper's *Impending Crisis of the South* (1857), was an all too effective argument by a nonslaveholding North Carolinian that slavery was disastrous to the non-slaveholding white majority in the South. Both books were not only denounced but violently suppressed in the South, while in the North they won wide audiences and helped harden antislavery sentiment.

Paradoxically, the South had more power in the federal government in the 1850s than it had had since Jeffersonian days. The campaign of 1852 demonstrated that the northern and southern wings of the Whig party were too far apart on the slavery question to hold together any longer, leaving the Democrats as the one great national party. Northern Democratic politicians competed against each other for promotion in the party and the federal government by going as far as they could toward satisfying southern demands and thereby winning southern support. Therefore the South came to have the dominant voice in the Democratic presidential administrations of Franklin Pierce and James Buchanan. As long as the Democrats remained a national party and the South's northern Democratic allies could win elections in a good part of the North, the South could in effect control the country and counteract the northern advantage in population and representation. But eventually the South, out of its insecurity, demanded more from its northern Democratic allies than they could grant without losing elections in the North.

What the South was demanding in the 1850s was the right for slavery to expand. This insistence grew out of complicated motives. This southern demand was in part simply the cotton-slavery imperialism of a prosperous and expansive social and economic system. The demand for slavery was also an effort to bolster the South's slipping proportion of representation in the federal government through the creation of additional slave states. Finally, the South was demanding that Northerners recognize the moral legitimacy of slavery by acknowledging its right to grow and thus relieve the white South from the intolerable burden of justifying and defending an unjustifiable and indefensible social system.

THE TERRITORIAL QUESTION

It seemed clear by the 1850s that there was no further room for new slave states within the territorial limits of the United States under the political arrangements that prevailed. The Missouri Compromise of 1820 barred slaves from the remaining unorganized parts of the Louisiana Purchase, the Oregon territory had been organized on free-soil principles, and geography seemed to prohibit slavery's spread over the arid wastes of the New Mexico and Utah territories.

Under these circumstances, expansionist Southerners turned their attention to the Caribbean area, and the Pierce administration attempted to purchase Cuba from Spain. This effort had the advantage of appealing on nonsectional grounds to a nationalistic "Young America" group who wanted to continue the expansionism of the 1840s. But when a trio of southern-oriented diplomats issued the Ostend Manifesto proposing that Cuba be seized if it could not be purchased, there was such a reaction in the North and in Spain that the Cuba project had to be dropped. Despite this setback, many Southerners continued to agitate throughout the 1850s for expansion into the Caribbean area and to support illegal filibustering expeditions that sought to overturn weak Central American governments and pave the way for American annexations.

With the outlook for foreign expansionism dim, a small group of southern politicians began a fateful effort to push slavery into that part of the Louisiana Purchase hitherto reserved as free soil. Democratic Senator Stephen A. Douglas of Illinois was anxious to pass a bill providing territorial government for the Kansas and Nebraska country, partly to facilitate the start of a transcontinental railroad that might terminate in his home town of Chicago. Senator David R. Atchison of Missouri, representing a slaveholding constituency across the Missouri River from the area in question, had staked his political life on a promise that his constituents would be able to take their slaves into the new territory. Atchison joined with a group of powerful southern Senators to insist that no territorial bill would pass unless it contained a clause repealing the Missouri Compromise prohibition of slavery. Douglas gave in to their demand, a weak President Pierce was persuaded to use all the power of the national administration to secure enough northern Democratic votes to pass the bill, and the Kansas-Nebraska Act of 1854 was the result.

Douglas argued that the act was simply an extension of the democratic "popular sovereignty" principle already applied to the New Mexico and Utah territories by the Compromise of 1850. But indignation blazed up in the North at this cynical abrogation of a sacred compromise and at the servile northern Democrats who obeyed an "aggressive slavocracy." While only a small minority of Northerners were disposed to interfere with slavery where it already existed, far more were ready to stop its further spread. With the Kansas-Nebraska Act, cotton-slavery imperialism provocatively challenged free-soil imperialism. The immediate response was the organization of a new sectional party in the North calling itself "Republican" and vowing its opposition to the least extension of the area of slavery.

Meanwhile Kansas, the more southerly of the two new territories, was filled with violence and bloodshed as proslavery and antislavery factions contended for control of the territorial government. New England abolitionists contributed guns and funds for free-soil immigrants, while "border ruffians" from Missouri crossed the river to furnish illegal ballots and armed support to the proslavery faction. When President Pierce again yielded to southern pressure and recognized a proslavery legislature elected largely by illegal voters from Missouri, the enraged free-soilers elected their own legislature and governor. A proslavery force raided the free-soil capital, and in retaliation, a fanatical free-soiler named John Brown invaded an isolated proslavery settlement and butchered five inoffensive residents. In the sporadic violence that followed, more than 200 people were killed.

In retrospect, the demand for repeal of the Missouri Compromise appears to have been a suicidal strategy for southern interests. Southern opinion generally was not strongly in favor of such a demand, and even many of the more radical Southerners admitted that slavery would probably never be established in any of the disputed territories. What the South was really demanding was an acknowledgment of its technical right to take slaves into all territories, an acknowledgment of the legitimacy of slavery. For the sake of this technical right, southern leaders put their northern Democratic allies in an untenable position in their home constituencies and called into existence a formidable antislavery party that would soon destroy their control of the federal government.

BUCHANAN RIDES THE STORM

The new Republican party, drawing heavily from former Whigs and outraged Democrats, grew by leaps and bounds in the North. As the presidential election of 1856 approached, the Democrats were also threatened by another new party, the Americans or Know-Nothings, who appealed to anti-immigrant, anti-Catholic sentiment. To meet this double challenge, the Democratic national convention dropped the discredited Pierce and nominated the cautious, conservative, and prosouthern James Buchanan of Pennsylvania. The new American party nominated ex-President Fillmore and drew a substantial vote, especially from former Whigs in the South, but carried only one state. The major feature of the election was the strong showing of the new Republican party, which carried all but five of the free states for its candidate John C. Frémont. Only by the lavish use of money in Pennsylvania and Indiana and by the support of an almost solid South did the Democrats squeak through with a bare electoral majority.

Meanwhile the attempt to apply the popular sovereignty principle was deepening the chaos in Kansas and Washington. Southerners were insisting that popular sovereignty did not allow the people of a territory to bar slavery until they came to draft a constitution preparatory to admission as a state. Shortly after Buchanan's inauguration in March, 1857, a southern majority on the Supreme Court upheld this southern contention in the celebrated case of Dred Scott. Chief Justice Roger B. Taney's opinion denied the slave Scott's contention that he had been made free by residence in the free territory of Iowa, saying that Congress could not bar slavery from the territories —and it was a logical inference that territorial legislatures could not either.

While northern opinion was reacting to this further evidence of slave power aggression, President Buchanan was trying to remove the issue from politics by pushing Kansas into statehood. Failing in his efforts to get a fair referendum on slavery in Kansas, the President unwisely succumbed to southern pressure and endorsed a proslavery state constitution drafted by a notoriously unrepresentative convention at Lecompton. At this point, Senator Douglas and a number of other northern Democrats, fighting for political survival at home, revolted against the President and blocked the admission of Kansas under the Lecompton Constitution.

At the height of the Kansas crisis in 1857, the country's nerves were further strained by a severe financial crisis. The Republicans capitalized on the hard times to broaden their appeal. The southern-dominated Democratic Congress had just passed the Tariff of 1857, reducing protection to the lowest level since 1812. It was easy to blame the depression on the new tariff and to win support from hard-hit manufacturers and industrial workers by promises of higher rates. At the same time, the Republicans made themselves more appealing to northwestern farmers by agitating for a homestead act giving free homesteads of 160 acres to actual settlers on the public lands. A wave of religious revivals following the financial crash further excited the public mind and intensified the North's moral sensitivity on the slavery question.

THE ELECTION OF 1860

Under these unsettling circumstances, the slavery debate began to be dominated by the approaching presidential election of 1860. Stephen A. Douglas of Illinois was the leading aspirant for the Democratic nomination and perhaps the only one who could win enough support in the North to be elected. But Douglas was in an exceedingly difficult dilemma, reflecting the dilemma of the Democratic party. In order to be nominated, he had to allay southern suspicions arising from his opposition to the Lecompton Constitution, but it was questionable whether he could allay these suspicions and win the nomination without taking a position so prosouthern that he would lose the subsequent election. And in the meantime, he had to win reelection to the Senate against the leading Illinois Republican, a shrewd Springfield lawyer named Abraham Lincoln.

In the famous series of debates between Douglas and Lincoln across Illinois in 1858, Douglas sought to escape his predicament by taking an ambiguous position. On the one hand, he maintained his doctrine of popular sovereignty, which would technically permit Southerners to take their slaves into the territories and deny territorial legislatures the right to bar slavery before statehood. But at the same time he assured the Illinois voters, in what came to be called the Freeport Doctrine, that slaves could never be successfully held in a territory unless the territorial legislature had passed a slave code or positive legislation for protecting and policing slave property. Douglas won the senatorial election by a narrow margin, but his Freeport Doctrine made him even less acceptable to Southerners as a presidential nominee.

By now southern demands were reaching an extreme of presumption and folly. The more radical Southerners had already begun to suspect that slavery, as Douglas claimed in the Freeport Doctrine, could not be sustained in the territories without a slave code. Now they moved beyond the claim that neither Congress nor territorial legislatures could bar slavery from the territories and began demanding that the federal government positively protect and guarantee slavery in the territories through enactment of a congressional slave code. Most Southerners were not insistent on this radical demand, and certainly very few Southerners had any real thought of taking slaves into any of the territories in any case. But as tension increased and excitement mounted, southern politicians feared to be outdone in defending their constituents' supposed interests, and the most extreme positions came to the fore. Southern insecurity had generated demands for more and more guarantees and assurances; these apparently aggressive movements of the slaveholding section had frightened the North into more determined resistance and spawned the Republican party; and this hardening resistance in the North had intensified southern insecurity and generated even greater demands.

Southern insecurity reached a peak of near hysteria in October, 1859, when the violent abolitionist John Brown, of Kansas fame, led a raid on the federal arsenal at Harper's Ferry, Virginia, seizing guns and ammunition with which he planned to arm a wholesale slave rebellion. Though Brown and his followers were quickly subdued, a paroxysm of terror ran through the South, and terror quickly turned to rage when it was learned that respectable antislavery people in the North had backed the plot.

Against this background, the Democratic national convention assembled at Charleston, South Carolina, in April, 1860. Radical Southerners insisted that the convention endorse their demand for a congressional slave code. When the pro-Douglas majority refused, after violent debate, the delegates from eight states of the lower South withdrew, and the convention had to adjourn. Two separate Democratic conventions then met in Baltimore, the northern-dominated one nominating Douglas and the southern-dominated one nominating John C. Breckinridge of Kentucky. Meanwhile, the Republicans, who had no support in the South, had met in Chicago to nominate Abraham Lincoln, and union-minded, old-line Whigs from the border states, calling themselves the Constitutional Union party, had put John Bell of Tennessee into the running as a fourth candidate. In effect, this four-way contest was not one election but two. Free-state voters chose between Lincoln and Douglas; in the slave states, the contest was between Bell and Breckinridge. At this critical moment, the American party system no longer operated in a nationwide context. In the realm of partisan politics, the erosion of unionism was all but complete.

Lincoln had no support *outside* the free states, but in the free states he made an almost clean sweep that was by itself enough for a majority in the electoral college (but only 39 percent of the popular vote). For the rest, Breckinridge carried most of the South handily; Bell won three border slave states; and Douglas, though running second to Lincoln in popular votes, won the electoral votes of only Missouri and half of New Jersey.

SECESSION

For years the small but steadily growing body of radical southern fire-eaters had been looking forward to this day, and they lost no time in making the most of their opportunity. South Carolina had been in a secessionist mood since the days of nullification, impatiently waiting for her stolid sister states to awaken to their danger. At last enough of the southern population was sufficiently aroused by the election of a "Black Republican," and South Carolina could lead the way. Hastily calling a state convention, the Palmetto State formally repealed its ratification of the federal constitution on December 20, 1860. Within six weeks, South Carolina was followed by the six Gulf States: Mississippi, Florida, Georgia, Alabama, Louisiana, and Texas.

As the border states hesitated, the waning Buchanan administration fretted in helpless impotence. The politicians at Washington scurried about seeking a formula for compromise, but the victorious Republicans would not listen to a proposal that countenanced the slightest extension of slavery, while the Southerners demanded at least a token concession on the territorial question. Meanwhile the seceded states sent delegates to Montgomery, Alabama, organized themselves as the Confederate States of America, and chose Jefferson Davis of Mississippi as their president.

CONFLICTING HISTORICAL VIEWPOINTS

6. What Caused the Civil War?

The Civil War is perhaps the best illustration of the ancient truism that the historian's view of the past is colored by his or her perception of the present. Southerners and Northerners debated the causes across regional lines. State-rightists, nationalists, and economic determinists offered their own predictable explanations for the catastrophe's origins.

The first scholarly assessment came from the pen of James F. Rhodes, a turn-of-the-century historian with a strong nationalist persuasion. In his History of the United States (7 vols., 1893–1906), Rhodes argued that the war was fought over the issue of slavery: "of the American Civil War it may safely be asserted [that] there was a single cause, slavery." Almost universally accepted for two decades, Rhodes's thesis was disputed and ultimately displaced during the 1920s and 1930s. But during the period of civil-rights activism following World War II, his interpretation won renewed support. In an authoritative modern reaffirmation of the slavery hypothesis, Allan Nevins concluded that "The main root of the conflict . . . was the problem of slavery with its complementary problem of race-adjustment." Nevins's magisterial Ordeal of the Union and The Emergence of Lincoln (4 vols., 1947–1950) also identified "minor roots," including constitutional, political, and economic factors. But the issue of slavery and the future of blacks in American society, he insisted, were fundamentally the causes of the Civil War.

On the eve of the Great Depression, Charles and Mary Beard argued that economic conflict, not slavery, caused the war. In The Rise of American Civilization (2 vols., 1927), the Beards viewed the conflict as one between rival forms of capitalism. According to this reform-minded husband-and-wife team, the Civil War was a "Second American Revolution" in which northern industrialists sought successfully to dominate southern agriculturists. Although Charles Beard would later abandon this interpretation, it has remained popular among radical scholars. Both William A. Williams's The Contours of American History (1961) and Barrington Moore's Social Origins of Dictatorship and Democracy (1966) offer variations on the Beardian theme.

Other historians interpreted the war as an inevitable clash of regional rivals. Arthur C. Cole, for example, argued in his The Irrepressible Conflict (1934) that the North and the South were two distinct civilizations, two separate societies drawn ineluctably into conflict by the very nature of their differences. But other scholars denied that there were irreconcilable ideological, institutional, or economic differences between the sections. Indeed, James G. Randall (The Civil War and Reconstruction, 1937), Avery Craven (The Repressible Conflict, 1939), and Kenneth Stampp (And the War Came, 1950) viewed the Civil War as an avoidable and needless conflict. Writing in the eras of World War II and the Cold War, these antiwar historians blamed blundering politicians and moral fanatics for a holocaust that should never have happened.

In one form or another, each of these major interpretations has supporters among the present generation of historians. For example, in The Impending Crisis (1976), the latest and perhaps the best synthesis of this much analyzed period, David Potter returns to the theme of Rhodes and Nevins. Although not arguing the issue of inevitability, Potter agrees that the institution of slavery lay at the heart of the problem. Exploring the paradoxical relationship between an ascendant American nationalism and a growing and disruptive sectionalism, he finds no basic or irresolvable ideological, economic, or cultural differences dividing North from South. The conflict, then, was one over values—values centering on the issue of slavery.

Perhaps inevitably the conflict that divided the Union more than a century ago continues to divide the scholarly community. As Thomas J. Pressly remarked in his analysis of how Americans Interpret Their Civil War *(1954), "the further the Civil War receded into the past, the greater the strength of the emotions with which these divergent viewpoints were upheld."*

FOR FURTHER READING

For economic development in the 1840s and 1850s, the references listed at the end of Chapter 9 will continue to be useful. Marcus Lee Hansen, in *The Atlantic Migration, 1607–1860* (1940),* gives a good account of the upsurge of immigration during these years. John R. Commons and others have written the standard *History of Labour in the United States* (4 vols., 1918–1935); and Hannah Josephson's *The Gold Threads* (1949) is a good account of the female workers in the New England textile mills. William O. Scroggs describes the Caribbean adventures of various Americans in *Filibusters and Financiers* (1916). The drift toward Civil War is traced by Avery O. Craven, in *The Growth of Southern Nationalism, 1848–1861* (1953), and by Roy F. Nichols, in *The Disruption of American Democracy* (1948).* In *Crisis of Fear* (1970), Steven A. Channing offers a superb account of the secession movement in South Carolina. Thomas B. Alexander has analyzed congressional voting in the 1850s as an index to *Sectional Stress and Party Strength* (1967); and Eric Foner's *Free Soil, Free Labor, Free Men* (1970) is a major study of early Republican ideology. The more illuminating biographies include: David Donald, *Charles Sumner and the Coming of the Civil War* (1950); George Fort Milton, *The Eve of Conflict: Stephen A. Douglas and the Needless War* (1934); Glyndon G. Van Deusen, *William Henry Seward* (1967); and Laura A. White, *Robert Barnwell Rhett* (1931). Indispensable to an understanding of secession is Ollinger Crenshaw's *The Slave States in the Presidential Election of 1860* (1945). Modern readers will gain much insight from those two famous books of the 1850s, Harriet Beecher Stowe's *Uncle Tom's Cabin* (1852)* and Hinton Rowan Helper's *The Impending Crisis of the South: How to Meet It* (1857).*

---

*Available in paperback edition.

8. PRESIDENTIAL ELECTIONS AND MAJOR EVENTS, 1860–1865

1860	**Abraham Lincoln** (Republican) elected over Stephen A. Douglas (Northern Democrat), John C. Breckinridge (Southern Democrat), and John Bell (Constitutional Unionist).
1860–1861	Seven states of the lower South secede and organize the Confederate States of America.
1861	Confederates bombard Fort Sumter, beginning the Civil War.
	Virginia, North Carolina, Tennessee, and Arkansas secede and join the Confederacy.
	Morrill Tariff. Substantial upward revision of duties, beginning a long period of high protection.
	Trent affair. Union naval officer seized two Confederate diplomats from a British vessel.
1862	Homestead Act provides free farms of 160 acres to actual settlers.
	Morrill Land Grant Act grants land to the states for agricultural and mechanical colleges.
	Pacific Railroad Act. Federal subsidies for a railroad from Omaha to California.
	Slavery abolished in the territories and the District of Columbia.
	Second Confiscation Act. Freeing escaped or captured slaves of Confederates.
1863	Lincoln's Emancipation Proclamation. Declaring free all slaves in Confederate areas.
	National Bank Ace, with a supplementary act of 1864, establishes a system of banks issuing a uniform paper currency based on holdings of federal bonds.
	Turning point of the war in July, when Union forces capture Vicksburg on the Mississippi and stop Lee's invasion at Gettysburg.
	Lincoln announces his "10 percent plan" for the easy restoration of the seceded states to the Union.
1864	Lincoln vetoes the Wade-Davis bill, containing a harsher congressional plan for restoration of the seceded states to the Union.
	Abraham Lincoln (Republican) reelected over George B. McClellan (Democrat).
1865	Lee surrenders to Grant at Appomattox Courthouse.
	Lincoln assassinated.
	The Thirteenth Amendment abolishes slavery throughout the United States.

The Civil War
1861–1865

15

When Abraham Lincoln arose to deliver his inaugural address on March 4, 1861, few people had any very clear idea of how the secession problem should be handled. Some voices in the North counseled letting the "erring sisters depart in peace." The abolitionist minority called for a holy war to free the slaves. Majority opinion in the North was increasingly convinced that the Union must somehow be preserved, but there was no clear mandate for military coercion of the seceded states. The war that finally came, like most wars, came not because anyone deliberately willed it, but out of a fortuitous chain of circumstances whose result reflected only imperfectly the conscious collective will of North or South. Insofar as a guiding will affected the outcome, it was the will of Abraham Lincoln.

LINCOLN AND THE SECESSION CRISIS

The new president was known to the country only as a lanky and apparently uncultivated lawyer-politician from the prairies of Illinois. He had won brief notice years earlier when his opposition to the Mexican War caused Illinois voters to repudiate him after a single term in Congress. Not until his debates with Douglas in the senatorial campaign of 1858 had he attracted national attention. Elected president by a minority of the voters, he had given little public indication of his policy in the months between the election and the inauguration. Actually he had blocked all efforts at compromise by privately opposing any arrangement that left the slightest room for the expansion of slavery. But this position could be put down to political expediency—compromise on the territorial question would have left the infant Republican party little reason for existence—and gave no clue as to what he would do when he assumed office.

Certainly Lincoln was not prepared to lead a crusade to free the slaves. He had insisted that slavery was wrong and that its expansion should be stopped so that the country might look forward to its eventual peaceful extinction. But he had repeatedly denied any disposition to interfere with slavery where it already existed. He had also denied in his debates with Douglas that he was "in favor of bringing about in any way the social and political equality of the white and black races." A "physical difference" would prevent the two races from ever living together on equal terms, he had said, and, therefore, "I, as much as any other man, am in favor of having the superior position assigned to the white race." He wanted slavery excluded from the territories so that "white men may find a home—may find some spot where they can . . . settle upon new soil and better their condition in life . . . as an outlet for *free white people everywhere.*"

The inaugural address revealed both a leader of unsuspected stature and a position around which northern opinion could rally. With an eloquence that no president since Jefferson had attained, Lincoln pleaded for preservation of the Union. "The mystic chords of memory," he said, "stretching from every battlefield and every patriot grave to every living heart and hearthstone all over this broad land, will yet swell the chorus of the Union, when again touched, as surely they will be, by the better angels of our nature." In trying to touch these chords, he reassured the South in the most positive terms that he would countenance no act against slavery in the states where it already existed.

But the address also had a vein of iron. The Union, said Lincoln, was perpetual, any violent acts against the authority of the United States were "insurrectionary or revolutionary," and these statements were to be taken "as the declared purpose of the Union that it *will* constitutionally defend and maintain itself." Though the federal government would not initiate hostilities, the president told the South, it would "hold, occupy, and possess" the federal forts and other property in the seceded states and collect the import duties there.

It is clear in retrospect that Lincoln thus committed himself to a course that led directly to one of the bloodiest wars in history. But war was not his purpose. Eight of the fifteen slave states were still in the Union. By refusing to recognize secession while at the same time declining to proceed forcibly against the secessionists, Lincoln was seeking to reinforce the manifest Unionist sentiment in the upper South. Apparently he wanted to keep the upper South from seceding, hoping that latent Unionism would eventually overcome secessionism in the seven seceded states of the lower South.

There were several difficulties with this union-saving strategy. One was that Lincoln exaggerated the strength of Unionist sentiment in the lower South. Another was the likelihood that the effort to hold the federal forts in the seceded states would lead to armed conflict. Armed conflict was the more likely because many of the secessionists were quite ready to provoke a crisis that would force the upper South to choose sides.

The issue of peace or war came to a focus in the harbor of Charleston, South Carolina. Practically all the federal forts and other property in the lower South had been taken over by the seceding states before Lincoln's inauguration. Of the few posts remaining in federal hands, the unfinished and lightly garrisoned Fort Sumter, located in the entrance to Charleston's harbor, had become the symbolic focus of the whole controversy over federal property. Sumter had sufficient supplies to hold out only six weeks, and a decision about its future could not be postponed. Lincoln finally informed the Confederate authorities that he was sending a naval expedition to reprovision Sumter. They in turn ordered their general at Charleston to demand the fort's immediate evacuation and, in case of refusal, to bombard it. The demand was made and refused, and on April 12, 1861, the Confederate shore batteries opened fire.

Lincoln responded by calling on the states for 75,000 troops. Rather than make war on their fellow Southerners, four states of the upper South—Virginia, North Carolina, Tennessee, and Arkansas—now reluctantly followed the lower South out of the Union. The four slave states of Delaware, Maryland, Kentucky, and Missouri remained with the Union, though the last two had strong secessionist movements and furnished many soldiers to the Confederacy. The tables were turned on the secessionists when the strongly Unionist western section of Virginia seceded from Virginia and laid the basis for the new state of West Virginia under the aegis of the Union. Meanwhile the Confederacy acted to consolidate the adhesion of the upper southern states by moving its capital from Montgomery to Richmond.

THE WAR BEGINS

A spirit of martial ardor swept over both sections in the spring of 1861. Northerners expected a short and easy war, while Southerners seemed oblivious to the overwhelming superiority in human and material resources against which they would have to contend. The 5.5 million free people of the 11 Confederate states faced a population of 22 million in the 23 Union states. The North had a four-to-one advantage in free males of fighting age and would muster twice as many soldiers. Even if one southern soldier was worth two Yankees (as Southerners loudly proclaimed), how were southern armies to be supplied and transported? The North had 80 percent of the country's factories and most of the coal and iron. Approximately 22,000 miles of railroad traversed the North as compared with 9,000 in the South, and the North's rail network included a series of vital trunk lines between East and West, while the sprawling southern regions were but circuitously and inefficiently bound together.

Under the circumstances, the South made a remarkable military showing. This was due in part to the advantage of fighting a defensive war. The North was compelled not only to invade but to occupy the South, and southern commanders had the additional advantage of shorter interior lines of communication for shifting troops from one front to another. Moreover, Jefferson Davis could utilize from the beginning a galaxy of outstanding generals, Albert Sidney Johnston, Joseph E. Johnston, Thomas J. ("Stonewall") Jackson, and, preeminently, Robert E. Lee; Lincoln spent several years trying a succession of variously unsatisfactory commanders before he found a really able one.

The Appalachian highlands, thrusting deep into the South, divided the theater of war into two zones. Throughout the conflict, the greatest public attention was focused on the East, where the rival armies menaced each other's capitals, only 100 miles apart. Here the Confederate armies, magnificently led by Joseph E. Johnston and then by Robert E. Lee, repeatedly repelled Union invasions aimed at Richmond. General Irvin McDowell's army was turned back at Bull Run in northern Virginia in July, 1861. Lincoln's next general, George B. McClellan, tried another tack, ferrying an enormous invasion force down Chesapeake Bay and up the York River to the eastern outskirts of Richmond only to be beaten off in the series of hard fought battles that constituted the Peninsula Campaign of May-June, 1862. Later that summer, Lee trounced another Union army led by John Pope in the second battle at Bull Run and followed up this victory with an audacious advance across the Potomac River into Maryland. McClellan caught up with him at Antietam Creek, some 50 miles northwest of Washington, in September, 1862 and in a closely contested battle inflicted so much damage that the Confederates had to withdraw to Virginia.

Back on his home ground, Lee was again invincible, defeating Ambrose E. Burnside at Fredericksburg in December and Joseph E. Hooker at nearby Chancellorsville the following May. Once again the great Confederate general sought to capitalize on his success by invading the North, gambling on the hope of a decisive victory that would cut the east-west trunk railroads in Maryland and Pennsylvania, imperil Washington, and persuade the North to make peace before its superiority in soldiers and material became irresistible. On July 1, 1863, Lee's 70,000 men and the 90,000 Union soldiers of George G. Meade faced each other from opposing ridges outside the little town of Gettysburg in southern Pennsylvania. For three days, wave after wave of Confederates swept up against the strong Unionist position, only barely failing to flood over it. Lee was again forced to retreat to Virginia, and the South's last hope of victory was gone.

While Lee's brilliant gamble was failing in the East, the Confederacy's military doom was being more plainly spelled out in the West. Here the Mississippi, Tennessee, and Cumberland rivers afforded natural invasion routes for the combined operations of Union gunboats and armies, and here an obscure Union commander, Ulysses S. Grant, steadily and inexorably crunched deeper and deeper into the South. Forts Henry and Donelson, guarding the Tennessee and Cumberland rivers, fell in February, 1862. Pressing on south up the Tennessee River, Grant inflicted a severe blow to the main Confederate army in the west at Shiloh in April and moved on into northern Mississippi. Meanwhile Union gunboats had steamed up the Mississippi from the Gulf to take New Orleans and down the Mississippi from the north to take Memphis. The last Confederate stronghold on the Mississippi—Vicksburg—fell to Grant in July, 1863 while Meade was turning back Lee at Gettysburg; thus the Confederacy was cut in two.

THE CONFEDERACY AT WAR

The burden of directing the Confederate war effort fell almost wholly on the shoulders of Jefferson Davis. Lacking able subordinates in his cabinet and in the Confederate Congress, Davis perhaps took on too much of the burden of detailed administration and sometimes exercised poor judgment in decisions about military strategy and commanding officers. But only an able and conscientious executive could have kept the Confederacy operating and its armies in the field under the staggering difficulties that he faced for as long as he did.

At the beginning of the war, Davis had high hopes of aid from Europe. France's Napoleon III was openly sympathetic as were the ruling upper classes in Great Britain, and both of these countries went so far as to recognize the Confederacy's belligerent status. But Davis was counting on the economic power of the South's cotton to produce more substantial aid—full diplomatic recognition, financial assistance, and perhaps even military intervention. The South might have built up large credits for the purchase of supplies in Europe by shipping its cotton abroad. Instead, the Confederate authorities placed an embargo on cotton exports, expecting that this would force British cotton mills to close and thus bring pressure on the British government to intervene more openly on behalf of the Confederacy. Unfortunately for the southerners, the British mills had a year's surplus of raw cotton on hand, some alternative sources of supply were available, and although some of the cotton mills eventually shut down, their unemployed workers remained sympathetic to the more democratic North and exerted their influence against any aid to the South.

The South's best chance to drive a wedge between Great Britain and the North came in November, 1861 when a United States naval vessel stopped the British ship *Trent* on the high seas and took off the Confederate diplomats James M. Mason and John Slidell. But the United States promptly released Mason and Slidell, and Lincoln's skillful minister in London, Charles Francis Adams, was increasingly successful in preventing the British from aiding the Confederacy either directly or indirectly. And France refused to act without British support.

Meanwhile Lincoln had ordered the Union navy to blockade southern ports; by the time the Confederacy decided to ship cotton to Europe in exchange for supplies, this was no longer possible. Cut off from all outside goods (except a trickle brought in by swift blockade runners), the Confederacy was increasingly hard put to supply its armies with munitions or its people with the ordinary necessities of life.

As the war wore on and as the Confederacy's prospects dimmed, the early enthusiasm was replaced by growing discouragement, apathy, and disaffection. The Confederate conscription law, which exempted overseers and owners of 20 slaves, was especially resented by poorer Southerners who began to say that this was "a rich man's war and a poor man's fight." Desertions became an increasingly serious problem. The South's state-rights tradition was also a source of weakness as fractious governors like Joseph E. Brown of Georgia and Zebulon B. Vance of North Carolina defied the policies of the Richmond government. It seems fair to conclude that the South's commitment to the war had been less than wholehearted in the beginning and that a growing disenchantment with it was a major factor in the Confederacy's eventual collapse.

LINCOLN AND THE WAR

Lincoln was having his problems too. The North had a large contingent of "Peace Democrats" who, as the war dragged unsuccessfully on, demanded a negotiated settlement. The draft law of 1863, from which the wealthy could escape by paying $300 or hiring a substitute, provoked a bloody two-day riot in New York City. At the other end of the political spectrum, Lincoln was ceaselessly hounded by a group of "radical" Republicans who wanted to make the war an antislavery crusade and who advocated a punitive policy toward the South. Under the leadership of people like Senator Charles Sumner of Massachusetts and Representative Thaddeus Stevens of Pennsylvania, the Radicals gained great power in Congress where they set up a Joint Committee on the Conduct of the War, which constantly criticized and interfered with the president's conduct of military operations.

The split between radical Republicans and moderate or administration Republicans was not related, however, to the series of major laws passed by the wartime Congresses. The Morrill Tariff Act of 1861 marked a turn toward higher protective duties, and subsequent legislation of 1862 and 1864 pushed duties to unprecedented levels, inaugurating an era of extravagant protectionism that would last into the twentieth century. The long fight for free land culminated in the Homestead Act of 1862, granting 160 acres to any family that wished to settle on the public domain. The Morrill Land Grant Act of 1862 donated public lands to the states for support of agricultural and mechanical colleges. In the same year Congress finally authorized the long projected transcontinental railroad, granting 30 million acres and millions in federal bonds to the Union Pacific and Central Pacific railroad companies to build a line from Omaha to the Sacramento River. By an act of 1863, Congress established a national banking system with member banks issuing a stable currency of uniform national bank notes on the basis of their holdings of federal bonds.

In passing these important measures to serve the interests of northern farmers and business enterprise, the Congress was simply legislating the Republican platform now that the Southerners were no longer there to oppose. None of these measures aroused the controversy in the Republican party that the subject of slavery created. Anxious to mollify the loyal slave states of Delaware, Maryland, Kentucky, and Missouri, Lincoln stoutly resisted doing anything to suggest that abolition of slavery was a northern war aim. In the fall of 1861, he removed the Radicals' favorite general, John C. Frémont, from command in Missouri for declaring that the slaves of rebels were free. Meanwhile he sought unsuccessfully to interest Congress and the loyal slave states in a plan of gradual, compensated emancipation with the federal government footing the bill.

The Radicals were determined to force the issue, and in 1862 pushed through Congress legislation abolishing slavery in the territories and in the District of Columbia. More important was the Second Confiscation Act of 1862, declaring forfeit the property of all persons supporting the rebellion and proclaiming escaped or captured slaves to be "forever free." By this time, Lincoln was becoming aware that an emancipation policy would be of value in helping to win the war, especially by gaining friends for the Union in Europe. Finally, on January 1, 1863, he issued his Emancipation Proclamation. This famous proclamation freed only those slaves living in rebel areas and justified the action on the grounds of "military necessity." Only as the Union armies advanced did the freedom proclaimed by the proclamation become an actuality for

the slaves. Not until 1865 did the Thirteenth Amendment, forbidding slavery throughout the country, become a part of the Constitution.

The Emancipation Proclamation did not allay the Radicals' suspicion of Lincoln,
but they failed to block his renomination for president in 1864. In this wartime
election, the Lincoln Republicans ran as the Union party, appealing to War Democrats
by nominating for vice-president Andrew Johnson, the Tennessee Senator who had
remained loyal to the Union. The regular Democratic nomination went to General
McClellan, many of whose supporters were calling for peace negotiations. The long
string of Union defeats in the East had so strengthened antiwar sentiment that Lincoln
might have been defeated but for some timely military successes in the West on the
eve of the election.

TOWARD APPOMATTOX

It is now clear that the fall of Vicksburg and Lee's failure at Gettysburg in July, 1863,
had destroyed the last chances of a Confederate victory. And by this time, after trying
a long succession of commanders, Lincoln had finally found a general who would
justify his confidence. Ulysses Grant, who had capped his doggedly successful western campaigns with the victory at Vicksburg, was called to the East and, in the spring
of 1864, was made general-in-chief of all the Union armies. Before leaving the West
he had consolidated Union control of Tennessee with a victory at Chattanooga. Now
his grand strategy was a two-pronged final offensive against the South with General
William T. Sherman leading one great Union army south from Chattanooga into
Georgia and Grant himself leading another south from Washington toward Richmond.

The twin offensives were launched simultaneously in May, 1864; the two Union
armies of around 100,000 each pressed back Confederate armies of around 60,000.
In the West, Sherman steadily pushed the Confederates south and by September won
the important rail center of Atlanta. Here he made his audacious decision to abandon
his line of supply and wage a war of destruction between Atlanta and the sea.
Devastating the countryside as he went, he was in Savannah by December, and the
Confederacy was further segmented. Turning north, Sherman reached Columbia,
South Carolina in February, 1865 and by March was in east central North Carolina.

By demoralizing the Confederate areas south of Virginia, Sherman greatly facilitated Grant's advance on Richmond. In the Spotsylvania Wilderness and at Spotsylvania Courthouse in May, 1864, Lee inflicted heavy casualties on the invading
Yankees as he had so often done in the past. But this Yankee general did not withdraw
to lick his wounds as had all his predecessors. By flanking movements, he kept
pressing south toward Richmond. At Cold Harbor, Lee again inflicted frightful losses
on the Union army, but still Grant pushed inexorably south, passing just east of
Richmond and crossing the James River. Lee managed to shield Richmond as Grant
moved around it to the south and southwest toward Petersburg. By June, the two
armies were entrenched facing each other in a long line bending from Richmond
southward around the southern side of Petersburg.

Grant simply would not let go, and as the siege went on through the summer and fall and winter his superiority in numbers began to tell. Remorselessly he kept extending his line to the west, and Lee's line became steadily thinner and more vulnerable as he had to keep stretching it farther. By April Lee could extend his line no more and had to pull out of his entrenchments, abandoning Richmond and Petersburg. But by this time Grant had cut off all the roads leading south over which Lee might effect a junction with the only remaining Confederate army of any strength. On April 9, 1865 at Appomattox Courthouse, Lee bowed to the inevitable and surrendered. One month later the fleeing Jefferson Davis was captured in disguise in Georgia and imprisoned at Fortress Monroe. The Confederacy was dead.

LINCOLN AND THE SOUTH

The treatment of the vanquished South had long since become a new bone of contention between Lincoln and the Radicals. Lincoln wished to bring the rebellious states back into full membership in the Union as rapidly and painlessly as possible. By the time Union forces occupied Arkansas in December, 1863, the president was ready with his "10 percent plan" of reconstruction. Under this plan he proposed to extend amnesty and restore confiscated property to all Confederates who would take a simple loyalty oath, excluding only high civil and military officers of the Confederacy or its states. As soon as 10 percent of a state's 1860 electorate had taken the oath, the state could write a new constitution and rejoin the Union.

The Radicals, however, feared with considerable reason that if the southern states were reconstructed on this basis, the old ruling class would return to power and the freed Negroes would be little better off than they had been under slavery. Anxious for a thorough reconstruction of southern society, they insisted that black men be given the ballot and that the old rebel leadership be effectively excluded from political life. As a counter to Lincoln's plan they secured the passage in 1864 of the Wade-Davis bill. This measure required a majority, rather than 10 percent, of the 1860 voters to take a loyalty oath before reconstruction could begin and further insisted on disfranchisement of ex-Confederate leaders.

Lincoln allowed the Wade-Davis bill to die by pocket veto, but the Radicals had one tactical advantage. A state would not be fully restored to the Union until its representatives were seated in Congress, and the Radical-controlled Congress had full power over the admission of members. This power the Radicals used to deny admission to the first southern representatives who appeared under Lincoln's 10 percent plan. In March, 1865, as the war drew to a close, they gave a further indication of their objectives by creating the Freedmen's Bureau to assist the ex-slaves in adjusting to freedom and to protect their rights in their new state.

The sharpening struggle between Lincoln and the Radicals was suddenly cut short on Good Friday, April 14, 1865, five days after Lee's surrender at Appomattox, when a demented actor and southern sympathizer, John Wilkes Booth, shot a fatal bullet into the president's head as he sat in a box at Ford's Theater.

A grieving nation suddenly discovered a great tragic hero. To Lincoln's strength and humility and eloquence and magnanimity was now added the quality of martyrdom. He had presided over the bloodiest war in the American experience, preserving the Union as the land of liberty and last best hope of humanity. Hesitantly and grudgingly, but in the end unmistakably, he had also made the war a struggle to include *all* male Americans within the sphere of American liberty. Yet the Emancipation Proclamation and the Thirteenth Amendment were only a beginning. It was Lincoln's Radical critics who saw most clearly that the task of completing emancipation still lay ahead, and even his great talents could hardly have been equal to this Herculean task. Perhaps it was a timely martyrdom that translated Abraham Lincoln—a man groping toward an ideal only dimly perceptible in his society and age—into the Great Emancipator. For a century and more to come, Lincoln, the symbol, would remind his fellow Americans that the egalitarian dream was still unfulfilled.

FOR FURTHER READING

The standard work on the Civil War era is Allan Nevins's *The War for the Union* (4 vols., 1959–1971), but James G. Randall and David Donald's *The Civil War and Reconstruction* (1961) and Peter J. Parish's *The American Civil War* (1975) are both important. Divergent interpretations of the North's reaction to secession are presented by David M. Potter in *Lincoln and His Party in the Secession Crisis* (1950),* and by Kenneth M. Stampp in *And the War Came* (1950). The northern conduct of the war is best followed through the biographies of Lincoln. Benjamin P. Thomas's *Abraham Lincoln* (1952) is generally considered the best one-volume study, but see also *With Malice Toward None* (1977) by Stephen B. Oates. For greater detail, see Albert J. Beveridge's *Abraham Lincoln, 1809–1858* (2 vols., 1928) and the chronologically successive volumes by James G. Randall (completed by Richard N. Current) on *Lincoln the President* (4 vols., 1945–1955).* Current has also written a fine interpretive essay on *The Lincoln Nobody Knows* (1958).* Special aspects of the North during the war are treated in: John Hope Franklin, *The Emancipation Proclamation* (1963); George M. Frederickson, *The Inner Civil War* (1965)*; James McPherson, *The Struggle for Equality* (1964); T. Harry Williams, *Lincoln and the Radicals* (1941)*; and T. Harry Williams, *Lincoln and His Generals* (1952).* The Negro's role in the struggle is analyzed in Dudley Cornish's *The Sable Arm* (1956) and Benjamin Quarles's *The Negro in the Civil War* (1953). Clement Eaton has written a *History of the Southern Confederacy* (1954);* Frank E. Vandiver's *Their Tattered Flags* (1970) is a sprightly political and military history of the secession regime; Rembert W. Patrick describes *Jefferson Davis and his Cabinet* (1944). The Confederacy's *King Cotton Diplomacy* (1931) is the subject of Frank L. Owsley, while D. P. Crook's *Diplomacy* (1975) examines the maneuverings of both sides. The military history of the war from the point of view of the northern armies may be followed in the vivid volumes by Bruce Catton: *Mr. Lincoln's Army* (1951),* *Glory Road* (1952),* and *A Stillness at Appomattox* (1954).* A more detailed and professional evaluation of the northern

---

*Available in paperback edition.

military effort through 1863, with greater attention to the western campaigns, is Kenneth P. Williams's *Lincoln Finds a General: A Military Study of the Civil War* (5 vols., 1949–1959). *The Gettysburg Campaign* (1968) is examined by Edwin B. Coddington. The fighting as viewed from the southern side is best followed in the distinguished studies by Douglas Southall Freeman: *R. E. Lee, a Biography* (4 vols., 1934–1935) and *Lee's Lieutenants* (3 vols., 1942–1944). Thomas L. Connelly, in *The Marble Man* (1977), critically examines the life and legend of Robert E. Lee. Tom Henderson Wells has written an excellent history of *The Confederate Navy* (1971). Also outstanding are two works by Frank E. Vandiver: *Rebel Brass* (1956) and *Mighty Stonewall* (1957). Bell I. Wiley has described *Confederate Women* (1975) and the common soldiers in *The Life of Johnny Reb* (1943) and *The Life of Billy Yank* (1952). Edmund Wilson's *Patriotic Gore* (1962) brilliantly portrays the human and literary dimensions of the era. Of the multitude of personal accounts of contemporaries, three very different ones may be singled out as having special interest: the *Personal Memoirs* (2 vols., 1885–1886) of General Grant; *A Diary from Dixie* (1905)* by Mary Boykin Chesnut; and *The Diary of Edmund Ruffin* (2 vols., 1972–1976), edited by William K. Scarborough.

Reconstructing the Union
1865–1890

16

In the generation after the Civil War, economic expansion absorbed most of the nation's energies. The people's attention, however, centered at first on a more traditional kind of problem, the Reconstruction of the Union and the new order in the defeated South. Not the least difficult of the questions they faced were those involving the rights of the freed slaves.

THE PROBLEM

The problems of Reconstruction were numerous. The most obvious, and easiest, problem was the physical rebuilding of shelled cities and ruined railroads. Harder to reconstruct was the defeated section's economic life. The South's industry was at a standstill; much of its farming land was lying idle. Its labor system was destroyed, investment capital was lacking, the savings of many people were wiped out by the collapse of Confederate currency and bonds. Beneath every other problem lay that of a new relation between the South's two races. All that was clear about the country's 4,500,000 blacks was that none of them remained a slave. Some 286,000 were Union soldiers; a few were settled on confiscated plantations in the Sea Islands off the Carolinas; and many were simply wandering, drifting from Union army camps to southern cities with great hopes and no means of support. Nearly everybody assumed that they were to continue to work on the land. A few radicals had suggested that they would become landowners, and the Sea Islands experiment raised some hopes. White Southerners assumed that blacks would work as laborers for white landowners.

In this politically minded country, most people approached such problems in political terms. By 1865, three southern states were already reconstructed under the easy terms offered by President Lincoln, which demanded only that 10 percent of the citizens take an oath of future loyalty and recognize that slavery was ended. Once this was done, elections were held for both state governments and federal Congress. But Congress refused to admit these delegates.

9. EVENTS OF RECONSTRUCTION

National	Date	General Tendency	State
Lincoln Plan announced.	1863	**Presidential Reconstruction**	Governments set up in Louisiana, Arkansas.
Wade-Davis Plan pocket-vetoed by Lincoln.	1864		
Lee surrenders. Lincoln shot. Johnson Plan announced.	1865		Governments partly functioning in Virginia, Tennessee.
Freedmen's Bureau bill and Civil Rights bill vetoed. Fourteenth Amendment submitted to states. Congressional elections: Radical gains.	1866		All remaining states reorganized under Johnson Plan.
Reconstruction Acts. Tenure of Office Act.	1867	**Height of Radical Reconstruction**	Tennessee readmitted. Military Rule in effect.
Impeachment of Johnson. Fourteenth Amendment in effect. Grant elected.	1868		North Carolina, South Carolina, Florida, Alabama, Louisiana, Arkansas readmitted under Radical governments.
Fifteenth Amendment in effect. First Enforcement Act.	1869	**Conflict**	Conservative government restored in Tennessee.
Congressional elections: Republican majorities reduced	1870		Virginia readmitted under moderate government. Moderate government restored in North Carolina. Mississippi, Texas, Georgia readmitted under radical government.
Second and third Enforcement Acts.	1871		Conservative government restored in Georgia.
Grant reelected.	1872		
	1873		
Congressional elections: Democrats gain control of House.	1874	**Restoration of White Rule**	Conservative government restored in Arkansas, Alabama, Texas.
Civil Rights Act (Declared invalid 1883).	1875		Conservative government restored in Mississippi. Federal troops removed from Louisiana, South Carolina.
Hayes-Tilden disputed election.	1876		Conservative government restored in Florida, South Carolina, Louisiana.
	1877		

To settle this difficulty, Americans turned to the Constitution. In this unheard-of situation, however, it offered little help. What was the status of a sovereign state that had seceded and been forced to return to the Union? Was it still a state, since secession had been illegal, or was it merely a conquered province? Who could decide: Congress or the president? The president was commander-in-chief of the armed forces and had the power to pardon. But Congress had the right to admit new states, to make rules for territories, and to judge the qualifications of its own members. Long before Lincoln's death, the two branches of government had been at loggerheads over these issues.

More important in the long run than even the constitutional question was the state of mind of three main groups: the ex-slaves, the defeated southern whites, and the citizens of the victorious North. Though able black leaders shortly appeared, most of the ex-slaves were not only illiterate but completely inexperienced, both in politics and in dealing with such economic institutions as wages and rent. Many pathetic stories are told about the strange hopes and fears of these displaced people. Yet the basic desires of the freed blacks were clear and by no means foolish. What they wanted was real freedom, and the signs of that freedom were the right to move around, access to education, and ownership of land.

Right after the war, according to northern travelers in the South, shock rather than bitterness was the most common state of mind among southern whites. With their institutions destroyed, what was to become of them? Most pressing of all, without slavery, how was the cotton going to be picked and planted? At first, many looked northward for their answers.

The third and largest group, the victorious northern whites, were by no means a united body. Nearly half were Democrats. Only a few Democrats had been willing to accept the breakup of the Union, but many had sharply criticized the conduct of the war and had opposed emancipation. The sole purpose of the fighting, the party's leaders had insisted, should have been the restoration of "the Union as it was." In the 1864 elections, the Democrats had lost some ground, yet they still mustered a formidable 45 percent of the votes.

Not even the Republicans were sure of what they wanted. The group called "Radicals" agreed that Lincoln had been too weak and lenient, but they agreed on little else. Republicans were also divided on such matters as the tariff and finance, and few had thought through the future status of the Negro.

Two paradoxes made constructive action inordinately difficult. First, slavery had been abolished and the ex-slaves armed by a nation that believed overwhelmingly in the inferiority of the Negro race. This belief, now discredited, was centuries old and almost universal. Even among the abolitionists, only a few had accepted the Negro as an intellectual and political equal. Only part of New England permitted Negroes to vote. Starting with Connecticut, Wisconsin, and Minnesota in 1865, one northern state after another continued to deny Negro suffrage in the years after the war.

Second, during Reconstruction the government had to undertake a program of drastic, even revolutionary measures. Yet nearly all nineteenth-century Americans had been taught that government action should be sharply limited. This had been said by

Jefferson, Jackson, and Lincoln. Schools and colleges taught as gospel truth the max-ims of *laissez-faire* political economy.

The choice faced by the North, in its simplest terms, was the choice offered to every victor: occupation or conciliation. All the feelings of nineteenth-century Ameri-cans were against continued military occupation. Somehow, most agreed, the South must be forced to see its errors and govern itself—according to northern ideas.

Yet to whom in the South could government be confided? To the ex-rebels who were, many Northerners believed, still rebels at heart? To the ex-slaves whom most Northerners regarded as members of an inferior race? Even if they were given the vote, the freedmen, inexperienced in politics and a minority in all but two states, could hardly govern alone. They would have to have the support either of a substantial number of southern whites or of sufficient occupying forces. With or without Negro suffrage, the same choice existed: conciliation or occupation.

PRESIDENTIAL RECONSTRUCTION

The first alternative, conciliation, was attempted under the authority of Presidents Lincoln and Johnson and is often referred to as Presidential Reconstruction. It is hard to tell how Lincoln's "10 percent plan" might have worked if it had been continued. As we have seen, this was already sharply challenged by Congress, and Lincoln himself had said it was only one of many possible devices. The Wade-Davis Bill, Congress's more drastic substitute, had been left unsigned by Lincoln.

Like Lincoln, Andrew Johnson embodied the log-cabin presidential tradition. He had been a tailor by trade and had learned to read only as an adult. A resident of eastern Tennessee, where slaves were few, and a former Jacksonian Democrat, he had been an outspoken opponent of secession and a lifelong enemy of the southern planter class. Yet he had no real commitment either to Negro rights or to the Republican party. Like Lincoln, Johnson was honest and able, but he proved completely lacking in Lincoln's gifts of patience and political realism.

Like his predecessor, Johnson started by offering amnesty to those who would sign an oath of allegiance. Exceptions to the offer, more numerous than in Lincoln's plan, included important Confederate officials and Confederates who owned more than $20,000 worth of property. This seemed to exclude from participation the leaders of the Old South. Those who had taken the oath were to vote for a constitu-tional convention in each state. The conventions were to repeal the state's ordinance of secession, abolish slavery, and repudiate the Confederate and state debts. Then the state could elect a new government and send representatives to Washington. By the end of 1865, all the states had actually passed through either the Lincoln or the Johnson version of this process, and in conservative and southern eyes, Reconstruc-tion was over.

Government was functioning in the South, and the people, black and white, were getting back to work. Yet much in the new order was deeply disturbing to northern opinion. Some of the reconstituted states elected prominent Confederates to state and federal office. Most enacted special "Black Codes" to regulate the conduct of freed Negroes. To former slaveholders, such rules seemed natural and necessary; to freed blacks and many northerners, they looked like the next thing to slavery. In some states, blacks were not allowed to assemble; in others, the labor of petty offenders could be sold at auction; in some, Negro children could be apprenticed to white men without the consent of indigent parents. Most of the codes provided for strictly enforced compulsory labor contracts. In South Carolina, the code spelled out the intent of such contracts: blacks were to engage only in agricultural labor or domestic service.

In 1865–1866, northern opinion was further affronted by outbreaks of racial violence in the South. Responsibility for race riots was of course disputed, but the victims nearly always turned out to be blacks or pro-black whites. To Radical Republicans, it seemed that life was not safe in the South for those who really supported a change in southern society, and this change they were determined to bring about. To some this was a moral duty; to others a political necessity.

In the spring of 1866, Congress extended the life of the Freedmen's Bureau, a wartime organization designed to supervise and aid the ex-slaves, and passed a Civil Rights Act prohibiting many kinds of discriminatory legislation. It also refused to admit the representatives of the new southern state governments. Clearly, the president could not hope to carry forward his policy without regard for such formidable opposition. Yet Johnson, like other presidents in other battles with Congress, seemed to grow steadily more stubborn. He blamed the race riots on Radicals, minimized southern denial of Negro rights, and pardoned thousands of southern leaders. In the spring of 1866, he vetoed both the Freedmen's Bureau bill and the Civil Rights Act.

By this time, Johnson had gained the support of Democrats and solidified the Republican party against him. In the fall, he toured the country, violently denouncing his opponents as traitors. In the November Congressional election, the voters gave their answer. The Republicans won two-thirds of both Houses and the Radical leadership moved into key positions of power. A new phase of Reconstruction was clearly at hand.

CONGRESSIONAL RECONSTRUCTION

During Congressional, or Radical, Reconstruction, the second alternative, military occupation, was finally given a trial. The purpose behind it was still reform; the South was to be occupied only until her society could be altered and a new electorate formed. This meant attempting something like social revolution, and it was clear that in this revolution blacks must play a major part.

The Freedmen's Bureau and Civil Rights bills, both repassed over the president's veto, established that the former slaves were to be protected by the federal government during a transitional state. They were not, however, to be given land; in this property-loving age only a few suggested such an extreme measure and local experiments in this direction were abandoned.

Federal protection for blacks already implied a change in the relation of the federal government and the states, and this change was spelled out in the Fourteenth Amendment submitted to Congress in June, 1866. The first section of this amendment provided that no state should infringe any citizen's "privileges or immunities," nor "deprive any person of life, liberty or property, without due process of law," nor deny to any person "the equal protection of the laws." Thus individuals were guaranteed by the *Union* against oppression by the *states.* (The Bill of Rights already protected individual liberties from the federal government.)

The second section of the amendment edged toward Negro suffrage. It provided that if a state denied the vote to any of its male inhabitants, its representation should be reduced accordingly. The third and fourth sections barred leading Confederates from Congress or federal office and forbade states to repudiate the federal or recognize the rebel debt. Obviously this all important amendment could not be ratified by three-fourths of the states without some southern support. As President Johnson urged southern states not to ratify, Congress moved on to still more drastic reconstruction action.

The First Reconstruction Act, passed in March, 1867, divided the South into five military districts, wiping out the existing state governments. Under military supervision, each state was to elect a constitutional convention. Delegates to these conventions would be chosen by vote of the whole male population, including the freed Negroes and excluding leading Confederates. Each constitution was to be ratified by a majority of the state's new electorate and approved by Congress. When the new state had ratified the Fourteenth Amendment, its representatives might be admitted to Congress. This act was clarified and tightened by further legislation, and in 1870 Radical Reconstruction was completed by the ratification of the Fifteenth Amendment, once and for all forbidding suffrage discrimination on the basis of "race, color, or previous condition of servitude."

All these actions were taken against the firm opposition of the president and in the face of the nearly certain disapproval of the Supreme Court. To safeguard Radical Reconstruction, Congress made the most drastic attempt in American history to establish the dominance of a single branch of government.

To disarm the court, Congress simply withdrew certain kinds of cases from Supreme Court jurisdiction, and the court prudently refrained from challenging this action. Johnson, however, could be rendered powerless only by impeachment and conviction for "treason, bribery, or other high crimes or misdemeanors." Failing after much effort to find serious evidence of "crimes," Congress saw its best chance for impeachment in the Tenure of Office Act passed in 1867. This act, of dubious constitutionality, forbade the removal of cabinet officers without congressional sanction. Johnson challenged it by trying to remove Secretary of War Edwin Stanton, an appointee of Lincoln. In the spring of 1868, the House of Representatives impeached the president in a long, confused, and shaky set of charges. Anger ran so high that his accusers failed by only one vote to secure the two-thirds of the Senate necessary for conviction.

RADICAL RECONSTRUCTION IN ACTION

How did the Radical program actually work in the South? To this crucial question, historians have developed two opposite answers. A generation ago, most accounts said that Radical Reconstruction had been a dreadful mistake. Southern state governments, dominated by ignorant blacks, self-seeking carpetbaggers, and despicable southern "scalawags" ("collaborationists" would be the modern term), had imposed a reign of terror, extravagance, and corruption. Finally, the South, supported by a revival of decent moderate opinion in the North, had risen in revolt and thrown off the yoke.

More recently this version has been challenged by an opposite one. According to this second, neo-Radical view, Radical Reconstruction was a long overdue attempt to bring justice and progress to the South. It was sustained in the South not only by federal forces but by determined black support. Its defeat was brought about by brutal terrorism and northern betrayal.

The truth about this abortive social revolution is various and complex. It is clear that some of the Radical governments were indeed both extravagant and blatantly corrupt. Yet extravagance and corruption were common in this period in northern states and cities. Moreover, the Radical governments scored some real accomplishments, bringing to the South broader suffrage (for whites as well as blacks), poor relief, and the beginnings of free, popular education.

Perhaps the key question to ask about Radical Reconstruction is whether it ever had a real chance of success; that is, could it have effected a permanent change in southern institutions and customs? The answer is complex. Successful Reconstruction would have demanded either prolonged northern occupation or some degree of cooperation between southern whites and blacks. For the first alternative, the northern people proved to have no enduring appetite. The second seemed more promising initially. Many southern whites did make an effort to accept the new situation (though many did not). Contrary to legend, many "scalawags" were well intentioned, just as many carpetbaggers were honest and many Negro leaders well informed and moderate. Yet any permanent alliance among these elements faced great difficulties. The cooperating southern whites were willing to accept black voting only under white leadership; the blacks demanded real political equality. Predictably, if not inevitably, the necessary coalition failed.

Violence against the Negroes and their political allies continued to break out on a larger and larger scale. At first determined to suppress the Ku Klux Klan and other terrorist organizations, Congress grew weary of the attempt. In one state after another, with differing degrees of forcible action, southern whites achieved victory at the polls. In 1877, when President Hayes withdrew the last federal troops, the cycle was complete; the South was again under the rule of native whites. At first, the new "lily-white" governments, mostly led by members of the prewar planter class, allowed blacks some token participation in politics. Then in the 1890s, governments claiming to represent poor whites came to power. Violently denouncing the alleged alliance of aristocrats and Negroes, these governments drove the southern blacks almost entirely out of politics. This was done partly by applying pressure and partly by enforcing ingenious suffrage requirements—grandfather clauses, literacy tests, and the like—against blacks and not against whites.

SOCIAL RECONSTRUCTION

Since blacks never received the "40 acres and a mule" for which they had longed in 1865, they had to work for white landowners. As money to pay them was lacking, the only possible solution was some form of tenantry. The result was the sharecrop and the crop-lien systems. Throughout the South, sharecroppers, both white and black, received their seed, tools, and staple necessities from landlords to whom they turned over a third or a half of their produce. Most, and often all, of the rest of the produce went to pay long-standing debts accumulated by the tenants at country stores or plantation commissaries with high monopoly prices and exorbitant rates of interest. The system was not slavery, and it got the crops planted and harvested. Yet the black farmer, forever in debt and unable to move, without education or political privileges, subject to white courts and terrorism, could hardly be called free. Indeed, recent research suggests that the shadow of slavery still darkened southern race relations as *peonage* (the use of laborers bound in servitude because of debt) was fairly widespread. To make matters worse, planter-class paternalism was supplanted by an increasingly virulent race hatred among whites who feared their inability to control completely their former slaves.

In the 1880s, the white-ruled South put on a spectacular drive for industry. Heavy inducements were offered to attract capital, and much was accomplished in developing steel, lumbering, tobacco, and, especially, textile industries. However, by the turn of the century, the region had barely held its own; the South's percentage of the nation's industry was about that of 1860. Even this, in a rapidly expanding economy, was a considerable achievement. But the price was heavy. In southern mill towns, disease and child labor were endemic. Most of the profits of industry were flowing out of the section. Until World War II, the South remained both poor and overwhelmingly agrarian.

Perhaps the saddest chapter in all American history is the general acceptance, in the North, of the failure of so much effort. Thirty years after the war, most people took for granted a southern system that included not only disfranchisement and rigid social segregation of the Negro but also recurrent violence. In 1892 and 1893, for example, more than 150 blacks were lynched each year, often with sadistic tortures.

How could the people who had defied the Fugitive Slave Act, fought the war, and voted for Radical Reconstruction accept this situation? For one thing, it was easy to emphasize the seamy side of Radical Reconstruction, the greed and corruption with which the process was sometimes executed. Moreover, most people were convinced that racial differences made political equality impossible. Government, according to nineteenth-century science and social science, could do very little to change customs or alter society. Thus a failure of northern resolve partly explains the failure of Reconstruction. The courts, Congress, the White House, and a popular majority all came, in time, to accept the view that white southerners knew best how to handle the race problem. It also seems likely that failure was built into the system itself. Federalism, whatever its other advantages, proved to be an imperfect instrument for the protection of black rights. As the experience of the post-World War II civil rights struggles suggests, the Fourteenth and Fifteenth amendments were often unenforceable in the face of adamant white opposition. The traditions of federalism, which required wide-ranging deference to local, state, and regional customs, seemed to deny effective enforcement of a colorblind constitution.

To the white community, however, the story had its bright side. A great Civil War had been settled without executions or confiscations, and the two sides were beginning to be reconciled. For much of the next century it was easy to forget that the black was paying most of the bill for this intersectional accord.

Responsive in its way to the drift of public opinion, the Supreme Court made its peace with the new situation. In the civil rights cases (1883), it decided that the Fourteenth Amendment did not prevent *individuals,* as opposed to states, from practicing discrimination. In *Plessy vs. Ferguson* (1896), the court held that "separate but equal" accommodations for Negroes in trains (and by implication in restaurants, hotels, and the like) did not violate their rights. Few inquired very carefully into whether accommodations were indeed equal.

The upshot, then, of the greatest struggle in American history seemed to be a tragic failure. Yet the story had not ended. The blacks had gained a few rights and a great many hopes. And neither in the North nor the South was the national conscience really at ease.

CONFLICTING HISTORICAL VIEWPOINTS

7. Was Reconstruction a Tragic Era?

Until the 1930s, historians generally agreed that Reconstruction was a period characterized by sordid motives and human depravity. It was the "Age of Hate," "The Blackout of Honest Government," "The Dreadful Decade," and "The Tragic Era." In 1939, however, Francis Butler Simkins, a distinguished southern scholar, urged his fellow historians to adopt "a more critical, creative, and tolerant attitude" toward the period. In a notable essay (Journal of Southern History, *1939*), *Simkins suggested that the traditional interpretation of Reconstruction was rooted in "the conviction that the Negro belongs to an innately inferior race."*

Until Simkins's time, most white students of Reconstruction did in fact approach their work with decidedly racist views. In the first serious history of the era, James Ford Rhodes's enormously influential History of the United States from the Compromise of 1850 *(7 vols., 1893–1906), blacks were described as "the most inferior race." Similarly, in John W. Burgess's* Reconstruction and the Constitution *(1902), blacks were characterized as inherently inferior beings incapable of "subjecting passion to reason." Although Rhodes and Burgess were sharply critical of the motives and actions of congressional Radicals, the traditional interpretation of Reconstruction is best identified with the work of William A. Dunning. A Columbia University scholar and the author of* Reconstruction, Political and Economic *(1907), Dunning and his many students uncovered a wealth of factual information about the period. But their work was seriously marred by their prosouthern and anti-Negro biases. They portrayed the postbellum scene in darkly tragic hues of unrelieved brutality, scandal, corruption, and licentiousness. According to the Dunningites, Reconstruction was not only unnecessary but harshly cruel to the prostrate South and ruthlessly exploitive of the ignorant ex-slaves.*

Black scholars—most notably W. E. B. Du Bois, author of Black Reconstruction

(1935)—vigorously disputed Dunning School conclusions. But in an age of virtually unchallenged white supremacy, few Caucasians thought to question simplistic characterizations of vindictive Radicals, venal carpetbaggers, reprobate scalawags, and barbarous darkies. A shift in the climate of racial opinion, however, ushered in a new era of Reconstruction historiography. Reflecting a growing national sensitivity to civil rights, historians since the 1930s have turned Dunning's conclusions inside out. First in a series of monographs and biographies, then later in such sweeping syntheses as John Hope Franklin's Reconstruction After the Civil War *(1961) and Kenneth Stampp's* The Era of Reconstruction *(1965), revisionists discarded racial stereotypes and viewed the postbellum period in a generally favorable light. According to these modern scholars, traditional studies grossly exaggerated not only the extent of corruption, fraud, and black rule, but even the length of Radical control. Indeed, to both Franklin and Stampp, Reconstruction was a tragic era only in that it failed to insure blacks economic, political, and social equality.*

At present the revisionists are clearly in the ascendancy. But as Stampp has written, the revisionist's "ultimate and inevitable fate is one day to have its own revisions revised."

FOR FURTHER READING

Herman Belz's *Reconstructing the Union* (1969) is a provocative study of Presidential Reconstruction. Representative traditional interpretations of Congressional Reconstruction include Walter L. Fleming's *The Sequel of Appomattox* (1919) and E. Merton Coulter's *The South During Reconstruction* (1947). H. K. Beale, in *The Critical Year* (1930), and E. L. McKitrick, in *Andrew Johnson and Reconstruction* (1960),* offer conflicting views of Lincoln's successor. La Wanda and John Cox's *Politics, Principle, and Prejudice* (1963),* David Donald's *The Politics of Reconstruction* (1965), and W. R. Brock's *An American Crisis: Congress and Reconstruction* (1963) are noteworthy revisionist works. Phillip S. Paludan's *A Covenant with Death* (1975) considers the failure of Reconstruction within a framework of law and tradition; James M. McPherson's subject is *The Abolitionist Legacy* (1975). Robert Cruden examines *The Negro in Reconstruction* (1969); and Hans L. Trefousse sympathetically analyzes *The Radical Republicans* (1969). There are numerous state studies, but among the best are: F. B. Simkins and R. H. Woody, *South Carolina During Reconstruction* (1932); Joel Williamson, *After Slavery* (1965); and V. L. Wharton, *The Negro in Mississippi, 1865–1890* (1947). James L. Roark's *Masters Without Slaves* (1977) examines planter life and thought during war and reconstruction. C. Vann Woodward's justly celebrated trilogy, *Reunion and Reaction* (1951),* *Origins of the New South* (1951),* and *The Strange Career of Jim Crow* (1955); Paul Gaston's *New South Creed* (1970); and George Tindall's *The Persistent Tradition in New South Politics* (1975) are valuable for understanding the South during the post-Reconstruction period. Stephan DeCanio, in *Agriculture in the Postbellum South* (1974), and Robert Ransom and Richard Sutch, in *One Kind of Freedom* (1977), offer strikingly different conclusions about the nature of the southern economy.

---

*Available in paperback edition.

The Triumph of American Industry
1865–1893

17

Like a vast and bloody wound, the Civil War seems to divide nineteenth-century American history into two parts. Yet America's industrial expansion, the most important development of the postwar years, was under way before the war and continued during it. This immense process would have taken place if slavery or secession had never been heard of and still would have transformed world history. American industrial growth was not unique: England had gone through a similar transformation earlier, Germany experienced an industrial transformation about the same time as the United States, and such transformations were under way before the end of the century in Japan and other countries. But American industrialization was larger in scale than that of any other country and perhaps transformed the national culture more profoundly.

"THE SECOND AMERICAN REVOLUTION"

As we have seen, America had long been exploiting her unique advantages for economic growth. Since 1815, the market revolution had been under way. Like no other country, America had within her own borders nearly all necessary raw materials, a rapidly expanding market, and a swelling labor force. By the 1850s, she also had an expanding and increasingly mechanized agriculture to feed her city workers, rich sources of capital, demonstrated inventive genius, and managerial skill. East of the Mississippi, the country already had an adequate transportation network. The American railroad system was the biggest in the world and the country's most important single industry, although American trains still ran on British rails.

Many historians have credited America's industrial spurt to the Civil War itself. Yet according to one index, *the value added by manufacturing,* (the difference between the value of raw materials before and after manufacturing), the century's largest percentage gains took place in prewar decades (see Table 10). Indeed, the view of the Civil War as a dramatic industrial watershed has been replaced by the view that

10. VALUE ADDED TO RAW MATERIALS BY MANUFACTURING IN SELECTED INDUSTRIES (1879 PRICES, IN BILLIONS OF DOLLARS)

Year	Total	Agriculture	Mining	Manufacturing	Construction
1899	11.75	3.92	0.55	6.26	1.02
1894	10.26	3.27	.39	5.48	1.12
1889	8.66	3.24	.35	4.16	.92
1884	7.30	3.00	.23	3.22	.86
1879	5.30	2.60	.15	1.96	.59
1874	4.30	1.98	.11	1.69	.52
1869	3.27	1.72	.07	1.08	.40
1859	2.69	1.49	.03	.86	.30
1854	2.32	1.32	.03	.68	.30
1849	1.66	.99	.02	.49	.16
1844	1.37	.94	.01	.29	.13
1839	1.09	.79	.01	.19	.11

Adapted from *Historical Statistics of the United States* (1960), p. 139.

economic growth occurred at a steadier long-term rate. Obviously, the war created certain immediate demands: woolen cloth for uniforms, shoes, blankets, and guns. Yet it can be argued that these necessities took productive resources away from more important endeavors. Indeed, one of America's great economic advantages in the nineteenth century was that *except* in the 1860s economic growth did not have to be shaped for military ends.

Another theory, advanced by Charles A. Beard and other historians, is that the Civil War was in reality a Second American Revolution in which industrialists, after several generations of frustrated effort, were able to capture control of the government and force it to do their will. Until the Civil War, the theory says, the southern-western agrarian majority prevailed, first in Jefferson's and then again in Jackson's time. Thus industry was unable to achieve either a sufficiently protective tariff, an adequate banking system, or (because of sectional bickering) a transcontinental railroad. But in the 1860s, the industrialists seized control of the government in a three-stage operation. First, the Republican party persuaded a part of the pivotal Midwest to support high tariffs by conceding free homesteads and other farmer-backed measures. Then, while the South was out of the Union and the agrarian majority correspondingly reduced, the representatives of industry jammed through Congress the legislation they had long wanted. Finally, through Radical Reconstruction, the South was kept out of the national councils while the industrialists' program was perfected and entrenched.

Through this daring seizure of power, American industrialists had achieved: (1)

a high protective tariff (beginning 1861); (2) a national banking system (1863) and the destruction of the state banks by punitive taxation (1865); (3) the right to import foreign laborers under contracts, signed abroad, which pledged their first year's wages for their transportation (1864; repealed 1868; practice outlawed 1884); and (4) a transcontinental railroad system lavishly supported by government land grants and loans (first legislation 1861). American industrialists were also said to acquire more complicated benefits from the system of wartime finance. Only a quarter of the costs of war were paid by taxation. The rest was handled by the sale of government bonds and issuance of *fiat money* (greenbacks). The bonds, which paid 6 and 7 percent interest, could sometimes be bought with greenbacks that sank, at their lowest, to less than half their face value. Yet the same bonds could be redeemed in gold. Thus smart investors could add 100 percent profit to the interest they had already received. Labor suffered severely from wartime inflation since wages lagged behind prices. Farmers suffered in the chronic deflation of the rest of the century. Only bankers and speculators profited throughout, the theory says, and the result of government policy was, as Hamilton had said it should be, the accumulation of capital for investment in industry.

Careful research has shown that this thesis of a Second American Revolution, carried out consciously in the interest of business and industry, is not valid. To begin with, industrialists and business people were by no means united either on the issues of the Civil War and Reconstruction or on the economic program just mentioned. The system of war finance grew in response to war emergency against the opposition of many powerful businesses. Inflation severely cut into interest on government bonds. After the war, few businesses were in favor of high tariff. Many of the politicians who demanded military rule for the South, like Thaddeus Stevens, were inflationists. The western banking community supported hard money and was generally in favor of a lenient policy toward the South. In short, the myth of an inside group, dictating economic policy in its own interests and using the slogans of war and Reconstruction to further its interests, must be discarded. In the minds of most people, including people in business, the war and Reconstruction were political and not economic struggles.

Yet it remains true, whether or not anybody planned it that way, that industry received important and unprecedented governmental support during the war, reached unprecedented heights in wartime, and continued to rise, with few interruptions, for the rest of the century. The railroads, in many ways the key to industrial expansion, were given very heavy support by the federal government and by some states. Much of this aid was in the form of the government's most plentiful asset—land.

The new banking and currency systems were, in the long run, unsatisfactory. Yet they served their wartime purpose for both government and industry. The greenback inflation helped pull the country out of depression and sparked the wartime boom. The national banking system provided a sound and uniform currency and also a steady market for government bonds, which were the basis for the new bank notes. Thus the government was provided with sufficient wartime revenue and could place with confidence its huge orders for munitions and supplies.

After the war, the needs of an expanding economy were less well met. The supply of money was often insufficient and bore no relation to the changing needs of business. The banking system was inflexible, and there was still no central authority with power to damp down booms and prevent panics. Business people, divided among themselves and often prisoners of rigid and obsolete economic theories, by no means agreed on what they wanted in the complex world of money and banking. If they had, they probably would have got it.

The triumph of industry was not a planned and masterful capture of the government, and the war itself may have had little to do with the rate of expansion. But by the 1880s, if not earlier, industrial enterprise was playing a new role in America, and contemporaries knew it. The change was partly cumulative and partly psychological. Before the war, industry had been a powerful competitor for public favor and attention. Now, its scale and achievements brought it clearly to the center of the stage. The great drama of exploiting, through private enterprise, the natural resources of a continent dominated the public imagination. For some time Congress, the Supreme Court, the press, and the pulpit gave business enterprise their unstinting support. State banks and sectional bickering about something as important as transcontinental railroads seemed memories of the distant past. So, for a time, did Jeffersonian prejudices against the growth of cities and factories.

CONDITIONS OF GROWTH

In many areas outside of politics, postwar conditions were even more favorable to industrial expansion than the conditions that had brought about the boom of the '50s. To begin with, the agricultural revolution that usually precedes and accompanies any industrial revolution continued to expand. It was becoming possible for fewer people to grow more food. Wheat is a major example. On the prairies of Illinois and Indiana, in the new and booming spring wheat belt of Minnesota and North Dakota, in the great valley of California, and, in good years, even on the dry plains of Montana, new varieties of wheat produced bigger and bigger crops. Farmers learned to use machinery on an ever-increasing scale. The harvester was followed by the twine binder and the steam thresher. Finally, on the biggest and richest farms, great combines pulled by steam engines harvested and threshed at once. Gigantic elevators stored the wheat at railheads and river ports. Some of it went from there to the new roller mills of flour-producing centers; Minneapolis alone shipped over 7 million barrels a year. Both wheat and flour were shipped abroad. American wheat became the mainstay of the British industrial population. European countries, worried about dependence on the United States, sent commissions to study American methods. Meanwhile the many expert speculators in American wheat kept an anxious eye on India, Russia, and Argentina.

Much the same story of geographical expansion, mechanization wherever possible, and entrance into an ever-widening market could be told, with important differences, of other American crops. Like Virginia tobacco in colonial times, American wheat, cotton, and cattle were part of a world economy. After 1870, farm prices in general would fall and farm problems would again become a major headache for politicians. But to those interested in increasing industrial production, more and cheaper food seemed nothing but good news.

The mineral resources necessary for industry turned out to be even more plentiful than anybody had suspected. Deposits of coal and iron, the main essentials for heavy industry, were found within transportable range in many places from the Appalachians to the Great Lakes. The center of copper production moved from Michigan to Montana and Arizona. Like the minerals, the timber of Wisconsin and the far Northwest seemed inexhaustible. The problem was not to save resources, but to multiply methods of using them ever faster.

Americans contributed more than their share to the technological advances needed by industrial society. Some crucial improvements in basic industry, like the Bessemer and open-hearth processes for steel production, were of combined European and American origin. Perhaps because of the needs of a continent-sized democracy, Americans excelled in the field of communication, producing the telephone, the typewriter, and the linotype. The problems of new cities brought further adaptations of worldwide scientific advance. By the 1890s, electric street railways were taking Americans to work, and electric lights were beginning to brighten their streets and houses. Population to operate the factories and swell the markets continued to pour in from Europe and Asia. Between 1870 and 1900, the population of the United States grew from 38,500,000 to 76,000,000. More than 12,000,000 of this increase came from immigration. Many wondered whether this flood could be absorbed, but the needs of industry for workers, plus the old American commitment to free immigration, beat back the doubters. The effect of so many newcomers on the occupational and social progress of the native-born population was mixed. Old-stock whites often found that the arrival of new workers pushed them up out of menial labor into clerical and white-collar positions. Blacks in the industrial centers, on the other hand, found that increased European immigration limited and undermined their occupational opportunities. The new immigrants themselves generally enjoyed little career mobility. Rarely organized in labor unions and often handicapped by language differences, the newcomers supplied the industrialists' demand for a cheap, stable work force.

Like people, money for investment flowed westward across the Atlantic. Most of the needed capital came, however, from American industry itself. It has been estimated that between 1869 and 1898 about 13 percent of the national income went into industrial expansion. This high figure reflects, in part, profitable and competitive innovation. In part, it reflects the energy and ability of the period's industrial capitalists, many of whom were more interested in expanding their vast and complex enterprises than in lavish living.

Nearly all conditions seemed to favor large-scale enterprise. Demand at first seemed inexhaustible. New urban populations with rising incomes needed consumer goods, and expanding agriculture and industry itself needed machines. Better transportation made it possible to concentrate on mechanization, which encouraged the growth of large operations, of bigness. In some industries, like steel, equipment became so expensive that only very big units could meet the fixed costs of production. Prices declined during the last half of the century, putting a premium on economic efficiency (sometimes, though not always, associated with large-scale production). Sharp depressions squeezed out weak competitors, underlining the disadvantages of cutthroat competition and suggesting the desirability of bringing rivals together into a single operation.

Bigness could take many forms. A great firm might seek to monopolize a single product, or a complex empire might tie together many related enterprises. (Carnegie's agglomeration, for instance, included iron and coal mines, shipping lines, steel plants, and rail factories.) Though many of the biggest firms were owned by single individuals or partnerships, the corporate form of organization was used more and more after 1875. It could draw most easily on wide sources of capital, and it could best evade regulation. When public hostility to bigness began to be a problem, "gentlemen's agreements" took the place of outright mergers, or able lawyers worked out new corporate forms like *trusts* (corporations that administer other companies and to whom the companies are legally committed) and *holding companies* (companies that hold controlling interests in the securities of a number of other companies).

One cause and result of bigness was the country's rich supply of managerial skill. No other profession, in the period, offered so much wealth and prestige, none was as attractive to ability and ambition as the management of industry, whether or not divorced from its ownership.

Except for their daring, one can find little in common among the great industrialists of the period. Some, like Carnegie, who rose from telegraph messenger to steel magnate, exemplified the traditional poor-boy-to-millionaire pattern; most, however, came from families well above the average in income and education. Some were ruthless pirates, indulging in every kind of misrepresentation and bribery, not hesitating to bring about disastrous panics in order to drive down the prices of stocks they wished to buy. Others were scrupulous Boston gentry who tolerated no associate whose moral character and probity were not impeccable. Some spent their money on Fifth Avenue palaces, baronial country estates, or Renaissance pictures. Many poured it out in unprecedented gifts for museums, libraries, and, above all, universities. A few hoarded it for future generations. But, most important, enough plowed it back into expanding production. In doing this, they were constantly assured by press and pulpit, they were benefiting the whole civilization.

THE ACHIEVEMENT

There was much reason for the widespread public admiration of the industrial accomplishment. Before the end of the century, industrial growth had: scattered factories from Michigan to Georgia; drawn workers for them from the farms and villages of the world; linked factories to mines, forests, and ports; and made the United States the greatest producer of wealth the world had ever seen.

The most spectacular accomplishment was railroad construction. The already dense network in the northeastern quarter of the country was consolidated and improved, and the wrecked southern roadbeds rebuilt. Daring engineers pushed five different railroads clear to the Pacific Coast, throwing steel bridges across the Mississippi, building tunnels and grades through the Rockies and the Sierras, crossing deserts where wood for ties and food for workers had to be brought from the East. Sometimes in regions of sparse population, the railroad lines played the role of the Virginia Company or the Ohio Company, transplanting people from the settled East to the western frontier. Everywhere in the West, the course of the railroads determined the future of the region. Towns that were bypassed faded away, while at main junctions and terminals whole new cities appeared. It is not surprising that the railroads dominated the politics of the period as they did its economy.

Steel, in midcentury a luxury product associated with fine cutlery, became the mainstay of the railroad age. Not only was it used for rails, locomotives, bridges, and cars, but also for mining machinery, oil drilling equipment, steam turbines, ships of the new navy, and girders for the first Chicago skyscrapers. By 1900, the United States produced as much steel as its next two competitors, England and Germany, combined; a year later the industry gave rise to the first billion-dollar merger. In a parallel development, oil, once a worthless by-product of the salt industry, became the nation's chief illuminant and lubricant as well as the source of the Standard Oil Trust, the Rockefeller fortune, and thereby the University of Chicago.

Change affected consumer goods as well as heavy industry. Shoe manufacture, a traditional trade of the artisan and homeworker, became dependent on highly complex machines rented from the monopolistic United Shoe Machinery Company. Chicago slaughterhouses and packing plants put the village butcher out of business. Long lines of cattle cars moved toward Chicago, refrigerator cars moved in the opposite direction, and meat millionaires built palaces on the lakefront.

Despite the large share of the new wealth that was plowed back into the industrial process, a great deal of it went to make life easier, more efficient, and more pleasant for millions of people. By the 1890s, the rapid rise of sports, the sharp increase in high school education, the flood of cheap magazines and popular novels, and even the bicycle craze (and the popular song that commemorated it forever) testified to the presence of a large, relatively leisured middle class. As for the industrial workers, their wage rates stayed about the same during the period while the cost of living dropped. Between 1865 and 1900, real wages rose by something like a half, and the average working day inched downward from 11 hours to 10. Were it not for the disastrous impact of seasonal and cyclical unemployment, one could conclude that the factory worker made important gains.

By the end of the century, the decisive stage in the process of industrialization and urbanization was completed. In the 1900 census, 40 percent of the people were counted as urban; that is, they lived in places with populations of 2,500 or more. The effects of urbanization, however, were not universal. The South and the western mountain and plain states were hardly touched by urbanization. As late as 1900, more people earned their living on farms than in factories. Yet in the regions of the Great Lakes, the Pacific Coast and the East, cities grew with astonishing speed. After 1870, streams of rural Europeans and Americans filled the nation's business and industrial centers, which grew at a pace without precedent in history. Much of this growth came in the decade of the 1880s, when the populations of more than 100 American cities doubled. By 1890 there were 26 cities with populations in excess of 100,000; by 1900 six of them had populations of over 1 million.

The principal lure was, of course, economic opportunity. But the city also promised such glamorous amenities as the incandescent light, the telephone, indoor plumbing, and trolley cars. Too often, however, the newcomers merely exchanged one form of poverty for another. Whatever its promises, the unplanned, unregulated, and haphazardly built nineteenth-century urban environment suffered painfully from growth. City landscape was scarred by slums; city poor were crowded into barrack-like wooden tenements; provisions for recreation, sanitation, fire and police protection, education, and even water supply were woefully inadequate to meet the needs of a multiplying population.

Before the 1890s, comparatively few tried to balance the costs of industrialization and urbanization against their benefits. Most Americans in these years assumed, as Jefferson had not, that factories and cities were not only good in themselves but peculiarly American. Such a change in a nation's way of life has to be paid for heavily, in one way or another, wherever it occurs—whether in Russia or England or America. Though in some ways industrialization was easier in this rich, expanding ocean-guarded republic than anywhere else, it had its costs. Later some people were to conclude that the moral, social, and psychological price of industrialization was as great as its tangible benefits.

Only in the mid-1890s, when the third of the period's racking depressions concentrated attention on the evils of the new way of life, did many Americans stop to regret the landmarks swept away, the traditional patterns destroyed, the difficult questions raised and not answered. But even then, nearly everybody knew that the gigantic process could never be stopped. In terms used by economists, the economy of the United States was now mature. In other terms, there was a lot of maturing still to come.

CONFLICTING HISTORICAL VIEWPOINTS

8. Were Industrialists Robber Barons?

During the social unrest of the late nineteenth and early twentieth centuries, the American entrepreneur was much maligned. As a class, one recent scholar has written, business people were often viewed in the populist and progressive eras as "avaricious rascals who habitually cheated and robbed investors and consumers, corrupted government, fought ruthlessly among themselves, and in general carried on predatory activities comparable to those of the robber barons of medieval Europe." Thus, the poet Walt Whitman lamented "the depravity of the business classes of our country" and *journalist Henry D. Lloyd* (Wealth Against Common-wealth, *1894*) *indicted the entire system of American capitalism for greed and graft and contempt for the common welfare. Among the severest critics of the captains of industry were such socialist writers as Gustavus Myers. In his indignant* History of Great American Fortunes *(1907), Myers portrayed post-Civil War entrepreneurs as unalloyed villains, grasping, ruthless and unscrupulous buccaneers who corrupted politics and crushed competition. Progressive scholars, although less doctrinaire, were scarcely more complimentary. While Frederick Jackson Turner carefully distin-guished western builders of new industry from eastern speculators in old enter-prises, and Charles and Mary Beard scrupulously acknowledged the creative results of business expansion, the business person nevertheless fared poorly in progressive writings. In their masterful synthesis of progressive historical interpretation,* The Rise of American Civilization *(2 vols., 1927), the Beards compared the industrialists of the Gilded Age to "military captains" and "feudal chieftains" who amassed vast per-sonal fortunes through "highly irregular and sometimes lawless methods, ruthless competition, menacing intrigues, and pitiless destruction of rivals."*

During the depression years of the 1930s, the business person's reputation sank even lower than the Dow Jones industrial averages. Capitalism, many scholars believed, was morally and fiscally bankrupt. When Matthew Josephson published his brilliant polemic, The Robber Barons, *in 1934, only a few intellectuals thought to quarrel with his epithet.*

But as the memory of the Great Depression faded so too did the concept of the robber baron. Indeed, since World War II the entrepreneur's stock in American historical writing has been decidedly bullish. In John D. Rockefeller: The Heroic Age of American Enterprise *(2 vols., 1940), the first major revisionist counterattack, Allan Nevins rehabilitated the reputation of one of the nation's most controversial indus-trialists. In this admiring study, and in a second biography of the same figure published 13 years later, Nevins conceded that Rockefeller had engaged in legally and morally questionable conduct, but he praised him nevertheless as a constructive innovator who brought order to the chaotic American industrial scene. Disputing Josephson's charges that greed was the industrialist's dominant motive, Nevins argued that post-Civil War industrial giants sought "competitive achievement, self-expression, and the imposition of their wills on a given environment." More re-cently, the works of Joseph F. Wall* (Andrew Carnegie, *1970) and Harold C. Livesay* (Andrew Carnegie and the Rise of Big Business, *1975) offer much the same kind of sympathetic conclusions about the genius of the American steel industry.*

With the notable exception of such New Left scholars as Gabriel Kolko (Rail-roads and Regulation 1877–1916, *1975), who reflect the radical anti-business tem-perament of the 1960s, most recent business historians reflect the moral relativism of these sympathetic interpretations. Writing in the World War II and Cold War eras, such entrepreneurial historians as Thomas C. Cochran and William Miller* (The Age of Enterprise, *1942), Alfred D. Chandler* (Strategy and Structure: Chapters in the History of the Industrial Enterprise, *1962), and Edward C. Kirkland* (Industry Comes of Age, *1961) have measured the industrialists by the standards of the society in which they lived and worked. While these historians clearly admire entrepreneurial genius, they have shown more interest in analyzing and describing the structure and nature of American industrialism than the moral character of the American industrialist.*

FOR FURTHER READING

Douglass C. North's nontechnical synthesis, *Growth and Welfare in the American Past* (1966), is an excellent point of departure for any study of economic development in the United States. Thomas C. Cochran's *Business in American Life* (1972) is a masterful overview by a mature scholar; and W. W. Rostow's *The Stages of Economic Growth* (1960) theorizes about the beginnings of industrialization and economic growth in America. Important histories of selected subjects include: T. C. Cochran, *Railroad Leaders, 1845–90* (1953); Peter Temin, *Iron and Steel in Nineteenth-Century America* (1964); and Lee Benson, *Merchants, Farmers, and Railroads* (1955). Arthur M. Schlesinger's *Rise of the City* (1933) is dated but still useful. More recent studies include Constance M. Green's *The Rise of Urban America* (1965) and Blake McKelvey's *The Urbanization of America* (1962). Thomas Bender's *Toward an Urban Vision* (1975) is a provocative intellectual history.

The Last West
1860–1890

18

While the United States was struggling with the tragic heritage of an old region, it was also confronting the problems of a new one. Between 1860 and 1890, with no time out for the Civil War, half the present area of the country was occupied and exploited. By 1860, settlers were fast filling up the eastern parts of Kansas and Nebraska. San Francisco and Sacramento were bustling towns, and farming was well established in the Willamette Valley of Oregon. Between these two distant borders—the Pacific settlements and the states just west of the Mississippi—lay a vast region of plains and mountains barely penetrated by European civilization.

Two things make this last and greatest West different from all earlier frontier regions. First, far more than ever before, this West was the frontier of an urban and industrial country. Second, its geography made it much less hospitable to settlers than any earlier American frontier.

PLAINS AND MOUNTAINS

From Jamestown to the Mississippi River, however hard were the conditions of frontier life, there had normally been enough rainfall for farming. Long accustomed to forest, pioneers of the last generation had encountered from northeastern Illinois to eastern Kansas rich prairies covered with tall grass and had learned to overcome their suspicion of treeless land. This was a lesson they were going to have to unlearn a little farther west.

Beyond the prairies lay the Great Plains, which begin at an invisible line of semiaridity that runs a wavering course, more or less close to the 98th meridian, from eastern North Dakota to the Texas Panhandle. Some of the area west of this line, particularly in its northeastern parts, could be profitably farmed by those who knew how. Westward toward the Rockies, however, the Plains grow steadily higher, drier, and less fertile. In 1860, nothing grew there but the short native grass, and aside from

11. WESTERN HISTORY, 1860–1895

Mining Rushes	Indian Wars	Miscellaneous Events	States (in Capitals) and Territories
		1858 Butterfield Overland Express (transcontinental stage route)	
1859 Nevada (gold and silver) Colorado (gold)		1859 Pony Express	1859 OREGON
1860–1866 Idaho (gold)			
		1861 Pacific Telegraph	1861 KANSAS, Colorado, Nevada, Dakota
1862 Arizona (gold) 1862–1864 Montana (gold)	1862 Massacre of whites, Minnesota	1862 Homestead Act	
			1863 Arizona, Idaho
	1864 Arapaho-Cheyenne War Massacre of Indians, Sand Creek, Colorado		1864 NEVADA, Montana
	1865–1867 War with Western Sioux		
		1866 Long Drive to Sedalia, Missouri	
1867 Wyoming (gold)	1867 Indian Peace Commission 1868 War on Southern Plains		1867 NEBRASKA 1868 Wyoming
		1869 Union Pacific Railroad completed	

1860

1865

1890

1865

1870

1875

1880

1885

1890

Mining
1873 Deeper portion of Comstock Lode, Nevada (richest strike ever)
1876 Black Hills, Dakota (gold)
1877 Leadville, Colorado (silver, lead)
1879 Tombstone, Arizona (silver)
1882 Butte, Montana (copper)

Wars / Indian Affairs
1871 War in Texas Panhandle
1874 Red River War
1875–1876 War in Black Hills
1877 Nez Percé uprising, Idaho
1885 Capture of Geronimo and end of Apache War
1887 Dawes Act
1889–1890 Ghost Dance, Battle of Wounded Knee

Acts / Economic
1873 Timber Culture Act
1874 Barbed wire patented
1877 Desert Land Act
1878 Timber and Stone Act
1882–1883 Santa Fe, Southern Pacific, and Northern Pacific routes completed
1885–1886 Disastrous winters, end of range cattle industry
1887 Drought and western farm crisis
1889 First Oklahoma rush
1893 Great Northern Railroad completed

Statehood
1876 COLORADO
1889 NORTH DAKOTA, SOUTH DAKOTA, MONTANA, WASHINGTON
1890 WYOMING, IDAHO

the soldiers who guarded the wagon trails at a few forts, it remained in the possession of its ancient inhabitants. These included the jackrabbit, antelope, coyote, and buffalo, all biologically adapted to live in arid country, and the Plains Indian, culturally adapted to live on the buffalo.

Beyond the Plains lay the Rockies, rich in minerals and long penetrated by fur trappers, and beyond them the intermountain plateaus, made up mostly of sage brush desert, jagged mountain ranges, and, in the Southwest, true desert dotted with cactus and mesquite. Some of the land in this forbidding province could be irrigated and used, as had been demonstrated by Spaniards on the Mexican borderlands and Mormons near the Great Salt Lake. Beyond these plateaus lay the Pacific mountain chains, first the Sierra Nevada and the Cascades, then the Coast Ranges, with rich valleys between.

The whole region had been given the bad name of the Great American Desert. Only the strongest motives could draw settlers into it. These motives were the same as those that had first drawn Europeans across the Atlantic: religious freedom (in the case of the Mormons), adventure, independence from one's neighbors, and, most common of all, desire for land and gold.

THE MINERS

Between 1859 and 1864, gold rushes occurred at scattered points in what later became the states of Nevada, Colorado, Idaho, Montana, and Arizona. One more major rush, to the Black Hills of South Dakota, took place in 1876. In each case, the boom went through the same stages. First, when a strike was reported, thousands of prospective miners—some greenhorns, some veterans of other mining booms—rushed to the spot. Within a short time merchants, gamblers, prostitutes, and plain bandits appeared to divert some of the wealth from the lucky minority. A certain amount of murder was tolerated, but claim jumping had to be prevented, and these remote communities soon worked out their own codes of mining law. Sometimes respectable citizens organized vigilante groups to bring about a semblance of rough justice. Before long, the diggings were worked out, at least as far as was possible with the picks or washing pans or sluice boxes of these first comers. Sometimes the mining towns were then abandoned, leaving only ghost towns. Sometimes a second metal would be found, and a second rush would take place, as in the cases of Colorado silver or Montana copper. Sometimes, as in Nevada in 1873, deeper digging would produce another bonanza. Often, after the raw surface metal was gone, organized exploitation with expensive machinery and deeper drilling would produce richer results. Meanwhile, the original prospectors, nearly always broke, would travel to some other likely wilderness in the United States, in Canada, in Alaska, or farther.

This haphazard but intense exploration of mineral resources doubled the world's gold supply, with important results for American political history. Silver production also increased sharply and created in a few western states a special economic interest that provided political power for more than half a century. In many cases, towns created to serve the needs of miners found other means of livelihood and survived when the mines closed. These new populations, scattered throughout the West, raised new problems, particularly those of transportation and protection against Indians.

TRANSPORTATION

The earlier Oregon migrants and California gold seekers traveled either around the Horn, across the Isthmus of Panama, or over the plains. Beginning in 1861, stage lines and wagon trains reached across the country. At the end of the 1850s, the enterprising firm of Russell, Majors and Waddell developed the spectacular pony express, which actually got letters from Independence, Missouri to San Francisco in ten days of fast relay riding. In 1861, this was displaced by a coast-to-coast telegraph line.

Meantime, the secession of the South had settled the old arguments about the route for a railway, and in 1862 work was started under heavy government subsidy. The Central Pacific climbed painfully east through the Sierra from Sacramento while the Union Pacific drove west along the wagon train route from Omaha via Cheyenne to South Pass. In 1869, while the nation celebrated, top-hatted dignitaries met at Promontory Point, Utah to watch the driving of the golden spike linking the two roads. For the next decade and a half, much of it a time of depression, the Union Pacific-Central Pacific remained the only through route from coast to coast. Then in the prosperous early 1880s, three more lines were completed: the Southern Pacific and the Santa Fe systems through the Southwest and the Northern Pacific from St. Paul to Portland. In 1893, a fourth road, the Great Northern, connected St. Paul and Seattle by a route still further north. This last road, unlike its competitors, was developed without government subsidy, chiefly by promoting the development of its region.

THE INDIAN TRAGEDY

Penetration of the plains and mountains by miners, migrants, and stage coaches had long since made Indian troubles inevitable. The long and bloody struggle for the last West is one of the least pleasant stories in American history. A peaceful solution of this conflict between an aggressive, expanding nineteenth-century civilization and a nomadic, stone-age culture dependent on vast hunting spaces was probably not possible. Yet, as in the case of Reconstruction, mistakes made a hard problem worse. Part of the fault lay with divided councils, civilian administrators squabbling with soldiers, soldiers disagreeing among themselves, and settlers arguing with eastern humanitarians. Part of the long tragedy arose from inevitable anger over traditional Indian methods of war. Yet no Indian atrocity was more grisly than such white actions as the Sand Creek massacre of 1864, when several hundred men, women, and children of a tribe trying to surrender were exterminated and their bodies mutilated by a detachment of U.S. troops.

Many Indians, from the Utes of the Great Basin and the Nez Percés of Idaho to the Modocs of northern California, fought the whites at one time or another. But the most serious opponents of frontier advance were the Sioux of the Northern Plains and the Apache of the Southwest. Divided into small, efficient war bands led by such resourceful leaders as Red Cloud and Crazy Horse, the Sioux proved remarkably adept at high-speed, mounted warfare. In position on their swift ponies, they were expert with the short bow and later with rifles, and they provided their white enemies with little more target than a heel and a hand. The Apaches, who had been fighting Mexicans for years, were equally dangerous and still more elusive in their own country of desert and rocky canyon.

The long struggle with the Plains Indians began with a Sioux massacre of whites in Minnesota in 1862. Fierce fighting with Sioux and many other tribes continued through the Civil War years and sporadically in the 1870s. The last serious Sioux war broke out in 1876 when the Dakota gold rush penetrated the Black Hills, recently guaranteed to the Indians. But as late as 1890, a messianic ghost dance ritual on the Northern Sioux reservation led to an uprising and one last tragic slaughter at Wounded Knee, South Dakota. Long before this, the Plains Indian's way of life had been destroyed with the slaughter of the buffalo. These animals, once among the most numerous in the world, were almost exterminated in the decade after 1870 by railroad hunters, sport shooters, and later by professionals catering to the eastern demand for hides. Meantime the Apache wars in the Southwest dragged on until Geronimo, the last important chief, was captured in 1885.

Ever since the Monroe administration, the government's official policy had been to move the Indians beyond the reach of the white frontier. Once not only Oklahoma but the whole plains area had been talked about as permanent Indian country. Inevitably, reservations had become smaller and more crowded with the advance of the settlers, and forced resettlement had to be supplemented with doles of beef, staples, and clothing.

As is often the case in American history, foolish and cruel policies eventually produced protest campaigns, some of them effective. As the Indian menace ebbed, eastern friends of the Indian argued with increasing effectiveness that a policy amounting to conquest and pauperization was not tolerable. The Indian, reformers argued, should be civilized and assimilated rather than maintained in primitive tribal condition. This accorded well with nineteenth-century social theory and also, at times, with the wish of western settlers to break up reservations. After a number of minor reforms, the Dawes Act of 1887 reversed Indian policy. Tribal authority and ownership of land was gradually to be extinguished, and reservation land was to be parceled out to individual Indians, each head of family receiving 160 acres. Such allotments were to be held in trust pending complete ownership after 25 years. Indians living in nontribal fashion were to become citizens. Land not so parceled out could be sold by the government to individual settlers with the proceeds of the sale going toward Indian education.

This well-intentioned statute proved disastrous to the Indians. Most of the reservation land went to white settlers. Tribal authority was destroyed, and individual Indians were often victimized by white neighbors. Some received allotments too soon; others were deprived of incentive by the waiting period. In 1934, government policy was reversed again by the Indian Reorganization Act, designed to protect what remained of tribal life.

THE OPEN RANGE

Before the Indians and buffaloes had quite vanished, the plains began to be occupied by the advance guard of the expanding American economy in the form of cattle. The range cattle industry, so much the staple of legend that the reality is hard to see, was actually a boom-and-bust episode typical of the period's economic history.

Longhorn cattle were developed in Texas, and from there the Anglo-American cowboy got his distinctive dress, his high-backed saddle, and some of his vocabulary. Feed was free on the unoccupied grassland, and the only thing lacking was a market. This was provided when railroads reached Kansas in the 1860s. Huge herds of steers could now be driven 1500 miles across the plains from Texas to Sedalia, Missouri or Abilene and Dodge City, Kansas. From there they could be shipped to packing centers. The long drive north from Texas was a dangerous and difficult business beset by Indians, angry homesteaders, diseases, drought, and the tendency of the animals themselves to panic and stampede. It is not surprising that when the herds were safely penned in the railhead towns the cowboys sometimes behaved like sailors in from a long voyage.

Texas longhorns were tough, wiry beasts, and it soon proved more profitable to drive them still farther and fatten them up on the open grasslands of western Kansas and Nebraska, the Dakotas, Wyoming, and even Montana. For a while, free grass, cheap cattle, and rising demand brought about boom conditions. Romance attracted such eastern dudes as Theodore Roosevelt, who had his fling as a rancher in South Dakota; 30 percent dividends attracted English syndicates. Soon, inevitably, even the vast plains became overcrowded. As in the mining camps, competition was regulated by semilegal codes. Cattle rancher associations divided up the government-owned unfenced range, regulated the annual roundup when new calves were separated and branded, and dealt summarily with rustlers.

By the early 1880s, two new enemies of the cattle industry appeared. The first of these was the prairie farmer advancing hopefully onto the dry plains and fencing the land. The second enemy was sheep. The sheep industry had spread from the New Mexico plateaus via the Colorado parks and Utah tablelands to the western plains. According to cattle owners, sheep cropped the range too close, destroyed turf with their hooves, and drove away by their lowly presence the superior and first-coming cattle.

The end of the open-range cattle industry came with the disastrous winters of 1885–1886 and 1886–1887 when the grass was hidden under deep snow and millions of cattle froze and starved. From this point on, the successful cattle ranchers abandoned the old wide-open ways, fenced the range, scientifically improved the herd, and put indignant cowboys to growing feed for the winter.

THE FARMERS

In the 30 years after the Civil War, more land was settled than in the whole of American history before that time. This great movement of population belonged only in part to the history of the Great Plains. Much of the new population completed the job of settling the fertile prairies. However, once the farmers solidly occupied eastern Kansas, Nebraska, and the Dakotas up to the line of semiaridity, they inevitably spilled over it into the Plains. Some tried their luck as far west as Wyoming and Montana. In many ways, the experience of these western settlers was like that of prairie farmers in the past generation. In other ways, both the new kind of country and the changing national economy made this last chapter of frontier farming different.

This was the first migration of farmers to take place since that great farmer victory, the passage of the Homestead Act of 1862. Under this law any head of family who lived on and cultivated his claim for five years could get title to 160 acres free. This amount of land seemed generous to legislators familiar with conditions farther east, but on the Great Plains, where farming cost more and was more risky, it was not enough to make a profitable venture. Later legislation made some attempt at adaptation to western realities. The Timber Culture Act of 1873 allowed a homesteader another 160 acres if the homesteader planted at least a quarter of it in trees. The Desert Land Act of 1877, lobbied through by cattle ranchers, allowed a prospective irrigator of dry lands to buy 649 acres for 25 cents an acre down. These irrigators would get title in three years on payment of the balance, provided they could prove they had irrigated a portion of the land. The Timber and Stone Act permitted the purchase of western lands not suitable for farming but valuable—sometimes very valuable—for timber or stone at the absurdly low price of $2.50 an acre.

All these laws, like many earlier American land laws, played into the hands of speculators; many of the laws invited fraud. Cattle, lumber, and land companies used their employees as false homesteaders and hired new immigrants for the same purpose. As the country was simply too big for the government to check up on everything that was happening, all but a small part of the land settled by farmers in this period was acquired not from the federal government directly but from intermediaries. Some land was acquired from land companies and some from western states that had received land under the Morrill Act for the purpose of promoting education.

The biggest of all the land sellers, however, were the railroads. The first transcontinentals and some other railroads had received enormous grants along their rights of way. Their main interest was not in revenue from direct sale of this land but in building the population in the areas they served. Thus railroads offered favorable terms, free inspection trips, agricultural information, and credit. They also advertised, and it is not surprising that the Great Plains sounded, in their promotional literature, a good deal like the Land of Canaan. Railroad agents together with state immigration bureaus and steamship line employees flooded Europe with leaflets about the low prices, phenomenal yields, and easy profits of western farming. In 1882, the peak year for this kind of migration, 105,000 Scandinavians and 250,000 Germans crossed the ocean, most of the former and many of the latter heading for western farms.

As farmers moved farther west they confronted a host of new problems. Where there were no trees, they had to spend their first winters in dugouts or houses made of thick plains sod. To keep warm, they had to burn buffalo or cattle dung, corncobs, or hay. Fencing presented a worse problem until the invention of barbed wire in 1874.

To make wells, farmers had to dig down hundreds of feet in the drier areas. To save what surface moisture there was, they had to learn to plow very deep and then harrow over the top to make a dust mulch. Finally, machines were needed to quickly harvest large areas in this region of dangerously changeable weather.

For fencing, for well machinery and windmills to pump the water, for steel or chilled-iron plows to break tough sod, for harvesters, threshers, and binders, as well as for land itself, the farmer needed credit. Fortunately or unfortunately, in the good times of the early 1880s, plenty of credit was available at high rates of interest. In the Red River Valley of Dakota as in the San Joaquin Valley of California, wheat ranches of scores of thousands of acres gave an early foretaste of industrialized agriculture. Elsewhere in the new areas, a more modest prosperity prevailed. Farmers built better houses; farming towns paved their streets and improved their schools. The price of land skyrocketed.

To many, it seemed that the Great American Desert had at last been conquered. Advances had been made in techniques of "dry farming" and in the use of new varieties of wheat that could resist drought and cold. The American farmer hoped that good times would continue indefinitely. Experts appeared who said that the climate of the plains was changing, that tree planting, irrigation, even the building of railroads and telegraphs were somehow bringing more rain.

Actually, the Great Plains were nearing the end of one of their regular cycles of relatively greater rainfall. In 1887, the first of a series of dry summers withered the crops in the fields. With this grim warning of trouble, credit stopped flowing westward and the boom collapsed. Many of those who had moved beyond the line of semiaridity hastened back in despair. Half the population of western Kansas disappeared in four years, and whole towns were deserted as Colorado mining towns had been when the ore veins ran out. This disaster, peculiar to the new region, ushered in a general agricultural depression, which in turn gave place to an overall financial collapse. And unlike other farm crises, this one could not be solved by offering new land at low prices. There was nowhere to go.

THE HERITAGE OF THE FRONTIER

In 1893, the historian Frederick Jackson Turner said that a period of American history had ended in 1890 with the disappearance of the frontier. So far, the frontier had molded American character. It had also, Turner and his followers believed, served as a safety valve for urban discontents. Without it, America would be very different.

Much of this "frontier theory" has been disputed. For instance, it has been pointed out that more government land was disposed of in the decade after 1890 than in the decade before. "Free land," moreover, had always been something of a delusion. Much had gone to speculators rather than directly to small farmers. It had always been particularly difficult for a city worker, without training, equipment, or credit, to "go west." In fact, since the Civil War at least, most people seeking to escape poverty had moved in the opposite direction, from the farm to the city.

Yet it was true, as Turner said, that the 1890 census for the first time found no

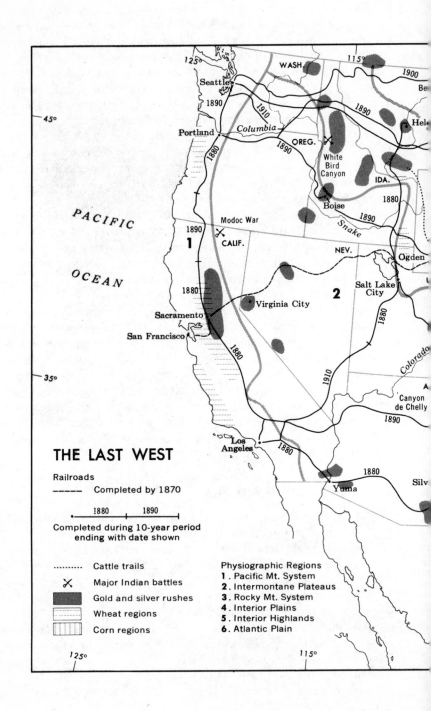

THE LAST WEST

Railroads

– – – – – Completed by 1870

|————|————|
1880   1890

Completed during 10-year period
ending with date shown

.... Cattle trails

✕ Major Indian battles

█ Gold and silver rushes

▓ Wheat regions

▦ Corn regions

Physiographic Regions
1. Pacific Mt. System
2. Intermontane Plateaus
3. Rocky Mt. System
4. Interior Plains
5. Interior Highlands
6. Atlantic Plain

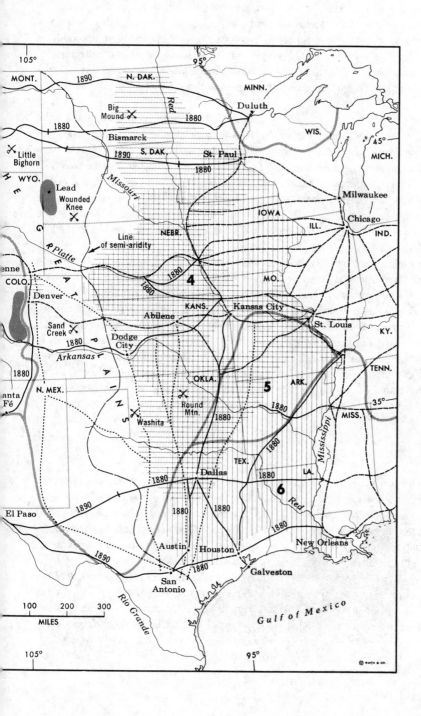

105°

MONT.
1890
N. DAK.
95°
MINN.

Big
Mound ✗
Red
1880
Duluth

1880
Bismarck
WIS.

Little
Bighorn ✗
1890
S. DAK.
St. Paul
45°
MICH.

WYO.
1880

Lead
Wounded
Knee ✗
Missouri
IOWA
Milwaukee

R Platte
NEBR.
ILL.
Chicago
IND.

Line
of semi-aridity
1880
4

COLO.
Denver
1880
MO.

Sand
Creek ✗
Abilene
KANS.
Kansas City
St. Louis
KY.

1880
Dodge
City
Arkansas

1880
OKLA.
5
ARK.
TENN.
35°

N. MEX.
Round
Mtn. ✗
1880
MISS.

anta
Fé
Washita ✗
1880
Mississippi

1880
TEX.
1880
LA.

El Paso
1890
Dallas
1880
6
Red

1880
1880
1890
1880

1890
Austin
Houston
New Orleans

San
Antonio
1880
Galveston

100   200   300
MILES
Rio Grande
Gulf of Mexico

105°
95°
© RMCN & CO.

GREAT PLAINS

continuous border beyond which the country was unsettled. It was true also that a great many people in the 1890s *felt* that a period was ending with the filling up of the West and that American problems in the future would be different and perhaps more difficult. While few historians agree with Turner that American individualism, egalitarianism, and nationalism come entirely from the West, few would deny that the American temperament owes something to both the reality and the legend of the frontier.

One obvious legacy of the West, and of this last West in particular, was a habit of violence. From vigilantes, frontier sheriffs, and cattle rancher associations, the West drew a tradition of rough justice. From mining camps and cowtowns and end-of-track railroad settlements, it drew another of just plain roughhouse. And in the twentieth century, violence sometimes hung on in still less attractive forms like the bloody labor wars of Colorado or the persistently high homicide rates of some western states. Perhaps violence was inseparable from some of the more attractive traits of the frontier legend—the devotion to individual freedom and equality we like to think of as western.

In politics, the West has shown certain consistent traits. Sometimes the western liking for innovation has made easterners think it radical. Four far-western states pioneered in women's suffrage. The Initiative and Referendum came from the West and so did that last extreme of egalitarianism, the popular recall of judicial decisions. Yet such vigorous ultraconservatives as senators McCarran of Nevada and Goldwater of Arizona are also characteristically western. Sometimes western radicalism and western conservatism are inextricably blended in the same people. What Westerners have in common, perhaps, is a fierce devotion to individual independence, a contempt for tradition, a willingness to try something new, and a delight above all in defying whatever mysterious forces are currently meant by the term "the East."

FOR FURTHER READING

R. A. Billington's *Westward Expansion* (1949) is a usable general history of the West; his *America's Frontier Heritage* (1966) offers a reappraisal of the Turner hypothesis; and his *Frederick Jackson Turner* (1973) is a magisterial biography. L. R. Hafen and C. C. Rister, in *Western America* (1941), give a detailed account of the trans-Mississippi region. Walter P. Webb's *The Great Plains* (1931)* is a fascinating and controversial interpretation of the region by a devoted native. Rodman Paul's *Mining Frontiers of the Far West, 1848–1880* (1963)* is the most scholarly overview of the subject but it does not supplant Mark Twain's *Roughing It* (1872).* J. D. W. Guice, in *The Rocky Mountain Bench* (1972), comments on the quality of frontier justice. Summaries of United States Indian policy in the period are L. B. Priest's *Uncle Sam's Stepchildren* (1942); Wilcomb E. Washburn's *Red Man's Land—White Man's Law: A Study of the Past and Present Status of the American Indian* (1971); and Francis

---

*Available in paperback edition.

Paul Prucha's *American Indian Policy in Crisis* (1976). Angie Debo's *A History of the Indians in the United States* (1970) and her *Geronimo* (1976) are both excellent; Dee Brown's *Bury My Heart at Wounded Knee* (1971) is a passionate account of the Indian wars; Stephen E. Ambrose's *Crazy Horse and Custer* (1975) is a study of the clash of cultures on the far western frontier; and Brian W. Dippie's *Custer's Last Stand* (1976) studies the anatomy of a great American myth. There are many books on the cattle kingdom, including: E. S. Osgood, *The Day of the Cattleman* (1929)*; E. E. Dale, *The Range Cattle Industry* (1930); and Louis Pelzer, *The Cattleman's Frontier* (1936). Studies by Joe B. Frantz and Julian E. Choate, Jr., *The American Cowboy* (1955); Philip Durham and Everett L. Jones, *The Negro Cowboys* (1965); and Charles W. Harris and Buck Raincy, eds., *The Cowboy* (1976) examine aspects of the much fabled western drover. The problems of the plains farmer are authoritatively discussed by F. A. Shannon in *The Farmer's Last Frontier* (1945) and effectively portrayed in the works of Hamlin Garland, especially *Main Travelled Roads* (1891).* The social history of the northern plains is discussed by Everett Dick, in *The Sod-House Frontier* (1937), and the special problems of the Scandinavian immigrant are depicted in Ole Rolvaag's *Giants in the Earth* (1927). R. M. Robbins, in *Our Landed Heritage* (1942),* surveys public land policy. Henry Nash Smith's *Virgin Land: The American West as Symbol and Myth* (1950)* is an important and highly sophisticated interpretation of the effect of the West on American thought and emotion.

12. THE INS VERSUS THE OUTS: AMERICAN POLITICS, 1868–1896

President	Presidential Vote (in thousands)		Representatives Elected			Major Tariff Legislation	Financial and Other Important Legislation	Business Conditions	
	R	D	R	D	Other				
1868 Grant R	3,013	2,707	149	63		1867 Reduction narrowly beaten.		To 1869 Moderate prosperity for agriculture. Moderate depression for industry.	1868
1870			134	104	5	Slight reductions.	1869 Resolution to pay bonds in coin. Bonds refunded at lower rates.	1869 Collapse of farm prices. 1869–1873 Moderate prosperity for industry.	1870
1872 Grant R	3,597	2,843	194	92	14	Ten percent off protected articles. Coffee, tea, free.	Most remaining internal taxes repealed. 1873 End of silver coinage. Greenback expansion vetoed.	1873 Panic.	1872
1874			109	169	14	1875 Ten percent cut restored.	1875 Resumption Act (greenbacks to be convertible 1879).	Depression →	1874

1876	**Hayes** *R*	4,037	4,284	140	*153*					**1876**
1878				130	*149*	14		Bland-Allison Act.		**1878**
								1879 Resumption (greenbacks convertible).	1879 **Recovery.**	
									Prosperity	
1880	**Garfield** *R*	4,453	4,414	*147*	135	11				**1880**
1882				118	*199*	10				**1882**
							1883 "Mongrel Tariff."	1883 Pendleton Act.		
1884	**Cleveland** *D*	4,850	4,880	140	*183*	2			**Panic and depression.**	**1884**
									1885 **Partial recovery.**	
1886				152	*169*	4				**1886**
							1887 Cleveland Tariff Message.	1887 Interstate Commerce Act.	1887 Collapse of farm prices. **Uneven prosperity**	
1888	**Harrison** *R*	5,447	5,538	*166*	159		Mills bill (reduction) passes House.			**1888**
								1889 Omnibus bill (4 western states).		
1890				88	*235*	9	McKinley Tariff (increase).	Sherman Anti-Trust Act and Sherman Silver Purchase Act.	**Minor panic.**	**1890**
1892	**Cleveland** *D*	5,183	5,555	127	*218*	11				**1892**
								1893 Repeal of Sherman Silver Purchase Act.	1893 **Major panic.**	
1894				*244*	105	7	Wilson-Gorman Tariff (slight reduction).			**1894**
									Depression	
1896	**McKinley** *R*	7,102	6,493	*204*	113	40				**1896**

The Political Parade
1868–1892

19

The politics of the generation after the Civil War is generally considered one of the least important and most sordid topics in American history. During this period, we have often been assured, the American people were concentrating on industrial development. Politics became a meaningless sideshow in which second-rate politicians made pompous speeches while special interests maneuvered for advantage behind the scenes. This picture has much truth in it, but it is not complete. Much was at stake politically, though the campaign slogans did not always reflect the real issues.

THE STAKES OF THE GAME

Political affairs were, for instance, deeply affected by the period's three depressions: the major one of 1873–1879, the minor one of the mid-1880s, and the collapse initiated by the panic of 1893. These depressions and related events, such as the fall of farm prices in 1869 and 1887, greatly influenced people's political behavior. They did not, however, produce effective governmental action. Only in the depression of the mid-1890s did demands for relief and remedy absorb political argument briefly, and even then the call for action was temporarily rejected. Throughout the period after 1868, depressions affected people mainly by motivating them to vote for the party out of power. They also influenced people's attitudes toward the two big economic arguments of the period, those over the tariff and over the currency.

According to the period's dominant economic theory, it was not part of the government's duty to interfere with the business cycle. Distress would always be remedied in the long run by the action of the invisible, all-powerful laws of political economy. The government's role in the economic sphere was simple: (1) it should raise enough money for its own modest wants by equitable means; (2) it should provide a sound currency; and (3) perhaps (there was disagreement on this point) it should seek to advance the national products in the international market. But the Civil

War had thrown these traditional economic functions way out of kilter. In its great need, the government had raised huge sums by any means available. It had placed internal taxes on everything in sight, from coal and iron to billiard tables. It had, for the first time, taxed incomes. Partly to make up for these taxes, it had increased the moderate prewar protective tariff. It had issued $450 million worth of fiat money, or greenbacks, and floated immense loans. Most people agreed that the problem was to get rid of these burdens and go back to the simple old ways. This proved harder than it sounded.

It was easy enough to remove the income tax and other internal taxes, and this was largely accomplished by 1872. It seemed obvious that the tariff came next. Many people thought that the high wartime rates constituted unfair favors to special interests and placed a heavy burden on consumers. At first, most politicians took it for granted that the rates must go down. Somehow, though, tariff reduction bills that passed one house tended to be amended piecemeal in the other and again in conference committee until they were no longer reduction bills.

Part of the difficulty lay in the nature of Congress, in which each member represented certain constituents and, consequently, very often a geographical and economic special interest. Each commodity was likely to have its own powerful advocate. It soon developed that the easiest way to compromise between two conflicting interests, such as raw wool and woolen textiles or raw sugar and refined sugar, was to do some kind of favor for each. Thus, despite many attempts, wartime rates were never substantially and permanently lowered. By 1890, the Republican party and a minority of the Democrats were openly committed to raising protection still higher, though the opposition continued to be both sizable and fervent. Certainly this issue was a real one; the rates on steel rails or woolens mattered a great deal to some people and the price of sugar to others.

A problem that accompanied the high tariff—and a strange one to modern readers—was the treasury surplus. Governmental functions were so comparatively simple that increased revenues could not easily be spent. Consequently too much of the limited supply of money accumulated in the treasury. One way to handle this problem was suggested by Grover Cleveland in 1888: lower the protective tariff. Other suggestions, however, proved more politically appealing. One could, for instance, lower the nonprotective tariff rates on articles like coffee, tea, or sugar that were not made in this country. This was done in 1872 and again in 1890. It had the advantage of reducing the income of the government only and not of private interests. And money could always be spent on veterans' pensions, river and harbor improvements, and subsidies to silver miners, railroad builders, and other powerful groups.

The other main economic argument arising from Civil War finance centered upon inflation. Right after the war, as we have seen, businesses were deeply divided on this matter and so were the still prosperous farmers. Gradually, however, as farm prices sank in the 1870s and then again in the late 1880s and 1890s, farm opinion turned toward inflation. At the same time, bankers, eastern editors, and some businesses became more and more convinced that tampering with the value of money was dishonest and invited disaster. Many economists today would agree that the country's money supply during the whole period was insufficient and inflexible. Certainly many contemporaries believed this as a result of their own bitter experiences.

Three main methods of encouraging inflation attracted widespread support. The first was the suggestion, sometimes called the Ohio Idea and incorporated in the Democratic platform in 1868, that the government bonds be paid in the fluctuating greenback currency instead of in gold. Congress turned down this suggestion decidedly in 1869, resolving to pay bondholders in "coin or its equivalent." It proved possible, however, to refund the bonds at lower than original rates of interest.

The next method of encouraging inflation centered upon the greenbacks, toward which there were different attitudes. One group said that more of the "money of the people" should be issued to relieve financial tightness. Another said that the existing greenbacks should be retired as fast as possible. A third, the group that won the argument, said that existing greenbacks should remain in circulation but no more should be issued. In 1875, Congress resolved that $300 million in greenbacks should be left in circulation, but that on January 1, 1879, greenbacks should be made redeemable in gold. Despite a rise, during the depression of the late 1870s, of angry demands for more greenbacks, this policy was carried out on time. In the good times of the early 1880s, agitation against this accomplished fact gradually declined.

The third inflation proposal to get a big following was the demand for "free" coinage of silver. Traditionally, gold and silver had been the basis of American money, and since 1834 the official ratio between the value of the two metals had been sixteen to one. Since this undervalued silver in terms of world prices, people had hoarded the silver dollars, which gradually disappeared. In 1873, the coinage of silver was quietly ended. In the decade after this, however, the huge silver strikes of the Far West greatly increased the supply of silver. If the silver dollar were to be coined at the old ratio, it would be the cheaper, and therefore the dominant, coin. This would expand the currency and also help the silver-mining interests, strategically located in under-populated western states and therefore disproportionately strong in the Senate.

The gold standard, the money of imperial Britain and of international bankers, was blamed for all the farmer's troubles. Pressure to go back to free coinage of silver at sixteen to one became almost irresistible, and twice Congress was forced to make a half-hearted concession to the silver forces. In 1878, the Bland-Allison Act directed the Treasury to purchase $2–4 million worth of silver bullion a month at market prices and to coin it into dollars. In 1890, the Sherman Silver Purchase Act required the purchase of the whole output of the silver mines and the issuance thereon of treasury notes. However, by action of the Secretary of the Treasury, these notes, like the silver dollars coined under the previous legislation, remained convertible into gold on demand; thus the gold standard was still intact.

Aside from the tariff and money, the main recurrent issue was political reform. From the late 1870s on, it became painfully clear that the government did not, as standard theory said it should, stay out of economic competition. Its favors in terms of tariffs and tax remissions and subsidies were bought by influence and even money. Some members of the well-established eastern middle class became deeply aroused on moral grounds. Perhaps they were alarmed also by the power of the new rich, who did not share their own traditions of public service. In any case, these essentially conservative reformers, Republican by normal allegiance but independent by conviction, became a surprisingly powerful influence. As parties were evenly balanced, professional politicians might hate the reforming "mugwumps" but could not ignore them.

The chief proposal of these reformers was the development of a federal civil service. This would end bribery and corruption, take the power of appointment away from unscrupulous politicians, and perhaps create a class of devoted, impartial public servants like those said to exist in England and Germany.

"Snivel service," as the indignant professional politicians called the movement, never achieved its ideal of completely just, impartial administration. It did, however, make it harder to get away with the kind of outright fraud and theft that had become common in the Grant administration. Some of the most powerful politicians of the day were kept out of the presidency because their records were not pure enough to satisfy the reform element. And after many frustrations, the civil service movement did finally secure, in 1883, the passage of the Pendleton Act. Under this, certain federal offices were filled by competitive examination. Since that time, presidents have frequently added to the number of offices under civil service, especially when the opposing party has been about to come to power. The increase of federal employees has, however, prevented reform from destroying traditional political methods.

Tariff, money, and reform were the most important of the obvious political issues, and, underlying these, business depressions played a big part in politics. On the surface, however, campaigns were fought over whatever false issue lent itself best to emotional slogans, torchlight parades, and bitter hatreds more or less forgotten between elections. The first of these false issues, sadly enough, was Reconstruction— a real and tragic problem subordinated to the political battle. While people lost interest in the fate of the southern Negro, Republican politicians "waved the bloody shirt," blaming their opponents for all the horrors of war. Conversely, southerners and Democrats dwelt on the horrors of Negro rule.

After attacks on rebels, blacks, and carpetbaggers began to pall, there were always Catholics, immigrants, and foreigners in general. One big section of the population could be counted on to respond to fear of the Pope, and another always cheered an attack on Great Britain. Finally, the war records, drinking habits, appearance, and marital life of leading candidates could be attacked.

THE RULES AND THE PLAYERS

Part of the explanation of the character of post-Civil War politics lies in two great political facts: the overwhelming power of Congress and the even division between the two great parties. In Reconstruction, Congress had broken the power of the executive. Real power was centered in the Senate. Powerful and arrogant, some leading senators had built nearly unbeatable personal political machines in their home states. Appointed at their behest, both state and federal officeholders could be assessed for campaign contributions. When this was theoretically outlawed by the Pendleton Act, local business interests could still be heavily tapped. Thus the right kind of governors and members of Congress would be elected, and a subservient legislature would send the real ruler of the state back again and again to the Senate. With the presidency weakened, there was no powerful advocate for general national needs, and politics had to be carried on by *logrolling*, that is, by the trading of one particular favor for another.

The Civil War and Reconstruction demoralized the Democratic party but by no means destroyed it. Though the Republicans held the presidency during most of the period, the Democrats actually won a popular plurality more often and controlled the lower house more than half the time. National elections often depended on a few thousand well-distributed votes.

Since no single interest group commanded a majority, each party had to appeal to many elements. The Republicans could count on the Union veterans and the blacks, when and where they could vote. Those business people who favored the high protective tariff voted Republican and so, usually, did believers in the gold standard (though many western Republicans were inflationists). In good times, midwestern farmers could be counted on for Republican votes. To a large group of respectable middle-class Protestants, it was unthinkable to vote Democratic. The clergyman who said in 1884 that the Democrats were the party of "Rum, Romanism, and Rebellion" went too far and may have lost the election for his candidate, but he voiced a stereotype many took for granted.

After Reconstruction, the Democrats started with the Solid South. Most immigrants in the coastal cities, neglected by Anglo-Saxon Republicans and helped by efficient Democratic bosses, were also safely Democratic. Western farmers and much of labor tended to vote Democratic when times were bad. Thus the Democrats were potentially a party of moderate protest, of agitation for low tariffs, and of cheap money. Yet in the East and Midwest as well as the South, some of the party leaders were ultrarespectable lawyers and business executives. This kind of conservative Democrat, often interested in foreign trade, might favor a low tariff but oppose any other kind of change as vigorously as any Republican.

Thus each party was divided. The Republican factions were three. The "Stalwarts" were all-out believers in party regularity and the bloody shirt. At the opposite extreme were the many Republican reformers. Between these two were the "Half-Breeds," much like the Stalwarts but less blatant. The Democrats included Bourbon reactionaries and near radicals. In presidential years, therefore, each party tended to select a colorless compromise candidate and write a meaningless platform. Precisely because it was necessary to play down divisive issues, it was necessary to play up personalities, scandals, and party regularity. In crucial states in tight years, even bribery and violence were not rare.

Did the system work well? The country and its industry expanded; the presidents and some other politicians were honest and reasonably able people. Party discipline, growing stronger through this period, got the government's essential business done and usually kept the most divisive issues out of politics. Interest groups were able to influence government but seldom dominated it altogether.

The system made for stability rather than innovation. In relatively peaceful times, it satisfied most people; when discontent raised its head, political habits had to change.

THE GRANT ERA

When Grant was elected in 1868, many people expected a dignified, masterly administration in the Washington tradition. Naturally, the chief national hero was flattered by politicians and big business. Equally naturally, Grant, who before the war had had little interest in politics and no experience of success, enjoyed the flattery. Originally inclined toward a lenient Reconstruction policy, he was skillfully maneuvered by the Radicals into their camp. His appointments dismayed his admirers. Though they included real leaders like Hamilton Fish, the New York aristocrat who became Secretary of State, they also included routine politicians, incompetents, seedy relatives of the Grants, military men out of jobs, and plain crooks. Grant's own honesty made his political naiveté all the more tragic.

In financial matters Grant was moderately conservative, vetoing a measure to increase the greenbacks but battling the Supreme Court to defend the validity of those in circulation. Secretary Fish handled foreign affairs with surprising effectiveness. In 1871, the difficult issues arising out of England's wartime friendliness to the Confederacy were sensibly settled by arbitration. To placate reformers, a Civil Service commission was set up, but it was not allowed to interfere with serious politics.

By 1872, the reformers were tired of Radical Reconstruction, irritated by the failure of tariff reduction, and disgusted by the administration's moral laxity. Determined to block Grant's reelection, they held a separate Liberal Republican convention and nominated for the presidency the veteran reformer and crusading editor Horace Greeley. Hoping to make a "new departure" and end the constant attacks on their patriotism, the Democrats nominated Greeley also. As a former Whig, Republican, and abolitionist, Greeley was a strange Democratic candidate. Vulnerable to ridicule for his many and sometimes contradictory causes, somehow a relic of the prewar past, Greeley was disastrously beaten.

With Grant reelected and reformers discredited, the way seemed clear for Stalwart domination. However, the Democrats captured the House of Representatives in the depression year 1874 and used their victory to investigate the administration. A sinister pattern was seen to repeat itself in one department after another: the purchase of political favors for money. Corruption of this sort touched great causes like the building of the Union Pacific; it honeycombed the Indian Service, the Freedmen's Bureau, and the collection of internal revenue; it touched ambassadors, cabinet members, and even the president's private secretary. In the face of investigation, the hero of Appomattox realized that something was the matter and apologized on the grounds of his own political inexperience.

THE DISPUTED ELECTION

In 1876, Republican regimes remained in power in only three southern states. With the South back on the Democratic side and many northerners hostile to the administration, it seemed likely that the Democrats would return to power. To prevent this unthinkable disaster, the Republicans nominated the honest and able, though rather uninspiring, Rutherford B. Hayes of Ohio. The Democrats also bid for the reformers by nominating Samuel J. Tilden, who as governor of New York had destroyed the grafting Boss Tweed ring in New York City.

Tilden won a sizable popular plurality, capturing New York and several other northern states in addition to the South. It seemed clear that he had won the election. The Republicans, however, claimed the votes of the three southern states still under carpetbagger rule: Florida, South Carolina, and Louisiana. In each of these states, the Democrats had intimidated Negroes and both parties had been guilty of other dubious practices. After a long and bitter dispute, the conflicting returns from these states were referred to an electoral commission which, acting on strictly party lines, gave the election to Hayes by one vote.

Certain Republicans had approached certain Democrats in advance to make sure this result would be accepted. The Compromise of 1877, as this has been called, somewhat resembles the prewar compromises. Like them, it was made by conservatives for the purpose of preventing trouble. Southern Democratic leaders were assured that, if they accepted Hayes's election, he would remove the troops from the remaining southern states and that the South would receive its share of railroad subsidies and similar federal favors. Conservative southern Democrats, many of them former Whigs who believed in supporting industry, had no love for the agrarian Democrats of the Northwest. The Republican conservatives, on the other hand, hoped to build up their party in the southern states. This hope did not mature, however, and by the next election, the bloody shirt was again waving in the breeze. One result of the compromise stood: the North was through intervening on behalf of the southern black. Once more white Southerners controlled the South.

THE PRESIDENTIAL SEESAW

Hayes made a serious effort to reform the federal bureaucracy, an effort that involved him in a bitter fight with the Stalwarts of his party but that did not go far enough to please the reformers. A financial conservative, he stood firm against inflation. A believer in the principle of a single presidential term, Hayes made too many enemies to be renominated even if he had changed his mind. After a stalemate between the Stalwart backers of a third term for Grant and the partisans of James G. Blaine, the oratorically gifted but somewhat tarnished "Plumed Knight" of the Half-Breeds, the nomination went to the moderately reform-minded James A. Garfield of Ohio. To placate the defeated Stalwarts, the Republicans gave the second place on the ticket to Chester A. Arthur of the New York Custom House, a perfect representative of machine politics. Garfield won a close election against General Winfield Scott Hancock and, like his predecessor, began struggling with the Stalwarts over patronage. On July 2, 1881, this promising president was shot by a crazy Stalwart office-seeker, he died on September 19.

To the surprise and dismay of some of his friends, Vice-President Arthur made a good president. Turning against his old cronies, he fought against corruption in the post office and machine politics in his own bailiwick. He backed the Pendleton Act, the first real civil service law, and even attempted to put through a thorough revision of the tariff. In this he failed, and the so-called Mongrel Tariff of 1883 was amended out of all reform meaning.

In 1884, the Half-Breeds finally pushed through the nomination of their hero, Blaine. The Democrats nominated Grover Cleveland, the stout and solid governor of New York, who had a reputation for honesty and independence. In a campaign that reached a peak of colorful scandal-mongering on both sides, Cleveland won. To the deep disgust of devoted Republicans, a number of "mugwump" reformers switched parties to support him.

To the horror of many Republicans, a Democrat was in power—for the first time since 1860. Actually, no disaster ensued; Cleveland dealt fairly effectively with the most obvious and immediate problems facing the government. One of these was the rising treasury surplus. Instead of dissipating this surplus through continually bigger pensions for veterans, a move that he courageously opposed, Cleveland insisted on tariff reduction. In 1887, using the most forthright language employed by any president since the war, he attacked the high tariff as the creator of oppressive monopolies and managed to push a tariff reform bill through the House of Representatives, though not the Senate.

The protective tariff, therefore, was the one national issue that played a big part in the campaign of 1888. The Republicans nominated the cold and correct Benjamin Harrison of Indiana, grandson of Old Tippecanoe. Since it was clear what was at stake, they were able to go farther than usual in "frying the fat," that is, wringing campaign contributions out of protected industries. Despite these and less savory tactics, Cleveland won a popular plurality; however, Harrison secured a majority of the electoral votes.

For some reason, the Harrison administration took this doubtful mandate as a green light for an extreme program along Stalwart lines. With liberal pension acts and rich pork-barrel appropriations for rivers and harbors, post offices, and the like, the new Congress launched a successful assault on the surplus in the old-fashioned manner. The administration leaders gave their cordial support to the complex and ultraprotectionist McKinley Tariff of 1890. To put this across, it was necessary to make several accommodating gestures toward the western critics of the administration. For the first time, the tariff offered protection to farm products as well as manufactures. The administration supported both the Sherman Silver Purchase Act and anti-monopoly legislation. The admission of six western states and an unsuccessful attempt to give Congress power to control southern elections completed the strategy of the administration high command.

In 1890, the Republicans were repudiated overwhelmingly in Congress, and, in

1892, Cleveland was vindicated by reelection. Despite the reappearance, however, of his corpulent and familiar figure, there were signs that the conventional pattern of politics was changing. In the heavily Democratic Congress there were several members of a new third party calling itself the People's party and demanding a whole list of radical reforms. Shortly after Cleveland's inauguration, a severe financial panic alarmed business people. This was only the beginning; the second Cleveland administration was to face a host of new problems at home and abroad. Or, more accurately, it would encounter old problems that could no longer be ignored.

FOR FURTHER READING

Matthew Josephson's *The Politicos* (1938) is dated but still fascinating, as is Herbert Agar's *The Price of Union* (1950). The best overview of the period is John A. Garraty's *The New Commonwealth, 1877–1890* (1968). H. Wayne Morgan's *From Hayes to McKinley* (1969) is an able synthesis of party politics in the gilded age; and Robert D. Marcus has offered an illuminating study of the *Grand Old Party* (1971). Daniel J. Rothman, in *Politics and Power* (1966), takes a close look at the Senate. Irwin Unger, in *The Greenback Era* (1964), skillfully relates financial controversy to political and ideological divisions. For the Grant administration, two biographies are very' helpful: William B. Hesseltine, *Ulysses S. Grant, Politician* (1935), and Allan Nevins, *Hamilton Fish: The Inner History of the Grant Administration* (1936). The disputed election is convincingly interpreted by C. Vann Woodward in *Reunion and Reaction* (1951); and both Vincent Desantis, in *Republicans Face the Southern Question* (1959), and Stanley Hirshson, in *Farewell to the Bloody Shirt* (1962), review Republican efforts to woo the white South. A full but rather uncritical account of a major figure of the period is Allan Nevins's *Grover Cleveland* (1932).

---

*Available in paperback edition.

The Ripening of Protest
1870–1896

20

In the 1890s, more than in any period before the 1930s, sharp criticism of American industrial and capitalist society broke through the bland surface of American political life. For a few years, conservative Americans were deeply alarmed by this and talked about the menace of revolution. It is hard for present-day Americans to understand the intensity of these fears. Most radical demands were for redress and not revolution; many were far from new.

One reason political feelings were so intense was that the two sides in most of the arguments did not speak each other's language. The representatives of discontent felt that they had been ignored and frustrated too long. Insistent on being heard, they often sounded more radical than they were. The conservatives, on the other hand, had long taken it for granted that serious discontent in America was impossible. When it appeared, they were deeply shocked.

DEFENDERS OF "LAISSEZ-FAIRE"

Educated Americans of the nineteenth century believed that human affairs were ruled by immutable law. The central law of political economy was that the general good would be best served by the pursuit of individual self-interest. If, under competition, there were difficulties or suffering in society, these were necessary spurs to effort. Rewards went to those who worked hard and deserved them, while poverty was almost always a punishment for vice and laziness. It was considered both foolish and immoral for the state or for any private organization to intervene in economic affairs.

These laws of political economy, said the textbooks, were the laws of God. They were also the laws of biology for those who accepted the new lessons of Darwinian evolution, which argued that human social organization was analogous to physical organisms in a free state of nature. According to the English social Darwinist Herbert Spencer and his American disciple and counterpart, William Graham Sumner of Yale

University, the unimpeded struggle for existence was the means by which the human race had reached its present high development. Interference through social action or state regulation would simply disrupt the natural processes, help the weak and unfit, injure the strong, and thereby slow the march of human progress. The argument was useful because of its obvious relevance to a business civilization and because it seemed to offer scientific confirmation of the values of competitive individualism. Supporters of *laissez-faire* often claimed that through free competition evolution took place under providential superintendence.

This doctrine of *laissez-faire* was taught by political economists, preached by clergy, and invoked by lawyers and judges. During the 1880s and 1890s, the Supreme Court gradually worked out an interpretation of the Fourteenth Amendment that made it a bastion of *laissez-faire*. The amendment prohibited states from depriving "any person of life, liberty, or property, without due process of law." "Liberty," the court said, included freedom of contract and "person" could mean a corporation. "Without due process of law" covered any sort of unreasonable or unnatural regulation (for example, regulation of hours of labor or railway rates). What was reasonable depended, of course, on the general knowledge of all educated persons; that is, on the doctrine of *laissez-faire*.

THE REVIVAL OF REFORM

Individualists by tradition, Americans were also reformers. If bad conditions existed, most people believed they could and should be changed. At first, the end of slavery and secession seemed to mean that all was well; gradually, with shocked surprise, many came to realize that this was not the case.

Some of the evils of the period, like recurrent corruption in government and fraud in business, raised no new moral problems; these things were recognizably evil and should be punished. Yet, under the new conditions, the line between legitimate competition and dishonesty was not easy to draw. Bribery was wrong, but tips to helpful public officials about likely investments and agreements to give special prices to favored insiders were borderline cases. Closely related to such problems was the old question of monopoly. Since Jackson's day or earlier, most Americans had disliked great accumulations of power. Many business persons and farmers began in the post-Civil War period to feel that great corporations were shutting the door to opportunity and endangering *laissez-faire* itself. Understandably the railroads, with their life-and-death power over shippers, drew the earliest fire. By the mid-1880s, when the Supreme Court began to strike down state regulatory laws, demand for national railroad legislation became overwhelming. In 1887, the Interstate Commerce Act forbade certain unfair practices, required that rates be both openly published and "reasonable," and set up a commission to investigate abuses and to appeal to the courts for redress.

In 1890, mounting demand for general antimonopoly legislation was met by the Sherman Anti-Trust Act. This law prohibited all contracts, combinations, or conspiracies that restrained interstate or foreign trade. Anglo-Saxon common law had long prohibited harmful restraint of trade, and many lawyers and business people believed, despite the language of the Sherman Act, that Congress did not intend to go beyond this traditional position. Argument arose as to what kinds of action were prohibited by the Sherman Act, and for the rest of the century, this statute, like the Interstate Commerce Act, remained ineffective. Both involved an interesting paradox that was to become increasingly common: government intervention to preserve *laissez-faire.*

Perhaps the biggest step in the revival of reform was the discovery of the problems of the city. Even those who believed that poverty was the fault of the poor found it impossible to ignore the epidemics that periodically spread from the slums or the fires that began in jerry-built tenements and spread to business blocks. Looking a little further, some middle-class Americans were amazed to find whole families living in single, airless, lightless rooms with unspeakable sanitation.

Many of those who did know about slum conditions were at first inclined to blame them on the slum dwellers, the new immigrants. In one of the great migrations of all history, about 14 million immigrants came to the United States in the last four decades of the century. Through the 1870s, most immigrants continued to come from northwestern Europe, particularly the British Isles, Germany, and Scandinavia. In the 1880s, however, southern and eastern Europeans started to appear in great numbers, and by the 1890s these new sources furnished the majority. Slavs from the Austro-Hungarian Empire, Italians from the poverty-stricken south, and Jews fleeing savage Russian persecution came, like American immigrants back to the Pilgrims, looking for liberty and opportunity. This was certainly in the best tradition of *laissez-faire,* and, moreover, was beneficial to expanding industry.

Many insisted that immigration, like other national problems, be left alone. Yet more and more voices were raised in favor of regulation. Some of the demand for a change in immigration policy was an expression of the ugliest forms of racial prejudice, but much came from other sources. Organized labor feared competition from destitute and hard-to-organize newcomers. Some conservatives worried about the menace to established tradition. To middle-class reformers, the new immigrants presented a perplexing picture. Often destitute, knowing no English, and disoriented by the sudden move from a familiar village to a raw metropolis, the newcomers tended naturally to stick together and to maintain their languages and customs. Equally naturally, they were easily organized for political purposes by bosses who could speak their language and attend to some of their immediate needs. Thus sections of New York and Chicago became, to middle-class Americans, as alien as Naples or Prague. Many people tended to approach the new immigrants with a curious mixture of emotions: compassion, missionary desire to uplift, fear, and resentment.

Whether demand for immigration restriction came from reformist or conservative sources or (as often) from both at once, the result was new government action in a new area. In 1882, Congress excluded Chinese laborers, a group especially disliked by organized labor. In the same year, convicts, paupers, and criminals were banned from entering the country—the list was later to include anarchists and other "undesirables." In 1885, the importation of contract labor was forbidden.

Fear of aliens, resentment of big business, and concern for the urban poor all increased sharply in periods of depression. When thousands of unemployed roamed the streets, it became harder to believe that poverty was always a punishment for vice or even that prices and production adjusted themselves automatically to social needs.

In each depression period, social violence dramatized the existence of discontent. In the railroad strikes of 1877, mobs took over and looted Pittsburgh and Baltimore until President Hayes sent troops. In 1886, a bomb thrown in the Chicago Haymarket provoked police reprisals and set off a public "anarchist scare." In 1892, the Homestead steel strike turned into a pitched battle between strikers and Pinkerton detectives. Horrified at such episodes, many shocked citizens demanded swift action to restore order and punish violence. This they got, but some went on to ask difficult questions. How could such things happen in America where everyone had an equal opportunity? What had gone wrong with the laws of free competition and inevitable progress?

Among the first flatly to challenge *laissez-faire* were certain Protestant ministers. Reacting to personal experiences of city conditions or social violence, some Christians found themselves unable to square the ethics of *laissez-faire* with the Gospel injunctions to love one's neighbor. By the early 1890s, many urban, middle-class congregations heard, to their surprise, that they should apply the law of love to labor relations and the relief of poverty. Some ministers went further than these general injunctions, urging that society be radically reconstructed according to what they considered Christian principles.

Up to this time, charitable relief had been administered through individual handouts or crowded and inadequate poorhouses. Midcentury believers in *laissez-faire* organized to secure charitable efficiency and to make sure that the unworthy poor got nothing and that nobody got enough to spoil his character. By 1890, however, a new group had appeared—the settlement workers. These men and women, of whom Jane Addams was the most famous, actually lived and worked in slum neighborhoods. Being "neighbors to the poor" tended to change their attitudes toward the causes and relief of poverty. At the same time, shocking descriptions of immigrant slums were spread by talented reporters like Jacob Riis, author of *How the Other Half Lives* (1890).

By the early 1890s, then, many middle-class Americans were finding it hard to accept altogether the theories of *laissez-faire*. On the left of this group were believers in drastic social change, like Edward Bellamy, author of the Utopian socialist novel *Looking Backward* (1888). Somewhat less radical was Henry George, perhaps the most influential American social theorist of the period. George traced all social evils to one single source: private gain from increase in land values. If this "unearned increment" were taken away from the landlord and used by society, it could be spent for social improvement. At the same time, labor and capital would be freed from an unjust burden and true individualism revived.

To the right of George were a host of academic theorists, among them Lester Frank Ward and Richard T. Ely, who denied that *laissez-faire* and unchecked competition had to be the sole laws of social evolution. A pioneer sociologist and first president of the American Sociological Society, Ward was a largely self-educated civil servant who late in life taught at Brown University. He challenged social Darwinist assumptions about the social development of the human animal with a reform Darwinism that preferred cooperation to conflict, rational choice to natural selection, purposeful intelligence to blind struggle. Although he did not deny the validity of evolutionary theory, Ward argued in *Dynamic Sociology* (1883) and *Applied Sociology* (1906) that human beings, by virtue of thought and will and through social planning and positive social action, could direct the processes of nature and alter their environment in beneficial ways. The "New School" economist Richard T. Ely, one of an emerging breed of European-educated American critics of *laissez-faire* capitalism and a founder of the American Economics Association, also embraced the agency of the state as an instrument for social progress. An unabashed meliorist, Ely was a reformer who never doubted that human beings, through government, could correct the worst ills of an urban and industrial society.

To the right of such theorists, and much more numerous, were people who had no answers to current problems and who still believed deeply in individualism but who found it harder and harder to believe that all was well.

ORGANIZED LABOR

Industrial workers did not need to be told that society was imperfect. While real wages advanced during the period, largely because of falling food prices, $1 to $1.50 a day (a common wage for unskilled labor) was hardly lavish and left absolutely no margin for illness, accident, or unemployment.

Yet would-be organizers faced great difficulties. Most managers of industry were frankly hostile to all labor unions, and large sections of the press and public shared this hostility. Frequent depressions made labor activity dangerous—there were thousands of unemployed to replace those who were fired and blacklisted. Above all, immigration meant the yearly arrival of thousands of new recruits to industry who were poor, inexperienced in the American labor market, and often willing to work for what they could get.

The first major postwar organizations attacked these problems in the idealistic spirit inherited from prewar reform movements. Up to about 1873, the most important organization was the National Labor Union, which was interested in greenback inflation and many other nonlabor causes. Not really sure of their feelings about wage systems, some of its leaders tried to start producers' cooperatives and made vague commitments to socialism. Others placed all their hopes on the eight-hour day. Its energies scattered, the NLU ceased to exist during the depression of the 1870s.

In the prosperous early 1880s, national attention was held by the Knights of Labor, an organization that had existed since 1869 but had now suddenly grown to three-quarters of a million members. Like the NLU, the organization was an industrial union interested in a host of causes including cooperatives and inflation. Though they officially disliked strikes and preferred arbitration, the loosely organized Knights found themselves involved in a series of major railroad strikes in 1884–1886. At first they scored surprising victories, but they ended by losing disastrously. Unfairly, they were associated by the alarmed public with the Haymarket bombing. In the depression of the 1890s, the organization perished. It had already failed to meet the competition of a new rival, the American Federation of Labor.

Samuel Gompers, founder of the new organization, was a cigar maker who had absorbed the craft tradition of his trade. Observing the Knights, he blamed their defeat on loose organization and political involvement. The AFL, which he founded under another name in 1881 and gave permanent structure in 1886, was organized strictly by craft (rather than by industry) and, deliberately or not, appealed mostly to skilled workers. Gompers emphasized what he called "pure and simple unionism," which meant the pursuit of higher wages, shorter hours, and union protection, including if possible the *closed shop* (restricting benefits to union members only). The proper methods by which to reach these goals were the strike and the boycott. From the government, the AFL primarily wanted protection of these methods, not ameliorative legislation. The organization did not oppose capitalism, refusing to support any overall social theory.

By adapting to existing conditions rather than fighting them, the AFL survived in the hostile world of the nineteenth century. It weathered the depression of the 1890s and by 1900 had half a million members and a limited measure of public recognition. It proved unable, however, to organize the large groups of immigrant workers in heavy industry. Many members of the labor movement, including a strong minority within the AFL itself, wanted to change the organization's nature—to add political activity to trade union methods, to abandon craft for industrial unions, and, above all, to "organize the unorganized." In the disturbed mid-1890s, this opposition got so strong that Gompers lost the leadership of the AFL for a year and only narrowly prevented the adoption of a socialist program.

THE FARMERS AND POPULISM

A basic problem of the farmers was the general decline of farm prices from 1870 to 1895. It took more and more cotton, corn, or wheat to pay the farmer's costs, including interest on debts. Part of the reason for declining prices was that vast areas of the world—Russia, Argentina, and Australia—were coming into competition with America. The farmer, however, tended to blame conditions closer to home. In the first place, the agriculturalist believed, the money supply was inadequate and inflexible. It had been wrong to retire the greenbacks, to decrease the number of bank notes in circulation, and, above all, to take silver out of the currency. Second, farmers blamed exploitation by intermediaries. Railroad and elevator rates were high and arbitrary, interest rates were going up, and the farmer was being milked by the farm implement monopoly. Protective tariffs (some farmers said) merely raised farmers' expenses without helping them.

In two regions, as we have seen, these chronic ills were augmented by local conditions. The overexpanded wheat farmers of the plains were hit by devastating droughts, and in 1887 an especially sharp price fall toppled their inflated credit structure. The South, in addition to suffering most of the ills of the West, had to bear the sharecrop and crop-lien system fastened on the section during the postwar short-age of capital. The southern farmer, moreover, suffered from the biracial system, though he did not usually recognize this. Only occasionally, and in only a few southern states, did white agrarian radicals make common cause with black farmers against railroads and landlords. More often the discontented whites blamed their troubles on their black neighbors and accused their enemies of being pro-Negro.

Farmers in the North and South often believed, as their ancestors had for centu-ries, that small farmers were by nature especially valuable and virtuous citizens, that at some time in the past things had been much better for them, and that their troubles were the result of deliberate Wall Street plots. Though conservative in many ways, farmers had an old tradition of calling on the government for help when they felt oppressed. In the late nineteenth century, their demands took two main forms: infla-tion to bring their prices up and regulation to bring their costs down. In the 1860s, the midwestern Grangers (members of the Patrons of Husbandry or Grange, an agricultural pressure group) helped secure state laws regulating railroads and elevators; some of these were invalidated in the 1880s by the Supreme Court. Farmers took part in many kinds of inflationary movements, including the greenback and silver struggles and various proposals to issue national currency on the basis of land or crops and lend it at low rates.

When acute farm crises hit at the end of the 1880s, the greatest existing farmer organizations were the two Farmers' Alliances of the North and South. In 1890, two senators and eight representatives were elected on straight Alliance tickets, in addition to a considerable number of closely sympathetic members of Congress. Encouraged, representatives of the northern and southern Alliances drew together during the next two years to form the People's party.

In their first national convention in Omaha in 1892, the Populists, as they were called, drew up a platform that summarized, in angry and dramatic language, most of the discontent of the period. It called for inflation by using legal tender notes, silver, and other methods. Railroad land grants were to be recovered, and aliens were to be forbidden land ownership. Railroads and telephone and telegraph industries were to be nationalized. In an effort to attract labor support, the platform called for the eight-hour day, immigration restriction, and the abolition of Pinkerton industrial detec-tives. Miscellaneous radical sentiment was cultivated by denunciation of land monop-oly, demand for the income tax, and a general statement that the powers of government should be extended as much as was necessary to secure the end of injustice and poverty. Finally, expressing the deep confidence in increased democracy of most American radicalism, the platform praised the *initiative* (a petition by which voters propose a law) and the *referendum* (the submission of a law to popular vote) and called for direct election of senators. Running on this platform, General James B. Weaver, the first Populist candidate for the presidency, received a million votes.

Stirred by this promising first effort, some hopeful radicals believed that the Populist movement was going to sweep to power, uniting all the diverse kinds of discontent, upsetting the two-party system as the Republicans had in 1856–1860, and driving out the monopolists and gold bugs.

CLEVELAND'S LAST STAND

Nothing could have been farther from the intentions of the man actually elected to the presidency in 1892. Grover Cleveland incarnated more completely than any politician of the period the doctrine of *laissez-faire*. When the Panic of 1893 swept banks and railroads into bankruptcy, when depression set in and unemployment mounted, he had no doubt of his duty. He must fight against the high tariff as always, but still harder against inflation. At all costs, demagogues and tamperers must be defeated to give natural forces a chance to bring recovery.

The immediate problem facing the administration was the danger of a lack of gold to meet treasury obligations. Gold had been drained away by the policies of the previous administration. The prohibitive rates of the McKinley Tariff had cut income. Outgo had been increased by political appropriations for rivers, harbors, pensions, and above all, payments for silver under the Sherman Silver Purchase Act. Cleveland put the administration's whole weight behind a drive to repeal this compromise measure. He won his objective but thereby permanently alienated the western wing of his party. As a result, he lacked the power to force tariff reduction through Congress. The Wilson-Gorman bill, thoroughly amended as usual in the Senate, brought little reduction in existing rates.

With the Silver Purchase Act repealed, the government was no longer obligated to buy the output of the silver mines, but it still had to exchange gold for the outstanding greenbacks and silver certificates. To meet the continuing gold drain, the administration resorted to selling government bonds for gold. Two issues were sold, with difficulty, on the open market. To sell a third, in February, 1895, the administration sought help in the same quarter that great corporations appealed to in time of stress. This was the international banking syndicate of Morgan, Belmont, and Rothschild. This group was accustomed to performing some of the functions carried out in other countries by central banks. It dealt with governments as equals and demanded high prices for its services. Drawing much of the necessary gold from abroad, the banking syndicate bought the entire bond issue on very profitable terms. The treasury reserve was saved for another year, at which time another public issue would become necessary.

This episode raised the pitch of popular emotion, which was already mounting fast. In the congressional elections of 1894, the Republican opposition swept Congress and the Populists increased their popular vote by 40 percent. In the same year the most serious strike of the period broke out in the model company town of Pullman, Illinois. While Pullman dividends had remained high, wages had been cut as much as 30 to 40 percent, and employees' rents had not been reduced. The desperate Pullman employees appealed for help, which they received from the American Railway Union, a new industrial union led by Eugene V. Debs. Around Chicago, ARU men started cutting Pullman cars out of trains, and the public began to fear a tie-up in its essential means of transportation.

Welcoming a showdown, the railroad General Managers' Association appealed to the administration. Cleveland's Attorney General, Richard Olney, himself a former railroad lawyer, secured an injunction (invoking among other laws the Sherman Anti-Trust Act) which forbade practically all strike activity. Under this injunction Debs went to jail. Meantime Cleveland sent federal troops to Chicago to maintain order, though the liberal governor of Illinois, John P. Altgeld, said this was unnecessary. When the troops arrived, riots did indeed break out.

Conservative fears were further aroused by unemployed "armies" that converged on Washington under the leadership of "general" Jacob Coxey and others. Actually these groups were not very large. Their intention was to demand such measures of relief as government loans to finance public work. This proposal seemed to the conservative press the height of extremism and absurdity. In Washington, Coxey was arrested for walking on the grass, and the armies peaceably melted away.

As if to complete the anger and frustration of the discontented, the Supreme Court in 1895 sustained the Debs injunction, threw out the very moderate income tax that had been attached to the Wilson-Gorman Tariff, and (in the Knight case) almost completely nullified, for the present, the Sherman Anti-Trust Act.

Still confident in his principles of *laissez-faire,* Cleveland spent much of his last two years in office fighting against a more active foreign policy. Shortly before the end of his term, he vetoed a bill requiring a literacy test for immigrants. Denounced as a traitor by western and southern Democrats, he was a hero to many eastern Republicans. Nevertheless, the Republican party looked forward to the election of 1896, expecting the president's unpopularity to give Republicans an easy return to power.

THE BATTLE OF 1896

William McKinley, nominated by the Republicans on a gold-standard, high-tariff platform, seemed the typical Republican statesman. A former governor of Ohio and a war veteran with impeccable moral principles, he was known mainly for the high tariff that bore his name. His candidacy was managed by his friend Mark Hanna, an Ohio manufacturer with great political gifts. The Democrats, meeting in Chicago, were swept off their feet by the famous "Cross-of-Gold" speech of William Jennings Bryan of Nebraska. Bryan was nominated and a platform adopted calling for free coinage of silver and a number of other reform measures.

For the first time since 1860, the parties were clearly divided on a single issue, and on that issue all the emotions of the period were focused. To one side, Bryan was a knight in armor rescuing the people. By the other, he was painted as an anarchist, an atheist, and a revolutionary. Actually Bryan reflected throughout his career the feelings of millions of Westerners, thoroughly traditional in religion and morality and by no means radical in politics. In 1896, many such solid and conventional citizens felt that they had been cheated out of their rights.

Yet when the votes were counted, the Republicans won. Bryan carried only the Solid South, the Great Plains, and the mountain West, losing the border states and the northern Mississippi Valley. There have been many explanations for this result, including a rise in farm prices just before the election and Republican pressure on factory workers. It seems to indicate, however, that the forces of discontent in 1896 were either not large enough or not united enough to win against a determined and skillful opponent. To some conservatives, McKinley's election seemed a narrow victory for sound principles, the end of a strange aberration, and a green light for prosperity. This impression was deepened when prosperity actually did return soon after the election. Discoveries in South Africa and Alaska increased the supply of gold. European crop failures and rising industrial production helped to raise the farmer's prices. For the next couple of decades, many farmers were comparatively well off. Those that were not usually sought redress through organization and bargaining rather than crusades.

In the South, similarly, normality of a sort returned. In North Carolina at the height of the Populist excitement some blacks had achieved political office. Now the frustrated agrarian radicals nearly all returned to militant segregationism, a position many of them had never left. For another two generations, Southerners stood united in defense of white supremacy.

In other respects, however, the forces of change were not as roundly defeated as it seemed. A small minority of determined radicals emerged from the Pullman strike and other defeats of the 1890s to provide articulate criticism of American society in the next generation. The Socialist party, formed in 1900, became something close to a coalition of American radicals under the leadership of Eugene V. Debs.

Few of the middle-class reformers who had been aroused by late-nineteenth-century problems returned immediately to a belief in *laissez-faire.* Though they did not agree on any overall social analysis or program, they continued to press for particular governmental actions to redress grievances. Thus the 1890s laid down the lines on which conservatives, liberals, and radicals would argue for the next half-century. In domestic controversy, and, also, as we shall see, in foreign policy, the second Cleveland administration marked both an end and a beginning.

CONFLICTING HISTORICAL VIEWPOINTS

9. Was Populism Constructive?

Until after World War II, historians were generally sympathetic to Populism. Openly critical of the values and excesses of a business civilization, such early scholars as Solon Buck (The Agrarian Crusade, 1920) and John D. Hicks (The Populist Revolt, 1931) saw much to admire in the Populist critique of industrializing America. In his enormously influential synthesis, Hicks portrayed the Populists as constructive liberal reformers in the tradition of Jefferson and Jackson. Although their programs failed and their movement disintegrated, Hicks concluded that they not only focused the nation's attention on many of its gravest problems but offered an agenda for twentieth-century reform.

Hicks's classic study remains the best point at which to begin a serious study of Populism. Comprehensive and insightful, it has never been surpassed as a general account of agrarian discontent. But during the 1950s, numerous revisionists ques-

tioned its interpretation. Disturbed by wartime fascism abroad and postwar McCarthyism at home, these scholars probed the darker side of Populism. Unlike Hicks, they fastened on its antisocial and negative rather than its constructive and positive features. In Populism, they discovered the antecedents of much that was distasteful and evil in American society. In an essay in The Radical Right *(Daniel Bell, ed., 1963), Peter Viereck, for example, found in Populism "a mania of xenophobia, Jew-baiting, intellectual-baiting, and thought-controlling lynch-spirit"; Victor Ferkiss uncovered "Populist Influences on American Fascism"* (Western Political Quarterly, *June 1957). The behavioral scientists were generally the most critical, but it was the historian Richard Hofstadter who offered the most persuasive revision of the Hicks thesis. In his Pulitzer Prize-winning* Age of Reform *(1955), this distinguished scholar acknowledged "much that is good and usable in our Populist past." Yet he noted much more that was retrograde and sinister. He faulted the benighted Populists for their chimerical remedies and romantic longings for a "lost agrarian Eden" as well as for their nativism, anti-Semitism, and paranoia—irrational obsessions that he believed foreshadowed twentieth-century authoritarianism.*

At its best, as in Hofstadter's work, revisionism presented a subtle and suggestive argument that enriched our knowledge of agrarian unrest. More often, however, Populism's critics were neither temperate nor convincing. Yet, while their conclusions said more about their fears for the present than about their understanding of the past, they did provoke a reexamination of the nature of Populism. In the 1960s, a decade of reawakened interest in radical causes, a body of widely varying studies emerged to rehabilitate the Populist image in scholarly literature. Among the first of these was C. Vann Woodward's "The Populist Heritage and the Intellectual" (American Scholar, *1959), a moderate and judicious essay that praised the southern Populists for their noble, but abortive, experiment in racial accommodation. Similarly, Walter Nugent's* The Tolerant Populists *(1963) celebrated broadminded Kansas agrarian reformers, and Norman Pollack's* The Populist Response to Industrial America *(1962) portrayed essentially humane and truly radical midwestern farmers who sought realistic solutions to the evils of industrialism. Robert F. Durden's* The Climax of Populism *(1965) denied that Populists were radical, but he absolved them of retrogressive and nativist tendencies; Michael Rogin's* The Intellectuals and McCarthy *(1967) used statistical methods to prove that Populism was not the ancestor of McCarthyism.*

The most recent celebration of Populist virtue is Lawrence Goodwyn's Democratic Promise: The Populist Moment in America *(1976). Although uncommonly passionate and tendentious, this important study has been widely hailed as the successor to Hick's* Populist Revolt, *a new standard history in its field. Praising the noble if unsuccessful effort of the Populists to build a "multisectional, black-white, urban-rural, farmer-labor coalition of democratic reform," Goodwyn viewed their movement as a valid alternative to both socialism and capitalism. Its legions were the architects of a "culture of generosity," the hopeful builders of a cooperative commonwealth, and the "last American reformers with authentic cultural credentials to solicit mass support for the idea of achieving the democratic organization of an industrialized society."*

FOR FURTHER READING

The most complete survey of the period's social thought is Sidney Fine's *Laissez-Faire and the General Welfare State* (1956), but Daniel Walker Howe's *Victorian America* (1976) is an important anthology. Daniel Aaron's *Men of Good Hope* (1951) is a series of essays on reformers. H. F. May, in *Protestant Churches and Industrial America* (1949), discusses the development of Protestant social criticism; and Jacob Henry Dorn's *Washington Gladden* (1967) examines a leading social critic. Rex Burns, in *Success in America* (1976), and I. G. Wyllie, in *The Self-Made Man in America* (1954), examine the impact of change on social thought and myth. The starting place for city problems is *The Rise of the City* (1933) by A. M. Schlesinger, Sr. Leo Hershkowitz's *Tweed's New York* (1977) is a brilliant revisionist defense of a much-maligned boss. Oscar Handlin, in *The Uprooted* (1951), and Philip Taylor, in *The Distant Magnet* (1971), convey the immigrant's point of view; while Thomas Pitkin, in *Keepers of the Gate* (1975), studies the reception of immigrants at Ellis Island. John Higham, in *Strangers in the Land* (1955), analyzes native hostility to immigrants; John S. Haller, Jr., in *Outcasts from Evolution* (1971), surveys scientific racism during the period; and both Paul F. Boller, Jr., in *American Thought in Transition* (1969), and Richard Hofstadter, in *Social Darwinism in American Thought* (1944), consider the impact of evolution on the Gilded Age. Harold C. Livesay's *Samuel Gompers and Organized Labor in America* (1978) is a good brief introduction to the early history of the AFL. A crucial farm problem is examined by George H. Miller in *Railroads and the Granger Laws* (1971), while Ari and Olive Hoogenboom offer a *History of the ICC* (1976). The campaign of 1896 is examined in several of the works in the essay above, but see also Paul W. Glad's *McKinley, Bryan, and the People* (1964).* Among the many fine autobiographies, see especially those of Jane Addams, Samuel Gompers, and William Allen White. The following are a sampling of innumerable biographies: C. A. Barker, *Henry George* (1955); Clifford H. Scott, *Lester Frank Ward* (1976); Paolo E. Coletta, *William Jennings Bryan* (3 vols., 1964–1971); C. Vann Woodward, *Tom Watson* (1938), on Southern Populism; and Ray Ginger, *The Bending Cross* (1949)* on Eugene V. Debs. Robert H. Wiebe's *The Search for Order, 1877–1920* (1967) is a penetrating analysis, useful for this chapter and the four following.

---

*Available in paperback edition.

Overseas Adventure
1898-1900

21

From the Peace of Ghent in 1814 until almost the end of the nineteenth century, the American nation remained aloof from international power politics. The United States was able to do so because of a fortunate combination of circumstances: the European balance of power, British control of the high seas, and growing American *potential* for armed resistance. Very few nineteenth-century Americans realized the transitory nature of this combination. Most believed that American freedom from foreign danger was permanent and "natural." The United States, Americans believed, was the greatest nation on earth. Following the advice of the founders, the republic chose to demonstrate this greatness only by peaceful growth.

Once colonial expansion was completed, public interest in foreign affairs, where it existed at all, concentrated on four traditional concerns. The first was a general sympathy for republican and constitutional institutions and a belief that the world was moving toward free government. Second, the public felt that the United States had a special interest in the western hemisphere since the Monroe Doctrine and should increasingly claim dominance in the Caribbean. Third, Americans had a special, and highly ambivalent, relationship with England. This led to frequent clashes over such issues as the boundaries of New World British possessions, American sympathy for Canadian rebellion, use of the Newfoundland fishing grounds, and British interest in Central America. These clashes often led to violent denunciation from both sides, but all were settled peaceably, usually by British concessions made partly in the interest of commerce. The fourth concern was the desire to expand foreign trade, especially in the Far East. Partly the unrealized dream of a commercial minority, this concern led to the establishment of relations with Japan, China, and Korea, the acquisition of a few tiny Pacific islands, and the development of a protectorate in Hawaii.

THE END OF ISOLATION

Historians have often seen the Spanish-American War of 1898 as a watershed, a clear departure from the past, the point of American emergence into world politics. Yet the extent of change can be exaggerated. All four of the traditional concerns mentioned above were involved in the crisis of the 1890s. There was no sudden increase of American might; since industrialization, the United States had been a potential great power. Nor did 1898 mark a sudden, permanent shift in popular interest. After a flurry of argument over imperialism, most Americans resumed, in the early twentieth century, their habitual concentration on home affairs. However, 1898 did mark something of a change in American commitments. From this point on, both the United States and the European powers assumed that America had some interest in world crises ranging from North Africa to the Far East.

Many reasons have been given for this change. The most obvious suggestion embodies the traditional economic interpretation of imperialism: the American economy had reached maturity and therefore America, like other advanced industrial countries, needed new raw materials and foreign markets. Many historians, arguing that the growing economy still absorbed most of the nation's productive energies, would deny any connection between American expansion abroad and internal American economic development. The connection, however, was frequently made by turn-of-the-century farmers and business people who, particularly after the depression of 1893, saw a relationship between domestic prosperity and foreign markets. Although most business leaders, like most citizens, were probably anticolonialists, there was nonetheless a highly articulate and influential group of business leaders who believed that industrial overproduction and recurrent panics required secure overseas markets and sources of natural supply. Similarly, western farmers, who were themselves business people and under pressure from mounting surpluses, frequently were among the expansionists who looked to outside markets for relief. It need not follow, of course, that American foreign policy was driven exclusively or even primarily by the engine of materialism, but the role of economic considerations in the tragicomedy of American expansion cannot be easily dismissed.

A second explanation for the new departures in foreign policy was the revival and restatement of the traditional idea of America's "manifest destiny" of expansion. But the change from continental to overseas expansionism needed new justifications. One of the most common arguments of late nineteenth-century expansionists was the idea of Anglo-Saxon "racial" superiority. In the 1890s, some claimed superiority over southern blacks and new immigrants; the claim was easily extended to subject races overseas. Sometimes racism was linked to a bastard variety of Darwinism. Strong races, it was alleged, needed warlike competition to maintain their virility. Fourth, expansion was urged as a religious duty by many, among them the Reverend Josiah Strong, whose best-selling *Our Country* (1886) called for the far-flung physical expansion of American Protestantism, the religion of the future, and of the moral, democratic society that went with it. Another special variety of expansionism was the navalism preached by Captain Alfred Thayer Mahan. Mahan argued that throughout history, national greatness had depended on overseas commerce with naval might to protect it. This greatness demanded not only the building of warships but also the acquisition of overseas harbors and coaling stations.

Some of these doctrines were advocated with great force by a group of able, highly placed young men, mostly of upper-class eastern background and typified by Senator Henry Cabot Lodge of Massachusetts and by Theodore Roosevelt. Roosevelt, a rising Republican politician, had already played spectacular roles as Civil Service Commissioner and then as Police Commissioner of New York City. In 1897, McKinley appointed him Assistant Secretary of the Navy. At this time, Roosevelt, a historian of American naval and Indian fighting, wholeheartedly believed that war—almost any war—would be useful. It would unite the country, take its mind off sordid issues, and develop the manly virtues in its young men.

Another less obvious cause of the change in American policy was the actual situation in great power politics. The imperial activities of the major European nations already engaged in a scramble for territory and influences in the world's under-developed regions whetted the American appetite for expansion. Having divided up Africa, the European powers were now eyeing the last two remaining areas for expansion: the Near East, occupied by the weak Turkish Empire, and the Far East, occupied by the still weaker empire of China. Each of these was too important to fall to any single power so the leading nations uneasily supported the independence of both, watching each other and staking out spheres of economic influence.

Since the German victory over France in 1871, the European continent had been dominated by Germany and its allies while Britain ruled the seas. In the 1890s, however, this pattern was breaking up. Germany, under its ambitious young ruler Wilhelm II, challenged Britain with a program of naval expansion. Britain, worried by this new menace and sensitive about many threats to her exposed, worldwide empire, was emerging from her stately isolation and looking around for allies. A new great power, Japan, was taking a hand in Far Eastern affairs and challenging traditional Russian interests in Korea and Manchuria. Everywhere the situation was fluid and dangerous. When a country with the potential might of the United States showed an interest in world politics, the country was inevitably seen as a menace by some powers and as a potential ally by others, whatever America's own intentions.

What happened in 1898 reflected all these forces. The United States first became involved in a minor war for a quite traditional objective: political liberty in the Western Hemisphere. The theater of war shifted to the Far East, and the old dream of Oriental commerce was reawakened along with the newer arguments for imperial expansion. Against its will and without quite realizing it, the United States became involved in great power politics through Far Eastern acquisitions.

FORERUNNERS OF EXPANSION, 1867-1890

Though most people in this period were not much interested in overseas adventure, some active political leaders as well as some propagandists promoted it. Most of this early expansionist activity involved the Caribbean or the Pacific.

William H. Seward, Andrew Johnson's Secretary of State and a vigorous expansionist since prewar days, bought Alaska from the Russian Empire in 1867. He also managed to secure for the United States the tiny Pacific island of Midway but failed in his attempt to acquire Caribbean bases. In the next administration, Grant passionately sought to annex the Dominican Republic. This dream was frustrated by his conservative Secretary of State, Hamilton Fish, who also narrowly prevented the country from intervening in the bloody Ten Years' War in Cuba (1868–1878).

A peak of popular isolationism was reached in the complacent 1880s. (Yet also in this decade, the United States acquired a formidable, modern "steel navy," supported in Congress as a means of coastal defense.) Republican James G. Blaine, who served as Secretary of State under Garfield (1881) and Harrison (1889–1892), struggled to reverse the isolationist trend. In both administrations, he wrangled with Britain, first over rights to build an Isthmian canal and then over protection of the fur seal herd in the Bering Sea. Like Seward, he tried unsuccessfully to acquire Caribbean bases.

Blaine was the first to broach the idea of Pan-Americanism, or unity of the western-hemisphere republics under American leadership. In 1885, he called the first Pan-American Conference, which actually met in 1889. This conference was ineffective, and the whole Pan-American venture was damaged by Blaine's high-handed efforts to settle South American disputes. It was still more seriously impaired when the United States, in 1891, seemed to threaten war with Chile over a waterfront riot in which two American sailors were killed.

The most important of this period's ventures took place in the Pacific. American interest in the distant and primitive Samoan archipelago was mainly naval. A clash with Germany led, in 1889, to the establishment of a peculiar Anglo-German-American dominion in Samoa.

American involvement in the Hawaiian Islands was more serious. Since the beginning of the century, the islands had been visited by American traders, whalers, and missionaries (in that order). Their descendants had become prosperous sugar planters who held the actual power in a picturesque native monarchy. From 1842 on, the United States repeatedly made it clear that it would resent European attempts on Hawaiian sovereignty. A treaty of 1875 allowed Hawaiian sugar free entry into the rich American market. Yet American contract labor laws did not affect the islands, and it was possible to make use of cheap Oriental workers. This idyllic situation, known affectionately in the islands as the Old Monarchy Days, was clearly too good to last.

In 1890, the McKinley Tariff put sugar on the free list, exposing Hawaiian producers to Caribbean competition, and gave a bounty to domestic sugar producers. In January, 1893, a strong-minded Hawaiian queen made a sudden effort to put the American oligarchy out of power and restore autocracy. This gave rise to a revolution. A republic resulted that promptly requested annexation to the United States.

The next month, however, Grover Cleveland became president. A staunch defender of tradition in both foreign and domestic affairs, Cleveland disliked anything that smacked of colonialism. When a presidential commission reported that the Hawaiian revolution had been improperly aided by Americans, Cleveland withdrew the annexation treaty from the Senate. Amid loud cries of outrage from thwarted expansionists, the Hawaiian Republic was forced to wait just outside the gate, much as the Texas Republic had been a half-century earlier.

The Venezuelan Affair of 1895 showed Cleveland in another traditional role, combining the old motifs of Anglophobia, anticolonialism, and desire for American dominance of the Caribbean. For some time the British had been trying to redraw a disputed boundary line between British Guiana and Venezuela. In 1895, when Britain rejected American pressure to submit to arbitration, Secretary of State Richard Olney sent a surprising note. The British were informed that any permanent union between a European and an American state was unnatural, that the United States was "practically sovereign in this hemisphere," and that, on certain subjects defined by America, her "fiat" was law. Anglophobes began calling for war, and for once the Cleveland administration found itself almost popular.

Preoccupied with the South African crisis and concerned about its lack of friends, Britain swallowed its pride and consented to arbitrate the issue. In the long run, Britain got about what it had wanted. While the episode hardly indicated that the United States was sovereign in the whole hemisphere, it did suggest that in the existing state of world politics, American power in the Caribbean might soon come to equal American sensitivity about that area.

In the long run, the most important problem of the Cleveland administration lay still closer, in Cuba. One of the few remnants of Spain's great American empire, Cuba was chronically rebellious; yet no Spanish government could afford to let it go. After the Ten Years' War ended in 1878, Cuba entered an interlude of comparative prosperity based in large part on sugar production for the American market. Cuban prosperity was assisted by the McKinley Tariff of 1890, which put sugar on the free list, and was impaired by the Wilson-Gorman Tariff's restoration of sugar duties in 1894. In 1895, a time of depression in Cuba as in the United States, another insurrection broke out. Far too insecure to handle wisely this difficult situation, the Spanish government talked of eventual concession and embarked on immediate repression. In Cuba, guerrilla methods were met by increasingly drastic reprisals.

Then as now, it was hard for the United States to ignore what went on so close to its shores. The Cuban rebels issued propaganda, raised money, and fitted out illegal expeditions from the United States. The United States had asserted special interest in Cuba since the days of Jefferson. Moreover, the American people throughout the nineteenth century had considered themselves the special patrons of antimonarchical revolutions. Spanish atrocities and Cuban suffering, exaggerated but not altogether false, were deplored in the new, ultrasensational newspapers of Joseph Pulitzer and William Randolph Hearst. Patriotic organizations, some labor groups, some reformers, and many members of Congress began to demand American action to end Spanish oppression in Cuba. Grimly, as it hung on to the gold standard, the Cleveland administration resisted the pressure for war, meanwhile pressing Spain to grant Cuban autonomy.

McKINLEY AND CUBA

William McKinley, inaugurated in 1897, represented a more expansionist party. Yet he was sincerely devoted to peace on religious grounds, and his administration was responsive to the wishes of the business community. Many conservative business people, feeling that sound government had been narrowly rescued from Bryanism, were heartily opposed to any further crusades, such as for Cuban liberty. The administration, after giving its first attention to securing the passage of the ultraprotectionist Dingley Tariff, attempted to calm the Cuban waters. At first, the outlook seemed promising as a new ministry in Spain was making gestures toward conciliation and autonomy. Both McKinley and the American minister at Madrid were optimistic when two accidents ended the possibility of peace.

First, Cubans intercepted and gave to the American press a letter from the Spanish minister in Washington. This incautiously (and inaccurately) described McKinley as a cheap popularity seeker. Second, and far more important, the American consul at Havana, disturbed at anti-American riots by pro-Spanish loyalists, persuaded the government to send the battleship *Maine* on a "courtesy visit." On February 16, 1898, McKinley received the appalling news that the *Maine* had been blown up and sunk in Havana harbor with a loss of over 260 American lives.

While the press and Congress screamed for vengeance and denounced the president for cowardly subservience to big business, McKinley still tried to preserve peace. The Spanish, who had everything to lose by war, expressed sympathy and regret and denied (correctly, it now appears) any knowledge of the disaster. On American demand, Spain abandoned its concentration camps for Cuban civilians, a method particularly distasteful to American opinion, and expressed willingness to conclude an armistice with the rebels. At first, however, the Spanish government could not bring itself to *request* such a truce, nor would it agree to American mediation if negotiations failed. Spain tried first to secure intervention by the European powers, some of whose rulers sympathized with her and disliked the republican upstart. However, American power, European disunion, and British opposition put serious international action out of the question. The European powers appealed to McKinley for moderation, and both the Pope and the powers put pressure on Spain for further concessions. Finally Spain agreed to request an armistice though not to accept American mediation.

But it was too late. Alarmed at a sudden swelling of public passion, reluctant to divide the country, and afraid that Congress might declare war against his will, McKinley on April 11 requested authority to use American troops to create stable government in Cuba. The final Spanish concession, of which he had learned the day before, was reported in an unnoticed sentence in his message. In a mood of patriotic exultation, Congress declared Cuba independent and demanded Spanish withdrawal. Then, to show the purity of American intentions, it added the "Teller Resolution" binding the United States not to annex Cuba.

VICTORY

Most Americans, watching Cuba with passionate indignation, did not know much about Spain's larger colony in the Far East, the Philippine Islands, where another colonial rebellion was under way. Theodore Roosevelt, as Assistant Secretary of the Navy, directed Commodore George Dewey to assemble the United States Asiatic

Squadron at Hong Kong and prepare, in the event of war over Cuba, to attack the Spanish fleet in Manila Bay. Apparently Roosevelt's purpose was military rather than expansionist: American rule of the Philippines was a possibility beyond even his imagination.

On May 1, Dewey attacked the Spanish fleet in Manila Harbor. Issuing his celebrated order—"you may fire when ready, Gridley"—he destroyed the enemy fleet of ten ships without the loss of an American life. This astounding victory (labeled by a jubilant press as "the greatest naval engagement of modern times") brought the Philippine question into being; it also left Dewey's squadron in a difficult position. Both friendly Britain and less friendly Germany also had naval forces in Manila Bay. Ashore, insurgent Filipinos confronted Spanish garrisons. The American fleet had brought the exiled leader Aguinaldo to the Philippines, but no American policy toward the rebellion had been defined. Finally a small American land force arrived. On the day after the war actually ended, the city of Manila surrendered to American troops, leaving insurgents and Spaniards disputing the rest of the archipelago.

Meantime in its original theater, the war went far less well at first. American coastal cities panicked at mythical rumors of Spanish raids, and mobilization proceeded with lamentable inefficiency. Still worse confusion marred the encampment of American forces in Florida and their embarkation for Cuba. Fortunately for the United States, Spanish equipment, tactics, and morale were in still worse shape.

After many misadventures, the remaining Spanish fleet was finally cornered in Santiago Bay. An American force, including Roosevelt's Rough Riders, a motley and horseless regiment of Ivy League polo players, cowboys, and western badmen, was landed nearby without opposition. A number of small but bloody engagements in the approaches to Santiago gave Americans, including Roosevelt, a chance to prove their courage under fire. On July 3, the decrepit Spanish fleet sailed bravely out of the harbor to meet certain destruction by naval gunfire, and on July 17 the city of Santiago surrendered, leaving the United States in control of Eastern Cuba. In early August, General Nelson A. Miles completed a nearly bloodless conquest of Spain's other American island, Puerto Rico, and the fighting ended.

The United States was not in an easy position. American forces occupied only one end of Cuba and one city in the Philippines. Dressed in blue winter uniforms, equipped with obsolete Springfield rifles, and fed on hardtack and repulsive canned meat (called by the press "embalmed beef"), American forces in Cuba were ridden with dysentery and malaria and threatened with yellow fever. Lieutenant Colonel Roosevelt, among others, was loudly demanding their recall. Even at home in the Florida camps, because of disgraceful neglect of sanitation, disease was spreading. (Many times more lives were lost by disease than by enemy action; of the 5,462 American dead, only 379 died in combat.)

Fortunately, Spain, without a navy and even more poorly prepared than the United States, had no hope of continuing hostilities, and on August 12, scarcely four months after war began, an armistice was signed. Secretary Hay pronounced it "a splendid little war." Colonel Roosevelt later declared: "It wasn't much of a war, but it was the best war we had."

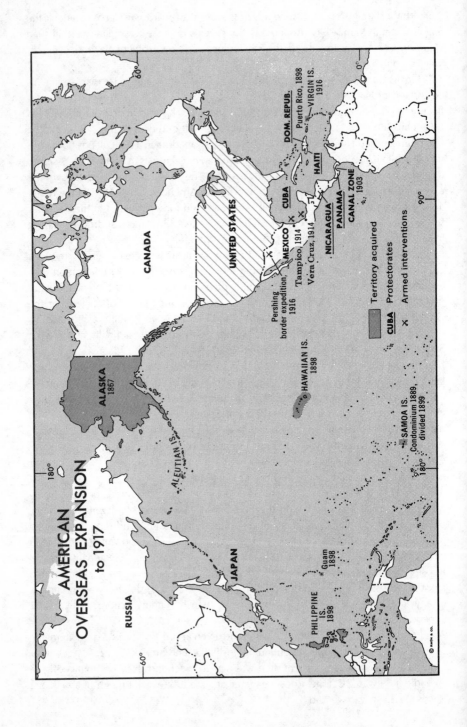

AMERICAN
OVERSEAS EXPANSION
to 1917

RUSSIA

JAPAN

PHILIPPINE
IS.
1898

Guam
1898

ALEUTIAN IS.

SAMOA IS.
Condominium 1889
divided 1899

ALASKA
1867

CANADA

UNITED STATES

HAWAIIAN IS.
1898

Pershing
border expedition,
1916

MEXICO
Tampico, 1914
Vera Cruz, 1914

NICARAGUA

Territory acquired

CUBA Protectorates

X Armed interventions

CUBA

HAITI

PANAMA
CANAL ZONE
1903

DOM. REPUB.
Puerto Rico, 1898
VIRGIN IS.
1916

PEACE AND EMPIRE

As armistice terms, the United States insisted that Spain withdraw from Cuba and cede to the United States Puerto Rico, an island in the Ladrones (Guam), and the city and harbor of Manila. The fate of the rest of the Philippines (more than 7,000 large and small islands with about 8 million people) was decided during the peace conference. At first reluctant to annex much distant territory, McKinley feared another upsurge of public opinion like that which had swept the country into war. Eventually he convinced himself that it was the duty of the United States to "uplift and civilize" the entire Philippines. Very reluctantly, Spain agreed to cede them in return for a payment of $20 million.

In the Senate, the treaty faced serious opposition from the anti-imperialists. This diverse coalition included most northern Democrats and the familiar minority of eastern, reform-minded Republicans. It brought together such contrasting individuals as Bryan, Cleveland, Andrew Carnegie, Samuel Gompers, and Mark Twain. Libertarians argued passionately that empire over subject peoples would violate the Declaration of Independence and the Monroe Doctrine. Others pointed out that the Constitution provided no way of governing territories never destined to become states. Racists insisted that Filipinos were unassimilable, and strategists argued, more persuasively, that a Far Eastern possession would endanger American security.

On the other side, it was argued that the flag, once planted overseas, should not be pulled down, that annexation represented the obvious will of God, and that it was America's duty to Christianize the Philippines (which were actually one of the principal outposts of Christianity in the Far East). The strong interest of Japan and Germany in the spoils of the Spanish empire furnished another argument (Germany eventually picked up the Caroline Islands and all the Ladrones or Marianas but Guam).

The business community, which had been generally opposed to war but was concerned for the expansion and protection of foreign trade, now tended to favor retention of the Philippines. This was partly for strategic reasons; both Hawaii and the Philippines would be useful if the United States was to resist European encroachment on China. Reluctantly the conservative Senate leadership agreed to go along with the president. Yet the opposing sides remained fairly even, and the treaty would not have passed had not Bryan, as head of the Democratic party, decided to support the treaty and fight the issue of annexation in the coming election.

In their 1900 convention, the Democrats declared that anti-imperialism was the "paramount issue"; the Republicans accepted the challenge. Theodore Roosevelt, one of the war's principal heroes, campaigned as McKinley's running mate. It cannot be proved that McKinley's solid victory constituted an endorsement of annexation, however. Many voted once more for the gold standard, the high tariff, and prosperity.

Perhaps the strongest real reason for retaining the Philippines was the lack of a clear alternative. It was obviously out of the question to suppress the revolt and return them to Spain, and nobody wanted to hand them to Germany or Japan. Disunited and in places uncivilized, the islands seemed unable to sustain independence without at least the protection of the United States. Yet many continued to feel that annexation was a mistake, both moral and strategic. If correct, perhaps the biggest mistake had been the initial occupation of Manila.

The imperialist tide, such as it was, carried with it not only the Philippines, Puerto Rico, and Guam, but also Hawaii and Samoa. McKinley had supported Hawaiian annexation since 1897. This was accomplished, by joint resolution of Congress rather than by treaty, only in August, 1898. Increased Far Eastern concern in general, Japanese interest in the islands in particular, and Hawaii's usefulness in wartime had furnished the decisive arguments. In 1900, the Samoan condominium was ended and the islands divided between Germany and the United States.

Meanwhile in Cuba, which the United States had sworn *not* to annex, American forces, performing a heroic job of cleaning up yellow fever, quarreled with their Cuban allies. In 1902, the forces were withdrawn, but not before the Platt Amendment making Cuba a virtual American protectorate was incorporated in American legislation, the Cuban constitution, and a Cuban-American treaty. This provided that Cuba might not impair its own independence or increase its public debt beyond its capacity. To safeguard either Cuban independence or a government that could maintain "life, property, and individual liberty," the United States was given the right to intervene, which it did in 1906 and several times thereafter. Finally, Cuba was required to sell or lease a naval station to the United States. Not until the Franklin Roosevelt administration was the Platt Amendment finally abrogated, leaving Cuba politically independent if still linked to the American economy.

America's imperial experience started unpleasantly when the Filipino insurgents, bitterly disappointed at not receiving independence, turned their guerrilla warfare against the United States. In the ensuing war, which lasted until 1902, some 5,000 Americans and at least 20,000 Filipinos died in battle or from disease. Like most troops fighting guerrilla enemies, American forces sometimes resorted to devastation, concentration camps, and even torture—the same methods for which America had denounced Spain. In a series of complex decisions, the Supreme Court underlined one of the anti-imperialist arguments by deciding that the Constitution did not necessarily apply in full vigor to "unincorporated territories" and that it was possible to levy tariffs on their products.

Despite these ironies, in the long run the American colonial record was a relatively good one. Everywhere strenuous work in education and sanitation was undertaken, and, despite the court decision, substantial free trade established. Movement toward popular government began with the establishment of a legislature in Puerto Rico in 1900. In 1901, civil government replaced military in the Philippines, which received an elective assembly in 1907. Thus the worst predictions of the anti-imperialists were not carried out; the United States did not turn, like Rome, from a republic to an empire. Neither did the hopes of the imperialists blossom; the resources of the Philippines remained substantially undeveloped, and poverty, in the Philippines and Puerto Rico, was ameliorated but by no means ended. In the twentieth century, most of the American people apparently gave little thought to their new acquisitions. In 1934, partly for ideological reasons and partly because of pressure from competing economic interests, Congress voted to give the Philippines their independence in ten years, and after World War II this pledge was carried out.

WORLD POWER

Thus the American venture into empire seems to have been a temporary enthusiasm. Yet its effects on foreign policy were profound and permanent. American hegemony in the Caribbean, already an accomplished fact, was underlined, and Britain, long the chief rival claimant, was glad to acknowledge it. In the second Hay-Pauncefote Treaty of 1901, England gave in to American demands for exclusive control of the proposed Isthmian canal, abrogating her own treaty rights to equality in this venture. Shortly afterward, Britain cheerfully cut her heavy overseas commitments by reducing her West Indian forces.

While Caribbean hegemony was almost inevitable in this era of frank great-power policing of the world, America's ventures in the Far East were far more controversial. To the vague and more or less sentimental interest in commercial equality and the independence of Asian states was added a large and vulnerable Far Eastern colony, menaced particularly by the rising power of Japan. Despite her growing naval strength, the United States lacked power to defend these distant commitments.

Since 1895, Japan and the European powers had been forcing China to surrender leased territories and establishing large additional spheres of economic influence. In 1899, Secretary of State John Hay, a friend of Roosevelt and a partisan of the new "large policy," stated traditional American policy in a fresh manner. Partly at the prompting of American commercial interests, he addressed identical notes to the six leading powers asking them to affirm equal treatment for foreign commerce within their spheres of interest in China. Though the answers were ambiguous, Hay announced that the world had accepted this Open Door policy.

In 1900, when the antiforeign Boxer Rebellion endangered the lives of foreigners in Peking, the United States joined an international rescue expedition. At this time, Hay broadened the Open Door policy by sending a second note affirming American support of Chinese territorial integrity and calling for commercial equality in all parts of the Chinese Empire, not just the spheres of European influence.

The Open Door policy pleased Americans and seemed far more in line with tradition than the acquisition of the Philippines. Yet the integrity of the huge, crumbling Chinese Empire added to the safety of the Philippines were big commitments, well beyond the actual, developed military power of the United States.

Inevitably, though tacitly, the course of events had drawn the nation closer to its old rival, Great Britain. During the Spanish War, when most European countries had resented America's chastisement of a proud European nation, Britain had supported the United States, and Rudyard Kipling, then the most popular Anglo-Saxon author, had urged America to "take up the white man's burden" of empire. Like the United States, Britain wanted the status quo maintained in the Far East as well as the Caribbean and welcomed help in achieving this objective. In many American circles, especially in the eastern upper class, the turn of the century saw a revival of sentiment for British friendship on cultural and even racial grounds. The pro-British tendency, however, was by no means shared by the whole American public, large sections of which disliked British policies in Ireland, India, and South Africa and still thought of England as the stronghold of monarchy and aristocracy. Yet as the great powers began to choose up sides for the world conflict of the twentieth century, there was probably never much doubt that a showdown would find America on the side of the Atlantic, rather than the Central European, powers.

After the turn of the century, most Americans were proud of the nation's new empire, fleet, and prestige and were glad that Washington was often consulted in times of international crisis. They by no means realized, however, that active world politics demanded serious—in the long run even tragic—commitments. For the first decade and a half of the twentieth century, American interest shifted back, for the most part, to its traditional concentration on economic growth and domestic political controversy.

CONFLICTING HISTORICAL VIEWPOINTS

10. Why Imperialism in 1898?

In 1968, at the very summit of the national debate over American interests in South-east Asia, the historian Walter LaFeber wrote (Texas Quarterly, Winter 1968): "The line from the conquest of the Philippines in 1898 to the attempted pacification of Vietnam . . . is not straight, but it is quite traceable." This interpretation of the events of 1898 was timely, but it was not new. Well before LaFeber's birth, Charles Beard had also concluded that America's turn-of-the-century imperialism was no accident but the result of "the present economic system."

While others, most notably Samuel Bemis (Diplomatic History of the United States, *1936), viewed the Asian adventure of the 1890s as "The Great Abberation," unplanned and unrepeated, Beard* (Rise of American Civilization, *1927;* Idea of National Interest, *1934) dismissed any "fortuitous aspects" in the events ending with the annexation of the Philippines. The road to empire, he never doubted, was paved with economic interest and the Americans who followed it to Manila were unabashed commercial expansionists. To the dean of the "Old Left" historians, then, American imperialism, the natural culmination of "over a century of commercial development," owed little "to fate, the accidents of history, the current of events, destiny, and the gifts of the gods." In this judgment, LaFeber, perhaps the most gifted of the New Left scholars, agreed. His* New Empire: American Expansion, 1860–1898 *(1963) emphasized "the economic forces which resulted in commercial and landed expansion," and his 1968 essay concluded that "the Spanish-American conflict can no longer be viewed as only a 'splendid little war.' It was a war to preserve the American system."*

The economic interpretation, although the oldest and most durable, has many critics. The most influential of these, Julius Pratt, author of The Expansionists of 1898

(1936), after painstaking examination of the commercial press, asserted that "an overwhelming preponderance of the vocal business interests of the country strongly desired peace." Conceding that the business community wanted an expanded overseas trade, he contended nonetheless that most of them became imperialists only after the Spanish American War began. To Pratt and many others of his persuasions, the Spanish American War, although spurred by a yellow press and a martial temper, was a war to liberate Cuba. To be sure it brought imperial opportunities that were welcomed by the business community—but these were windfalls.

The question, of course, remains: Why imperialism? By reading these works and those listed below, the student can perhaps formulate his or her own answer.

FOR FURTHER READING

An informative, reliable history of recent American foreign policy is Richard W. Leopold's *The Growth of American Foreign Policy* (1962). Charles S. Campbell's *Transformation of American Foreign Relations* (1976) is admirable synthesis of scholarly work in the period from 1865 to 1900. An excellent account of the emergence of the United States into power politics is Ernest R. May's *Imperial Democracy* (1961); H. Wayne Morgan, in *America's Road to Empire* (1965), is critical of both May and the economic determinists. David Healy's *U.S. Expansionism* (1970) generally concurs with the LaFeber thesis. R. L. Beisner, in *Twelve Against Empire* (1968), and E. B. Tompkins, in *Anti-Imperialism in the United States* (1970), focus on the opponents of expansion. A lively and sometimes penetrating history of the McKinley administration is Margaret Leech's *In the Days of McKinley* (1959). It should be compared to Howard Wayne Morgan's provocative but not influential biography, *William McKinley and His America* (1963). Tyler Dennett, in *John Hay* (1933), Kenton J. Clymer, in *John Hay,* and Charles S. Campbell, in *Special Business Interests and the Open Door Policy* (1951), illuminate an important chapter in American foreign policy. Both Walter Millis's *The Martial Spirit* (1931) and Graham A. Comas's *An Army for Empire* (1971) are useful studies of the Spanish-American War; H. G. Rickover, in *How the Battleship Maine was Destroyed* (1976), traces the disaster to an internal and accidental explosion; and Frank Freidel's *The Splendid Little War* (1958) is a highly entertaining pictorial history. Edmond Morris's *The Rise of Theodore Roosevelt* (1979) and the Roosevelt biographies listed in later chapters will also prove useful for this topic.

13. THE PROGRESSIVE ERA

	President	Domestic Events	Foreign Policy: Europe, Asia	Foreign Policy: Latin America	
1898			Spanish-American War. 1899 Open Door Policy. Boxer Rebellion		1898
1900	McKinley *R* (September 6, 1901, assassinated)	Gold Standard Act.			1900
1902		Newlands Reclamation Act. 1903 Elkins Act. Coal strike settled. Panic of 1903.		1901 Platt Amendment. Venezuela Incident. 1903 Panama Affair.	1902
1904	Roosevelt *R*	Northern Securities case.	1905 Russo-Japanese War and Peace of Portsmouth. Algeciras Conference on Morocco. 1907 "Gentlemen's Agreement" on Japanese immigration. Root-Takahira Agreement.	"Roosevelt Corollary"	1904
1906		Hepburn Act. Pure Food and Drug Act. 1907 Panic.			1906
1908	Taft *R*	Conservation conference. 1909 Payne-Aldrich Tariff. Mann-Elkins Act. 1911 "Rule of Reason" decisions.			1908
1910			1911 Chinese Railway Consortium.	Mexican Revolution.	1910
1912	Wilson *D*			1913 "Watchful Waiting" in Mexico.	1912
1914		1913 Underwood Tariff. Federal Reserve Act. Federal Trade Commission Act. Clayton Anti-Trust Act.	(August) War in Europe. 1915 (May) *Lusitania* sunk. (May) United States threat and German concession on submarine warfare.	Tampico and Vera Cruz incidents.	1914
1916	Wilson *D*	Federal Farm Loan Act. Adamson Act.		Mexican border warfare	1916

Roosevelt and
the Progressive Era
1901–1908

22

On September 6, 1901, President William McKinley, a moderately conservative statesman, was shot by an anarchist. When he died a week later, the young and dynamic Theodore Roosevelt became president. This tragic incident is often taken to be the beginning of a new period of progressive reform that lasted until World War I. Actually, of course, the Progressive Era was not brought on by the assassin's bullet. Its sources lay deep in the economic, social, and moral history of the country.

THE MATURE ECONOMY

By 1900, the American economy was relatively mature. It was no longer necessary to concentrate all resources and efforts on the expansion of productive capacity. Production continued to increase fairly rapidly in the new century but not at the fantastic rate of the previous period.

Progressivism owed some of its nature, if not its existence, to the fact that the period 1901–1914 was one of relatively stable prosperity. There was no prolonged depression like those of the 1870s or 1890s but only two brief financial panics (1903 and 1907). The farmer, that perennial stepchild of the American economy, entered one of few periods of relative contentment. Of course, many farmers were continually having a hard struggle, and some farm evils like tenancy were still increasing. But average farm income, for a change, was moving upward. This was partly because city population, at home and abroad, was increasing faster than farm acreage. By 1900, only 35 percent of Americans lived on farms.

For some of the new urban population, crowded into slums and immigrant ghettos, things were less than cheerful. Real wages for industrial labor rose more slowly than in earlier decades. Never were social contrasts more extreme, from the still uninhibited multimillionaire, with a Fifth Avenue palace and a 50-room Newport cottage, to the tubercular child in the cotton mill or the garment worker in the tenement sweatshop. America led the world in the number of industrial accidents. Thus it is only with careful qualification that one can call the Progressive Era a time of contentment. It is more nearly correct to call it a period of hope, especially for the politically articulate middle class.

Business consolidation reached a peak at about the turn of the century. Contrary to progressive fears, rising monopoly did not stifle competition; innovation and expansion kept it in check. During the Progressive Era, the largest firms retained but did not increase their share of the nation's industry. However, this was enough to make big business the main target of criticism. Its defenders argued that not all consequences of bigness were bad; for instance, there was more money for such advances as electrification and research laboratories. Public relations and advertising received much attention and so did the new "Scientific Management" movement of Frederick W. Taylor. Taylor, originally an engineer, urged that each movement of each worker be made as efficient as possible through close study, minute division of function, and rigorous supervision. Working toward similar objectives with less theory, Henry Ford began production of his Model T in 1909. By 1914, he was producing a quarter of a million cars a year.

One aspect of business consolidation that received a great deal of attention was the tendency toward banker control. Only a dozen great investment houses, led by that of J. P. Morgan, could float the securities necessary for the period's gigantic mergers, like that of U.S. Steel in 1901. These private bankers, controlling insurance and trust companies as well as industries and railroads, could draw on a large part of the national savings. When necessary, they could supplement their resources with those of their foreign connections. Thus they could perform many of the functions of supervision and stabilization traditionally carried out by official central banks; in a sense, Morgan was the successor of Nicholas Biddle. Conscientiously, Morgan and his allies tried to end cutthroat competition, prevent risky investment, and rescue sick industries before their financial collapse. In return, they exacted not only high fees but control. Through seats on the governing boards of railroads, steel companies, and many other corporations, they could enforce their own ideas of sound operation on a large part of American business.

These functions, however useful, were not without their costs. Sometimes the bankers were unimaginative and unenterprising (they were very reluctant, for instance, to back automobile manufacturers). They did not worry much about working conditions in the industries they controlled. And as the period's two panics testify, they did not always achieve the stability at which they aimed. Even if the bankers of the age of Morgan had been perfect, however, they would not have been popular. The main single complaint of progressives was directed against what they regarded as immoral and irresponsible power, and this was personified by the mighty, invisible "Money Trust."

THE PROGRESSIVE MIND

Antimonopoly feelings were as old as the Republic, and most of the rest of the progressive ideology was a continuation of the previous period's social criticism.

Settlement workers were still discovering urban poverty; ministers were still reinterpreting Christianity in terms of social reform; social scientists were still challenging the basis of nineteenth-century individualist morality. But the discontent of the early twentieth century had a new tone, and this tone was set by a cheerful, though not a complacent, middle class. Careful study has shown that the leaders of early twentieth-century progressivism tended to be fairly prosperous professionals or members of the business community in their early forties, usually Anglo-Saxon and Protestant, often motivated by personal ambition as well as moral indignation.

Side by side with progressivism, radicalism was also flourishing. In the century's first decade, the Socialist party elected many local officials and one congressman. In 1912, its presidential candidate, Eugene Debs, got 6 percent of the popular vote. Such Socialist intellectuals as Upton Sinclair and Jack London confidently predicted a socialist America in the near future. On the far left, the syndicalist Industrial Workers of the World (IWW), uncompromising advocates of class conflict, organized western miners and lumberjacks. In 1912, the IWW began to spread to eastern textile towns.

Except when frightened by such episodes as the Colorado mine wars or the *Los Angeles Times* bombing of 1911, middle-class progressives refused to be deeply alarmed by the rise of radicalism. Only a few of the most hopeful and fearful Americans believed that revolution was close. Theodore Roosevelt, who had stormed about the menace of anarchism in 1896, could find a good word in 1908 for some socialists. The Socialist party itself was sharply divided between advocates of gradual and immediate change. Neither fear nor personal suffering played much part in the motives of progressive leaders. Undoubtedly, concern about the high cost of living helped to turn the thoughts of some toward the trusts and the tariff. Many sympathized with the plight of the urban poor. Yet even such obvious evils as child labor and slums looked different in a period without major depressions. Problems like these were not considered proofs of society's failure, but calls to action. And for most progressives, the most pressing questions were not humanitarian but moral and political.

First, progressives wanted to end corruption, to throw out the crooks and return power to "good citizens" like themselves. Second, they wanted to control "big business," not in the interest of socialism but in the interest of free enterprise. Some of them wanted to break up large combinations. Others concluded that "the trusts" should be allowed to exist under close supervision or that there should be some kind of partnership between government and business.

Because they found life in America good, progressives wanted to preserve its promise for the future. They rejected the determinism that had been common in the late nineteenth century. Science, government, and the public morality were all changing, and changing for the better. There were no such things as immutable laws, except (for most progressives) concerning moral fundamentals. Following William James, who died in 1910, the pragmatic school of philosophy argued that particular judgments should be made on the basis of concrete consequences rather than according to general metaphysical principles. In educational theory, John Dewey and his followers insisted that children should be taught to solve the problems that arose in their own environment instead of being instructed in the wisdom of the past. The law and even the Constitution were reinterpreted as guides to action rather than unchanging codes.

At the height of the Progressive Era, people talked not only of the New Freedom of Woodrow Wilson or the New Nationalism of Theodore Roosevelt, but also of the new literature, the new psychology, even the "new woman."

REFORM AND MINORITY RIGHTS

Optimism gave these middle-class reformers much of their confidence and courage. It also blinded many of them to some of the most difficult contemporary problems. Most progressives seemed strangely unconcerned, for example, about racial injustice. A few of them, including Oswald Villard, Lillian Wald, Jane Addams, and Clarence Darrow agitated openly for Negro rights and even joined the black militant W. E. B. Du Bois in organizing the National Association for the Advancement of Colored People (NAACP) in 1909. But progressivism was largely for whites only, and most of its adherents shared the nearly universal belief that blacks were inherently inferior and socially unassimilable. A similar attitude applied to the new immigrants who flowed after 1890 in a great human tide from southern and eastern Europe into the nation's cities. Although appalled by conditions in the urban slums, otherwise humane and tolerant reformers rarely questioned nativistic assumptions, and some of them were in fact in the vanguard of the immigrant restriction movement.

Many Progressive leaders, Presidents Roosevelt and Wilson among them, were reluctant and belated supporters of women's suffrage. Yet these reform years proved more beneficial to women than to blacks. By 1896, the four Western states of Wyoming, Utah, Colorado, and Idaho had granted women the vote. But no further gains were made until suffragists in Washington and California won referendums in 1910 and 1911. Despairing of success through state-by-state action, the "woman movement" (as it was then often called) swung its considerable energies behind the "Anthony Amendment" to enfranchise all adult women at a single stroke. The movement's modern origins dated from 1848, but not until the National American Woman Suffrage Association (NAWSA) was formed from two rival organizations in 1890 was there significant unity of action. Led first by Elizabeth Cady Stanton and Susan B. Anthony and after 1900 by Carrie Chapman Catt and Anna Howard Shaw, NAWSA focused on federal legislation. Essentially middle-class and moderate, the association sometimes cooperated and sometimes clashed with such radical feminists as Alice Paul and Lucy Burns of the Congressional Union (later called the Woman's Party). But in the end, suffragists of all persuasions won; the Nineteenth Amendment cleared Congress during 1919 and was ratified and became law on August 26, 1920.

THE PROGRESSIVE ACCOMPLISHMENT

Reform started with the exposure of evil. A vogue for sensational accounts of corruption and monopoly began with books like Henry Demarest Lloyd's attack on Standard Oil (*Wealth against Commonwealth,* 1894). The new fashion was taken up by sensational newspapers like those of Hearst and by a new crop of popular, cheap, ably edited magazines led by *McClure's.* For a while one could hardly pick up a periodical without running into a heavily documented exposure of the city traction ring or the patent medicine trust. Muckrakers, as Roosevelt called the new journalists, attacked big business, the unions, the churches, the press itself, state and city government, and finally the U.S. Senate. While many people read the muckrakers for sheer excitement, some were stirred to action.

Some of the most important progressive crusades started outside politics in such fields as charity organization, education reform, or juvenile courts (concern for the young was characteristic). Sooner or later, however, most concrete accomplishments had to be registered in political action.

The first progressive political offensive was directed against the most obvious target: America's swollen cities, where grafting utilities and protected vice were all too obvious. City reform got under way in the 1890s, and in the first decade of the century many cities moved from boss rule to reform. Some moved back soon enough, but often the cycle left a heritage of public waterworks, public or highly regulated street railways, tenement laws, and playgrounds.

Still more was accomplished in the states, perhaps the most important laboratories of reform. In 1900, Robert M. La Follette, one of the most militant and uncompromising progressive leaders, became governor of Wisconsin. Working closely with experts from the state university, he made Wisconsin a "laboratory of democracy." Reformers won control of one state after another in the Middle West and then in the Far West and East. Even in the South, where reform was often allied with anti-Negro demagoguery, the progressive movement demonstrated vitality. Typical state reforms included a great many devices intended to keep the bosses and railroads out of power and "the people" in control. These included the direct primary, the secret ballot, and even preferential popular choice of U.S. senators, still officially chosen by legislatures. Beginning in Oregon, a number of western states put lawmaking directly in the hands of the people through the initiative and referendum.

States were pioneers in such economic measures as close regulation of railroads, utilities, and trusts, progressive taxation, and conservation of natural resources. Labor legislation passed by states included worker's compensation laws for accident cases, child labor laws, and laws establishing maximum hours and minimum wages for women. (Laws regulating men's labor conditions were sometimes overturned by the courts and always strongly opposed as interference with individual liberty.) By 1917, two-thirds of the states, pushed by fervent reformers, had prohibited alcoholic liquors.

Obviously, many of these measures needed to be completed by federal action, and ambitious progressive leaders were eager to move from state capitals to Washington. In 1906, La Follette himself joined what muckrakers called the "millionaire's club," the U.S. Senate. With other progressive senators, he played a major part in pushing presidents toward reform.

THE PROGRESSIVE HERO

Theodore Roosevelt's inauguration did not cause the Progressive Era, but it was a major event in it. For the first time since Jackson, a president became the most popular

American. For the first time since Lincoln, a president stretched the powers of his office. Like Jefferson and Franklin Roosevelt, Theodore Roosevelt was harder to understand than he seemed. On the surface he was noisy, impulsive, and even violent, given to dramatic phrases like "the square deal" and "the strenuous life." He liked to lay down the law about literature, science, or personal morality. At times he acted rashly, as when he discharged without honor three divisions of highly decorated black soldiers on unfounded charges of rioting at Brownsville, Texas. Most of his impulsiveness came either early or late in his career or was confined to minor issues. His major decisions as president were usually shrewd compromises.

An informal, confident aristocrat, Roosevelt indulged in pillow fights with his children and dragged sweating diplomats on rocky scrambles. This delighted the public and by no means compromised the dignity of the presidential office. A consistent nationalist, Roosevelt took it for granted that the president of the United States was the equal not only of foreign emperors but of domestic millionaires. A born politician, he never quite lost touch either with radicals like Lincoln Steffens or extreme conservatives like Senator Nelson Aldrich. To each, he managed to appear as a defender against the other. Like all good politicians, Roosevelt as president was a master of timing. When he became president, he reassured shocked conservatives by announcing his continuance of McKinley's policies and cabinet. At the same time, he put out a trial balloon by denouncing the trusts and moved further in that direction when public response was favorable. In 1904, he easily defeated a conservative Democrat, Judge Alton B. Parker, for reelection. President in his own right and conscious of the progressive tide throughout the country, he moved further toward reform objectives. Then in 1907, when the financial panic seemed to demand caution, he followed the suggestions of J. P. Morgan. Finally, in 1908–1909, about to leave office, he called for a host of drastic reform measures. This accomplished nothing immediately but left a program that his successors could not ignore.

The actual domestic accomplishments of Roosevelt were important but less important than his demonstration of the possibilities of the presidency. Despite his reputation as a trustbuster, Roosevelt was never hostile to big business as such. He disliked practices he considered dishonest and deeply resented defiance of the federal government. His first request in his December, 1901 message to Congress was for the creation of a Department of Commerce and Labor, including a Bureau of Corporations that would collect information about abuses committed by interstate industries. This moderate measure passed against heavy opposition. In 1902, Wall Street was startled to learn that the administration was going to sue the Northern Securities Company, a typical Morgan-sponsored railroad merger, under the neglected and emasculated Anti-Trust Law. Though the administration won this suit and later others, Roosevelt never placed much confidence in sudden punitive assaults against particular mergers. Wanting to prevent unethical practice rather than sheer bigness, he would have preferred (but did not get) legislation providing for the registration and more orderly regulation of all interstate business.

In 1902, the administration had to deal with a bitter anthracite coal strike. Though bituminous supplies were ample, the press played up the prospects of a desperate fuel shortage. Instead of simply sending troops to the coal fields to "restore order" after the manner of Cleveland, Roosevelt called both parties to the White House. Unwilling to concede equality to their opponents, the operators adamantly refused to discuss concessions. This angered Roosevelt who began looking into the possibilities of using the army to mine coal, a threat that went well beyond any known presidential powers. After much pressure, the operators agreed to the appointment of a mixed arbitration commission, and in March, 1903, this group made its award. It gave the miners a 10 percent raise but denied them several of their other objectives, including union recognition. Trouble in the coal fields was long to continue, but a precedent had been established for a new kind of presidential action.

In his second administration, Roosevelt had to deal with the demands of the growing group of midwestern Progressive Republicans in Congress. Of all these demands, the most overdue was railroad regulation. The Elkins Act of 1903, supported by the railroads themselves, had forbidden special rebates to large customers, but the Interstate Commerce Commission was still hamstrung in any effort to regulate rates. After a long process of presidential pressure and compromise, Congress passed the Hepburn Act in 1906. This measure gave the Commission power to set aside existing schedules and determine reasonable rates pending court review. The commission could also prescribe uniform bookkeeping practices to enable it to keep track of operations, and its jurisdiction was strengthened in other ways. It did not, however, receive the power to make an evaluation of railroad property as a basis for rate making, an omission that bitterly disappointed Senator La Follette. Similarly, the Federal Pure Food and Drug Act and Meat Inspection Act of the same year gave progressives only part of what they wanted. Some of the worst practices of packers and patent medicine producers were ended, but fraudulent advertising was not prohibited.

Roosevelt, a believer in outdoor life and a vigorous champion of the national interest, prided himself most of all on his efforts for conservation of natural resources. For three centuries Americans had devoted themselves to exploiting their lumber, minerals, and other wealth as rapidly as possible. Now many were becoming conscious of the possibilities of exhaustion as well as the inefficiency and immorality of indiscriminate private appropriation. Under an act passed in 1891 but so far used only a moderate amount, Roosevelt withdrew enormous areas from public entry and set them aside as National Forests. Water power and mineral sites were also withdrawn, and Roosevelt gave his backing to federal construction of irrigation works under the Newlands Act (1902).

Here as elsewhere, the president's chief service was probably the exercise of his talent for publicity. A White House conference of notables and a well-staffed national commission reported on the complex problems of land, water, forest, timber, and mineral conservation. A devoted core of conservationists was built up, led by Roosevelt's friend Gifford Pinchot, head of the Federal Forestry Service. Yet opposition by western interests accustomed to private use of public resources continued to be formidable, and conservationists secured only a start toward their goals.

The considerable list of reforms *not* undertaken by the Roosevelt administration was headed by tariff reform. Tariff revision was increasingly demanded by midwestern progressives, whose constituents had always been divided in their opinions on the tariff and were now hurt by foreign reprisals against American agricultural products. The president, however, could never really interest himself passionately in the tariff. Besides, any move in the matter was sure to split the Republican party. So this, with much other unfinished business, was left to Roosevelt's unlucky successor.

IN DANGEROUS WATERS

In foreign policy, Roosevelt seemed in his element. An old expansionist, he was both better informed about foreign policy than any recent president and more interested in it. More than most progressives, he seemed to understand the relationship between power and objectives. Yet here, more often than in his domestic policy, he betrayed a tendency to rashness. In contradiction to his much quoted adage, Roosevelt did not always speak softly and his stick was sometimes not big enough.

Roosevelt, like many European contemporaries, believed that the world had to be benevolently but firmly supervised by the enlightened great powers. Though he was occasionally irritated by the British, he took it for granted that the Anglo-Saxon powers, as equals and friends, should lead the procession. Then came the other Western European nations, and then a newcomer Roosevelt greatly respected for its martial virtues, Japan.

Part of the job of the enlightened nations was to prevent major wars. Roosevelt still believed that a manly willingness to fight was part of the essential moral equipment of nations and individuals. Force was still justified to enforce "progress" on backward peoples, and each great nation must retain the right to protect its vital interests. With these important qualifications, Roosevelt supported some of the goals of the contemporary peace movement. He furthered the work of The Hague conferences on world peace, the establishment of a world court, and the negotiation of treaties for the arbitration of most disputes.

The most obvious accomplishment of the administration was its continued and rapid movement toward American domination of the Central American and Caribbean areas. The Hay-Pauncefote negotiations, under way before Roosevelt took office, cleared away British objections to an American-controlled Isthmian canal. Congress had decided that the best route lay through Nicaragua where the United States had obtained treaty rights to build a canal. However, powerful and somewhat shabby private interests, concerned in part with protecting the investment of the nearly defunct French Panama Canal Company, persuaded the Senate to shift to the Panama route. When the Republic of Colombia, which owned Panama, refused to accept American terms, Roosevelt regarded it as an inadmissible blocking of progress by a backward nation.

A revolution in the Isthmus, carried out with American cognizance and naval protection, made Panama an independent republic. With the new country, the United States immediately negotiated a very favorable treaty providing for American "use, occupation, and control" of a Canal Zone. The French company got its money,

Panama got $10 million, work started on the canal, and Roosevelt saw the whole affair as one of his great successes. His critics have said, however, that the episode left deep resentment in Latin America, that the canal could have been built in Nicaragua, and that it could have been built in Panama without a revolution if Roosevelt had shown a little more patience in his negotiations with Colombia.

In 1902, Venezuela, once more the center of an international incident, refused to pay its international debts. Britain and Germany both reacted as great powers usually did in such circumstances. Their ships blockaded and even bombarded Venezuelan ports until the Venezuelan dictator agreed to arbitrate his government's obligations. Secretly but forcefully, Roosevelt warned the powers to end their naval action. When Germany was slow in complying, Roosevelt backed his warning with a display of naval force.

In Roosevelt's view, if the United States objected to intervention by others in the Caribbean, the United States had a duty when necessary to police that area itself. In 1904, when the Dominican Republic found itself in similar financial straits, Roosevelt moved in. Against the Senate's opposition, he made an arrangement under which the United States collected Dominican customs, paid the country's creditors, and put its government on an allowance. This was done so successfully and even tactfully that neither Europe nor Latin America objected. Roosevelt accompanied his action with a series of characteristic and sweeping statements constituting a new corollary to the Monroe Doctrine and claiming the right of intervention to prevent "chronic wrongdoing" in the western hemisphere.

Under Roosevelt's immediate successors, this "Roosevelt Corollary" was interpreted with less restraint. The relatively conservative Taft administration tried to push American capital into Caribbean countries with the idea of subsequent protection by force. The liberal Wilson administration repudiated this kind of "Dollar Diplomacy" but itself intervened far more forcibly to secure good government. By World War I, the Caribbean appeared an American lake. The United States owned Puerto Rico and the Virgin Islands (bought from Denmark in 1917), controlled the Canal Zone, had a formal protectorate over Cuba under the Platt Amendment, and had liberal precedent for armed intervention elsewhere in the area. Later during the Hoover and Franklin Roosevelt administrations, the United States gradually modified its policies in an effort to overcome Latin American resentment, formally abandoning all claims to the right of unilateral intervention.

The other area of increased American activity was the Far East. China, unmilitary and unprogressive, did not meet Roosevelt's standards for being a civilized nation. Thus he had no objection in principle to foreign enterprise there. Like Hay, however, he objected to exclusive control by foreign powers of commercial opportunity in any part of Chinese territory. His suspicion was deeply aroused by Russian domination of Manchuria. When Russia and Japan went to war in 1905 over rival interests in Korea and Manchuria, Roosevelt gave strong diplomatic support to Japan.

The Russo-Japanese War, like the Spanish-American War, was a smashing defeat of a European by a non-European power with considerable effects on the world balance. With the Russian fleets destroyed and Russia facing revolution, Japan yet lacked resources for continuing the war until Russia surrendered completely. Thus both powers accepted Roosevelt's mediation and gathered to make peace at Portsmouth, New Hampshire. Delighted at his novel role, Roosevelt handled the negotiations with considerable skill. Yet the Peace of Portsmouth, which gave Japan important territorial gains but denied her a money indemnity, proved unpopular in the victorious country.

Roosevelt's hopes for a stable balance in the Far East were defeated, and his major Far Eastern problem during the rest of his term in office was the rising power of Japan. His policies were a characteristic compound of realism, tact, and bravado. Since he could not prevent it, he accepted Japanese domination in Korea and took no action when Japan began to divide control of Manchuria with her defeated enemy, Russia. When California and particularly San Francisco started discriminating harshly against Japanese immigrants, Roosevelt put federal pressure on them to desist. At the same time, he negotiated the "Gentleman's Agreement" (1907) whereby Japan barred emigration of laborers to America. In 1906, he sent the U.S. fleet, by now the world's third largest, on a trip around the world. Its stop in Tokyo Bay, a daring and imaginative gesture, was a complete social success. More or less in return for all this hard work, Roosevelt was able to secure the Root-Takahira Agreement of 1908. In this, both countries agreed to respect equal opportunity for foreign commerce in China, Chinese territorial integrity, and each other's Far Eastern possessions. For the present, this certainly seemed to guarantee the safety of the Philippines. How far it protected Japanese mainland gains was not clear.

In 1906, when France and Germany were at loggerheads over Morocco, Roosevelt helped persuade his friend the German kaiser to accept a settlement that left France dominant.

Never had the United States been taken so seriously in world politics. Yet despite Roosevelt's imagination and skill, it is not clear that in the long run his work greatly advanced either American interests or world peace. United States hegemony in Central America, a fact in any case, had been underlined with unnecessary roughness. In the Far East, Japan had replaced Russia as the principal potential threat, and neither the Open Door nor the integrity of China looked much more secure. American commitments in this area still exceeded American power. Throughout the world, the United States had swung a little further toward alignment with the developing Anglo-French-Russian-Japanese entente. The American people, delighted with the country's increased prestige, still often ignored the dangerous realities of foreign policy.

Such carping, however, was little heard at the end of Roosevelt's term of office in 1908–1909. In an unguarded moment at the time of his election in 1904, he had promised not to seek another term. Undoubtedly regretting this, he easily forced the Republican party to accept as his successor his friend and Secretary of War, William Howard Taft. Campaigning against the two-time loser Bryan on a platform of the Roosevelt policies, Taft won easily. Saying goodbye to his "tennis cabinet" and his ambassadorial cronies but not to the nation's affections, Roosevelt departed on an African big-game hunt to be followed by a triumphal tour of European capitals.

CONFLICTING HISTORICAL VIEWPOINTS

11. Who Were the Progressives?

Few phenomena of American history are more controversial than the Progressive movement. For more than six decades, scholars have offered conflicting answers to such questions as: Why did the movement begin and end when it did? What were its major objectives? Was its impact on the national experience salutary or otherwise? What was its relationship to other reform movements before and since? On these topics there is so little agreement among historians that Peter Filene has written "An Obituary for the 'Progressive Movement' " (American Quarterly, *Spring 1970), arguing provocatively that the very concept should be abandoned as a figment of the scholarly imagination.*

The nature of this continuing historiographical debate is perhaps best suggested by conflicting assessments, of the social origins of the reformers. In his analysis of The Progressive Movement *(1915), Parke De Witt, the first scholar to study progressivism, accepted the interpretation offered by the reformers themselves. Like them, he viewed their movement as an uncompromising onslaught against big business. The period, he concluded, was one of conflict between "the people" and "the interests." Essentially the same idea pervaded the two most famous historical studies written during the 1920s. Vernon L. Parrington's* Main Currents in American Thought *(3 vols., 1927–30) and Charles and Mary Beard's* The Rise of American Civilization *(1927) viewed progressivism as the lineal descendant of a reform tradition that stretched back in American history to the age of Jefferson and Jackson. Pitting the masses against business moguls and crooked politicians, the movement was the twentieth-century phase of the age-old struggle between democracy and aristocracy, equality and privilege. The Progressives, then, were the people themselves, rank-and-file, democrats with a small* d, *who waged the battle for reform in defense of their national birthright.*

Writing from within the progressive frame of reference, such scholars as De Witt, Parrington, and Beard were, in effect, involved participants whose sympathetic and simplistic analysis of progressivism was not shared by historians of subsequent generations. The events of the 1920s and 1930s offered new historical vantage points from which to view the movement. To those who lived through the political reaction of "Normalcy" and the economic crisis of the Great Depression, progressivism generally seemed less idealistic and much less effective than earlier scholars assumed. As early as 1932, John Chamberlain, a young Marxist, studied the era closely and then bade Farewell to Reform. *The progressives, he concluded, were nostalgic conservatives seeking to restore a simpler past, not liberal reformers responding to the challenges of industrialism and urbanism. Although Harold U. Faulkner could still celebrate progressivism as* The Quest for Social Justice *(1931), most scholars from Chamberlain's time forward shared his doubts about the nature of the movement.*

Thus both George Mowry's The California Progressives *(1951) and Richard Hofstadter's* The Age of Reform *(1955) portrayed the era as one in which the urban middle class sought to restore its position of leadership. The progressives were not selfless crusaders for popular democracy, these scholars affirmed, but bourgeois victims of status anxiety. Drawn from the old and established professional elite (lawyers, educators, ministers, editors), whose standards of morality and order had been offended by political bosses and a floodtide of new immigrants and whose influence had been eclipsed by a rising new class of industrial and financial plutocrats, the progressives struggled to restore traditional standards of probity and to regain their lost power and deference.*

In a vein somewhat different from Mowry and Hofstadter, Samuel P. Hays, in The Response to Industrialism, 1885–1914 *(1957), and Robert Wiebes in* Businessmen and Reform *(1962), cast additional doubts on the traditional view that progressivism was basically a people's crusade against big business. In fact, both argued that so-called "special interests" often favored meaningful reforms that "the people" opposed. In their view, the progressives were neither disinterested do-gooders nor disquieted bourgeois but realistic conservatives, a new class of bureaucratic-minded professionals who sought to bring order and efficiency to a chaotic and wasteful society.* The Search for Order, 1877–1920 *(1967), Wiebes's second book and the most systematic expression of this interpretation, suggested that in their quest for stability and system, the "new middle class" progressives often found ready allies in big corporate managers.*

Not all recent scholars trace the social origins of reform to the middle class. J. Joseph Huthmacher (Mississippi Valley Historical Review, *1962) and Michael Paul Rogin and John L. Shover* (Political Change in California, *1970) emphasize working-class (particularly Catholic and immigrant) support for progressive programs. David P. Thelen, in* The New Citizenship *(1972), went further to argue the futility of attributing social movements to particular social groups. Noting that Wisconsin Progressives, not unlike their conservative critics, drew their ranks from farmers, workers, professionals, and business people, he emphasized issues more than classes and concluded that "no particular manner of man became a progressive."*

Since World War II, then, historians have redefined the sources of progressivism and its relationship to the business community. Although delineating the conservative tendencies inherent in the progressive mind, most scholars still accept the traditional equation of progressivism with reform. New Left historians, however, have denied even that. Gabriel Kolko, for example, has described the movement as The Triumph of Conservatism *(1963). In his view, the progressives were not reformers at all and the chief characteristic of the era was not orderly change in the public interest but complete control by business interests. Clearly, Kolko's is a minority view, but his total inversion of the traditional interpretation serves as a telling reminder that history is art not science.*

FOR FURTHER READING

George Mowry's *The Era of Theodore Roosevelt* (1958)* is a good survey. The best single book on Roosevelt himself is probably still H. F. Pringle's *Theodore Roosevelt* (1931).* It can be supplemented by *Roosevelt's Autobiography* (1921), J. M. Blum's

---

*Available in paperback edition.

penetrating sketch, *The Republican Roosevelt* (1954),* and W. H. Harbaugh's *Power and Responsibility* (1961). Other specimens of the very rich biographical literature are Lincoln Steffens's fascinating and untrustworthy *Autobiography* (2 vols., 1931); William Allen White's solid and revealing *Autobiography* (1946); Daniel Levine's *Jane Addams and the Liberal Tradition* (1971); William F. Holmes's *The White Chief: James Kimble Vardaman* (1970); and David P. Thelen's brief *Robert M. La Follette and the Insurgent Spirit* (1976). *The Socialist Party of America* (1955) is David Shannon's subject; and in *We Shall Be All* (1969), Melvin Dubofsky dissects the IWW. Important statements on race relations in an age of reform include: R. S. Baker, *Following the Color Line* (1908)*; Temple Kirby, *Darkness at the Dawning* (1972); Ann J. Lane, *The Brownsville Affair* (1971); August Meier, *Negro Thought in America, 1880–1915* (1963); and David W. Southern, *The Malignant Heritage* (1968). Both Aileen S. Kraditor, in *The Ideas of the Woman Suffrage Movement, 1890–1920* (1965), and William O'Neill, in *Everyone Was Brave* (1969)* focus on a second facet of the struggle for human rights. In *Progressive Cities* (1977), Bradley Robert Rice traces the development of the commission form of government. The intellectual history of the period is outlined in Henry S. Commager's *The American Mind* (1952), and some important aspects of it are interpreted by Morton G. White in *Social Thought in America* (1949). James M. Gilbert, in *Work Without Salvation* (1977), and Daniel T. Rodgers, in *The Work Ethic in Industrial America* (1978),. examine middle-class concerns with the alienation of labor in the new industrial order. Roosevelt's foreign policy is examined by Howard K. Beale in *Theodore Roosevelt and the Rise of America to World Power* (1956). The story of the interoceanic waterway is told by David McCullough in *Path Between the Seas* (1977) and by Walter La Feber in *The Panama Canal* (1978). Delber L. McKee, in *Chinese Exclusion versus the Open Door* (1977), portrays one aspect of American immigration policy.

The Peak of Progressivism
1909–1917

23

In 1908, William Howard Taft, proclaiming his devotion to Roosevelt's progressive policies, was an easy winner over the perennial William Jennings Bryan. Pointing to Taft's experience in government—as a judge, as first civil governor of the Philippines, as Secretary of War and presidential troubleshooter—Roosevelt and others predicted an outstanding administration. Taft had experience in every relevant area but that which proved most important: democratic politics.

TAFT AND THE PROGRESSIVES

Later, seeking reasons for the administration's relative failure, critics were to caricature Taft as a fat and lazy reactionary. Actually, Taft was handicapped not so much by his 300 pounds as by his conception of the presidency. His devotion to the Roosevelt policies was genuine, and he worked hard for causes he believed in. But he was convinced that the president should stay within his constitutional role and not stretch it as had every successful president since Jackson. And in showdowns, he could not help preferring decent and polite conservatives to most progressives with their radical rhetoric and their disregard of constitutional niceties.

Perhaps no Republican president coming to power in 1909 could have been successful. Since the Panic of 1907, times had been a little less prosperous, and the growing progressive movement demanded more and more drastic action about the major unsolved problems: trust control, taxes, tariffs. Roosevelt, sometimes sidestepping these issues, had managed to avoid an outright split between Republican reformers and Republican conservatives. Yet even his political magic could not have prevented a clash much longer. "Standpat" conservatives still controlled the party machinery while ambitious, aggressive Republican progressives, mostly from the Midwest, were increasing their strength in both houses of Congress with every election.

Blaming the rising cost of living on the sky-high Dingley Tariff, many western progressives demanded a tariff cut. Once more a moderate tariff reduction bill sailed through the House only to be modified sharply upward in the Senate. Taft, who was squarely on record for tariff reduction and had succeeded in toning down the bill's worst excesses, believed that the resultant compromise was the best that could be secured. But the progressives charged him with betrayal and stung him into saying, in September, 1909, that the new Payne-Aldrich Tariff was the best the Republican party had ever passed. At the same time, he failed to support the progressives in their successful attack against the power of Speaker Joseph G. Cannon. (Taft disliked Cannon but wanted his support for the tariff bill.) And because Taft and his Secretary of the Interior Richard A. Ballinger were slower-going and more legal-minded in their attitude toward conservation of natural resources, many progressives feared that they were betraying the national domain to private interests. By the spring of 1910, Taft was seen in some progressive circles as a reactionary and a traitor to the Roosevelt heritage.

Despite the president's political ineptitude, it can be argued that his administration brought about more solid progressive accomplishments than Roosevelt's. The Taft years saw the introduction of two progressive amendments to the Constitution, the Sixteenth (income tax) and the Seventeenth (direct election of senators). Taft had little to do with the latter, but he played an important part in initiating the income tax amendment, potentially the period's most revolutionary change in government.

Progressive legislation that passed during Taft's presidency, much of it with his support, included the Mann-Elkins Act strengthening the Interstate Commerce Commission, the Postal Savings and Parcel Post acts, the establishment of a federal Bureau of Mines and a Children's Bureau, and the separation of the Labor from the Commerce Department. Still more impressive is the fact that Taft's administration brought more than twice as many antitrust suits as that of his spectacularly trust-busting predecessor. Roosevelt had lost confidence early in the possibility of halting consolidation and believed instead in federal regulation to prevent unfair competition and deliberate moves toward actual monopoly. Approximately the same doctrine was enunciated by the Supreme Court in the Standard Oil and American Tobacco Company decisions of 1912, distinguishing between unreasonable and reasonable restraint of trade. Precisely because Taft was more conservative than Roosevelt, he believed more strongly in enforcing the Sherman Anti-Trust Act, assuming that it meant what it said. In the fall of 1911, Taft infuriated Roosevelt by moving against U.S. Steel. J. P. Morgan, who controlled the giant steel corporation, had cooperated with Roosevelt in trying to control the Panic of 1907, and Roosevelt had promised that the steel company would not be sued for acquiring Tennessee Coal and Iron in that crisis. But the Taft administration, apparently repudiating his promise, named the purchase as part of the grounds for the suit.

Like Taft's domestic policy, his foreign policy amounted to a shift of emphasis that seemed to his critics a betrayal of principle. Roosevelt had believed in American political—and, when necessary, military—intervention abroad to protect political stability and the balance of power. Within the limits of these objectives, he had favored American capital export. Taft and his Secretary of State, Philander Knox, believed frankly in using American foreign investment as an instrument of policy. Positive efforts to further private foreign ventures were expected to lead both to peace and to the welfare of the recipient countries.

However, the administration's ventures in what its critics called "Dollar Diplomacy" did not seem to work out as expected. In the Caribbean, Taft's program involved him in unpopular military ventures, while in the Far East it led to a startling departure from realism. Roosevelt, after trying various tacks in Far Eastern policy, had finally come to recognize some of the limitations of American power in the area, especially with reference to the rising might of Japan. Taft and Knox insisted on trying to force American participation in Chinese railway development and made a further effort to internationalize Japan's economic ventures in Manchuria. This policy angered Japan and other foreign powers, failed to sustain Chinese integrity, won only grudging and temporary support from American capital, and was reversed by Taft's successor.

Even the most benign aspects of Taft's foreign policy turned out badly in political terms. His long and vigorous negotiations for tariff reciprocity with Canada were regarded by many midwesterners as an effort to sell out western agriculture for the benefit of eastern industry. When he finally pushed a Canadian reciprocity treaty through the Senate, the Canadians, alarmed by loose American talk of eventual annexation, rejected it. Earnestly devoted to peace, the president negotiated treaties with Great Britain and France promising to arbitrate all differences, even those involving vital interests and national honor. Ardent nationalists were alarmed and the treaties were amended into meaninglessness in the Senate.

REPUBLICANS AND PROGRESSIVES, 1910–1912

From early in 1910 Taft, stung by progressive criticism, threw the administration's powers, including patronage, against the progressive wing of his own party in the primary elections. In turn, progressives denounced "Dollar Diplomacy," tariff betrayal, and conservation setbacks. The result of the congressional elections was a bad beating for the Republican party as a whole and particularly severe losses for the Taft-backed eastern conservatives. From this point on Democrats controlled the House of Representatives and a Democratic-insurgent Republican coalition controlled the Senate. Needless to say, the rest of Taft's term was a torment to him, and it became increasingly clear that he could not count on renomination, let alone reelection.

In January, 1911, the insurgents formed the Progressive Republican League, apparently backing Senator La Follette for the nomination. La Follette, showing signs of nervous collapse at an important public function, gave progressive Republicans an excuse to switch their allegiance to their real leader. For all but a few, this was the most popular living American, Theodore Roosevelt.

When he had first emerged from the African jungle in the spring of 1910, Roosevelt had heard from Pinchot and others about the administration's misdeeds. Yet when he arrived back in America after a triumphal tour of Europe, he refrained from directly criticizing his successor and former close friend. At the same time, he expressed far more radical sentiments than he had ever uttered before. In a famous speech at Osawatomie, Kansas in August, 1910, Roosevelt announced that all property should henceforth be held subject to the right of the community to regulate to whatever degree the public interest might require. This sort of language deeply alarmed the increasingly conservative president.

After congressional debacle and the steel suit, Roosevelt began openly attacking Taft, and the president, hurt beyond bearing, referred to "political emotionalists or neurotics" with unmistakable reference. Nobody was surprised when in February, 1912, Roosevelt, at the urging of seven progressive Republican governors, announced that his hat was in the presidential ring.

Waging a vigorous primary campaign for the Republican nomination, Roosevelt roundly defeated Taft in those states that had adopted the new direct primary system. Taft, however, controlled the southern Republicans and the party machinery. Using much the same tactics that Roosevelt had used to nominate Taft in 1908, the Taft forces controlled the Republican convention, decided disputes in the president's favor, and secured Taft's renomination. Amid scenes of weeping, singing, and fighting, Roosevelt's furious followers withdrew to form their own organization and nominate their hero.

The founders of the new Progressive Party included social reformers like Jane Addams, a few of the more daring western progressive politicians, and some representatives of the New Business who were urging on businesses an increase of social responsibility and self-regulation.

Some of the most fervent admirers of the new party were young intellectuals who had been influenced by Herbert Croly's *The Promise of American Life*. This book, published in 1909 and warmly praised by Roosevelt himself, called for a frank abandonment of Jeffersonian individualism and traditional *laissez-faire*. The new American progressivism, it urged, should harness and not destroy the creative powers of giant industry. Government, making use of a new, highly trained elite, should aim at something like a renaissance, at once political and intellectual.

The Progressive platform showed the influence of all these elements. It called for a long list of social legislation, including prohibition of child labor, minimum wages for women, and social insurance. It repeatedly advocated "scientific" and "efficient" government, particularly with reference to conservation and the regulation of business. While it favored international peace, its foreign policy sections were distinctly nationalistic. Showing the influence of western progressives, it backed the initiative, referendum, and recall; direct election of senators; preferential primaries for the presidency; women's suffrage; and even (to the horror of Taft and his friends) popular recall of some judicial decisions.

Surprisingly radical on many matters, the Progressive Party was distinctly moderate on two. A strong antitrust plank was sidetracked in favor of an appeal for "constructive regulation." Not only was the platform silent on black rights, but Roosevelt acquiesced in the exclusion of blacks from progressive organizations in the South.

The Progressive Party of 1912 was more than a group of Roosevelt-worshipers. It was an attempt to adapt traditional American liberalism to fit new conditions and combine new and old ideas. Its uneasy mixture of practicality and moral uplift foreshadowed the business reform ideology of the 1920s, and many of its proposals were to find their echoes in the New Deal.

Despite the cheers and tears, Roosevelt's exciting venture turned out badly for his supporters and himself. It deepened the Republican split, for the time handing over the party to the old guard. It destroyed Roosevelt's own very important role in American politics, and it set back the necessary job of adapting traditional liberalism to twentieth-century realities. From Roosevelt's own point of view (or Taft's), it had one further bad result: it brought the Democrats to power.

WILSON AND THE PRESIDENCY

Woodrow Wilson, the Democratic candidate in 1912, was born and brought up in the South. The son of a Presbyterian preacher, he became a political scientist and historian. In 1902, he was chosen president of Princeton. In this position, he was at first a distinguished success, but he became entangled in some fierce and complicated battles over university policy. To Wilson, at least, these were fights for moral principle, and he became discouraged when he was fought to a stalemate in 1910. In that year the Democratic politicians of New Jersey invited him to run for the governorship.

Up to this time, Wilson's expressed opinions on public issues had been moderately conservative, and he had been tagged by some rich and influential Democrats as a possible savior of the party from "Bryanism." To the surprise and dismay of the New Jersey bosses, Wilson took the campaign and state party away from them, revealing himself as an ardent and idealistic progressive. As governor, he equipped New Jersey, the "mother of trusts," with a full set of up-to-date regulatory legislation. An obvious presidential hopeful by this time, Wilson carefully conciliated Bryan and other progressives while retaining the support of some conservative elements in the party. In a fierce convention battle, he took the party's nomination at a time when the Republican split made election probable.

Wilson's campaign speeches were as progressive as Roosevelt's but different both in style and content. Where Roosevelt was emotional and combative, Wilson was controlled. Where Roosevelt called for frank recognition of big business and governmental regulation, Wilson insisted on the restoration of opportunity and open-market competition. This too, of course, would mean an immediate increase in government intervention but only for the purpose of assisting the underdog. In a series of glowing orations, Wilson insisted that his program would usher in a New Freedom instead of Roosevelt's New Nationalism.

With the support of an undivided party Wilson was an easy winner, though he was backed by only 42 percent of the popular vote. His party, long out of power, was a curious combination of city immigrants, western followers of Bryan, eastern banking and business interests, and the more than ever Solid South. Some Republicans honestly doubted whether such a group, led by an impractical professor, could govern.

These doubters misjudged both party and president. Able leadership could, up to a point, overcome Democratic divisions as Roosevelt had once overcome Republican divisions, and Wilson was not only an experienced politician but a daring student of American political institutions. The president, he thought, could become an equivalent of the British prime minister, using both party organization and personal popular support to force his own program through the legislative branch.

From their initial doubts, many progressives turned, in Wilson's first months in office, to amazed enthusiasm. Yet in his career thus far, Wilson had shown weaknesses as well as strong points. He demanded complete support from his friends and in showdowns was likely to find his opponents wicked and perverse. Wanting to believe his own program and point of view completely right, he could become bitter and reckless when menaced with defeat. In times of adversity, his intensity and devotion could become handicaps. In his first administration, however, they were superb assets.

In office, Wilson moved immediately against the most formidable redoubts, the tariff and banking. With the help of Republican progressives, he forced through *both* houses of Congress the Underwood Tariff, reducing the rates to about the level of pre-Civil War days and extending the free list. The tariff bill included a moderate income tax, at last clearly constitutional.

The country's banking and currency system, dating from 1863 and earlier, was unsatisfactory to different groups for opposite reasons. Many lamented the absence of a central bank able to control interest and rediscount rates, to mobilize reserves in a crisis, and thus to mitigate America's all too frequent financial panics. On the other hand, according to a widespread progressive belief currently reinforced by congressional investigation, the "Money Trust," dominated by certain private bankers and especially by J. P. Morgan, had far too much power over American credit and therefore over American economic development. Moreover, for 50 years, a large section of American opinion had believed that the ups and downs of the American economy were partly caused by the inadequacy and inflexibility of the national currency.

Steering with great adroitness between advocates and enemies of a central bank and between believers in public and private control, Wilson, with the help of Bryan and others, secured the passage of the Federal Reserve Act of 1913. This measure divided the country into Federal Reserve Districts. In each, there was to be a Federal Reserve Association that national banks must join and other banks might. A district Federal Reserve Bank was to be owned by the member banks and governed by a mixed public-private board. Each Federal Reserve Bank would receive the cash reserves of its member banks, grant loans to them, and rediscount their business and some agricultural paper. On the basis of the rediscounted business obligations, the Federal Reserve Banks would issue a new kind of currency, Federal Reserve Notes, which would be partly covered by a gold reserve of 40 percent of their value. The worth of these notes was expected to fluctuate with the needs of business since they were based mostly on business transactions. Federal Reserve Banks would pool resources in times of threatened panic. The whole system was to be supervised by a presidentially appointed Federal Reserve Board, which could raise or lower rediscount rates and thus exert some control over the availability of credit. While the new system by no means solved all America's long-standing banking and currency problems, it was the most satisfactory compromise between efficiency and decentralization that had been developed thus far. After some initial hostility, it was accepted by banking and business.

The third major accomplishment of Wilson's first years, the new trust legislation, was a more doubtful success. It was a compromise between the programs of the New Freedom and the New Nationalism, with a surprisingly large element of the latter. The Federal Trade Commission Act established a presidentially appointed five-person board with power to investigate corporate practice and issue cease-and-desist orders against unfair methods of competition. While its findings were conclusive, its orders could be appealed to the courts.

The Clayton Anti-Trust Act prohibited specific practices such as discriminatory prices, tying agreements, interlocking directorates, or purchase by one firm of stock in another. Such actions, however, were to be illegal only when they tended toward substantially lessening competition, which meant when the courts said they did.

According to the Clayton Act's labor clauses (hailed by Samuel Gompers of the AFL as "Labor's Magna Carta"), labor was not to be considered a commodity, labor and farm organizations were not to come under the antitrust law's definition of restraint of trade, and the power of courts to issue labor injunctions was (rather cautiously) restricted. Like the act's other clauses, these were somewhat imprecise and their meaning was whittled down in the courts. Yet the Wilson trust legislation looked formidable, and some business leaders began to consult the government before making moves toward consolidation.

With these major bills passed, the president made it clear that he believed he had accomplished his principal reform objectives. In 1914 and 1915 he seemed to go out of his way to conciliate business and conservative opinion. He refused support for either women's suffrage or child labor legislation, opposed federal loans for farmers, and sanctioned racially segregated facilities in federal departments. Many progressives in both parties were disheartened by Wilson's "conservative progressivism," especially when reform candidates lost heavily in the congressional elections of 1914.

In 1916, however, perhaps partly because a new election was pending and the Democrats had to attract some Roosevelt voters, the administration turned much more toward progressive reform. Louis J. Brandeis, the prominent antitrust lawyer and progressive intellectual, was appointed to the Supreme Court amid a storm of conservative criticism. Wilson reversed his earlier position and backed a Federal Farm Loan Act providing long-term rural credits and an act prohibiting interstate shipment of goods made by child labor (later held unconstitutional). The dollar-matching principle (federal appropriations to match state expenditures) was extended from agricultural experiment stations to an automobile highway program and (after the election) to vocational education. Finally, forgetting his *laissez-faire* principles under the pressure of foreign crisis and the threat of a serious railroad strike, Wilson supported the Adamson Act establishing an eight-hour day on the railroads. Thus the Wilson administration, enacting a program not altogether unlike that sponsored by Roosevelt in 1912, represented the culmination of the whole movement of reform that had begun in the 1890s.

WILSONIAN FOREIGN POLICY

To the skepticism and amusement of much of the world, Wilson made many sincere and idealistic pronouncements about foreign policy. He was determined to support and increase American power and prestige but only for the benefit of all humanity and only according to the most scrupulous methods. Some have seen in this intention a standard for foreign policy never equaled; others have found in it a misunderstanding of the nature and limits of power. To some extent, Wilson's purposes were supported by the new Secretary of State, William Jennings Bryan, perhaps the first pacifist to serve as foreign minister of a great power.

Much of Wilson's early foreign policy involved a startling denial of immediate national interest and was carried out amid loud outcries of nationalist indignation. Economic intervention in China was abandoned; the Philippines and Puerto Rico were given more self-government; and the United States, acknowledging treaty obligations previously denied, stopped discriminating against foreign shipping in the Panama Canal tolls.

In apparent contradiction to this policy of abstention, interventions in the Caribbean were more frequent and bloody than ever before and the United States became involved in what looked like aggression in Mexico. The contradiction was deeply ironic: the Caribbean interventions were aimed at political reform of the area and the Mexican involvement was the result of an altruistic effort to support Mexican democracy.

In 1910, one of the major revolutions of the twentieth century overthrew Porfirio Diaz, the bloody but efficient dictator of Mexico. American investors, who had $2 billion at stake and had gotten along very well with Diaz, were alarmed. When Diaz's liberal successor was murdered, the Taft administration seemed ready to support the new conservative president, Victoriano Huerta. Wilson, however, committed the United States to oppose Huerta without regard to material interests on the grounds that he had come to power by violence.

Instead of making Huerta's opponents grateful, Wilson's attempt at intervention in favor of Mexican democracy came close to uniting all Mexican factions against the United States. Always concerned to back American prestige, Wilson supported an admiral who demanded abject apology over a minor incident involving American sailors at Tampico in 1915. In the same year, the United States Navy, in order to prevent delivery of German munitions for Huerta, bombarded and occupied the port of Vera Cruz. Wilson was rescued from his increasingly untenable position when the major Latin American powers agreed to mediate. An international conference at Niagara Falls resulted in the coming to power of Huerta's main opponent, Venustiano Carranza, who was by this time no friend of the Wilson administration.

Even then, Wilson's Mexican troubles were not finished. Francisco Villa, a picturesque bandit who might be described as a cross between Robin Hood and Jesse James, shot up American border towns, killing American citizens. In 1916, Wilson sent General John J. Pershing into Mexico in pursuit of Villa. Though Villa was a rebel against the Carranza government, the American action was bitterly resented throughout Mexico, and war between the two countries seemed close. When entry into a larger war became imminent in 1917, the United States had to withdraw the expeditionary force. To Mexicans, America had become the enemy of the very revolution Wilson wanted to assist and guide.

THE MEANING OF PROGRESSIVISM

The progressive movement had not solved the problems of foreign policy. It had not produced, or tried to produce, any new social system. It had made only the barest beginning toward the redistribution of wealth or the control of private accumulations of power. While ultraconservatives lamented the end of free enterprise, the million or so Americans who wanted to move toward socialism were impatient with progressive caution. Despite the efforts of Southern white progressives, the South still lagged far behind the rest of the country in health and wealth. The deepest rooted American form of inequality was almost untouched, North or South. In the face of massive discrimination, many Negroes accepted the program of Booker T. Washington, who counseled the temporary acceptance of social discrimination and the adoption of modest economic goals. Only a few Negro intellectuals, led by W. E. B. Du Bois, demanded complete equality. In 1909, after a peculiarly savage race riot in Springfield, Illinois, a group of white progressives joined Du Bois to form the National Association for the Advancement of Colored People (NAACP) and press this neglected cause.

Some of the things progressives had accomplished proved impermanent. It was plain to close observers, even before 1917, that the reform fervor was declining and the opposition gathering strength. Soon, in wartime, much of the progressive program was to take on a different meaning, and in the postwar decade many progressive enactments were to be emasculated or abandoned.

Yet some permanent gains had been made. Big business, neither destroyed nor much weakened, was never again as defiant of public opinion as it had been. Immensely valuable national resources had been saved for the future. New paths for possible later government action were made possible by the income tax and other measures. Outside the arena of politics, dedicated reformers, now little remembered, left countless monuments in the shape of playgrounds, schools, clinics, and parks. In architecture, poetry, social science, and psychology, innovation had characterized the Progressive Era. In some fields, indeed, intellectual experiment begun in the Progressive Era was eventually to lead in disturbing directions, pointing far beyond the optimistic reform spirit of the prewar years.

More important than any concrete accomplishment of the progressive movement was its general reassertion of the will to adapt. Like other countries, America had been confronted by the huge problems of industrial civilization. In the face of this challenge, the country had not failed to find resources of courage and vitality. More than anyone yet realized, these resources were to prove indispensable in the coming decades.

FOR FURTHER READING

H. F. Pringle's *William Howard Taft* (2 vols., 1939) and Paolo E. Coletta's *The Presidency of William Howard Taft* (1973) are both interesting and sympathetic biographies. W. V. and Marie V. Scholes examine *The Foreign Policies of the Taft Administration* (1970). Russell B. Nye describes the rise and character of *Midwestern Progressive Politics* (1951).* The best account of Roosevelt's Bull Moose movement is G. E. Mowry's, *Theodore Roosevelt and the Progressive Movement* (1946).* Of the immense literature on Wilson, the most valuable long biography is that being written in several volumes by Arthur Link. Link summarizes Wilson's first administration admirably in his *Woodrow Wilson and the Progressive Era, 1910–1917* (1954).* John A. Garraty's *Woodrow Wilson* (1965) is an excellent brief biography, and John M. Blum's *Woodrow Wilson and the Politics of Morality* (1956) is a sprightly interpretation. There are good biographies of nearly all major figures. Henry F. May's *The End of American Innocence* (1959) and the more popular *Progressive Years* (1975) by William O'Neill look at the period's intellectual history.

---

*Available in paperback edition.

14. THE WAR AND THE TWENTIES

President	Political Events	Economic Conditions	Foreign Policy	Miscellaneous	
1916 Wilson D		1914 Depression. 1915–1916 Recovery: war orders.		1915 Movie, "Birth of a Nation."	1916
1918	Republicans win Senate.	1917–1918 War prosperity.	1917 (April) War declared. (January) Fourteen Points. (November) Armistice.		1918
	1919 (September) Wilson's collapse.	1919 Inflationary boom strikes.	1919 (June) Versailles Treaty signed.	1919 Red Scare. First regular radio station. Sinclair Lewis, *Main Street.*	
1920 Harding R	Prohibition and women's suffrage in effect.	Deflation and depression.	(March) Treaty finally defeated in Senate.	19th Amendment	1920
	1921 Immigration quotas established.	1921 Depression.	1921–1922 Washington Conference.		
1922	Fordney-McCumber Tariff. Progressive gains in Congress.	Recovery.			1922

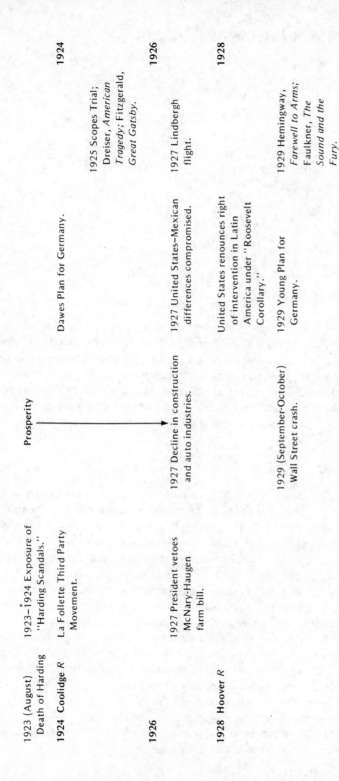

1923 (August) Death of Harding

1923–1924 Exposure of "Harding Scandals."

1924 Coolidge *R*

La Follette Third Party Movement.

1924

Dawes Plan for Germany.

1925 Scopes Trial; Dreiser, *American Tragedy*; Fitzgerald, *Great Gatsby*.

Prosperity →

1926

1926

1927 President vetoes McNary-Haugen farm bill.

1927 Decline in construction and auto industries.

1927 United States–Mexican differences compromised.

1927 Lindbergh flight.

1928 Hoover *R*

1928

United States renounces right of intervention in Latin America under "Roosevelt Corollary."

1929 Young Plan for Germany.

1929 (September-October) Wall Street crash.

1929 Hemingway, *Farewell to Arms*; Faulkner, *The Sound and the Fury*.

The First Overseas War

24

The war that began in August, 1914, brought to an end a century of relative peace, apparent democratic progress, and European domination of the world. It helped to bring about the first Communist revolution. For the United States it ushered in a period of economic world power and political isolation. It brought far greater steps toward governmental direction of the economy than most progressives had dreamed of. All this drastic innovation produced intense emotional confusion: Americans moved in a rapid zigzag from neutrality to crusading excitement to disillusion and revulsion.

THE WAR AND AMERICA

In 1914, most Americans found it hard to understand why all Europe went to war over the murder by a Serb of the heir to the throne of Austria-Hungary. Actually, the European great powers, all heavily armed, had long been engaged in a struggle for empire and prestige. They were organized in two huge, approximately equal alliances, each fearful of the other. One consisted of the two Central European empires of Germany and Austria-Hungary (with the doubtful adherence of Italy); the other consisted of Britain, France, and Russia. When Austria-Hungary, afraid of the disintegration of its multinational empire, demanded severe punishment of Serbia, Germany backed its ally's demands. Russia felt it necessary to assist Serbia, and France was linked to Russia. When Germany invaded France through Belgium (whose neutrality had been internationally guaranteed), England came somewhat reluctantly into the war. Later the Central Powers were joined by Turkey and Bulgaria; the Western Allies by Italy, Japan, Greece, Rumania, and other countries.

When war broke out, most Americans believed their country could and should stay out of it. Many quoted, or misquoted, the founders on the subject of foreign entanglements. To many progressives, war was associated with reaction, and to the socialist minority it was a product of dying capitalism.

Yet few managed to follow completely President Wilson's advice to remain neutral in thought. Most of the eastern, Anglo-Saxon elite of the nation, including a great many editors and journalists, deeply valued British law and literature and identified their own values with Western European civilization. Still larger groups felt a vague traditional sympathy with France and a genuine moral outrage over the invasion of Belgium. Some influential individuals argued, on less emotional grounds, that American safety depended on British control of the Atlantic Ocean. The drift of American foreign policy for two decades had been toward cooperation with Britain. Thus much Allied war propaganda fell on already friendly ears.

Not all Americans, however, favored the Allies. Many, including most Irish-Americans and many Midwesterners, continued to associate Britain with empire, aristocracy, and oligarchy. To the well-organized and articulate German-American minority, the Fatherland was an innocent victim of Allied encirclement.

Even more clearly than in Jefferson's day, real neutrality was made difficult by America's economic importance and geographic position. In 1914, the country was entering a depression, and war orders promised recovery. From the beginning, America took the traditional and legally correct position that all belligerents were free to buy supplies. Because of British naval power, only the Allies could tap American resources, which they desperately needed. Originally inclined to insist on cash sales in the interests of neutrality, Wilson and Secretary Bryan early withdrew their opposition to loans and bank credits. By 1915, American industry was booming, and American prosperity was bound up in Allied success. A German victory, an embargo on munitions, a prohibition of loans, or a sudden peace would have meant financial crisis.

Undoubtedly this economic involvement influenced some American opinion. Yet business, and particularly big business, was by no means dominant in the formation of American foreign policy. Some progressives were against whatever business leaders supported. And the president, who bore the responsibility for foreign-policy decisions, had demonstrated in the Mexican crisis a deep hostility to "selfish interests." While Wilson loved British culture and disliked German militarism, he was determined to maintain peace. He was also determined, as always, to defend America's national honor and her power. Both were essential to the overriding goal: the promotion of worldwide democratic progress. The president's most influential advisers, including his close friend Edward M. House, tended strongly in a pro-Allied direction.

Thus the forces affecting American policy were fairly evenly balanced. Most Americans wanted to stay out, and most hoped for Allied victory. Neither economic interest nor Allied sympathy was strong enough to counter the traditional dislike of becoming involved in Europe's troubles. Perplexed by conflicting emotions, many Americans responded most clearly to surging nationalism. Only a direct challenge to American rights and feelings could tip the balance toward war. This challenge arose out of a familiar problem: neutral rights at sea.

Once again, as in the time of Napoleon, a great land power and a great sea power were fighting an all-out war. Each preferred to remain on good terms with America, the world's most powerful neutral. Yet neither, in the long run, could afford to give up any weapon necessary to victory. The British, as expected, used their navy to blockade Germany and deny her essential supplies. The Germans, to cut off British supplies, turned to a new weapon, the submarine.

Enormously effective, the submarine was also vulnerable. Traditionally, a blockading warship was supposed to warn an enemy merchant vessel and remove passengers and crew before sinking her. If, however, a submarine surfaced to warn its victim, it could fairly easily be sunk by an armed merchant ship. In at least one famous case, a German submarine that had surfaced for this purpose was sunk by a British decoy ship, disguised as an American merchant vessel. Thus the Germans, throughout the war, faced a difficult choice. They could not use their only effective sea weapon in the only effective manner without killing civilians. Yet killing civilians, in 1914, was still regarded by world opinion as illegal and brutal. Submarine warfare, which might bring Germany victory, could at the same time add to Germany's enemies and thereby bring defeat.

In dealing with blockade and counterblockade, the Wilson administration had three possible choices, none of which was without its advocates. The first was strict neutrality, favored by Bryan, by many congressional Democrats, and by much midwestern opinion. Of the many methods proposed to implement such a policy, the most plausible was to prohibit American citizens from traveling on armed ships and thus to prevent the most dangerous kind of incidents. Under this plan, protests against both German and British blockade excesses would be filed for postwar negotiation. This policy, or any policy of abandoning or diminishing American neutral rights, was rejected by Wilson on grounds of national honor.

The opposite extreme would have been to intervene, early and frankly, on the Allied side. This would not only have ended the dilemma about neutral rights, it would have shortened the war and given America a more decisive voice in the peace. It was advocated by Theodore Roosevelt, which hardly recommended it to Wilson. Such a choice was completely contrary to tradition and would have divided the country disastrously.

The third choice, and one that attracted Wilson from time to time, was American mediation, either to moderate the war or to end it. Mediation efforts took two forms. The first was an effort to induce Britain to modify her blockade or cease from arming merchant vessels in return for German abandonment or modification of submarine warfare. The second was the attempt to persuade both belligerents to state negotiable war aims.

Both kinds of effort at mediation, sporadically pursued and probably illusory, had clearly failed by 1916. Neither side was willing permanently to abandon weapons it considered essential, and neither would abandon the prospect of victory. As the bloodshed mounted, so did fear and hatred, until compromise became impossible even to imagine.

For America to force peace before this process had gone too far, it would have had to threaten both sides with losing the war. Only a threat to cut off munitions could have compelled Britain to abandon her own war aims. To make such a threat and carry it out might have resulted in German victory. It was clear that the Wilson administration, in a showdown, was unlikely to take such action against the side most Americans preferred. To force Germany to make peace, on the other hand, it would have been necessary to threaten actual intervention on the Allied side. Only a heavily armed America, with a united or docile public opinion, could have made such a policy work. Really effective mediation was made impossible by the whole nature of the American political system. Thus the policy actually adopted was, and perhaps had to be, a constantly shifting compromise among the three alternatives: neutrality, intervention, and mediation.

FROM NEUTRALITY TO WAR IN FOUR ACTS

The first stage of American policy, from the outbreak of war to February, 1915, was characterized by benevolent neutrality toward England. After the shocking invasion of Belgium, the Germans gave little direct offense, while the British blockade became increasingly rigid. Contraband of war was gradually extended to cover most commodities, neutral ships were stopped at sea and taken to port for search, and trade with other neutrals who might transship to Germany was severely rationed. Yet American protests were moderate in tone, British concessions considerable, and, most important, no American was killed. The United States accepted without much ill feeling even the British proclamation of a mined war zone in the North Sea, where few American ships went.

The second stage, running from February, 1915 until May, 1916, was dominated by German submarine warfare. In February, Germany proclaimed a submarine war zone around the British Isles, cutting the main Atlantic sea lanes. From this point on, the U.S. administration refused to accept the legality of submarine warfare and announced that Germany would be held to "strict accountability" for American losses.

On May 7, 1915, the oceanliner Lusitania, unarmed but carrying some war cargo, was sunk off the Irish coast. Of the 1198 passengers drowned, 128 were Americans. In a series of very strong notes, Wilson demanded that Germany accept responsibility for these losses and abandon its methods of submarine war. After repeated warnings, partial or temporary German concessions, and further sinkings, Wilson, in March, 1916, made it clear that a continuation of unrestricted submarine warfare would mean a break in German-American relations. This clearly implied war, and Germany, somewhat grudgingly, promised that henceforth her raiders would warn before sinking. This seemed a major American victory. The nation was, however, practically committed to go to war if and when Germany changed her mind. To give some meaning to his implied threats of force, Wilson gave his backing, in late 1915, to a preparedness program including increased army and navy appropriations and heavy new taxes.

The third stage, from May, 1916 to February, 1917, brought somewhat less tense relations with Germany, increased irritation against England, and the peak of Wilson's efforts for a negotiated peace. In this period Britain, hard pressed in war and confident of American tolerance, stepped up her enforcement of the blockade. American mail was searched, and American firms believed to have dealt with Germany were black-listed and barred from British trade. Wilson found these actions almost intolerable, and Congress made gestures of retaliation.

In November, Wilson narrowly won reelection against Charles Evans Hughes, a moderate Republican progressive running with the support of a reunited (and largely conservative) party. In the campaign Wilson was attacked by both isolationists and interventionists. His own partisans, however, pointed to his success in keeping America out of war as well as to his recently increased domestic progressivism.

Once reelected, Wilson made his most ambitious effort at mediation, a public request to both sides for a statement of war aims. When this effort failed and it became clear that neither side was interested in compromise, Wilson became increasingly disillusioned with the Allied cause. On January 22, in an eloquent speech, he declared that the world's only hope lay in a "Peace without Victory" for either side.

The fourth and final phase started a week later when Germany, where military pressures had finally defeated civilian resistance, announced the resumption of unrestricted submarine warfare against neutral and belligerent vessels alike. Wilson had no alternative but to break relations, yet he still refused to ask for war. On March 1, the administration released to the press an intercepted German note proposing, in the event of war with the United States, an alliance with Mexico to recover lost territories and an effort to persuade Japan to switch sides. Meantime Wilson, despite a filibuster by Robert M. La Follette and other antiwar progressives, started arming American ships. Only at the beginning of April, after a series of new sinkings, did Wilson finally ask for and get from Congress a declaration of war against Germany.

AMERICA AT WAR: PATRIOTISM AND DISCONTENT

Though many Americans had expected limited, almost painless participation in the war, the state of the Allied war effort in 1917 made this impossible. Germany was sinking British ships faster than they could be built, the French army was exhausted and mutinous, and Russia was convulsed by revolution.

The first Russian Revolution in March, 1917 had caused America to welcome Russia joyfully into the ranks of democratic and constitutional states. In November, however, the Bolsheviks with their slogan of "land, bread, and peace" had overthrown the moderate Kerensky government, and Russia embarked on the Soviet road. In March they signed a treaty with Germany, surrendering large territories and freeing German troops for a one-front war. Germany thus began a series of immense offensives that threatened to defeat the Allies before American help could become effective.

Faced with this desperate necessity, the United States built a conscript army of more than 3,500,000 and by November, 1918, had shipped 2,000,000 soldiers overseas without losses. American naval forces greatly reduced the submarine menace. American ground forces in France played a distinguished and probably decisive part in the bloody operations of 1918, in which the German offensives were finally met and the German armies rolled back.

To do all this, it was necessary to regiment to a new degree the vast economic power of an essentially civilian country. Money for huge loans to the Allies as well as for America's war effort was raised by a fairly democratic system of war finance. About one-third of the total needed was raised by taxes as compared to about one-fifth in the Civil War. For this purpose, incomes and corporate profits were taxed at unheard-of rates. In 1918, incomes of over $1 million were assessed a total tax of 77 percent. (In 1913, a top rate of 7 percent had seemed high.) Federal war bonds were sold to 65 million customers in four great drives. Even so, the war was financed partly by inflation and mostly through expansion of bank credit by action of the new Federal Reserve System.

After fumbling with various regulatory devices in the first war winter, Congress in the spring of 1918 gave the president almost dictatorial powers over the war economy. Under him, 500 war agencies policed the productive effort. The War Industries Board allocated raw materials, determined priorities, and standardized products. The War Labor Board opposed strikes and lockouts but promoted union recognition, the eight-hour day, and uniform wages. The Food Administration under Herbert Hoover guaranteed the purchase of and set the prices for major farm commodities, thereby greatly increasing food production. The Fuel Board and the Shipping Administration similarly increased production in their spheres. The railroads were taken over and efficiently run by the Railway Administration.

By 1918, the United States had a fairly efficient regulated economy. Some advanced progressives talked cheerfully of war socialism and prophesied that these gains for collectivism would not be lost. Most citizens, however, were probably restive under this new system and were held in line only by wartime patriotism. Business objected to high taxes, resented labor's gains, and in general disliked being told what to do. Farmers, faring well, resented the fixing of prices that had never been set in periods of depression. Yet despite its widespread unpopularity, governmental direction of the war economy marked a momentous step in a generally continuing direction. There was no return to *laissez-faire,* if indeed *laissez-faire* had ever existed. After the war, the government was to act as a partner to business, and later, under the New Deal, wartime precedents were to be invoked for other kinds of intervention.

Equally great steps, with equally momentous consequences, were taken in the field of manipulating public opinion. Despite evidence of public enthusiasm, the government was apparently disquieted about national unity. The Committee on Public Information blanketed the country with pamphlets and speeches about the goals of the war. Cracking down on opposition, the Post Office barred antiwar publications from the mails. A Sedition Act passed in 1918 forbade abusive language about the American form of government, flag, or uniform and acts bringing into contempt the form of government or the Constitution. About 1,500 persons, including most of the leadership of the Socialist party, were imprisoned for sedition. States and private organizations went much further than the federal government in war hysteria. The German language was driven from the schools, German music was eliminated from concerts, and religious pacifists were physically abused. In some places, the slightest criticism of the administration or the Allies was considered punishable disloyalty. A reaction to all this emotion was inevitable. For the future, both the possibilities and the dangers of mobilizing emotion had been demonstrated.

Even considering measures of compulsion, popular support of the war was extraordinarily general. Yet beneath this unity lay discontent. This was indicated in the congressional elections of 1918 when Wilson, calling for the election of a Democratic Congress as an endorsement of his war leadership, received instead a Republican majority in both houses.

Yet despite growing disaffection with the war and Wilson's conduct of it, the popular mood in America contrasted sharply with that in Europe, where the indescribable horrors of war were a direct and daily reality, wasting both landscape and population. Whatever their other sacrifices, few American civilians knew or understood the remote and hideous world of the Western Front, a world of barbed wire and rat-infested trenches, of rotting corpses, crowded field hospitals, poison gas, and shrapnel. At war's end, the nation proudly noted that the weight of its arms and troops tipped the balance in the Allied favor. While this was true enough, the price paid in American lives was relatively small. In an intense six months of fighting, the United States sustained about 100,000 combat-related deaths, about half in battle and half to disease. By contrast, in four years the Russian combat dead numbered 1,700,000, the French 1,400,000, the British 900,000. Indeed, both sides sacrificed a half-generation of their young men in the bloodiest and most costly war in history.

THE FAILURE OF A WILSONIAN PEACE

On its entry into the war, America, democratic and free from either war guilt or aggressive ambitions, was recognized as the most effective Allied representative. Wilson became the worldwide prophet of a democratic peace. On January 8, 1918, he outlined to Congress his famous Fourteen Points.

The first five of these were general liberal formulae: open treaty making, freedom of the seas, removal of trade barriers, arms reduction, and impartial adjustment of colonial claims in the interest of the natives. Most of the rest of the points were concerned with the readjustment of boundaries in the interest of the Wilsonian principle of national self-determination even for small nations. The final point, the most important to Wilson, provided for an association of nations to maintain the peace. A number of the Fourteen Points were contrary to provisions in the secret treaties already negotiated among the Allies. Wilson knew of these treaties but ignored them, doubtless believing that he could force the Allies to abandon them.

On October 6, Germany, her military situation hopeless, asked Wilson for an armistice based on his announced program. Despite Allied objections, the Fourteen Points were accepted as the basis for peace, with some reservations. On November 11, military authorities finished negotiating an armistice that disarmed Germany and made further resistance impossible.

In January, 1919, at Paris, the victorious Allies started negotiating among themselves the peace terms to be imposed on Germany. Accompanied by an undistinguished peace delegation and a large corps of experts, Wilson left for Paris. Frantic ovations throughout Europe apparently convinced him that it was his mission, alone, to force a just peace on the world. Actually, his power was limited by two powerful opponents, the Allies and the Senate Republicans. Like Germany, Wilson had to fight a two-front war. Insisting from the outset that the covenant of the League of Nations be part of the Treaty, Wilson made a quick trip to Washington and found more than a third of the Senate lined up against the covenant in its negotiated form. Returning to Paris, he had to face the Allied leaders with weakened bargaining powers. These leaders of state, bound by the secret treaties, were also understandably determined to secure their nations against further attack and to make Germany pay for the long struggle. Despite a courageous fight, Wilson had to make many concessions. To Italy he had to concede sizable German-speaking border areas. Japan secured not only Germany's island colonies (which were to play a crucial part in World War II), but also, against Chinese opposition, German interests in the Shantung Peninsula. To France, who desired the actual dismemberment of Germany, Wilson had to concede very severe terms regarding the defeated nation. Germany was stripped of colonies and merchant marine, disarmed, and forced to surrender border areas. Perhaps more important, Germany was required to admit its guilt for the war as a basis for reparations, whose sum would be fixed later by the Allies.

With hindsight it is easy to see the inadequacies of the Versailles settlement. Too harsh to be a reconciliation, it was illusory as a restoration of Anglo-French world hegemony. Japan was thwarted, China chaotic, the colonial world restive, and all nonwhites irritated by the failure of a clause affirming racial equality. Bolshevik Russia was proclaiming world revolution, and Communist revolutions seemed to threaten both Asia and Central Europe. With somewhat confused aims and limited American participation, Allied forces invaded Russian territory during her years of upheaval and civil war.

To Wilson, exhausted and implacable, all the faults of the Versailles settlement were compensated for by the gains for self-determination and above all by the establishment of the League of Nations. This would, he hoped, supervise the administration of former German colonies by their new masters under the mandate system. It would secure the reduction of armaments, preserve the independence and integrity of all nations, mediate disputes, and even use force against those resorting to war. For this great hope, Wilson came home to fight.

At first, the treaty's chances looked good. Wilson's prestige was still great, and the idea of a League of Nations had long attracted American support. Yet the treaty aroused many kinds of opposition. Among its enemies were the disappointed minorities of German, Italian, and Irish descent, isolationists who feared that the League would involve America in European affairs, liberals who objected to the compromises of democratic principle, and, vaguer but crucially important, many Americans already reacting against wartime enthusiasm and sacrifice.

The Senate, where the struggle centered, was divided into three groups: (1) loyal Wilsonian Democrats, in favor of the treaty and the League; (2) a group of about a dozen senators, including La Follette, Borah, and Johnson of California, who were "Irreconcilable," all-out foes of both issues; and (3) "Reservationists" who were inclined to accept the treaty with certain changes defining and restricting the authority of the League.

In the long struggle, opposition to the treaty was marshaled by Henry Cabot Lodge, an enemy of Wilson and a master tactician. In order to attract the crucial Reservationists, Lodge proposed not rejection but alteration of the treaty. The changes were carefully calculated to sound plausible but to be unacceptable to Wilson. Lodge knew his opponent. Wilson forbade Democrats to accept the reservations, thus making impossible a two-thirds majority. Without reservations, the treaty was opposed by Irreconcilables and Reservationists; with reservations, it was opposed by Irreconcilables and loyal Democrats.

Refusing to accept defeat, Wilson embarked on a nationwide speaking tour. The people, he said, must not allow the Senate to "break the heart of the world" by rejecting the treaty. Prematurely aged and emotionally exhausted, Wilson broke down in the midst of his tour and had to be taken back to Washington. There he suffered a severe stroke and was partly incapacitated for the rest of his presidency. Sick, isolated, but grimly determined, he continued to forbid his followers to compromise. Though the Allies were by now willing to accept the reservations, Wilson's loyal followers rejected them, and the treaty failed to get ratification.

Once more Wilson appealed to the final authority, announcing in the spring of 1920 that the coming presidential election would constitute a "solemn referendum" on the treaty. In the campaign, the Democratic candidate, Governor James M. Cox of Ohio, supported the treaty and the League. The Republican candidate, Senator Warren G. Harding of the same state, opposed it only ambiguously, and some of his supporters favored it equally vaguely.

Harding won by the most sweeping majority since Monroe. It is impossible to prove that the election constituted a real referendum on foreign policy. It was certainly affected by many domestic issues, including the breakdown of Wilson and, to a considerable extent, of his administration. In another sense, however, the election of 1920 was a major decision; the campaign, the press, and the results indicated that the American people wanted a president as little like Woodrow Wilson as possible, and this is what they got.

The United States, a country with a long isolationist tradition, had been moving for a generation toward world leadership. Now its efforts had decided a world war, and its leader had dominated a world settlement. In 1920, the people, exhausted by this break with the past and disillusioned by its results, determined to do their best to return to familiar, cherished ways.

CONFLICTING HISTORICAL VIEWPOINTS

12. Why Did America Enter World War I?

Contemporary accounts of U.S. intervention in World War I were generally favorable to Wilsonian policies. The war was a noble and necessary war, many first-hand observers agreed, and Americans could take pride and satisfaction in their role in it. Reinforcing this initial view were two semi-autobiographical publications: Burton Hendrick, ed., The Life and Letters of Walter H. Page *(3 vols., 1922–26) and Charles Seymour,* The Intimate Papers of Colonel House *(4 vols., 1926–28). Both House and Page had helped shape American policy and neither questioned the wisdom of U.S. intervention.*

A revisionist interpretation, however, was not long in developing. Disillusioned by the failures of Wilson's peace and threatened by the gathering clouds of war in Europe and Asia, many Americans in the 1920s and 1930s traced the nation's involvement not to idealism or self-interest, but to folly, sentimentalism, and greed. Scholarly advocates of this view included Harry E. Barnes (Genesis of the World War, 1926), *C. Hartley Grattan* (Why We Fought, 1929), *and C. C. Tansill* (America Goes to War, 1938), *all of whom argued that Wilson's policies were neither wise, necessary, nor beneficial to the United States. In their accounts, U.S. intervention was attributed to the pernicious influences of misguided Wilsonian Anglophiles, skillful British propagandists, and grasping American munitions makers and international bankers.*

Although the revisionist view was in many ways an accurate reflection of popular, or at least congressional, sentiment during the postwar and depression years, it has not been widely accepted by historians. A more satisfactory argument was offered by Charles Seymour, whose American Diplomacy during World War I *(1934) has been called "the first historian's history of intervention." Treating American involvement as a historical problem rather than a moral issue, this Yale professor asserted that Wilson, although pro-ally, struggled valiantly to remain neutral. Anticipating such relatively recent interpretations as Arthur Link's* Wilson the Diplomatist *(1957) and Ernest May's* The World War and American Isolation *(1959), Seymour concluded that Wilson had little choice but to lead the nation into war. In the final analysis, he believed, the German submarine was the cause of American intervention. In close agreement, Link and May have stressed the tragedy of Wilson's dilemma and the limited range of his alternatives. While they, too, endeavored to avoid judgment, their studies stress the essential correctness of presidential policy.*

Also critical of revisionism were such "realist" historians as George Kennan (American Diplomacy, 1950) *and Robert Osgood* (Idealism and Self-Interest in America's Foreign Policy, 1953) *who argued that in 1917 the United States entered the right war for the wrong reasons. Having experienced the Second World War, realists doubted that the United States could have avoided the First. Their primary complaint, then, was not that Wilson carried the nation into war, but that he did so in the name of morality and legality, not national security and self-interest.*

Radical historians, on the other hand, denied that American intervention could be attributed to altruism and idealism. In their view, the war was waged not to make the world safe for democracy, but to make the world's markets safe for American economic expansion. Although perhaps best argued in William A. Williams's The Tragedy of American Foreign Policy *(1962), a subtle and challenging variation on this theme is presented in N. Gordon Levine's* Woodrow Wilson and World Politics *(1968). According to this scholar, it was Wilson's aim to build "a new rational international-capitalist order, safe from war and revolution and open to [American] commercial and moral expansion."*

FOR FURTHER READING

In addition to the studies mentioned above, students interested in the diplomacy of American interventionism should consult Thomas A. Bailey and Paul B. Ryan's *The Lusitania Disaster* (1975) and Patrick Devlin's *Too Proud to Fight* (1974). The social history of the home front can be found in P. W. Slosson's *The Great Crusade and After, 1914–1928* (1937). The wartime state of civil liberties is described by Zachariah Chafee, Jr., in *Free Speech in the United States* (1941), and wartime repression is put in a wider context by William Preston, Jr., in *Aliens and Dissenters* (1963). The misuse of history by wartime historians is examined by Carol S. Gruber in *Mars and Minerva* (1975), and by George T. Blakey in *Historians on the Home-front* (1971). The plight of German-Americans is detailed by Frederick C. Luebke in *Bonds of Loyalty* (1974). The rejection of the treaty is examined in T. A. Bailey's *Wilson and the Peacemakers* (1947)*; and Ralph Stone has written an able account of *The Irreconcilables* (1971).* The beginnings of Soviet-American relations are described by G. F. Kennan in *Russia Leaves the War* (1956)* and *The Decision to Intervene* (1958).* Jean-Baptiste Duroselle's *From Wilson to Roosevelt* (1960, translated 1963)* is an excellent French account of American foreign policy.

---

*Available in paperback edition.

The Twenties: Prosperity and Social Change

25

The postwar decade is thought of today in at least three ways. It was the Jazz Age, the roaring twenties, the romantic heyday of flappers and flivvers. It was also the period of Republican prosperity, conservatism, and isolation. Further, it was the period of Hemingway, Fitzgerald, and T. S. Eliot, a time of literary experiment and creation.

These paradoxical elements are not entirely the inventions of historians; even at the time, America looked different to different kinds of people. Entrepreneurs and farmers, Freudians and fundamentalists were all reacting at different rates and in different ways to a changing social and economic order. Some changes, like industrialization and urbanization, had been going on a long time and were now accelerated. Others, like the importation of challenging new ideas (among them psychoanalysis and relativity), had begun before the war. Still others were direct results of the war, which was itself a traumatic break with national tradition.

Some Americans accepted change willingly; others fought every departure from the good old ways. Still others, perhaps most notably Henry Ford, accepted innovation in some areas, like technology and transportation, and fought it in others, like manners and morals. Even for the most conservative, however, tradition seemed hard to define, let alone restore.

Fortunately, this time of flux was cushioned by good fortune. For many Americans, the 1920s were years of peace and prosperity—the last to occur for a long time.

THE FAILURE OF WILSONIANISM, 1918–1920

The first postwar years were by no means placid. The fight over the treaty was only one aspect of a frustrating struggle to liquidate the war. In 1919, many advanced progressives and labor leaders were talking about planned and masterful nationwide reconstruction and even predicting the nationalization of basic industries. Actually, nothing was farther from popular demand or administration intent. From the armistice on, government contracts were canceled, employees dismissed, and regulatory powers abandoned. Soldiers were rapidly discharged with only minimum provisions for reemployment.

Congress abandoned regulation and reform less rapidly than the administration. Immediately after the war, two progressive causes reached nationwide victory. The Eighteenth (prohibition) Amendment, pushed hard by the Methodist Church and the Anti-Saloon League, was passed through a combination of moral zeal, desire to conserve resources, and dislike of German-American brewers. In October, 1919, the Volstead Act, passed over Wilson's veto, ended forever (most of its friends and enemies thought) the manufacture, sale, transportation, or possession of intoxicating beverages. In the same year, the Nineteenth Amendment made women's suffrage a nationwide reality.

In dismantling controls, the postwar Congress had a mixed record. The railroads, returned to private hands by the administration, were placed under stringent regulation by the Esch-Cummins Act of 1920. This law's purpose, however, was partly to promote rather than prevent consolidation into fewer systems. From then on, the railroad industry, threatened with truck and bus competition and in places overbuilt, was treated more as an invalid and less as a tyrannical giant. The government-built merchant marine was returned to private interests, and here too subsidy was more needed than control. In the vital area of water power, Congress, in 1920, established a new regulatory agency, the Federal Power Commission, to license development and operation.

For the most part, however, the wartime directed economy was dismantled without planning and without disaster. In the spring of 1919, after a very brief postwar slump, business began to pick up. At the time, the upturn was credited to unsatisfied consumer demand, but today economists point to government spending, temporarily continued in the form of loans to the Allies and European relief operations. Rapidly, recovery turned into speculative boom, as wholesale prices rose by about 30 percent.

Instead of Imperial Germany, the main public enemy in 1919 seemed to be the high cost of living. Salaried people were badly pinched, and labor was restive about the possibility of maintaining wartime gains in organization and real wages. Four million workers, more than ever before, took part in strikes. In most of these, including a coal strike and a bitter and bloody steel strike, the unions were beaten. Government and articulate public opinion sided strongly with employers.

Along the nation's troubled racial front there was also violence and disorder. Beginning with the savage East St. Louis riot of 1917 and climaxing with a violent eruption in Chicago during the Red Summer of 1919, American cities began a painfully uneasy adjustment to the growing presence of new waves of black migrants. Pushed out of the South by discrimination and violence and drawn to northern industrial centers by wartime employment and the promise of a better life, blacks by the thousands came to occupy the blighted slums of Buffalo, Chicago, Cleveland, Detroit, New York, and other cities. In time, these black newcomers found somewhat better economic, political, and educational opportunities. But during the war and its aftermath, their presence was bitterly resented by whites who feared social equality and job competition. There were at least 26 urban race conflicts during the Red Summer, and in Chicago alone a chain of white violence, black counterviolence, and official repression left 23 blacks dead and thousands more homeless. Outraged by these bloody encounters—and the 83 lynchings of 1919—the NAACP and allied organizations launched a campaign that resulted in 1921 in the first antilynching bill ever passed by the House of Representatives. In the Senate, however, a Southern filibuster prevented its passage. During the postwar decade, lynch mobs killed at least 330 Americans, nearly all of them southern blacks.

Many white citizens blamed racial unrest, strikes, the high cost of living, and foreign crises on one simple cause: radical conspiracy. The Third International, calling from Moscow for world revolution, was echoed by the two new tiny American Communist parties. A few bombings, believed to be of anarchist origin, roused public emotions. Many conservative citizens feared, and a few ardent radicals hoped, that revolution was at hand.

In the fall of 1919, Attorney General A. Mitchell Palmer, formerly regarded a Wilsonian progressive, organized his famous series of raids on alleged foreign radical organizations. In the worst of these, thousands of people were arrested with little regard for legal procedure and sometimes treated with considerable brutality. Practically no evidence of dangerous revolutionary activity was uncovered, but many zealous individuals, organizations, and governmental units turned their hostility from Germans to radicals. The New York legislature expelled five duly-elected Socialist representatives, and a drastic sedition bill, carrying the death penalty in certain cases, was introduced (but never passed) in Congress. In one of the last episodes of the Red Scare, two philosophical anarchists named Nicola Sacco and Bartolomeo Vanzetti were arrested for a robbery and murder that few liberals believed they had committed. Despite impassioned agitation for their release, the two men were finally executed in 1927. They were posthumously pardoned half a century later.

Well before this execution, in fact before the end of 1920, the Red Scare had begun to ebb. For several years, however, fear of the alien, the dissenter, and the nonconformist showed itself in other ways: in race riots and lynchings, in anti-Semitic whisperings, in crusades against alarming ideas, and in suspicion of foreigners. All these tendencies played a part in the growth of the Ku Klux Klan, a new, secret organization founded in 1915 in imitation of its Reconstruction namesake. The Klan, stronger in the West than the South and with surprising strength in some of the nation's larger cities, was militantly anti-Catholic, antiforeign, and antiliberal. At its height in the early 1920s, thousands joined in sheeted parades, perhaps 5 million enrolled as members, and at least two states came under its political control. Only in the mid-1920s, when most kinds of hysteria gave way to complacency, did the Klan lose strength.

In 1919–1920, many Americans came to associate Wilsonian idealism with frustrated hopes and divisive emotions, with the unsolved problems of Europe, with war propaganda and foreign entanglements, and with the high cost of living and the Red Menace. Even the most devoted Wilsonians had to admit a shattering contrast between the vigorous leader of 1913 or the inspired prophet of 1917 and the sick, stubborn, old man of 1919, presiding over an administration zealous in hounding radicals but helpless in dealing with social or economic problems. It is not surprising that the country turned with relief toward a leadership as different as possible.

READJUSTMENT AND NEW DIRECTIONS, 1920–1924

Warren G. Harding was a small-town editor, a regular McKinley and Taft Republican, and a handsome, genial man with a modest intellectual endowment and undemanding moral standards. Conceivably, he was more forceful and able, and less the bumbling misfit, than several generations of historians have portrayed him to be. But even his most sympathetic biographer concedes that his term of office was scarred by gross mismanagement. To his credit, he announced a plan to staff his administration with his party's "best minds." A few of these were secured, including Charles Evans Hughes, the new Secretary of State; Herbert Hoover, Secretary of Commerce; and possibly Andrew Mellon, the Pittsburgh aluminum king who became Secretary of the Treasury. In too many cases, though, the administration was staffed with party hacks and presidential cronies in a manner reminiscent of the Grant Era. A major center of power was the famous "little house on K Street" where members of the so-called "Ohio Gang" played poker and avoided Prohibition. Harding's heterogeneous group of the talented and the tawdry made decisions of great importance, most of them highly popular in their time.

In his campaign, Harding, whose oratory rarely rose above the platitudinous, avoided defining his foreign policy. Much of the Republican party was bitterly isolationist, yet an important faction, including ex-President Taft, insisted that a new administration work out a less offensive substitute for the League of Nations. Whatever the election really meant (and clearly it was no "solemn referendum" on the League), Harding drew from it the conclusion that American entry into the League was a dead issue. U.S. membership in the World Court, which Harding and his Republican successors favored, was blocked by ultraisolationist forces in the press and the Senate.

Despite the strength of isolationist feelings, real isolation was impossible. In the Far East, the original home of the Open Door Policy and the traditional center of Republican foreign interest, a new settlement was urgently necessary. During the war, Japan had taken large steps toward the domination of China and military hegemony in East Asia. Traditional American commitments to Chinese territorial integrity and the Open Door still ran well beyond America's military power. In the winter of 1921, an international conference in Washington, sometimes referred to as a Republican Versailles, struggled with the related problems of disarmament and the Far East.

In a series of interlocking treaties the United States attained the following objectives: (1) Japanese expansion was rolled back; (2) the embarrassing Anglo-Japanese Alliance was terminated; (3) the status quo in the Far East and the integrity of China were guaranteed by all major powers concerned except Russia; (4) the major naval powers agreed to curtail construction of capital ships, with Japan limited to three-fifths of the naval power of each of the Big Two (Britain and the United States). In return for these advantages the United States surrendered the possibility of naval superiority and agreed not to fortify her possessions in the western Pacific. Much later, in an age of renewed Japanese aggression, these concessions were to be denounced. At the time, however, the United States was in no mood either for an arms race or for contesting Japan's control of the western Pacific area. The Washington Settlement seemed a great success, and Japanese-American relations relaxed.

It proved impossible to remain aloof even from Europe. The United States had made huge loans to the Allied nations both during and right after the war. These were viewed by Europeans as American contributions to the common struggle and by most Americans as legitimate business obligations. Not without recrimination, the United States negotiated a series of funding agreements extending payment over 25 years with rates of interest scaled down according to ability to pay.

Payment by any scheme turned out to present almost insoluble problems. Sufficient gold was not available, and large imports of European goods were promptly rendered impossible. True to Republican traditions, formed during a period of infant American industry and devoutly upheld long after, Congress, in 1922, enacted the steeply protective Fordney-McCumber Tariff.

To many Europeans, debt payments to the United States seemed inseparably connected with German reparation payments to the former Allies. But in 1923, the Germans, racked by inflation and resentful of the sole war guilt principle on which reparations were based, defaulted. France promptly occupied the industrial Ruhr and was challenged by passive resistance from the German population. This situation, clearly threatening prosperity and peace, was a major test for the new foreign policy, and the test was passed. An international commission of experts, headed by an American banker, negotiated the Dawes Plan in 1923, and six years later a like group worked out the similar Young Plan. The basis of these plans was (1) successively scaled-down German payments, (2) stabilization of the German currency, and (3) an international loan to Germany to make these steps possible.

The greatest industrial nation in the world, now also the greatest creditor, could not stay aloof from world affairs. Instead, private investment was substituted for other forms of intervention. American investors, acting more or less in response to State Department suggestions, sustained the German Republic, helped the relatively moderate banker and industrialist regime in Japan, contested Near Eastern oil areas with the British and French, and supported congenial governments in Latin America. Because this was done in the name of profit rather than politics and, above all, because military force was invoked only in minor Caribbean instances, the administration could quote with satisfaction the antientanglement advice of the founders.

Antiforeign emotions were appeased by a drastic change in immigration policy. Well before the war, fear and dislike of "The New Immigration" from southern and eastern Europe had been spread by alarmist propaganda, and pseudoscientists continued to cite head measurements of Slavs and Latins to demonstrate "criminal tendencies." Unions had long opposed the admission of cheap labor, and the advance of technology had made a mass of unskilled workers less important to industrialists. The war and the Red Scare had spread suspicion of aliens, and Congress in 1921–1924 took a series of actions designed both to decrease sharply the number of immigrants and to swing back the balance to a majority of north European peoples. In its 1924 version, the new legislation established a quota system limiting immigration from each country to 2 percent of its proportion of resident aliens according to the census of 1890. To the anger of the Japanese, a special provision totally excluded Orientals as "aliens ineligible to citizenship." This decision, which reduced immigration from a flood to a trickle, broke decisively with a major American tradition and wounded the feelings of important minorities. In the long run, however, its results were far different from those intended by some of its supporters. The end of free immigration, like the disappearance of the frontier, lessened the wide-open, competitive, mobile tendencies of American life. It also speeded assimilation. Without the familiar flood of desperate, exploitable new arrivals, the foreign-born and their children were to insist with increasing force on a full place in American life and politics.

The economic policies of the Harding administration were developed in a time of instability. Late in 1920, the postwar boom turned into depression as government supports of basic commodity prices ended and European demand temporarily fell off. In the face of plummeting prices and mounting unemployment, government policy was simple: to do everything possible to encourage business leadership. Secretary Mellon called for strict economy and proposed sharp cuts in taxes on profits and high incomes. (Interestingly, Congress gave him only part of what he asked.) The administration continued the Wilson policy of withdrawal from all forms of government economic enterprise and cooperated still more fully with industry's drive to "discipline" organized labor. Hoover's Department of Commerce strove to further foreign investment and encouraged the formation of trade associations to prevent price cutting and other "unfair" competition. Pro-business appointments to the courts and the new regulatory commissions ended any threat of unsympathetic regulation.

Whether or not because of government policy, recovery began in 1922 and became well-established in 1923. The fact that this depression ended quickly, without government action except for encouraging business, was to affect the thinking of many people at the outset of a greater depression a few years later.

One major exception to the encouraging economic tendency was the plight of the farmer. Once more production was far outrunning effective demand, and prices were falling disastrously. During the war, with demand unlimited and prices regulated by the government, farmers had prospered. Right after the war, a land boom had sustained at least the more fortunate. But in the 1920s, with bumper crops to sell, mechanization putting a premium on efficiency, and European and world competition increasing sharply, most farmers were in trouble. Large sections of the country were again confronted with the familiar problems of unpayable mortgages and rapidly increasing tenancy. A series of farm organizations, from the semisocialist Non-Partisan League of North Dakota to the more conservative Farm Bureau Federation, once more voiced demands for relief. In Congress the powerful Farm Bloc secured considerable relief legislation of familiar kinds such as encouragement of cooperatives, facilitation of credit, and regulation of packers and speculators.

Farmers were not the only people to show their discontent with the Harding policies. Prewar progressivism, with its underdog sympathies and anti–big-business emotions, lived on in the hearts of millions of teachers, preachers, social workers, unionists, and others. In the new postwar circumstances, however, both high morale and unity seemed hard for progressives to attain.

In 1922, the most promising of a series of progressive coalitions took shape in the form of the Conference for Progressive Political Action, a federation of farm organizations, discontented labor groups, moderate Socialists, and assorted Bull Moosers and other progressives. In the congressional elections of 1922, the CPPA scored some startling successes. Harding Republicans lost many seats both to Democrats and progressive Republicans.

In the new Congress, investigations disclosed a series of scandals equaled only in the Grant administration. Harding cronies in the Veterans' Bureau and a number of other agencies had been dispensing favors for financial inducements. The worst revelation was that government oil lands, held for naval needs, had been transferred in a series of maneuvers to a group of private speculators. Still popular but grievously betrayed by his own friends, the president fell ill in the course of returning from an Alaskan junket. On August 2, 1923, he died of a stroke in San Francisco. To his party's good fortune, he was replaced by Vice-President Calvin Coolidge, a tradition-minded Yankee who seemed the perfect incarnation of conventional Republican morality. In all fairness, this taciturn Vermonter (the most cruelly caricatured of presidents) was not entirely the political cipher of the Coolidge joke. He was, in fact, conventional, uninspiring, and perhaps even mediocre. But there was much in his public career that was both virtuous and admirable, and he brought to the office more knowledge of domestic and foreign affairs than has often been conceded by his critics.

In 1922–1924, many people thought that the Harding scandals and the progressive gains foreshadowed a political upheaval. The CPPA backed the redoubtable Robert M. La Follette as a "Progressive" presidential candidate. The La Follette platform had, to be sure, a rather old-fashioned ring for 1924: antimonopoly, public ownership of railroads, conservation, farm relief, and curbing of the Supreme Court. The Wisconsin Senator, whose antiwar record was now an asset in his own section, looked formidable enough to frighten conservatives. The Republicans, renominating Coolidge on a status quo platform, denounced La Follette and his supporters as extreme radicals. Meanwhile the Democrats, deeply divided by their old agrarian-urban split, bogged down in a deadlocked convention and emerged with an unpromising conservative candidate, John W. Davis.

The result of the election was a Coolidge landslide. La Follette, without adequate organization or large funds, scored 16.5 percent of the popular vote and ran ahead of Davis in many western states. Yet after the election, his disparate coalition fell apart. Progressivism, for the moment, seemed negative and old-fashioned. The election seemed a green light for business prosperity and its political friends.

THE NEW ERA AND ITS CRITICS

For the rest of the decade, American prosperity was the center of attention both for complacent natives and jealous or admiring foreigners. The principal basis for the good times was an increase in productivity based on advances in technology and management. Between 1923 and 1929, the output per worker-hour in manufacturing rose 32 percent. The basic industrial plant and transportation systems were by then largely adequate; much of the expansion could go into the kind of production that people notice most easily. The most spectacular advances took place in the production of electric power and light and of durable consumers goods and in the construction of both suburban houses and urban skyscrapers. By 1929, one American in five had an automobile. Radios, household appliances, and prepared foods were almost equally part of the new way of life.

Changing patterns of consumption, stimulated by mass advertising and assisted by time payments, seemed to render obsolete the old "Puritan virtues" of hard work, abstinence, and saving. Leisure and enjoyment became not only permissible but almost obligatory. From perplexing foreign problems and dull domestic politics, public attention turned to the lives of movie stars, the exploits of athletes, or the heroism of aviators like Charles Lindbergh who flew the Atlantic alone in 1927 and immediately became the most popular American.

The new prosperity brought with it a new ideology. Business, according to its enthusiasts, had accomplished the dreams of past radicals without coercion or hatred. Poverty and war were both overcome, and cutthroat competition had been replaced by cooperation and service. The new business leader was committed to high wages and deeply interested in employee welfare. Thus there was no further use for divisive labor unions or impractical political radicalism.

Actually the results of the new prosperity were less than Utopian. While farm prices rose a little from the postwar depression level, farmers as a whole, whose per capita income in 1929 was roughly one-third that of the national average, failed to regain their prewar purchasing power. Real wages rose sharply but not in proportion either to productivity or profits. In 1929, the average factory worker made less than $1,500 a year, and 71 percent of all American families got less than $2,500. (By contrast, the combined income of the richest 0.1 percent equaled that of the poorest 42 percent.) Even if these figures are multiplied to represent post-World War II purchasing power, they fall far short of universal well-being. Large groups, such as coal or textile workers, southern small farmers, and blacks, remained in real poverty.

Later, many critics were to point out that the New Era's prosperity was as unsound as it was uneven. Business consolidation, though it did not usually attain the outright monopoly that had alarmed people earlier, often led to dangerous practices. Prices were often inflexible, and insider groups sometimes built crazy pyramids of holding companies. In the late 1920s, too much money was going into outright speculation in land or stocks and not enough into genuinely productive investment. Worst of all, there was a serious maldistribution of income that put too little money in the paychecks of the average consumer.

Even at the time, important minorities refused to join in the chorus of complacency. Surviving congressional progressives, led by Senator George Norris of Nebraska, prevented the administration from turning over to private interests the government-built nitrate plants on the Tennessee River. (In turn, Coolidge and his successor were able to block Norris's own plan for a government-run Tennessee dam and power system.) Prodded by the Farm Bloc, Congress passed ambitious farm relief laws. Of these, the most discussed was the McNary-Haugen bill, vetoed in 1927. This was a complex scheme providing for government purchase and sale abroad of surplus farm commodities.

Perhaps the most important dissenters in the Coolidge era expressed themselves in ways that had nothing to do with politics. Many people of rural and small-town upbringing were uneasy about the new free and easy ways of living and appalled by the alleged wildness of the younger generation. Some called for a return to sobriety, simplicity, and tradition; some swelled the ranks of Protestant religious fundamentalism. Two generations after the Darwinian controversy, the state of Tennessee passed a law against teaching in the schools that humans descended from "lower animals." In 1925, when this law was challenged by shocked liberals in the famous Scopes trial in the mountain community of Dayton, no less a public figure than William Jennings Bryan appeared to champion a literal interpretation of Genesis.

At the opposite extreme from the Fundamentalists but equally hostile to the dominant business ideology, were the literary intellectuals and their followers. With the war, their exuberant rebellion against moral and esthetic conventions had turned to a far deeper kind of alienation. Repelled by postwar intolerance and equally disgusted by what seemed to them the materialism and conformity of the Coolidge era, many of the most literate Americans worried out loud about the fate of American civilization. Some roundly denounced the country and withdrew to the sophistication of Paris or the primitivism of Mexico or Spain.

The most intelligent of the discontented realized that more was at stake than any set of national mores. Old questions, put in new forms, were raising doubts about human nature itself. Americans were confronting problems common to all people but particularly distressing to those who inherited a tradition of individual freedom. To some popular behaviorist psychologists, the human person was a bundle of predictable and controllable responses to physical stimuli. To Freudians, human beings were ruled by emotional drives far below the level of consciousness. Neither view seemed to offer much hope to those who cared most for individual freedom. Squarely confronting these and other intellectual challenges, some Americans produced excellent and profoundly serious novels or poems. Others laid the foundation for a deeper and richer criticism of contemporary civilization than had yet been possible.

Perhaps no group indulged more fully in this spirit of national self-criticism and personal re-evaluation, and no group more fully explored the failures of American society, than Afro-Americans. The black literati of the Harlem Renaissance shared the discontented white intellectuals' distaste for bourgeois values and joined their insurrection against traditional literary forms. But the alienation of the black artists seemed more firmly rooted in the day-to-day realities of American life. In a rich outpouring of poems and novels, they celebrated the emergence of a "New Negro"—race-proud and militant, impatient with white injustice, determined to fight for basic human dignity. Joined by a confident new generation of black musicians, dancers, painters, and actors, they struggled to work out a new attitude toward blackness and the cultural heritage of their African past. In a parallel development, the inarticulate black denizens of the nation's industrial slums found a symbol of race pride in the exotic figure of Marcus Garvey and his Universal Negro Improvement Association. Unlike either Booker T. Washington or W. E. B. Du Bois, Garvey stirred the imagination of the impoverished black masses. His back-to-Africa movement, like his dream of an African Empire, died in embryo. But his immense popularity (estimates of his following range from one to four million) exposed as perhaps never before the depths of Afro-American despair.

The discontent of some of the nation's intellectuals and the dissatisfaction of much of its black minority were not widely shared by other segments of the population. Indeed, traditional "lost generation" accounts have doubtless exaggerated the degree and the depth of alienation and dissaffection among even the most discerning and sensitive elements of society. Everybody was not happy or rich in the mid-1920s, but prosperity was still a substantial fact, and those who were the most satisfied were also the most influential. More people than ever before moved to the suburbs, drove to the beach, or dreamed of a summer in Europe. Prosperity could be measured not only in baseball gate receipts but in such substantial terms as houses, schools, and hospitals. What civilization, complacent citizens could legitimately ask, had ever done so much for so many?

Ignoring his critics, President Coolidge continued to issue his laconic and reassuring statements, take his afternoon naps, continue the probusiness policies but without the corruption of his predecessor, and remain generally popular. The federal government persisted in trimming its costs. (States were spending more and more on highways.) In 1926, Secretary Mellon was finally able to put over his full program of tax relief for the wealthy.

In foreign affairs, success seemed equally conclusive. In Europe, the mid-1920s were an era of apparent economic stabilization, of Franco-German rapprochement, and of increased prestige for the League of Nations. Despite congressional suspicion, the administration was able to develop a habit of unofficial cooperation with the League for many purposes. In Mexico, where conflict between the forces of social revolution and American business interests dragged on, the Coolidge administration managed to compromise serious differences over subsoil oil rights.

Americans of the New Era believed that they could attain not only permanent prosperity, but lasting international peace. Barred by Congress from toying with collective security, the Coolidge administration made further but generally unsuccessful efforts to negotiate disarmament in 1927, an effort carried on by Hoover with somewhat more success in 1930. In August, 1928, largely through American efforts, 15 nations signed the Kellogg-Briand Pact renouncing war as an instrument of national policy. Like Prohibition, this innocuous measure was widely popular among the hopeful. Nearly all nations adhered to it during the remaining interval before the Second World War.

SMITH AND HOOVER

Neither foreign policy nor domestic economic argument played a major part in the presidential campaign of 1928. On the surface, the issues of this contest were personal; at a deeper level it involved the most divisive group loyalties. Herbert Hoover, the Republican nominee, was presented as a self-made engineer, a nonpolitical expert administrator, and a major spokesman of the new business outlook. The Democratic candidate, Alfred E. Smith of New York, though no radical, was known as a friend of the underprivileged and a champion, during the Red Scare, of civil liberties. The only major issue on which the two sharply differed was Prohibition.

This issue symbolized the real division between supporters of the two men. In many rural and Protestant areas, Prohibition was still regarded as at least a hopeful attack on a great evil, demanding the support of all respectable people. To many city dwellers, on the other hand, it was associated with lawlessness, gangsterism, and puritanical prejudice. Hoover had the conventional presidential background of Protestantism and rural poverty. Smith was a Catholic, a "wet" (opposed prohibition), and a city product with a New York accent. Without concrete issues, the campaign was fought to a large extent in terms of stereotypes and prejudices.

On the surface, the result was another Republican landslide. Hoover carried several states of the Democratic but Protestant and rural South. Yet later students of history have noticed that the big cities voted far more heavily Democratic than in previous twentieth-century elections. Despite his religion and his origins, Smith also scored significant Democratic gains in a number of discontented western farm regions. In the Smith vote, some historians have found the beginnings of the unbeatable Democratic coalition of the New Deal years. However, recent scholarship questions the concept of an "Al Smith Revolution" of 1928 as the necessary precursor to the "Roosevelt Revolution" of the 1930s. Although the Smith vote was impressive, the Depression still remains the primary explanation for Roosevelt's victory in 1932.

In 1929, to most people, the new administration seemed to promise increased efficiency and broader humanitarianism within the framework of the Harding-Coolidge policies. Yet Hoover, the ablest of the three postwar presidents, encountered disaster at home and menace abroad. Whether one looked at the 1920s with nostalgia or distaste, they were soon to seem a strange interlude in the tragic and turbulent history of the twentieth century. It was perhaps just as well that the United States had enjoyed an interlude of peace and prosperity, however illusory, between two times of appalling and challenging crisis.

CONFLICTING HISTORICAL VIEWPOINTS

13. Were the Twenties Roaring and Reactionary?

Few decades in American history have suffered more superficial analysis than the 1920s. In popular thought and in all too many serious works of history, the years between the armistice and the crash have been described—after a contemporary newspaper advertisement for a motion picture—as years of "beautiful jazz babies, champagne baths, midnight revels, [and] petting parties in the purple dawn." Most studies of the postwar decade, like the talkies, are animated by stock characters typecast as "flaming youth," "discontented intellectuals," or "self-complacent Babbits."

This conception of the 1920s as the "Jazz Age" of a "lost generation" was the work of many hands. But its chief architect was the self-styled "retrospective journalist" Frederick Lewis Allen, whose Only Yesterday *(1931) is probably the most readable and most read account of the decade. In Allen's view, "The Twenties" was a unique segment of American life with an atmosphere and style of its own. Isolated somehow from its past and curiously unconnected to its future, the decade was a frivolous interlude in which a nation, on the rebound from Wilsonian idealism, plunged into "a revolution of manners and morals."*

Allen's portrait, however impressionistic and superficial, profoundly influenced a generation of historians who viewed the period (when they viewed it at all) as an unfortunate interregnum between progressivism and the New Deal. The two best overviews of the period, William E. Leuchtenburg's lively social history (The Perils of Prosperity, *1958) and John D. Hick's political, economic, and diplomatic survey* (Republican Ascendancy, *1960), emphasize the decade's more frivolous and retrograde impulses. In the late 1950s, however, more subtle and complex images of the 1920s began to emerge. While in the popular mind the decade remained the "fantastic interim," or "the era of wonderful nonsense," growing numbers of scholars became skeptical about conventional emphasis on the spectacular, the bizarre, and the unique. Upon close examination, many found continuity as well as change in the postwar decade. Parting the traditional curtain of speakeasies, marathon dances, and raccoon coats, they perceived what Arthur Link has called "the exciting new frontier of American historical writing."*

A good example of this new view is Roderick Nash's Nervous Generation *(1970), which did much to mute the roar in the "roaring twenties." A survey of formal thought and popular culture, this recent study pointedly deemphasized the degenerate bohemian and the flagpole sitter and argued that the period was notable for neither disillusioned cynicism nor happy revelry.*

Similarly, recent political and diplomatic histories no longer teem with one-dimensional political Philistines and resolute isolationists. Arthur Link (American Historical Review, *July 1959) and Clark Chambers* (Seedtime of Reform, *1963), for example, revealed powerful reform currents at work in a decade once presumed to be pervasively conservative. Robert K. Murray* (The Harding Era, *1969), Donald McCoy* (Calvin Coolidge, *1967), and David Burner* (Herbert Hoover, *1978), among others, have offered provocative new studies of these Republican presidents that help dispel familiar, oversimple notions and that differ sharply in important particulars from earlier and markedly less sympathetic biographies. And foreign relations specialists, most notably William A. Williams, have challenged "The Legend of Isolationism in the 1920s"* (Science and Society, *Winter 1954).*

Thus, in the past decade or so, historical perceptions of the 1920s have been altered. Although many areas of sharp disagreement remain, there is now broad scholarly discontent with "Jazz Age" stereotypes. However enjoyable and enchant-

ing, the traditional, breezy survey à la Allen lacked the depth and complexity historians now bring to their analyses of the 1919–1929 decennium.

FOR FURTHER READING

The works mentioned above by Allen, Leuchtenburg, and Hicks, however flawed in emphasis, are still useful introductions to the period. Francis Russell's *Shadow of Blooming Grove* (1968) and William Allen White's *Puritan in Babylon* (1938) are readable biographies of Harding and Coolidge.

Economic history is excellently summarized by George Soule in *Prosperity Decade* (1947).* Irving Bernstein's *The Lean Years* (1960)* is a revealing history of labor from 1921 to 1933. Foreign policy is illuminated by Selig Adler in *The Isolationist Impulse* (1957).* Robert K. Murray examines the *Red Scare* (1955)*; Kenneth T. Jackson surveys *The Ku Klux Klan in the City* (1967); and Ray Ginger's *Six Days or Forever* (1958) analyzes the Scopes trial. Garvey's career is the subject of E. David Cronon's *Black Moses* (1955)*; and Nathan Huggins has surveyed the *Harlem Renaissance* (1971). An influential contemporary sample of American society is R. S. and H. M. Lynd's *Middletown* (1929).* President Hoover's Research Committee on Social Trends summarizes a great mass of interesting material in *Recent Social Trends* (2 vols., 1933). Andrew Sinclair's *Prohibition* (1962) and Norman H. Clark's *Deliver us From Evil* (1976) are both provocative interpretations of the "noble experiment." James J. Fink, in *The Car Culture* (1975), examines the rise of American "automobility"; and Marshall Smelser's *The Life that Ruth Built* (1975) is a biography of a popular legend. For literary history, the best source is contemporary writing, and the best introductions are Alfred Kazin's *On Native Grounds* (1942) and Malcom Cowley's *Exile's Return* (1951). Darwin Payne's biography of Frederick Lewis Allen, *The Man of Only Yesterday* (1975), offers a portrait of one arbiter of the decade's taste.

---

*Available in paperback edition.

15. THE NEW DEAL

	Labor	Agriculture	Business and Industrial Recovery	Relief	Reform	Miscellaneous
1932			Reconstruction Finance Corporation established.	Relief and Construction Act. Federal Home Loan Bank Act.		Bonus March. Election of Roosevelt.
1933	Section 7A of NIRA.	Agricultural Adjustment Act. Farm Credit Act.	Thomas Amendment to AAA (inflation). Emergency Banking Act. Economy Act. Beer and Wine Revenue Act. Banking Act of 1933 (guaranteed deposits). National Industrial Recovery Act.	Civilian Conservation Corps. Federal Emergency Relief Act. Home Owners Loan Act. Public Works Administration. Civil Works Administration.	Tennessee Valley Authority. Federal Securities Act.	Twenty-first Amendment (Repeal of Prohibition).

Year	Labor	Agriculture	Currency & Trade	Relief	Finance	Foreign / Political	Year
1934		Cotton Control Act. Federal Farm Bankruptcy Act.	Gold Reserve Act. Silver Purchase Act. Trade Agreement Act (reciprocal trade treaties).	Civil Works Emergency Relief Act.	Securities Exchange Act. National Housing Act.	Johnson Act.	1934
1935	National Labor Relations (Wagner) Act.	Resettlement Administration. Relief Electrification Administration.		Works Progress Administration and National Youth Administration.	Banking Act of 1935. Social Security Act. Public Utility Holding Company Act. Revenue Act. (wealth tax).	First Neutrality Act.	1935
1936		Soil Conservation and Domestic Allotment Act.				Neutrality Act extended. Soldier's Bonus. Roosevelt reelected.	1936
1937		Farm Security Administration.			Court Reorganization Act (not passed). Wagner-Steagall Housing Act.	Neutrality Act revised. Depression (fall).	1937
1938	Fair Labor Standards Act.	Agricultural Adjustment Act of 1938.				Billion dollar naval expansion. Republican gains in Congress.	1938

Depression and Social Experiment
1929–1938

26

In the summer of 1929, while stock prices rose beyond all relation to earnings or dividends, most industrial and financial experts predicted nothing but permanent prosperity. Signs of trouble, including declines in both construction and automobiles, the two key industries of the New Era, were generally ignored. In September, the market hesitated nervously, and then, in late October, a devastating series of crashes canceled 40 percent of the paper values of common stocks.

Despite the continuing optimism of government and business leaders, the crash of 1929 was not a mere correction of inflated values. Like the panics of 1873 and 1893, it turned into severe and prolonged depression. In the years from 1929 to 1933, as stock prices fell ever lower and confidence evaporated, manufacturing production was halved and building nearly stopped. Banks and businesses failed; farm income, already low, was cut in half; worst of all, unemployment grew steadily. By 1932, it was variously estimated at from 13 to 17 million. American prosperity, and with it the spirit of the New Era, had disappeared.

The impact of the great depression on those who lived through it is hard to exaggerate. At the lowest economic level, the unemployed faced the threat of actual starvation when charities, cities, and states ran out of relief funds. Apple selling and bread lines became common sights; shanty towns sprang up on the edge of cities; men and women were sometimes seen pawing through restaurant garbage. At the opposite end of the scale, some respected financiers were caught misusing investors' funds. Only a few killed themselves or fled to Europe, but both bankers and big business in general rapidly lost public prestige. In the large, previously contented middle class, people unused to disaster lost savings, houses, jobs, and hope. Even those who suffered no personal privation found it hard to dispel fear. Anyone might be the next victim of a disaster nobody understood.

Why did catastrophe paralyze the richest and most productive country in the world? At the time, many blamed some of the more obvious weak spots in the economy: the loose and ill-coordinated banking structure and the irresponsible financial manipulation that had piled one holding company on another. Later, New Dealers insisted that Republican policies had crippled foreign trade, encouraged inequality and concentration, fostered the boom and then clung doggedly to financial conservatism after the crash. On the other hand, President Hoover was always to believe that the depression was almost beaten when the election of a Democrat destroyed business confidence. In the long run, many historians have concluded that the fault lay in the unsoundness and inadequacy of the previous decade's prosperity. In the 1920s, prosperity depended as never before on mass consumption. Yet inequality and a too rigid price structure limited consumption. By 1929, effective demand for automobiles and some other products was apparently about filled. Attractive outlets seemed to be lacking for really large-scale investment. In other words, the prosperity of part of one country in a poor world could not continue. The New Era picture of liberal and progressive American capitalism, while not without truth, was not true enough.

HOOVER AND THE DEPRESSION

On coming to office in 1929, President Hoover found himself confronted by two familiar problems of the twenties: farm relief and the tariff. Each of these grew more difficult with the coming of depression.

Like Coolidge, Hoover fought off Farm Bloc proposals that seemed to involve subsidy and price fixing. In their place, Hoover secured the passage of a complex measure establishing a Federal Farm Board empowered to promote such time-honored remedies as cooperative marketing. By 1930, the "Stabilization Corporations" also created by this law were buying and storing surplus wheat and cotton. Already the government was up to its neck in nondisposable surpluses, and prices were still going down.

As part of his farm program, Hoover proposed another old panacea—tariffs—on agricultural products. This led Congress to further demands for industrial protection and the enactment of the Smoot-Hawley Tariff, signed by Hoover despite the protest of more than 1,000 economists. The high rates of this measure ended all prospects of reviving foreign trade.

In his measures, specifically designed to fight the depression, President Hoover, the elected representative of New Era know-how, broke sharply with the past. When Secretary Mellon recommended that the government allow prices and wages to fall until recovery set in according to traditional *laissez-faire* formulae, Hoover decided that such a drastic purge might kill the delicate patient. His first action, following New Era doctrine rather than nineteenth-century economic theory, was to call conferences of leaders in business, which urged employers to maintain wages and production. When this proved ineffective, Hoover used available government machinery to cut taxes, liberalize credit, and prop farm prices.

By 1930, the administration turned to more drastic remedies. In that year, however, the long-brewing revolt against the Republicans was speeded by depression, and Hoover lost the support of Congress. Many administration measures failed, but the president managed to secure large public works appropriations and measures to refinance home mortgages and further stimulate credit. A new agency, the Reconstruction Finance Corporation, lent large sums to banks, railroads, and businesses and also eventually to states, cities, and agricultural credit corporations. To stem international financial disaster, Hoover called successfully in 1931 for a one-year moratorium on German reparations and Allied debt payments.

Thus, in a major break with the past, the Hoover administration assumed governmental responsibility for fighting an economic crisis. Yet the Hoover measures, sweeping and large scale as some of them seemed by the standards of the twenties, were not adequate to the dimensions of the crisis. Moreover, the president flatly refused to meet two widespread demands. First, he declined to countenance currency inflation. Second, he fought all measures designed to provide direct federal responsibility for unemployment relief. Either of these actions, he sincerely believed, would have grave effects on American tradition and character.

As the plight of the unemployed became desperate, Hoover was wrongly seen as heartless. By 1932, dejection, apathy, and bad luck seemed to have destroyed the administration's earlier vigor. In that year, a "Bonus Army" of unemployed servicemen assembled in Washington to demand immediate cash payoff of 20-year insurance policies provided for World War veterans by legislation in 1924. Panicking at a minor threat to order, the administration directed the Army to destroy the veterans' camp with tanks and tear gas. This episode helped to make Hoover, a sensitive man, the worst-hated president since Cleveland. Although not without personal warmth and humor in his private life, the public Hoover too often appeared to be a dour and dogmatic technocrat, aloof, uncompassionate, more troubled by falling corporate profits than soaring unemployment. Whether through political inexperience or through limitations of personality, the hapless president lost the confidence of the nation and never managed to project the jaunty, crowd-winning confidence or the style of easy leadership that endeared his Democratic successor to a generation of depression-weary voters. Having forecast during the campaign "the day when poverty would be banished from the nation," his very name quickly became the byword of personal misfortune and mass suffering. In a matter of months, his reputation collapsed, and the "great humanitarian" of 1928 became the scapegoat of the nation's worst economic disaster. His reelection was obviously unlikely.

The Democratic candidate to succeed him, Governor Franklin D. Roosevelt of New York, was little known to most of the public. A Hudson River aristocrat from the Democratic branch of his family, he had been influenced by his cousin Theodore as well as by Wilson, whom he had served as Assistant Secretary of the Navy. After a sacrifice campaign for the vice-presidency in 1920, Roosevelt had been crippled by poliomyelitis. Nonetheless, he had remained active in Democratic politics and in 1928, bucking a Republican trend, had succeeded Smith as governor of New York, where he had tackled depression problems with considerable energy.

The trait the public immediately saw in the new Roosevelt was a gay, unflappable confidence that seemed a welcome opposite to Hoover's dogged gloom. What lay beneath this self-assurance is a question on which observers never agreed. To Roosevelt's critics, his cheerful nonchalance, his willingness to experiment, his tolerance of contradictions, and his impatience with theory meant superficiality and arrogance. To his admirers, however, his flexibility seemed to reflect a bedrock of courage and a genuine humanitarian and religious concern for the underdog. Either way, FDR's energy, his zest for life and leadership, and most of all his infectious optimism were welcomed by a dispirited people.

Nominated by adroit maneuvers in a close convention, Roosevelt pledged drastic action to end the depression. What sort of action was not clear; while Roosevelt called for public power development and other progressive reforms, he also pledged a 25 percent cut in spending and evaded the tariff question. Hoover, meanwhile, asked the people to sustain his own battle with the depression and grimly predicted disaster if his opponent won. The result was hardly in doubt; the Roosevelt landslide approximately equaled the Hoover victory of 1928.

During the interregnum before the new administration could take over in March, Hoover tried hard to persuade the president-elect to commit himself to a balanced budget, maintenance of the gold standard, and other central Republican policies. Roosevelt committed himself to nothing and was blamed by Republicans for a further economic downturn. In February, the Governor of Michigan announced a bank holiday to prevent financial collapse, and other states followed suit. By Inauguration Day, all banks were shut and some cities turned to issuing temporary currency. In the Midwest, farmers resorted to old methods of semiviolent protest against a hopeless situation; milk trucks were overturned and mortgage sales forcibly halted. Unemployed vagrants, many of them boys, were roaming the country. As never before, the stage was set for masterful presidential action.

THE FIRST NEW DEAL

In his arresting inaugural, Roosevelt promised that he would, if necessary, ask for powers to fight the depression equal to those given presidents in wartime. America's resources were adequate for the task ahead; the only thing it had to fear was "fear itself." Resounding with confidence and vigor, the speech committed the administration to no single course. For a while, nearly all Americans, from bankers to tenant farmers and unemployed, counted on Roosevelt to give them their demands. The New Deal, taking various forms through the next years, is best understood as a continuing experimental response to these demands. Behind each measure demanded by the president lay group pressures, party needs, presidential advisers, and congressional blocs. To understand fully the New Deal, one would have to understand two profound mysteries: American society and Franklin D. Roosevelt.

In the spring of 1933, Congress passed a series of administration measures with unheard-of speed. Roosevelt later summarized his objectives as "Relief, Recovery, and Reform," and this First New Deal can be described in terms of these "Three Rs."

Relief for the country's most urgent needs started with legislation to open and sustain the sounder banks, leaving the weaker ones shut. Direct federal help for the unemployed began with the Civilian Conservation Corps, which set young men to work on reforestation and other conservation projects. Larger unemployment relief programs included federal grants to states and plans for vast public works. Relief for home and farm owners was the main purpose of further legislation to refinance mortgages.

Recovery of the economy called forth the most spectacular measures of the First New Deal, measures that demonstrated its lack of consistent economic theory. Approaches to recovery included the Economy Act, which reflected the traditional belief that government spending somehow caused economic decline; the Trade Agreements Act, which gave the president power to negotiate low-tariff agreements in order to revive foreign trade; and even the Beer and Wine Revenue Act, which legalized one promising industry. (By the end of the year, the 21st Amendment swept away Prohibition completely.) The most important recovery programs of the First New Deal, however, relied on two main methods: first, raising prices by restricting output and controlling competition; and second, inflating the dollar, now irresistibly demanded by western Democrats.

During the campaign, Roosevelt and some of his advisers had declared that the expansion of the American economy, like that of the frontier, was finished. In the future, better distribution and planned production would replace violent competition. This theory owed something to Herbert Croly and the Bull Moose movement and something to Herbert Hoover and the trade associations of the 1920s. The ambitious National Industrial Recovery Act (NIRA) gave industry the legal right to agree on binding codes of common practice. These codes would, it was hoped, end sharp practices, unfair treatment of labor, and unjust, below-cost cuts in prices. How much they would permit prices to *rise* was never clearly settled. To make such agreements possible, the antitrust laws were suspended. To compensate for this favor to industry, workers were promised in the famous Section 7A of the NIRA the right "to organize and bargain collectively through representatives of their own choosing . . . free from the interference, restraint, or coercion of employers. . . ."

Reflecting a somewhat similar purpose, the Agricultural Adjustment Act (AAA) of 1933 sought primarily to raise farm prices by many and complex methods. Its most striking feature was a system of subsidies to be given farmers who agreed to decrease production. Such payments were to be financed by taxes on the industries that processed agricultural products.

Inflation, the other principal recovery device, was provided for in an amendment to the AAA, sponsored by Senator Elmer Thomas of Oklahoma, who remembered Bryan's crusade against gold. The Thomas Amendment gave the president power to inflate the currency in many ways. Moving reluctantly at first, Roosevelt took the dollar off gold, sanctioned special measures to support the price of silver, and eventually stabilized the currency at about 60 percent of its former value.

Reform—that is, deliberate effort to render the social system more just or humane—could be seen in the new programs to regulate stock exchanges and investment banking, in the labor clause of the NIRA, and, most clearly of all, in the Tennessee Valley Authority. This daring project, bringing to fruition the long frustrated dreams of Senator Norris and other progressives, was designed to remodel a whole river system by building a series of dams. Among its objectives were cheap power and fertilizer, flood control, soil and forest conservation, the improvement of inland waterways, and new recreational areas. Reform and recovery were both objectives of the National Housing Act of 1934, which provided insurance of loans to promote repair and modernization of homes, farms, and small plants.

NEW DEMANDS AND
A SECOND NEW DEAL, 1934–1936

Through these and other laws, the First New Deal seemed to have scored a qualified success. Its first actions brought a sharp rise in production and prices. Then the rate of recovery slowed, and people realized that the depression had not disappeared. The elections of 1934, increasing the already large Democratic majorities, showed clearly that a majority approved the administration's efforts. Yet more was needed; the First New Deal had brought to light a whole series of new demands.

Farmers had benefited from price rises but were still distressed. Some of them had been disturbed by the destruction of crops and animals undertaken as an emergency measure in time of surplus. Then in 1934, the worst drought in the nation's history threatened to change surplus to shortage. Thousands of tenants and sharecroppers were driven from the land and left destitute. In part caused by the drought, this also seemed in part to be caused by the AAA, which encouraged landlords to mechanize and cut acreage. So far, it seemed to many angry small farmers, the New Deal farm program had helped the richest most.

The unemployed demanded faster relief than was provided by the cautious handling of public works. Organized labor, which had reached a low point in 1933, took new courage from Section 7A with its guarantees of freedom to organize. But as new millions rushed into the ill-prepared unions, hard problems arose. Employers, many of them still hostile to "outside" organizations, thought that Section 7A had authorized them to form more or less docile company unions. Workers insisted that only national organizations could be effective. The National Labor Board, formed by the president to arbitrate multiplying controversies, lacked both authority and consistent policy.

Business and industry, at first eager for New Deal help and willing to promise drastic reform, had become restless with partial recovery. Despite gains made through NIRA codes, many business leaders resented excessive government interference in the details of their operations. Some hoped to exclude the government altogether and make the program into one of simple business self-regulation on the Hoover pattern. On the other hand, progressives were charging that big business already dominated the codes and gouged consumers. Worried liberals, looking both at NIRA and AAA, doubted increasingly whether raising prices and cutting production was the best answer to widespread scarcity.

Thus the administration, which had tried to please everybody, found itself attacked from right and left. Conservatives looked back with nostalgia at the probusiness policies of the Republican years or lamented the end of *laissez-faire* and traditional individualism. Just below the surface of some of the most fervent complaints ran an undercurrent of fear that the balance of power in the country was shifting away from those who ought to be in charge, in the direction of the shiftless, the irresponsible, and the foreign born. Not a few outraged citizens concluded that the whole New Deal was a conspiracy against free enterprise, sound money, and American tradition and even that it was secretly aiming at ushering in socialism or communism.

At the other extreme, the tiny Communist party of the United States had made some progress. It was aided in 1935 by a sharp change in the international Communist line. Instead of denouncing all non-Communist efforts at reform as insipid and useless, Communists were now to call for a "United Front" and to make every effort to work with "progressives" and "anti-Fascists." During the period from 1935 to 1939, while this line endured, the Communist movement achieved some influence among American intellectuals and among some elements of labor. More important than actual Communist gains, which remained numerically small, was the conviction, or half-conviction, fairly widespread among intellectuals, that capitalism could not recover.

Still more important in practical politics was the rapid spread of economic panaceas. Most of these appealed, as in the past, to disgruntled rural and small town people, and most involved a combination of currency tinkering and old-fashioned anti–big-business rhetoric. Among them were the Townsend Plan for liberal old-age pensions; the inflationary suggestions of Father Coughlin, the radio priest who denounced international bankers in speeches with anti-Semitic overtones; the sweeping production-for-use plan of Upton Sinclair in California; and the glittering, enticing "Every Man a King" proposal of Huey P. Long, a talented, ruthless spokesman of the dispossessed who made himself governor and near-dictator of Louisiana. All these plans, however illusory, gained their strength from two undeniable truths. First, the richest country in the world had too many poor people. Second, the New Deal had not yet produced a convincing remedy.

In response to all these pressures, the president, supported by new advisers, backed a new set of measures. This Second New Deal, often seen as more radical than the first, was not really aimed at systematic alteration of the economic or social system. Indeed, one important group of young men who prepared it were under the influence of Louis D. Brandeis, who had helped to prepare Woodrow Wilson's "New Freedom" program and had imbued his followers with a dislike of bigness and a fervent belief in competition and diversity. The Second New Deal contained no measures aimed at direct regulation of business on the scale of the NIRA and none whose objectives were as sweeping as those of the TVA. Its main object, like that of its predecessor, was to get the economy going and to correct in the process some obvious injustices. Some of its measures had the further, highly traditional purpose of breaking up concentrations of power.

The new measures were sometimes proclaimed in combative tones. Often they were carried through with hard-boiled political efficiency. Quite obviously, some of them reflected the demands of newly articulate groups. It is not surprising that some members of the business community, remembering the placid 1920s, were both resentful and alarmed. To many young people and to believers in social experiment, on the other hand, the Second New Deal brought a time of heady excitement, when almost any goal seemed possible, and almost any method worth a try.

In the sphere of unemployment relief, the administration committed itself to the principle of providing work rather than handouts. A special agency, the National Youth Administration, provided employment for unemployed youths and assisted students to stay in college. The Second New Deal's principal relief agency was the gigantic Works Progress Administration administered by the former social worker Harry Hopkins, a devoted, self-sacrificing, and sometimes ruthless New Dealer. The WPA built roads, schools, parks, and countless other projects. In addition to construction workers, it employed actors, painters, musicians, and writers. Astounded conservatives and delighted liberals found the federal government sponsoring symphony concerts, excellent guidebooks, colossal murals of varying quality, and the production of plays, some of them experimental and some left-wing.

Existing farm programs were supplemented by efforts to help the neglected poorest farmers. The Resettlement Administration tried to move families from submarginal land, and the Rural Electrification Administration brought power lines to areas not served by private utilities.

In the Social Security Act, the United States, entering the field much later than other leading industrial countries, laid the foundations for a system of old-age, unemployment, and disability insurance financed largely by employer and employee contributions. The Revenue Act of 1935, though whittled down in Congress, sharply increased taxes on high incomes, corporations, and estates. The Banking Act of 1935 increased the power of the Federal Reserve Board to buy and sell government securities in the open market for stabilization purposes, and the Public Utility Holding Company Act restricted the practice of piling one company on another in the fashion popular in the late 1920s.

Finally, as the new labor problems became more and more pressing, the president, in 1935, gave his backing to a bill long advocated by Senator Robert F. Wagner of New York. The Wagner Act outlawed employer coercion and support of company unions. Henceforth an employer was required to bargain with the union chosen by a majority of his employees in government-supervised, secret-ballot elections.

Sweeping changes in the size and shape of organized labor were partly a cause and partly an effect of new government policies. Since NIRA days, organizers had turned their attention to the long-unorganized millions in such great industries as steel, automobiles, rubber, and textiles. Inevitably, swelling numbers and this change of direction strained the traditional craft organization of the American Federation of Labor. Led by John L. Lewis, the colorful and domineering head of the United Mine Workers, a group of rebels formed within the AFL a Committee for Industrial Organization. This group, expelled in November, 1935, became in 1938 the independent Congress of Industrial Organizations.

In a series of hard-fought, sometimes bloody, strikes, the CIO attacked the long-defended bastions of American heavy industry. This time the outcome of labor warfare was a sweeping union victory. Beginning wth the surrender of U.S. Steel and General Motors in 1937, America's most powerful corporations were to make agreements with CIO unions. Already, by that year, organized labor had grown from a depression low of under 3 million to more than 7 million, and it was still growing fast.

Not only the size but the nature of the American labor movement was changed. Most of it, unlike the labor movements of other industrial countries, continued to accept the capitalist system of production. (An important faction of the CIO, later to be expelled, was under Communist influence.) But American labor by the mid-1930s was far more deeply committed to political action to further its social objectives than it had been before.

In 1936, the Republicans, sharply denouncing the New Deal, nominated Alfred M. Landon, the moderately liberal governor of Kansas, to oppose Roosevelt. In a victory that surpassed all but Harding's, Roosevelt got more than 60 percent of the popular vote and carried all states but Maine and Vermont. In this election, the Democrats were supported for the first time by an emerging, powerful, but unstable coalition consisting of labor, most farmers, recent immigrants, blacks, and the South; while the Republicans had the support of most people in business. Though this pattern was to vary from election to election with changing circumstances, it would affect American politics for more than a generation.

DEADLOCK AND A THIRD NEW DEAL, 1937–1938

Despite this resounding election victory in 1936, the New Deal in 1937 and 1938 ran into a series of partial defeats. The first was in its conflict with the Supreme Court. In its sessions of 1935 and 1936, the court had overturned a number of important New Deal statutes, sometimes in five-to-four decisions. These included the National Industrial Recovery Act and the processing tax of the Agricultural Adjustment Act. According to a majority of the court, Congress during the New Deal had unconstitutionally delegated detailed legislative power to administrative agencies (as in the NIRA) and had gravely misinterpreted the taxing power, the interstate commerce clause, and other parts of the Constitution.

To the president and many New Dealers, the court majority seemed to be interpreting the Constitution in a rigid and reactionary manner. Concluding that it would be impossibly slow and difficult to amend the Constitution, Roosevelt, in February, 1937, unveiled a drastic proposal for changing the court's personnel. One justice was to be added for every member who failed to retire after age 70. Some people were shocked by this attack on the court, and many disliked the president's unsuccessful attempt to present his plan as part of an innocuous program for judicial efficiency. While argument raged fiercely, the court itself took a hand in the struggle. A number of important New Deal statutes were suddenly sustained, and one conservative justice voluntarily retired. This made court reform seem less urgent, and despite the president's refusal to compromise, the bill was defeated in Senate committee.

In the long run, the change in the court's attitude constituted a major New Deal victory and ushered in a long period of increase in the government's power for social and economic legislation. Yet the prestige of the Supreme Court as an institution survived; that of the president was sharply damaged.

Presidential prestige was further injured by the onset of a new depression. In the summer of 1936, production, profits, and wages (though not employment) edged toward the levels of 1929. Apparently this was partly because of large government spending for New Deal purposes and for payment of the veterans' bonus (finally provided by Congress over Roosevelt's veto in 1936). The president, worried about deficits and mounting debt, acted to tighten credit and cut the budget, particularly WPA funds. In the fall, a sudden collapse seemed to bring back conditions of 1932. Farm prices headed down again, unemployment grew, and some critics concluded that the administration had failed to find a solution for the depression.

Whether this was true or not, the New Deal proved in 1937–1938 that it had not lost its energy. Expenditures were sharply increased for relief, public works, and, under the Wagner-Steagall bill, for public housing. Whereas earlier governmental expenditures had usually been defended only as humanitarian necessities, now spending was advocated partly as a means of inducing recovery. This reflected the increasing influence among economists, in and out of the administration, of the theories of the English economist J. M. Keynes. Keynes argued impressively that in time of depression, deficit spending by government was necessary in order to induce recovery and "prime the pump" of private investment.

Partly to further recovery by breaking up price fixing (a direct reversal of the First New Deal's objective), antitrust prosecutions were vigorously increased. A new Farm Security Administration tried hard to help the tenant farmers and migratory workers who were still America's most poverty-stricken people. A new AAA sought to raise all farm income by many devices, including new measures for crop restriction and government loans on stored surplus crops. Finally, the Fair Labor Standards Act of June, 1938, made possible by the Supreme Court's new attitude, established modest minimum wages and maximum hours for most employees and killed that old and tough enemy of American progressives, child labor. Some of the innovations of this last New Deal, including compensatory spending and wage regulation, proved to be among the most permanent and substantial changes brought about in the whole period.

THE MEANING OF THE NEW DEAL

The 1938 congressional elections ended the New Deal period. Not only did conservative Republicans gain sharply in the West, but conservative Democrats in the South beat off Roosevelt's daring attempt to defeat them and thereby turn the Democratic party into a clear-cut New Deal organization. Though Roosevelt remained popular and existing New Deal measures remained in effect, further concerted or rapid reform action was impossible. For the next quarter-century, the same conservative coalition was normally to control Congress.

Why did the New Deal lose momentum in 1938? Most obviously, foreign crisis began to draw the country's attention away from domestic reform. Yet many have blamed the slowdown partly on the program's own shortcomings, particularly its shifting approach to economic problems, its effort to combine incompatible groups of supporters, and its dependence on Roosevelt's personal leadership. It had certainly failed to solve one of the country's most serious problems; in 1938, there were still 10 million unemployed. Government spending seemed to be the only really successful way of stimulating recovery, and agriculture still depended on heavy subsidies.

Yet when Americans looked abroad, they could feel some reason for pride. No country had solved the problems of modern industrial society with complete success, and several, struggling with those problems, had lost political freedom. Without revolution, without even major constitutional change, the American republic had taken on a big new responsibility. So far, its function had been at most to provide a favorable environment for private economic action and to regulate when necessary. Now, in the face of economic collapse, first Hoover and then Roosevelt had made the government responsible for reaching and maintaining adequate prosperity.

Some of the most important changes brought about by the New Deal were social rather than economic and incidental rather than programmatic. Domination of American society by an elite made up of the native, urban upper-middle class, a domination never secure and never official but long partially effective, had become impossible.

To many who remember these years, however, the most important fact was neither the big accomplishments, the big failures, nor the hidden social changes. It was rather the revival of creativity, daring, and hope, qualities that were to be badly needed in the decades just ahead.

CONFLICTING HISTORICAL VIEWPOINTS

14. How New Was the New Deal?

To many conservative observers, the New Deal was a destructive experiment in socialism. Al Smith angrily denounced the "Brain-Trusters" as Marxists in Jeffersonian clothing, and Herbert Hoover shuddered when he contemplated the horrors of "New Deal collectivism." Yet, with the exception of Edgar Robinson—whose deprecatory The Roosevelt Leadership *(1955) is read largely for its novelty—this contemporary judgment has found no support among historians. Whatever else it was, scholars generally agreed, the New Deal was not socialism. Richard Hofstadter* (Age of Reform, *1955) called it the "New Departure" and Carl Degler* (Out of Our Past, *1959) termed it the "Third American Revolution." They both agreed that the New Deal departed in fundamental ways from the American reform tradition, but neither viewed it as particularly radical or dangerous. The New Deal was something of a break with the past, these liberal scholars argued, but it was also an essentially constructive and healthy response to the challenge of the Great Depression.*

The argument for benign discontinuity was widely, although not universally, accepted. Many distinguished historians, including Arthur Link, Henry Steele Commager, and Eric Goldman, believed that Roosevelt's programs evolved naturally from traditional American reform impulses. In Rendezvous with Destiny *(1952),*

Goldman discovered the New Deal's antecedents in the ideas and policies of Theodore Roosevelt, Woodrow Wilson, and even Herbert Hoover. The roots of the New Deal, he concluded, were firmly fixed in the soil of traditional American values.

Although once heatedly debated, the revolution-evolution controversy is no longer an issue dividing the scholarly community. In recent years, historians have worried less about the origins of the New Deal and more about its effectiveness. Liberal sympathizers, most notably Arthur M. Schlesinger, Jr., have cast the Roosevelt administration in a most favorable light. Sharply contrasting New Deal dynamism with the static "Old Order," Schlesinger's brilliant Age of Roosevelt *(3 vols., 1957–60) portrayed FDR as a common-sense democrat who spurned "dogmatic absolutes" and sought a middle way between the extremes of "chaos and tyranny,"* laissez-faire *and collectivism. Other liberal scholars, including James MacGregor Burns (*Roosevelt: The Lion and the Fox, *1956) and William E. Leuchtenburg (*Franklin D. Roosevelt and the New Deal, *1963), however, were less laudatory. Although generally favorable, Leuchtenburg focused on the limited effects of New Deal recovery and reform measures; Burns, though not without sympathy for Roosevelt, faulted the Democratic president for failing to embrace Keynesian economics and to recast his party as the party of reform.*

More recently, radical scholars offered vastly more damning analyses. Such New Left scholars as Howard Zinn (ed., New Deal Thought, *1966) and Barton J. Bernstein (ed.,* Towards a New Past, *1967) attempted to expose the poverty of the New Deal imagination and the essential conservatism of its leadership. In their view, Roosevelt was the creature of corporate capitalism; he failed to solve the problems of the depression, and he made no effort to create an equitable society.*

The radical interpretation has won much support among younger historians who find little that was bold or innovative in the New Deal record. Many older scholars, however, have attacked the New Left for measuring the past with the yardstick of the present.

FOR FURTHER READING

President Hoover's revealing *Memoirs* (3 vols., 1951–1952) describe his own administration well and comment without admiration on the policies of his successor. Arthur M. Schlesinger, Jr., in *The Crisis of the Old Order* (1957) provides an unflattering portrait of Republican leadership from a liberal Democratic point of view. The more sympathetic studies of Harris Gaylord Warren (*Herbert Hoover,* 1967), Joan Hoff Wilson (*Herbert Hoover,* 1975), and David Burner (*Herbert Hoover,* 1978), reflect an emerging revisionist consensus of the first depression president. The 1929 debacle and the onset of depression are illuminated by John Kenneth Galbraith in *The Great Crash* (1954) and by Peter Temin, in *Did Monetary Forces Cause the Great Depression?* (1976). *The Bonus March* (1971) is analyzed by Roger Daniels; Hoover's long lame-duck period is the subject of Jordan A. Schwarz, in *The Interregnum of Despair* (1970). The Roosevelt literature is exceptionally full. Frank Freidel's *Launching of the New Deal* (1973), the fourth and latest volume in his multivolume *Franklin D. Roosevelt* (1952–) is indispensable for the early years of FDR's leadership. It should be supplemented with the more comprehensive studies by Burns, Leuchtenburg, and Schlesinger. Some of the most interesting and contradictory works are those by FDR's contemporaries. Compare, for example, Francis Perkins's *The Roosevelt I Knew* (1948) and Raymond Moley's *After Seven Years* (1939). Lyle W. Dorsett, in *Franklin D. Roosevelt and the City Bosses* (1977), considers the impact of New Deal welfare programs upon urban machine politics. Dixon Wecter's *The Age of the Great Depression* (1948) is an introduction to the period's fascinating social history. Studs Terkel's *Hard Times* (1970) contains many personal accounts. Of an enormous literature on American Marxism in the 1930s, one of the most readable and understanding accounts is Murray Kempton's *Part of Our Time* (1955).* In *Turbulent Years* (1970), Irving Bernstein writes brilliantly of the labor movement; in *American Welfare Capitalism, 1880-1940* (1976), Stuart D. Brandes briefly considers an important facet of corporate union-busting; and in *Cry from the Cotton* (1971), Donald Grubbs focuses sympathetically on southern tenant farmers. Aspects of the era's intellectual history are detailed by C. C. Alexander, in *Nationalism in American Thought, 1930–1945* (1969),* and by Arthur A. Ekirch, Jr., in *Ideologies and Utopias* (1969). Otis L. Graham, Jr.'s *An Encore for Reform* (1967)* is a sensitive examination of the relation between the New Deal and the Progressive Era.

---

*Available in paperback edition.

The Reversal of Foreign Policy
1931–1941

27

During most of the 1930s, American attention was centered on domestic problems. Yet foreign events, occurring in the same period, were to affect the United States even more profoundly than the New Deal. The fragile international order established at Versailles and propped by prosperity broke down. Aggressive military states threatened to dominate Europe and Asia. To meet this challenge, America moved from relative disarmament to colossal military power, and American opinion swung from an extreme of isolationism to unprecedented acceptance of worldwide commitment. This commitment was to prove permanent, and under its stress American tradition and society were to be profoundly altered.

THE BREAKDOWN OF ORDER, 1931–1933

When Hoover took office, he intended to carry on, with only slight revision, the foreign policies of the New Era. More internationalist in outlook than Coolidge, he carried much further the policy begun under Coolidge of substituting conciliation for intervention in Latin America. Cautiously, the Hoover administration moved closer to cooperation with the League of Nations. In any efforts to preserve world peace, however, he was determined to stick to noncoercive political or economic methods. At the London Conference of 1930, the administration worked hard, with some success, to reduce further naval armament according to the pattern set by the Washington Conference of 1921. This was the last victory for disarmament. The effort to limit land armies at Geneva in 1932–1933 resulted in complete failure. By that time, the very idea of arms limitation was rejected by several powerful states.

The Versailles order in Europe had always been unstable. With American power withdrawn, France and England confronted Fascist Italy, Communist Russia, and defeated, unstable Germany. If these discontented powers were to be united and armed, their strength could outweigh that of the defenders of the status quo.

In the late 1920s, the Central European order was upheld to some extent by American investment. In 1931, partly because of the withdrawal of American funds, a major Austrian bank failed, and panic threatened to spread to Germany. To prevent further collapse, Hoover suggested a one-year suspension of payments of both German war reparations and Allied debts to the United States. After a damaging delay caused by French suspicions, this "Hoover moratorium" was accepted. Frightened by the growing power of the aggressive Hitler movement in Germany, the Western Allies finally, in 1932, agreed to cancel almost all reparations—but they were too late to save the German Republic. The United States refused to cancel war debts in a parallel manner. While most countries paid the first installments due after the end of the moratorium, these were, in most cases, the last payments made.

In 1931, Britain, the home of *laissez-faire* economics, found it necessary to abandon the gold standard for a managed currency, and many other countries promptly followed suit. Hoping to restore currency stability, the United States helped plan a World Economic Conference that would give first priority to exchange stabilization.

The most dramatic collapse of international order occurred in the Far East. Since the Washington Conference, Japan had been ruled by conservative cabinets, and American-Japanese relations had been relatively good at this time. The Japanese military, however, were becoming increasingly angry at arms limitation and civilian control. Since Theodore Roosevelt's Treaty of Portsmouth, Japan had possessed railroad and port rights in Manchuria, where many Japanese saw an opportunity to acquire raw materials and living space. In 1931, taking advantage of incidents in Manchuria produced by rising Chinese nationalism, the Japanese army embarked on a program of conquest in this vast, nominally Chinese region. This action, carried out apparently against the will of the civilian government in Tokyo, violated not only the League Covenant but also the Republican security structure, consisting of the Washington Nine-Power Treaty and the Kellogg Peace Pact. The Open Door and Chinese integrity, moreover, were part of Republican tradition.

Thus Hoover had to act, but once more American commitments in the Far East outran American power. Furthermore, the deepest beliefs of the Quaker president ruled out either military reprisal or cooperation with the League in economic sanctions. In addition, England, whose collaboration would have been necessary for effective action, had no wish to provoke Japanese threats to its own huge Asian holdings. Resorting to purely moral force, Secretary of State Stimson announced that the United States would not recognize any situation brought about by force in violation of the Open Door or Chinese integrity. After much hesitation, the League took a somewhat similar stand, advising its members not to recognize the Japanese puppet state of Manchukuo. Neither the so-called Stimson Non-Recognition Doctrine nor world disapproval deterred Japan in Manchuria, although Japan did withdraw from a brief military occupation of Shanghai undertaken in 1932 in retaliation for a Chinese boycott. At the same time, despite Hoover's abhorrence of coercive international action, the United States had become further involved in the defense of the crumbling international order.

THE NEW DEAL AND THE WORLD, 1933–1937

In the first years of the New Deal, American isolationism reached its peak. To the disillusion of the 1920s was added the new disillusion of the depression. A host of plays, movies, and novels depicted the horrors of war, and in 1935 a Senate investigation seemed to show that munition makers caused most wars for the sake of sordid profits. Many Americans believed that European propagandists had made a sucker of the United States in 1917 and were trying to do it again. At the same time, our former allies were defaulting on their obligations and failing to sustain their own League. (Throughout the decade, European appeasement and American isolationism were called on to justify each other.)

Traditional suspicion of Europe was only one of a number of components, all powerful and some mutually contradictory, of the isolationist frame of mind. Many young people were deeply affected by pacifism, and some liberals wanted to concentrate on building a good society at home. On the other hand, conservatives were suspicious of foreign threats to American tradition. Many Midwesterners and most Irish-Americans maintained their historic suspicion of British imperialism.

In the early years of the New Deal, Roosevelt failed to challenge the dominant isolationist creed, though as a follower of Wilson and his cousin Theodore, he could hardly accept it. He was primarily concerned with getting his program of national economic reform through Congress and into action, and he badly needed the support of midwestern isolationist progressives. Thus he refrained from opposing such measures as the Johnson Act of 1934, which forbade loans to nations in default.

As Japanese expansion slowed down to assimilate its gains, American-Japanese relations seemed to improve. And though nearly all Americans disliked the brutal Hitler regime that took power in Germany in 1933, few proposed to do anything about it.

In cooperation with some isolationists or continentalists, Roosevelt backed a modest program of naval building and continued the program of cementing good relations with Latin America. The nonintervention policy was not only restated, but backed in practice by abandonment of the right of intervention in Panama and Cuba. Expropriation by Mexico of the property of United States oil companies was accepted and compensation agreed on. At the Inter-American Conference of 1936, intervention by one state in the affairs of another was condemned, and mutual consultation provided for in case of threats to the peace of the hemisphere. This Good Neighbor Policy, though it by no means ended all Latin American suspicion of the United States, was to produce good results in wartime when most of the Latin American countries were to be first friendly neutrals and then allies.

In economic matters, the main drive of the early New Deal was nationalistic. In order to save his own program of raising prices through currency inflation, Roosevelt abruptly reversed his early approval of exchange stabilization and, in so doing, broke up the World Economic Conference in London. On the other hand, Cordell Hull, the new Secretary of State, had a deep southern-Democratic belief in lower tariffs, and Roosevelt succeeded in getting congressional backing for the Hull program. From

1934 on, the administration had and used authority to negotiate mutual tariff reductions through reciprocal trade treaties. Hope for a revival of international trade was also involved in Roosevelt's decision in 1933 to recognize Soviet Russia. This action, long prevented by ideological hostility, was supported by political realists and business leaders who prophesied (mistakenly) a major expansion of Russian-American trade.

American isolationist policies were little changed by the new challenges to world order that occurred in the mid-1930s. In 1935, Mussolini's Italy invaded Ethiopia, and in the same year Adolf Hitler felt strong enough to remilitarize Germany in defiance of the Versailles Treaty. In the next year, German troops marched into the Rhineland where the same treaty prohibited their presence. In July, 1936, Francisco Franco opened a Fascist rebellion against the republican government of Spain, and in 1936–1937 the Berlin-Rome-Tokyo Axis united the major dissatisfied, essentially aggressive states. All these actions were dealt with ineffectually by the Western European powers. In the Ethiopian affair, the League invoked only half-hearted sanctions, England condoned German rearmament in a naval treaty, and western countries, through a policy of "nonintervention," denied munitions to the Spanish government. Turning increasingly to the left, that government got some aid from Russia while the Spanish rebels were more effectively supported by Germany and Italy.

American policy toward these crises was dominated by a determination to keep out of war rather than to keep war from occurring. The neutrality legislation of 1935–1937 was designed to prevent the particular kinds of mistakes that were believed to have drawn America into World War I. The first neutrality law, passed in 1935, forbade arms shipments to all belligerents, rejecting an administration wish to discriminate between aggressor and victim. In the Ethiopian crisis, this was supplemented by a "moral embargo" on oil, the commodity most needed by Mussolini. American refusal to take stronger action gave an excuse for the League to refuse an outright oil embargo. The second neutrality law (1936) forbade loans to belligerents. In 1937, a congressional resolution, requested by the president, extended the application of the neutrality system from international war to the Civil War in Spain, thus shutting off American arms from the Loyalist government and helping to ensure Franco's success. Finally, the neutrality law of 1937 made the existing prohibitions permanent and, in addition, forbade American travel on belligerent ships. It also gave the president power, for two years, to list commodities other than munitions that belligerents would be required to pay for and transport in their own ships (the cash-and-carry provision). Thus the United States had reversed the policies of Woodrow Wilson and returned to something like those of Jefferson. Neutral rights were waived in order to stay out of war. It seemed clear to the aggressive nations that they had little to fear from American counteraction, as long as America itself was not attacked.

DEEPENING CRISIS AND
CAUTIOUS CHANGE IN POLICY, 1937–1939

Once more, a shift in American policy was brought on by events in Asia, not Europe. Japan, which had continued to press from Manchuria into North China until 1933, made a truce in that year. In 1937, fighting broke out again near the Peiping-Tientsin railway for which Japan had certain treaty privileges. Since the ensuing war, though full scale, was undeclared, the American neutrality legislation was not automatically applied. Partly in order not to cut off arms to China, and partly to keep some anti-Japanese action in reserve, Roosevelt refrained from invoking the neutrality laws, and America shipped some war materials to each belligerent. However, in October, 1937, Roosevelt expressed his feelings about Japanese action with new vigor. Referring to a "spreading epidemic of world lawlessness," he suggested that aggressors be "quarantined."

Alarmed isolationist reaction made it plain to the president that he had moved beyond public opinion. The United States joined in the League of Nations' condemnation of Japanese action but opposed sanctions. In December, when Japanese planes sank an American gunboat on the Yangtze, apologies were accepted without much excitement. Once more, world disapproval without action failed to deter Japan, and its forces proceeded to bomb and occupy the principal Chinese cities. By 1938, it had set up a puppet government in China and committed itself fatefully to the establishment of a New Order in East Asia.

Lacking a clear European policy, the United States played only a minor role in the major European events of this period, periodically and fruitlessly appealing for moderation and conciliation. In 1938, Hitler absorbed Austria and began threatening Czechoslovakia. This led to the Munich Agreement among Britain, France, Italy, and Germany, which forced Czechoslovakia to surrender certain strategic frontier districts inhabited by German-speaking people. This settlement was brutally nullified in March, 1939 when Hitler took over the rest of Czechoslovakia. During the same spring Italy invaded Albania, while Hitler seized the Lithuanian town of Memel and unmistakably began threatening Poland. This time, however, Britain and France guaranteed the prospective victim, and it became evident that major war was imminent.

Roosevelt, who shared this opinion, believed also that Britain and France could win with American material help. He therefore called for a cautious and moderate program of rearmament mainly on the basis of continental naval and air defense. He also asked Congress to repeal the arms embargo in order to make it possible for belligerents to buy American munitions on a cash-and-carry basis. Though most press opinion favored this action, it was defeated by isolationists in Congress. This was to be their last major victory.

In the summer of 1939, while Britain and France were making a half-hearted effort to make a defensive alliance with Russia, Stalin instead suddenly concluded pacts of trade and nonaggression with Hitler. This apparently left Germany free to attack Poland without becoming involved in a major two-front war, and on September 1, Hitler's troops crossed the Polish frontier. France and England, this time, declared war as they had promised. Poland, destined to be the most tragic victim of World War II, was quickly overrun. As German troops advanced through western Poland, Russian troops occupied the eastern part of the country.

Now that war was a fact, Roosevelt was able (in November, 1939) to prevail on Congress to repeal the arms embargo and place shipments of both munitions and other commodities on a cash-and-carry basis. Once more, as in 1914, the Western Allies were free to come and get American arms, provided that they could pay cash and provide shipping. This seemed enough to assure western victory without further American commitment. Most observers predicted that the major belligerents would settle into a long stalemate, confronting each other in "impregnable" Maginot and Siegfried lines.

CATASTROPHE AND THE END OF NEUTRALITY, 1940–1941

In the spring of 1940, the stalemate war came to a sudden end as the Germans conquered first Denmark and Norway and then the Low Countries. In a lightning assault from Belgium, mobile German units poured into France and in a month had crushed and demoralized the French army, supposed by many to be the world's strongest. It seemed as if there was no possible resistance to the new German combination of parachutists, dive-bombers, and tanks. On June 22, France surrendered. The Germans occupied half the country, leaving the collaborationist government at Vichy in charge of the rest.

Thinking he had won his war, Hitler hoped that England would make a compromise peace. Instead, though isolated and almost without land armament, the British replaced their ineffective premier with Winston Churchill, who announced his determination not only to resist but ultimately to destroy the Nazi regime. In the ensuing battle of Britain, though British cities were heavily bombed, the Royal Air Force defeated the German effort to clear the way for invasion. It began to seem possible once more that American support might sustain England, and many Americans wanted to do this at all costs. Others, however, insisted that the most important objective still was to keep America out of war.

In the ensuing foreign policy argument, one of the most important in American history, both sides were made up of diverse elements. On the anti-interventionist side with the traditional midwestern isolationists were: Anglophobes, including many Irish-Americans; people who thought Britain's cause hopeless; pacifists; young people who had heard with horror about the intolerance and hate generated by World War I; middle-aged people who had shared the postwar disillusionment; progressive reformers reluctant to give up domestic objectives; and some, but not by any means all, of those who disliked Roosevelt because of his domestic policies. This diverse coalition was supported by the small group influenced by the Communist party, which had supported collective security until 1939 and was to support war after 1941, but which was isolationist during the two years of the German-Soviet alliance. Those who favored drastic action in support of Britain included, as in 1914, many influential Americans conscious of deep ties to British culture. These were joined by those who were outraged by atrocity stories, this time true, about Nazi barbarism. Most important, perhaps, were the increasing numbers who felt that American security would be seriously threatened by Nazi control of the Atlantic.

Most Americans, probably, were neither isolationists nor outright interventionists.

Most wanted to help Britain and also to stay out of the war. The decisive question was which of these last objectives was the more important. Before the fall of France, opinion polls seemed to show that most Americans wanted first of all to keep out of war. After it, the majority gradually shifted; most concluded that British survival came first. This decision, however, was neither universal nor clear-cut, and the administration did not help to clarify the choice.

Insofar as one can understand Roosevelt's policy, he appeared by no means neutral in his sympathies and clearly wanted to contribute as much material aid as possible to Britain. This policy, he said, would keep America out of war. At first, he doubtless believed that this *would* be so, and until very late he hoped that it *might* be the case. Always conscious of the dangers of hostile public reaction, and once more desperately anxious to put over his program, he continued to say that America would stay out of war when he must have known that this was no longer certain. Whether a franker policy would have had better results, either at the time or in the long run, will long be debated.

The steps taken by the administration, and approved by a majority of Congress and public opinion, were drastic enough. In May, Roosevelt called for a $1 billion defense appropriation and for airplane production of 50,000 a year. At Charlottesville on June 10, he promised continued material help to "opponents of force." In September, by executive agreement, he traded 50 over-age destroyers, desperately needed by Britain, for defense bases in British Western Hemisphere possessions. In the same month, Congress adopted the first peacetime conscription law in American history.

In the fall of 1940, foreign policy argument was channeled into an election campaign. Because of the national emergency, the Democrats broke the anti-third-term tradition to renominate Roosevelt. His opponent Wendell Willkie, though a utility company president who had fought TVA, was a representative of the liberal wing of the Republican party. Accepting much of the New Deal, Willkie attacked mismanagement and bureaucracy. Since Willkie accepted the necessity of aiding Britain and since both candidates promised that America would stay out of actual foreign war, there was little difference on foreign policy. In the closest victory of his presidential career, Roosevelt got 55 percent of the popular vote.

Once more securely in office, Roosevelt asked for and got a still more binding commitment to British victory. In March, Congress passed the lend-lease bill, giving the president authority to transfer equipment, rather than money, directly to nations whose defense was vital to that of the United States. In response to urgent appeals from the beleaguered British, munitions were furnished in enormous quantity. In the spring of 1941, British and American staff officers discussed common strategy in the event of American belligerency. In August Roosevelt and Churchill, meeting at sea, committed themselves to the liberal principles of the Atlantic Charter, promising a free and warless world "after the final destruction of the Nazi tyranny."

Committed to Hitler's defeat, America could not allow its shipments of munitions to be destroyed by the increasingly powerful German submarine offensive. In the summer of 1941, the United States entered into undeclared naval warfare with Germany. American ships reported submarine sightings to the British. American troops occupied Greenland and Iceland, and America began convoying British and American shipping to Iceland, halfway across the Atlantic. Sinkings occurred, and in September Roosevelt, denouncing German "piracy," ordered American naval vessels to "shoot on sight."

Meanwhile the nature of the war in Europe had profoundly changed. Unable to knock Britain out of the war before American deliveries became effective, Hitler decided to secure his continental flank. Germany already controlled Hungary, Rumania, and Bulgaria, and in April, 1941 its armies conquered Yugoslavia and Greece. Germany's moves toward the East intensified Hitler's growing difficulties with his quasi-ally, Stalin. In June, 1941, the Germans invaded the Soviet Union, penetrating so deeply that it looked for some months as if they would win another major victory. Promptly both Churchill and Roosevelt announced that any enemy of Hitler was a friend of theirs, and lend-lease aid to Russia began. While Russian participation stimulated anti-interventionism in some quarters, it reduced it in others. For the first time, it seemed, a coalition existed that could actually destroy the Nazis, and the United States was a member of it in all but actual land fighting.

For some time, Roosevelt had concluded that official American participation in war would be desirable, and a majority of the public had decided, according to the polls, that war would be preferable to British defeat. Hitler, however, was by no means eager to provoke further American intervention and add another great power to his already formidable list of opponents. Once more, the crucial development came from the other side of the world.

WAR WITH JAPAN

In the Far East also, the Hitler breakthrough of 1940 precipitated great changes. To Japan, it seemed to offer a last chance to consolidate her new East Asian order and thereby to end the costly and indecisive "China incident." By moving southward toward the colonies of occupied France and Holland and hard-pressed Britain, Japan could secure needed supplies of oil, rubber, and tin.

So far, Roosevelt, concentrating on the European danger and not eager for involvement on another front, had continued the rather ambiguous U.S. policy toward Japan with one important change. In July, 1939, the United States threatened future economic measures by giving a six-months' notice of the abrogation of her 1911 commercial treaty with Japan. In July, 1940, sensing that a Japanese forward movement was at hand, the president prohibited the export of some kinds of oil and scrap metal. Later measures tightened this embargo and increased the pressure on Japan to find alternate sources.

In September, 1940, the Japanese, with Hitler's diplomatic assistance, forced the Vichy government to concede ports and bases in the northern part of French Indochina. In September, Germany, Italy, and Japan signed the Tripartite Pact, obliging each to help the other in case of attack by any power not now at war. Since a special article excluded Russia, this could mean only the United States.

There were still, however, powerful Japanese who hoped to achieve Japan's goals without war with America. Through much of 1941, the attitudes of both countries were set forth in a series of negotiations. Japan was willing, at most, to refrain from armed aggression in Southeast Asia and even to "interpret" in America's favor the promises of the Tripartite Pact. But to pay for peace in the Far East, even in the event of war with Germany, the United States would have had to restore Japanese-American trade, help Japan to obtain oil supplies from the Netherlands East Indies, and recognize (or at least cease to obstruct) her new order in China. The United States was unwilling to accept these terms and offered instead to restore trade and help Japan gain some of its economic goals provided it gave up its military objectives both in Southeast Asia and China. Once more, the American commitment to the Open Door and Chinese integrity assumed enormous importance.

In July of 1941, Japanese forces moved into southern Indochina and clearly headed for Malaya and the Dutch East Indies. Roosevelt promptly responded by freezing all Japanese funds in the United States. In August, still hopeful of keeping the United States neutral, Prince Konoye, the Japanese premier, requested a "Pacific Conference" with Roosevelt. Though Konoye suggested the possibility of further important concessions, Roosevelt refused to meet unless there was some preliminary agreement on basic issues. In October, the Konoye government fell, and the new Tojo government prepared for war.

Well before the complex Washington discussions of November, 1941, the positions of each side had been made clear, and the two positions had proved incompatible. The American government considered trying to gain time by presenting proposals for a temporary Pacific truce, but decided against this. Knowing that an attack was at hand, the Americans restated for the record their earlier position. On December 7, 1941, Japanese planes attacked and severely crippled the American fleet at Pearl Harbor. The next day, Congress declared war, and three days later Germany and Italy declared war on the United States.

Later, Roosevelt was much criticized, first for not pursuing further the effort for peace with Japan and second for not preventing the Pearl Harbor disaster. It was argued bitterly that his real objective was to force Japan to attack the United States and thereby to get America into war with Hitler by the "back door."

Probably, a real compromise with Japanese ambition, short of surrender of old American commitments and betrayal of American allies, would have been difficult to achieve. It is arguable, however, that a Roosevelt-Konoye meeting might have gained time and, less plausibly, that it might have strengthened the opponents of Japanese militarism. As for the second charge, it seems that by late November, 1941, the American government had decided that war was inevitable and that further stalling would be of no use. Roosevelt knew before December 7 that a Japanese movement was actually under way and indeed warnings were sent to American Pacific bases to that effect. Apparently because an attack was expected farther west, the warnings to Pearl Harbor were insufficiently frequent and emphatic, and defensive action was neglected. Thus a small cloud remained over the official version of the Pearl Harbor incident. At the time, however, the Japanese "sneak attack" united the American people for war as nothing else could have.

FOR FURTHER READING

An able study of *American Diplomacy in the Great Depression* (1957) is offered by Robert H. Ferrell. Lloyd Gardner examines *Economic Aspects of New Deal Diplomacy* (1964). The most formidable attacks on the Roosevelt foreign policy are Charles A. Beard's *President Roosevelt and the Coming of the War* (1948) and C. C. Tansill's *Back Door to War* (1952). Wayne S. Cole, in *Charles A. Lindbergh* (1974) and Thomas C. Kennedy, in *Charles A. Beard and American Foreign Policy* (1975), examine the work of two prestigious opponents of American interventionism. Roosevelt is defended by Basil Rauch in *Roosevelt: From Munich to Pearl Harbor* (1950). W. L. Langer and S. E. Gleason's *The Challenge to Isolation, 1937–1940 (1952)** and *The Undeclared War, 1940–1941* (1953)* are well-documented and informative studies, generally favorable to U.S. policy. Other notable accounts include: Donald Drummond, *The Passing of American Neutrality* (1955); Robert Divine, *The Illusion of Neutrality* (1962); and Roberta Wohlstetter, *Pearl Harbor: Warning and Decision* (1962). American relations with Japan are assessed by Herbert Feis in *The Road to Pearl Harbor* (1950)* and by Paul Schroeder in *The Axis Alliance and Japanese-American Relations, 1941* (1958). Richard Triana has studied *American Diplomacy and the Spanish Civil War* (1968); and in *Prelude to Downfall* (1967), Saul Friedlander surveys American relations with Nazi Germany on the eve of war.

---

*Available in paperback edition.

War for the World
1941–1945

28

FROM DEFEAT TO VICTORY, 1941–1944

Through the winter and spring of 1941–1942, the United States confronted its most serious challenge since 1861. One headline after another reported successful Japanese invasions: Malaya, Guam, Wake, Hong Kong, Singapore, the Dutch East Indies, Burma, the Western Aleutians. On May 6, 1942, the last organized American forces in the Philippines surrendered at Corregidor. The New Order in Greater East Asia was almost a fact. Any counteroffensive against Japan, it seemed, would have to conquer concentric rings of islands scattered over vast ocean areas.

Hitler, meanwhile, held firmly the productive power of Western Europe. His first invasion of Russia was turned back in the winter of 1941 after reaching the outskirts of Moscow. His second, beginning in June, 1942, reached deep into the Caucasus and entered Stalingrad on the Volga. Britain was threatened with the collapse of her Atlantic supply line. Sinkings mounted after American entry, many of them occurring within sight of American coastal cities. The worst fears of western leaders were that Russia would collapse and Britain starve long before American power became really effective.

Already Anglo-American staff conferences had decided that the main Allied offensive must be directed against Germany, the more formidable enemy, while a holding action was carried on in the Pacific. But any offensive seemed a long way away, and even a holding action was not immediately apparent.

By summer and fall of 1942, more hopeful news began to appear. Japanese naval power, checked at the Coral Sea in May, was ended as an offensive threat at Midway in June. In August, American troops began a grim and bloody offensive in the Solomon Islands. In October, the British stopped the German drive toward Suez at El Alamein; the next month, American forces landed in North Africa and began fighting German troops. In the gigantic battle of Stalingrad, the Russians captured a German army and began the reconquest of the vast territories they had lost.

16. WORLD WAR II

	Diplomatic	Pacific Theater	European Theater	Home Front
1939—OUTBREAK	March 14 Germany annexes Czechoslovakia. March 31 Anglo-French pledge to Poland. August 23 German-Russian Pact.		September 1 Germany invades Poland. October 14 Russia invades Finland.	November 4 Neutrality Act of 1939 (cash and carry).
1940—DISASTER	September 3 United States–British "Destroyer Deal." September 27 Japan-Germany-Italy Tripartite Pact.	September 22 Japan gets bases in French Indochina.	April 9 Germany invades Norway, Denmark. May 10 Germany invades Benelux. June 22 German-French armistice. August–September Battle of Britain.	September 16 Selective Service. November 5 Roosevelt defeats Willkie.
1941—INTERVENTION	July 26 United States freezes Japanese funds. August 14 "Atlantic Charter" statement by Roosevelt and Churchill. November United States–Japanese Washington negotiations.	July 24 Japan occupies French Indochina. December 7 Pearl Harbor.	April Germany invades Greece, Yugoslavia. April–May United States extends protective action in Atlantic. June 22 Germany invades Russia. September 11 "Shoot on sight" order in Atlantic.	March 11 Lend-Lease Act. November 17 Neutrality Acts repealed. December 8 Declaration of War.
1942—LOW POINT	May Molotov in Washington. June Churchill in Washington. August Moscow Conference (Stalin, Churchill, Harriman).	February 15 Singapore surrenders. May 6 Corregidor surrenders. May 7–8 Coral Sea. June 3–6 Midway. August–February Guadalcanal.	January–June German offensive in North Africa. Summer German offensive in Russia. September–February Stalingrad. November 4 El Alamein. November 8 U.S. landings in North Africa.	January 30 Office of Price Administration established. February–March Japanese–American "relocation." November Republican gains in Congress. December 2 First self-sustaining nuclear reaction (Chicago).

16. WORLD WAR II (continued)

	Diplomatic	Pacific Theater	European Theater	Home Front
1943—ALLIED UNITY	**January 14–24** Casablanca Conference (Roosevelt, Churchill). **August 11–24** Quebec Conference (Roosevelt, Churchill). **November 22–26** Cairo Conference (Roosevelt, Churchill, Chiang). **November 28– December 1** Teheran Conference (Roosevelt, Churchill, Stalin).	**Throughout year** Allied gains in South Pacific (Solomons, New Guinea). **November 21** United States invades Gilberts (Tarawa) (start of central Pacific offensive).	**January–May** Allied victory in North Africa. **July–December** Russian offensive. **July 10** Sicily invaded. **September 9** Italy invaded (Salerno).	**November 5** Senate resolution for international organization.
1944—VICTORY IN SIGHT	**July 1–22** UN Monetary and Financial Conference (Bretton Woods). **August 21–October 7** Dumbarton Oaks Conference (plans UN). **October 9–18** Second Quebec Conference.	**January 31** Marshalls invaded. **June 18** Marianas invaded. **October 23–25** Philippine Sea. **November 24** Beginning of air attack on Tokyo.	**June 6** Normandy invaded. **July 25** St. Lô breakthrough. **September 12** United States enters Germany. **December** "Battle of the Bulge" (German counteroffensive).	United States reaches twice Axis war production. **November 7** Roosevelt defeats Dewey.
1945—THE ATOMIC AGE	**February 4–11** Yalta Conference. **April 23–June 26** San Francisco UN Conference. **July 17–August 2** Potsdam Conference (July 26, ultimatum to Japan). **September 2** Japan surrenders.	**February** Manila recaptured. **February–March** Iwo Jima. **April–June** Okinawa. **August 6** Hiroshima. **August 9** Nagasaki. **August 14** V-J Day.	**March 7** Rhine crossed. **April 25** United States and Soviet forces meet on Elbe. **May 8** V-E Day.	**April 12** Roosevelt dies. **July 16** First atomic bomb exploded, Alamogordo, New Mexico.

In 1943, the Allies passed decisively to the offensive. After hard fighting, German forces were cleared from Africa, and in the summer and fall Anglo-American forces invaded Sicily and Italy. Though Mussolini fell from power and Italy surrendered, the Italian dictator escaped, and bitter German resistance formed in central Italy. In the Pacific War, the island-hopping strategy provided the means of American victory. Sea and air power made it possible to isolate and bypass Japanese garrisons; it would not be necessary to reconquer the vast Japanese holdings one by one. Bitter fighting brought control of the Solomons, and in November the battle of Tarawa began the Central Pacific campaign.

By this time, the technique of amphibious warfare was so highly developed that it became possible to land on any hostile shore with sufficient preparation, provided one was willing to accept immense casualties. The crucial difficulty was maintaining a beachhead after landing. This was borne out in June of 1944 in the long-awaited landing in Normandy. This attack on the heavily defended French coast, the greatest amphibious operation in history, was seriously endangered by bad weather and stubborn resistance. By the end of July, however, a breakthrough at St. Lô ended the Normandy campaign and opened the campaign of France. American tank units were able to sweep around the defenders as German forces had in 1940. By November most of France and Belgium had been liberated by Anglo-American forces, but in December a fierce counterattack surprised Americans in the Ardennes Forest.

On the eastern front in 1944, the Russians entered Poland, Yugoslavia, Hungary, and even East Prussia. In the Pacific the island-hopping campaign continued through the Marshalls, Marianas, and Carolines. In November, bombers from the Marianas began devastating raids on the Japanese home islands. In the Philippines, American reentry brought on the greatest naval battle in history at Leyte Gulf, where the remaining power of the Japanese navy was broken. By the end of the year, though much fighting remained in Europe and on the Pacific, victory and the problems of victory were clearly in sight.

THE HOME FRONT

Perhaps the greatest single factor in this victory was American production of ships, tanks, planes, and the infinitely varied tools of modern war. In 1941, though the buildup had begun, there was still a long way to go. Shipments to Britain had depleted American supplies, and once more it proved difficult to organize American economy and society for war production. The gigantic task was handled with all the best and worst features of New Deal government: with imagination and vast scale and also with a full complement of reversals, reorganizations, bureaucratic battles, bottlenecks, and waste. Yet by 1943, the huge machine was operating, and by 1944 America was producing double the combined total of the Axis countries.

This goal was won, moreover, without the extreme measures of coercion urged by some experts. There was no single production "czar," and there was no draft of labor. Adjustment of incentive seemed to work far better than totalitarian force. Industrialists received very high rewards in depreciation allowances and government construction of war plants. Yet corporation profits and high individual incomes were again taxed at confiscatory rates. Business, and especially big business, played a major part in planning, accepting a partnership with the government as it had in World War I and had not in the New Deal period. Labor strikes, much denounced in the press, were actually few in proportion to the work force. Labor kept the gains of the New Deal, including a 40-hour week with time and a half for overtime. Earnings rose rapidly, and unions expanded from 10 to nearly 15 million members.

The biggest wartime gains of all went to some of the previously depressed farmers. Their continued strength in Congress pushed the regulated farm prices up to 110 percent of parity, and government efforts to keep food prices down were at first only partly successful. While 17 percent of the farm population moved to the cities, the income of the remainder went sharply up, and so did their production.

While many people in Europe and Asia were starving, American consumers had to cut down their driving, go without new cars, and accept rationing of food and some other products. From 1943 on, control of most prices was reasonably successful. Not only was there no real civilian suffering, but many people—especially people previously deprived—lived and ate better than ever before.

Not the long efforts of the New Deal, but the incidental effects of war brought prosperity and, with it, fundamental social change. Apparently, the mechanism of economic growth was government spending on a new scale. In 1936, the biggest New Deal spending year, a federal outlay of $8 billion had caused many citizens to worry about the foundations of the Republic. In 1945, when federal expenditures reached $98 billion, unemployment practically vanished and the country seemed to reach new levels of production and prosperity. High wages and farm prices, together with war taxes, produced a greater measure of economic equality than had ever existed. As war industry redistributed the population, the Pacific Coast gained wealth and power. With full employment, blacks were accepted in some kinds of jobs previously closed to them, and the federal government, through the Fair Employment Practices Commission, began to concern itself with equality of employment. Blacks and southern whites both migrated in large numbers to industrial cities. Thus northern racial problems grew more intense, while southern racial mores began very slowly to shift.

Many of the changes accelerated or begun during the war were to prove permanent. Neither wages, prices, employment, government expenditure, nor taxes were to return to prewar levels. Control of inflation, as well as prevention of depression, had become a major governmental concern. In addition to strictly economic fields, government was deeply involved in race relations, public information, and the promotion of scientific endeavor. Perhaps most fateful of all, the size, political influence, and economic importance of the armed forces in this most unmilitary of nations had been expanded. Few Americans guessed that this time demilitarization was to prove elusive.

In politics, the war seemed superficially to bring unity. Since America had been attacked, overt opposition to the war was negligible. Startling worldwide commitments seemed to be accepted, and many said that isolationism had died at Pearl Harbor. In contrast to 1917, unity seemed to exist without hysteria. Civil liberties were generally preserved with one large exception: 117,000 Americans of Japanese ancestry, two-thirds of them citizens, were moved from their West Coast homes first to barbed-wire temporary camps and then to isolated relocation centers in the interior. Though most were resettled in the East or Midwest before the war was over and some eventually received financial compensation for their losses, the scars of this ruthless and unnecessary action remained.

If there was less overt opposition and less hysteria than in World War I, there was also less idealistic enthusiasm. The Four Freedoms, Henry A. Wallace's glowing picture of a "Century of the Common Man," Wendell Willkie's commitment to "One World" were highly effective in liberal circles. None of these, however, came as close to producing a nationwide response as Wilson's appeal to "make the world safe for democracy." For many Americans, this was less a crusade than (as Roosevelt called it) a "War for Survival."

American opinion, deeply divided in 1941 over both the New Deal and Roosevelt's interventionist foreign policy, was not magically reunited in wartime. But division had to manifest itself in indirect ways—in hostility to the Europe-first policy, resentment of price control, exaggeration of strikes, and (despite much countereffort) criticism of the Allies. Some liberals attacked the government for its tactical compromises with Vichy or alleged tenderness toward the British Empire. A larger group remained deeply suspicious of collaboration with Russia, and a still larger faction was determined to prevent the postwar survival of the New Deal.

In 1942, the Republicans sharply increased their strength in Congress. In 1944 Roosevelt, like Lincoln, won a wartime election, this time against the rather ineffective opposition of Thomas E. Dewey, and in the same year many archisolationists lost their seats in Congress. Thus Franklin Roosevelt, again like Lincoln, retained the decision-making power of a wartime president. But for this he paid a price. It was necessary —or so he decided—to postpone discussion not only of important unsettled domestic controversies, but also of some of the thorniest unresolved international problems. The only goal on which all could agree was military victory.

THE GREAT ALLIANCE

In international relations, as in so many fields, World War II seemed to reverse American precedents. In World War I, America had been gingerly cobelligerent; now she was a full-fledged ally bound to refuse a separate peace. She took the lead in the efforts to make the wartime international coalition into a new international organization. Both public opinion and this time even the Senate seemed heartily to back the proposal for a new United Nations.

President Roosevelt placed his major hopes both for victory and postwar stability on the "Four Policemen": Britain, China, Russia, and the United States. But only with Britain was real cooperation achieved. Similar national traditions plus the mutual admiration of Roosevelt and Churchill helped to make the Anglo-American war effort the most successful combined operation in history; yet even here major differences appeared.

The Americans were used to thinking of war in terms of an all-out drive for victory followed by a return to peace and normality. The British had some experience of victory's delusions and costs. Many of the American leaders were suspicious of British efforts to cling to empire. Above all, Roosevelt and Churchill differed in the later stages of the war over Russian relations.

In 1942, American political and military leaders demanded an immediate cross-channel invasion of Europe, partly to prevent collapse of the eastern front. Churchill accepted the necessity of such an operation in the future, but thought it impossible without further buildup and fought hard for diversionary operations in southern Europe. After 1943, his reasons were partly political: western penetration of the Balkans and Central Europe would prevent Russian domination of these areas. This argument was settled by compromise. To Stalin's chagrin, the Normandy invasion was put off until 1944, while the North African and Italian campaigns represented a partial concession to Churchill's views. A Balkan front was never opened.

Roosevelt's program for making China a great power was a complete failure. Chiang Kai-shek's Nationalist government shared control of the huge country with a well-intrenched Communist movement, and each side fought the other as well as Japan. Exhausted by long war, the Nationalist government was further weakened by corruption. Neither General Joseph Stilwell nor anybody else could bring about a major Chinese contribution to victory. Yet at Cairo in November, 1943, Roosevelt, Churchill, and Chiang agreed that after the war China would get back Manchuria as well as Formosa and the Pescadores. The first of these pledges was largely nullified by the Yalta Agreement, and the second was to be the source of endless trouble.

By far the most difficult relationship was, of course, with Russia. America began this wartime association with a recent past of deep hostility toward that nation. During the period of the Russo-German Pact, American opinion had been outraged by Russia's moves into eastern Poland and Rumania; by her absorption of the three small Baltic states—Latvia, Lithuania, and Estonia; and, above all, by her Winter War with Finland, who had refused to surrender certain border districts considered by Russia necessary to her own defense. With the German-Russian break, however, both Roosevelt and Churchill immediately saw the possible importance of Russian contributions to the war. To help keep Germany occupied in the east, America sent Russia lend-lease aid amounting to $11 billion. Temperamentally optimistic and used to thinking in terms of only one opponent at a time, many Americans managed to convince themselves that Russian society and government had fundamentally changed. Russia and America were to remain friendly after the war, and this friendship was to be the mainstay of world peace. This opinion was held by Roosevelt and by his principal advisers, liberal and conservative, civilian and military.

Through 1943, some success was achieved in shaping common military objectives. Good feeling reached its height in late November, 1943, when Roosevelt, Stalin, and Churchill met at Teheran, Persia. There the coming offensive against Hitler was roughly coordinated. It was agreed that German military power must be permanently eliminated, perhaps by division of the country. In Yugoslavia, Allied aid was to go only to Tito, the Communist leader of one branch of the underground. Both the eastern

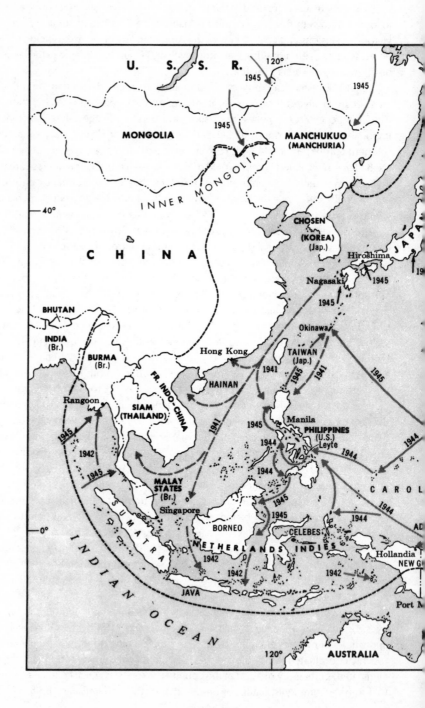

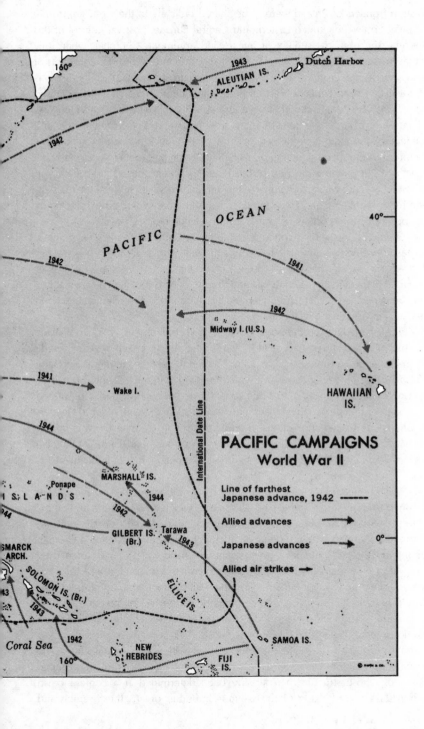

160°

1943   Dutch Harbor
ALEUTIAN IS.

1942

PACIFIC   OCEAN   40°

1942   1941

1942
Midway I. (U.S.)

1941   Wake I.   HAWAIIAN
IS.

1944

PACIFIC CAMPAIGNS
World War II

MARSHALL IS.
Ponape
I S. L A N D S   1944
44   1942
GILBERT IS.   Tarawa
(Br.)   1943

Line of farthest
Japanese advance, 1942   -------

Allied advances   →

Japanese advances   ⇢

Allied air strikes   →

0°

SMARCK
ARCH.

SOLOMON IS. (Br.)
43
1943

ELLICE IS.

Coral Sea   1942   SAMOA IS.

160°   NEW
HEBRIDES   FIJI
IS.

International Date Line

and western frontiers of Poland were to be shifted radically to the west. From here on, as Soviet armies penetrated Eastern and Central Europe, postwar control of this area became the principal subject of inter-Allied argument. Churchill, while fully aware that Russia's losses entitled her to some security and even more conscious of her unquestioned power in the area, wanted to bargain sharply with Stalin. He was willing, for instance, to concede Russian predominance in Rumania and Bulgaria in return for British predominance in Greece and equality in Yugoslavia and Hungary. Poland presented a harder problem. Russian forces had set up a government in Poland independent of the exile government in London; the latter had contributed large fighting forces to the Allied side, and on its behalf Britain had gone to war. Churchill was willing to put pressure on the London Poles to accept the realities of Russian power, but he was not willing to recognize the unqualified sovereignty of the Russian-supported Polish government. He wanted to use Allied bargaining power, including troop dispositions, to secure as favorable a Polish settlement as possible.

Roosevelt was unwilling to concur completely in Churchill's policy of firmness. He too was concerned about Polish freedom and could not ignore the strong feelings of Polish-Americans. Yet he was aware also of America's historic dislike of power politics. Eager to mediate between Russia and Britain, overconfident of his own ability to charm and persuade Stalin, he continued his effort to build a future based on genuine Russian-American collaboration.

This effort shaped the most important of the Allied conferences, which took place at Yalta, in the Crimea, in February, 1945. By this time, the approach of victory made it necessary to agree on some concrete plans. Though the political future of Germany was left undecided, it was agreed that it would be divided into four zones of military occupation. Stalin here conceded that one zone, formed out of previously constituted western zones, would be occupied by France, now back in the war under the leadership of Charles de Gaulle and jealous of equal treatment. Germany, it was further agreed, would pay heavy reparations in the form of goods and labor. At Russian insistence, the United States agreed on a figure of $20 billion, half of it for Russia, as a basis for future discussion.

The Polish boundaries agreed on at Teheran were confirmed. This meant that Russia gained large territories in the east, to some of which it had historic and ethnic claims. In the west, Poland was to be liberally compensated with German territory, though the final German-Polish boundary settlement was postponed until a German peace conference. The Communist government in Poland was to be broadened by the inclusion of new members from the exile government in London and from the underground. Free and secret elections, in which all democratic parties could take part, would be held as soon as possible. Similarly, in the rest of liberated Europe, interim governments would be formed on a basis "broadly representative of all democratic elements," and free elections would be held as early as possible.

Another section of the Yalta Agreement dealt with world organization. The nations united against the Axis were to meet in the United States to form an organization, some of whose structure had already been determined at a conference in Dumbarton Oaks in Washington. Of the two most important organs, the Assembly and the Security Council, the latter was to act by unanimity alone. This "veto" provision, much criticized later, was desired by the United States as well as by Russia. The new organization would not, it was recognized, be in a position to coerce great powers; its effectiveness would depend on the close collaboration of the major states.

Finally, by a secret section of the agreement, Russia was obligated to enter the war against Japan within two or three months after the defeat of Germany. For this Russia was to receive liberal compensation. The status quo was to be recognized in Outer Mongolia, a Soviet puppet state nominally a part of China. Russia was to get back what it had lost to Japan in the Treaty of Portsmouth, including railroad and port concessions in Manchuria and possession of the southern portion of the huge island of Sakhalin. Russia would also receive the Kurile Islands north of Japan. Roosevelt was to "take measures" to secure the concurrence of Chiang Kai-shek in these terms, which would, however, be "unquestionably fulfilled."

In later years, the Yalta Agreement was to be subject to bitter criticism that made two cases against it. The first of these cases was idealistic and humanitarian. America conceded forced labor as part of German reparations and, despite many pious references in the text to the "principles of the Atlantic Charter," disposed of millions of people without their consent. Moreover, important rights in Asia, which the United States had refused to concede to Japanese pressure, were handed over to Russia without consulting China.

The second criticism of the agreement was concerned with the postwar balance of power. The complete destruction of German power and the concession of new Polish boundaries brought Russian armies into the heart of Europe and left Russia potentially dominant on that continent, while the Far Eastern terms brought Russia back into the crucial Manchurian region. Thus one potentially hostile great power was substituted for another in each area.

Defenders of the Yalta Agreement on the basis of power politics have answered these criticisms mainly by pointing to the current military situation. The Russians were in occupation of much of Poland and the Balkans. Anglo-American forces were not within reach of these areas and had no way of getting there. American Pacific commanders, expecting a fanatical resistance in the Japanese home islands and wrongly informed about the size of Japanese forces in Manchuria, were demanding that Russia be brought into the Far Eastern war.

The moral indictment of Yalta has been answered in several ways. First, defenders have pointed out that the hope for collaboration with Russia was a hope for world peace, noble and natural however unrealistic. The incredible Nazi atrocities, increasingly exposed by the reconquest of occupied territory, did not dispose America to be tender-hearted about German rights or to think about resurrecting German power. These disclosures served also to take American attention away from the brutality of some Russian behavior in Poland and elsewhere. Second, it has been argued that the provisions regarding free elections in Poland and other reconquered countries would have safeguarded democratic principles if they had been carried out by Russia after Yalta. Finally, the objectors have been reminded that the Far Eastern provisions were accepted by Chiang, when he learned of them, with little protest. The Soviet Union shortly concluded a treaty with Nationalist China promising to support only the Chiang regime as the central Chinese government.

Taken together, these defensive arguments explain many things. The errors of Yalta were not caused by treason, as extremists later alleged, but by optimism. Yet even the best that can be said is not entirely reassuring. Certainly the agreement did not meet the standards of idealism that America had so often invoked in the past, even when power to enforce these ideals was lacking (as in Manchuria in 1931). On the other hand, if the Yalta Agreement is to be judged in terms of hard-boiled realism, it can hardly be called an American success.

Nonetheless, when Roosevelt returned from his long journey, exhausted but triumphant, most Americans gratefully accepted his heartfelt statements that a future of democracy and peace had been assured. In the months after Yalta, Russian actions in some parts of Eastern Europe made it clear that such phrases as "free elections" and "all democratic elements" had different meanings East and West. There was no possibility that Russia would allow hostile elements to hold power in the most important border countries. In some of these, notably Poland and Rumania, it was equally impossible to form governments at once democratically chosen and friendly to Russia. When American commanders discussed with German agents in Switzerland possible surrender terms for German forces in Italy, the Russians made it clear that they suspected the United States of plotting to shut them out of peace negotiations. Depressed by increasing friction, Roosevelt began to doubt the future he had planned. Before these doubts could lead to action, however, he died (of a cerebral hemorrhage on April 12).

Most Americans, and nearly all Europeans, believed that a great leader was lost. Surely they were right; Roosevelt's confidence and optimism had been as important in war as they had been earlier in depression. His mistakes had flowed from the same great qualities.

FROM YALTA TO HIROSHIMA

The victory of 1945 was clouded by Allied dissent and darkened by cruelty and destruction. In the spring of that year, however, this was not apparent to the American people, and even the president's death failed to spoil the news of success on every front. In Europe, the German counteroffensive was stopped at Bastogne, Belgium before the end of 1944. By March, 1945, American forces had crossed the Rhine. In early April, when American troops reached the Elbe, General Eisenhower decided on military grounds not to push forward toward Berlin, but first to make sure of the Southern Alpine redoubt where it was believed that the Nazis might make a last stand. This decision, communicated to Stalin, was protested by Churchill. It was, however, upheld by Truman, the new president, on the basis of prior agreements among the Allies on zones of occupation. A little later, Eisenhower refused to press toward Prague, and the Russians occupied both Central European capitals. On May 1, while Soviet troops were entering Berlin, Hitler killed himself, and three days later Germany surrendered to England, Russia, and the United States.

As American forces drew closer to the Japanese home islands, they continued to meet fierce resistance. No Pacific battles were harder fought than Iwo Jima in February or Okinawa in May. Off the latter island, as in the Philippines, Japan made use of a strange and effective weapon, the suicide plane. Hundreds of pilots dove deliberately at American ships. This and other fanatical behavior convinced most Americans that they were in for a desperate fight in Japan itself.

Actually, Japan's resistance was almost at an end. American submarines had cut off necessary supplies, and since November American bombers had inflicted terrible destruction. In June, the Japanese war cabinet fell, and a new government began unsuccessfully to seek Russian mediation.

President Harry Truman and Winston Churchill, meeting at Potsdam, demanded on July 26 that Japan surrender. If Japan did, they promised, the Japanese would neither be destroyed nor enslaved; if it did not it would meet "utter destruction." Since Truman had received word of the first explosion of an atomic bomb, he was in a position to carry out this threat. It had long been decided that the new weapon would be used against the enemy for maximum effect, rather than being dropped first on uninhabited territory as a warning. Some of the president's advisers believed that use of the new weapon would greatly increase the power of the United States in the postwar settlement, particularly in relations with the Soviet Union. On August 6, an atomic bomb was dropped on the city of Hiroshima. On the 8th, Russia hurriedly entered the war in advance of the agreed time. On August 8, another atomic bomb hit Nagasaki, and on August 14 Japan agreed to the Potsdam terms. A formal surrender was signed aboard the *Missouri* in Tokyo Bay, September 2.

Even in the euphoria of victory celebrations, some Americans could not avoid asking themselves how it happened that their country, with its deeply humanitarian traditions, had been the first to use history's most terrible weapon. The Hiroshima bomb killed 80,000 people and injured many more, some of whom died horribly in the ensuing weeks and months. Yet in 1915, the United States had been genuinely outraged by the death of 1,198 civilians on the *Lusitania*. Throughout the 1930s, and as recently as 1939, American's had denounced aerial bombing of civilian populations.

The advent of the atomic bomb typified several tendencies, good and bad, that ran through the history of the war. It was, in the first place, a typical result of the American civilian war effort. It depended on a bold decision based on immensely complex science and engineering. It was conceived by scientists from many countries, some of them refugees. Thus it was a product of a liberal society associated with some of the best American traditions.

At the same time, its use in war was the climax of a period of mounting inhumanity for which all major nations bore some responsibility. The worst atrocity of the period was the systematic German annihilation of 6 million Jews. In places, Russian treatment of political and national minorities was almost as bad. Bombing of cities was carried out by Axis nations from Shanghai in 1932 to Rotterdam in 1940. City destruction was carried to new lengths by Britain and America in Germany, in 1943–1944, when 300,000 civilians were killed. The American fire bombings of Japan

RECONQUEST OF EUROPE
World War II

Allied advances
German counter offensive

0   150   300
MILES

killed about 330,000 people. Thus the annihilation of two cities in 1945 could be taken for granted by callous people, while more sensitive ones defended the action as a means of shortening the war and thus reducing both Japanese and American losses in the long run.

Postwar examination by American experts seemed to indicate that Japanese resistance had been almost over before Hiroshima. (Somewhat similarly, precision bombing of industries and transport turned out to have been far more decisive than city destruction in Germany.) But whatever the military or other judgments on the use of the atomic bomb in 1945, its existence became henceforth a major and incalculably frightening fact.

Thus the United States came to the end of a period of great and revolutionary achievement. From a policy of isolation it had emerged to a stance of worldwide involvement. It had helped to build a great alliance, and through this and its productive and military achievements, the United States had helped destroy perhaps the worst regime in history. All this had been accomplished without dictatorship, without the destruction of either economic or political liberty at home.

The price for these great achievements started with a million American casualties, but that was only a beginning. Millions of people in Europe and Asia were starving in their ruins. Hate and fear were rampant as never before in modern history. Another totalitarian state had been brought to immense worldwide power. The peaceful, democratic world promised by Roosevelt, and by Wilson before him, seemed no-where in sight.

CONFLICTING HISTORICAL VIEWPOINTS

15. Why was the Atom Bomb Used on Japan?

Soon after the destruction of Hiroshima and Nagasaki, President Truman's mother commented: "I'm glad Harry decided to end the war. He's no slow person. He gets where he's going in short order." But where was he going? More particularly, was the decision to level the Japanese cities purely a military one, or did it have political and diplomatic dimensions as well? Was the use of the "ultimate weapon" designed to defeat Tokyo or to intimidate Moscow? In short, did the Cold War with Russia begin before the hot one with Japan ended?

For a decade and more, these questions have stirred scholarly debate. In Truman's own Memoirs *(Vol. I, 1955) and the writings of his Secretary of War, Henry L. Stimson* (Harpers Magazine, *February 1947), the decision to bomb the island nation was described purely in humanitarian and military terms. In Stimson's words, the nuclear devices were used "in order to end the war in the shortest possible time and to avoid the enormous losses of human life which otherwise confronted us. . . ." Some scholars, however, questioned the candor of the president and his secretary. Among the earliest to do so was P. M. S. Blackett, a British physicist whose* Fear, War, and the Bomb *(1948) asserted that "the dropping of the atomic bomb was not so much the last military act of the second world war as the first major operation of the cold diplomatic war with Russia."*

Blackett's conclusion won support from Gar Alperovitz, a Harvard scholar and one time State Department employee who sharply criticized the Truman administration's Atomic Diplomacy *(1965). Drawing heavily upon Stimson's own diaries, he addressed the question of "the influence of the bomb on certain questions of diplomacy." Admittedly, the reverse question—"the influence of diplomacy upon the decision to use the bomb"—could not be answered from available sources. Yet he found evidence that "strongly suggests"—and he so implied in much of his book —that the weapon was used chiefly to demonstrate American power and, thereby, to make Russia more manageable in Central and Eastern Europe.*

The critics of Truman's "atomic diplomacy" have critics of their own. Michael Amrine, author of The Great Decision *(1959) and other studies of American atomic policy, condemned Alperovitz as a "cold-blooded cousin of . . . Dr. Strangelove," and charged that his thesis was based on unsubstantiated and highly convoluted conjecture. The distinguished diplomatic historian Herbert Feis agreed with Amrine. In his own study,* The Atomic Bomb and the End of World War II *(1966), a revision of an earlier work entitled* Japan Subdued *(1961), Feis concluded that Secretaries Stimson and Byrnes were aware that the A-bomb might not only "subdue the Japanese" but also "monitor Russian behavior." He warned, however, that this awareness should not be "distorted" into accusations of "atomic blackmail," saying "the impelling reason for the decision to use [the bomb] was military."*

The most recent and balanced addition to the controversy is Martin Sherwin's A World Destroyed *(1975), a thoughtful analysis of the complex interactions of science, policy, and diplomacy. Although placing himself closer to Alperovitz than to Feis, Sherwin disputed the revisionist thesis that the bomb was used primarily, if not exclusively, to impress the Russians. The American nuclear arsenal was created solely to win the war, he argued, and Truman used it to that end. But Sherwin also believed that both Roosevelt and Truman intended to wage atomic diplomacy against the Russians. Discovering an unsuspected degree of continuity in American wartime and postwar policies, he contended that Roosevelt, perhaps not less than Truman, shared Churchill's deep suspicions of Stalin's intentions. Together, the wartime president and prime minister secretly plotted to retain exclusive control of atomic energy as insurance against postwar Soviet ambitions. The Anglo-American partnership died with Roosevelt, but his successor continued short-sighted wartime nuclear policies that, in Sherwin's view, contributed to the origins of the Cold War. Thus, whether through cause or effect, the end of one war and the beginning of another were one.*

FOR FURTHER READING

For military and diplomatic history, probably the single most valuable work is Churchill's monumental though not infallible *The Second World War* (6 vols., 1948–1953).* American involvement is traced in detail by A. R. Buchanan in *The United*

---

*Available in paperback edition.

States and World War II (2 vols., 1964). Walter Millis's *Arms and Men* (1956)* is a humane and enlightened study of American military policy from the beginning and is especially valuable for this period. Robert A. Divine's *Roosevelt and World War II* (1969) is brief and sympathetic; while James MacGregor Burns's *Roosevelt: The Soldier of Freedom* (1970) is more detailed and critical. The tangle of Washington bureaus is to some extent unraveled by Eliot Janeway in *The Struggle for Survival* (1951). Richard Polenberg, in *War and Society* (1972), and John Morton Blum, in *V Was for Victory* (1976), contribute to an understanding of the homefront. The tragic tale of Japanese-American internment is told by Roger Daniels in *Concentration Camps USA* (1971), and by Michi Weglyn in *Years of Infamy* (1976). Lawrence S. Wittner examines the peace movement during and after the war in *Rebels Against War* (1969). One of the most thorough accounts of inter-Allied negotiations is Herbert Feis's *Churchill, Roosevelt, Stalin* (1957).* Robert Sherwood's *Roosevelt and Hopkins* (2 vols., 1948)* gives a highly favorable picture of the American effort to achieve good relations with Russia. Chester Wilmot, in *The Struggle for Europe* (1952),* provides a stimulating and intelligent English criticism of American strategy and diplomacy. Diane Shaver Clemens, in *Yalta* (1970),* offers a revisionist view. Among important memoirs are those of Secretaries of State Cordell Hull, Edward R. Stettinius, and James F. Byrnes; of Admiral William D. Leahy; and of Generals Dwight D. Eisenhower* and Omar Bradley.*

17. THE TRUMAN YEARS

	Domestic	The Atom	Europe	Asia
1945	April 12 Death of FDR. November Coal strike.	Baruch Plan rejected. McMahon Act (AEC).	July 17–August 2 Potsdam Conference. August 21 End of lend-lease. November 20–October 1 Nuremburg trial.	August 14 Sino-Soviet Treaty. December Beginning of Marshall mission to China.
1946	June–November End of price controls. November 5 Republicans capture both Houses.		November 4–December 12 Foreign ministers complete treaties with German allies (ratified 1947).	January–April Iran incident.
1947	March 22 Truman loyalty program. June 23 Taft-Hartley Act. July 26 National Security Act.		March 12 Truman Doctrine (aid to Greece and Turkey). June 5 Marshall Plan announced. November–December London Conference (Britain, Russia, United States) breaks up over German question.	January End of Marshall mission to China.
1948	June Selective Service revised. November 2 Truman defeats Dewey.		February Communist coup, Czechoslovakia. June Yugoslav-Russian break. June 24 Berlin blockade begins.	May 15 Israel independent, recognized by United States.

1949	January 20 "Point Four" announced. Chinese Nationalist defeated. December 8 Chiang to Formosa.	April 4 North Atlantic Treaty. May Russians agree to end Berlin blockade.	First Russian atomic explosion	October 14 Smith Act convictions.	1949
1950	January Acheson "defense perimeter" speech. June 25 North Korean attack. November 26 Chinese attack in Korea.		United States starts work on hydrogen bomb.	January 21 Hiss convicted. February 9 McCarthy attacks State Department. September 23 McCarran Act. November 7 Republican election gains. December Hoover attacks Truman foreign policy.	1950
1951	April 11 MacArthur recalled. July 10 Korean Peace talks open. September 8 Japanese Peace Treaty.	April 2 Eisenhower Headquarters in Paris opens.		1951–1952 Corruption disclosures, foreign policy and communism argument.	1951
1952		August 2 West German peace Contract (occupation ends).	British atomic explosion. United States hydrogen explosion.	April 8 Truman seizes steel mills. June 30 McCarran-Walter (Immigration) Act. November 4 Eisenhower defeats Stevenson.	1952

Neither Peace nor War, 1946–1952

29

After World War II, American history became impossible to separate from world history. The scene grew too large for a historian to grasp, just as events were too complex for contemporaries to understand. Yet the American people who lived through these years had not changed overnight. Both their traditions and their leaders had been formed in a period of relative safety and isolation.

THE END OF THE GREAT ALLIANCE

The first postwar president, Harry S. Truman, seemed particularly old-fashioned. He looked to many like a small-town machine politician. He was this, but he was also much more. Truman had to make some of the most tremendous and dangerous decisions in the history of the United States. He made all with courage and some with great intelligence. Sometimes hot tempered, inclined to tolerate unreliable cronies, he possessed a deep sense of American history and a profound understanding of the responsibilities of his office.

When Truman found himself president in April, 1945, he confronted an alarming world. The United States was the only remaining great power under constitutional government. England's might and wealth were nearing exhaustion; Western Europe was wrecked and impoverished; Germany was a disputed battleground. In the Far East, both the old colonial order and Japan's New Order were about to disappear, and almost everywhere nationalists and Communists were preparing to struggle for power.

The collapse of the Grand Alliance of World War II began in Eastern and Central Europe where Russia had military strength and was determined that its approaches should be guarded by friendly nations. At first Soviet occupation policies varied from country to country, but it shortly became apparent that serious opposition to Russian interests would not be permitted. Russian policies were harshest in Poland and Rumania, where Russian interests were crucial and anti-Russian sympathies widespread.

While Russian domination of Eastern Europe became more rigid, the Stalin dictatorship was becoming harsher in Russia. Western European economies were faltering and Communist parties, still under Moscow's control, were both active and formidable in France and Italy. Rightly or wrongly, American policy makers feared not only the consolidation but the extension westward of Russian power. On their part, the Soviets, drawing upon memories stretching back at least to the post-World War I Allied intervention in Russia, viewed the western powers with great suspicion.

To counter this perceived danger from the east, American choices were limited. The Churchill policy of frank division of Europe into spheres of influence had been rejected by Roosevelt and was not revived by Truman. The extent of the Roosevelt policy of conciliation toward the Russians has doubtless been exaggerated, but all western overtures seemed to lead only to misunderstanding and frustration. Liberals hoped to settle all disputes through the United Nations, but the veto provision made coercion of a great power impossible. At the other extreme, some wanted to use the power of the United States to challenge Russian gains and to push toward the illusory, traditional American goals of political democracy and the Open Door everywhere. For such purposes, America had a choice of economic or military weapons. Economic pressure was applied clumsily in 1945, when the United States abruptly cut off lend-lease and lost a Russian request for a loan. With its armies being demobilized, America still had the monopoly of the atomic weapon, and there were those who wanted to threaten, at least, to use it. Yet a policy of preventive war was politically impossible and, to most Americans, morally repellent. The only remaining possibility, given the American world view, was some policy of limited resistance. In 1945–1947, the American government moved gradually in this direction.

During the first months under Truman, the wartime alliance seemed to work in some areas. At Potsdam, in July, 1945, Truman met Stalin and Churchill (replaced during the conference by Clement Attlee of the British Labor Party). The Potsdam Conference sent an ultimatum to Japan and agreed on a complex set of principles for the government of Germany by the Allied Powers. Unable to agree on Eastern European problems, the Big Three turned them over to future meetings of foreign ministers. From 1945–1947, these ministers managed with much difficulty to draw up treaties with the German allies, and the United States reluctantly recognized the Soviet-oriented regimes in Hungary, Rumania, and Bulgaria. An International Military Tribunal, sitting at Nuremberg in 1945–1946, condemned 12 major Nazi war criminals, military and civilian, to death. A similar international court, meeting in Tokyo in 1946–1948, resulted in the hanging of seven Japanese war leaders.

In these years, however, strained relations were more common than agreement. In March, 1946, Winston Churchill warned at Fulton, Missouri that an "Iron Curtain" had cut Europe in two and that Stalin, who did not want war, might gain his objectives without it. At first received with some hostility, Churchill's thesis seemed more plausible to Americans as tensions tightened.

The earliest and most difficult impasse took place in Germany. The agreed provisions for four-power government there had been based on an assumption of continued East-West cooperation. Under a situation of East-West disagreement, the provisions proved to be absurdly impractical. Berlin, the German capital, was to be governed by the four powers jointly. Though it lay 100 miles inside the agreed Russian zone, no definite access routes from the west were provided.

According to the Potsdam agreement, Germany was to be denazified, demilitarized, stripped of its war-making power, and left with a standard of living no better than that of the average for Europe (at that time very low). Though no central German government was to be set up for the present, the country was to be administered as an economic unit through the agreement of the four zonal administrations. Though the final amount of reparations was not set, removal of German industrial equipment was to commence. In addition to what it removed from its own zone, Russia, which had suffered frightful destruction at German hands, was to receive 25 percent of the equipment removed from the western zones, part of which was to be paid for by shipments of German food and raw materials from the Russian zone. For the present, the United States went ahead with this program, including the dismantling of German industry.

It was soon clear that completely different social systems were emerging in the eastern and western zones. As German productive facilities were further weakened, it proved difficult to feed the West German population, swollen by 12 million refugees from the east. Promised food from the Russian zone was not forthcoming.

In 1946, the United States announced a change in policy, including upward revision of German production, eventual political unification of Germany on a decentralized basis, and reexamination of the German-Polish frontier. To quiet Russian fears, the United States offered to guarantee German disarmament for 25 or even 40 years. This offer was promptly refused. In January, 1947, Britain and America agreed to join their zones. Later that spring, a foreign ministers' conference completely failed to agree about reparations, and the deadlock over Germany was complete.

At about the same time, a dramatic plan for international control of atomic energy, drawn up by a committee headed by Bernard Baruch, the veteran financier, was rejected by a suspicious Soviet Union. The Baruch plan called for destruction of American bombs only after international inspection and control had become effective, while the Soviet Union demanded immediate destruction. Meanwhile the Russians, with the aid (perhaps unnecessary) of espionage, were working hard on their own atomic weapon. In August, 1946, Congress created its own system for tight government control of American atomic research and development by an Atomic Energy Commission.

In 1946 and 1947, the strategic Middle East was threatened by Russian demands on Iran for oil concessions and on Turkey for border changes and joint control of the Black Sea straits. The Truman administration responded vigorously, and Russia withdrew her troops from Iran in the spring of 1946. The pressure on Turkey continued intermittently while in Greece the conservative government, supported by English troops, was attacked by indigenous Communist guerrillas, assisted by Greece's Communist neighbor, Yugoslavia. In February, 1947, the British government, strained to the economic breaking point, informed the United States that it would have to withdraw from Greece. Fearing the consequences of Soviet control of the Middle East, and dreading the collapse of the Western European economy, Truman decided on a course of major and independent American action.

CONTAINMENT IN EUROPE, 1947–1949

The new policy of containment was described by George F. Kennan of the State Department in 1947. Soviet policy, Kennan said, was dominated by a belief in the inevitable triumph of communism. World Communist victory, while it might be pursued with patience, could not be abandoned as an objective without a fundamental change in the Soviet system. Such a change might eventually be induced if the United States (1) demonstrated to the world its own vitality and (2) frustrated Soviet plans by the patient application of counterforce wherever necessary.

Counterforce was first applied under the "Truman Doctrine" announced in March of 1947. Calling for economic and military help for people menaced by armed minorities or outside pressures, Truman persuaded Congress to appropriate funds for Greece and also for Turkey. The withdrawal of Yugoslav assistance to the Greek guerrillas, together with American military aid, allowed the Greek government to defeat the Communist insurgents. But having committed itself to counterrevolutionary policies, the United States found itself propping up an undemocratic and unpopular regime. In the years ahead, this pattern of American support for anti-Communist but reactionary governments would become a familiar one.

In June the United States proposed a more general program for European economic relief. In a speech at Harvard, General George Marshall, then Secretary of State, offered to assist the recovery of all European nations, including the Communist ones. Russia denied her satellites this opportunity, but the Western European countries willingly presented a united recovery plan. After considerable debate, Congress (which probably would not have supported a bill that included aid for Communist nations) established the European Cooperation Administration, and in the next three years, more than $10 billion were appropriated for its purposes. This "Marshall Plan" was the greatest success of American postwar policy. It laid the basis for the startling European recovery and unprecedented European unity of the 1950s. And because it provided credits rather than cash, it promoted one of the greatest peacetime economic booms in U.S. history.

Naturally, these American actions produced sharp Russian reactions. The Communist parties of Western Europe, through strikes and political agitation, tried hard though unsuccessfully to make the Marshall Plan a failure. Communist control of Eastern Europe tightened, and in February, 1948, Communists in a *coup d'état* took over Czechoslovakia, a country already aligned with Russia in foreign policy but governed by a coalition. This event, which deeply alarmed Europeans, was partly balanced by a break between Yugoslavia (hitherto the most important European Communist satellite) and the Soviet Union. From then on Tito's realm was to be Communist but independent in foreign policy. This development might, it seemed, indicate one road toward the disintegration of Stalin's empire, and alleged Titoists were ruthlessly eliminated in all Communist-bloc states. Although American policy makers were slow to recognize it, the Yugoslav-Soviet split also demonstrated that Communism was less monolithic than most western leaders had once believed.

In the summer of 1948, Russia decided on drastic countermoves in the crucial German area. Reacting ostensibly to a reform of the currency in the western zones, but perhaps more fundamentally to an American move to promote a permanent consolidation of the three western zones, Russia announced that the division of Germany ended all reason for western presence in Berlin. Russian forces cut all surface communication between West Germany and the former capital, threatening with starvation the city's western garrisons and West Berlin's 2 million pro-Western inhabitants. This threat, the gravest to world peace so far, was met by flying supplies into Berlin in American planes. In May, 1949, the Russians suddenly decided to end the blockade, but the division of Germany was already complete. In September, the (West) German Federal Republic was proclaimed at Bonn, and in the following month the (East) German Democratic Republic was created with its capital East Berlin. Thus the most difficult American-Russian problem had taken a new shape. It was obvious that most Germans wanted their country united and preferred western alignment. It was equally obvious that the Russians would not allow a united Germany to join the western bloc.

Alarmed by the Berlin threat and encouraged by economic revival, the European countries made gestures toward unity and asked for American commitments. In April, 1949, the United States broke with its ancient dislike of binding alliances and signed a treaty of mutual defense with 13 nations of Western Europe. Later this North Atlantic Treaty was signed by Greece and Turkey.

Obviously, such commitments to defend vast areas demanded military means. In July, 1947, the National Security Act overhauled the defense establishment, creating the office of Secretary of Defense, the National Security Council, the Central Intelligence Agency, and other new organizations. In June, 1948, Selective Service was revived and at the same time two bomber groups, capable of delivering nuclear bombs, were sent to air bases in Britain.

Despite these steps, the United States had only begun to build forces sufficient for a sustained worldwide power struggle. Congress was still reluctant to make very large appropriations, and the president was determined to make further cuts. Up to 1950, defense expenditure was limited to $15 billion, and the armed forces to little over a million troops. This meant that the nation was still depending heavily on the atomic bomb. In September, 1949, a Russian nuclear explosion announced the end of American atomic monopoly. In the winter of 1949–1950 the administration decided to begin work on the hydrogen bomb, which would be far more devastating than any existing weapon.

Thus by 1949, the United States had adopted, in theory and practice, the policy of containment. It was not clear whether the United States was bound to undertake counteraction in *any* area of Communist activity or only in those areas where resistance seemed promising. This problem was to cause immense difficulty later. So far, however, the most obvious threat had been to Western Europe, and here there was no doubt of America's commitment. The United States was bound to support its

European allies with economic might and also, if necessary, with weapons of incredible and unknown powers of destruction. Despite vigorous debate, public opinion apparently supported this commitment more fully than it had approved resistance to the Nazis before 1940.

THE NEW AMERICAN SOCIETY, 1945–1949

In domestic as in foreign affairs, the first Truman years were a time of profound change, of conflict, and of considerable success. Remembering 1921 and 1929, many people predicted a postwar depression. Instead, it soon became apparent that the most serious economic problems were to be shortages and inflation. Price controls, fairly efficient in the last years of the war, were mostly destroyed in the summer and fall of 1946 in a long wrangle between the president, who favored them, and the Congress, which distrusted them. Between December, 1945 and December, 1947, prices rose by about a third.

As in 1919, organized labor wanted to protect its wartime gains and defend wages against inflation. This time its efforts were successful. In several rounds of strikes beginning in 1946, unions achieved compromise settlements with employers, usually providing considerable wage increases for which the consumers paid most of the bill in higher prices. For the first time in American labor history, a period of major strikes passed almost without violence. Yet both the public and the administration were concerned about the growing power of labor to bring the economy to a standstill. In 1946, the government briefly took over the coal mines, and Truman threatened to have the army run the railroads if necessary.

By no means placid, postwar American society was richer and more productive than any in history. America's gross national product in the prosperous year 1929 had been worth a little over $100 billion and in the depression had fallen below $70 billion. By 1948, it was above $174 billion (using the same dollar value) and only beginning a spectacular upward movement.

At first, prosperity was apparently stimulated by pent-up consumer demand. Undoubtedly, federal spending for European relief and other purposes helped sustain it. From the wartime peak of $98 billion, federal spending fell to $33 billion by 1948, as against the $3 billion which had seemed normal in the 1920s. In the gloomy 1930s, certain economists had said that booms were unlikely to be sustained in the future either by a rising birthrate or new industries. Now they were proved wrong by a spectacular "baby boom" and by important new developments in such fields as electronics and aviation.

Once more, as in the 1920s, representatives of American capitalism claimed that it had outstripped the dreams of past radicals. This was at least more nearly true than it had been in the earlier period. Continued high taxes and high wages were redistributing wealth to a significant degree. While farm income once more started downward after 1947, wages continued to rise and so did the share that workers had in the country's total net income. While some corporations were huge and powerful, all business including small business had grown. Most people did not believe that the gloomy predictions of 1900 trustbusters were about to be fulfilled. Competition did not seem to be disappearing.

Compared to the early 1920s, the new postwar period saw far less hostile reaction to national and racial minorities partly, no doubt, because there were fewer foreign-born Americans. All too slowly, blacks made some important advances. Truman began the desegregation of the armed forces and called, in 1948, for a series of civil rights measures.

The "G. I. Bill of Rights" sent thousands of veterans to college who would never otherwise have gone. It was arguable that the postwar American society, with its vast new middle class, its burgeoning suburbs, and its high-paid labor, was not only the richest but the most equalitarian society the world had seen. Yet, when one looked into the pockets of poverty that lay beneath the rich surface, one found many people who did not share in the new well-being. Among these were small farmers, technologically displaced workers, the old, the mentally deficient, and, despite all advances, most blacks.

These paradoxical facts shaped the politics of the postwar period. Most Americans, not directly affected by the new kinds of distress, wanted neither to abandon the New Deal nor to extend it. Thus both left and right were frustrated, and the political pendulum swung indecisively, almost regularly, back and forth between a moderately conservative Congress and a surprisingly liberal president.

In September, 1945, Truman called for a long list of reform measures that he called the "Fair Deal." These included higher minimum wages and broader social security, public housing and slum clearance, more regional development along TVA lines, federal assistance to education and health protection, and an attack on racial discrimination in employment. The familiar Southern-Democrat-Republican coalition frustrated most of these aims. Yet the Employment Act of 1946 marked official acceptance of federal responsibility for the maintenance of maximum employment.

In 1946, during the peak of inflation and strikes, the Republicans gained control of both houses of Congress. Liberals predicted disaster, yet few New Deal laws were repealed. One important new measure, the Taft-Hartley Act, indicated a conservative swing in labor policy but regulated unions much less strictly than many conservatives wanted (it outlawed the closed but not the union shop). The same Republican 80th Congress, denounced by Truman for frustrating his Fair Deal, cooperated remarkably with his foreign policy.

As the election of 1948 approached, most people underrated both Harry Truman and his chances. While conservatives disliked the Fair Deal, labor and liberals were tired of Truman's peppery intervention in strikes and longed for a leader of Roosevelt's inspirational gifts. The Democratic party itself seemed to be falling apart. The left wing threatened to follow Henry A. Wallace, who roundly denounced Truman's foreign policy for unnecessary hostility to Russia. A strong civil rights bill in the platform brought the secession of many conservative Southerners, who supported the "Dixiecrat" movement of Governor J. Strom Thurmond of South Carolina. The confident Republicans, once more fighting their right wing, renominated Governor Dewey of New York.

Actually, the situation was less unfavorable to Truman than it seemed. The people were not yet deeply divided about foreign policy, and some had resented the tendency of a Republican Congress to frustrate reform and curb labor. The two Democratic secessions actually proved advantageous. Wallace's well-intentioned protest movement compromised and thus doomed to insignificance by its Communist supporters, drew antiradical fire away from the Fair Deal. Thurmond carried only four Deep South states, and his candidacy helped keep northern blacks in the Democratic camp. The Democrats regained control of Congress.

Jubilantly, the president called once more for the enactment of the Fair Deal, to which he added a new farm program, civil rights measures, and repeal of the Taft-Hartley Act. He called also for a new "Point Four" in foreign policy, providing for American technical assistance to the vast underdeveloped areas of the world. Congress passed some of the milder Fair Deal measures in such familiar fields as minimum wages, social security, and housing. But there were no new TVAs, no dramatic new farm program, and no drastic revision of the Taft-Hartley Act. Point Four operations were commenced with an appropriation of $35 million for all Asia, Africa, and Latin America.

If they looked to history, rather than to their highest hopes, for their standards of comparison, Americans had some reason to be pleased with their government's record in the first four postwar years. At home, they had achieved great prosperity and retained sufficient political unity. Abroad they had assumed vast responsibilities and scored some successes. But in the middle of the century, this relatively cheerful picture was shattered by unforeseen events.

CHALLENGE IN ASIA, 1949–1951

In 1949–1950, as in 1941, disaster struck not in Europe, where American policies and commitments were fairly clear, but in the Far East, where both goals and responsibilities were cloudy.

The only major success in this area was the occupation of Japan, where American power was not seriously contested by Russia. Issuing his orders through the Emperor and receiving a surprising degree of cooperation from the Japanese, General MacArthur carried through with considerable success a program of remaking Japanese government and society on democratic and pacifist lines.

In China, at the end of the war, the inept and unpopular government of Chiang Kai-shek faced a well-entrenched, experienced, and armed Communist opposition which controlled about a fourth of the Chinese population. Russia, which occupied Manchuria as a result of her brief war with Japan, recognized the Chiang government as sovereign throughout China, including Manchuria. Stalin's forces gave limited assistance to the Chinese Communists but turned over the Manchurian cities to Nationalist garrisons often flown in from the south by America. (It is by no means certain that Stalin, at this time, wanted a Communist success in China, which would provide him with a powerful rival in the Communist world.)

In the era of high hopes and Roosevelt-Stalin accords, many American observers,

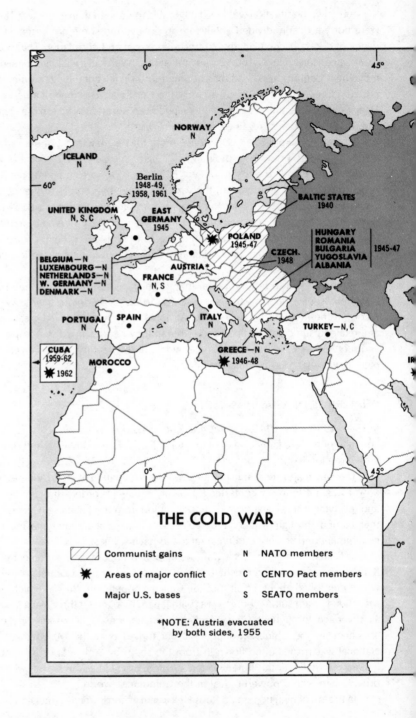

ICELAND
N

NORWAY
N

Berlin
1948-49,
1958, 1961

BALTIC STATES
1940

UNITED KINGDOM
N, S, C

EAST
GERMANY
1945

POLAND
1945-47

HUNGARY
ROMANIA
BULGARIA   1945-47
YUGOSLAVIA
ALBANIA

BELGIUM — N
LUXEMBOURG — N
NETHERLANDS — N
W. GERMANY — N
DENMARK — N

CZECH.
1948

AUSTRIA*

FRANCE
N, S

PORTUGAL
N

SPAIN

ITALY
N

TURKEY — N, C

CUBA
1959-62

1962

MOROCCO

GREECE — N
1946-48

IR

THE COLD WAR

Communist gains

N   NATO members

Areas of major conflict

C   CENTO Pact members

Major U.S. bases

S   SEATO members

*NOTE: Austria evacuated
by both sides, 1955

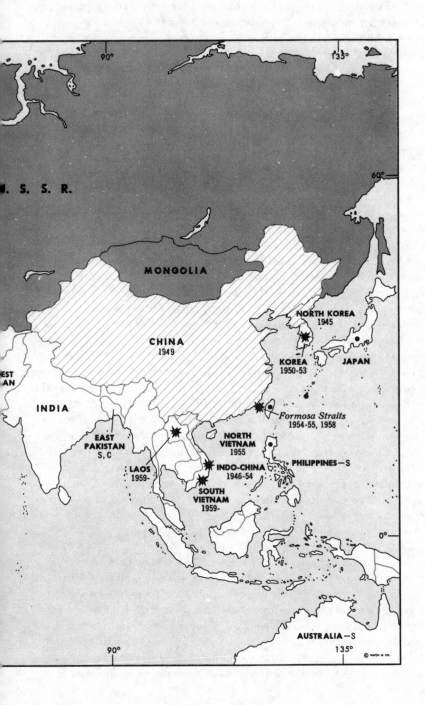

not all of them left-wing, found the Chinese Communists efficient and honest and the Nationalists corrupt and hopeless. Some advocated an effort to produce a coalition government. Encouraged by a few gestures in this direction from both Chinese sides, Truman sent General Marshall to try to bring about such a union and temporarily cut off the supply of American arms. By December, 1946, Marshall concluded that the task was hopeless and asked to be recalled.

After the Marshall mission, limited aid to Chiang was resumed, with little effect. In 1949, the Nationalist armies disintegrated, the Communists captured city after city, and in December Chiang's government moved to the island of Formosa. Suddenly the American people awoke to the fact that China, whose integrity America had long upheld, was now indeed united but under hostile control. From the Baltic to the Yellow Sea over the whole vast Eurasian mainland, Communists were in power. Time would prove, however, that Communist unity was more apparent than real.

Later, many argued that America should have given Chiang more active support. At the time, very few demanded the kind of massive commitment that would have been necessary to keep the tottering Nationalists in power. Here as elsewhere, the faults of American policy were to a large extent the result of traditional American optimism. Roosevelt's program for making Nationalist China a great power, Truman's hope for Nationalist-Communist coalition, and later suggestions that Chiang could have been sustained with a little more effort were all equally unrealistic.

Many Americans were genuinely shocked at events for which they were unprepared. Neoisolationists and Asia-firsters blamed the Roosevelt policies for the disaster, and some partisans saw in the loss of China a means of ending Republican defeat.

Accused not only of mistaken judgment but also of deliberate treason, Truman and his Secretary of State, Dean Acheson, insisted that the Chinese Nationalists were to blame for their own defeat, and the president announced that the United States would not get involved in Chinese civil war in behalf of Formosa. And in January, 1950, Secretary Acheson made a speech defining a broad American "defense perimeter" in the Pacific—very broad but covering neither Formosa nor Korea. This raised in a new form the most difficult problem concerning the containment policy. *Any* announced boundary for American intervention might seem to invite Communist attack in the area left outside. Was the only answer American commitment *everywhere?* Or was it possible, in a democratic country, to decide for or against action in each case without advance commitment or public preparation?

The next challenge came in Korea, where postwar zones of Russian and American military occupation had solidified into hostile political entities. On June 25, 1950, the (Communist) North Koreans crossed the South Korean border in force. Truman, instantly assuming that the Cold War had been globalized, ordered the dispatch of supplies to South Korean troops and also directed the Seventh Fleet to move into the straits between China and Formosa, with orders to prevent attack by either side. Meanwhile the United States brought the North Korean aggression before the Security Council. Since Russia happened to be boycotting this body and could not cast its veto, the council demanded North Korean withdrawal and urged its members to assist South Korea.

In obedience to this order, and also to sustain a regime created and fostered by the United States, President Truman first sent to Korea American air and sea forces and then ground troops under General MacArthur. Fifteen other nations sent small contingents to the UN army in Korea. Thus the situation was an ambiguous one; MacArthur was nominally in command of an international army under UN orders. Actually, his army was made up of 90 percent Americans and South Koreans. Thus the international "police action" was also an American war. It turned into a bloody and frustrating struggle with profound effects on American foreign and domestic policy.

At first, the North Koreans swept the raw American troops southward. In September, holding only a small area around the port of Pusan, the UN force started a northward counterdrive. By a brilliant landing behind enemy lines at Inchon, near Seoul, MacArthur achieved a major victory. This raised the question of whether the UN troops would stop at the old boundary or push on to unify the nation under the South Korean government (both Korean governments claimed to represent the whole peninsula). When the General Assembly resolved that its aim was to create a "unified, independent, and democratic Korea" MacArthur's troops crossed the 38th parallel and drove northward toward the Chinese boundary at the Yalu River, which MacArthur was forbidden to cross. Though President Nehru of India and others warned of possible Chinese intervention, General MacArthur assured President Truman that this was most unlikely. At the end of November, however, Chinese troops surprised the UN army near the Yalu, inflicted a severe defeat, and started a drive southward against stiff resistance.

Chagrined at what he called a new war, MacArthur demanded but was refused new measures to win it. These included permission to bomb the "privileged sanctuary" in China from which Chinese troops and some Russian-made planes were coming, the use of Chinese Nationalist troops from Formosa, and an all-out commitment to victory over the new enemy, with or without the support of America's European allies. When MacArthur carried his protest to the extent of press interviews and letters to members of the Republican opposition, Truman recalled his insubordinate general.

This bold action, taken by Truman to protect what he considered the all-important control of the president over foreign policy, precipitated an angry debate. At first, the public seemed to side with the general's eloquent demand for complete victory. Defenders of the administration, however, stuck to their position that an all-out war with China would be disastrous. In Korea, the line between the two sides was stabilized at about the old border between North and South, and in July, 1950, American representatives began a long, frustrating effort to negotiate peace with the Chinese and North Koreans.

Limited but determined military resistance in Korea was part of a developing American policy, based on an increasing fear of worldwide Communist aggression, and a determination to avoid all-out war. In 1950–1951, only partly for Korean purposes, the military budget was quadrupled and the armed forces increased to 3,500,000. In Europe, where recovery was now well under way, American aid shifted from an economic to a military emphasis. At American suggestions, the North Atlantic

Treaty Organization decided to build a combined Western European force to deter possible Russian attack. Headquarters were established in Paris, and once more Eisenhower was placed in supreme command of an allied army.

Almost inevitably, European rearmament raised the question of contributions from West Germany, the most exposed and now the most prosperous European state. A separate German army was still an intolerable idea to the French and other victims of the Nazis. In 1952, following a French suggestion, the Western European nations formed a European Defense Community in which national components, including a German one, would be placed under a single command.

Japan had proved an important "sanctuary" during the Korean action, and in September the United States signed a peace treaty dropping all restrictions on Japanese economic growth or even rearmament. Japan, however, in an act rare among modern nations, refused to rearm. A separate security treaty gave American forces the right to remain in Japan. At about the same time, the United States signed mutual defense treaties with the Philippines, Australia, and New Zealand.

Thus the Korean War, following the Berlin blockade and the Russian atomic explosion, changed the nature and degree of American commitments once more. American action had turned back North Korea's southward thrust without bringing about a third world war. For this achievement, a heavy price had been paid and not all of it by Americans. The postwar conflict, once centered in Eastern and Central Europe, now spanned the globe. The United States had lost 25,000 men, Korea was devastated, and the Korean civilian population, North and South, had suffered staggering losses. Yet it seemed that victory, or even an end of the fighting, was not in sight. Instead of guarding a limited defense perimeter, the United States seemed to have undertaken to resist Communist advances in even the most remote and difficult theaters. Europe seemed permanently divided, and the German question farther than ever from solution. War had brought its usual accompaniment of conscription, inflation (comparatively moderate), and high taxes. Military expansion seemed to threaten more than ever the traditional civilian character of American society and government. Both America and Russia were known to be developing the hydrogen bomb, potentially 1,000 times more powerful than the weapon that had destroyed Hiroshima. It is not surprising that the American people, most of whom remembered years of apparent security, were very deeply disturbed.

CONFUSION, HYSTERIA, AND THE END OF THE TRUMAN ERA

Popular unrest first took the form of a new debate over foreign policy, similar in some ways to those of 1898–1900, 1914–1917, and 1939–1941, but more violent than any of them. Some extremists argued that the whole diplomacy of Roosevelt and Truman had been part of one gigantic plot, including the New Deal, Pearl Harbor, the buildup of Russia, the sellout of China, and war without victory in Korea. Less violent critics of the administration argued, as former President Hoover did in 1950, that it was a mistake for America to make any commitments on the continents of Europe or Asia.

Senator Taft and others called for a reliance on air power rather than ground troops, and many urged that timid or uncooperative allies be disregarded. On the other hand, the somewhat demoralized liberals maintained that the real mistake had been support of corrupt and reactionary regimes or reliance on military rather than economic methods of defense against communism.

Though none of these arguments held up very well in an extreme form, discontent was not to be dismissed lightly. Nobody knew just where, if anywhere, were the limits of American commitment, and the long-run positive goals of foreign policy were not clear. American "cold war" resistance had been improvised to meet unforeseen threats. Attempts to provide this resistance with a theory were not altogether convincing, and its opponents offered no clearly feasible alternatives. Thus the argument centered, increasingly and disastrously, on one emotional issue: Communists in government.

Unfortunately, neither the facts nor the arguments affecting this issue were simple. Liberals had in the past appealed to free speech, and it was true that the United States, since its beginnings, had normally tolerated advocacy of revolution. But free speech, even revolutionary speech, did not clearly cover new forms of secret political activity. No earlier radical group had been under the control of a foreign great power. And it was not quite clear whether, during a cold war, wartime or peacetime precedents should govern.

Between 1941 and 1945, when Communists throughout the world were supporting the anti-Hitler alliance, some Communists had found employment in Washington, usually in low-echelon jobs. A few of these had been exploited by the Soviet Union for espionage. In some intellectual circles and in sections of organized labor, the Communist party had regained a portion of the strength it had held in the 1930s. These facts, exposed and greatly exaggerated at the moment Americans were dying in a frustrating war with Communists in Korea, produced an explosive reaction.

Responding to early disclosures of Communist activity, Truman established a government loyalty program in March, 1947. Employees were investigated by the FBI, and those found disloyal (later, also those considered "security risks") were discharged. Despite efforts for fairness, the novel and secret character of this program led to some abuses and much uneasiness. Turning from the problem of secret infiltration to a quite different area, Truman's Justice Department started in 1948 to prosecute the leaders of the American Communist party under the Smith Act of 1940, which forbade advocacy of, or conspiracy to advocate, forcible revolution.

Though these actions were disapproved by many liberals, they were not enough to pacify current fears. Designed in part to departisanize the Red issue, they were used to legitimize a wider witch hunt. The demand for more drastic measures arose partly from the House of Representatives' Committee on Un-American Activities whose methods had long drawn liberal criticism. The most spectacular, though not the only or the clearest, case of communism in government arose in this Committee in 1948 when Whittaker Chambers, an ex-Communist, accused Alger Hiss of having been a Communist and, a little later, of having engaged in espionage.

Hiss, a brilliant and widely admired young man, had held a moderately influential

State Department post and had attended the Yalta Conference. Nearly all liberals believed him innocent, and President Truman referred to the Committee's work as a "Red Herring." Yet Chambers's melodramatic and baffling charge proved very hard to refute, and recent evidence seems clearly to implicate Hiss in at least low-level espionage activities. In 1950, Hiss was finally convicted in court, not of espionage but of perjury in his denial of Chambers's charges. Still more alarming to the public was the discovery that spies had been operating in wartime atomic installations. The threat of annihilation was added to the loss of China as a result of Communist conspiracy.

In 1950, Congress passed, over Truman's veto, the McCarran Internal Security bill, which among many drastic provisions required the registration of Communist organizations and provided that *suspected* subversives could be interned, without trial, by presidential order in time of "internal security emergency." In 1952, the McCarran-Walter bill severely increased political restrictions on immigration. And in 1950, when fear of communism had reached its peak, the Communist issue was discovered by its great promotional genius, Senator Joseph McCarthy of Wisconsin.

Charging that many Communists (the number varied) were employed in the State Department and moving on to attack as traitors General Marshall and Secretary Acheson, McCarthy succeeded in creating a wide following and an unparalleled amount of public alarm and confusion. In the congressional elections of 1950, the new political technique of extreme, unsupported charges seemed to work remarkably well, as critics of McCarthy went down in defeat and clever politicians adopted his tactics. As in the anti-German hysteria of World War I, states, cities, and private organizations took up the crusade. Soon self-appointed groups were purging libraries, harassing teachers, and listing dangerous television stars. For a time, it seemed as if traditional individual freedom, decency, and common sense were to be sacrificed in the search for a complete, impossible security.

In this disturbing atmosphere, the 1952 election campaign began. In April, when a threatened steel strike seemed to threaten paralysis, Truman seized the steel plants, an action held unconstitutional in June. A series of sordid political scandals in the administration, not enormous by Harding or Grant standards but still disturbing, began to be exposed. Opposition extremists spread the picture of an incompetent president, surrounded by traitors and crooks, committed to a hopeless war.

Actually, in the summer of 1952, the nation's right-wing extremists received their severest blow when the Republican convention nominated not a McCarthyite demagogue and not even the widely respected conservative Senator Taft but General Eisenhower. The General, long identified with both the Roosevelt and the Truman foreign policies, could hardly lend himself to McCarthy's charges of "Twenty Years of Treason." Eisenhower did, however, support all Republican candidates, including McCarthy, while he confined himself to more moderate discussions of "the mess in Washington" or at most "creeping socialism." In foreign policy, the Republicans promised both peace and victory. John Foster Dulles, their leading foreign policy spokesman, promised that Republicans would roll back communism instead of merely containing it. Near the end of the campaign, Eisenhower promised that if elected he would fly to Korea and bring the war to an end.

The Democrats nominated the eloquent Governor of Illinois, Adlai Stevenson, who aroused immense liberal enthusiasm but proved unable to stem the Republican tide. Surprisingly, the overwhelming Eisenhower victory failed to produce much change in Congress, where Republicans barely gained a two-house majority. Ironically, the first election of a Republican president since Hoover guaranteed that there would be no sharp change in American foreign policy.

CONFLICTING HISTORICAL VIEWPOINTS

16. Who Started the Cold War?

The governments of the Soviet Union and the United States have offered remarkably similar explanations for the origins of the Cold War. Each side has characterized the conflict as a morality play in which the other is cast as the villain. Both have presumed to act in the name of the world's "peace-loving" peoples, and each portrayed the other as an imperialist power bent on global conquest.

Articulated initially by top officials in the Truman administration, including George F. Kennan (Foreign Affairs Quarterly, July 1947), head of the State Department Policy Planning Staff, the official American interpretation of Cold War origins was not seriously questioned by most historians in the United States until the 1960s. Although scholarly accounts were often less hysterical than those by journalists and other popular writers, historians generally agreed that Russia's aggressive designs threatened the stability of the postwar world. Indeed, one of the most methodical and authoritative apologists for American diplomacy was Herbert Feis, a State Department adviser-turned-historian. In a series of books (Roosevelt-Churchill-Stalin, 1953; Between War and Peace, 1960; The Atomic Bomb and the End of World War II, 1966; and From Trust to Terror, 1970), Feis argued that in its Cold War policies the United States was merely responding to a Russian challenge. Fomenting revolution and seeking conquest, the Soviet state, he believed, shattered the Grand Alliance, violated its Yalta Agreements, and forced a reluctant and war-weary United States to assume the leadership of a threatened "free world."

Although the orthodox view dominated popular and scholarly writing throughout the 1950s, there were from the beginning of the Cold War a few precocious dissenters who raised disturbing questions about American policy. Years before popular disenchantment with the war in Vietnam found reflection in a multitude of revisionist attacks on American postwar policy, the philosopher-journalist Walter Lippmann (The Cold War, 1947) questioned the rationale for containment. And such "realist" historians as Hans Morgenthau (In Defense of the National Interest, 1951) and William McNeill (America, Britain, and Russia, 1953) offered early challenges to prevailing assumptions of exclusive Russian guilt. But the first systematic revision of the traditional interpretation was probably William A. Williams's American-Russian Relations, 1871–1947 (1952). In this volume and in such later works as The Tragedy of American Policy (1959) and The Contours of American History (1961), Williams attributed the onset of the Cold War to the dollar diplomacy of the United States. Linking American foreign policy to the "needs" of American capitalism, he viewed containment as the latest manifestation of a traditional American diplomacy of economic expansionism dating at least from the days of the Open Door. American counterrevolutionary activities, then, were designed not to contain Communist aggression but to promote commercial penetration of Eastern Europe.

In recent years, Williams's thesis has been documented and extended by a number of New Left scholars. In The Politics of War (1968) and The Roots of American Foreign Policy (1969), Gabriel Kolko, for example, has offered the least temperature indictment of American policy yet available. Although typical of much New Left scholarship on the period, Kolko's work is more extreme than studies by such thoughtful radicals as Walter LaFeber and Lloyd Gardner. In his balanced America, Russia, and the Cold War (1967), LaFeber surveyed the entire era and concluded that both powers must share the blame for the war of nerves. In Architects of Illusion (1970), Gardner was also highly critical of American policy shapers, but he too conceded that "neither side could fully control events, or even freely respond to them in many instances."

The critics of revisionism are numerous, and many historians reject the economic determinism of the New Left. But recent scholars have shown little willingness to defend the simple pieties of the orthodox interpretation. Thus in The United States and the Origin of the Cold War (1972), and more recently in Russia, the Soviet Union, and the United States (1978), the most persuasive antirevisionist counterattacks now available, John L. Gaddis concluded that "leaders of both super-powers sought peace" and that "neither side can bear sole responsibility for the onset of the Cold War." Clearly, although the question of Cold War origins remains open, there is now widespread scholarly belief that the orthodox answer is no longer satisfactory.

FOR FURTHER READING

Among general histories of the period, Herbert Agar's The Price of Power (1957)* is thoughtful and very brief, and Eric F. Goldman's The Crucial Decade (1956)* is colorful and anecdotal. F. L. Allen, in The Big Change (1952),* points out some of the differences between this period and the previous postwar era. The origin of the Cold War is the subject of several of the books discussed in the essay above. Two able but differing interpretations of American involvement in the struggle are John W. Spanier's American Foreign Policy Since World War II (1960)* and Louis J. Halle's The Cold War As History (1967). Good, brief overviews include John Lukacs's A History of the Cold War (1961)* and Norman Graebner's Cold War Diplomacy, 1945–1960 (1962).* Robert James Maddox's The New Left and the Origins of the Cold War (1973) is harshly critical of revisionist scholarship. The memoirs of Truman and Kennan are indispensable and Dean Acheson's Present at the Creation (1969)

---

*Available in paperback edition.

is outstanding. Students interested in exploring the Soviet point of view should read *History of the USA since World War I* (1976), by N. Sivachyou and E. Yazkov, a tendentious challenge to "bourgeois" history. Robert Griffith, in *The Politics of Fear* (1970), and Richard M. Fried, in *Men Against McCarthy* (1976), consider aspects of the McCarthy phenomenon. William F. Buckley and L. Brent Bozell's *McCarthy and His Enemies* (1959) is a spirited defense of the Wisconsin senator. Allen Weinstein, in *Perjury* (1978), and John Cabot Smith, in *Alger Hiss* (1976), offer opposing answers to the celebrated Hiss question. Perhaps the best introduction to the Truman administration is the Missouri president's own *Memoirs* (2 vols., 1955–1956),* but these volumes should be supplemented by: Barton J. Bernstein, ed., *Politics and Policies of the Truman Administration* (1970); Alonzo Hamby, *Beyond the New Deal: Harry S. Truman and American Liberalism* (1973); Robert J. Donovan, *Conflict and Crisis: The Presidency of Harry S. Truman* (1977); Maeva Marcus, *Truman and the Steel Seizure Case* (1977); and William C. Berman, *The Politics of Civil Rights in the Truman Administration* (1970).

18. MODERN REPUBLICANISM

	Domestic	Space and the Atom	Europe	Asia, Latin America, and Africa	
1952	November Eisenhower elected.	November 1 Eniwetok hydrogen explosion (United States).		December Eisenhower visits Korea.	1952
1953	1953–1954 McCarthyism. Recession.	August 20 Russian H-bomb.	March 5 Stalin's death. June Riots in East Berlin. August 30 France rejects EDC.	July 27 Korean armistice.	1953
1954	April–June Army-McCarthy hearings. May 17 Supreme Court outlaws school segregation. November Democrats capture Congress.	March 1 Bikini H-bomb (United States).		May–June Guatemala Crisis. July 21 Geneva Agreement. September 8 SEATO Pact.	1954
1955	July 11 Dixon-Yates contract cancelled.		May 15 Austrian Peace Treaty. July 18–23 Geneva meeting (Eisenhower, Bulganin).		1955
1956	November Eisenhower elected with Democratic Congress.	Stevenson proposes H-bomb ban.	February Khrushchev denounces Stalin crimes. October–November Hungarian insurrection.	October Suez Crisis.	1956
1957	Recession. September 24 Troops to Little Rock. Civil Rights Act.	May 15 British H-bomb. October 4 Sputnik.	March 28 European Common Market.	January 5 "Eisenhower Doctrine" in Middle East.	1957
1958	November Democratic gains in Congress.	January 31 United States satellite. March 31 Russia suspends tests (United States follows).		May Lebanon Crisis.	1958
1959	July Steel strike.	September 13 Soviet "Lunik" hits moon.	September Khrushchev visits United States.	February 16 Castro premier of Cuba. June Tokyo riots.	1959
1960	Recession. November Kennedy elected.	February 11 French atomic explosion. July 20 Polaris sub launches missile.	May U2 incident. November West Berlin threatened	June 30 Congo independent; civil war. August Laos Crisis.	1960

Modern Republicanism
1953–1960

30

Some Americans had hoped, and others had feared, that the Eisenhower administration would sharply change American foreign policy and reshape post-New Deal American society. It did neither. In nearly every sphere, the history of the administration seemed to go through three stages: first, announcement of sweeping change; second, reversion, with overwhelming public approval, to a slightly modified version of earlier policies; finally, frustration and renewed crisis. One explanation of this cycle is not hard to find. In the circumstances confronting American policy-makers of this period, real alternatives were few, and completely satisfactory solutions impossible. Yet the American people did not give up easily their search for security and contentment. In 1953, many wanted a change; in the middle 1950s, most believed that they had found security; by the end of the decade, it was apparent that they had not.

Dwight D. Eisenhower had been trained all his life for war, yet nobody questioned his devotion to peace. Far from bringing to the White House a habit of command, he was devoted to consultation and consensus. A moderate conservative, he was thwarted more by the right wing of his own party than by the opposition. Unwilling to use fully his political power, he remained, despite overwhelming personal popularity, an ineffective party leader.

FROM REACTION TO COMPLACENCY

In 1953, fear of domestic subversion reached panic proportions. The federal security program was drastically tightened, while congressional committees searched for disloyalty in education, entertainment, and private foundations. For a while, Senator McCarthy, now chairman of the Committee on Government Operations, seemed the most powerful individual in Washington. Far from admitting that Republican victory had ended the danger of Communist infiltration, he intensified his accusations. The State Department, long his principal victim, seemed to have surrendered. Officials who criticized the senator were suspended, and books that offended him were removed from American information libraries and destroyed (sometimes their authors were called to Washington and harshly grilled). Two junior members of McCarthy's staff junketed through Europe issuing portentous reports on the loyalty of senior American officials after talking briefly with shady foreign informants. Civil servants and even army officers were encouraged to disobey their superiors and disclose confidential information. The morale of federal employees sank dangerously, and some of America's staunchest friends abroad were dismayed.

In 1954, the senator fell from power as rapidly as he had risen. The president had shown signs of disquiet, and, perhaps more important, the public was beginning to be bored. A prolonged and complicated controversy with the Department of the Army resulted in a series of television hearings in which McCarthy's manners and methods shocked the public. Finally a select committee of the Senate condemned his conduct as contradictory to senatorial traditions. Discredited and comparatively ignored, McCarthy died in May, 1957.

Later in the decade, the Supreme Court, presided over by Earl Warren, a liberal Republican, delivered a number of decisions that restricted the scope of congressional committees and in other ways reaffirmed the importance of traditional individual freedoms. At the polls, the congressional elections of 1954 demonstrated that the "Red issue" had lost its potency, and in 1956 it was hardly used. In the prosperity and complacency of the middle Eisenhower years, hysteria died down more quickly than it might have under more vigorous counterattack. Yet the costs of tolerating McCarthyism were high. An ugly image had been presented to the world, sections of the government service had been demoralized, and some important issues of foreign policy seemed to have been placed beyond the range of effective discussion. As McCarthyism waned, a shrill minority on the Far Right added Eisenhower and Warren to their list of worldwide conspirators.

In the same period, the administration's economic and social policies shifted from right to center. At the outset, many cabinet members were wealthy business executives, the conservative Senator Taft apparently wielded great power in Congress, and the president's own pronouncements on domestic matters were highly conservative. Senator Taft died in July, 1953. In the winter of 1953–1954, a recession set in causing the Treasury Department to modify its conservative, anti-inflation policies. Without drastic government action, recovery came swiftly, and in the mid-1950s an unparalleled prosperity prevailed. Despite this fact and despite the president's great and continuing popularity, Democrats recovered and kept control of Congress throughout the Eisenhower administrations. With the Korean War over and the McCarthy hysteria abated, it became clear that the country's dominant mood had not changed greatly since the Truman years. Few Americans wanted to dismantle the New Deal, and few wanted radical new departures. Under these circumstances, the Eisenhower instinct for compromise and conciliation had free rein.

In the prosperous mid-1950s, the political pattern seemed to consist of (1) administration friendliness to business, (2) administration efforts, seldom strikingly successful, to promote economy and decentralization, and (3) compromises between president and Congress in support of moderate, familiar kinds of reform programs. Efforts to win business confidence included tax concessions, increased "partnership" of government and private enterprise in the development of public power and even nonmilitary atomic energy, and support for state, rather than federal, control of tideland oil resources. On the other hand, Eisenhower's first Republican Congress created the Department of Health, Education, and Welfare, extended social security, and gave moderate support to public housing. Even after the Democrats recovered control, few measures more startling than these were passed. Such controversial programs as health insurance or federal support of education were regularly defeated or heavily amended.

A major effort to change the direction of New Deal and Fair Deal farm policies was made by Ezra Taft Benson, Eisenhower's conservative Secretary of Agriculture. Amid loud outcries from farm representatives, price supports were made "flexible" rather than rigid; that is, they were lowered. Yet, since farm income was declining, many New Dealish measures, including a "Soil Bank" scheme to reduce acreage, received administration support. Neither farm subsidies nor the farm problem seemed at all likely to disappear.

A surprisingly vigorous program of antitrust prosecutions and various efforts to help small business failed to achieve a significant movement in the direction of *laissez-faire.* Government spending, so long denounced as the road to socialism, was cut back only moderately after the Korean War. It remained higher than the 1950 post-World War II low of $45 billion and by 1957 was to reach a new peacetime high of $82 billion. Government decisions of many kinds continued to affect every part of the economy. To the president's obvious distress, it became clear that this fact played vast temptations in the way of competing interests. In 1955, the Dixon-Yates contract, an effort to provide for private construction of a huge power plant for Memphis, proved to be improperly negotiated and was canceled by Eisenhower. The next year disclosures of attempted bribery of a senator forced the president to veto a bill to exempt natural gas producers from federal rate control.

The most important advance of the period, that made by blacks, was not a product of executive action. Despite some recent gains, in 1952 blacks were still generally subject to enforced segregation in the South, and throughout the nation they were far behind whites in jobs, income, housing, education, and health. In 1954, the Supreme Court reversed its 1896 position on segregation. Until now, "separate but [nominally] equal" treatment of blacks in transportation, recreation, and education had been legal. Now segregation, specifically in education, was pronounced inherently unequal. The decision produced fierce defiance in the South, where massive resistance campaigns were led by highly influential private Citizens' Councils. Only in the border states did effective school desegregation begin. Despite his personal misgivings about the court's decision, Eisenhower supported it in the name of constitutional duty. In 1957, he sent federal troops to Little Rock, Arkansas, where Governor Orval Faubus, alleging fear of mob action, was using state guards to obstruct court-ordered integration of the high school. In 1957, Congress passed the first Civil Rights Act since 1875. It created a Civil Rights Commission with power to investigate denial of voting rights or equal protection of the law. Under this and later legislation, the federal government began a cautious effort to protect black voting in the South.

More important than any government action was the new determination of southern blacks to achieve equality for themselves. In 1955, the blacks of Montgomery, Alabama, under the leadership of Martin Luther King, Jr., an eloquent young minister, achieved the desegregation of the bus system through a determined boycott. Similar efforts, carried on with remarkable discipline in a spirit of passive resistance, made further gains in desegregating transportation, restaurants, and housing. More progress was made by the southern black than in any decade since Reconstruction. Yet violent resistance continued and frustrations were many. By the end of the decade, it was clear that the hardest problems for blacks lay in the swelling slums of northern cities, islands of poverty in a sea of wealth.

In its social effects, Eisenhower prosperity had something in common with Coolidge prosperity. Like the 1920s, the 1940s and 1950s added large numbers of citizens to the complacent, suburban, moderately conservative ranks of the middle class. As in the 1920s, however, the culture of prosperity excluded some people and was repudiated by others.

Until nearly the end of the decade, few middle-class citizens noticed that a large minority remained poor. Esthetic blight and moral sluggishness were the main targets of criticism. Perhaps the most obvious failure of America—here the critics were repeating strictures made since the 1880s and 1890s—was the cities. Traffic choked them, old slums disgraced them, and new jerry-built housing spread from their edges into the countryside. In the slums and, more shockingly, in some wealthy suburbs, juvenile delinquents expressed their confusion and frustration in acts of violence.

As in the 1920s, intellectuals denounced dullness and conformity. The successor of Babbitt was the "Organization Man" who was said to live and breathe in the cheerful, noncontroversial manner prescribed by the head office on the basis of personality research. To repudiate, defy, and outrage this monster seemed to a few serious people the main need of the hour. "Beatniks," bearded and bizarre, proclaimed a new religion of defeat and withdrawal rather than defiance.

To most Americans, however, Eisenhower prosperity and its genial symbol were apparently highly satisfactory. An unassuming president who left many administrative decisions to his subordinates, praised free enterprise, disowned corruption, and cooperated with a cautiously reformist Congress seemed to fit the needs of the hour. Surely one of these needs, though hardly the only one, was for reassurance and rest after decades of fierce controversy. Despite a heart attack in 1955, Eisenhower was renominated in 1956 and scored a landslide victory over a visibly less confident Adlai Stevenson.

FROM MASSIVE RETALIATION TO PEACEFUL COEXISTENCE

In 1952, many Republicans had denounced war, government spending, and appeasement. Some had promised in contrast peace, economy, and a rollback of world communism. The difficulties of this commitment were made greater by a change in the tactics of the opponent. In March, 1953, Joseph Stalin died. Nikita Khrushchev, who emerged as Russia's new leader, repeatedly proclaimed a relaxation of the Russian police state and a foreign policy of peaceful competition with capitalism. The main theater of this competition was to be the underdeveloped countries just emerging from colonial rule. In many of these countries, the new, comparatively "soft" Communist line, coupled with unquestionable Russian technological achievement, seemed far more effective than Stalin's steamroller technique.

During most of Eisenhower's presidency, foreign policy was to a large extent formed by Secretary of State John Foster Dulles. Dulles, a tactless man of formidable knowledge and consistency, distrusted Russia's intermittent gestures of conciliation. American power, he believed, was sufficient to defeat and not merely to contain the Communist enemy. Sometimes alarming America's allies with statements about going to the brink of war, he was more aware than he sounded of the limits of action.

Anti-Communist militance plus Republican traditions of economy led to the proclamation of a new military policy. Instead of reacting to local Communist threats with expensive and indecisive ground wars, America, Dulles said, would from now on rely on "massive retaliation" at times and places of its own choosing. Expenditures and ground troops would be cut back, while nuclear weapons would be further developed and the air arm expanded. This would provide, as the newspapers soon put it, "more bang for a buck." Corollaries of this "New Look" in military policy were tight alliances and the development of a string of air bases abroad from Spain to Iran. NATO armies in Europe would be equipped with tactical atomic weapons.

The new policies drew heavy criticism abroad and at home. Critics charged that they would make American resistance to aggression impossible except in cases justifying all-out nuclear war. This became even harder to contemplate as American tests made clear the colossal destructiveness of the H-bomb, and scientists made conflicting statements about the effect of fallout on cancer, leukemia, and birth deformities. In October, 1954, Eisenhower, who had seldom echoed Dulles's bellicose pronouncements, said that war had become obsolete under modern circumstances. Since the Russians were saying much the same thing, the world breathed a little easier.

The new military-diplomatic policies were severely tested in the Far East. Carrying out a campaign promise, the administration succeeded in negotiating a Korean peace on approximately the same terms Truman had been willing to accept. The massive retaliation policy may have contributed something to Communist willingness to sign, since Dulles announced that if war persisted it could not be confined to the Korean Peninsula. Prisoners of war were allowed, as both Truman and Eisenhower had insisted, to choose whether or not to go home, and a large number of Communist soldiers chose to go to Formosa. The Korean peninsula was left divided, leaving America committed to assist and defend an economically and politically shaky South Korean state.

With peace in Korea, attention shifted southward to Indochina where since 1945 the French had been fighting a bloody and unsuccessful war against the Viet Minh independence movement, by now solidly under Communist leadership. The United

States had been skeptical about colonialism here as elsewhere but, since the Korean War, had been supporting the French more and more heavily with money and material. In March, 1954, it suddenly became clear that northern Indochina could no longer be held unless the United States committed at least its air power. Both Dulles and Eisenhower proclaimed that the loss of Indochina would lead to Communist domination of all South Asia. Prospects of joint American-British intervention were explored by Dulles without success. Some of the administration's military advisers suggested the use of small atomic weapons; Vice-president Nixon suggested that it might be necessary to risk "putting our boys in."

Examined closely, American intervention in Indochina seemed a dubious prospect. Dispatch of American troops to fight a jungle war, right after the unpopular Korean episode, would contradict administration pronouncements. Air power alone would be difficult to use in Indochina. According to the new military doctrine, this seemed to make a clear case for massive retaliation against the centers of opposing power, presumably Moscow and Peking. This terrible alternative was not to be considered, and Eisenhower, overruling his military advisers, decided against even local air assistance to the French.

In May, the fall of the fortress of Dienbienphu forced the French to move toward settlement of the war. Though the United States took no direct part in the Geneva Conference among Russia, China, Britain, France, and the Indochinese states, Washington accepted its complex and fateful results. The Geneva agreements recognized the three states of Laos, Cambodia, and Vietnam. The last was divided at the 17th Parallel, with the Viet Minh holding the north and the French-backed Saigon government the south. In two years, internationally supervised elections were to be held throughout Vietnam. Meantime, military forces were to be regrouped and populations exchanged. Military bases of any country, the introduction of new military forces, and adherence to military alliances were forbidden on both sides of the line. Observance of the agreements was to be supervised by a commission representing India, Poland, and Canada.

As had happened in the divisions of Korea and Germany, separate governments developed in the two parts of Vietnam. The insecure government in the South refused, with American approval, to carry out the scheduled election, arguing that proper supervision in the Communist north was impossible. Eisenhower later admitted that with the Communist leader, Ho Chi Minh, the likely victor of such an election, the time was not right for democracy in Southeast Asia. Of the new states, Communist North Vietnam was the strongest, neutral Cambodia leaned toward friendship with China, and Laos and South Vietnam, both weak and internally divided, were added to the long list of possible American responsibilities.

One of the administration's early acts was to carry out Republican promises to "unleash Chiang Kai-shek." The Seventh Fleet, patrolling the Straits of Formosa mainly to protect Chiang's Nationalists against mainland assault, was instructed to present no opposition to attacks in the other direction. But in 1954 the Chinese Communists loudly proclaimed their intention of capturing Formosa, which, quoting the Cairo Declaration of 1943, they insisted was part of China. It had long been clear that the

United States would not allow Formosa to fall, and it had just assisted in the movement of former Communist soldiers to this retreat. American policy was less clear toward the tiny islands that were within ten miles of the Chinese coast, which the Nationalists had garrisoned. When mainland batteries began shelling these offshore islands, the United States announced that America would defend them *if* the assault seemed to be part of an attack on Formosa itself. In a treaty with Chiang, the United States pledged to defend Formosa and the Pescadores, while Chiang promised not to invade the mainland without United States consent. Thus the brief "unleashing" was ended.

In September, 1954, the United States signed the SEATO treaty of military alliance, modeled on the Atlantic Pact, with Britain, France, Australia, New Zealand, the Philippines, Pakistan, and Thailand. A special protocol extended the treaty's coverage to Laos, Cambodia, and South Vietnam. Thus a Far Eastern policy not much unlike that of Truman had emerged. The United States had divided two crucial areas with the Communists and guaranteed the resulting status quo. The Formosa Straits, like Korea in 1950, were an area of great danger where the limits of American commitment were not clear.

The Eisenhower policies were further tested in a new theater, the Middle East, whose problems to some extent typified those of the entire underdeveloped two-thirds of the world. More and more, it began to be said that the outcome of the world struggle for power lay not in Europe or East Asia but in the vast, backward, impoverished, restless countries of Africa, southern and western Asia, and Latin America. Clearly, American power could not replace that of the European empires that had until recently provided most of these areas with one kind of stability. In many of the new countries, governments were unstable and economies both unjust and unstable. An intensive effort to understand and assist them was widely urged. Yet America's whole past made it difficult for its people to understand the needs and feelings of the most impoverished and oppressed people.

In the Middle East, American policy was influenced by two special concerns. One was the region's immensely important oil resources, long defended by Britain and coveted by Russia. The other was a special kind of commitment to the new state of Israel. The American Jewish community contributed heavily to Israel's support, and most Americans admired the courage of the tiny state, which not only defended its independence against heavy odds, but welcomed all survivors of Hitler's death camps. Most of Israel's Moslem neighbors, particularly the displaced Palestinians, hated the Israelis as interlopers and refused to accept the new state's existence.

The United States fostered, but did not join, the Baghdad Pact signed in 1954 by Great Britain, Turkey, Pakistan, Iraq, and Iran. America agreed also to assist President Nasser, the Egyptian dictator who aspired to Pan-Arab leadership, to build a huge dam on the upper Nile. But when Nasser seemed to bargain for Russian support as well, the American offer to build the dam was suddenly withdrawn. Nasser promptly seized this excuse to nationalize the French-built, British-and-French-owned Suez Canal, which had been for generations the lifeline of the British Empire and was now a funnel for vitally needed European supplies of oil. At the end of October, 1956, Egypt was attacked by Israel, Britain, and France. Siding against her traditional allies, America condemned this use of force. American pressure, in strange combination with Russian threats of intervention, forced a humiliating British-French withdrawal.

Alarmed at declining western prestige and strong signs of Soviet interest in the Middle East, the president, in January, 1957, persuaded Congress to endorse the "Eisenhower Doctrine." This authorized the president to provide military assistance to Middle Eastern nations requesting aid against Communist aggression. This pledge proved difficult to implement. Within two years, crises occurred in Jordan, Syria, and Iraq. Each, however, involved the threat of a Communist coup from within rather than the threat of external aggression, and American help was not sought. In July, 1958, the United States did send troops to Lebanon, whose president had requested them. At the end of the Eisenhower era, conditions in the Middle East seemed a little less dangerous despite the baffling dilemmas of American policy. So far, nationalism in this area seemed to be gaining on communism.

In Europe, where the president was personally popular, the program for collective defense ran into serious difficulties. The NATO scheme had been formulated when Stalinist threats and Far Eastern aggression had alarmed the European nations. Now, with the Korean peace and the new Russian tone of conciliation, immediate fear of Communism subsided. In some circles, not all of them left-wing, fear of possible American rashness and consequent nuclear war took its place. Moreover, Europeans, like many Americans, were more interested in their own burgeoning prosperity than in problems of defense.

In August, 1954, the European Defense Community scheme, a French suggestion heartily endorsed by the United States, was killed by the French parliament. Secretary Dulles angrily threatened an "agonizing reappraisal" of American policy, which seemed to suggest withdrawal of American forces or perhaps making a separate arrangement with Germany. Under British leadership, the European nations in 1955 developed a complex substitute. Germany was invited to provide a limited proportion of NATO troops. The (West) German Federal Republic received full sovereignty, was guaranteed by France, England, and the United States, and promised not to pursue reunification by force. West Germany still claimed the lost eastern territories, West Berlin was still isolated, and no Central European settlement came near being acceptable to both sides. As yet, the dream of making Western Europe a single major military power was a failure.

Ironically, while America's relations with her European allies deteriorated, her relations with her major antagonist moved from unexampled harshness to unexampled mutual toleration. At the outset of his administration, Eisenhower announced that Russian goodwill could be demonstrated by a Korean peace and an Austrian peace treaty. Not only the first but, to everybody's surprise, the second condition was satisfied. In 1955, Austria was evacuated and became an independent, neutral, Western-oriented nation. Russia made peace with Yugoslavia without forcing a Yugoslav return to the orthodox Communist fold and recognized West Germany. At a major Communist congress in 1956, Khrushchev denounced the crimes of the Stalin period in startling terms. Western skepticism about the new Russian line was lessened when the Chinese began to denounce it as a betrayal of Leninism.

In the summer of 1955, while the new line was still unfolding, Eisenhower consented to meet with the British, French, and Russian heads of government at Geneva. While the conference settled no outstanding problems, its most dramatic moment came with Eisenhower's suggestion of an "open sky" formula under which each side would receive full military information from the other and be free to verify it by aerial inspection. Acceptance of this proposal, either by Russia or by the American Congress, was doubtful. Yet an exchange of military information seemed a promising avenue toward peace and became a recurrent goal of American policy. The new "spirit of Geneva" seemed for a while more important than concrete negotiations, as America and Russia exchanged delegations of ballerinas, farmers, and other ambassadors of goodwill. The Dulles policy of massive retaliation was dead, and even the Truman policy of building collective resistance became harder to implement.

If the new Soviet line raised problems for western policy, it raised still harder ones for Stalin's heirs, who had no thought of abandoning Stalin's East European gains. From Warsaw to Berlin, people longed to test the limits of the new policies. Some remembered that Secretary Dulles had promised American support for liberation. But in 1953, strikes and riots in East Germany produced no American action. In 1956, Poland, a country especially important to the United States because of immigration, daringly defied the Russians and established a regime that, while still Communist and part of the Eastern alliance, offered considerably greater liberty of expression. Taking the cue, and tragically taking it too seriously, the Hungarians revolted with greater violence and seemed on the point of leaving the Soviet sphere altogether. After considerable initial hesitation, Russian troops brutally suppressed the revolt. Later, its leaders were executed. Since the United States took no action, it seemed that liberation was as dead a policy as massive retaliation.

Despite these disturbing events, the United States apparently entered Eisenhower's second term in a cheerful and optimistic mood. Within two years new threats at home and abroad made optimism far more difficult.

THE END OF COMPLACENCY, 1957–1960

The administration's troubles began with an economic downturn in late 1957. This recession, more serious than its postwar predecessors, focused attention on three problems. The first of these was unemployment, which hovered around 5 percent, declining only slightly with economic upturns. The second problem was the rate of American economic growth, which was far slower than that of either Russia or Western Europe. The third was the American balance of payments. Declining European purchases and continuing American arms and aid programs were causing an outflow of gold and threatening American capacity to maintain its massive responsibilities.

Aside from these immediate problems, analysis began to show more and more clearly that Eisenhower prosperity, impressive as it was, had never spread to all the people. The war and the early Cold War periods, with their colossal new government expenditures, high taxes, and demand for labor, had benefited the lower economic groups most. The group considered poor by economists had shrunk from something like two-thirds of the people in the depression to about one-fourth in 1953. Since then, while the well-to-do group had grown sharply, the proportion of poor had remained about the same, and their share in the national income had decreased. The poor quarter of a rich society was too easy to overlook and neglect. Most of the disadvantaged were untrained and undereducated, and automation was rapidly lessening demand for unskilled labor. Many were old, and many were black. Neither unions, social security, nor housing legislation seemed to reach the problems of these rejected people. Even an economic upturn might pass them by.

These moral, social, and economic challenges did not become clear overnight. It was obvious enough that distress existed in some areas (like West Virginia coal fields and big-city slums) and that the economy had lost some of its drive. At the same time the administration was wounded when Sherman Adams, Eisenhower's chief administrative aide, was forced to resign after disclosure of his acceptance of improper gifts from favor-seeking cronies. Rumors of corruption, the fact of recession, and worry about foreign policy were registered in the election of 1958. Democrats, and especially liberal Democrats, scored their biggest gains since 1936. The president accepted this blow with good grace and continued to cooperate with Speaker Sam Rayburn and Majority Leader Lyndon Johnson, the moderate Democratic leaders in Congress.

Abroad, challenges and disasters mounted dramatically from 1957. In October of that year, the Russians placed in orbit their "sputnik," the first earth satellite of human manufacture. This was not only a major feat of applied science, but also a demonstration of military power. Russia had already boasted that it possessed an intercontinental ballistic missile capable of delivering a nuclear warhead anywhere. Now this claim seemed probably true. Sputnik set off a wave of American self-criticism, which tended to exaggerate the achievements of Soviet education, science, and weapons as much as these had been underrated earlier.

Many tasks were quickly accomplished to remedy the American lag in rocket building and the penetration of space. In January, 1958, a small American satellite was put in orbit, and in November the Air Force fired a huge rocket 6,000 miles into space. Probably the strongest American answer to the Soviet lead was the firing of a rocket from the "Polaris" submarine in July, 1960. Like the competition between European powers from the sixteenth to the nineteenth centuries, the "space race" had both a peaceful and a warlike aspect. It was a new field for "peaceful competition" in which each country spent vast resources for scientific and exploratory prestige. It was also a sinister and complex struggle for military superiority and particularly for possession of mobile, hard-to-destroy, and infinitely powerful nuclear weapons. Whoever was ahead, it was clear that the terms for American foreign policy had changed. America's historic invulnerability was gone; war would mean immediate and vast destruction in the United States as well as in enemy territory.

In confronting the new threat, the administration was handicapped by the fatal disease (1957) and death (1959) of Secretary Dulles. No new policy seemed at hand to replace his consistent though unsuccessful and unrealistic system. And the Soviet

Union, full of self-confidence, intensified both the conciliatory and the belligerent phases of its policies. American-Russian negotiations about disarmament and an end to nuclear tests continued under immense pressure from alarmed world opinion. In 1958 both countries announced a temporary cessation of testing, but the Soviet Union, which acted first, got most of the credit. In November of that year, Khruschev, apparently pressured by hard-liners within his own government and party, renewed Russian pressure on Berlin. In the absence of an acceptable settlement, he announced, Russia would in six months sign a peace treaty with East Germany that would turn over the Berlin approaches to the most intractable and rigid of the satellite states. From time to time in the next years, the deadline was extended, but the threat remained. Pressing hard for negotiations on the Berlin issue, Khrushchev secured an invitation to visit the United States in September, 1959. Once more nothing was settled, but an atmosphere of strained cordiality was maintained.

Making a further concession, Eisenhower agreed to meet Khruschev in Paris in May, 1960, without preliminary lower-level negotiations that the United States had earlier demanded. Just as the meeting was getting under way, the Russians shot down an American spy plane 1,300 miles inside Russian territory. At first, American officials denied the charge of espionage, but the pilot, who had been captured, confessed. Contrary to international custom in such matters, the administration now acknowledged and justified the practice of secret photographic flights over Russian territory. Dramatically, Khruschev demanded an impossibly abject apology from the president and, in its absence, angrily broke off the Paris meeting and withdrew an invitation for a presidential return visit to Russia.

In Asia, affairs went little better. Communist China bombed the offshore islands again in 1958 and bloodily subdued autonomous Tibet in 1959. Immediately after the Paris fiasco, an Eisenhower visit to Japan had to be postponed because of student riots against a Japanese-American security treaty. In Laos and South Vietnam, Communist guerrilla movements seemed to be stronger than non-Communist governments.

In Algeria, prolonged insurrection absorbed the energies of France and threatened the United States with a difficult choice between anticolonialism and a traditional alliance. Further south in Africa, the French, British, and Belgian empires were liquidated with great rapidity, leaving in their wake many large and small nations, mostly lacking experienced leaders of viable economies. In one of the weakest and largest of these, the former Belgian Congo, disintegration threatened to spread East-West conflict to a new theater.

Most distressing of all to Americans were the developments in Latin America. Since the wartime triumphs of the Good Neighbor Policy, little had been accomplished in this region by American diplomacy. Despite statements of democratic solidarity, both the Truman and Eisenhower administrations had made cordial gestures toward oppressive military regimes. The most spectacular action of the Eisenhower administration in the region, applauded at home but reviving memories of intervention among Latin Americans, had been to assist a right-wing coup against a pro-Communist government in Guatemala. No program like the Marshall Plan had been developed to complement political with economic action, and the region's desperate economic problems were steadily growing more acute. In 1958, Vice-President Richard Nixon, touring Peru and Venezuela, was the target of violent hostile demonstrations.

In January, 1959, in Cuba, the guerrilla forces of Fidel Castro triumphed over the government of Fulgencio Batista. Many Americans sympathized with the Castro movement's program of needed economic reform and blamed American policy for close relations with the previous right-wing regime. But before long, executions and confiscations in the island seemed to indicate that Castro was drawing closer to the Communist bloc. By the end of the Eisenhower administration, American investments in Cuba were confiscated, American trade nearly cut off, and Castro's violently anti-American and by now pro-Soviet movement was threatening to attract support throughout the poorer regions of the hemisphere.

Probably the position of the United States in 1960, difficult as it was, seemed even worse because of the apparent lull of the mid-1950s. Straining for a vanished security, the American people still felt a deep affection for the immensely likable president, while at the same time they repudiated his party in Congress and increasingly criticized his policies.

This situation was dramatized, as so much of American history has been, in a presidential campaign. Richard Nixon, Eisenhower's vice-president, received the Republican nomination with the president's nominal blessings and campaigned on the administration's record. Senator John F. Kennedy of Massachusetts, 44 years old, able, rich, and Catholic, promised sweeping change and vigorous forward movement. The outcome of the election, a hairline Kennedy victory, proved difficult to analyze. It seemed to demonstrate that (1) the obvious ability, political skill, and vigor of Senator Kennedy impressed the public; (2) a great many people, though many fewer than in 1928, still voted according to historic ethnic and religious loyalty; and (3) the American people, though shaken from the complacency of 1956, were still not in the mood for large-scale new departures. This last point was underlined by the congressional elections. Democrats retained control, but Republicans and conservatives of both parties registered gains. Thus the Kennedy administration came to power in no position to implement the bold new programs it had promised.

In 1960, critics of the Eisenhower administration pointed out, correctly, that eight years of "Modern Republicanism" had failed to solve the critical domestic and foreign problems that faced the country. Its defenders argued, also correctly, that peace had been preserved, general prosperity maintained despite brief recessions, and the political atmosphere somewhat improved. In the tragic years ahead, Eisenhower's more vigorous successors were to achieve few more complete victories, and some of the unsolved problems were to become more intractable.

CONFLICTING HISTORICAL VIEWPOINTS

17. Was Eisenhower a "Good" President?

In 1960, the comedian Mort Sahl urged Americans to vote "no" in November and keep the White House vacant four more years. Many laughed at Sahl's remark—

but many more would have welcomed the chance (denied them by the Twenty-second Amendment) to elect "Ike" to a third term. The political appeal of the old general was as broad as his grin was infectious. Loved and trusted as no other postwar president has been, the affable, avuncular Eisenhower was his party's best vote getter since Warren G. Harding and one of the most popular chief executives of this century. But did he measure up to the standards of presidential greatness? Was he an able administrator, an effective party spokesman? Was he an inspiring national leader and an adroit opinion shaper in the national interest? The published answers to these questions, the studies of the Eisenhower presidency, are numerous and contradictory.

Among contemporary judgments, the most favorable include Kevin McCann's campaign tract, The Man From Abilene *(1952); the "official" biographies of Robert Donovan* (Eisenhower, *1956) and Merlo Pusey,* (Eisenhower the President, *1965); and the highly partisan but perceptive works of Arthur Larson,* A Republican Looks at His Party *(1956) and* Eisenhower *(1968). Pusey, for example, found Eisenhower's years in office to be "buoyant, forward-moving, and fruitful." Comparing Eisenhower to Lincoln, he forecast for the soldier-president "a great and distinctive place" in the national memory. Although somewhat more critical, Larson, who served as Eisenhower's speech writer, friend, and adviser, agreed that Ike "unquestionably ranks among the great presidents."*

On the other hand, Emmet J. Hughes, another White House insider, expressed profound disillusionment with the Eisenhower presidency in his memoir, Ordeal of Power *(1962). Echoing the harsh judgments of the journalists Marquis Childs* (Eisenhower, Captive Hero, *1958) and William Shannon* (Commentary, November *1958), Hughes portrayed a president lacking in both skill and vision—and even lacking in understanding of the office he held. With Childs, he found him "indifferent and hesitant," a "weak president" who recalled the diffident James Buchanan more than the assertive Lincoln; with Shannon, he saw Eisenhower as a caretaker presiding over the "great Postponement."*

These conflicting images mirror contemporary stereotypes of the 34th president. To the great mass of the American people, he symbolized all that was right about America; to liberals and intellectuals, he seemed to be a politically naive but revered mediocrity who squandered his popularity and abdicated executive leadership. Today, the stereotypes remain, but new and more subtle interpretations are emerging. In the aftermath of Vietnam and Watergate, traditional liberal assumptions about the virtues of dynamic presidential leadership have been challenged. Although once faulted for his "Whiggery," Eisenhower is now often praised for his fidelity to the doctrine of separation of powers and his spirit of partnership with Congress. New Left scholars and writers with radical affinities have praised his restraint in handling international crises. Murray Kempton has decried "The Underestimation of Dwight D. Eisenhower" (Esquire, September *1967); Gary Wills* (Nixon Agonistes, *1969) has pronounced him a "political genius"; and William O'Neill* (Coming Apart, *1971), in a work often harshly critical of both John Kennedy and Lyndon Johnson, saved his warmest praise for Ike.*

Doubtless, some of these recent assessments have gone too far. Yet they reflect growing dissatisfaction with two-dimensional portraits of Eisenhower as either heroic statesman or political innocent. And they affirm, as Richard Nixon once did, that this soldier in politics was "far more complex and devious . . . than most people realized."

The most persuasive reassessment, and the first major biography by a scholar, is Herbert Parmet's Eisenhower and the American Crusades *(1972). Sparing in its use of both encomiums and epithets, this well-balanced yet favorable study described a conservative but generally constructive chief executive who gave a grateful people what they thought they needed. Although more certain and knowledgeable in foreign than in domestic affairs, Parmet's Eisenhower was an astute politician and a worthy and dignified if not exceptional president, who left office with a "remarkable record" and "enormous popularity." "To label him a great or good or even a weak President misses the point. He was merely necessary."*

FOR FURTHER READING

In addition to the studies by Larson, Hughes, and Parmet mentioned above, the most valuable departure points for a study of the Eisenhower administration are: Charles C. Alexander, *Holding the Line* (1975), and Robert L. Branyan and Lawrence H. Larsen, eds., *The Eisenhower Administration: A Documentary History* (2 vols., 1971). Peter Lyon's *Eisenhower: Portrait of the Hero* (1974) is a full and competent biography, and Gary W. Reichard's *Reaffirmation of Republicanism* (1975) closely examines Eisenhower's relations with his first Congress. Eisenhower's own memoirs* are less helpful than Sherman Adams, *Firsthand Report* (1961). Accounts of the administration's foreign policy include Richard Goold-Adams's sympathetic biography of Dulles, *The Time of Power* (1962), and Townsend Hoopes's critical *The Devil and John Foster Dulles* (1973). Richard E. Neustadt, in *Presidential Power* (1960),* offers interesting insights into the powers and limitations of the presidency under Truman and Eisenhower. Stuart G. Brown's *Conscience in Politics* (1961),* and John Bartlow Martin's *Adlai Stevenson of Illinois* (1975) are studies of the era's leading also-ran. Richard Kluger's *Simple Justice* (1975) is a vivid history of *Brown* vs. *Board of Education;* N. V. Bartley, in *The Rise of Massive Resistance* (1969), and Neil R. McMillen, in *The Citizens' Council* (1971), chronicle southern reactions to the *Brown* ruling; and Benjamin Muse's *Ten Years of Prelude* (1964) is a good overview of the first decade of the civil rights struggle. The facts of the period's economic history are accurately and simply presented by Herman P. Miller in *Rich Man, Poor Man* (1964).* Influential interpretations of the period's economic problems include J. K. Galbraith's *The Affluent Society* (1958)* and Michael Harrington's *The Other America* (1962)*. The social and intellectual impact of American affluence is suggestively treated by David Potter in *People of Plenty* (1954). Samuel Lubell, in *The Revolt of the Moderates* (1965),* interprets the political situation just before Eisenhower's reelection, and Theodore H. White, in *The Making of the President, 1960* (1961),* analyzes Kennedy's victory.

---

*Available in paperback edition.

Promise and Frustration
1960–1968

31

In the first years of the 1960s, it seemed as though many of the promises of recent American history were to receive their fruition. While affluence increased, major efforts were made to alleviate the distress of the poor and to further the drive of blacks toward full equality. Abroad, the power of the United States seemed to increase and division among its enemies promised greater successes than ever. Yet, through the decade, doubts increased not only about victory in these goals but about many of the premises on which the efforts depended. By 1968, Americans were clearly casting about for new goals and new programs, and few answers were readily available.

IN SEARCH OF THE NEW FRONTIER

Despite Kennedy's narrow victory, his administration opened in an atmosphere of hope. Cool, rational, urbane, the president put together a brilliant staff and set about the task he had defined as "getting America moving again." More consciously than any predecessor, Kennedy, with the help of his attractive wife, tried to improve not only the political and economic order, but the American style of life, calling artists, writers, and intellectuals to the White House a little in the manner of a European monarch.

Kennedy's administration opened in a time of economic sluggishness, with 6 percent of the labor force unemployed. The president was thoroughly persuaded by his economic advisers that a strong drive for expansion was in order, including deficit financing if necessary. Here as elsewhere, however, he was limited by public and congressional opposition. He was further constricted by the less obvious problem, growing more severe during the decade, of the balance of payments. American receipts from investment and export sales were falling short of expenditures, private and public, military and civilian.

Seeking to speed up the economy without impairing confidence in the dollar or

19. THE KENNEDY-JOHNSON YEARS

	Black Revolution	Other Domestic	Vietnam War	Other Foreign	
1961	Freedom Riders.	January Kennedy inaugurated.	December Kennedy pledges help to South Vietnam.	April Bay of Pigs. August Berlin wall.	1961
1962	October Troops to Oxford, Mississippi.	April Steel price dispute. November Election; slight Republican gains.		October Cuban missile crisis.	1962
1963	April–May Birmingham incidents. August March on Washington.	September Tax cut passed. November 22 Kennedy shot.	November Fall of Diem.	August Above-ground test-ban treaty signed.	1963
1964	January Poll tax amendment. June 3 Civil rights workers murdered in Mississippi. July Civil Rights Act.	August Economic Opportunity Act. November Johnson wins election.	August Tonkin Gulf incident.	October Chinese atomic bomb.	1964
1965	August Voting Rights Act. Watts riots.	July Medicare enacted.	February Bombing of North Vietnam begins. June U.S. troops in combat.	April U.S. troops to Dominican Republic.	1965
1966	January Robert C. Weaver, first black cabinet member. Black Power movement.	November Election; Republican gains.	June Bombing of Hanoi, Haiphong.	July France withdraws from NATO command organization.	1966
1967	June Thurgood Marshall appointed to Supreme Court. July Riots in Newark, Detroit.		January U.S. offensive. September Elections in South Vietnam.	June Israeli-Arab War.	1967
1968	April 4 Martin Luther King shot. April 10 Civil Rights Bill passed.	June 5 Robert Kennedy shot. November Nixon elected president.	February Viet Cong offensive. May Paris peace talks. November 1 Bombing of North Vietnam ended.	August Soviet invasion of Czechoslovakia.	1968

unduly antagonizing the Congress, the administration began by pushing through bills of a kind familiar since the New Deal, such as assistance for slum clearance and increases in social security payments and the minimum wage. Federal expenditures, both military and civilian, were cautiously accelerated. Tax reform offered increased incentives for investment and modernization in industry. Finally, after an alarming stock slump in 1962, the administration succeeded in the following year in persuading Congress to pass a $10 billion tax cut. This action, in a time of rising expenditures, marked a new degree of federal commitment to Keynesian policies. By 1963, the national growth rate had nearly doubled and employment, income, and wages had all risen sharply.

One major concern that went with business upturn was inflation. The limited powers of the administration to deal with this threat were supplemented by constant appeals for restraint both in wages and prices and by the issuance of "guidelines" for industry. In 1962, a sudden price rise by U.S. Steel was followed by most other steel firms. Angrily, the president applied maximum pressure and the rise was rescinded. At the cost of considerable business resentment, price increases in general were held to a minimum.

While the administration's economic policies were moderately successful, Kennedy was less successful in attacking the country's persistent social problems, especially those connected with poverty. Administration bills for medical care for the aged under social security, for federal support for education, and for urban renewal were defeated. These and other antipoverty measures were seen by the president as a major goal for his second term.

In confronting the country's worst social problem, black inequality, Kennedy was sharply limited by the dominant congressional coalition of Southern Democrats and generally conservative Republicans. Defeated in several legislative battles, fearing to tie up all domestic and foreign action in a filibuster, the administration relied mainly on executive action. Negroes were increasingly appointed to office, pressure against discrimination was applied through government purchasing policies, and after some hesitation a presidential order forbade discrimination in federally financed housing. Robert Kennedy, the president's brother whom he appointed Attorney General, vigorously attacked the problem of Negro voting rights in the South.

As in the previous administration, the most important advances were made through the increasingly militant, though still nonviolent movement of Southern blacks, now strongly supported by college students, clergy, and other white sympathizers from the North and opposed in the South by threats and mounting violence. By the end of 1962, the efforts of "freedom riders," supported by the Attorney General against violent white resistance, achieved the end of segregation in transportation. In October, 1962, federal troops were sent to Oxford, Mississippi when mob violence and the resistance of the governor of the state threatened to bar a Negro, James Meredith, from the state university. The threat of similar action prevailed the following year in Alabama, and university desegregation was under way in all states.

The year 1963 saw the peak of the peaceful victories of the civil rights movement and the beginning of a new stage. Violent resistance sharply increased; in Birmingham, police dogs were used against marchers, and four black girls were killed in the bombing of a church; in Jackson, Mississippi, Medgar Evers, a moderate black civil rights worker, was killed in front of his house. In June, the president, eloquently proclaiming a state of moral crisis in the nation, committed the government more fully than at any time since Reconstruction to the achievement of equality. A new civil rights bill attacking particularly discrimination in public accommodations was introduced in Congress as a major administration objective. In August, the nation seemed profoundly impressed by a peaceful march of a quarter of a million people in Washington, under the leadership of Martin Luther King.

Superficially, it seemed that great and peaceful progress was being made on this old and crucial front, and there was no doubt that opportunities increased for many blacks, especially those with skills and education. Yet the economic gaps between most blacks and most whites were not lessened, the city ghettoes remained almost unaffected, and there were signs that some blacks were losing their patience with moderate leadership. It was also clear that a large and determined white minority was ready to fight with all weapons against real social equality for the black population.

KENNEDY AND THE WORLD

Perhaps the most important international fact of the whole decade of the 1960s was a steady deterioration of the two great alliances formed by America and Russia in the early Cold War period. In 1960, Russia withdrew technicians from China, and during the rest of the decade Russian-Chinese hostility mounted sharply. From time to time, serious efforts to increase their independence appeared in Soviet satellites in Eastern Europe, and in Russia itself intellectuals fought an uphill fight for freedom of expression. While neither party dictatorship in Russia nor Russian control of Eastern Europe was ended, Russian freedom of action was limited. This situation had some obvious advantages for American policy. It also meant, however, that Russian leaders felt the need of some major success, either peaceful or military, to consolidate their leadership in a divided Communist world.

The western alliances put together under Truman and Eisenhower were at least equally insecure. Like his predecessors, Kennedy tried to promote European economic and military unification. Partly with this in mind, he persuaded Congress in September, 1962 to adopt a Trade Expansion Act, allowing the president to negotiate tariff reductions up to 50 percent in order to deal with the European Common Market. France, under General de Gaulle, insisted on maintaining an independent and highly nationalistic stance. In January, 1963, de Gaulle blocked England's effort to enter the European Common Market. Insisting on a separate French nuclear force, de Gaulle likewise resisted European military unification and refused to join in efforts for nuclear disarmament. England, generally loyal to its special relationship with the United States despite many disagreements, found itself increasingly unable to play the role of Great Power, especially in the Far East. Japan, America's principal ally in that region, continued to prosper without arming, under American protection. Without solid alliances, a stable balance of power, or a really powerful international organization, Kennedy, like his predecessors and successor, dealt with each crisis as it arose according to the means available.

In military terms, the means increased. Robert F. McNamara, the spectacularly talented Secretary of Defense, imposed modern administrative techniques and the Kennedy policies on the massive military establishment with remarkable success. Whatever remained of Dulles's reliance on massive retaliation was scrapped in favor of a balanced development of the ability to respond appropriately to all kinds of threats, whether nuclear, conventional, or guerrilla. The mistaken impression of Russian superiority in missiles gave way to a clear American preponderance in most kinds of armament. Rocket development was further demonstrated by somewhat belated successes in putting astronauts into orbit. In the various theaters of foreign policy, both America's new might and its limitations were to be clearly shown.

Far more than its predecessors, the Kennedy administration turned its attention to the problems of the impoverished and unstable "Third World." The Peace Corps recruited young Americans for service in regions that needed their efforts, while, less successfully, the president tried to persuade Congress to provide massive aid for struggling economies. A special effort to promote unity, economic development, and nonrevolutionary social change in Latin America was given the name of the "Alliance for Progress." Though only the barest beginning was made in the social and economic goals of the alliance, goodwill was increased. Willingness to tolerate diversity and neutrality led to some other successes, especially in relations with African states. A Chinese attack on Indian borders in 1962 led India to turn a friendlier face toward America.

One of America's closest neighbors, Cuba, remained on unfriendly terms. In April, 1961, Kennedy reluctantly acquiesced in a project developed under the Eisenhower Administration for backing an invasion by anti-Castro exiles, recruited and trained secretly with American help. Misled as to the extent of support likely in Cuba, the administration provided logistical assistance but refused decisive military help. The resulting humiliating defeat increased Kennedy's suspicion of military adventure and expert military advice. On the other hand, it raised the hopes of Cuba's Soviet ally for an easy success.

The truculent side of Khrushchev's changeable policy was shown at the West's most vulnerable point, Berlin. In a meeting with Kennedy in Vienna in June, 1961, Khrushchev refused to give up his threat to negotiate a treaty with East Germany that would have the effect of ending the occupation rights of the Western Allies. Kennedy let it be known that the defense of Berlin was an American commitment even to the extent of nuclear war. In August, 1961, Communist forces built a wall physically dividing the city in half, and preventing the escape of East Germans to the West.

In the opinion of Kennedy and his key advisers, an effort for a clearer victory in Berlin was one major reason for Khrushchev's next major challenge to America, which led the world nearer to major war than it had been since 1945. In August, 1962, American reconnaissance planes reported that the Soviet Union, contrary to repeated and specific assurances, was building in Cuba sites for short-range missiles (220 miles) capable of striking the southern-most reaches of the United States with nuclear warheads. Probably viewed by the Cubans as defensive, these weapons, once their presence became known, required vigorous action from the White House (particularly on the eve of a Congressional election).

In a series of tense meetings, the president and his advisers debated various responses ranging from pacific to belligerent. Characteristically, Kennedy chose neither extreme. On the one hand, the administration was unwilling to propose, under pressure, the reciprocal withdrawal of Russian missiles from Cuba and American missiles from Italy and Turkey. (Actually, the latter bases, rated obsolete, were soon quietly withdrawn; missile-carrying submarines were regarded as less vulnerable.) On the other hand, Kennedy also rejected an immediate though limited airstrike recommended by his military advisers and others. Instead he announced that he had ordered American warships to stop and search vessels coming to Cuba that might contain offensive weapons. In case this proved insufficient, he ordered military concentrations preparatory to possible invasion of the island, which might mean a direct clash with Russian personnel at missile bases.

To Khrushchev, Kennedy offered a pledge not to invade Cuba if Russian offensive weapons were withdrawn under inspection. To the world's relief, Khrushchev accepted Kennedy's terms. Russian ships heading for Cuba with missiles aboard were turned around and missiles already present were removed under American aerial surveillance. Gratifyingly, both the Organization of American States and America's European allies backed Kennedy's action. For the moment, it seemed as though American boldness, together with Russian realism, had produced not only an American victory but a better chance for peace. Refraining from any tendency to gloat over its success, the Kennedy administration increasingly stressed the advantages, to both sides, of Soviet-American disengagement. It had been the single most dangerous moment in the Cold War; Kennedy partisans saw it as his finest hour.

The most urgent peaceful task was to end the threat of nuclear annihilation. In 1958, as part of the last rapprochement, both great powers had suspended nuclear testing pending disarmament talks. In the fall of 1961, the Soviet Union resumed testing, exploding the largest bombs yet, and America felt it necessary to follow suit. In 1963, however, a complex and determined American diplomatic effort produced a treaty banning atmospheric, but not underground tests. Ratified by the Senate despite conservative fears, this treaty was signed by Russia, the United States, Britain, and many other countries, not including either France or China. Further measures of relaxation were promised, and in October the United States agreed to a large sale of wheat to the Soviet Union.

These important if limited foreign policy successes failed to end the world's tensions, which showed themselves in the most acute form in Southeast Asia, apparently a remote and peripheral concern of the United States and yet the very place where the United States had challenged a potential enemy in 1941. In Laos, where neither Communists nor anti-Communists seemed fiercely determined, Kennedy abandoned Eisenhower's highly unsuccessful support of a right-wing faction for a policy, approved by the Soviet Union, of supporting a tripartite coalition. In Vietnam, however, even such a partial and unstable compromise was impossible.

In South Vietnam, the Eisenhower Administration had given diplomatic and military assistance to the relatively vigorous, though corrupt, unpopular, and dictatorial government of Ngo Dinh Diem, whose support came mainly from the landlords and the Catholic minority, swollen by refugees from the Communist North. In 1960, insurgents, led in part by Communist guerrillas who had fought France, formed the National Liberation Front (called by its opponents the Viet Cong), and North Vietnam announced its support of their cause. Unwilling to see the Communists win, and never fully comprehending the nature of Asian postcolonial struggles, the Kennedy administration increased American military aid to Diem. By 1962, progovernment officials were being assassinated by the Viet Cong, villagers were being removed to military hamlets by the government, guerrillas were being infiltrated from the North, and helicopters manned by American military "advisers" were firing on insurgents. In 1963, the American public suddenly began to realize that the United States had become involved in a peculiarly brutal war that its side was not winning. Following rebellion by the large and militant Buddhist faction against the South Vietnamese government, the United States withdrew its support, and in November Diem was assassinated and his government fell, giving place to a series of governments that were neither more successful nor much more popular than his. The dilemma for American policy epitomized a question long awaiting answer: what should be done in the case of a Communist insurrection, with considerable popular support, against a weak and unpopular government in a militarily unpromising terrain?

Kennedy was not to decide this question, and there are indications both that he found the prospect of American defeat unacceptable and that he thought further American commitment of troops to a failing cause a mistake. In the fall of 1963, his administration seemed to be characterized by great promise, resting on a limited record of solid accomplishment against odds. The Democrats had held their slim lead in the congressional elections of 1962, and the president's staff was planning confidently for his reelection. An increased margin of victory would, they thought, bring further advances against poverty at home and the threat of war abroad. On November 22, 1963, the president was shot dead in Dallas, Texas. His successor announced: "I am not going to be the president who saw Southeast Asia go the way of China."

THE GREAT SOCIETY

Nobody could have presented a greater contrast to the cool, rational, slightly aloof Kennedy than his successor, Lyndon B. Johnson. Tense, ambitious, hard-driving, gregarious, and earthy, Johnson had risen to wealth and political power through the hard school of Texas politics. His enemies considered him unscrupulous and coarse. In the opening days of his administration, however, most Americans were reassured by his emphasis on familiar programs of domestic reform. Modeling his approach on that of Franklin Roosevelt, clearly concentrating on domestic affairs and particularly on the problems of poverty, Johnson made clear his intent to build a new and workable consensus, the first since New Deal days. While courting business and Congress, the president hoped to retain the support of Kennedy liberals. The administration's brightest hope was that the first wholly Southern president since the Civil War could reconcile the South to the advancement of blacks. Committing himself to this cause more eloquently than to any other, Johnson succeeded in pushing through in 1964 Kennedy's Civil Rights bill, which included further support for blacks in voting rights, education, job opportunities, and above all, public accommodations. A further massive tax reduction gave rise to record economic advance. The Economic Opportunities Act spelled out Kennedy's proposal for a "War on Poverty" in terms of job training, grants to cities, and other measures. As the election of 1964 approached, Johnson gave the impression of masterful success.

Conservative Republicans, restive since New Deal days with moderate candidates of the Eisenhower variety, nominated Senator Barry Goldwater of Arizona in a convention whose highly organized antiliberal fervor alarmed many Republican liberals. Goldwater, a personally attractive and forthright man, had at various times proposed such measures as sale of the Tennessee Valley Authority, repeal of the Income Tax Amendment, and making Social Security voluntary. In the campaign, he seemed to suggest that local military commanders be allowed to make independent decisions concerning the use of tactical atomic weapons. To cheering audiences, Goldwater denounced big government, the rising crime rate, and declining morals. The president campaigned on his record, presented as a reassuring combination of reform at home and steadfast, moderate resistance to aggression abroad. In the biggest landslide since 1936, Johnson carried all but six states.

With the Democratic majorities in Congress handsomely increased, it seemed that the power of the conservative Republican-Southern Democrat coalition had been broken for the first time since 1938. Unlike Truman and Kennedy, neither of whom possessed his political skill, Johnson was able to push through a coordinated reform program. Laws passed in 1965 and 1966, too many even to list, centered around four crucial fronts. Black equality was promoted by a stricter voting rights act and other measures. (Johnson also appointed the first black cabinet member and the first black Supreme Court Justice.) Kennedy's bill for medical care for the aged was successfully pushed through, breaking a long taboo against federal support of health care. Ancient sectarian opposition to federal aid to education was also overcome, and the president, largely self-educated, seemed to take special pride in bills to assist schooling at all levels. Finally, the complex problem of urban poverty was further attacked through such innovations as rent subsidies and demonstration cities. Not unjustly, the president claimed the most spectacular legislative record since Franklin Roosevelt's famous "hundred days" in 1933.

THE AGONY OF POWER

Despite these achievements, it was apparent by the middle of the decade that America, potentially a great society, was actually a divided and confused one. In both foreign and domestic affairs, the Johnson administration inherited the unsolved problems and shifting balances of the last decades. In both spheres, old policies were pushed to new lengths. In both, increased commitments seemed, by 1965 or 1966, to bring increased frustration.

The disintegration of the two great alliances continued to offer a strange mixture of menace and opportunity. By 1966, de Gaulle had announced France's withdrawal from the NATO military organization. China, at last a nuclear power but torn by domestic turmoil, was denouncing Russian revisionism as bitterly as it attacked American imperialism. And indeed the two greatest powers, Russia and the United States, seemed to be continuing their gingerly rapprochement. Johnson was able, in the wake of Kennedy's test-ban treaty, to push through a dubious Congress a consular treaty and finally, in 1968, to get Russian agreement to a treaty against the further spread of nuclear weapons.

To both great powers, the restless and impoverished Third World seemed to present impossible problems. The Alliance for Progress failed to solve Latin America's economic or political problems, and in one instance the president reverted to older methods. In the Dominican Republic, where the liberal government was overthrown by a military coup in 1963, a revolt against the new military regime threatened civil war in 1965. Stating reasons ranging from protection of American lives to preventing a triumph of Castroism, Johnson sent 22,000 troops to the island. Fortunately a compromise among contending factions eventually produced a regime with some claim to legitimacy. Yet the Johnson action was denounced as high-handed both in Latin America and by liberals at home.

The problems of power were most tragically illustrated, however, in the bloody, baffling struggle in Vietnam. Coming to power in the aftermath of Diem's fall, with the South Vietnamese government weak, the NLF increasingly formidable, and North Vietnamese involvement increasing, Johnson in effect had only two possible courses: to increase the American effort or to accept an unfavorable solution. In retrospect, it seems clear that Johnson, however reluctant to be a war president, never contemplated the latter alternative.

In August, 1964, a U.S. destroyer cruising in the Tonkin Gulf in an area of recent South Vietnamese naval action, was attacked—once inside North Vietnamese territorial waters and, according to disputed evidence, a second time in international waters —by North Vietnamese torpedo boats. Ordering retaliatory action, the administration requested and got from Congress authorization for whatever further military action might prove necessary to repel attacks on American forces or provide assistance to Southeast Asian states who requested it. During the campaign and after, Johnson emphasized the limited character of the reprisals taken; his critics soon charged, however, that the Senate had been duped into granting what the administration readily admitted was the "functional equivalent" of a declaration of war. The Tonkin Gulf resolution, whatever the circumstances of its passage, provided crucial justification for more drastic actions taken later. As the folksy president sometimes admitted, the document was "like Grandma's nightshirt— it covered everything." In February, 1965, an attack on an American barracks was made the occasion for retaliatory air raids on North Vietnam. Gradually the aerial offensive against the North shifted from transport to factories and fuel dumps and included buildings in the center of large cities. The raids were defended less in terms of specific reprisals and more as part of an effort to stop troop infiltration into the South or to force North Vietnam to negotiate by showing that victory was impossible. Partly in support of the air offensive, American ground troops were increased until, by 1968, they reached one-half million men engaged in an effort to search for guerrillas and destroy them throughout the country.

By 1967, it was clear that this massive effort was very far from successful. The South Vietnamese government, despite American efforts to broaden its base, was opposed by large parts of the population. Not only was the infiltration of Northern troops increasing, but American efforts to secure parts of the country and there promote agrarian reform were failing. Repeated and complex suggestions of negotiation failed to produce plausible compromise terms. To the North Vietnamese, the struggle in the South was part of a civil war in which the United States had no right to intervene. To the defenders of American policy, the war was the defense of an independent nation. Between these two premises, compromise proved impossible.

At home, as the casualties mounted (25,000 Americans had died in Vietnam by 1968) and the end seemed no nearer, the war was denounced more widely and more intensely than any American war since 1865. Opponents included powerful senators, much of the press, large sections of the liberal clergy, and a large number of fervent and articulate young people. On the left of the antiwar movement, some critics insisted that the Vietnam war was part of a long pattern of American aggression, that the administration had no intention of negotiating and desired permanent bases, and that the outcome would be war with China and possibly Russia. Other critics, some of whom by no means accepted all or even any of these statements, believed the war impossible to win, and incompatible either with the needs of domestic policy or the effort of worldwide stability. Still others were appalled by the very heavy bombing of both halves of Vietnam (by 1968, America had dropped a greater tonnage of bombs on Vietnam than had been dropped on Europe and Asia together in World War II), by the use of napalm and fragmentation bombs, by the forcible relocation of villages, and by the chemical destruction of crops and forests. The minimum demands of the growing antiwar movement were the end of bombing in the North, recognition that the NLF must play a part in the government of the South, and the scaling down of operations. Defenders of the administration, while insisting that they were willing to negotiate and denying any intention of carrying the war to the North, insisted that South Vietnam must be defended. They insisted that Communist success in Vietnam would mean the spread of Communist power through Southeast Asia, the collapse of American efforts everywhere to prevent the expansion of communism, especially through Chinese-style guerrilla wars, and, immediately, bloody reprisals against government supporters in South Vietnam. The president argued that the failure to defeat Hanoi threatened the security of Hawaii and even San Francisco.

A TIME OF TROUBLES, 1966–1968

By 1967, it was apparent that the unsuccessful war in Vietnam was only one of a number of desperate and divisive problems facing the United States. Not one was new, though all were presented in newly acute form.

The most serious disaffection was that of the black minority. While both civil rights progress and violent resistance to it continued in the South, a series of cataclysmic events turned the nation's attention to the Northern Negro ghettoes. In August, 1965, a riot in Watts, a black section of Los Angeles, resulted in 34 deaths and 30 hours of looting and arson. For the next three years, scenes of burning buildings, helmeted troops, and even tanks moving down city streets became almost commonplace on American television screens. The worst disturbances took place in Newark (23 killed) and Detroit (43 killed) in July of 1967, but few major cities escaped violence altogether. Immediate origins differed, usually involving some real or fancied action by police such as the shooting of a fleeing petty criminal or even the arrest of a Negro. Nearly always firebombs and sniping (whose incidence was usually exaggerated) were answered by drastic police action. As the smoke cleared, it always became evident that the dead and injured were mostly blacks, and that property destroyed was in black slums.

In 1967, President Johnson appointed a commission, apparently of rather conservative cast, to investigate these disturbances, and early in 1968 the commission made a startling report. The underlying cause of the riots, it flatly declared, was white racism resulting in pervasive discrimination. In the ghettoes, unemployment, inadequate and humiliating welfare systems, and long experience of police hostility had resulted in complete frustration. To counter the threat of a completely and permanently divided society, the commission called for an unprecedented national commitment to a complex series of remedies, including further measures to encourage of education, employment, and housing construction and a shift from the welfare system to income support.

Many hostile and genuinely frightened whites, on the other hand—and especially those who lived on the outskirts of the black ghettoes—demanded instead new measures of suppression. Though most Negroes, according to the polls, still believed in integration, a growing minority of militants subscribed to the new slogan of Black Power, which could mean anything from bloc voting and separate economic development to outright separatism. In a few central cities, relations between police and black militants threatened to approach the level of civil war, and suburban housewives took up pistol practice in preparation for its spread. On April 4, 1968, Martin Luther King, the leading black advocate of nonviolence, was murdered by a white man in Memphis, Tennessee. The immediate results of this tragic event included a great outpouring of expressions of grief and guilt, riots in 125 cities including Washington, D.C., and the passage of a civil rights bill including an open housing provision. The president decided, however, that the national mood made it inadvisable to appeal for the kind of comprehensive program called for by his commission.

A parallel and in some ways remarkably similar social problem, sexual discrimination, was also thrust upon the national conscience in the 1960s. In 1963, a presidential commission reported widespread discrimination against women workers, who comprised more than a third of the nation's labor force. That same year, Betty Friedan's *The Feminine Mystique* forcefully attacked the socialization process whereby woman's role was defined exclusively as wife and mother. Neither publication attracted immediate widespread public attention, yet both were symptoms of the awakening of feminism from a slumber of four decades. Having won the vote, the women's movement, after nearly a century of vitality, had collapsed during the 1920s. It was reborn, however, amid the passions of the 1960s. Stirred by student protests and the civil rights and antiwar movements, women activists again addressed the problems of their sex. Although the resulting feminist resurgence seemed to take the nation by surprise, the grievances expressed were all too apparent. The Nineteenth Amendment had enfranchised women but it had not redefined her role in home and society. Nor had it opened the way to educational and employment equality. In the four decades since the suffrage amendment was ratified, women's position relative to men had in fact deteriorated in important areas. A smaller percentage of the nation's college students, both graduate and undergraduate, were women in 1960 than in 1920 or 1930. Well-intentioned but often arbitrary "protective legislation" denied them access to some desirable occupations; they had only limited access to managerial and executive positions; they were generally denied equal pay for equal work.

To attack these injustices Friedan and several other women formed in 1966 the National Organization of Woman (NOW), a worthy successor to Susan B. Anthony's and Carrie Chapman Catt's NAWSA. NOW, which proved attractive primarily to middle-class white professional and business women, represented the moderate wing of the Women's Liberation movement. Often identified as the "feminist's NAACP," it waged a dignified program of public education and lobbied for more equitable state and local legislation. Younger activists, often those associated with the New Left, however, were generally critical of NOW and formed their own radical groups. Among these small and often factious units, the most notable was probably WITCH (at first Women's International Terrorist Conspiracy from Hell, but later sometimes called Women Infuriated at Taking Care of Hoodlums or Women Inspired to Commit Herstory), a tiny but shrill, loosely knit "non-organization" that employed guerrilla theater to dramatize sexual injustice.

Whatever their persuasions, the new feminists, like their sisters of a half-century before, faced the ridicule and hostility of tradition-minded men and women who either argued that woman's place was defined by biology or that sexual equality would destroy the institutions of marriage and family. Yet, there was some triumph as well as much abuse. At the most abstract level, sexual bigotry was not routed, but it retreated a little as women in growing numbers became sensitive to sexual issues. More particularly, governments, both state and federal, began to respond to this new sensitivity. Title VII of the 1964 Civil Rights Act forbade both sexual and racial job discrimination; HEW sponsored "affirmative action" programs for women as well as minorities; Congress enacted in 1972 (not ratified by all the states by 1980) an Equal

Rights Amendment to the Constitution; the Supreme Court in 1973 issued a remarkably liberal abortion ruling. To be sure, sexism, like racism, possessed subtleties that seemed to defy government solution. Yet the status of women had indisputably improved during the first decade of women's liberation.

A very different kind of protest in this age of change and unrest was that of certain articulate sections of youth. In the summer of 1964, a number of northern university students had gone to Mississippi to take a militant part in the civil rights movement. The violence they encountered inevitably led to a loss of respect for all authority, and the success of nonviolent methods suggested new kinds of power. The University of California at Berkeley, in 1964, was the scene of the first major student sit-in, which grew out of an argument over limits on student on-campus political activity. Almost completely successful in securing its immediate objectives in Berkeley, the new student movement spread rapidly to other campuses throughout the country. Shifting objectives (free speech, student participation in control of university education, increased numbers of black students and faculty) were accompanied by increasingly militant tactics, sometimes resulting in violent clashes with police. More and more, grievances seemed to center on the Vietnam war, regarded by many articulate young people as an American aggression. Divided in their emotions about all these causes, most Americans at least understood what they were about. Far more baffling was a new youth ideology, partly shared with the still more militant students of Europe and Asia, far transcending politics, often expressed in bizarre gestures, and centering its attack on the frustrations inherent in all highly organized societies. Still more alarming than even the most extreme militance was its polar opposite, a widespread tendency toward withdrawal and passivity, often symbolized by a cult of drugs. Curiously, many adults seemed unable to distinguish between the hippie counterculture and the most nihilistic forms of youthful rebellion. The public's attention was captured by defiant gestures and particularly by such dramatic events as the clash between students and police which led to the temporary closing of Columbia University in the spring of 1968. Deeper, more important changes of attitude toward such important matters as sex, family, and career were understood more slowly.

Riots in the ghettoes, demonstrations on the campuses, and a major rise in nonpolitical crime (its dimensions disputed but its reality undeniable) tightened the tensions of another disaffected minority, the right wing. Outraged by youthful protest and black militance and confused by a rising chorus of complaints from such previously inarticulate groups as Indians, homosexuals, welfare recipients, migrant workers, and radical women, these anxious patriots feared a social and moral breakdown. Viewing this new age of protest as part of a dangerous departure from traditional religious and political standards, they demanded the restoration of "law and order" and the suppression of dissent.

Fears and frustrations at home seemed to be accompanied by new dangers abroad. In February, 1968, the Viet Cong and North Vietnamese launched an offensive that produced heavy fighting and widespread destruction in the major South Vietnamese cities, including Saigon. As it became apparent that four years of increased American commitment had not made it possible even to secure the allied capital, and as Communist attacks and American counter measures completed the destruction of some "friendly" towns, the peace movement gained new recruits and overt demands for further military commitment seemed almost to disappear. Yet it was possible, as some observers pointed out, to see this offensive as a major, even a decisive defeat for the Communists. The people of South Vietnam did not, as expected, rally to their support, nor did the Saigon government collapse, and the losses of the attackers were of a size not long to be borne.

In June, 1967, the eruption of war between Israel and the Arabs threatened to produce another East-West confrontation, with Moscow supporting the attack on a country to which America was committed. A smashing Israeli victory prevented immediate disaster, but American powerlessness in this crisis seemed to demonstrate that the nation could not afford to commit its principal effort to the peripheral, frustrating war in Vietnam. In January, 1968, the American reconnaissance ship Pueblo was captured by North Koreans off the Korean coast. Militant counteraction, demanded by a few, would have risked the opening of still another front.

So far, surprisingly enough, relations between Moscow and Washington had continued ever since the Eisenhower administration to combine conventional verbal hostility with some minimum measure of actual cooperation. In August, Soviet forces suddenly invaded Czechoslovakia, whose Communist government had been edging toward political and intellectual freedom, and the Soviet government forced Prague to reverse its program of reform. In the wake of this event, either a revival of great-power combination or a turn towards isolationism seemed possible. What was clear was that new priorities were needed; the foreign policy, which had been dominant since 1947, of limited response to Communist pressure anywhere in the world, was increasingly difficult to defend.

In times of crisis, Americans usually turned to the White House, but this time the presidency itself seemed to be suffering a crisis of authority. Despite Lyndon Johnson's reputation as a political wizard, his popularity polls declined sporadically from a high 80 percent to a disastrous 35 percent in the fall of 1968. In 1966, Democratic election losses had reinstated the conservative Republican-Southern Democrat coalition in power in Congress. The new realities were shown by drastic cuts in foreign aid and in funds for such administration social programs as medicare and open housing. By the time of the 1968 presidential campaign, presidential appointments (including that of a new Chief Justice) were being rejected and even the treaty for stopping the spread of nuclear weapons was stalled in the Senate.

Thus the Johnson administration, which had brought to fruition many of the hopes of the New Deal and pushed to new lengths the foreign policy of resistance to communism, was ending in frustration on both fronts. Consensus had become deep division, and even the spectacular and unparalleled Johnson prosperity was being threatened by a sharp upturn in prices. With relief as well as trepidation, the people turned to the traditional electoral remedy.

A CHANGE OF LEADERSHIP

Despite his lost prestige, most people took it for granted that the president could command the nomination of his own party and that this would make him a formidable contender against Richard Nixon, the probable Republican nominee. This assumption was challenged first by Senator Eugene McCarthy of Minnesota who, sharply attacking the president's Vietnam policy, got 42 percent of the Democratic vote in the New Hampshire primary. A few days later, Robert Kennedy, already an outspoken critic of the war, announced his own candidacy on a program of opposition to the war and commitment to a drastic attack on ghetto poverty. The two antiwar candidates neatly divided the potential Democratic opposition. While McCarthy's courage and low-key style drew the ardent support of many students and intellectuals, Kennedy's name and record drew equally fervent crowds in black and other minority centers, and professional Democratic political leaders watched him with rapidly increasing interest.

The expected Democratic showdown, however, never materialized. Sensing the futility of his own candidacy, an increasingly unpopular Lyndon Johnson announced on March 31 a halt in the bombing of North Vietnam, called for a negotiated settlement, and declared he would not seek reelection. In June, Robert Kennedy, during a celebration of his important but narrow victory over McCarthy in the California primary, was murdered by an obscure assassin. Kennedy's death dealt a staggering blow to the party's antiwar forces. In August, Vice-President Hubert Humphrey, a domestic liberal and staunch supporter of Johnson's war policies, easily defeated McCarthy on the first ballot for the Democratic nomination. In the streets outside the convention hall, angry and frustrated antiwar demonstrators, a few of whom hoped to disrupt the proceedings within, were clubbed by police while the world watched. Reflecting the growing polarization of American society, many citizens expressed shock and outrage at police overreaction, while many others applauded police containment of an unruly and unwashed mob of dissidents. Few could doubt, however, that the noisy melee contrasted sharply with the well-managed Republican convention in July. Amid apparent order and restraint, the GOP in Miami passed over such early contenders as George Romney, Nelson Rockefeller, and Ronald Reagan to nominate Richard Nixon and his running mate, Spiro T. Agnew, an obscure border state conservative favorite of the party's increasingly vital southern wing.

During the ensuing months, Nixon and Humphrey, neither of them a popular figure nor an eloquent speaker, engaged in a colorless campaign of partisanship and personality. Both candidates stressed "law and order" and supported the negotiations then proceeding unproductively with the North Vietnamese in Paris. Humphrey belatedly tried to dissociate himself from Johnson's war policies, and Nixon spoke vaguely of a "secret plan" to end the fighting. But in the end, Humphrey had little choice but to run on the record of a discredited administration, and Nixon fell back on his customary strategy of attacking his opponent without offering concrete proposals of his own. Faced with seemingly unattractive alternatives, many mainstream voters picked the least objectionable candidate. But a substantial body of alienated citizens elected to leave the two-party system. The articulate but impotent far-left minority either boycotted the election or cast protest ballots for radical candidates; the disaffected right, far more formidable, turned to American Independent party candidate George C. Wallace, a former Alabama governor and staunch segregationist. Advocating drastic action against black militants and student radicals and supporting saturation bombing of North Vietnam, Wallace and his ticket mate, retired Air Force General Curtis E. LeMay, developed remarkable strength outside the South, particularly among blue-collar workers and noncollege youth. Although he carried only five southern states, Wallace polled a larger percentage (13.5 percent) of the total vote than any third party candidate since 1912. The balloting was unusually close between the major party candidates. Humphrey, struggling vainly to shore up the crumbling Democratic coalition, commanded the Eastern cities and the minorities, especially Negroes. But he lost the upper South and the election to Nixon, who swept the traditionally Republican strongholds of the Middle and Far West. Yet despite the shattering of the Johnson consensus of 1964 and an apparent shift to the right, there was little cause for jubilation in the GOP. By election day, early predictions of an easy Republican triumph had eroded to a hairline victory. Nixon's share (43.4 percent) of the total popular vote was smaller than any president since Woodrow Wilson. For the first time since Zachary Taylor in 1848, a newly elected president faced an opposition Congress. Indisputably, a nation divided by war and tormented by fear of violence and race had repudiated the party in power. But the incoming administration faced seemingly insurmountable domestic and foreign problems without a popular mandate and without congressional support.

FOR FURTHER READING

William L. O'Neill's *Coming Apart* (1971) is a splendid "informal" history of the 1960s. Two first-rate books by members of Kennedy's staff are A. M. Schlesinger, Jr.'s *A Thousand Days* (1965) and T. C. Sorenson's *Kennedy* (1965). Bruce Miroff's *Pragmatic Illusions* (1976) is critical of the Kennedy leadership; Carl Brauer's *John F. Kennedy and the Second Reconstruction* (1977) is more sympathetic. Tom Wicker, in *JFK and LBJ* (1968), offers balanced assessments of both presidents. Alfred Steinberg's *Sam Johnson's Boy* (1968) is an informative, hostile biography of President Johnson; while Hugh Sidey's *A Very Personal Presidency* (1968) is a penetrating critical essay on Johnson's presidential style. Johnson guardedly speaks for himself in *The Vantage Point* (1971).* Rowland Evans and Robert Novak's *Lyndon B. Johnson* (1966) and Eric F. Goldman's *The Tragedy of Lyndon Johnson* (1968) are highly suggestive assessments; Doris Kerns, in *Lyndon Johnson and the American Dream*

---

*Available in paperback edition.

(1976), provides a psychobiography. *The Great Society Reader* (Marvin E. Gettleman and David Mermelstein, eds., 1967) is useful but partisan. Analyses of the Johnson-Goldwater and Nixon-Humphrey races include Theodore H. White's *The Making of the President* studies for 1964 and 1968 (1965, 1969), and Lewis Chester et al., *An American Melodrama: The Presidential Campaign of 1968* (1969). The judicial activism of the Supreme Court is assessed by John D. Weaver in *Warren: The Man, the Court, the Era* (1967); while Victor Navasky has dissected *Kennedy Justice* (1971). Benjamin Muse portrays *The American Negro Revolution* (1968); Malcolm X has written a moving *Autobiography* (1966); Alphonso Pinkney analyzes black nationalist movements in *Red, Black and Green* (1976); and John Hersey, in the *Algiers Motel Incident* (1968), has focused on a ghetto riot. Richard Maxwell Brown's *Strain of Violence* (1975) and Hugh Davis Graham and Ted R. Gurr's *Violence in America* (1969) contribute to an understanding of an unhappy American tradition. Kirkpatrick Sale sympathetically analyzes *SDS* (1973); Irwin Unger's history of the New Left, *The Movement* (1974), is generally critical; and Theodore Roszak charts the *Making of a Counter Culture* (1969).* Judith Hole and Ellen Levine examine the *Rebirth of Feminism* (1971); and Gayle Graham Yates explains *What Women Want* (1975). One chilling Cold War drama is presented by both Herbert Dinerstein, in *The Making of a Missile Crisis* (1976), and by Robert F. Kennedy, in *Thirteen Days* (1969). Perhaps the best overview of the Vietnam quagmire is Chester L. Cooper's *The Lost Crusade* (1970). Other highly suggestive statements include: Bernard Fall, *Two Vietnams,* 2nd ed. rev. (1967); J. William Fulbright, ed., *The Vietnam Hearings* (1966); David Halberstam, *The Best and the Brightest* (1972); Neil Sheehan, ed., *The Pentagon Papers* (1971); and Francis Fitzgerald, *Fire in the Lake* (1972).

20. 1969–1980

	Domestic	Southeast Asia	Middle East	Other Foreign
1969	**January** Nixon inaugurated. **June** Burger replaces Warren as Chief Justice. **August** Family Assistance Plan proposed. **October** Vietnam mobilization demonstration.	**Spring** Secret U.S. bombing of Cambodia begins. **April** Peak U.S. troop strength in Vietnam. **August** Phased troop withdrawal begins.		**July** Nixon Doctrine proposes reduced American presence in Asia.
1970	**May** Campus disorders; Kent State killings. **November** Midterm elections; modest Democratic gains. **June** Pentagon Papers leaked to press.	**April** U.S. and ARVN force invade Cambodia.		
1971	**January** Nixon proclaims New American Revolution. **August** New Economic Policy announced; 90–day wage and price freeze imposed. **November** Phase II economic plan activated.	**January–March** U.S. supports ARVN incursion into Laos.		**October** Red China admitted to UN with U.S. support. **August** "Ping pong" diplomacy with Red China. **December** First devaluation of dollar.
1972	**May** Wallace assassination attempt. **June** Watergate burglary coverup begins. **October** Revenue sharing bill enacted. **November** Nixon reelection landslide.	**Spring** Haiphong harbor mined; Hanoi bombed. **October** Kissinger announces "peace is at hand." **December** Renewed bombing of North Vietnam.		**February** Nixon's Peking summit. **May** Nixon's Moscow summit; SALT I.

1973	May–August Senate Watergate hearings. **October** Agnew resigns; Nixon fires Special Prosecutor; agrees to surrender tapes. **December** Ford becomes vice-president.	**January** Paris accords end U.S. involvement in Vietnam. **August** Bombing of Cambodia halted.	**October** Arab-Israeli -War. Arab oil boycott. **September** Kissinger becomes Secretary of State.
1974	**February-August** House impeachment investigation. **August** Supreme Court orders tape surrender; Nixon resigns; Ford sworn in; Nixon pardoned. **November** Midterm elections; Democratic gains.		
1975	Winter-Spring 10 percent unemployment.	**April** Khmer Rouge take Phnom-Penh; Vietcong seize Saigon. **May** Mayaguez incident.	**Summer** Independence of Mozambique and Angola. **August** Helsinki accord.
1976	**July–August** Carter and Ford nominated. **November** Carter elected.		**Autumn** Rhodesian crisis.
1977	**January** Carter inaugurated; pardoned draft evaders. **June** Haldeman and Mitchell entered prison. July prime interest rate reached 6.75 percent.		

20. 1969–1980 (continued)

	Domestic	Southeast Asia	Middle East	Other Foreign	
1978	May Wallace left politics. June California's Proposition 13 passed; Supreme Court Bakke ruling. November Energy bill enacted; midterm elections, Democratic majority held. Annual inflation rate exceeded 9 percent.		September Camp David accords. November Shah imposed martial law.	April Panama treaty ratified.	1978
1979	March ERA deadline extended. May "Draft Kennedy" started. September Prime rate reached 13 percent. October Department of Energy created. December Carter announced reelection bid. Annual oil company profits up 100 to 200+ percent; gasoline prices rose 60 percent; inflation rose 13.3 percent.		January–February Shah toppled; Islamic Republic proclaimed. November U.S. embassy seized in Iran. December Soviets invade Afghanistan.	January U.S. "normalized" relations with Red China, severed relations with Taiwan. June–July SALT II signed; Senate debate began. September Soviet combat brigade in Cuba.	1979
1980	February–March inflation and prime rate exceeded 18 percent; Carter proposed "drastic" budget cuts. Reagan elected.		U.S. breaks relations with Iran, threatens military action.	Senate SALT II considerations suspended; U.S. restricted trade to USSR; U.S. boycotted Moscow Olympics.	1980

Crises of Confidence
1969–1980

32

OF DECADES (IMMEDIATELY) PAST

In perhaps the most memorable inaugural address since Lincoln's second, John F. Kennedy challenged Americans to "ask not what your country can do for you—ask what you can do for your country." A dozen years later, in apparently conscious evocation of that refrain, Richard M. Nixon chose the occasion of his own second inauguration in January 1973 to urge the nation to "ask—not just what will government do for me, but what can I do for myself." However similar, the words, of course, carried very different meaning—a difference marked by 12 years of change and turmoil; a difference clearly reflected in the contrasting personal styles and (rather less starkly contrasting) social philosophies of the two chief executives. But the two inaugural admonitions might also suggest, in ways unintended by either president, the differing tempers of the decades upon which they left their marks.

Very likely the 1960s will be recorded in the book of popular thought as a time when American public figures were assassinated with alarming frequency; when campus ROTC buildings and inner-city ghettos went up in smoke; when disruptive racial confrontations and violent student demonstrations overshadowed all other issues of national concern; when the "love generation," the unkempt children of the middle class, withdrew to a workless counterculture of acid rock, psychedelic drugs, and wanton sexuality. To not a few observers then and now, it was a decade when the social turbulence of the young and the disaffected strained the bonds of national cohesion. Yet for all of the social nihilism of the times, the '60s were not merely years of rebellion and dissent. The Age of Protest, as it has been called, was also a period of social concern and moral commitment, a time of national soul-searching in which the United States addressed some of its more pressing social ills. To be sure, in the harsh light of recent national experience, the millenial aspirations of the decade's social planners and political activists now seem naive. Too often the problems they addressed defied solution. Civil rights legislation and affirmative action programs did not, and perhaps could not, produce a color-blind society. The War on Poverty proved to be much less than "unconditional," and the dizzying welter of agencies and programs it enlisted did not, as Lyndon Johnson hoped, "throttle want" in an otherwise affluent society. Similarly, organizations as disparate as the National Organization of Women, the National Farm Workers' Association, and the American Indian Movement articulated minority grievances. But for women, Chicanos, and Indians, scarcely less than for blacks, the benefits of American justice and opportunity remained unequally distributed. Yet the failures of the 1960s can be, and indeed have been, unduly emphasized. However ephemeral the "sensibility of the sixties," the decade stands as one of the great ages of American reform, a time of overdue and enduring achievements in such areas as school desegregation and minority rights, education, environmental and consumer protection, health and welfare. Nor should it be forgotten that because of the social activism of the passionate visionaries of the 1960s the burdens of class, race, and sex are today less oppressive than ever before.

In the '70s, however, retrenchment, not reform, was the watchword. Many of the cultural affectations of the '60s (including the informality of dress and lifestyle) and even some of the social mores (the casual approach to sex and drugs) found easy acceptance. Yet the political tone of the '70s was demonstrably different. A change in the guard brought Nixon and Gerald Ford to the office held by Kennedy and Johnson. Although neither was an inflexible idealogue, these conservative Republican chief executives, like the "Middle Americans" they presumed to represent, had little taste for social experimentation. However else it would be known, the period following Nixon's inauguration in January, 1969 would not be known as a season of reform.

The expiration of the Great Society was quickly followed by the collapse of the peace movement. Despite the widespread popular outrage occasioned by the American invasions of Cambodia (1970) and Laos (1971), the antiwar movement lost its momentum as Nixon began the phased troop withdrawals that brought more than half a million American soldiers home from South Vietnam between the elections of 1968 and 1972. In the spring of 1970 student demonstrators on 448 campuses were either on strike or had closed down their institutions. Several years later, as the war ended and the Selective Service System gave way to an all-volunteer army, the focus of student concern was more often the grade-point average than international peace.

The student left, including the Students for a Democratic Society (SDS) and its offshoot, the Youth International Party (Yippie), also abruptly disappeared with the war that had done so much to nourish it. Its leaders, the youthful rebels who set out to destroy "the establishment" in the '60s, often sought to join it in the '70s. "Last year, Jerry Rubin came here and told us to pull this rotten system up by the roots," one puzzled undergraduate at the University of Rochester reported in 1971. "This year, he came here and told us to register to vote in the primary." Older if not always wiser, not a few of the radical youth leaders of the '60s turned from the politics of confrontation to what Yippie spokesman Rubin called the "inner revolution of the '70s." Rubin himself experimented with "a smorgasbord course in New Consciousness," which included seemingly everthing from Gestalt therapy, bioenergetics, and est to jogging, health foods, yoga, and acupuncture. Following this exhausting therapeutic regimen, he wrote a new book, *Growing (Up) at Thirty-Seven* (1976) and became a Wall Street securities analyst. His Yippie colleague, Abbie Hoffman, author of the 1968 publication *Revolution for the Hell of It,* went underground for a time to avoid imprisonment on drug charges and then dropped out of politics. SDS founder Tom Hayden, in business suit and necktie, ran unsuccessfully for the U.S. Senate; his codefendant in the "Chicago Eight" conspiracy trial, Panther party leader Bobby Seal, tried and failed to be elected mayor of Oakland, California. Others turned to Oriental mysticism, among them Hayden's former SDS associate, Rennie Davis, who bought a Mercedes and became the disciple of teenage guru Maharaj Ji. Still others joined former Panther official Eldridge Cleaver, former Nixon hatchet man Charles Colson, and President James Earl Carter as "born again" Christians.

The decade of the '70s had its popular movements, of course. But after 1970 even protest very often assumed distinctively conservative forms. Singer Anita Bryant led a crusade against civil rights for homosexuals; conservative Republican Howard Jarvis won voter support for California's Proposition 13, which slashed property taxes, severely limited state spending for social purposes, and launched a nationwide "tax revolt." Antifeminist Phyllis Schlafly organized a national "Stop ERA" movement that threatened once again to block the ratification of an amendment that was first introduced in Congress in 1923.Organizations calling themselves Fascinating Womanhood and Total Woman were formed by female activists to mobilize tradition-minded women who opposed the women's rights movement. "Right to Lifers" agitated for an antiabortion amendment. The affirmative action programs of professional schools and corporations were challenged by whites who alleged that quotas designed to provide new opportunities for minorities constituted "reverse discrimination."

Such were the crusades of the 1970s. To one degree or another, all were legitimate expressions of the concerns of broad categories of a diverse body politic. But collectively they seemed to reflect the cramped spirit of a decade that was somehow less hopeful, less expansive, and perhaps even less generous than the one before.

THE ME DECADE, THE AGE OF NO CONFIDENCE

The apparently divergent contours of the '60s and '70s could also be charted in ways that transcended the merely political. As noted elsewhere in this volume, the historian's tendency to periodize, to make the past intelligible to the present by organizing it into manageable blocks of time, has its hazards. History, it seems worth repeating, is an all but seamless web; its developments are notable more often for continuity than for change. At close range, what appears distinctive in human conduct and institutions more often than not loses its particularity when viewed from a longer perspective. Still the temptation to find peculiar meaning in current events is irresistible. The '70s were not half over before self-styled "new journalist" Tom Wolfe labeled it the "Me Decade." Wolfe, who won an enthusiastic readership with such "pop analyses" of the '60s scene as his *Pump House Gang* (1968) and *The Electric Kool-Aid Acid Test* (1968), found in the 1970s a new "alchemical dream" which promised not to make base metals into gold but to remake oneself. The spirit of the

'70s, he averred, was most clearly seen in the "Me movements," in est, Arica, and Scientology; in encounter sessions, assertiveness training, Oriental meditations groups, and charismatic Christianity; in the new national passion for "changing one's personality—remaking, remodeling, elevating, and polishing one's very self . . . (Me!)"

In a lighter vein, political humorist Russell Baker, the Peter Finley Dunne of his generation, deplored "the growing public absorption in the hedonism of public pleasure and private consumption—the hunt for the ideal restaurant, the perfect head of lettuce, the totally satisfying relationship." Articles in *Esquire, New Yorker,* and *Harper's* diagnosed the narcissistic preoccupation of the '70s. In a characteristic lament, one writer described "the world view emerging among us centered solely on self, and with individual survival as its sole good." In *The Culture of Narcissism* (1978), the most fully developed cultural analysis of the politically quiescent and socially passive '70s, the historian Christopher Lasch similarly argued that "Americans have retreated to purely personal preoccupations." Following the political turmoil and social dissidence of the recent past—the campus disorders, the inner-city riots, the drug excesses, the street crimes, the political scandals, the war in Southeast Asia— "people have convinced themselves," Lasch observed, "that what matters is psychic self-improvement: getting in touch with their feelings, eating health foods, taking lessons in ballet or belly dancing, immersing themselves in the wisdom of the East, jogging, learning how to 'relate,' overcoming the 'fear of pleasure.' " In the judgment of not a few contemporary observers, then, Americans of the '70s turned from the war on poverty and the peace movement, from political passion and social commitment, to join Jerry Rubin in a "journey into myself," to self-discovery, psychic growth and intimate encounters, to what Lasch called "strategies of narcissistic survival."

Inevitably, commentators found it easier to describe than to explain the apparently different sensibilities of the two decades immediately past. Few doubted, however, the importance of demography. The youth culture of the '60s was, by all accounts, a by-product of the postwar baby boom. For reasons not yet satisfactorily explained, the period immediately following World War II was one of unprecedented population growth in the United States. Between 1948 and 1953 the number of births rose by nearly 50 percent. By the mid-'50s the boom crested. By 1960, again for reasons not fully understood, the total number of births began to drop sharply. By the mid-'70s the "population bomb" was defused and the nation approached what demographers called ZPG, zero population growth.

But the baby-boom generation was not so easily dispensed with. A disproportionate bulge in the nation's population curve, it passed through the 14- to 24-year-old age category in the 1960s. (In 1960 the center of population gravity in the United States was the 35 to 40 age group; by 1965, the center had shifted to age 17.) In a less demanding age, in one less vexed by issues of race and war, the social impact of this extraordinary cohort might have been very different. But the postwar generation reached late adolescence and early adulthood at a critical moment in American history, and it gave that decade of youthful rebellion its special character. By the '70s, a decade of falling birth rates had pushed upward the center of population gravity. Inexorably, the youth of the '60s, like Jerry Rubin and Rennie Davis, reached the dread age of 30. Population dynamics do not in themselves determine social behavior. But they can help to define shifting styles in the recent past and to identify the chromatic flaw in the title of one of the counterculture's most talked-about books, Charles Reich's *The Greening of America*. In 1970, when that publication appeared, the distinct and rebellious youth culture, harbinger of what Reich hoped would be 'Consciousness III,'' was already subsiding. In the decade that followed, America was not so much greening as graying.

The character of the "Me Decade" was also linked to what the historian Henry Steele Commager called the "Age of No Confidence." In fact, the two concepts were but the two faces of a single coin. Lasch's subtitle—"American Life in an Age of Diminishing Expectations"—suggested, and other social analysts generally agreed, that the culture of narcissism, the new ethic of self-preservation, reflected the erosion of the postwar optimism of the 1950s and 1960s. In 1941, Henry Luce, publisher of *Time, Life,* and *Fortune,* proclaimed the advent of the "American Century," an age in which "the most powerful and vital nation" would go unchallenged in a world it would dominate "for such purposes" and by "such means" as it alone saw fit. Nothing in the American past seemed to suggest otherwise. Throughout the nearly four centuries of their New World experience, Americans shared the exuberant faith of the Puritan leader John Winthrop that their's was a "Citty Upon a Hill" with "the eies of all people Uppon us." With Thomas Jefferson, they believed that they were the chosen people of a "New Israel." This sense of American exceptionalism, which suggested that the nation stood somehow apart from the tawdry stream of human history, survived and in fact was embellished by the Second World War. Virtually alone among the world's great nations, the United States emerged from the most terrible of wars not only unscathed but with its wealth and power enhanced.

But the American Century lasted only a generation. As the '60s ended, traditional presumptions of American omnicompetence and omnipotence were in tatters. Heretofore confident of their nation's role as both global police officer and moral preceptor, Americans now faced defeat in Vietnam and declining influence around the world. Never doubting the strength of the "almighty dollar" or the seemingly perpetual expansion of their Gross National Product, they soon were awash in a flood of economic ills—unchecked and apparently uncheckable inflation, economic stagnation, declining productivity rates, staggering trade deficits, and a sharply devalued dollar. Following the Arab oil boycott of 1973 came a creeping awareness that the United States was dangerously dependent on uncertain, rapidly depleting, and ruinously expensive foreign energy supplies. As the energy crisis of the '70s unfolded, the American people—who with roughly 6 per cent of the world's people produced about one-third of its goods and consumed more than one-third of its petroleum—slowly, reluctantly, and only imperfectly came to understand what the impending exhaustion of nonrenewable natural resources could mean to an industrial society and its economy.

The unsettling news of the '70s, then, was that the United States, too, lived in a world of limits—limited world influence, limited economic growth, limited natural resources, limited expectations for a better future. At least since the enlightenment, the spirit of western humanity has been elevated by faith in progress, the assumption that human society was, if not perfectable, at least infinitely meliorable. Despite the stubborn persistence of evidence to the contrary, western bourgeois democracies in general and the American nation in particular enjoyed a sense of limitless possibilities. In the last century that optimism was profoundly and repeatedly tested by thinkers from Darwin to Spengler. More concretely, the indescribable horrors of two world wars, the spread of totalitarianism, the Nazi holocaust, the threat of nuclear destruction, the contagion of world lawlessness and terrorism—all suggested that whatever its state of grace, humanity's course was not inevitably upward.

Unremarkably, in the face of such dangers and uncertainties, the sanguine western spirit sagged noticeably. Indeed even the Americans, those seemingly incurable optimists, began to feel this malaise in the '70s. With the end of the American Century at hand, with the American Dream of unlimited abundance now subject to doubt, the American people began uneasily to discard comfortable myths about their own virtue and uniqueness.

It would be imprudent to forget that by definition contemporary historical writing is shortsighted. The instant analyses of the '70s will be challenged by those who enjoy greater perspective. Future writers may well find thitherto unsuspected social purpose in the "Me Decade." Very likely, as present confusions recede in time, the configurations of the "Culture of Narcissism" and the "Age of No Confidence" will seem overdrawn. Of course, those who would know tomorrow's views must wait for tomorrow. Yet for the moment, by every outward sign, Thomas Jefferson's "chosen people," the 220 million inhabitants of the "Citty Upon a Hill," appeared to be engaged in the disquieting task of joining the human race. Had they more confidence in their political leaders, that task might have been less unnerving.

NIXON AND THE NEW FEDERALISM

Of the three men who occupied the White House in the 1970s, Richard Milhous Nixon alone was indisputably well qualified for the presidency. A veteran of both houses of Congress, a two-term vice-president well versed in the system and process of American politics, a widely traveled expert in foreign affairs, he brought experience and intellect to the Oval Office. His public personality and presidential style, however, contrasted sharply with those of his post-World War II predecessors. He did not share Harry Truman's identification with the common person, and he lacked Dwight Eisenhower's affability and personal charm. He was unblessed by either John Kennedy's urbanity and wit or Lyndon Johnson's disarming folksiness. Usually reserved and formal, by nature reclusive, he was a political loner and one of the most aloof and isolated presidents in American history. Although he was an enthusiastic sports fan and the self-styled apostle of Middle America, he was a politician strangely ill at ease with people. Suspicious of the news media, he rarely held press conferences; uncomfortable in the public eye, he maintained a low presidential profile and spent much of his time away from Washington and the demands of bureaucracy, press, and

Congress. Intense and hardworking, he preferred to labor in the isolation of Camp David, Maryland, the presidential retreat, or in the privacy of his sun-washed villas in San Clemente, California and Key Biscayne, Florida. Generally concentrating on one large issue at a time, he made decisions alone or in the select company of a few trusted aides. Not an avid reader, he neither skimmed newspapers nor watched network television news programs. His major source of outside information was a daily news summary produced by members of his staff. He chose a predominantly conservative and reasonably competent but undistinguished cabinet and, with the exception of Attorney General John Mitchell, generally denied it access to the Oval Office. Although he delegated power and responsibility in enormous blocks, it fell not to the heads of the traditional executive departments but to an inner circle of highly trusted subordinates led by presidential assistants H. Robert Haldeman and John D. Ehrlichman. Derisively called the "Disneyland Mafia" and "The Germans," even by White House staffers, these political amateurs had few contacts with either party or Congress, and little knowledge of, or experience in, public affairs. In the end, it seemed apparent that their most conspicuous qualification was intense personal loyalty to the president. Jealously protective of his time and energies, they erected around him a "Berlin Wall" that was rarely penetrated even by cabinet members, top Republican officials, or congressional leaders. As one disgruntled speech writer observed late in Nixon's first term, the 37th president operated in a "soundproof, shockproof bubble."

Even before assuming office, Nixon revealed that foreign affairs would be his principal concern. "I've always thought this country could run itself domestically without a president," he said during the campaign. "All you need is a competent cabinet to run the country at home." True to his word, he gave international issues, particularly the war in Vietnam, top priority throughout his first term. But one other legacy of the Johnson administration, a runaway economy, required an enormous amount of presidential attention. Having promised the nation both "guns and butter," the Democratic president had refused to seek a tax increase to finance the rapidly escalating war in Southeast Asia. The result by 1968 was a raging inflation that threatened not only the value of the dollar, but the nation's role as a great power and the quality of life in the United States.

The Republican administration's response to this economic crisis was a cautious monetary and fiscal "game plan" that proved inadequate. By tightening the money supply and balancing the budget, the president and his advisers hoped to curb inflation without economic controls or even wage-price guidelines. Instead, inflation continued unabated, while unemployment rose sharply, the stock market sagged, and corporate profits fell. Taking note of the seemingly impossible—simultaneous recession and inflation—Democratic critics and outside economists labeled these policies "Nixonomics." Not until August, 1971, did the administration abandon its free market measures for a bolder "New Economic Policy." Then, proclaiming himself a Keynesian, the president briefly froze prices and wages, adopted budgetary deficits (the largest in peacetime history), and pursued a fitful course that moved from stringent controls to voluntary restraints to a second price freeze and renewed controls. Lurching from one policy to the next and back again in what one eminent economist called "schizoid economics," the administration failed to slow inflation or restore stability. Although a temporary respite in 1972 deprived the Democrats of an election issue, economic problems reached crisis proportions early in Nixon's second term. By mid-1973, as the president imposed his second price freeze in 15 months and prepared to reinstitute stringent price controls, corporate profits and wages were soaring, the stock market was in a prolonged slump, and consumer costs, especially for food, were spiraling at a rate unequaled since the early post-World War II period. By that date, the administration had already twice devalued the dollar in a desperate attempt to offset mounting trade deficits by improving the competitive position of American goods on foreign markets.

In large part, the administration's erratic economic policies were rooted in the president's own stalwart Republicanism. Despite his use of economic activism, he remained to the end a devoted free marketeer. That same traditional conservatism also placed him directly at odds with the liberal social programs of his Democratic predecessors. Although administration officials periodically urged tough antistrike legislation and Nixon vetoed a minimum wage bill (1973), there was no serious threat to New Deal programs. But early in his first term, it was clear that Nixon viewed many Great Society programs as both unwise and unworkable.

When the Democratically controlled 91st Congress convened, the Republican administration offered it broad policy aims rather than specific programs. In good Republican fashion, the President proposed to decentralize authority over federal programs and emphasized local solutions for local problems. But acting upon the advice of Daniel Patrick Moynihan, his urban affairs adviser, he delayed immediate action. A liberal Democrat who had served as Assistant Secretary of Labor under both Kennedy and Johnson, Moynihan argued that a wholesale dismantlement of the Great Society would further divide a nation already torn by an unpopular war, a rising crime rate, and domestic unrest. Lacking a program of his own and accepting momentarily the argument for continuity, Nixon gave the Great Society a reprieve. To the astonishment of critics and supporters alike, bills authorizing the extension of Johnson's antipoverty programs, including such favorite conservative targets as Job Corps and Model Cities, won presidential support and were enacted by Congress.

The President also shocked his party's right wing in August, 1969, when in a television address he unveiled his Family Assistance Payments plan to provide every American family with a guaranteed annual income of at least $1,600. Although cloaked in conservative rhetoric, FAP was a remarkably liberal scheme developed largely by Moynihan. Months later, the former Harvard professor's influence was felt once again when Nixon appealed for "a decade of government reform such as this nation has not witnessed in half a century." Embracing reform as his "watchword," the president urged congressional consideration of tax and welfare reforms, a full-employment budget, and new federal initiatives against hunger and environmental decay. In his State of the Union message in January, 1971, he proclaimed the advent of a "New American Revolution . . . as profound, as far-reaching, as exciting as that first revolution 200 years ago."

But it was not revolution but counterrevolution that Nixon seemed to favor. A tireless spokesman for such traditional values as self-reliance and hard work, a harsh critic of the "permissive society," he would not be Moynihan's Disraeli, implementing domestic programs that even liberals dared not touch. Whatever his watchword, his personal instincts and political philosophy favored retrenchment and consolidation, not innovation and reform. He signed a limited Tax Reform Act of 1969, but he resisted a modest and successful congressional effort to reduce the oil depletion allowance. He created the Environmental Protection Agency and signed the Water Quality Improvement Act (1970), but administration policies, particularly its support of the supersonic transport and the Alaskan pipeline, frequently enraged environmentalists both in and out of Congress. Moreover, in the face of mounting conservative opposition, he quietly dropped FAP and his proposal for a modest national health program. Indeed, at midpassage, the administration's first-term course was firmly fixed. Having drifted uncertainly at first, it now moved with growing confidence away from the "New American Revolution," away from the twentieth century trend toward big government, in the direction of the "New Federalism."

Offered early in 1970 as a framework for the administration's policies, the "New Federalism" promised "to reverse the flow of power and resources from the states and communities to Washington." To begin the process, the White House proposed the "sharing" of federal revenues with city, county, and state governments. Congressional leaders, fearing a dilution of their powers to control the federal purse, hesitated at first. But in October, 1972, under heavy pressure from the administration, Congress enacted a measure to return to local governments over a five-year period $30.2 billion in federal revenues. As he signed the bill at a ceremony in front of Philadelphia's Independence Hall, a deeply satisfied president declared that with this enactment the New Federalism began the "renewal" of the federal system. The nation's financially hard pressed city governments, however, quickly learned to their dismay that revenue sharing was not a windfall. In his budget proposals for fiscal 1974, the frugal Republican chief executive moved to slash previously budgeted federal grants for social services and community development. The crisis of the cities, he said, had passed.

But well before he offered his austerity budget of 1974, Nixon was already battling congressional spending. To cut federal expenditures and reduce federal commitments he spent much of his first-term domestic energy beating back appropriation bills for social programs. When he failed, he used his veto (19 times during the 92nd Congress alone); when his vetoes were overridden, he simply refused to spend congressionally authorized funds. Nevertheless, as his first term ended, Richard Nixon continued to preside over a social service state. During four years of his leadership, the nation's food stamp program more than quadrupled; loans to small businesses more than tripled; subsidies for the arts and low-cost housing grew markedly; and new service agencies, including the Office of Child Development and the Office of Consumer Affairs, proliferated.

The administration's conservatism, although emerging slowly in legislative areas, was immediately apparent in areas largely outside congressional control. Fulfilling a campaign promise to appoint a no-nonsense attorney general, Nixon named John Mitchell, his campaign manager and former law partner, to head the Department of

Justice. Gruff and taciturn, Mitchell served until his resignation (to manage Nixon's reelection campaign) in 1972 as the stern symbol of the administration's unwavering devotion to "law and order." With one eye fixed on the nation's soaring crime rate and another on the mood of the electorate (particularly on Wallace's 13 percent), he sponsored a controversial "no-knock" crime law for predominantly black Washington, D.C.; advocated preventive detention and stop-and-frisk laws; claimed an unrestricted government right to eavesdrop electronically on suspected security risks; dealt harshly with antiwar demonstrators; and prosecuted a motley body of radicals and political dissidents on charges ranging from conspiracy to espionage. Although the Supreme Court ruled against unrestricted electronic surveillance and civil libertarians objected to the "no-knock" statute and the apparent harassment of political dissenters, many Americans, perhaps most, believed that severe measures were required to stem the rising incidence of criminal violence and civil disorder. The crime rate, however, continued to climb.

Fear of crime was but one facet of a pervasive national malaise that had emerged gradually in the late 1960s as the nation's most salient political issue. However troubled by the stalemate in Vietnam, the American people seemed more deeply disturbed by such domestic ills as drug abuse, racial disorder, and violent protest. Identified originally as the Wallace "backlash" but later more accurately described as the "Social Issue," this widespread dysphoria portended, some analysts believed, a fundamental national political realignment. Indeed, White House strategists viewed the Social Issue as the cement for a majority Republican coalition of the unyoung, the unpoor, and the unblack. In the first test of that strategy, the midterm elections of 1970, the results were inconclusive. The administration's campaign to unseat the "Radical-Liberals" of the Democratic party produced some truly memorable vice-presidential billingsgate (critics called Spiro T. Agnew's colorful epithets "Agnew-isms") but not a Republican Congress. However much they disliked "scroungy student dissenters," "pusillanimous pussyfooters," "sniveling hand-wringers," and the "effete corps of impudent snobs," the voters themselves seemed as concerned with runaway inflation as with the Social Issue. On election day, the GOP won two new seats in the Senate but lost a total of nine congressional seats and eleven governorships. Despite White House claims of a stunning victory, the Democrats remained firmly in control of both houses of Congress.

In the administration's grand design for a new Republican coalition, the conservative white voters of the South were of central importance. Increasingly disenchanted by the liberal, "pro-Negro" policies of the national Democratic party, white southerners admired Nixon more than any recent president. He did not sweep the region in 1968, but he dominated the Upper South and, without Wallace in the running, could easily have carried every southern state except Texas. To an administration that prided itself on its capacity to play political "hard ball" it seemed only logical to absorb Wallace's strength by openly courting the troubled South.

This "Southern Strategy," of course, ran directly counter to Afro-American aspirations. Despite the race chauvinism of youthful black militants and a growing black emphasis on separate economic and cultural development, the vast majority of the nation's Negro minority still dreamed of assimilation in a colorblind society. Black fears were aroused by Nixon's blistering attacks on "forced integration" and "busing"; and widespread black skepticism met his preinaugural promise to do "more for the Negro than any president has ever done." Negroes expected the worst from this Republican administration, and their suspicions were not altogether without foundation. In one of the most significant shifts of his administration, Nixon reversed his predecessors' policy of executive engagement in the civil rights struggle. In 1969, for the first time since World War II, the Justice Department sought court-ordered delays in southern desegregation. It relaxed government compliance standards and shifted the burden of civil rights enforcement to the courts. Perhaps most telling of all, it attempted, though without success, to block the extension of the most efficacious federal civil rights statute, the Voting Rights Act of 1965. Still there was no major rollback of Negro freedoms. The New Nationalism mirrored increasing white impatience with black demands for rapid social change. Yet the achievements of the past remained secure, and all but the most persistent vestiges of lily-white public education vanished from the South. Moreover, Nixon supported an act extending the life of the Civil Rights Commission and resisted southern pressures to restore federal tax exemptions for all-white private schools. His pledge to curb federal spending took precedence over his pledge to promote "black capitalism" through federal loans and subsidies. But in his Philadelphia Plan of 1970, he exercised executive authority to impose racial quotas on traditionally all-white construction unions. These were modest achievements. Ironically, however, the administration's performance in the area of civil rights was stronger than either the president or his critics cared to admit.

In his judicial appointments Nixon broke more sharply with the policies of his immediate predecessors. Harshly critical of liberal judicial activism, the Republican president sought to remake the court in his own conservative image. Although he failed in two attempts to appoint conservative southerners with segregationist records to the Supreme Court, he filled four high court vacancies with judicial conservatives. Joined by one and sometimes two of the other five justices, the Nixon appointees (perhaps only one of whom was a genuine "strict constructionist") were expected to reverse nearly two decades of Warren Court liberal activism. Once again, however, there was more continuity than seemed immediately apparent. The decisions of the reconstituted court neither expanded nor eroded basic civil liberties and rights. Contrary to White House wishes, it ruled in favor of abortion and against state aid to parochial education. Its principal departures from earlier high court rulings came in a tougher attitude toward criminals and pornography.

TOWARD A GENERATION OF PEACE

The caution and ambivalence that so often marked Nixon's domestic policies found no parallel in his bold handling of international affairs. Promising a "full generation of peace" through negotiation not confrontation, he moved quickly to "normalize" relations with the Peoples' Republic of China and the Soviet Union. In both cases, détente was complicated by the president's reputation as an intractable cold warrior.

A vigorous Red-hunter during his congressional career, he had often found his political opponents "soft" on communism. As vice-president, he engaged Khrushchev in "kitchen debates" in Moscow and Camp David, and in 1954 urged massive air strikes in defense of beleaguered French forces at Dienbienphu. Yet, though initially viewed by Kremlin leaders as the most belligerent in a long line of anti-Communist presidents, he proved more sophisticated and flexible than any of his post-World War II predecessors in his dealings with Communist nations. Placing ideology aside, he pursued a policy of realism based on the ancient maxim that nations have no permanent friends or enemies, only permanent interests. In this exercise in *Realpolitik,* Nixon was to an extraordinary degree his own Secretary of State. He was assisted at every turn, however, by Henry Kissinger, a former Harvard professor, director of the National Security Council, and perhaps the most remarkable foreign policy adviser ever to serve the White House. Kissinger did not formally become head of the Department of State until 1973, but he was in fact the nation's chief diplomat throughout the first term.

The most spectacular examples of the new realism in American diplomacy came in 1972. In February of that year, while a nation of television viewers watched via satellite, the president journeyed to Peking to lay the groundwork for a resumption of Sino-American relations. Although denied recognition by the United States and its western allies since the rise to dominance of Mao Tse-tung in 1949, mainland China was a major power armed with nuclear weapons and populated by one-fifth of the world's people. In 1971, the Peoples' Republic was admitted to the United Nations with American support, and, over ineffectual American opposition, Chiang Kai-shek's Nationalist regime was ousted. In a second internationally televised summit meeting, Nixon became the first president ever to set foot on Soviet soil when he conferred in Moscow in May, 1972, with Soviet party leader Leonid Brezhnev. A year later, a second Nixon-Brezhnev meeting occurred in Washington amid rising hopes of a permanent "thaw" in the Cold War. Seasoned diplomatic observers cautioned that other summits had been followed by deteriorating relations, and ultraconservatives, Vice-President Agnew among them, were alarmed by the open camaraderie between the nation's chief executive and the leaders of its postwar adversaries. But the president declared that "1972 has been a year of more achievement for peace than any year since the end of World War II," and most Americans believed him.

The Peking-Moscow summits, although enormously important as symbols, were less important than the substantive agreements they represented. As Nixon's second term began, China and the United States had not exchanged formal diplomatic recognition, but relations between the two nations were vastly improved and a cultural and economic exchange was underway. The first phase of the Strategic Arms Limitation Talks (SALT) with the Soviets brought no agreement on the control of offensive nuclear weapons, but a SALT I agreement limiting defensive or antiballistic missile systems was signed. Moreover, the two nations had signed a massive trade agreement, as well as agreements of cooperation in such areas as cancer research and space exploration, and were negotiating a "Mutual and Balanced Force Reduction" for Europe.

The apparent ease with which these spectacular breakthroughs were accomplished was deceptive. Soviet-American rapprochement was at best tenuous; divergent East-West interests in the Middle East and subequatorial Africa soon threatened renewed tensions. In the first major test of détente, the Yom Kippur war of 1973, revenge-minded Egyptians attacked Israel to recover territories lost in the 1967 war. Both sides quickly sought help. The Russians aided the Egyptians and the United States supplied Israel, but a larger international crisis was avoided when the big powers forced a cease-fire. This uneasy peace was an immediate triumph for the Nixon-Kissinger policy. The administration achieved better relations with the Arab states without either offending Israel or seriously impairing relations with the Soviets. Yet a long-range solution was not in sight. The strategic location and mineral riches of the Middle East made it a likely setting for continued East-West rivalry. Further to the south, Soviet interests likewise posed a threat to American ambitions for an independent but prowestern black Africa. The collapse of Portuguese colonialism in Angola and Mozambique and black restiveness under minority white rule in Rhodesia and South Africa piqued the interests of both major powers and offered new challenges to détente. These and other international developments suggested that to Nixon and Kissinger local issues in Asia, Africa, and the Middle East held scant importance of their own. Superpower relationships were the administration's passion; little outside the question of relative Soviet-American advantage seemed to matter.

In 1972 the administration's most pressing problems remained in Vietnam. Elected on a campaign pledge to end the war and win the peace by a "secret plan," Nixon sought an early conclusion to the fighting through negotiations in Paris with the North Vietnamese. When these talks, underway since the autumn of 1968, proved unproductive, the president shifted to a policy of "Vietnamization." Designed to "de-Americanize" the war by transferring American combat responsibility in Vietnam to ARVN soldiers, the policy reversed a decade of accelerating troop strength by gradually withdrawing American forces. Although the success of Vietnamization and the future of the wobbly Saigon regime remained in doubt, troop withdrawals continued throughout the first term. From a peak strength of 550,000 in April, 1969, the number of American soldiers fell to 27,000 in early 1973, and American annual combat deaths dropped from a 1968 high of 14,592 to only 300 in 1972.

Yet even as American involvement in Vietnam declined, the war was carried to other theaters in Southeast Asia. In secret missions unknown to even congressional leaders and the Secretary of the Air Force, American aircraft bombed communist "sanctuaries" inside Cambodia throughout most of 1969 and well into the spring of 1970. On April 30, 1970, U.S. and South Vietnamese soldiers invaded Cambodia, and the following winter ARVN troops with American air support moved into Laos. Although defended by military brass and White House officials as necessary to disrupt enemy supply lines and purchase time for Vietnamization—and therefore vital to American withdrawal—these limited but much criticized incursions provoked domestic disorders in tragic proportions. The antiwar movement, recently lulled by massive troop withdrawals and falling casualty figures, erupted in protest against the Cambodian invasion. On campuses across the country, students picketed and struck, and at riot-torn Kent State four of them were killed by Ohio national guardsmen. The bloodletting at Kent, soon followed by a similar though unrelated tragedy at all-black

Jackson State College in Mississippi, brought a sense of renewed urgency to the peace movement. But a substantial majority of the voters remained steadfast in support of the president's conduct of the war. To the dismay of a growing body of congressional "doves," the people evidently accepted Nixon's argument that he could shorten the war by widening it.

In the end it was negotiation, not Vietnamization, that ended American participation in the struggle. Fresh from stunning triumphs in Peking and Moscow, Kissinger returned from Paris in October, 1972 to announce that "peace is at hand." Yet, though popular hopes and the stock market soared, the carnage continued for three long months. During the Christmas season, when it appeared that the October agreements had unraveled, the president dispatched wave upon wave of B-52s to rain bombs in unprecedented tonnage on Hanoi and Haiphong. At last, however, late in January, 1973, the longest war in U.S. history ended. The Paris Accords, signed by the United States, North and South Vietnam, and the National Liberation Front, provided for a supervised cease-fire, complete American withdrawal, and a prisoner exchange. Yet even as the nation celebrated Nixon's "peace with honor," the U.S. air war over Cambodia continued. Not until mid-August, 1973, after Congress moved to terminate funds for all military operations in Southeast Asia, did the commander in chief halt the round-the-clock bombing sorties against the enemies of Lon Nol's corrupt military regime in Phnom-Penh. With neither Congress nor the public willing to support further the ineffective anti-Communist governments in Southeast Asia, Nixon's successor, Gerald Ford, proved incapable of delivering promised military support to Cambodia and South Vietnam. In April 1975, Cambodia fell to the Khmer Rouge. Later that month, the South Vietnamese regime also surrendered to Communist insurgents. Following a hasty and controversial evacuation of American personnel and Vietnamese children from Saigon, the long American nightmare in Southeast Asia ended.

"WHITE HOUSE HORRORS"

The administration's foreign policy successes offset early Republican fears of a one-term Nixon presidency. The president's popularity had slumped markedly following the midterm elections of 1970. Early in 1971, opinion pollsters revealed, he trailed Senator Edmund S. Muskie of Maine in public esteem. Popular enthusiasm for Nixon's "peace initiatives" abroad and favorable developments at home, however, soon brought renewed hopes. During the early months of 1972, the good news from Peking and Moscow was matched by a dramatic, though temporary, economic upswing that brought new jobs and stabilized prices. Soon thereafter, Muskie's bid for the Democratic nomination was crippled by a feeble showing in the hotly contested Democratic primaries; and in May Wallace's threat to Nixon's southern support was eliminated when the Alabamian was critically wounded in an assassination attempt. Then in July, an army of enthusiastic and idealistic amateurs capitalized on recent party reforms and seized control of the Democratic convention to nominate Senator George McGovern, a left-leaning South Dakotan whose issues were immediate peace in Vietnam, reduced military spending, and sweeping tax and welfare reforms. In a campaign effort remarkable only for its blunders, McGovern was quickly branded by Republicans and conservative Democrats as the candidate of "amnesty, acid, and abortion." His efforts to brand the Nixon administration as the "most corrupt in American history" proved ineffectual. On election day, as many of his party's traditional leaders feared, he led the Democrats to their worst humiliation in half a century.

Only half of the eligible voters (some 55 percent) turned out, but among those who did Nixon was a clear favorite. Awarding him every state but Massachusetts and the District of Columbia, the electorate submerged Nixon's opponent in a sea of electoral (521 to 17) and popular (60.7 percent) votes.

It was a triumph almost without precedent. Except for Lyndon Johnson's landslide of 1964, no president ever polled a larger popular majority; except for Franklin Roosevelt's record-shattering sweep of 1936, no president ever won more electoral votes. Indeed, Nixon ran so well among blue-collar workers, union members, ethnics, and Catholics that he carried fully 37 percent of all the votes cast by Democrats— a record unequaled even by Dwight Eisenhower. Still, Nixon's was a personal rather than a party victory. As they had in 1968, ticket-splitting voters returned solid Democratic majorites to both houses of Congress. Losing only twelve seats in the house (243–192), the Democrats gained two additional Senate seats (57–43) and a majority of the nation's governorships. Clearly McGovern had lost, but the Republicans had not won.

But if the mandate of 1972 was uncertain, Richard Nixon's second term intentions were not. Having built a "structure of peace" through détente abroad, he would now restructure the nation's domestic priorities by diffusing federal responsibilities for local problems and decreasing federal spending for social programs. Although perhaps not sounding a full retreat from the Kennedy-Johnson "war on poverty," he was surely advocating a drastically revised battle plan. "Visionary" and "inherently unworkable" federal programs for urban renewal, personnel training, vocational education, and housing subsidies were to be eliminated or sharply curtailed. The nation's rudimentary health-care program for the aged could stay, but such Great Society agencies as the Office of Economic Opportunity and such programs as Model Cities, Job Corps, Community Action, and Neighborhood Youth could not. By so economizing, the government could hope not only to ease mounting inflationary and tax pressures, but free additional monies for revenue-sharing grants to hard pressed city halls and state houses.

To the surprise of no one, least of all the president, the New Federalism proved no more appealing to the Democratically controlled 93rd Congress than it had to the 92nd. Indeed, the dominant mood in Washington as the new Congress convened was one of combat. Lawmakers from both parties were angered by apparent executive usurpations of legislative prerogatives. In the tradition of a succession of strong chief executives, Nixon, despite his self-styled strict constructionism, had governed in the grand manner. Without either the advice or consent of Congress, he had invaded Cambodia and Laos, mined the harbor of Haiphong, and resumed saturation bombing of Hanoi. He had invoked executive privilege to shield White House policymakers from congressional inquiry and impounded congressionally authorized funds slated for programs he opposed. Although precedents for such extraordinary assertions of presidential authority were numerous, aroused congressional leaders were now urging redress of the imbalance of power. There was, then, every indication that the executive-legislative stalemate of the first Nixon administration would become in the second a power struggle of historic importance. At stake, it appeared, was the doctrine of checks and balances itself.

As it turned out, however, the overriding issue of Nixon's second term was the abuse, not the accretion, of executive power. During the campaign of 1972, two White House aides were arrested for their roles in a conspiracy to burglarize and implant illegal wire taps in Democratic National Committee headquarters in Washington's elegant Watergate Building. Although Democrats accused the White House of "political espionage," the president and his chief aides denied executive involvement and dismissed the incident as a "third-rate burglary attempt." Vice-President Agnew even suggested that the Democrats had burgled their own National Committee. The voters, for the most part, showed little interest, and in November the unseemly affair, like the presidential aspiration of Senator McGovern, was buried in the Nixon landslide.

Or so it seemed until early in 1973, when congressional investigators, aided by a courageous federal judge and a vigorous press, began exposing a sordid family of White House scandals that shocked the nation and raised profoundly disturbing questions about Nixon's capacity and fitness for leadership. Almost daily throughout the spring and summer, evidence mounted of official misconduct and lawlessness. By autumn, most of what Attorney General Mitchell later called the "White House horrors" were fully in view. Nixon's popularity collapsed, and for the first time in more than a century there was serious talk in Congress of the impeachment of a president.

At the heart of the Nixon scandals lay, of course, the Watergate break-in and subsequent efforts by highly placed administration officials to limit the investigation and conceal or destroy evidence. But there were also allegations that the White House, or its Committee for the Re-Election of the President, engaged in: (1) unethical and illegal campaign practices ranging from "dirty tricks" against Democratic hopefuls to the extortion of illegal contributions from corporations and interest groups desiring government favors; (2) efforts to politicize such nominally independent and traditionally nonpartisan government agencies as the Federal Bureau of Investigation (FBI) and the Internal Revenue Service; and (3) illegal and wide-ranging domestic security and intelligence gathering operations. Additionally, there were charges that Nixon's income and property taxes were not in order, that his estates in California and Florida were acquired under questionable circumstances, and that federal funds (totaling nearly $10 million) spent on improvements for these private dwellings often had little to do with presidential security. Quite apart from the scandal, there were also allegations of constitutional abuses, including: the misuse of impoundment and executive privileges; the secret and unauthorized air war against Cambodia; the continued conduct of the war in Southeast Asia after the repeal of the Gulf of Tonkin Resolution. To some of Nixon's harshest critics, these too were impeachable offenses. To most

Americans, however, these assertions of independent presidential power apparently lay well within the broad range of permissable executive discretion.

Initially the White House tried to ignore the uproar, then it issued a series of general denials of executive wrongdoing. But each presidential statement seemed to raise more questions than it answered. There was, moreover, little discernible White House cooperation with the several investigations into its alleged misconduct. Invoking the doctrines of separation of powers and executive privilege, Nixon at first refused even to permit his aides to testify before the Select Senate Committee on Presidential Campaign Activities. Under mounting congressional pressure, he reversed this position but refused investigators access to secret White House tape recordings of selected presidential conversations and telephone calls. When these were subpoenaed by the Justice Department's independent special prosecutor, the president fought compliance through two federal courts, promising obedience only to a "definitive" ruling of the Supreme Court. After months of negotiation and litigation, Nixon agreed to turn over the disputed material—but not before he had fired the special prosecutor and forced the resignation of Attorney General Elliot Richardson, and not before Congress moved toward his impeachment. To the nation's astonishment, however, the surrendered tapes did not contain two of the conversations presumed by investigators to be most relevant to the inquiry. Moreover, one of the seven remaining tapes contained a mysterious 18-1/2 minute erasure at a crucial point. The president's lawyers attributed these critical gaps in the evidence to inadequacies in White House recording equipment and to secretarial error. But evidence rapidly accumulated to prove that Nixon himself was engaged in a conspiracy to obstruct justice by concealing evidence.

In July, 1974, a unanimous Supreme Court, acting upon a second special prosecutor's request, ordered the White House to surrender tape recordings of 64 key presidential conversations. Following the release of this incriminating material, the House Judiciary Committee voted to recommend three articles of impeachment to the House of Representatives. Charged with obstruction of justice, abuse of power, and contempt for constitutional procedures on a scale without parallel in American history, Nixon seemed headed for imminent impeachment. His last line of defense apparently lay in the Senate where, many believed, conservatives of both parties might marshal enough support to deny the two-thirds of the votes necessary for conviction. On August 8, however, the beleaguered president bowed to the urging of top party and White House officials and announced his resignation. Although still denying criminal action, he acknowledged that the loss of public confidence rendered him incapable of effective leadership. Once returned to private life, the man Henry Kissinger called "lonely and tormented," the first American chief executive to resign in disgrace continued to assert that he had been victimized by the zeal of his friends and the malice of his enemies.

FORD'S INTERLUDE

And thus Gerald Ford became the 38th president. In every respect, his ascent was as incredible as Nixon's fall. A veteran congressman from Michigan and former House minority leader whose highest political ambition was to be speaker, Ford became the first vice-president to assume office under the Twenty-Fifth Amendment and the first nonelected president. He had, as he said, "received the vote of no one."

Thoroughly decent, open, and gregarious, Ford quickly restored public confidence in the basic integrity of the presidency. But he failed to provide convincing leadership. As a congressman, he was popular on both sides of the congressional aisle but had left no mark on the House. Indeed, his record as a lackluster, partisan, and thoroughly conventional representative seemed to hold little promise for an inspired presidency. Promising an "open" administration, he worked hard to offset public disenchantment with the frequently devious and secretive ways of his immediate predecessors. His many press conferences and public statements, however, often seemed more notable for clumsiness of speech than cogency of expression. Despite a law degree from a prestigious eastern university, a broad segment of the press and public wondered openly if he was intelligent enough to be president. His impolitic and seemingly hasty decision to pardon Nixon, without an admission of guilt from the former president or even a full disclosure of his misdeeds, stirred public controversy and raised the question of a double standard of justice. Some who remembered Ford's earlier efforts to derail the congressional Watergate investigation, cried "corrupt bargain." Others believed that unconditional immunity from prosecution for Nixon should be accompanied by equal presidential compassion for Vietnam-era draft evaders. Ford provided a program of conditional amnesty, however, that required two years of alternate government service for the youthful protestors who refused induction.

Plagued by unpopular early decisions and widespread doubts about his aptitude for executive leadership, the likeable new president confronted a bewildering array of international and domestic problems during his two years in office. Despite administration forecasts and a temporary upturn of the business cycle in 1972, the United States in 1974 suffered its worst recession in four decades. A "stagflated" economy of high unemployment and high inflation was further vexed by a continuing petroleum shortage that promised soaring energy costs and greater dependence on uncertain foreign supply. There were scandals in the FBI and CIA (Central Intelligence Agency) ranging from revelations of burglary and illegal surveillance to foreign coups d'état and assassination plots. Abroad, there were crises seemingly without number: a continuing and volatile Arab-Israeli standoff, ominous Soviet ambitions in the Middle East and sub-Saharan Africa, the final collapse of America's Southeast Asian allies, a Marxist-oriented revolution in Portugal, a transfer of power in post-Franco Spain, near-anarchy and the growth of Communist strength in Italy, and the diminishing influence and growing isolation of the United States in the UN General Assembly.

In responding to these disquieting problems, Ford rarely veered from Nixon's course. More conservative and less flexible than Nixon, he vetoed more legislation in one year than Herbert Hoover did in four. More solicitous toward corporations than to civil rights, he pursued traditional Republican monetary and fiscal policies, warned against overly stringent controls on either intelligence agencies or private enterprise, and continued to support both the principle of détente and unprecedented peacetime defense spending. In matters of style and personality, Ford differed markedly from Nixon; yet his policies and programs were very nearly the same. He was, most Americans seemed to believe, a likeable mediocrity.

During Senate confirmation hearings in 1974, then Vice-President-designate Ford disavowed any ambition to be president. Upon Nixon's resignation, however, he soon reconsidered. Though few thought his chances good, he sought election in 1976. Even White House officials viewed him as an underdog. Personally popular but not widely hailed for his executive talents, Ford seemed to lack even the traditional advantages of incumbency. He had served half of Nixon's second term, but he had not developed a national nor even a statewide constituency. Michigan's Fifth District contained the largest electorate he had ever faced at one time. His early campaign organization was remarkably inept; the candidate himself seemed curiously "unpresidential" in his electioneering.

But even these difficulties appeared minor when compared to his party's weaknesses. Although the GOP had won four of the past seven presidential elections, it had dominated Congress only twice since 1932. It had been a minority party since the Great Depression and could now claim the allegiance of only 22 percent of the electorate. Only 19 of the nation's 50 state governors were Republicans. In control of the White House since 1969, the party had delivered peace but neither prosperity nor economic stability. Its claim to be the law-and-order party had been mocked by the gross misdeeds of a Republican president, his vice-president, and two attorneys general. A sensational, if minor, sex scandal involving Democratic Congressmen had not fully expunged the stain of Watergate. Moreover, Republican unity was threatened throughout the spring and well into the summer by the party's small but bellicose extreme right wing. Led by former Governor Ronald Reagan of California, the arch-conservatives demonstrated surprising strength in the primaries, and in one of the least decorous Republican conventions in memory, they dictated a platform that repudiated many of Ford's policies and very nearly blocked his nomination. Given these circumstances, it seemed unremarkable that the conservative Gerald Ford attempted to expropriate the memory of liberal Harry Truman, an accidental president and underdog who overcame party disunity and popular doubt to win election in his own right.

The Democrats, having at least superficially healed the wounds of the McGovern debacle, engaged in their customarily spirited preconvention contest. A profusion of candidates (variously labeled as conservatives, hawks, liberals, populists, and progressives) entered the hotly contested primaries, while former nominees McGovern and Humphrey stood by expectantly. No obvious favorite emerged, but voter indifference eliminated a dozen competitors by convention time, leaving a single practical choice. This was Jimmy Carter of Georgia, a deeply religious retired naval officer, engineer, peanut farmer, and former governor of Georgia whose dazzling smile and meteoric rise from the obscurity of a southern statehouse to a first ballot nomination marked him as the most interesting political phenomenon since John Kennedy.

In the campaign that followed, Carter quickly lost most of a substantial early lead. Both candidates made major mistakes; both were often ineffective on the stump.

Carter struggled against a stubborn reputation for vagueness on the issues; Ford remained too often on the defensive. Although Ford was clearly favored by most conservatives and Carter won the unenthusiastic support of most liberals, the differences between two candidates who promised honest government, military preparedness, and a balanced budget were more apparent than real. In the end, it seemed to be a contest between one candidate who could not shake his reputation as a "bumbler" and another who offered little more than inexperience and the pledge "I'll never lie to you." It produced, most commentators agreed, fewer issues, more yawns, and a lower voter turnout than any presidential election in recent memory. On election day, Carter carried the South and enough large middlewestern and eastern states to win a slim electoral (294) and popular (51 percent) majority. It was hardly a landslide; it may even have been a party rather than a personal victory. Yet Carter's popular vote margin could be compared favorably to those of the victors in 1948, 1960, and 1968. Conceivably, normally Democratic votes cast for independent candidate Eugene McCarthy cost Carter the electoral ballots for four large states. In congressional and gubernatorial races, the electorate once again showed a clear preference for Democratic candidates.

OUTSIDER IN WASHINGTON

President James Earl Carter, Jr. preferred that the nation call him Jimmy. With seemingly little more to recommend him than unshakable self-confidence and vaulting ambition, he broke onto the national scene as an agribusinessman, a self-proclaimed "outsider" with no Washington experience, a private citizen who made much of the fact that he was not a professional politician. Until his inauguration as the 39th president, Carter's governmental experience was limited to one term each as state senator and governor of Georgia. Yet in a nation disenchanted with the "imperial presidency" and still reeling from the shock of the Nixon scandals, Carter's very inexperience was at first a political asset. In the presidential campaign he had shrewdly capitalized on Watergate. From the Oval Office he urged Americans to "trust me" and cultivated an image of righteous candor. In the spirit of Jefferson, that other gentleman farmer from the South, he took pains to demonstrate that he, too, had the common touch. The pomp and ceremony so characteristic of Nixon's presidency were ostentatiously abandoned. On inauguration day, following ceremonies at the capitol, he refused the presidential limousine and walked down Pennsylvania Avenue hand in hand with the First Lady to the White House. Thereafter he chose to ride in a relatively plain sedan. In his first televised address, a "fireside chat," he appeared in cardigan and open shirt. He wore denims and polo shirts at congressional picnics, briefly banished the musical flourishes of "Hail to the Chief" at official functions, and conferred frequently and easily with the press. He held town meetings in out-of-the-way places and stayed overnight in the modest homes of "ordinary" Americans. He even sent his eight-year-old daughter to an inner-city public school. For his White House staff, he chose close associates from Georgia, notably Hamilton Jordan, who became chief of staff, and Jody Powell, press secretary. Young and casual, Jordan and

Powell projected the same open-faced honesty as the president and seemed undismayed when the press good-naturedly called them, in the southern fashion, "good ole boys." In time, as the wounds of Watergate healed, such self-conscious symbolism came to seem gratuitous. Gradually, a less accessible, less informal chief executive emerged, sometimes to the strains of "Hail to the Chief." Yet this least pretentious of all recent presidents must be credited for his effort to strip the presidency of its more imperial forms.

However engaging his personal style, Carter's popular support was small and very soft. In the election his majority was slim and unenthusiastic. During his second year in office his approval rating fell to 40 percent. By 1979 he was less popular than Nixon at his lowest point. Indeed, not since Truman's nadir in 1946 had the popular favor of any president dropped so low so fast. Aside from the self-evident fact that Carter, like Ford, somehow failed to offer convincing leadership, there was no single explanation for this threatening development. Some thought him to be the victim of his own efforts to demystify the presidency; some said he was a weak swimmer out of his depth. Others thought him the legatee of the popular resentment and mistrust of his predecessors; a few believed that he came to be president at a time when the nation's problems were insoluble, when its bloated bureaucracy and its unruly political institutions were unmanageable. But for whatever reason, Carter seemed likely to be the first president since Herbert Hoover to be denied a second term.

Yet by all accounts, he was an earnest, intelligent, hardworking president who lacked neither courage nor character. To provide the practical experience he and his staff so obviously lacked, he brought to his side a number of old Washington hands, including such members of the foreign policy establishment as Secretary of State Cyrus Vance and Secretary of Defense Harold Brown, and such seasoned bureaucrats as Health, Education, and Welfare Secretary Joseph Califano and Energy Secretary James Schlesinger. With the assistance of these and other members of a generally gifted cabinet (which included two women, one of whom was black) he identified and sought solutions for some of the nation's knottiest problems. Yet his tangible achievements were few. His detailed and technically sound proposals for long overdue tax, welfare, and civil service reforms, his bill to create a consumer protection agency, his hospital-cost containment measure got nowhere. He did manage to trim a costly congressional pork barrel for dam and water projects and to win support for new Departments of Education and Energy. But his energy bill, the "centerpiece" of his domestic program, encountered withering fire from the oil and gas lobby. By shifting the measure's emphasis from conservation to development and from consumer compensation to investment incentives, Congress satisfied the demands of powerful private interests, but it passed a bill that was anything but the "moral equivalent of war" promised by a frustrated president. In its final form, the energy bill provided appreciable reductions in neither of the two most critical areas: domestic consumption and foreign dependence.

In other areas of the economy the administration's record was worse—the worst, argued James Reston, dean of the Washington press corps, since Herbert Hoover. During the campaign Carter identified recession as the nation's foremost domestic

problem. In his term an assortment of ills identified with a troubled economy con-
tinuted unabated: unemployment (particularly for black teenagers but also for nonwhites generally); declining investment, savings, and productivity levels; stagnated or
declining after-tax earnings; mounting trade deficits. But it was high and variable
inflation—which in early 1980 threatened to reach an annual rate of 20 percent—that
proved to be the curse of the '70s and Carter's greatest political liability. Spurred by
sharply rising food, fuel, housing, and transportation costs, consumer prices doubled
between 1967 and 1978. Between 1973 and 1978, the cost of automobiles jumped
72 percent and new homes 67 percent; in 1979 gasoline prices rose 60 percent.

Carter's approach to the crisis of double-digit inflation was hesitant, belated, and
fully as conservative as his Republican predecessors. Convinced that mandatory
"wage and price controls have never worked in peacetime," he did not find a
workable alternative. In 1978 he proposed voluntary guidelines (7 per cent) and
created a Council on Wage and Price Stability to monitor the results. This was not
strong medicine and the patient got worse. The Consumer Price Index rose 13.3
percent in 1979; early the following year both inflation and interest rates topped 18
percent. In March, 1980, midway through the presidential primaries, Carter imposed
a modest federal gasoline tax to discourage consumption and new credit restraints on
consumer borrowing. Although he had submitted his budget to Congress only weeks
before, he now recommended "drastic" spending cuts to balance (for the first time
since 1969 and only the second time in more than two decades) the federal books
in fiscal 1981.

Such halfway measures promised no immediate relief. Economists generally
agreed on little, but there was substantial agreement that a balanced budget, whatever
its salutary long-range psychological effects, would have little impact (perhaps as little
as 2 percent) on a runaway wage-price spiral in 1981. Short of fundamental structural
changes in the economy, many believed a deep recession to be the most effective way
to slow inflation. Some thought Carter's policies were designed to produce just that.
Seizing the moment, conservatives argued the case for fiscal austerity, particularly in
the area of social spending. Labor leaders, the congressional black caucus, and liberals
in general expressed the well-grounded fear that the weight of the government's
stability program would rest most heavily on the bottom rail, on low-income earners,
on the relatively poor and powerless. Few expected Congress to slash federal spending
for veterans' benefits, farm subsidies, or defense. By general consent, the massive
"entitlement programs," including Social Security and Medicare, were untouchable.

In foreign affairs the Georgia president often proceeded more imaginatively.
Although committed to the ideals of détente, Carter indicated early that his administra-
tion would be less devoted to traditional balance-of-power geopolitics than to human
rights. The practical limitations of such a policy, however, often proved embarrassing.
Despite a decade-long thaw in the Cold War, conflicting Soviet-American interests in
Africa, Asia, the Middle East, and Latin America often seemed to dictate continued
U.S. support for repressive anti-Communist regimes. Nor was the president's support
for "prisoners of conscience" in the USSR always consistent with his desire for
Soviet-American cooperation in controlling the arms race. Anti-Soviet "hardliners,"

supporters of Kissinger-style *realpolitik,* and other critics of the "idealism" of Carter's foreign policy decried his "naiveté." Not a few cried, "I told you so" when, following the Soviet invasion of Afghanistan in December, 1979, he offered military aid to and alliance with Mohammad Zia ul-Haq, president and dictator of Pakistan. Yet despite such backsliding, despite the unattractive trade-offs apparently required by a dangerous world, Carter more than any other chief executive since World War II tried to practice the human rights doctrine the nation preached.

Nor were the administration's other successes inconsequential. In an act of singularly bold and personal diplomacy, he brought together President Anwar Sadat of Egypt and Prime Minister Menachem Begin of Israel for direct negotiations that resulted in the historic Camp David accords. Although hopes for a full resolution of the Middle East crisis were not realized, Carter's initiative marked the first real breakthrough in Arab-Israeli relations since the October War of 1973.

Farther to the East, following through on initiatives begun by his predecessors, he completed the process of "normalizing" relations with the People's Republic of China. He also completed negotiations for a treaty that would gradually transfer control of the Panama Canal to Panamanian authority. That agreement, which permitted American military protection of an otherwise internationally neutral Isthmain waterway, met conservative opposition and barely won the two-thirds Senate majority required for ratification.

Administration efforts to win early confirmation of the SALT II agreement were less successful. The SALT process, begun by Nixon and Kissinger in the heyday of détente, was a confusing issue to the average American who had little understanding of the arcane terminology and sophisticated hardware of modern nuclear defense systems. Generally favored by a people who wanted peace, the process was nonetheless complicated by a pervasive American mistrust of the Soviet Union and by a growing fear that the United States was no longer militarily superior to its principal Cold War adversary. Some arms experts opposed SALT II on grounds that its limits were too high, that it would accelerate rather than slow the race for strategic advantage. But others, including influential, hawkish Senator Henry Jackson, argued that the Carter administration had been outbargained by the sharp traders of the Kremlin, whose military budget was thought to be 40 to 60 percent greater than that of the United States. On balance, the treaty seemed to promise some measure of arms stability at a time when the Soviets had the edge in ICBMs and submarine missiles but the United States had a substantial lead in long-range strategic bombers and nuclear warheads.

Arguments of comparative advantage, however, quickly became moot. Troubled from the outset by Soviet interests in the affairs of such third-world nations as Ethiopia, South Yemen, and Angola—and in late 1979, by the discovery of a Soviet combat brigade in Cuba—the treaty ratification process was derailed by events in Afghanistan in December, 1979. Whatever the intention (and veteran Kremlinologists could not agree whether the move was "defensive" or "offensive" in character), SALT II and détente itself were imperiled by the Soviet decision to occupy this hapless Islamic neighbor to the south. To be sure, the Afghans, through a succession of pro-Soviet governments, had been closely allied to the USSR for a decade or more. But this was the first Soviet military action since World War II outside the Warsaw Pact countries. Given the political and religious turmoil then sweeping much of the Islamic crescent, given the proximity of the oil fields in Iran, given traditional Russian designs on the warm waters of the Persian Gulf, the Carter administration could not have ignored this latest example of Soviet "adventurism." Not since the Cuban missile crisis of 1962 had Soviet-American relations been so strained. With cold war fevers rising, further consideration of SALT II was delayed indefinitely, and the president announced an embargo of American grain and high technology exports to Russia and an American boycott of the summer 1980 Olympics in Moscow.

But nothing quickened the nation's martial spirit more than the seizure of U.S. diplomatic personnel by fanatically anti-American militants in Teheran. Once praised by Carter as an "island of stability," the oil-rich kingdom of Iran, with its repressive and staunchly pro-American Shah, was toppled by religious and cultural fundamentalists bent on the creation of an Islamic republic. In November, 1979, with the apparent support of the revolution's elderly spiritual leader, the austere and (to westerners) inscrutable Ayatollah Khomeini, youthful militants stormed the American Embassy taking some 65 hostages and demanding the return of the Shah then temporarily in exile in the United States.

The administration's response to this egregious violation of international conventions was restrained. Dismissing immediate military action as counterproductive, it applied economic and international pressure, but did not at first sever diplomatic relations. In time the embassy's black and women employees were released. But despite the censure of a nearly unanimous world community, the constructive intervention of the United Nations and the World Court, and the urgings of duly constituted but impotent secular officials of Iran, the militants and their patron, the aging Ayatollah, refused further compromise and kept more than 50 Americans in captivity. Having apparently exhausted all practical remedies save the resort to arms, the president risked a hazardous rescue mission in May 1980 that ended in a desert near Teheran with an equipment failure and death for eight American commandos. Thereafter the United States could do little but writhe in the frustrations of a helpless giant and wait for the long-promised Iranian parliament to assemble and debate the issue. Because the hostage issue—and the fierce anti-Americanism it represented—was apparently the only glue that held together an otherwise chaotic regime, it was widely believed that the problem could drag on indefinitely.

For Jimmy Carter, who had often questioned the Cold War expedient that brought American aid to counterrevolutionary regimes no matter how autocratic, the situation was surely ironical. Now, in an American election year, in a Near Eastern theocracy halfway round the world, sentiment raged against the "American devils" who had propped up the Shah, trained SAVAK, his dread secret police, and supplied the arms he sometimes turned on his own people. To be sure, Carter had stood by the Shah after it was clear that most Iranians did not. But it was a cruel fate that forced this champion of human rights to reap the bitter harvest of a policy he had so eloquently disavowed.

ELECTION 1980

Carter began his reelection campaign in trying circumstances. Having promised the moon in 1976, he had to run on his own uninspiring record in 1980. During his tenure the national estate had, if anything, deteriorated further. His pledges for domestic reform were largely unfulfilled. Both government spending and the national debt had grown, despite his promises to the contrary. Voter confidence in his economic policies fell lower than the dollar on the world's monetary exchanges. Pollsters reported that his approval ratings were below that of any president since the introduction of modern opinion-sampling methods. Republican, independent, and not a few Democratic voters dismissed him as ineffectual. Members of his own party launched a "Dump Carter" movement in order to deny what seemed likely to be a Republican victory in November. The Americans for Democratic Action called him a "warmed-over Ford," and his administration "the governing wing of the Republican party." Yet even as the primary season began, the president's popularity rebounded dramatically, if only temporarily.

This remarkable recovery owed nearly everything to the estimable advantages of incumbency. While two Democratic and a half-dozen Republican opponents began a bruising delegate scramble that would carry the survivors through 37 states by national convention time, Carter stayed in the White House, conspicuously monitoring conditions in the Near East, conferring with advisers about Afghanistan and Iran. For a time, this "Rose Garden" strategy worked. But the national propensity to close ranks behind a president in times of international trouble was soon offset by a worsening economic crisis at home. As the hostage problem continued without solution and popular indignation over Soviet troops in Afghanistan cooled, pocketbook concerns eclipsed all others. Months before the election, the issues of virulent inflation and impending recession became foremost on voters' minds.

Even so, the campaign stirred little enthusiasm. Carter easily denied the challenge of his Democratic rivals. California Governor Jerry Brown, who had beaten Carter in several 1976 primaries, withdrew early. Senator Edward M. Kennedy, heir apparent to the legend of Camelot, entered the race at the head of a promising "Draft Kennedy" movement only to fade when he could not shake popular doubts about his character or ability. Among the Republicans, former Governor Ronald Reagan of California, with relative ease, outdistanced a field of candidates, including: Senator Howard Baker of Tennessee, Senator Robert Dole of Kansas, former Governor (and ex-Democrat) John Connally of Texas, former Ambassador and CIA Director George Bush of Connecticut, and Congressman John Anderson of Illinois. Although personally attractive, the aging (69-year-old) ultraconservative Reagan was thought by many seasoned campaign watchers to be less "electable" than such relative moderates as Baker or Bush or the liberal, maverick Anderson, whose appeal reached to independents, disaffected Democrats, and college students. Yet, the Californian was the favorite of party stalwarts and he won a first-ballot nomination. As expected, the disgruntled Anderson declared his candidacy on an independent ticket.

These, then, were the alternatives produced by one of the world's longest, most expensive, and most cumbersome electoral processes: a doomed, although attractive, third-party candidate; an incumbent president whose domestic and international leadership inspired no discernible confidence; and a former movie star who had held no administrative position since 1974 and who had experience in neither Washington nor foreign affairs. As the campaign progressed, voter apathy suggested an emerging recognition that the qualities required to win major-party nominations and elections were not necessarily the same qualities required to solve national problems or to govern effectively. On election day scarcely half of the electorate voted, but among those who did Reagan was the clear favorite. Garnering 51 percent of the votes, he outpolled Carter and Anderson combined and won an electoral vote landslide. The badly routed Democrats managed to retain the House, but the Republicans for the first time since 1952 won control of the Senate. Although there was little serious talk of a "mandate," the magnitude of the conservative sweep was impressive. Among the Democratic casualties were such leading Senate liberals as Idaho's Frank Church and South Dakota's George McGovern, both targeted for defeat by Protestant fundamentalists and other "New Right" interest groups. Political analysts generally agreed that Reagan benefitted heavily from the hostage issue and an election-eve debate with Carter. Most also believed that the pendulum of public opinion was moving sharply to the right.

With their election behind them, the people of the United States confronted a third and uncertain century in their national experience. Abroad, international rivalries and the arms race continued unabated. Mounting East-West tensions threatened a fragile Soviet-American rapprochement, and the prospects for President Nixon's "generation of peace" seemed less than bright. The world's nuclear stockpile loomed ever more ominously as a growing legion of nations developed the technical wherewithal to destroy humanity. At home, staggeringly high prices, a lower growth rate, depleting energy supplies, and despoiled natural resources foreshadowed not only changing consumption patterns but diminishing affluence. Not least of all, the nation confronted these challenges at a moment of declining popular faith in government. In the course of a decade marked by internal and international setbacks, its elected officials and political institutions had been unable to reverse what President Carter called "the crisis of confidence . . . that is threatening the very fabric of America."

Yet, as they looked toward the 200th birthday of their constitution, the citizens of the world's oldest republic had no reason to doubt their own remarkable capacities for self-renewal. However somber the national mood, however uncertain the future, they had cause to believe in the essential worth of their own national heritage, in the vitality of their basic institutions, in the fundamental strength of their economy, and in their ability to survive as a free and united people in a perilous world.

CONFLICTING HISTORICAL VIEWPOINTS

18. Is the Presidency too Powerful?

Soon after the ratification of the Constitution, Thomas Jefferson advised his friend and protégé, James Madison, that "the tyranny of the legislature is really the danger most to be feared and will continue to be so for many years to come. The tyranny of the executive power will come in its turn, but at a more distant period." Some two centuries later, following the extraordinary assertions of presidential power by Lyndon Johnson and Richard Nixon, a growing number of scholars believed that Jefferson's "more distant period" was at hand. In recent decades, they argued, the presidency had been unduly exalted; the presidents had grown too aloof, too arrogant, too neglectful of congressional prerogatives. In this view, the system of constitutional checks and balances devised by the founders no longer effectively restrained executive authority. In the words of one political scientist, the man in the Oval Office had been elevated from "Servant to Sun King."

The Vietnam War and the Watergate scandals were the most flagrant and frequently cited examples of a runaway presidency. Yet most scholars agreed that Johnson's wholesale escalation of the undeclared war in Southeast Asia, Nixon's secret bombing of Cambodia, or even John Mitchell's "White House horrors" were not so much aberrations as a culmination of the twentieth-century tendency toward presidential aggrandizement. The roots of the activist presidency could be traced to the bold examples of such assertive chief executives as Andrew Jackson and Abraham Lincoln—and more recently to Theodore Roosevelt and Woodrow Wilson, the first of the so-called "modern presidents." But closer in time and in importance was the growth of presidential power since the New Deal. In a period of almost uninterrupted crises, stretching from the depression of the 1930s to the threat of nuclear destruction in the 1960s, executive authority in such critical areas as the economy and foreign policy had expanded enormously.

Until the intrusions of Vietnam and Watergate, scholars generally agreed that these developments were both inevitable and constitutional. In an increasingly complex and threatening world, they concluded, the nation's welfare and security required a strong president. The legislative process was properly deliberative and inherently slow. Only the president enjoyed the capacity for centralized leadership; only he possessed the control of information and communication demanded by a modern nation in a troubled world. This view, noted the political scientist Thomas E. Cronin (Congressional Record, October 5, 1956), became "textbook orthodoxy." It was forcefully advocated by such eminent students of American government as Clinton Rossiter (The American Presidency, 1956), Lewis W. Koenig (The Chief Executive, 1964), and James MacGregor Burns (Presidential Government, 1965). Perhaps the most influential spokesman for executive domination was Richard E. Neustadt, whose Presidential Power (1960) characterized the president as the "Great Initiator" of both domestic and foreign policy and the "Final Arbiter" in matters of war. The standard in its field for nearly a decade, this popular book has been aptly called "a latter-day version of Machiavelli's Prince," a primer for chief executives who would maximize their power.

Amid the disillusionments of war and scandal, however, this expansive view fell rapidly into scholarly disfavor. Even without the example of Watergate, Neustadt (Alliance Politics, 1970) became more cautious in his claims for presidential power. Alarmed by the president's seemingly unchecked capacity to wage war, some writers called the office a "Frankenstein monster"; an increasing number expressed fear that the ship of state had listed dangerously to its presidential side. Almost overnight a new scholarly concensus emerged as even many of the former aggrandizers became the new critics of executive authority. Among the most provocative of these was the historian Arthur M. Schlesinger, Jr., whose widely read Imperial Presidency *(1973) elegantly lamented the development in the office of the American president of "the most absolute monarch (with the possible exception of Mao Tse-tung of China) among the great powers of the world." Although in earlier works Schlesinger had, by his own admission, contributed to the "rise of the presidential mystique," he now attacked the "cult" of presidential activism and argued for a return to a "properly balanced" system of executive restraint and legislative responsibility.*

And so the pendulum swings. Taken together these sharply diverging schools of presidential analysis—the one dominant in the 1960s, the other emerging fullblown in the 1970s—provide as neat an example of the importance of perspective to the interpretative process as the student is likely to find. With the Nixon excesses so near to mind, scholars who once lauded Theodore Roosevelt for his sweeping theory of executive "stewardship" or faulted Dwight Eisenhower for his unseemly "Whiggery" fell under the spell of the two-century old mandate for separated powers. Similarly, in the aftermath of Vietnam, historians and political scientists who once praised Franklin Roosevelt and Harry Truman for their bold foreign policy initiatives became critical of executive usurpations in the areas of war and treaty making. Students baffled by these shifting currents of opinion need only recall that the first lesson of revisionism is humility.

FOR FURTHER READING

Those who would chart the social contours of the '70s should perhaps begin with the decade's journalism, its newspapers and periodicals. Other suggestive and widely varying points of departure include the books by Jerry Rubin and especially Christopher Lasch mentioned in the text, Tom Wolfe's *Mauve Gloves & Madmen, Clutter & Vine* (1976), and Jim Hougan's *Decadence* (1975). On the nature of the presidency see, in addition to the studies cited in the essay above: Norman C. Thomas, ed., *The Presidency in Contemporary Context* (1975); Charles W. Dunn, ed., *The Future of the American Presidency* (1975); and William M. Goldsmith, *The Growth of Presidential Power,* 3 vols. (1974). Rowland Evans and Robert D. Novak have written authoritatively about *Nixon in the White House* (1971). Jules Witcover, in *The Resurrection of Richard Nixon* (1970); Ralph De Toledano, in *One Man Alone* (1969); and Garry Wills, in *Nixon Agonistes* (1970)* offer varied assessments of the man and his politics. John Osborne's several *Nixon Watch* studies (1970, 1971, 1972) are often incisive. Nixon tells his own story in *Six Crises* (1962) and *Memoirs* (1978). Books by disgruntled "insiders" include: Leon E. Panetta, *Bring Us Together: The Nixon Team and the Civil Rights Retreat* (1971), and Richard J. Whalen, *Catch the Falling Flag: A Republican's Challenge to His Party* (1972). James Keogh's *President Nixon and the Press* (1972) supports the administration's views on media bias. Theo Lippman, Jr. provides an unflattering portrait of *Spiro Agnew's America* (1972); and Daniel Moynihan writes knowingly of *The Politics of a Guaranteed Income* (1973).

---

*Available in paperback edition.

Kevin Phillips candidly, but unofficially, discusses the Nixon administration's election strategy in *The Emerging Republican Majority* (1969); and Richard M. Scammon and Ben J. Wattenberg analyze the mood of the electorate in *The Real Majority* (1970). Reg Murphy and Hal Gulliver offer an unfriendly appraisal of *The Southern Strategy* (1971); and George Tindall, in *The Disruption of the Solid South* (1972), places that strategy in its proper historical perspective. Nixon's efforts to remake the Supreme Court are analyzed by James F. Simon in *In His Own Image* (1972), and by Louis M. Kohlmeier in *"God Save This Honorable Court!"* (1972). Henry Kissinger, in *American Foreign Policy* (1969), outlines the administration's objectives in a formulative stage, and the first volume of his autobiography, *White House Years* (1979), carries the story through Nixon's first term. These should be supplemented by: Virginia Brodine and Mark Selden, eds., *Open Secret: The Kissinger-Nixon Doctrine in Asia* (1972);* David Landau, *Kissinger: Uses of Power* (1972); Marvin and Bernard Kalb, *Kissinger* (1974); and Robert Osgood, et al., *Retreat from Empire* (1973). Theodore H. White reports on the *Making of the President* (1972). Of Watergate books there is seemingly no end. Among the more useful are: Bob Woodward and Carl Bernstein, *All the President's Men* (1974) and *Final Days* (1976); Theodore White, *Breach of Faith* (1975); John Sirica, *To Set the Record Straight* (1976); and Jonathan Schell, *Time of Illusion* (1976). Jerald ter Horst writes of *Gerald Ford and the Future of the Presidency* (1974). Jules Witcover, in *Marathon* (1977), details Carter's election in 1976; James Wooten, in *Dasher* (1978), examines Carter's past. Bruce Mazlish and Edwin Diamond's *Jimmy Carter* (1979) is "psychobiography"; and Clark Mollenhoff's *The President Who Failed* (1979) is unfriendly in the extreme.

Name Index

Subject Index